Logic Design

Logic Design

K. Venkataraju
Professor
Department of Electronics & Communication
Brindavan College of Engineering
Bangalore

TECHSAR™
NEW DELHI

Published and Printed by

Techsar Pvt. Ltd.
4435-36/7, Ansari Road, Daryaganj,
New Delhi - 110 002 (India)
E-mail: tech_info@techsarworld.com
Website: www.techsarworld.com

ISBN: 978-93-84588-30-4

Reprint 2025

Dedicated
to my grandchildren
Aryan and Tania

Preface

This book gives an insight into the analysis and design of combinational and sequential systems. Both combinational and sequential systems are used extensively in digital systems.

The concepts and principles of the digital systems are vividly explained. There are eight chapters which are structured logically and integrated around the central theme of analysis and design of digital systems.

This book starts with the definition of combinational logic and explains canonical forms and process of generation of switching equations from truth tables. Simplification of Boolean expressions using Karnaugh maps is dealt with comprehensively with pertinent examples.

In chapter 2, simplification of Boolean functions using Quine-McCluskey minimization technique and map entered variable technique is illustrated with examples clearly specifying the steps involved in a comprehensive way.

A general approach to design of combinational logic circuits is given in chapter 3. A methodology is described as to how to carry out a step-by-step approach in designing a digital system. Decoders and encoders are described comprehensively.

Digital multiplexers and their applications as Boolean function generators are dealt with in chapter 4. Adders, subtractors, look ahead carry adders and binary comparators are explained in precise terms and one can easily comprehend the concepts.

In chapter 5, the latches and flip-flops are explained in a coherent and systematic manner. Then master slave flip-flops including edge triggered flip-flops are described in detail.

Characteristic equations of different types of flip-flops are discussed in chapter 6. Registers and their applications are described in a concise way. Binary ripple counters, synchronous counters, and counters based on shift registers are illustrated with appropriate examples. Design of synchronous counters and synchronous mod-6 counters using clocked *SR*, *JK*, *D* and *T* flip-flops are described.

Mealy and Moore Models are discussed with block diagrams in chapter 7. Synchronous sequential circuit analysis is described with a number of graded examples.

Chapter 8 begins with the concept of state diagram and its construction. Counter design based on state tables and state diagrams are elaborated with suitable examples.

This book will be useful for engineering undergraduate students, practising engineers and consultants.

K.Venkataraju

Acknowledgements

The author gratefully acknowledges the encouragement given by Dr. Majed.A.A. Sabha, Chairman, Brindavan Group of Institutions, Bangalore.

My sincere thanks are due to Mr. C.M. Lingappa Chairman, Jnana Vikas Institute of Technology Wg. Cdr. P.K. Ramamurthy, Director, JVIT and Dr. S.K. Srivastava, Principal, JVIT for their encouragement and support.

My sincere gratitude is due to Dr. K.U. Muthu, Dean and Dr. V. Ramarajan, Professor, Brindavan College of Engineering, Bangalore, for their motivation and guidance to write this book.

I appreciate the sincere efforts of Mr. K.S. Ramprasad and Mr. A.N. Viswanatha Rao, Scientists of DRDO in reviewing the manuscript and I profoundly thank them for their suggestions.

I sincearely thank Prof. G. Venkatesha, Dr. Sasikumar, Prof. Dinesh, Dr. Ravikumar and Prof. Sumitra, Brindavan College of Engineering, Bangalore for their valuable support. My thanks are due to my colleagues, Electronics and Communication department, Brindavan College of Engineering, Bangalore for their encouragement.

I must acknowledge all the encouragement and support from my wife Usha, sons Ravi and Sibi and daughter-in-law Maya.

K. Venkataraju

Preamble

This course gives the basic modules of logic design such as simplification of Boolean equations, analysis of combinational circuits, design of combinational circuits, analysis of sequential circuits and design of sequential circuits. It aims at determination of various steps in logic design sequence, design of decoders and encoders, design of multiplexers, adders, subtractors, design of flip-flops, latches, design of registers, shift resisters, counters, analysis and design of synchronous sequential circuits and construction of state diagrams.

Programme Outcome Addressed

(a) Graduates will demonstrate an ability to identify, formulate and solve logic design problems.
(b) Graduates will be able to communicate effectively in both verbal and written form.
(c) Graduates will develop confidence in self education and ability for lifelong learning.
(d) Graduates can participate and succeed in competitive examinations.

Competence

At the end of the course, the students will be able to:

(1) Simplify Boolean functions using Karnaugh maps, Quine-McCluskey minimization technique or Map Entered Variable method.
(2) Analyse and design decoders and encoders including priority encoders.
(3) Analyse and design multiplexers, adders, subtractors and binary comparators and to known how these devices are applied for problem solving.
(4) Understand sequential circuits like latches and flip-flops and design of flip-flops for different applications.
(5) Derive characteristic equations of different flip-flops and design of registers, synchronous and asynchronous counters.
(6) Design of sequential circuits like Mealy and Moore circuits and analyse the synchronous sequential circuits.
(7) Construct state diagrams and design of synchronous counters.

Course Articulation Matrix

Course Learning	Activities	Programme Outcomes										
		a	*b*	*c*	*d*	*e*	*f*	*g*	*h*	*i*	*g*	*k*
CLO 1	2, 5, 6, 7, 8, 11	*H*	*H*		*H*		*M*		*H*		*L*	*M*
CLO 2	2, 5, 6, 7, 8, 11	*H*	*H*		*H*		*M*		*H*		*M*	*H*
CLO 3	2, 5, 6, 7, 8, 11	*H*	*H*		*H*		*M*		*H*		*M*	*H*
CLO 4	2, 5, 6, 7, 8, 11	*H*	*H*		*M*		*M*		*H*		*L*	*H*
CLO 5	2, 5, 6, 7, 8, 11	*H*	*H*				*M*		*H*		*M*	*H*
CLO 6	1, 3, 5, 6, 7, 8, 10	*M*	*M*	*M*			*M*		*H*		*M*	*H*
CLO 7	2, 5, 6, 7, 8, 11	*H*	*H*				*M*		*H*		*M*	*H*
CLO 8	1, 2, 5, 6, 7, 8, 10, 11	*H*	*H*				*M*		*H*		*M*	*H*

L: Low M: Medium H: High

Activities to be selected

1. Course Seminar
2. Course Project
3. Case Studies
4. Technical Events
5. Assignments
6. Quiz
7. Internal Assessment Tests
8. Viva Voce
9. Subject Proficiency/ Skill Assessment
10. Demonstration/Presentation
11. Tutorial Classes

Programme Outcomes

Level of Achievement of Programme Outcome

POS	Students graduating from Electronics & Communication Engineering discipline will be expected and prepared to exercise the skills and abilities as listed below.
a	Ability to apply knowledge of mathematics science and engineering
b	Ability to identify, formulate and solve engineering problems in electrical science
c	Ability to design and conduct experiments analyse and interpret data
d	Ability to design systems to meet the given specifications
e	Ability to demonstrate skills in multidisciplinary environment
f	Ability to use modern engineering tools to analyse engineering problems
g	Ability to demonstrate knowledge of professionalism and ethics
h	Ability to communicate effectively in both verbal and written form
i	Ability to develop the acumen and awareness of the impact of engineering solutions on society
j	Recognition of the need for and an ability to engage in lifelong learning
k	Develop ability to attempt and succeed in competitive exams

Assessment Pattern

Sl No.	Bloom's Category	Test 1	Test 2	Test 3/Semester end Exam
1.	Remember	10	10	10
2.	Understand	10	10	10
3.	Apply	80	80	80

Concept Map

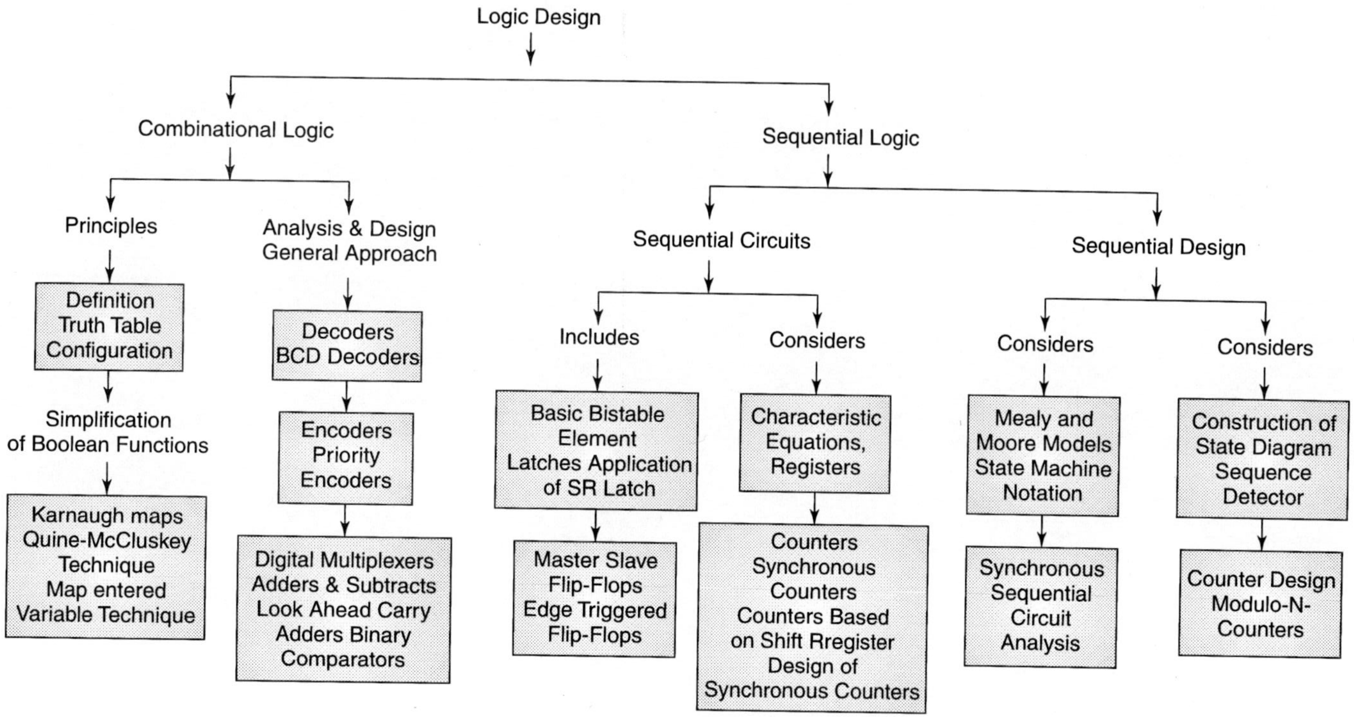
Logic Design
Combinational Logic
Sequential Logic
Principles
Analysis & Design General Approach
Sequential Circuits
Sequential Design
Definition Truth Table Configuration
Simplification of Boolean Functions
Karnaugh maps Quine-McCluskey Technique Map entered Variable Technique
Decoders BCD Decoders
Encoders Priority Encoders
Digital Multiplexers Adders & Subtracts Look Ahead Carry Adders Binary Comparators
Includes
Considers
Basic Bistable Element Latches Application of SR Latch
Master Slave Flip-Flops Edge Triggered Flip-Flops
Characteristic Equations, Registers
Counters Synchronous Counters Counters Based on Shift Rregister Design of Synchronous Counters
Considers
Considers
Mealy and Moore Models State Machine Notation
Synchronous Sequential Circuit Analysis
Construction of State Diagram Sequence Detector
Counter Design Modulo-N-Counters

Course Document

DEPARTMENT OF ELECTRONICS AND COMMUNICATION ENGINEERING

Course Name: Logic Design *Code : ES 33*
Total Contact Hours: 52 *Semester : 03*

Course Objectives

The main objectives are to:

- Provide an insight to the principles of combinational and sequential logic.
- Provide systematic and comprehensive treatment of components of combinational and sequential logic circuits and techniques for designing digital systems using these components.
- Provide a strong foundation for advanced industry-relevant course in digital system design, which includes VLSI, microprocessors and embedded microcontrollers.
- Present real-world examples to give the learner a feel of how digital system design is practiced.

Course Learning Outcomes (CLOs)

At the end of the course, the student should be able to

CLO 1 Formulate logic function expressions and obtain their minimal SOP and POS forms of function of 3, 4 and 5 variables using Boolean algebra postulates and Karnaugh maps.

CLO 2 Construct Quine-McCluskey tables and obtain minimal SOP and POS forms of functions with any number of variables using Quine-McCluskey method and map entered variable method.

CLO 3 Design arithmetic and combinational logic circuits using gates, encoders and decoders.

CLO 4 Design arithmetic and combinational logic circuits using adders, subtractors, multiplexers and binary comparators.

CLO 5 Understand sequential circuits like latches, flip-flops and construct specified synchronous or asynchronous sequential logic circuits using appropriate flip-flops.

CLO 6 Determine the characteristic equations and design and analyze shift registers, synchronous and asynchronous counters.

CLO 7 Design of sequential circuits like Mealy and Moore circuits and analysis of synchronous sequential circuits.

CLO 8 Construct state diagrams and design of synchronous counters.

CHAPTER 1

Course Code & Title: *ES 33 & Logic Design*

Topic Name : Principles of Combinational Logic-I *Topic No: 1 N/L Hours:* 6

Topic Level Objectives (TLOs)

1. Introduce logic functions, their canonical forms and the standard terminology used in combinational logic.
2. Introduce basic gates, building blocks of combinational logic.
3. Provide a systematic treatment of postulates of Boolean algebra.
4. Construct truth table.
5. Construct Karnaugh maps.
6. Introduce simplification of switching functions.

Intended Learning Outcomes (ILOs)

After successful completion of the topic, the learner will be able to

1. Formulate a logical function expression from a real-world problem definition
2. Recognize if a logic function is in SOP and POS form.
3. Recognize if a logic function is in canonical form.
4. Distinguish between minterms and maxterms.
5. Explain and prove DeMorgan's Theorem.
6. Demostrate conversion of product terms into minterms and sum terms into maxterms.
7. Demonstrate minimization of logic functions using fundamental postulates.
8. Illustrate Karnaugh map technique to simplify logic functions with 3, 4 and 5 variables.
9. Construct Karnaugh maps to include incompletely specified functions.
10. Illustrate Karnaugh map technique to simplify maxterm expression.

CHAPTER 2

Course Code & Title: *ES 33 & Logic Design*

Topic Name : Principles of Combinational Logic-II *Topic No: 2 N/L Hours: 7*

Topic Level Objectives (TLOs)

1. Explain Quine-McCluskey Minimization technique.
2. Describe Quine-McCluskey technique using don't-care terms.
3. Explain Reduced Prime Implicant Table.
4. Introduce simplification of switching functions using Quine-McCluskey method and map entered variable method.

Intended Learning Outcomes (ILOs)

After successful completion of the topic, the learner will be able to

1. Compose Quine-McCluskey minimization tables, form implicant groups and derive minimal logic functions.
2. Demonstrate the use of Quine-McCluskey minimization technique for functions having don't-care terms.
3. Compose reduced prime implicant tables.
4. Explain map entered variable method of function minimization.

CHAPTER 3

Course Code & Title : *ES 33 & Logic Design*
Topic Name : Analysis and Design of Combinational Logic-I *Topic No : 3 N/L Hours : 6*

Topic Level Objectives (TLOs)

1. Formulate general approach to analysis and design of combinational logic.
2. Introduce encoders and decoders.
3. Introduce BCD decoders and priority encoders.
4. Provide comprehensive treatment of the methods and philosophy of design and analysis of digital circuits using modular combinational logic.

Intended Learning Outcomes (ILOs)

After successful completion of the topic, the learner will be able to

1. Explain the function of a decoder.
2. Design decoders in general and BCD decoders in particular.
3. Explain the function of an encoder.
4. Design different types of encoders including decimal to BCD encoders.
5. Design of priority encoders like 8 line to 3 line priority encoder, 4 line to 2 line priority encoder.

CHAPTER 4

Course Code & Title : *ES 33 & Logic Design*

Topic Name : Analysis and Design of Combinational Logic-II *Topic No : 4 N/L Hours : 7*

Topic Level Objectives (TLOs)

1. Introduce multiplexers, adders, subtractors and binary comparators.
2. Demonstrate multiplexers as Boolean function generators.
3. Demonstrate cascading full adders.
4. Introduce Look Ahead carry adder.
5. Provide comprehensive treatment of the methods and philosophy of design and analysis of digital circuits using modular combinational logic.

Intended Learning Outcomes (ILOs)

After successful completion of the topic, the learner will be able to

1. Explain the function of digital multiplexers.
2. Demonstrate the use of multiplexers as Boolean function generators.
3. Explain the function of adders and subtractors.
4. Design half and full adders and subtractors.
5. Demonstrate cascading of full adders.
6. Design Look Ahead carry adders and explain them.
7. Design binary comparators of 1 bit, 2 bits and 4 bits.

CHAPTER 5

Course Code & Title: *ES 33 & Logic Design*

Topic Name : Sequential *Topic No : 5 N/L Hours: 7*

Topic Level Objectives (TLOs)

1. Explain the basic bistable elements and latches.
2. Explain the application of SR latch.
3. Introduce all types of flip-flops.

Intended Learning Outcomes (ILOs)

After successful completion of the topic, the learner will be able to

1. Understand the basic bistable element.
2. Understand the SR latch and its applications.
3. Construct a switch debouncer.

4. Explain the $S'R'$ latch, gated SR latch and the gated D latch
5. Explain the master slave SR flip-flop.
6. Explain the master slave JK flip-flop.
7. Explain the edge triggered flip-flop.
8. Explain the positive and negative edge triggered D flip-flop.

CHAPTER 6

Course Code & Tittle: *ES 33 & Logic Design*
Topic Name : Sequential Circuits-2 *Topic No : 6 N/L Hours : 7*

Topic Level Objectives (TLOs)

1. Provide comprehensive treatment of the methods and philosophy of design and analysis of asynchronous sequential circuits using flip-flops.
2. Provide comprehensive treatment of the methods and philosophy of design and analysis of synchronous sequential circuits using flip-flips.

Intended Learning Outcomes (ILOs)

After successful completion of the topic, the learner will be able to

1. Derive the characteristic equations of the following flip-flops : SR, JK, T and D.
2. Understand registers, shift registers and counters.
3. Construct binary ripple counters and synchronous binary counters.
4. Construct Johnson counter and ring counters based on shift registers.
5. Design a synchronous counter using different types of flip-flops.
6. Design a synchronous Mod-6 counter using clocked JK, SR, D and T flip-flops.

CHAPTER 7

Course Code & Title : *ES 33 & Logic Design*
Topic Name : Sequential Design-1 *Topic No 7 N/L Hours : 7*

Topic Level Objectives (TLOs)

1. Introduce the concept of Mealy and Moore models of sequential circuits.
2. Introduce the concept of state machine notation.
3. Analyse synchronous sequential circuits.
4. Provide comprehensive treatment of the methods of design and analysis of finite state machines.

Intended Learning Outcomes (ILOs)

After successful completion of the topic, the learner will be able to

1. Explain Mealy and Moore models.
2. Explain the behaviour of a state machine.
3. Construct a state machine model from word description.
4. Analyse and design synchronous sequential circuits.
5. Analyse and design asynchronous sequential circuits.
6. Design a sequential circuit for a given state diagram.

CHAPTER 8

Course Code & Title: *ES 33 & Logic Design*
Topic Name : Sequential Design-2 *Topic No : 8 N/L Hours : 6*

Topic Level Objectives (TLOs)

1. Introduce the concept of state assignment.
2. Provide comprehensive treatment of the methods of design and analysis of counters.

Intended Learning Outcomes (ILOs)

1. Construct state diagrams for specified machine behaviours.
2. Design of Modulo-N counters.
3. Design of synchronous counters using *SR*, *JK*, *D* and *T* flip-flops to count a particular sequence.

Contents

CHAPTER 1

Principles of Combinational Logic-1

1.1 DEFINITION OF COMBINATIONAL LOGIC

The combinational circuits are logic circuits, the output of which at a given time is a function of the inputs at that time. Figure 1.1 shows a combinational logic model.

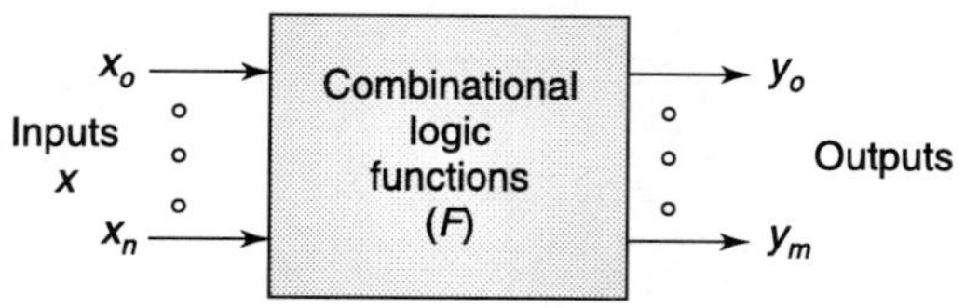

Fig. 1.1 Combinational logic model

Let x be the set of all input variables (x_0, x_1 ... x_n) and y be the set of all output variables (y_0, y_1 ... y_m). The combinational function, F, operates on the input variable set X and produces the output variable set Y. The output variables are not fed back to the input. We can say that $Y = F(X)$.

1.2 GENERAL LOGIC DESIGN SEQUENCE

Figure 1.2 gives six steps through which one can design a product from a problem statement.

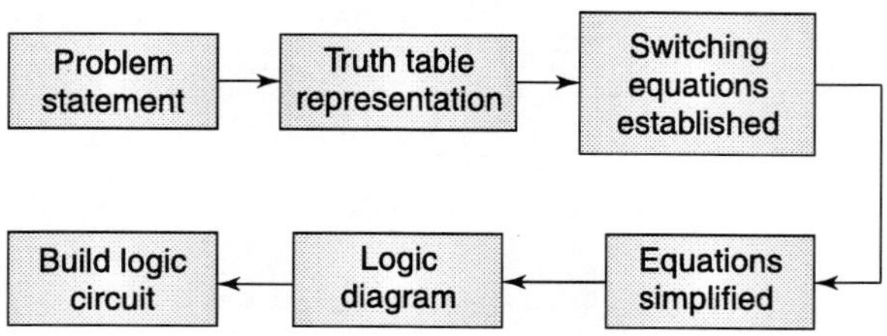

Fig. 1.2 General logic design sequence

Once the problem has been clearly specified, truth table can be constructed taking all the possible inputs and outputs. Then from truth table, switching equations can be written. Next step is to simplify the equations using techniques like Karnaugh maps (hance forward K-map). From the simplified equations, logic diagram can be drawn. Once the logic diagram is available, a logic circuit can be built.

1.3 TRUTH TABLE CONSTRUCTION

Given a clearly specified problem statement, we can easily decide the number of inputs, number of outputs and construct a truth table.

Example 1.1 Construct a truth table for a system with four inputs, output is true indicating when a majority of the inputs is true.

Solution Let us take the four inputs as *A*, *B*, *C*, *D* and output as *Y*. When the majority of inputs, *A*, *B*, *C*, *D* is true, i.e., if more than two inputs are true, output *Y* is true.

Four inputs will take sixteen different combinations. Now, let us construct the truth table as shown in Fig. 1.3.

Inputs				Output
A	*B*	*C*	*D*	*Y*
0	0	0	0	0
0	0	0	1	0
0	0	1	0	0
0	0	1	1	0
0	1	0	0	0
0	1	0	1	0
0	1	1	0	0
0	1	1	1	1
1	0	0	0	0
1	0	0	1	0
1	0	1	0	0
1	0	1	1	1
1	1	0	0	0
1	1	0	1	1
1	1	1	0	1
1	1	1	1	1

Fig. 1.3 Truth table for example 1.1

Example 1.2 Give the truth table representation of a system which consists of two two-bit numbers as its inputs and generates an output to indicate, when the sum of the two numbers is even.

Solution There are two two-bit numbers. Hence, there are four inputs. Let us say the inputs as *A*, *B*, *C*, *D* with *AB* & *CD* being the two-bit numbers. The sum of these two two-bit numbers may be odd or even. If it is even the output is indicated as 1. Let us call the output *Y*. For example, let

AB be 10 and *CD* be 10. The sum will be 10 + 10 = 100(4). The output is even. So the output *Y* is 1. The truth table is constructed as shown in Fig. 1.4.

Inputs				Output
A	B	C	D	Y
0	0	0	0	1
0	0	0	1	0
0	0	1	0	1
0	0	1	1	0
0	1	0	0	1
0	1	0	1	1
0	1	1	0	0
0	1	1	1	1
1	0	0	0	1
1	0	0	1	0
1	0	1	0	1
1	0	1	1	0
1	1	0	0	0
1	1	0	1	1
1	1	1	0	0
1	1	1	1	1

Fig. 1.4 Truth table for example 1.2

1.4 SWITCHING EQUATIONS

For each input variable combination that produces a logical 1 in a truth table, output column can form a term in a Boolean switching equation. Next step in design sequence is deriving switching equations from the truth table. Let us consider the truth table in Fig. 1.1. The output variable *Y* is a logical 1 in five cases: $(\overline{A}, B, C, D)$ $(A, \overline{B}, C, D)$ $(A, B, \overline{C}, D)$ $(A, B, C, \overline{D})$ and (A, B, C, D). The remaining input variable combinations cause output *Y* to be logical 0.

A Boolean equation can be written that includes all the input variable combinations for which the output *Y* is a logical 1. Each term in the equation is formed by ANDing the input variables. Each AND term is then ORed with the other AND terms to complete the output Boolean equation.

Let us come back to the truth table in Fig. 1.1.

The output equation can be written as

$$Y = \overline{A}BCD + A\overline{B}CD + AB\overline{C}D + ABC\overline{D} + ABCD.$$

Let us define some of the terms used in Boolean equations.

Literal: A literal is a Boolean variable or its complement. If X is a binary variable, X or $\overline{X}$ would be literal.

Product term: A product term is a literal or the logical product (AND) of multiple literals. If X, Y are binary variables, then the product term may be X, XY, $\overline{X}Y$, etc.

Sum term: A sum term is a literal or the logical (OR) of multiple literals. If x, y are binary variables, then the sum term may be x, $x + y$, $\bar{x} + y$, etc.

Sum of products: A sum of products (SOP) is the logical OR of multiple product terms. If x, y and z are binary variables, then $\bar{x}y + \bar{x} + yz + xyz$ is a sum of product term.

Product of sums: A product of sums (POS) is the logical AND of multiple OR terms. If x, y and z are binary variables, $(x + y)(\bar{x} + y + z)(\bar{y} + z)$ is a POS term.

Minterm: A minterm is a special case product (AND) term. A minterm is a product term that contains all the input variables that make up a Boolean expression.

Maxterm: A maxterm is a special case sum (OR) term. A maxterm is a sumterm that contains all the input variables that make up a Boolean expression.

Canonical sum of products: A canonical sum of products is a complete set of minterms that defines when an output variable is a logical 1. Each minterm corresponds to the row in the truth table where the output function is 1.

Canonical product of sums: A canonical product of sums is a complete set of maxterms that defines when an output is a logical 0. Each maxterm corresponds to a row in the truth table where the output function is 0.

Minterm and maxterm designations: Let x, y, z be the input variables. If all the input variables are 0, the minterm is $\bar{x}\,\bar{y}\,\bar{z}$ which is designated as m_0. Similarly, the maxterm is $x + y + z$ which is designated as M_0. Figure 1.5 gives the minterm and maxterm designations for three variables x, y, z.

Input variables			Minterm		Maxterm	
x	y	z	Term	Designation	Term	Designation
0	0	0	$\bar{x}\,\bar{y}\,\bar{z}$	m_0	$x + y + z$	M_0
0	0	1	$\bar{x}\,\bar{y}\,z$	m_1	$x + y + \bar{z}$	M_1
0	1	0	$\bar{x}\,y\,\bar{z}$	m_2	$x + \bar{y} + z$	M_2
0	1	1	$\bar{x}\,y\,z$	m_3	$x + \bar{y} + \bar{z}$	M_3
1	0	0	$x\,\bar{y}\,\bar{z}$	m_4	$\bar{x} + y + z$	M_4
1	0	1	$x\,\bar{y}\,z$	m_5	$\bar{x} + y + \bar{z}$	M_5
1	1	0	$x\,y\,\bar{z}$	m_6	$\bar{x} + \bar{y} + z$	M_6
1	1	1	$x\,y\,z$	m_7	$\bar{x} + \bar{y} + \bar{z}$	M_7

Fig. 1.5 Minterm and maxterm designations

Canonical forms: Canonical forms are special cases of SOP and POS forms. They are also called minterms and maxterms.

To convert an SOP equation into canonical form using Boolean algebra, we carry out the following steps:

1. Find out the missing variables in each AND term.
2. AND the missing term and its complement with the original AND term.
3. Expand the term by application of the property of distribution.

Let us take a function of three variables x, y, z and product term as $x\,y$. In the AND term xy the missing variable is z.

As per step 2, this becomes $xy\,(z + \bar{z})$ as $(z + \bar{z}) = 1$, the original AND term value is not changed.

As per step 3, this becomes $xyz + xy\bar{z}$

To convert a POS equation into canonical form using Boolean algebra, we carry out the following steps:

1. Find out the missing variables in each OR term.
2. OR the missing term and its complement with the original OR term.
3. Expand the term by application of property of distribution.

For example, let us take a function of three variables x, y, z and the sum term as $(x + y)$.

step 1: In the sum term, the missing variable is Z.

step 2: The sum term becomes $x + y + z\bar{z}$ as $z\bar{z} = 0$. The original OR term is not changed.

step 3: The sum term is expanded to $(x + y + z)\,(x + y + \bar{z})$.

Example 1.3 Convert the given expression into proper canonical form:

$$F(A, B, C) = AC + AB + BC$$

Solution In the first product term AC, B is missing and in the second product term AB, C is missing and in the third product term BC, A is missing.

Now
$$F(A, B, C) = AC\,(B + \bar{B}) + AB\,(C + \bar{C}) + BC\,(A + \bar{A})$$
$$= ACB + AC\bar{B} + ABC + AB\bar{C} + BCA + BC\bar{A}$$

Rearranging, we get

$$F(A, B, C) = ABC + A\bar{B}C + ABC + AB\bar{C} + ABC + \bar{A}BC$$

The term ABC occurs three times, so eliminating the repeated terms, we get

$$F(A, B, C) = ABC + \bar{A}BC + A\bar{B}C + AB\bar{C}$$

Example 1.4 Convert the given expression into proper canonical form:

$$F(a, b, c) = a\bar{b} + a\bar{c} + bc$$

Solution Let us use the missing variable and its complement.

$$F(a, b, c) = a\bar{b}(c + \bar{c}) + a\bar{c}(b + \bar{b}) + bc(a + \bar{a})$$
$$= a\bar{b}c + a\bar{b}\bar{c} + a\bar{c}b + a\bar{c}\bar{b} + bca + bc\bar{a}$$

Rearranging, we get

$$F(a, b, c) = a\overline{b}c + \underline{a\overline{b}\overline{c}} + ab\overline{c} + \underline{a\overline{b}\overline{c}} + abc + \overline{a}bc$$

Eliminating repeated terms, we get

$$F(a, b, c) = a\overline{b}c + a\overline{b}\overline{c} + ab\overline{c} + abc + \overline{a}bc$$

Example 1.5 Convert the following equation into proper canonical form:

$$F(w, x, y, z) = \overline{w}y + xz$$

Solution

$$F(w, x, y, z) = \overline{w}y + (x + \overline{x})(z + \overline{z}) + xz(w + \overline{w})(y + \overline{y})$$

$$= \underline{\overline{w}yxz} + \underline{\overline{w}yx\overline{z}} + \overline{w}y\,\overline{x}z + \underline{\overline{w}yx\overline{z}} + xzwy + xzw\overline{y} + \underline{xz\overline{w}y} + xz\overline{w}\,\overline{y}$$

Eliminating repeated terms,

$$F(w, x, y, z) = \overline{w}xyz + \overline{w}xy\overline{z} + \overline{w}\,\overline{x}yz + wxyz + wx\overline{y}z + \overline{w}x\overline{y}z$$

Example 1.6 Convert the following equation into canonical form:

$$f(A, B, C, D) = \overline{A}\,\overline{B}D + AB\overline{C}\,\overline{D} + \overline{A}BD + ABC\overline{D}$$

Solution

$$f(A, B, C, D) = \overline{A}\,\overline{B}D(C + \overline{C}) + AB\overline{C}\,\overline{D} + \overline{A}BD(C + \overline{C}) + ABC\overline{D}$$

$$= \overline{A}\,\overline{B}DC + \overline{A}\,\overline{B}D\overline{C} + AB\overline{C}\,\overline{D} + \overline{A}BDC + \overline{A}BD\overline{C} + ABC\overline{D}$$

There are no repeated terms. Hence,

$$f(A, B, C, D) = \overline{A}\,\overline{B}CD + \overline{A}\,\overline{B}\,\overline{C}D + AB\overline{C}\,\overline{D} + \overline{A}BCD + \overline{A}B\overline{C}D + ABC\overline{D}$$

Example 1.7 Convert the following POS equation into proper canonical form:

$$f(a, b, c) = (a + b)(\overline{b} + \overline{c})$$

Solution

$$f(a, b, c) = (a + \overline{b} + c\overline{c})(\overline{b} + c + a\overline{a})$$

$$= \underline{(a + \overline{b} + c)}(a + \overline{b} + \overline{c})\underline{(a + \overline{b} + c)}(\overline{a} + \overline{b} + c)$$

Eliminating the repeated term, we get

$$f(a, b, c) = (a + \overline{b} + c)(a + \overline{b} + \overline{c})(\overline{a} + \overline{b} + c)$$

Example 1.8 Convert the following POS equation into proper canonical form:

$$f(A, B, C, D) = (A + \overline{B} + C)(\overline{A} + D)$$

Solution

$$f(A, B, C, D) = (A + \overline{B} + C + D\overline{D})(\overline{A} + B\overline{B} + C\overline{C} + D)$$

$$= (A + \overline{B} + C + D)(A + \overline{B} + C + \overline{D})$$

$$(\overline{A} + B + C + D)(\overline{A} + B + \overline{C} + D)$$

$$(\overline{A} + \overline{B} + C + D)\ (\overline{A} + \overline{B} + \overline{C} + D)$$

There are no repeated terms. Hence,

$$f(A, B, C, D) = (A + \overline{B} + C + D)\ (A + \overline{B} + C + \overline{D})$$
$$(\overline{A} + B + C + D)\ (\overline{A} + B + \overline{C} + D)$$
$$(\overline{A} + \overline{B} + C + D)\ (\overline{A} + \overline{B} + \overline{C} + D)$$

Switching equations can be written using the minterm or maxterm numerical designation instead of writing the variable names. Even the m and M designations can be dropped and decimal equivalent value for the term can be written directly.

If the canonical SOP equation is

$$f(A, B, C) = A\overline{B}\,\overline{C} + A\overline{B}C + \overline{A}BC + ABC + \overline{A}\,\overline{B}C$$
$$= m_4 + m_5 + m_3 + m_7 + m_1$$

We can represent $f(A, B, C)$ in decimal notation as

$$f(A, B, C) = \Sigma\ (4, 5, 3, 7, 1)$$

where Σ indicates that it is sum of products canonical form. Likewise, π indicates that it is a product of sums canonical form. It is to be noted that maxterms are the complements of minterms.

Consider example 1.1, truth table. The minterm expression for the output variable Y is

$$Y = f(A, B, C, D) = \overline{A}BCD + A\overline{B}CD + AB\overline{C}D + ABC\overline{D} + ABCD$$
$$= \Sigma\ (7, 11, 13, 14, 15)$$

A maxterm representation for the same output variable Y is obtained by ORing together the set of input variables for which the output variable is 0. Each maxterm is ANDed with the other maxterms to obtain the output equation.

$$Y = f(A, B, C, D) = (A + B + C + D)\ (A + B + C + \overline{D})\ (A + B + \overline{C} + D)$$
$$(A + B + \overline{C} + \overline{D})\ (A + \overline{B} + C + D)\ (A + \overline{B} + C + \overline{D})$$
$$(\overline{A} + B + C + \overline{D})\ (\overline{A} + B + C + D)\ (\overline{A} + B + C + \overline{D})\ (\overline{A} + B + \overline{C} + D)$$
$$(\overline{A} + \overline{B} + C + D)$$
$$Y = \pi\ (0, 1, 2, 3, 4, 5, 6, 8, 9, 10, 12)$$

Example 1.9 Express the following SOP equations in a minterm list (decimal notation) form:

(i) $$f(A, B, C) = A\overline{B}C + \overline{A}B\overline{C} + ABC$$

(ii) $f(a, b, c, d) = \bar{a}b\bar{c}d + abcd + a\bar{b}\bar{c}d + \bar{a}bcd$

Solution (i) $A\bar{B}C = 101 = 5 \quad \bar{A}B\bar{C} = 010 = 2 \quad ABC = 111 = 7$

$$f(A, B, C) = \Sigma\,(5, 2, 7) = \Sigma\,(2, 5, 7)$$

(ii) $\bar{a}b\bar{c}d = 0101 = 5 \quad abcd = 1111 = 15 \quad a\bar{b}\bar{c}d = 1001 = 9$

$$\bar{a}bcd = 0111 = 7$$

$$f(a, b, c, d) = \Sigma\,(5, 15, 9, 7) = \Sigma\,(5, 7, 9, 15)$$

Example 1.10 Express the following POS equations in a maxterm list (decimal notation) form:

(i) $f(A, B, C) = (\bar{a} + b + c)\,(a + \bar{b} + \bar{c})\,(\bar{a} + b + \bar{c})$

(ii) $f(a, b, c, d) = (\bar{a} + b + c + \bar{d})\,(a + \bar{b} + \bar{c} + d)\,(\bar{a} + b + \bar{c} + d)\,(a + b + c + d)$

Solution (i) $\bar{a} + b + c = 100 = 4 \qquad a + \bar{b} + \bar{c} = 011 = 3 \qquad \bar{a} + b + \bar{c} = 101 = 5$

$$f(A, B, C) = \pi\,(4, 3, 5) = \pi\,(3, 4, 5)$$

(ii) $f(a, b, c, d) = (\bar{a} + b + c + \bar{d})\,(a + \bar{b} + \bar{c} + d)\,(\bar{a} + b + \bar{c} + d)\,(a + b + c + d)$

$$\bar{a} + b + c + \bar{d} = 1001 = 9 \qquad a + \bar{b} + \bar{c} + d = 0110 = 6$$

$$\bar{a} + b + \bar{c} + d = 1010 = 10 \qquad a + b + c + d = 0000 = 0$$

$$f(a, b, c, d) = \pi\,(9, 6, 10, 0) = \pi\,(0, 6, 9, 10)$$

1.5 KARNAUGH MAPS

After deriving switching equations from truth table, the next step in the logic design sequence is simplification of switching equations. Simplification of equations reduces the amount of hardware circuits needed to realise a function. This, in turn, reduces the number of gates and gate inputs which reduces the number of integrated circuits. Finally, this results in cost reduction and improvement in reliability.

How do we simplify switching equations?

We can use Boolean algebra but the process is tedious and cumbersome. What we need is a systematic approach for finding and eliminating any redundancies in the switching equation.

K-map is a systematic method to simplify equations. It is a matrix of squares. Each square represents a minterm or maxterm from a Boolean equation. The arrangement of the matrix squares permits identification of input variable redundancies which facilitates reduction of output equation.

If an equation contains a minterm then a 1 is entered into the square representing the minterm. A maxterm is represented by a 0. K-map squares are so arranged that it identifities group of minterms that contains redundant variables of the form of $x+\bar{x}=1$. For example, $ab+a\bar{b}=a(b+\bar{b})=a$. The adjacent squares are differing by one bit from each other and are logically adjacent.

One variable K-map: A one variable map relates to a function of one variable. For example, $f(x) = x$ for which truth table and K-map are shown in Fig. 1.6.

Square	x	f (x)
0	0	0
1	1	1

Truth table

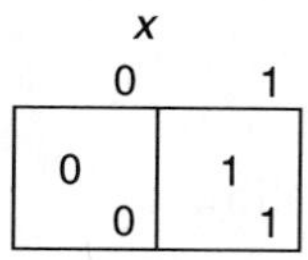

K-map

Fig. 1.6 Truth table and K-map for $f(x) = x$

The squares are numbered as 0 and 1 in lower right hand corner depending on the input variable.

Square No.	x	y	f (xy)
0	0	0	0
1	0	1	1
2	1	0	1
3	1	1	0

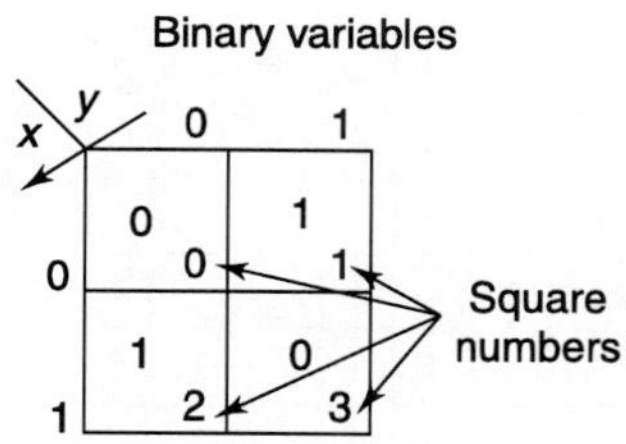

Fig. 1.7 Truth table and K-map for $f(x, y) = \bar{x}y + x\bar{y}$

Two-variable K-map: Let us consider a two-variable function $f(x, y) = \bar{x}y + x\bar{y}$ for which the truth table and K-map are shown in Fig. 1.7

Square No.	x	y	z	f (x, y, z)
0	0	0	0	0
1	0	0	1	0
2	0	1	0	1
3	0	1	1	0
4	1	0	0	1
5	1	0	1	0
6	1	1	0	1
7	1	1	1	1

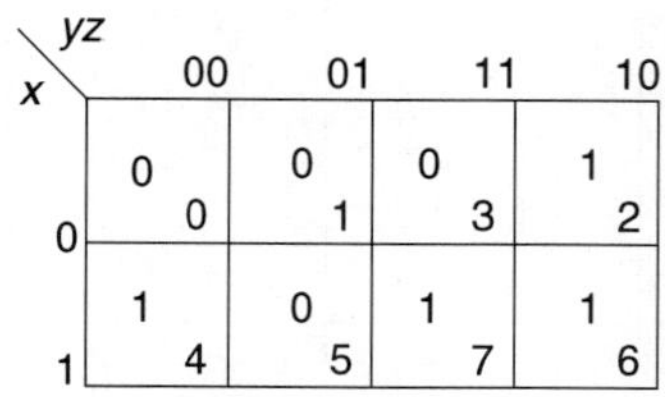

Fig. 1.8 Truth table and K-map for $f(x, y, z) = \Sigma(2, 4, 6, 7)$

Three-variable K-map: Let us consider a three-variable function $f(x, y, z) = xy\bar{z} + x\bar{y}\bar{z} + \bar{x}y\bar{z} + xyz$, for which truth table and K-map are shown in Fig. 1.8.

All the minterms for which the output function is 1, form the SOP, i.e., $\Sigma(2, 4, 6, 7) = \bar{x}y\bar{z} + x\bar{y}\bar{z} + xy\bar{z} + xyz$ The adjacent squares differ by only one bit between them. Between square (0) and square (1), yz variables change from $\bar{y}\bar{z}$ to $\bar{y}z$. Only variable z changes from $\bar{z}$ to z. Between square (1) and square (3), *yz* variables change from $\bar{y}z$ to yz. Only variable *y* changes form $\bar{y}$ to *y*. Similarly, between square (0) and square (2), *yz* variables change form $\bar{y}\bar{z}$ to $y\bar{z}$. Only variable *y* changes from $\bar{y}$ to *y*. For all the squares (0), (1), (3) and (2), variable *x* is 0. Therefore, there is no change in variable *x*.

Now consider square (0) and square (4). *yz* variables remain same, i.e., $00 = \bar{y}\bar{z}$, whereas variable *x* changes from 0 to 1, i.e., $\bar{x}$ to *x*. this means that between square (0) and square (4), there is only one variable change.

Hence, we can conclude as follows:

Square (0) is adjacent to squares (1), (2) and (4).

Square (4) is adjacent to squares (0), (5) and (6).

Square (2) is adjacent to squares (0), (3) and (6).

Square (6) is adjacent to squares (2), (7) and (4).

Square No.	*w*	*x*	*y*	*z*	*f* (*w*, *x*, *y*, *z*)
0	0	0	0	0	1
1	0	0	0	1	0
2	0	0	1	0	1
3	0	0	1	1	0
4	0	1	0	0	0
5	0	1	0	1	0
6	0	1	1	0	1
7	0	1	1	1	0
8	1	0	0	0	0
9	1	0	0	1	1
10	1	0	1	0	0
11	1	0	1	1	0
12	1	1	0	0	0
13	1	1	0	1	1
14	1	1	1	0	0
15	1	1	1	1	1

wx \ *yz*	00	01	11	10
00	1 [0]	0 [1]	0 [3]	1 [2]
01	0 [4]	0 [5]	0 [7]	1 [6]
11	0 [12]	1 [13]	1 [15]	0 [14]
10	0 [8]	1 [9]	0 [11]	0 [10]

Fig. 1.9 Truth table and K-map for *f* (*w*, *x*, *y*, *z*) Σ (0, 2, 6, 9, 13, 15)

Four-variable K-map: Let us consider a four-variable function *f* (*w*, *x*, *y*, *z*) = Σ (0, 2, 6, 9, 13, 15)

Figure 1.9 shows the truth table and K-map for the above function. From the K-map, the adjacent squares are identified as follows:

Square (0) is adjacent to squares (4), (1), (2) and (8).

Square (8) is adjacent to squares (0), (9), (10) and (12).

Square (7) is adjacent to squares (5), (6), (3) and (15) and so on.

Now, we know how to represent Boolean function on the K-map. Minterms are marked by 1s and maxterms are marked by 0s. Once the function is plotted on the K-map, we have to group the adjacent squares of 1s or 0s in group of 2, group of 4, group of 8 and group of 16. Grouping facilitates elimination of 1, 2, 3 or 4 variables.

Group of 2 eliminates 1 variable.

Group of 4 eliminates 2 variables.

Group of 8 eliminates 3 variable and so on.

When adjacent 1s are grouped, we get the result in SOP form and when adjacent 0s are grouped, we get the result in POS form.

In order to simplify Boolean expression, we have to represent the minterms on the K-map and look for the highest group formation, and then next lower and so on. To simplify 4-variable K-map, start with group of 16, next, group of 8, next, group of 4, next group of 2 and finally individual minterms.

Prime Implicants: Any single minterm or permitted group of minterms is called an implicant of an output function. A prime implicant is a group of minterms that cannot be combined with any other minterms or groups.

Example 1.11 Simplify $Y = f(a, b, c) = \Sigma\,(0, 1, 4, 5)$

Solution A three-variable K-map is drawn as shown in Fig. 1.10.

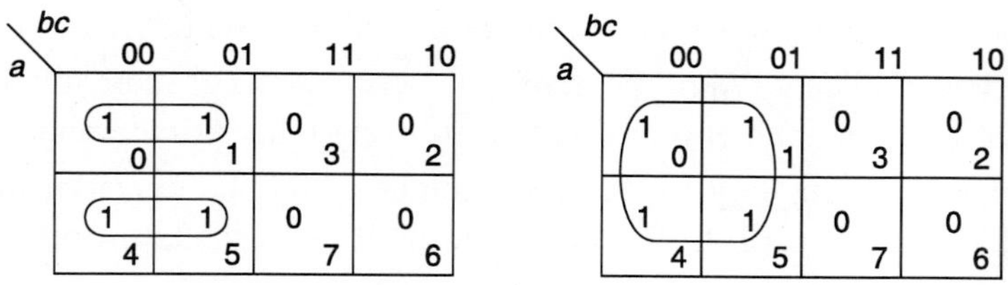

Fig. 1.10 K-maps for Σ (0, 1, 4, 5)

1s have been entered on the K-map on squares (0), (1), (4) and (5). To simplify the given equation, we have to look for logically adjacent groups. Here, squares (0) and (1) can be grouped together and squares (4) and (5) can be grouped together as shown. We observe that the two groups of two minterms each are implicants.

Also we observe each implicant (0, 1) and (4, 5), is adjacent to each other. Hence, group of four minterms is grouped together The prime implicant consists of four minterms {0, 1, 4, 5} grouped together.

For a group of four minterms, two variables get eliminated. Here, variable *a* is having both 0 and 1 in the group. Hence, *a* gets eliminated. Variable *b* has got 0 in all the minterms of the group. So, variable *b* remains as $\bar{b}$.

Variable *c* is having both 0 and 1 in the group. Hence *c* gets eliminated. So finally what remains is $\bar{b}$.

The equation $f(a, b, c) = \Sigma\,(0, 1, 4, 5)$ gets simplified to $\bar{b}$

Example 1.12 Simplify the following expression using K-map. Implement the simplified expression using the gates as indicated. $f(a, b, c, d) = \Sigma m\,(0, 1, 2, 5, 6, 7, 8, 9, 10, 13, 14, 15)$ using only NAND gates. (VTU – June 2013)

Solution

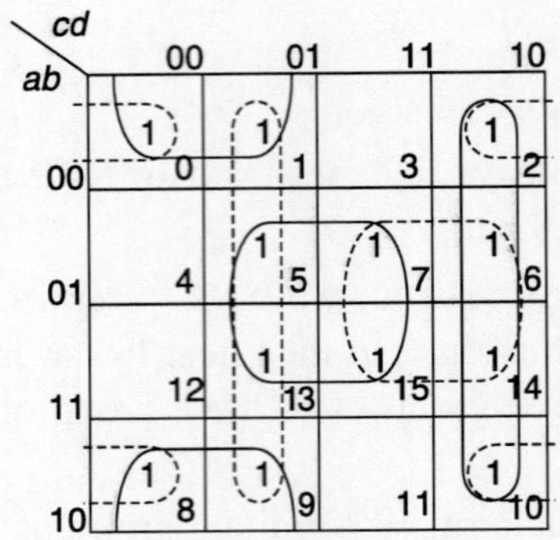

Fig. 1.11 K-map for example 1.12

From Fig. 1.11, we find that there are six prime implicants (PI), i.e., there are six groups of each of four minterms. Here, in the K-map, three prime implicants are shown in thick lines and the other three are shown in dotted lines.

The three prime implicants shown in thick lines are called essential prime implicants (EPI).

An essential prime implicant is a prime implicant in which one or more minterms are unique, that is, it contains at least one minterm not contained in any other prime implicant.

The simplified expression for $f(a, b, c, d)$ includes only the essential prime implicants {5, 7, 13, 15}, {0, 1, 8, 9} and {2, 6, 10, 14} because all of its minterms are covered by these three prime implicants.

EPI {5, 7, 13, 15} gives simplified expression bd.

EPI {0, 1, 8, 9} gives simplified expression $\bar{b}\bar{c}$.

EPI {2, 6, 10, 14} gives simplified expression $c\bar{d}$.

Final simplified expression for $f(a, b, c, d)$ is,

$$f(a, b, c, d) = bd + \bar{b}\bar{c} + c\bar{d}$$

Let us implement the simplified expression using basic gates which is shown in Fig. 1.12.

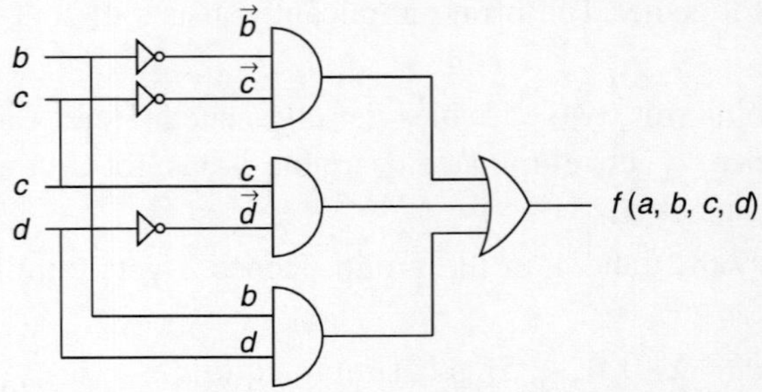

Fig. 1.12 Implementation of logic circuit using basic gates

Now, let us convert the inverters into NAND gates as well as AND-OR gates into NAND-NAND gates as shown in Fig. 1.13.

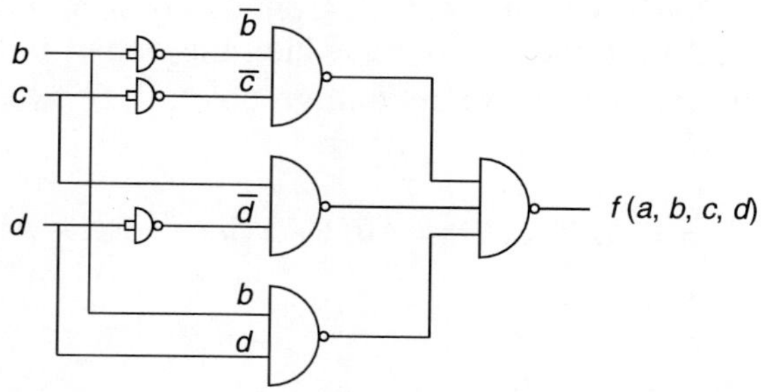

Fig. 1.13 Implementation of logic circuit using NAND gates

In this example, we observe that the three dotted groups also form as EPIs. These dotted three EPIs (they also cover the entire set of minterms) form another solution for the same problem. So, the EPIs are {0, 2, 8, 10}, {1, 5, 13, 9} and {7, 6, 15, 14} So, alternate solution for $f(a, b, c, d)$ is

$$f(a, b, c, d) = \overline{b}\,\overline{d} + \overline{c}d + bc$$

Example 1.13 Design a logic circuit that has 4 inputs, the output will only be high, when the majority of the inputs is high. Use Karnaugh map to simplify. (VTU – June 2013)

Inputs				Output
A	B	C	D	Y
0	0	0	0	0
0	0	0	1	0
0	0	1	0	0
0	0	1	1	0
0	1	0	0	0
0	1	0	1	0
0	1	1	0	0
0	1	1	1	1
1	0	0	0	0
1	0	0	1	0
1	0	1	0	0
1	0	1	1	1
1	1	0	0	0
1	1	0	1	1
1	1	1	0	1
1	1	1	1	1

Fig. 1.14 Truth table for example 1.13

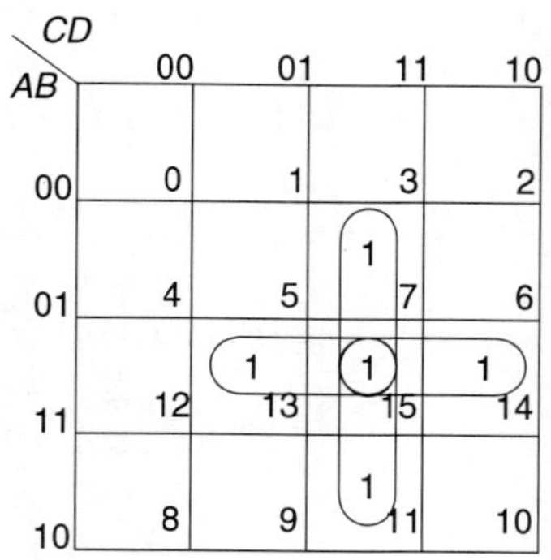

Fig. 1.15 K-map for example 1.13

Solution The truth table for the problem statement is shown in Fig. 1.14 and the K-map is shown in Fig. 1.15.

When majority of the inputs, i.e., more than 2 inputs are true, then output is true, i.e., minterms 7, 11, 13, 14 and 15 are the inputs for which the output is high. Correspondingly K-map is plotted and groups are formed. We get four groups each of two minterms.

Simplified expression is

$$Y = f(A, B, C, D) = ABD + BCD + ABC + ACD$$

Logic circuit is shown in Fig. 1.16.

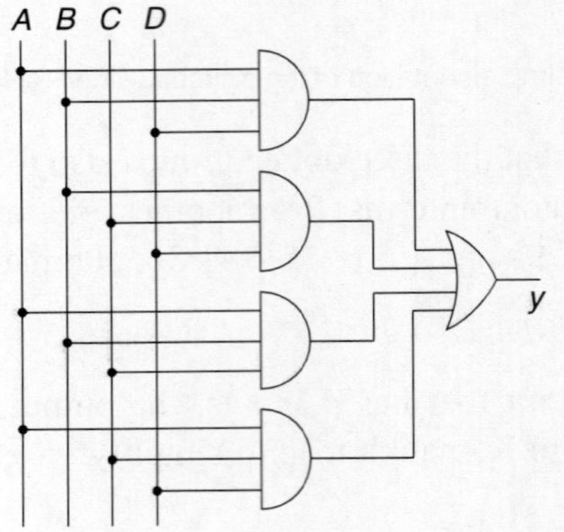

Fig. 1.16 Logic circuit for example 1.13

Example 1.14 Use a K-map to simplify the following functions:

(i) $f(A, B, C, D) = (A + B + \overline{C})(\overline{B} + \overline{D})(\overline{A} + C)(B + C)$

(ii) $f(A, B, C, D) = \pi\,(1, 2, 4, 5, 7, 8, 10, 11, 13, 14)$ (VTU – Dec 2012)

Solution (i) $f(A, B, C, D) = (A + B + \overline{C})(\overline{B} + \overline{D})(\overline{A} + C)(B + C)$

$$A + B + \overline{C} = A + B + \overline{C} + D\overline{D}$$

$$= \underset{2}{(A + B + \overline{C} + D)}\ \underset{3}{(A + B + \overline{C} + \overline{D})}$$

$$\overline{B} + \overline{D} = \overline{B} + \overline{D} + A\overline{A} + C\overline{C}$$

$$= (\overline{B} + \overline{D} + A)(\overline{B} + \overline{D} + \overline{A}) + C\overline{C}$$

$$= \underset{5}{(\overline{B} + \overline{D} + A + C)}\ \underset{7}{(\overline{B} + \overline{D} + A + \overline{C})}$$

$$\underset{13}{(\overline{B} + \overline{D} + \overline{A} + C)}\ \underset{15}{(\overline{B} + \overline{D} + \overline{A} + \overline{C})}$$

$$\bar{A} + C = \bar{A} + C + B\bar{B} + D\bar{D}$$

$$= (\bar{A} + C + B)\,(\bar{A} + C + \bar{B}) + D\bar{D}$$

$$= \underset{8}{(\bar{A} + C + B + D)}\,\underset{9}{(\bar{A} + C + B + \bar{D})}\,\underset{12}{(\bar{A} + C + \bar{B} + D)}$$

$$\underset{13}{(\bar{A} + C + \bar{B} + \bar{D})}$$

$$B + C = B + C + A\bar{A} + D\bar{D}$$

$$= (B + C + A)\,(B + C + \bar{A}) + D\bar{D}$$

$$= \underset{0}{(B + C + A + D)}\,\underset{1}{(B + C + A + \bar{D})}\,\underset{8}{(B + C + \bar{A} + D)}$$

$$\underset{9}{(B + C + \bar{A} + \bar{D})}$$

Now, rearranging and eliminating repeated terms,

$$f(A, B, C, D) = \underset{2}{(A + B + \bar{C} + D)}\,\underset{3}{(A + B + \bar{C} + \bar{D})}\,\underset{5}{(\bar{B} + \bar{D} + A + C)}$$

$$= \underset{7}{(\bar{B} + \bar{D} + A + \bar{C})}\,\underset{13}{(\bar{B} + \bar{D} + \bar{A}\,C)}\,\underset{15}{(\bar{B} + \bar{D} + \bar{A} + \bar{C})}$$

$$= \underset{8}{(\bar{A} + B + C + D)}\,\underset{9}{(\bar{A} + B + C + \bar{D})}\,\underset{12}{(\bar{A} + \bar{B} + C + D)}$$

$$= \underset{0}{(A + B + C + D)}\,\underset{1}{(A + B + C + \bar{D})}$$

$$f(A, B, C, D) = \pi\,(0, 1, 2, 3, 5, 7, 8, 9, 12, 13, 15)$$

Now K-map for the Boolean function is drawn. Since this is POS function, 0s, are grouped Alternately, POS function can be converted into SOP function. Hence, above POS function is converted into the following SOP function:

$$f(A, B, C, D) = \Sigma\,(4, 6, 10, 11)$$

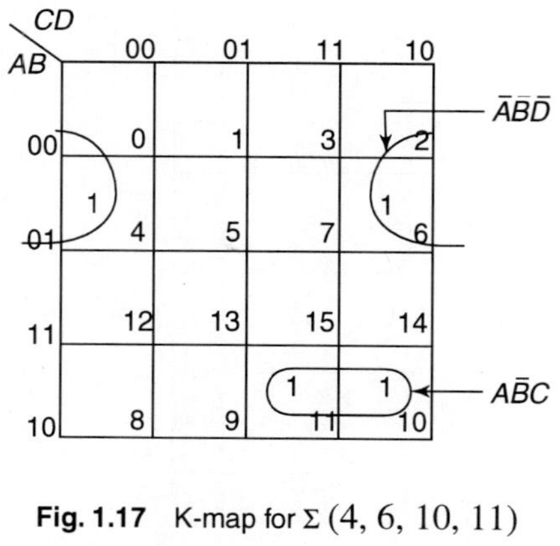

Fig. 1.17 K-map for $\Sigma\,(4, 6, 10, 11)$

The K-map is shown in Fig. 1.17. There are 2 EPIs, namely, {4, 6}, {10, 11}. All the minterms are covered by these two EPIs.

Hence, the simplified equation is

$$f(A, B, C, D) = \overline{A}B\overline{D} + A\overline{B}C$$

(ii) $$f(A, B, C, D) = \pi\,(1, 2, 4, 5, 7, 8, 10, 11, 13, 14)$$

The above POS function can be converted into SOP equation. The SOP equation is

$$f(A, B, C, D) = \Sigma\,(0, 3, 6, 9, 12, 15)$$

Now K-map is drawn for the above SOP equation as shown in Fig. 1.18.

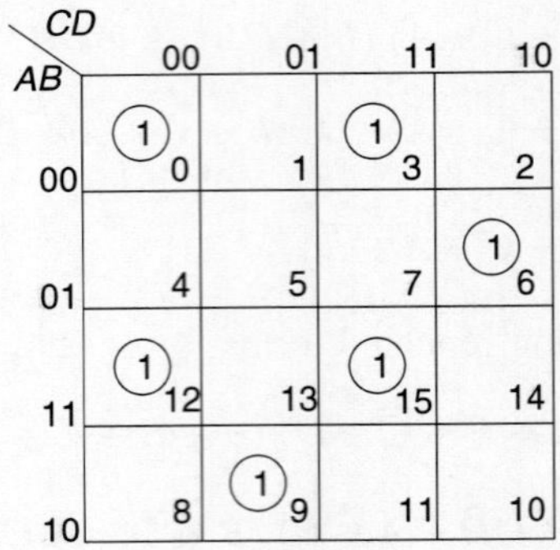

Fig. 1.18 K-map for example 1.14(ii)

From K-map it is observed that no grouping is possible. Hence,

$$f(A, B, C, D) = \overline{A}\,\overline{B}\,\overline{C}\,\overline{D} + \overline{A}\,\overline{B}CD + \overline{A}BCD + A\overline{B}\,\overline{C}D + AB\overline{C}\,\overline{D} + ABCD$$

Example 1.15 Design a three-input, one-output minimal two-level gate combinational circuit which has an output equal to 1 when majority of its inputs are at logic 1 and has an output equal to 0 when majority of its inputs are at logic 0. (VTU – Dec 2012), (VTU – Dec 2013)

Solution The truth table is constructed for the above problem as shown in Fig. 1.19 and K-map is shown in Fig. 1.20.

Inputs			Output
A	*B*	*C*	*Y*
0	0	0	0
0	0	1	0
0	1	0	0
0	1	1	1
1	0	0	0
1	0	1	1
1	1	0	1
1	1	1	1

Fig. 1.19 Truth table for example 1.15

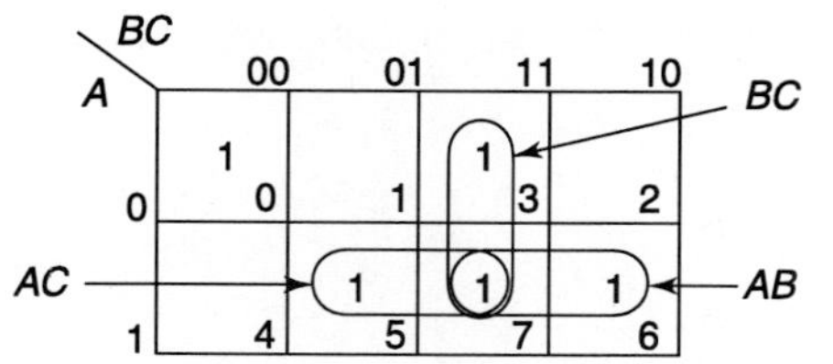

Fig. 1.20 K-map for minimal sum for solved example 1.15

From truth table, the function Y is written as

$$Y = f(A, B, C) = \Sigma (3, 5, 6, 7)$$

The simplified expression for $f(A, B, C)$ is

$$Y = f(A, B, C) = AB + BC + AC$$

The logic circuit for minimal sum implementation is shown in Fig. 1.21.

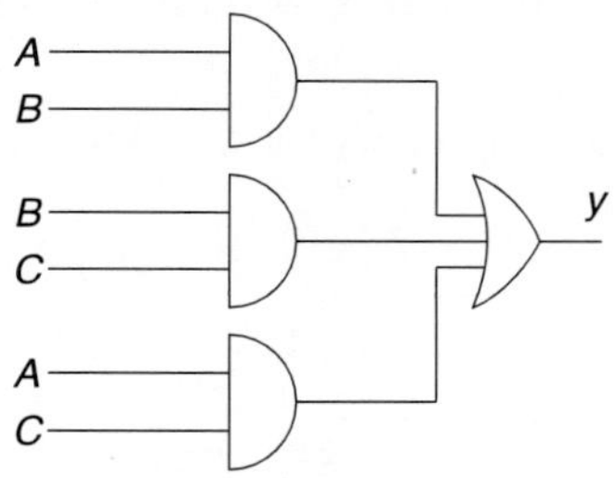

Fig. 1.21 Logic circuit implementation for minimal sum

Now, we observe that there are 3, two-input AND gates and 1, three-input OR gate. The total number of gate inputs is 9. If number of gate inputs is the criterion considered for minimal circuit, let us also consider the minimal product circuit. K-map for minimal product is shown in Fig. 1.22.

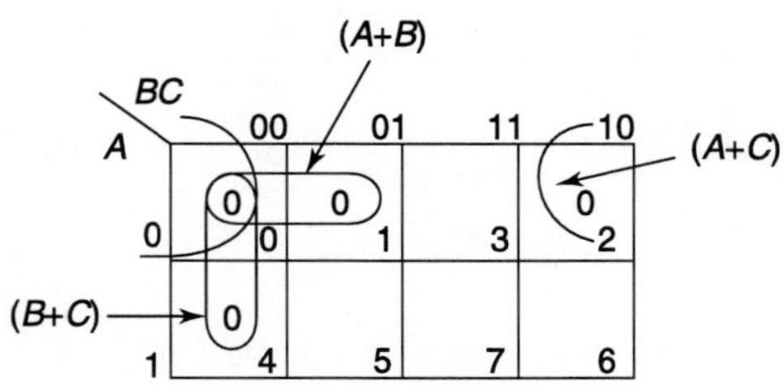

Fig. 1.22 K-map for minimal product for solved example 1.15

Minimal product is obtained by grouping 0-squares. We get three groups each of two squares having output 0. The simplified expression is written as

$$Y = f(A, B, C) = (A + B)(B + C)(A + C)$$

The logic circuit for minimal product implementation is shown in Fig. 1.23.

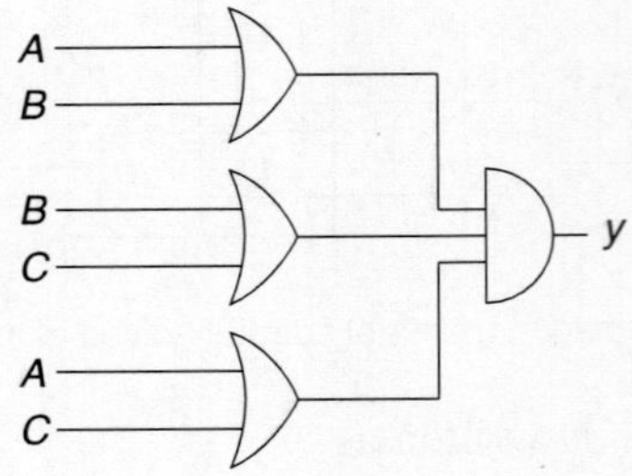

Fig. 1.23 Logic circuit implementation for minimal product

Now, we observe that there are 3, two-input OR gates and 1, three-input AND gate. The total number of gate inputs is 9.

For both minimal sum and minimal product implementation of logic circuits, the number of gate inputs is 9. Hence, either one of these will be the minimal circuit. Any one circuit will satisfy the requirement.

Example 1.16 Find the essential prime implicants for the Boolean expression by using K-map.

$$f(W, X, Y, Z) = \Sigma m\,(1, 3, 6, 7, 8, 9, 10, 12, 13, 14)$$

K-map for $f(W, X, Y, Z)$ is shown in Fig. 1.24. (VTU – Dec 2012)

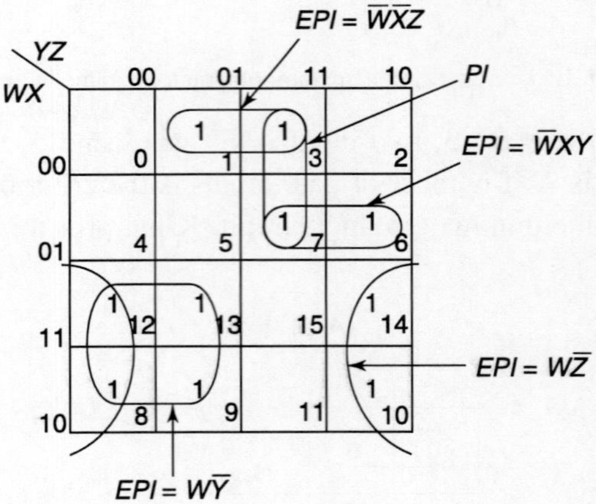

Fig. 1.24 K-map for example 1.16

Solution From the K-map, we observe that there are 4 EPIs (essential prime implicants) which cover all the minterms of the function. The simplified expression is written as:

$$f(W, X, Y, Z) = W\overline{Y} + W\overline{Z} + \overline{W}XY + \overline{W}\,\overline{X}Z$$

Example 1.17 Using K-map, determine the minimal sum of product expression and realize the simplified expression using only NAND gates.

$$f(w, x, y, z) = \pi M(0, 2, 3, 7, 8, 9, 10) \qquad \text{(VTU – Aug 2004)}$$

Solution The problem given is POS expression. Let us convert into SOP expression. We get

$$f(w, x, y, z) = \Sigma m(1, 4, 5, 6, 11, 12, 13, 14, 15)$$

Now let us draw the K-map using the minterms the K-map is shown in Fig. 1.25.

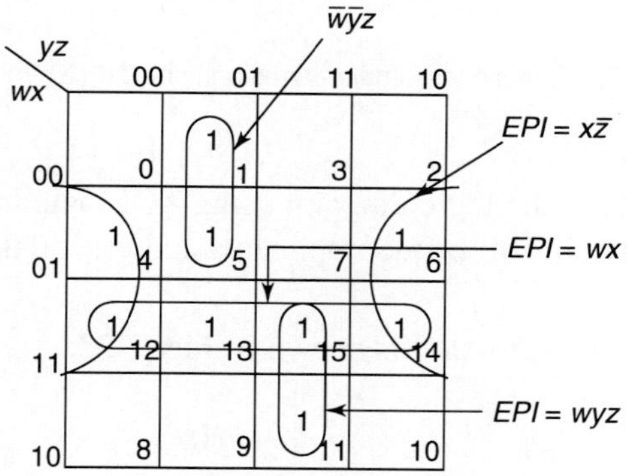

Fig. 1.25 K-map for example 1.17

The simplified expression is written as

$$f(w, x, y, z) = wx + x\bar{z} + \bar{w}\bar{y}z + wyz$$

We can implement the logic circuit for the simplified expression using basic gates.

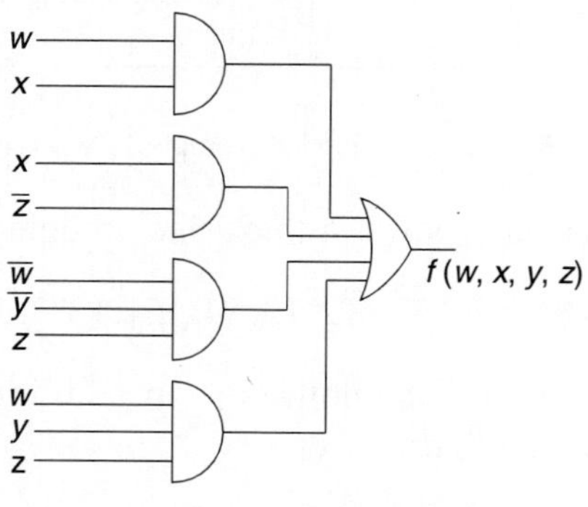

Fig. 1.26 Logic circuit using basic gates

We can implement the above logic circuit by using only NAND gates, by replacing AND-OR gates by NAND-NAND gates. Logic circuit implementation by using only NAND gates is shown in Fig. 1.27.

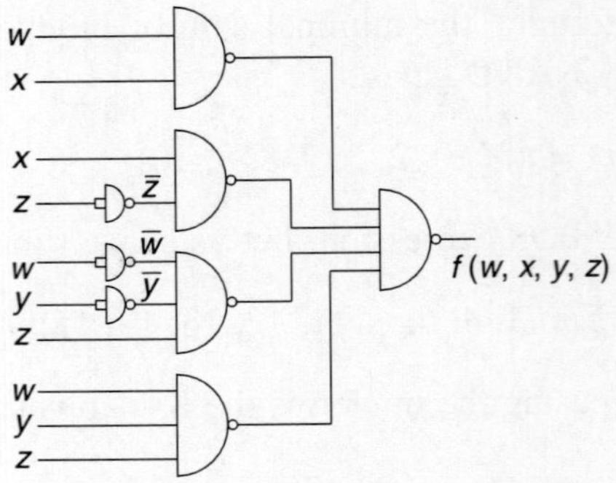

Fig. 1.27 Logic circuit implementation using NAND gates

Example 1.18 $f(a, b, c, d) = \Sigma m\ (1, 2, 3, 5, 6, 7, 11, 12, 13, 14, 15)$.

For the above expression (i) draw the logic diagram using AOI logic for minimal sum and obtain minimal sum using K-map, (ii) find all prime implicants and essential prime implicants.

(VTU – Aug 2005)

Solution K-map for the above expression is shown in Fig. 1.28.

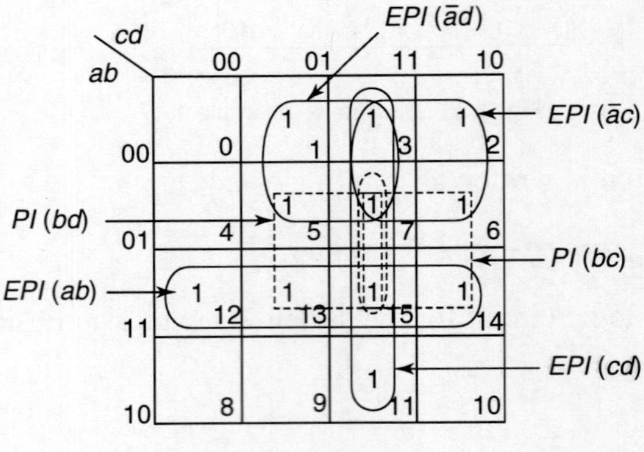

Fig. 1.28 K-map for example 1.18

The essential prime implicants are shown in thick line groupings.

$$\text{EPIs} = ab, cd, \bar{a}d, \bar{a}c\ \{12, 13, 14, 15\}, \{3, 7, 15, 11\}, \{1, 3, 5, 7\}, \{2, 3, 6, 7\}$$

Essential prime implicants are prime implicants. In addition there are two other prime implicants which are shown in dotted lines.

Hence, $\quad \text{PIs} = ab,\ cd,\ \bar{a}c,\ \bar{a}d,\ bc,\ bd$

$$\text{Minimal sum} = f(a, b, c, d) = ab + cd + \bar{a}c + \bar{a}d.$$

Logic diagram using AOI (AND, OR, INVERTER) logic is shown in Fig. 1.29.

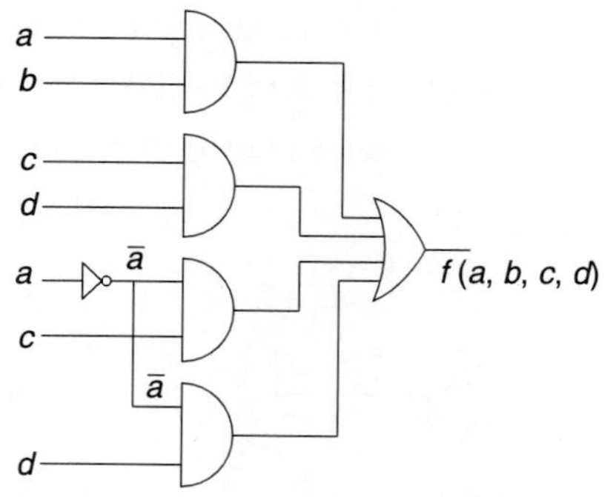

Fig. 1.29 Logic diagram for example 1.18

Example 1.19 Give sum of product and product of sum circuit for,

$$f(A, B, C, D) = \Sigma m\,(6, 8, 9, 10, 11, 12, 13, 14, 15)$$

Solution K-map for the above problem is drawn as shown in Fig. 1.30 (SOP).

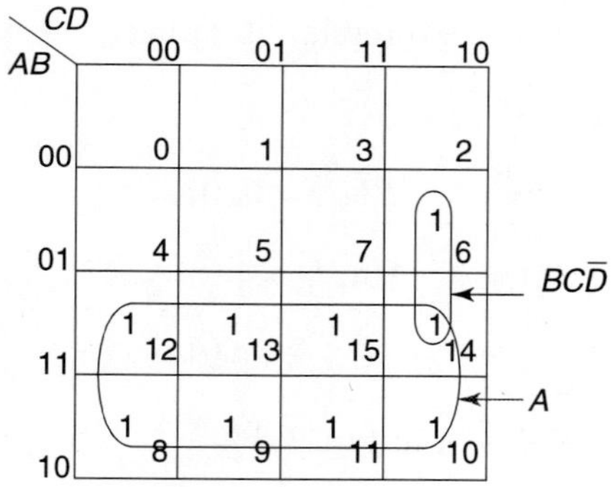

Fig. 1.30 K-map for Σ (6, 8, 9, 10, 11, 12, 13, 14, 15)

The sum of product solution is $f(A, B, C, D) = A + BC\bar{D}$. The logic circuit for SOP is shown in Fig. 1.31.

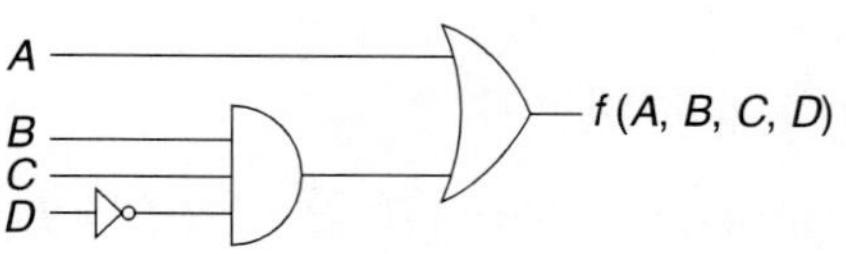

Fig. 1.31 Logic circuit for $f(A, B, C, D) = A + BC\bar{D}$

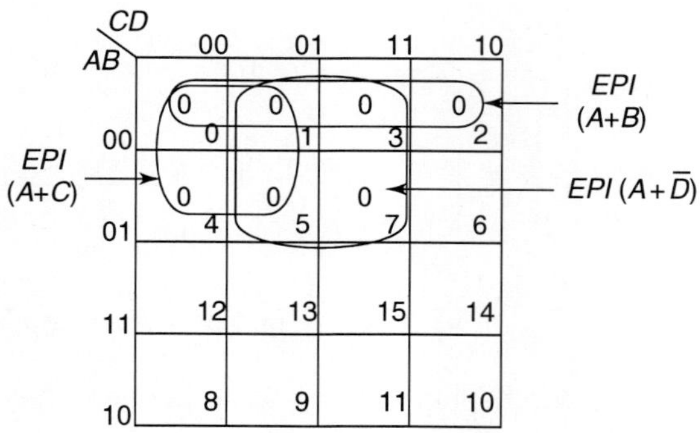

Fig. 1.32 K-map for π (0, 1, 2, 3, 4, 5, 7)

Product of sum is found out by drawing K-map using maxterms as shown in Fig. 1.32.

$$f(A, B, C, D) = (A + B)(A + C)(A + \overline{D})$$

The logic circuit for product of sum (POS) is shown in Fig. 1.33.

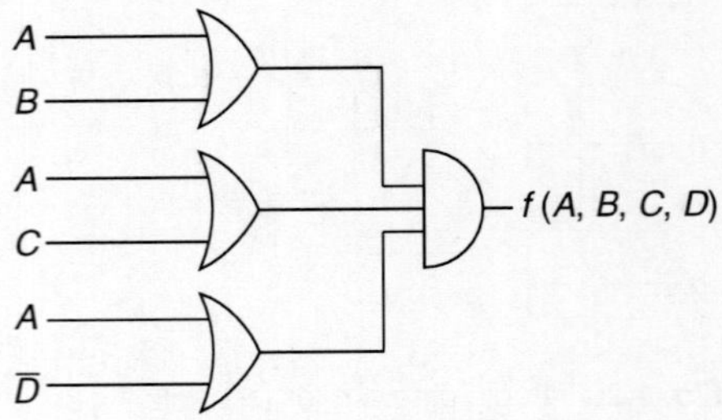

Fig. 1.33 Logic circuit for $f(A, B, C, D) = \pi\,(0, 1, 2, 3, 4, 5, 7)$

Example 1.20 Minimize the expression

$$\overline{Y} = \overline{A}B\overline{C}\,\overline{D} + \overline{A}B\overline{C}D + AB\overline{C}\,\overline{D} + AB\overline{C}D + A\overline{B}\,\overline{C}D + \overline{A}\,\overline{B}C\overline{D} \qquad \text{(VTU – Dec 2013)}$$

Solution Firstly, let us write the above expression in terms of decimal minterms. Hence,

$$\overline{Y} = \Sigma m\,(4, 5, 12, 13, 9, 2)$$

$$(\quad \overline{A}B\overline{C}\,\overline{D} = 100 = 4, \quad \overline{A}B\overline{C}D = 0101 = 5,$$

$$AB\overline{C}\,\overline{D} = 1100 = 12, AB\overline{C}D = 1101 = 13,$$

$$A\overline{B}\,\overline{C}D = 1001 = 9, \overline{A}\,\overline{B}C\overline{D} = 0010 = 2)$$

Now let us draw the K-map as shown in Fig. 1.34.

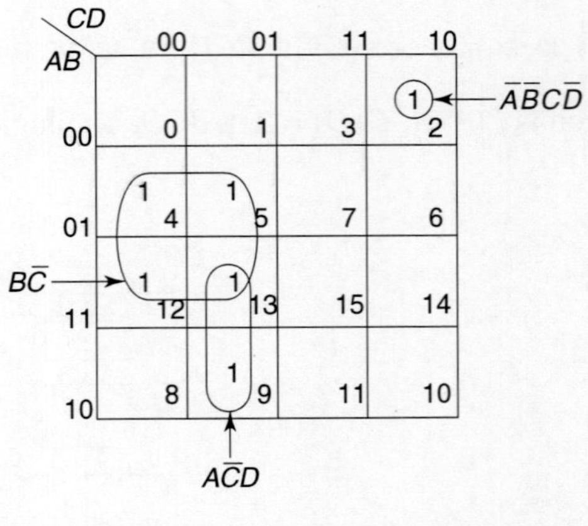

Fig. 1.34 K-map for $\overline{Y} = \Sigma m\,(4, 5, 12, 13, 9, 2)$

From the K-map, we can write the simplified expression as $\overline{Y} = \overline{A}\,\overline{B}C\overline{D} + A\overline{C}D + B\overline{C}$

Example 1.21 Simplify the function using K-map

$$Y = f(a, b, c, d) = \pi M\,(0, 4, 5, 7, 8, 9, 11, 12, 13, 15).$$

Write the simplified SOP and POS expression. (VTU – June 2012)

Solution K-map is drawn for the above expression using maxterms.

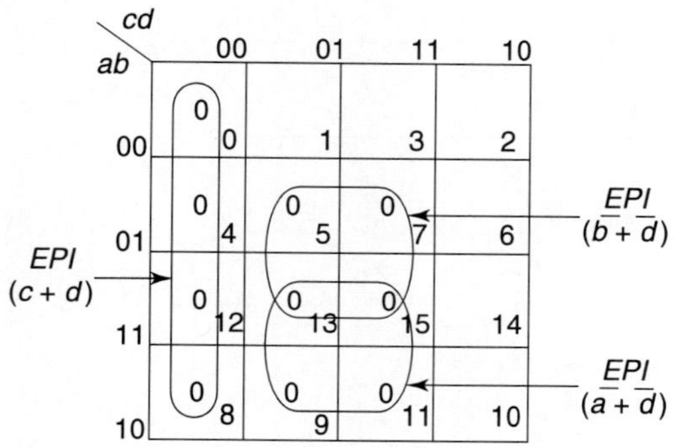

Fig. 1.35 K-map for πM (0, 4, 5, 7, 8, 9, 11, 12, 13, 15)

The simplified POS expression is

$$Y = f(a, b, c, d) = (c + d)\,(\bar{a} + \bar{d})\,(\bar{b} + \bar{d})$$

The expression is converted into SOP form.

$$Y = f(a, b, c, d) = \Sigma m\,(1, 2, 3, 6, 10, 14)$$

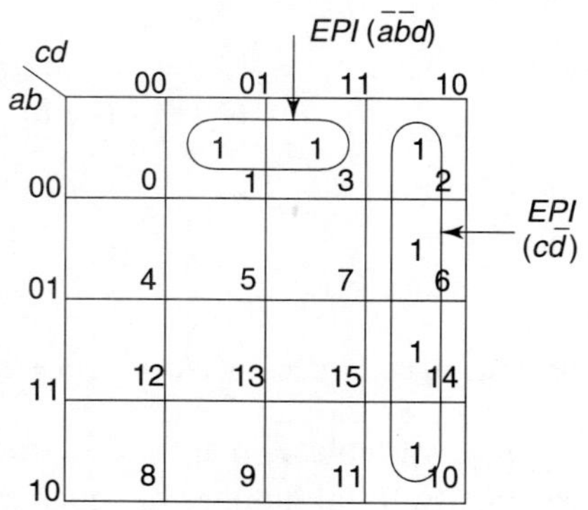

Fig. 1.36 K-map for Σm (1, 2, 3, 6, 10, 14)

The simplified SOP expression is

$$Y = f(a, b, c, d) = \bar{a}\bar{b}d + c\bar{d}$$

Example 1.22 Simplify by using K-map and realize the circuit using basic gates.

$$f(a, b, c, d) = \pi\,(2, 3, 4, 6, 7, 10, 11, 12) \qquad \text{(VTU – June 2011)}$$

Solution

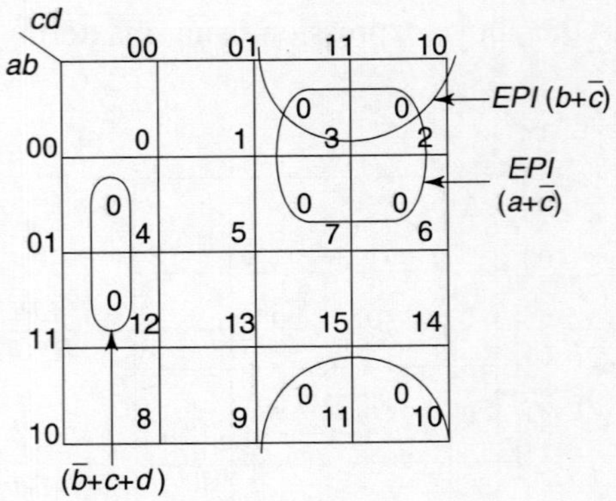

Fig. 1.37 K-map for π (2, 3, 4, 6, 7, 10, 11, 12)

From the K-map, we observe that there are three EPIs.

Hence $f(a, b, c, d) = (\bar{b} + c + d)\,(b + \bar{c})\,(a + \bar{c})$

The logic circuit is realized using basic gates as shown in Fig. 1.38.

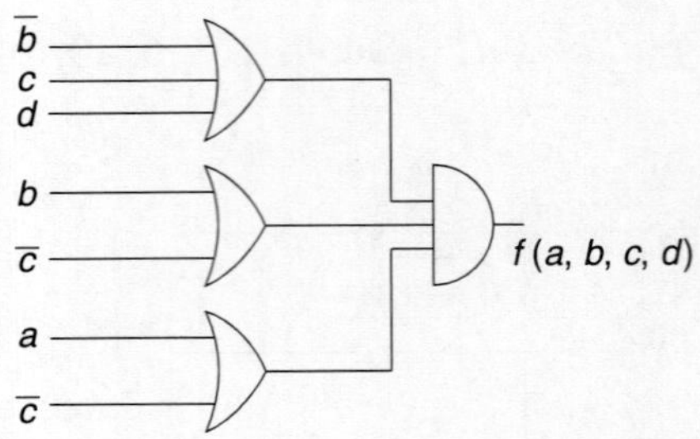

Fig. 1.38 Realization of circuit using basic gates for $f(a, b, c, d) = (\bar{b} + c + d)\,(b + \bar{c})\,(a + \bar{c})$

Five-Variable Karnaugh Map: Five-variable K-map is constructed by having two variables vertically and three variables horizontally. Total number of squares will be ($2^5 = 32$) 32. We use stacked numbering version of K-map. The general five-variable K-map is shown in Fig. 1.39. The right half of the map (squares 16 to 31) is viewed as sliding over the left half of the map. Square 0 will be below square 4. Hence, they are adjacent. Similarly, square 8 will be adjacent to 12, square 2 will be adjacent to square 6 and square 10 will be adjacent to 14 and so on.

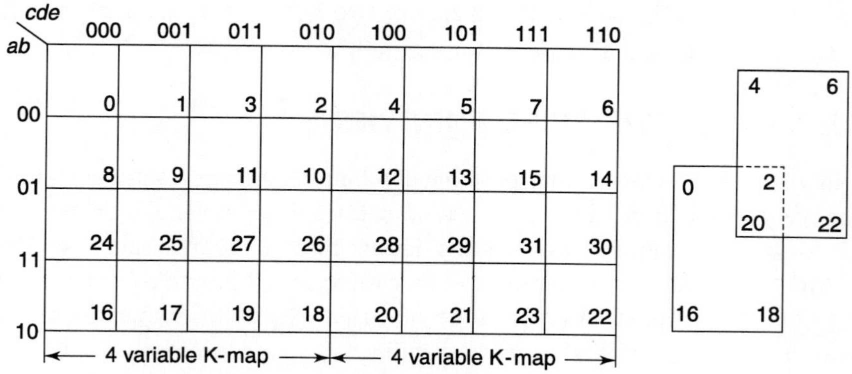

Fig. 1.39 Stacked version of five-variable K-map

Example 1.23 Simplify $f(v, w, x, y, z) = \Sigma\ (5, 7, 13, 15, 21, 23, 29, 31)$

K-map for the Boolean function is shown in Fig. 1.40.

Solution From K-map we observe that

$$f(v, w, x, y, z) = xz$$

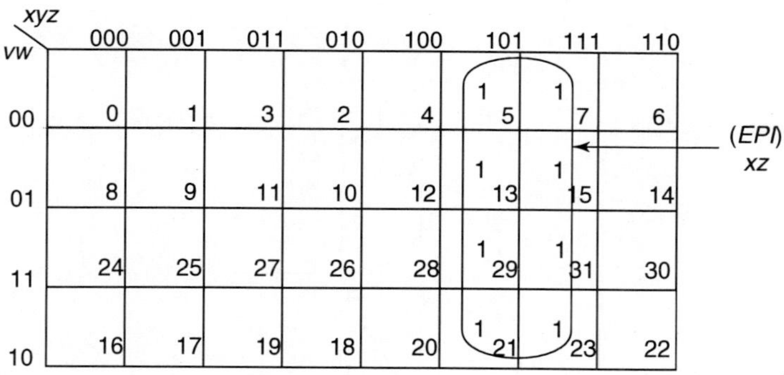

Fig. 1.40 K-map for Σ (5, 7, 13, 15, 21, 23, 29, 31)

Example 1.24 Simplify

$$f(a, b, c, d, e) = \Sigma\ (4, 5, 6, 7, 9, 11, 13, 15, 25, 27, 29, 31)$$

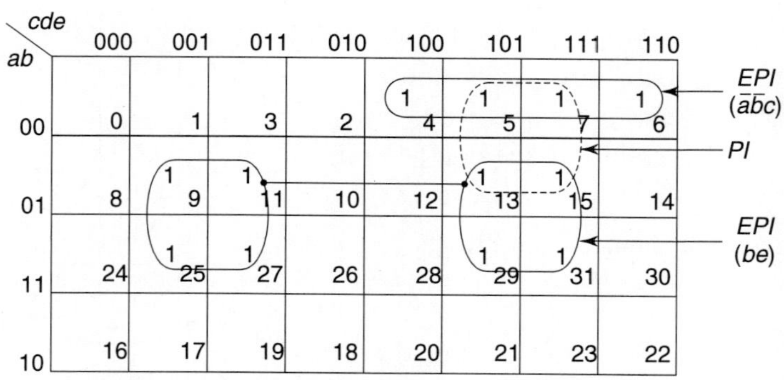

Fig. 1.41 K-map for Σ (4, 5, 6, 7, 9, 11, 13, 15, 25, 27, 29, 31)

Solution We observe form the K-map that there are two EPIs which cover all the minterms.

$$f(a, b, c, d, e) = \bar{a}\bar{b}c + bc$$

1.6 INCOMPLETELY SPECIFIED FUNCTIONS

When an output value is known for every possible combination of input variables, the function is said to be completely specified. Sometimes, all combinations of input variables cannot occur. Then output value is not known for those combinations. In this case, function is said to be incompletely specified. The truth table does not generate an output value for all possible combinations of input variables. The minterms or maxterms which are not used as part of output function are called don't-care terms. They can be used as 1 or 0 depending on our requirement.

Example 1.25 Simplify the following expression using K-map. Implement the simplified expression using basic gates.

$$f(w,x,y,z) = \Sigma m\,(2, 3, 4, 5, 13, 15) + \Sigma d\,(8, 9, 10, 11) \qquad \text{(VTU – June 2010)}$$

Solution The minterms (2, 3, 4, 5, 13, 15) are marked as 1s in K-map. The don't-care terms 8, 9, 10 and 11 are considered *d*. They will be considered 1s, so that they will be grouped along with 1s. Hence, we get better grouping to reduce the expression.

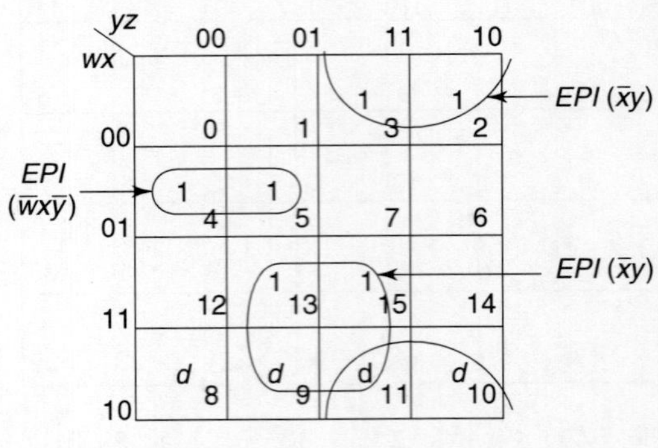

Fig. 1.42 K-map for Σm (2, 3, 4, 5, 13, 15) + Σd (8, 9, 10, 11)

The minterms (9, 11, 13, 15) are grouped as EPIs. Here, don't-care terms are combined with 1s to form groups. Similarly, don't-care terms are combined with 1s to form EPI {2, 3, 10, 11}. Square 8 is also a don't-care term. It is not used in forming groups. Hence, the necessity to reduce or simplify the expression makes don't-care terms to be used or not.

Don't-care terms alone cannot form groups. Hence, $f(wxyz) = wz + \bar{x}y + \bar{w}x\bar{y}$

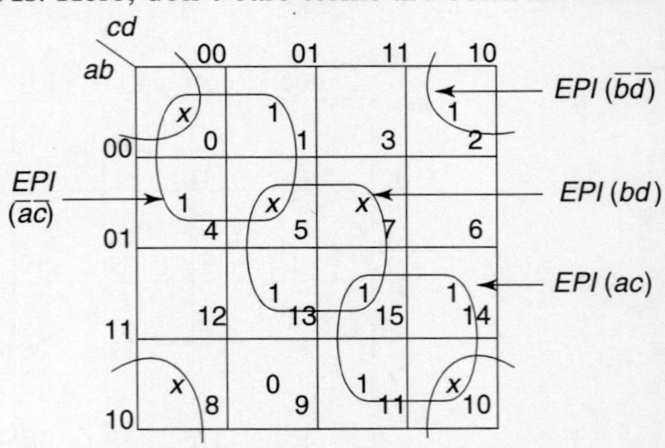

Fig. 1.43 K-map for Σm (1, 2, 4, 11, 13, 14, 15) + *dc* (0, 5, 7, 8, 10)

Example 1.26 Simplify $f(a, b, c, d)\ \Sigma m\ (1, 2, 4, 11, 13, 14, 15) + dc\ (0, 5, 7, 8, 10)$ using K-map technique. (VTU – Dec 2011)

Solution Here x is used as don't-care term as d is one of the variables. It is observed from the K-map which is shown in Fig. 1.43 that there are 4 EPIs of four minterms each. The simplified expression is

$$f(a, b, c, d) = \bar{a}\bar{c} + ac + bd + \bar{b}\bar{d}.$$

Example 1.27 Obtain a minimal SOP expression for the function $f(a, b, c, d, e) = \Sigma m\ (3, 7, 11, 12, 13, 14, 15, 16, 18) + dc\ (24, 25, 26, 27, 28, 29, 30, 31)$ using K-map method. (VTU – Dec 2011)

Solution

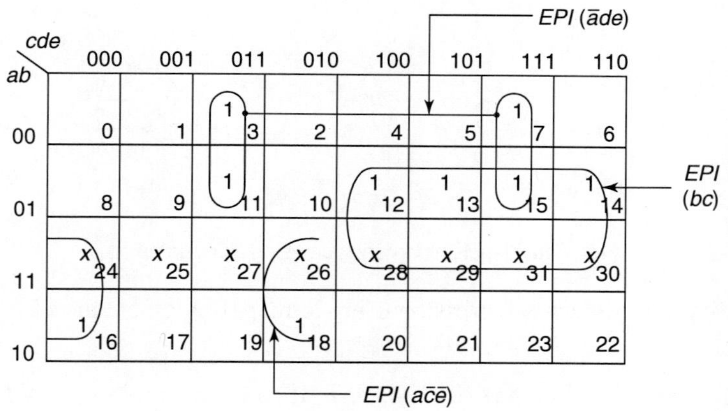

Fig. 1.44 K-map for $f(a, b, c, d, e)$

Here x is used as don't care term. 3 EPIs are formed as shown in Fig. 1.44. The simplified expression is $f(a, b, c, d) = bc + \bar{a}dc + a\bar{c}\bar{e}$.

Example 1.28 Simplify the following expression using K-map. Implement the simplified expression using the gates as indicated.

$f(A, B, C, D) = \pi M\ (0, 3, 4, 7, 8, 10, 12, 14) + \Sigma d\ (2, 6)$ using only NOR gates. (VTU – June 2013), (VTU – Dec 2013)

Solution

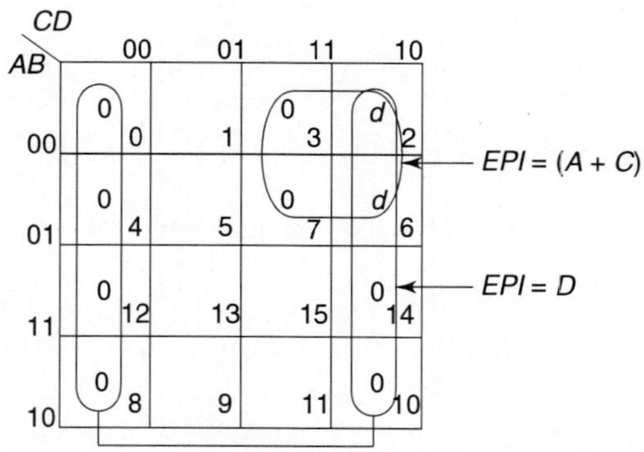

Fig. 1.45 K-map for $\pi M\ (0, 3, 4, 7, 8, 10, 12, 14)$

From the K-map, we observe that there are two EPIs. Hence, the simplified expression is

$$f(A, B, C, D) = D(A + \overline{C})$$

First, let us implement the above expression using basic gates as shown in Fig. 1.46.

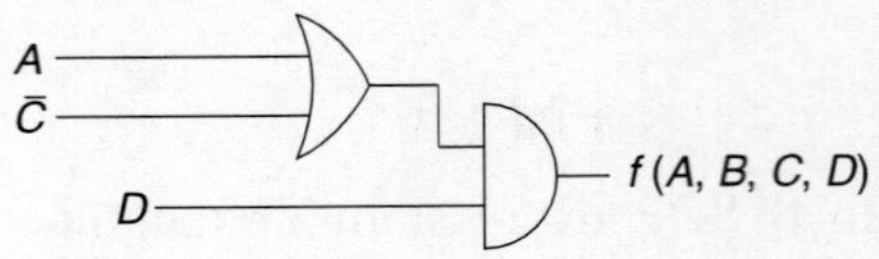

For conversion to NOR gates, put a bubble on the output of OR gates and on the inputs of AND gate.

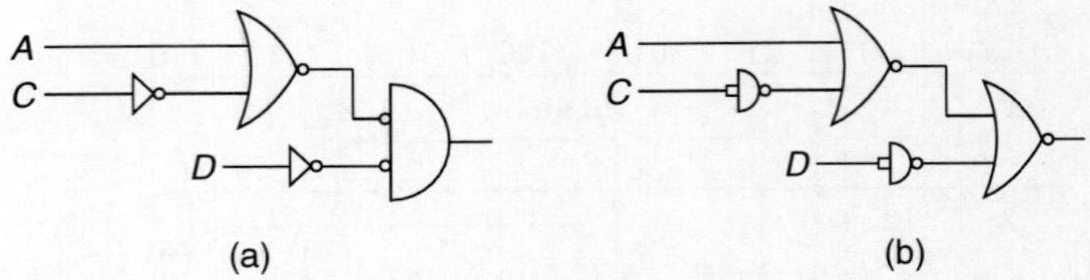

Fig. 1.46 Final implementation using NOR gates

Example 1.29 Simplify the following expression using K-map. Implement the simplified expression using basic gates.

$$f(a, b, c, d) = \pi M(2, 3, 4, 6, 7, 10, 11, 12)$$ (VTU – June 2010) (VTU – June 2011)

Solution

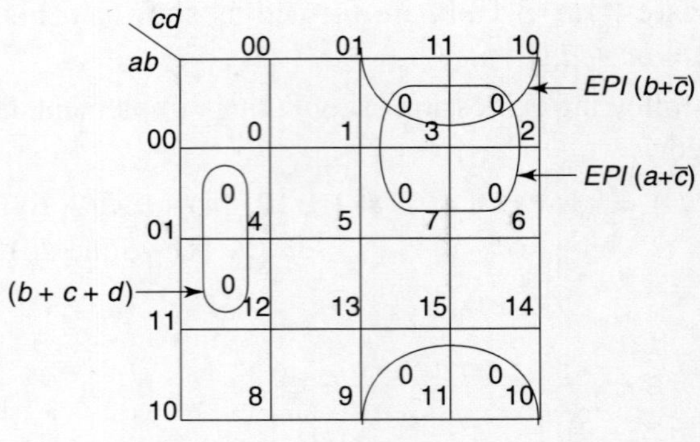

Fig. 1.47 K-map for πM (2, 3, 4, 6, 7, 10, 11, 12)

Solution K-map is drawn with maxterm 0s as shown in Fig. 1.47.

The simplified expression is

$$f(a, b, c, d) = (\overline{b} + c + d)(b + \overline{c})(a + \overline{c})$$

Example 1.30 Find all the minimal sums and minimal products for the following incomplete Boolean functions using K-maps.

$$f(a, b, c, d) = \pi\,(1, 2, 3, 4, 9, 10) + \pi d\,(0, 14, 15)$$

Solution Karnaugh map is constructed for the above function using the maxterms.

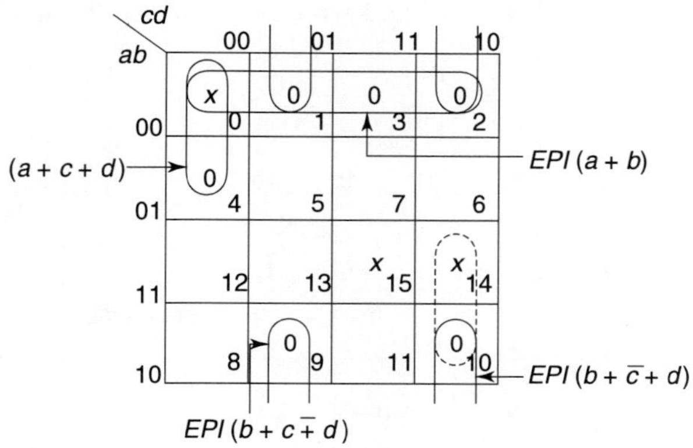

Fig. 1.48 K-map for π (1, 2, 3, 4, 9, 10) + πd (0, 14, 15)

Minimal product is $(a + b)(a + c + d)(b + c + \bar{d})(b + \bar{c} + d)$.

Now let us construct K-map for minimal sum using 1s.

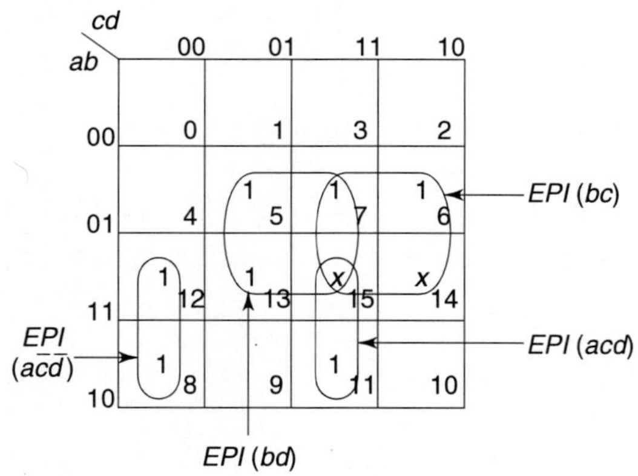

Fig. 1.49 K-map for Σ (5, 6, 7, 8, 11, 12, 13) + d (0, 14, 15)

There are 4 EPIs. Hence, minimal sum is

$$f(a, b, c, d) = bc + bd + acd + a\bar{c}\bar{d}$$

K-maps for minimal product and minimal sum are shown in Fig. 1.48 and Fig. 1.49.

1.7 SIMPLIFYING MAXTERM EQUATIONS

The procedure for simplifying maxterm equations is similar to the procedure for simplifying minterms except that instead of 1s, 0s are loaded into the map and grouped to form PIs. Reading the map is different which will be shown in the examples.

Example 1.31 Simplify $f(a, b, c, d) = \pi\ (0, 4, 5, 7, 8, 9, 11, 12, 13, 15)$

K-map is constructed as shown in Fig. 1.50 and we observe that there are three EPIs. Each one of them is four variable maxterm.

Solution

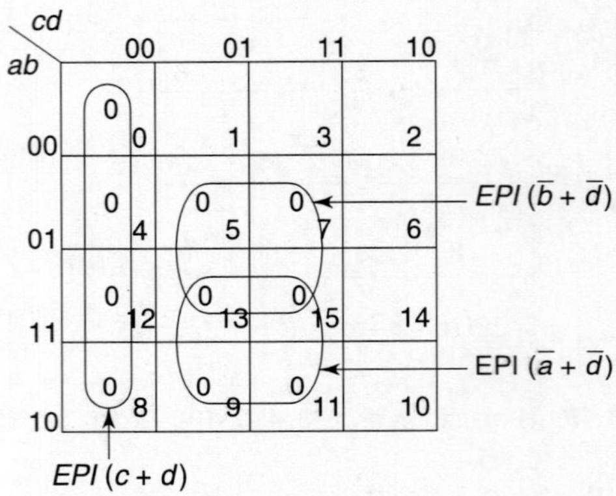

Fig. 1.50 K-map for π (0, 4, 5, 7, 8, 9, 11, 12, 13, 15)

There are three EPIs {0, 4, 12, 8}, {9, 11, 13, 15} and {5, 7, 13, 15}.

The simplified expression is

$$f(a, b, c, d) = (c + d)\ (\bar{a} + \bar{d})\ (\bar{b} + \bar{d})$$

Example 1.32 Simplify $f(w, x, y, z) = \pi\ (0, 2, 6, 11, 13, 15) + \pi d\ (1, 9, 10, 14)$

Solution K-map is constructed for the above Boolean function as shown in Fig. 1.51.

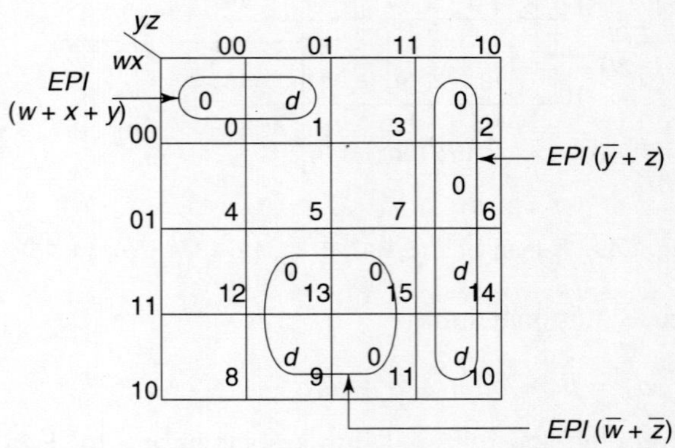

Fig. 1.51 K-map for π (0, 2, 6, 11, 13, 15) + πd (1, 9, 10, 14)

There are three EPIs. The simplified expression is

$$f(w, x, y, z) = (w + x + y)(\overline{w} + \overline{z})(\overline{y} + z)$$

Example 1.33 Write down all the minimal sums and minimal products of the following incomplete function using K-maps.

$$f(a, b, c, d) = \pi\,(0, 3, 4, 11, 13) + \pi d\,(2, 6, 8, 9, 10)$$

Solution Minimal product is obtained by entering 0s in K-map and grouping them as shown in Fig. 1.52.

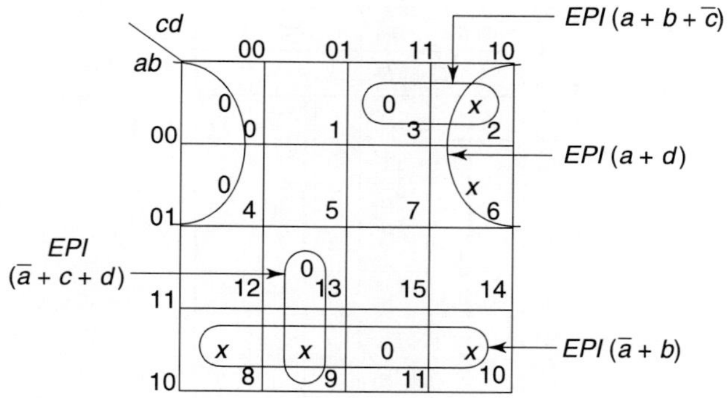

Fig. 1.52 K-map for π (0, 3, 4, 11, 13) + πd (2, 6, 8, 9, 10)

Minimal product of $f(a, b, c, d)$

$$= (\overline{a} + c + \overline{d})(a + b + \overline{c})(a + d)(\overline{a} + b)$$

Minimal sum is obtained by entering 1s in K-map and grouping them as shown in Fig. 1.53.

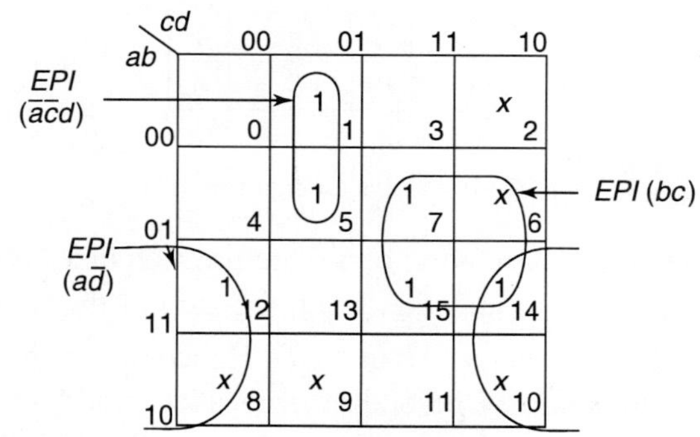

Fig. 1.53 K-map for minimal sum of π (0, 3, 4, 11, 13) + πd (2, 6, 8, 9, 10)

Minimal sum of $f(a, b, c, d)$

$$= bc + a\overline{d} + \overline{a}\overline{c}d$$

Example 1.34 Develop a truth table for a system which accepts two 2-bit binary numbers and generates three outputs. The first output indicates when the 2 numbers differ by 2 or more, the second output indicates when the 2 numbers are identical and the third output indicates when the first number exceeds the second number.

Solution There are two 2-bit numbers as inputs. Hence, there are four inputs. Let us say the inputs as *A*, *B*, *C*, *D* and *AB* will be the first two-bit number and *CD* will be the second two-bit number. There are three outputs which we may call *X*, *Y*, *Z*. *X* is the output when *AB* and *CD* differ by 2 or more. *Y* is the output when *AB* and *CD* are identical and *Z* is the output when the *AB* exceeds *CD*. The truth table is constructed as shown in Fig. 1.54.

Inputs				Outputs		
A	*B*	*C*	*D*	*X*	*Y*	*Z*
0	0	0	0	0	1	0
0	0	0	1	0	0	0
0	0	1	0	1	0	0
0	0	1	1	1	0	0
0	1	0	0	0	0	1
0	1	0	1	0	1	0
0	1	1	0	0	0	0
0	1	1	1	1	0	0
1	0	0	0	1	0	1
1	0	0	1	0	0	1
1	0	1	0	0	1	0
1	0	1	1	0	0	0
1	1	0	0	1	0	1
1	1	0	1	1	0	1
1	1	1	0	0	0	1
1	1	1	1	0	1	0

Fig. 1.54 Truth table for example 1.34

Example 1.35 Give the truth table representation of a system which takes two 2-bit binary numbers as its inputs and generates an output to indicate, when the sum of the two numbers is odd.

Let us take two 2-bit binary numbers as *AB* and *CD*. Hence, there are four inputs. *A*, *B*, *C*, *D*. The sum of these two 2-bit numbers may be odd or even. If it is odd, the output is indicated as 1. Let us call the output as *Y*. For example, let *AB* be 01 and *CD* be 11. The sum will be $01^{(1)}$ + $11^{(3)} = 100^{(4)}$. The output is not odd. So the output *Y* is 0. The truth table is constructed as shown in Fig. 1.55.

Inputs				Output
A	B	C	D	Y
0	0	0	0	0
0	0	0	1	1
0	0	1	0	0
0	0	1	1	1
0	1	0	0	1
0	1	0	1	0
0	1	1	0	1
0	1	1	1	0
1	0	0	0	0
1	0	0	1	1
1	0	1	0	0
1	0	1	1	1
1	1	0	0	1
1	1	0	1	0
1	1	1	0	1
1	1	1	1	0

Fig. 1.55 Truth table for example 1.35

Example 1.36 Convert the given expression into proper canonical form

$$F(A, B, C) = A + ABC$$

In the first term, B and C are missing. Hence, we have to AND product term with (missing terms + their complements)

Hence, $F(A, B, C) = A(B + \overline{B})(C + \overline{C}) + ABC$

$$= ABC + AB\overline{C} + A\overline{B}C + A\overline{B}\,\overline{C} + ABC$$

Eliminating repeated product terms, we get

$F(A, B, C) = ABC + AB\overline{C} + A\overline{B}C + A\overline{B}\,\overline{C}$

Example 1.37 Convert the given expression into proper canonical form.

$F(A, B, C) = (A + B)(B + C)(A + C)$

We will find the missing literal in each sum term. We have to OR the sum term with (missing literal * its complement)

$\therefore \quad F(A, B, C) = (A + B) + (C \cdot \overline{C})(B + C) + (A \cdot \overline{A})(A + C) + (B + \overline{B})$

Since $A + BC = (A + B)(A + C)$, the above expression may be rewritten as

$F(A, B, C) = (A + B + C)(A + B + \overline{C})(B + C + A)(B + C + \overline{A})(A + C + B)$
$(A + C + \overline{B})$

Eliminating repeated sum terms such as $(A + B + C)$,

we have $F(A, B, C) = (A + B + C)(A + B + \overline{C})(\overline{A} + B + C)(A + \overline{B} + C)$

Example 1.38 Simplify $f(A, B, C, D) = \Sigma(0, 1, 2, 3, 10, 11, 12, 13, 14, 15)$

Using K-map

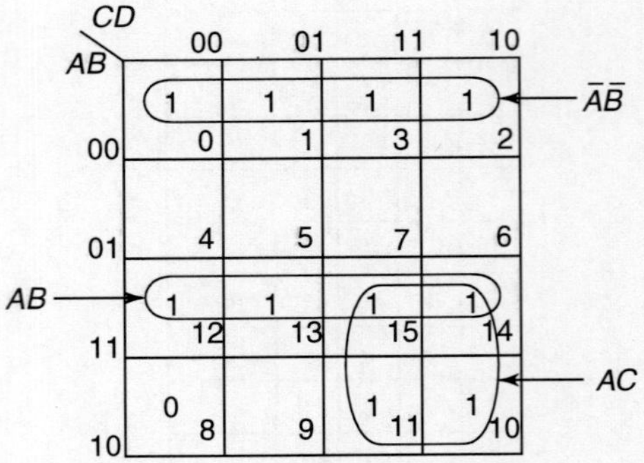

Fig. 1.56 K-map for example 1.38

K-map is constructed for the above function as shown in Fig. 1.56. The grouping is done as shown.

From K-map, it is seen that there are three prime implicants $\overline{A}\,\overline{B}$, AB & AC.

Hence, the simplified expression is

$f(A, B, C, D) = \overline{A}\,\overline{B} + AB + AC.$

Example 1.39 Find all the prime implicants of the function

$f(a, b, c, d) = \Sigma(7, 9, 12, 13, 14, 15) + \Sigma d(4, 11)$

K-map is constructed for the above function as shown in Fig. 1.57.

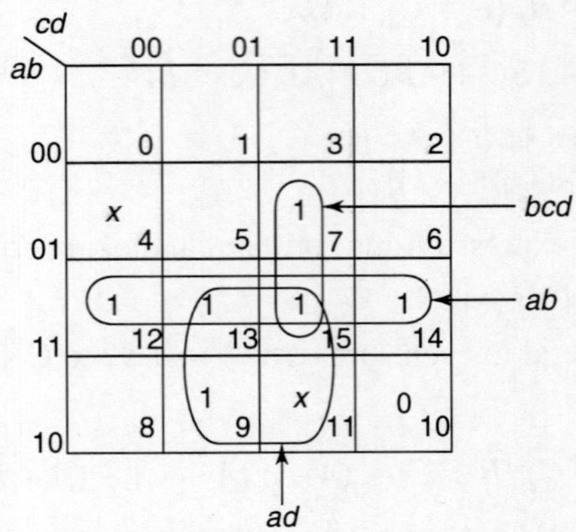

Fig. 1.57 K-map for example 1.39

The grouping is done including don't-care terms. The prime implicants are shown in Figure.

The prime implicants of the function $f(a, b, c, d)$ are ab, ad and bcd.

Example 1.40 Find minimal sum and minimal product for the following function using K-map. $f(a, b, c, d)\ \Sigma m(6, 7, 9, 10, 13) + d_c(1, 4, 5, 11, 15)$

$$f(a, b, c, d) = \Sigma m(6, 7, 9, 10, 13) + d_c(1, 4, 5, 11, 15)$$

K-map for minimal sum (SOP) form is constructed as shown in Fig. 1.58. The grouping is done using minterms and don't-care terms.

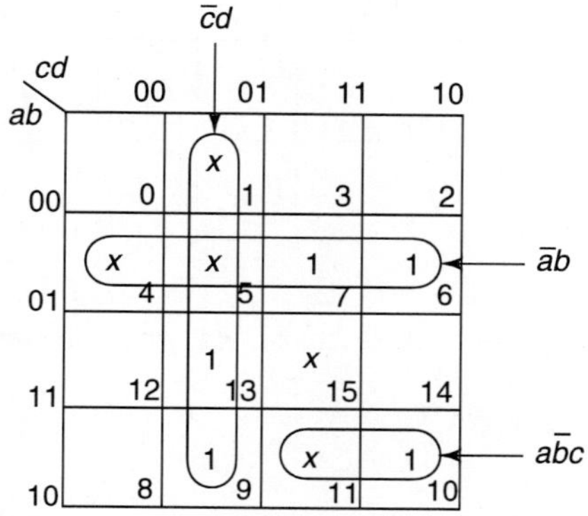

Fig. 1.58 K-map for minimal sum for example 1.40

Minimal sum = $\bar{a}b + \bar{c}d + a\bar{b}c$

K-map for minimal product (POS) form is constructed as shown in Fig. 1.59. The grouping is done using maxterms and don't-care terms.

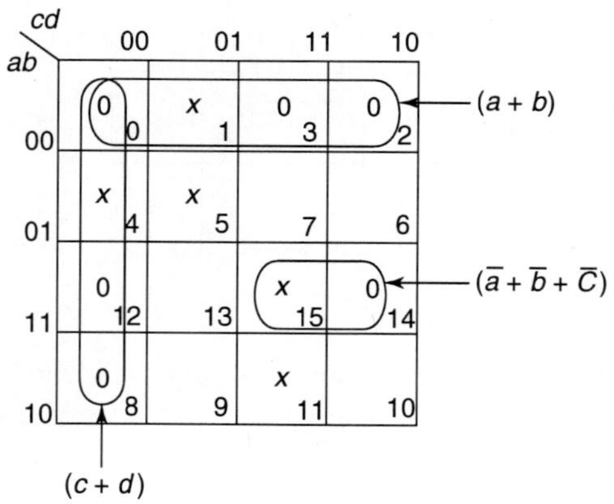

Fig. 1.59 K-map for minimal product for example 1.40.

Minimal product = $(a + b)\ (c + d)\ (\bar{a} + \bar{b} + \bar{c})$

Example 1.41 Using K-maps, determine the minimal sums and minimal products for $f(w, x, y, z) = \Sigma m(0, 1, 3, 7, 8, 12) + d_c(5, 10, 13, 14)$. Is your answer unique?

$$f(w, x, y, z) = \Sigma m(0, 1, 3, 7, 8, 12) + d_c(5, 10, 13, 14)$$

K-map is constructed using minterms and don't-care terms. Grouping is done as shown in Fig. 1.60.

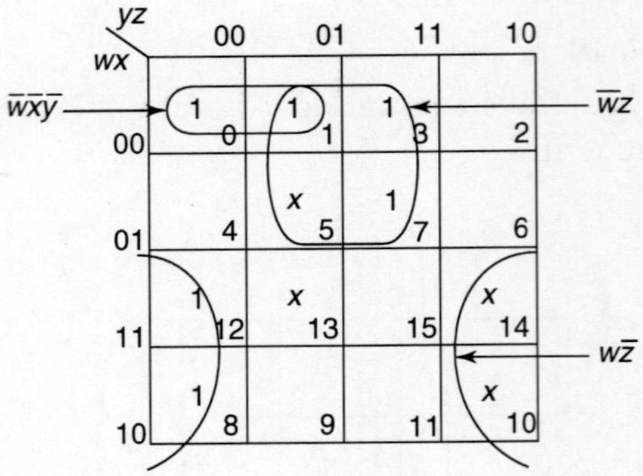

Fig. 1.60 K-map for example 1.41 using minterms.

Hence, $f(w, x, y, z) = \overline{w}z + w\overline{z} + \overline{w}\,\overline{x}\,\overline{y}$

This is SOP form.

In order to get minimal product, we have to use maxterms and don't-care terms. Grouping is done as shown in Fig. 1.61.

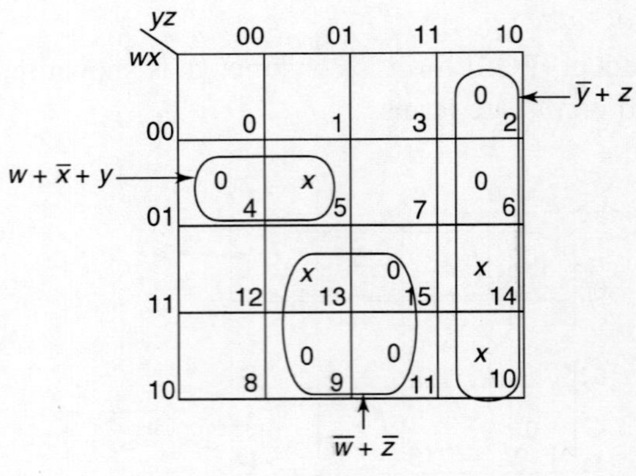

Fig. 1.61 K-map for example 1.41 using maxterms.

Hence, using maxterms, we get

$f(w, x, y, z) = (w + \overline{x} + y)\,(\overline{w} + \overline{z})\,(\overline{y} + z)$

This is in POS form. (or)

Alternately, we can use 0s as 1s and get a solution and complement it to get POS solution.

$\overline{f} = \overline{w}x\overline{y} + wz + y\overline{z}$

Complementing it

$$f = \overline{\overline{f}} = \overline{\overline{w}x\overline{y} + wz + y\overline{z}}$$

$$= (\overline{wx\overline{y}})\ (\overline{wz})\ (\overline{y\overline{z}})$$

$$= (\overline{w} + \overline{x} + y)\ (\overline{w} + \overline{z})\ (\overline{y} + z) \text{ (POS form)}$$

The answer is unique.

Example 1.42 Show that $A \odot B \odot C \odot D$

$$= \Sigma m(0, 3, 5, 6, 9, 10, 12, 15)$$

The given function is $\Sigma m(0, 3, 5, 6, 9, 10, 12, 15)$

Let us construct the K-map using the minterms. K-map is shown in Fig. 1.62.

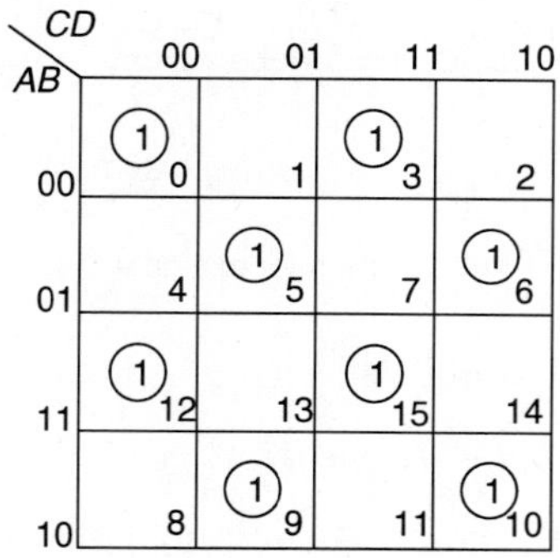

Fig. 1.62 K-map for example 1.42

From K-map, we see that there is no group that can be formed.

Hence, we get the function

$$f = \Sigma m(0, 3, 5, 6, 9, 10, 12, 15)$$

$$= \overline{A}\,\overline{B}\,\overline{C}\,\overline{D} + \overline{A}\,\overline{B}CD + \overline{A}B\overline{C}D + \overline{A}BC\overline{D} + AB\overline{C}\,\overline{D} + ABCD + A\overline{B}\,\overline{C}D + A\overline{B}C\overline{D}$$

$$= \overline{A}\,\overline{B}(\overline{C}\,\overline{D} + CD) + \overline{A}B(\overline{C}D + C\overline{D}) + AB(\overline{C}\,\overline{D} + CD) + A\overline{B}(\overline{C}D + C\overline{D})$$

$$= (\overline{A}\,\overline{B} + AB)\ (\overline{C}\,\overline{D} + CD) + (\overline{A}B + A\overline{B})\ (\overline{C}D + C\overline{D})$$

$$= (A \odot B)\ (C \odot D) + \overline{A \odot B}\ (\overline{C \odot D})$$

$$= A \odot B \odot C \odot D$$

Hence, it is proved that

$$A \odot B \odot C \odot D = \Sigma m(0, 3, 5, 6, 9, 10, 12, 15)$$

Example 1.43 Simplify the given function using K-map $\Sigma m(0, 2, 3, 10, 11, 12, 13, 16, 17, 18, 19, 20, 21, 26, 27)$.

Solution This is five variable function. The K-map for the Boolean function is shown in Fig. 1.63. Let the function be $f(a, b, c, d, e)$

$$f(a, b, c, d, e) = \Sigma m(0, 2, 3, 10, 11, 12, 13, 16, 17, 18, 19, 20, 21, 26, 27)$$

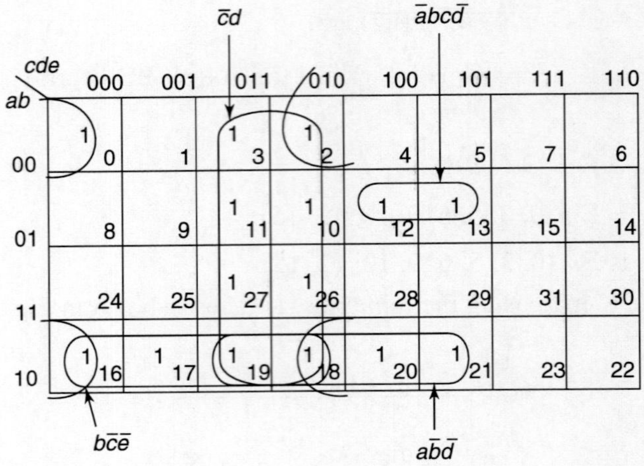

Fig. 1.63 K-map for example 1.43.

The grouping is done as shown in Fig. 1.63.

Hence, $f(a, b, c, d, e) = \bar{c}d + a\bar{b}\bar{d} + b\bar{c}\bar{e} + \bar{a}bc\bar{d}$.

Example 1.44 Design a three-input, one-output minimal two-level gate combinational circuit which has an output equal to 1 when majority of its inputs are at logic 1 and has an output equal to 0 when majority of its inputs are at logic 0. (VTU – June 2014)

Solution: Let the three inputs be A, B and C and the output be Y. Let us make a table consisting of all combinations of inputs and output. The table is shown in Fig. 1.64.

Inputs			Output
A	*B*	*C*	*Y*
0	0	0	0
0	0	1	0
0	1	0	0
0	1	1	1
1	0	0	0
1	0	1	1
1	1	0	1
1	1	1	1

Fig. 1.64 Input/output table for example 1.44

The K-map for minimal sum is shown in Fig. 1.65.

$$f(A, B, C) = AB + BC + CA$$

The two-level minimal sum implementation is shown in Fig. 1.66.

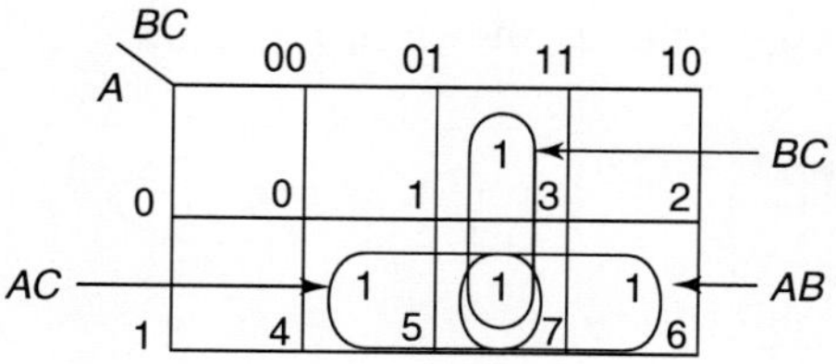

Fig. 1.65 K-map for minimal sum for example 1.44.

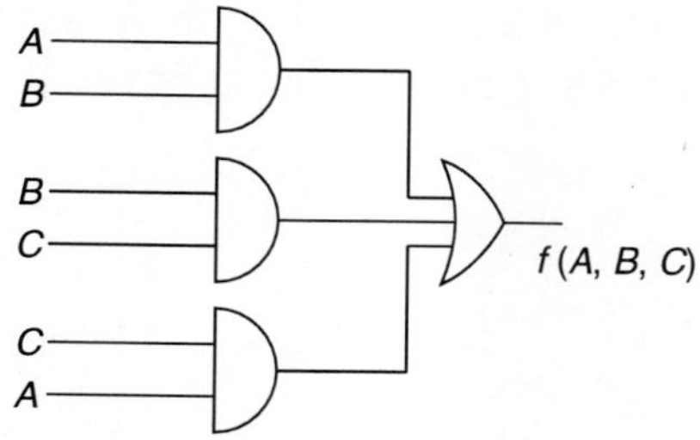

Fig. 1.66 Two-level minimal sum implementation for example 1.44.

The K-map for minimal product is shown in Fig. 1.67.

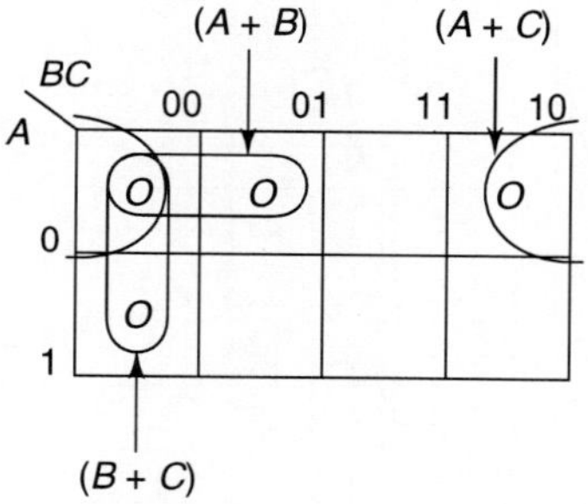

Fig. 1.67 K-map for minimal product for example 1.44.

From K-map it is seen that

$$f(A, B, C) = (A + B)\ (B + C)\ (C + A)$$

The two-level minimal product implementation is shown in Fig. 1.68.

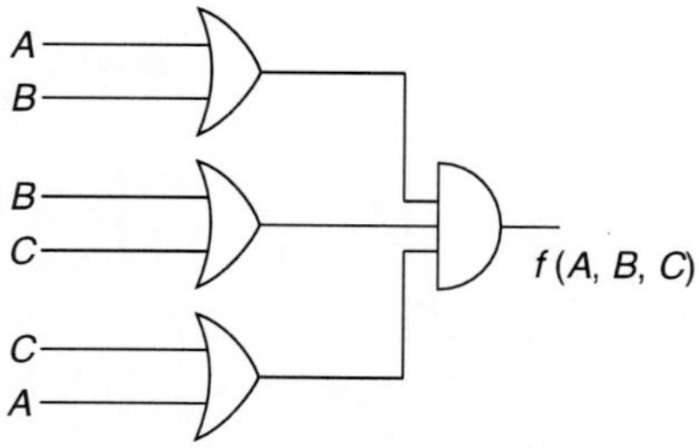

Fig. 1.68 Two level minimal product implementation for example 1.44.

Example 1.45 $A_8A_4A_2A_1$ is an 8421 *BCD* input to a logic circuit whose output is a 1 when $A_8 = 0$, $A_4 = 0$ and $A_2 = 1$ or when $A_8 = 0$ and $A_4 = 1$. Design the simplest possible logic circuit. (VTU – June 2014)

There are 4 inputs which give 16 different input combinations. A table is constructed using the 16 different input combinations and the corresponding output as shown in Fig. 1.69.

Inputs				Output
A_8	A_4	A_2	A_1	Y
0	0	0	0	0
0	0	0	1	0
0	0	1	0	1
0	0	1	1	1
0	1	0	0	1
0	1	0	1	1
0	1	1	0	1
0	1	1	1	1
1	0	0	0	0
1	0	0	1	0
1	0	1	0	0
1	0	1	1	0
1	1	0	0	0
1	1	0	1	0
1	1	1	0	0
1	1	1	1	0

Fig. 1.69 Input/output table for example 1.45

From the input/output table let us construct K-map as shown in Fig. 1.70. First let us construct K-map for minimal sum.

We find from the K-map for minimal sum that $Y = f(A_8, A_4, A_2, A_1) = \overline{A}_8\, A_2 + \overline{A}_8\, A_4$.

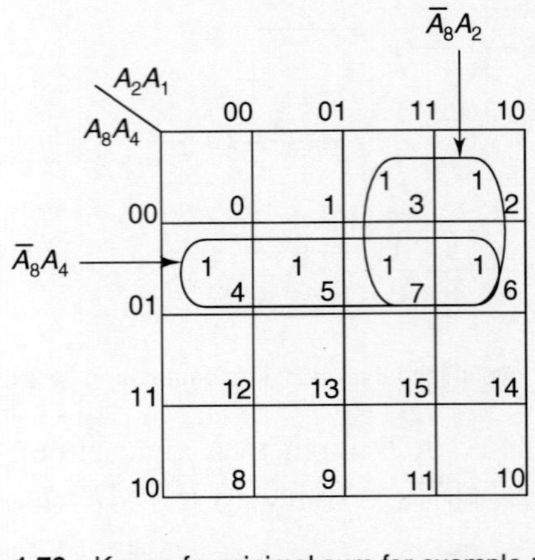

Fig. 1.70 K-map for minimal sum for example 1.45

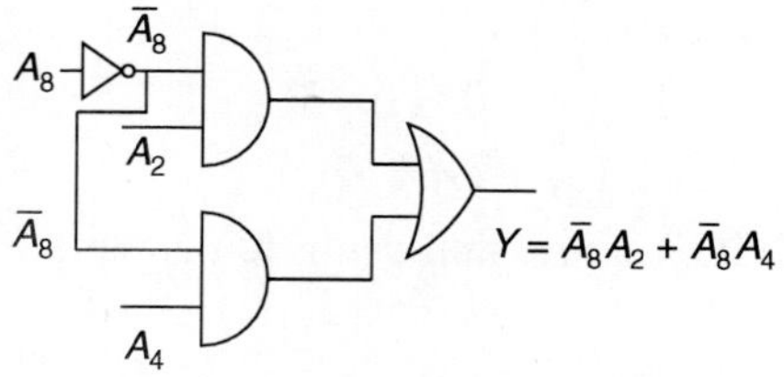

Fig. 1.71 Simple logic circuit for minimal sum.

The simplest possible logic circuit for the minimal sum is shown in Fig. 1.71.

EXERCISE

1. Convert the given expressions in standard SOP from.
   (i) $f(A, B, C) = A + AB + CB$
   (ii) $f(P, Q, R) = PQ + R + PR$
2. Convert the given expressions in standard SOP form.
$$F = AB + \overline{C}D + A\overline{B}C$$
3. Express the following expressions in standard POS form:
   (i) $f(A, B, C) = (A + B)(B + C)$
   (ii) $f(A, B, C) = (A + \overline{B})(A + C)$
4. Transform each of the following canonical expressions into its other canonical form in decimal notation:
   (i) $f(x, y, z) = \Sigma m(1, 3, 5)$
   (ii) $f(w, x, y, z) = \pi m(0, 2, 5, 6, 7, 8, 9, 11, 12)$
5. Simplify the following functions using K-map:
   (i) $f(A, B, C, D) = \overline{A}\overline{B}C + AD + B\overline{D} + C\overline{D} + A\overline{C} + \overline{A}\,\overline{B}$
   (ii) $f(A, B, C, D) = \pi(1, 2, 4, 5, 7, 8, 10, 11, 13, 14)$
6. Design combinational circuit to check for even parity of four bits. *A* logic-1 output is required when four bits do not constitute an even parity.
7. Design a combinational circuit that accepts inputs as 3-bit number and generates an output binary number equal to square of the input number. Realize the logic circuit using only NAND gates.
8. Simplify using K-map:
$$F(w, x, y, z) = \Sigma m(0, 1, 4, 5, 6, 8, 9, 12, 13, 14)$$
9. Using K-map obtain the minimal sum of products and the minimal product of sums form of the function $f(a, b, c, d) = \Sigma(1, 2, 3, 5, 6, 7, 8, 13)$.
10. Implement the following function using K-map:
    $F(A, B, C, D, E) = [\Sigma m(0, 2, 4, 6, 8, 16, 18, 20, 22, 24, 26, 28, 30) + d(3, 7, 11, 15, 19, 23, 27, 31)$

11. Simplify the following using K-map:
    (i) $f(ABCD) = \pi M(0, 1, 2, 3, 4, 6, 10, 11, 13)$
    (ii) $f(ABCD) = \Sigma m(1, 3, 7, 11, 15) + \Sigma d(0, 2, 5)$
12. Determine the minimal SOP expression using K-map and realise it using 2 input NAND gates.

$$f(A, B, C, D, E) = \overline{C}\,\overline{D} + \overline{B}C\overline{D} + ABD + AB\overline{C} + B\overline{C}D + \overline{A}BD$$

13. The input to a combinational logic circuit is a valid single digit BCD data. Design the logic circuit using minimum hardware to detect whenever a number greater than 5 appears at the output.
14. Using a K-map to reduce each expression to a minimum sum of products form
    (i) $y = \overline{A}\,\overline{B}\,\overline{C}\,\overline{D} + \overline{A}\,\overline{B}\,\overline{C}D + ABCD + ABC\overline{D}$
    (ii) $y = \overline{A}B(\overline{C}\,\overline{D} + \overline{C}D) + AB\,(\overline{C}\,\overline{D} + \overline{C}D) + A\overline{B}\,\overline{C}D$
15. Show that $A \odot B \odot C \odot D = \Sigma m(0, 3, 5, 6, 9, 10, 12, 15)$
16. Design a combinational circuit for 3-bit even parity generator and implement it using NAND gates only.
17. Using K-maps, determine the minimal sums and minimal products for $f(w, x, y, z) = \Sigma m(0, 1, 3, 7, 8, 12) + dc(5, 10, 13, 14)$. Is your answer unique?
18. $f(a, b, c, d) = \Sigma m(1, 2, 3, 5, 6, 7, 11, 12, 13, 14, 15)$ for the above expression.
    (i) Draw the logic diagram using AOI Logic for minimal sum. Obtain minimal sum using K-map.
    (ii) Find all the prime implicants and essential prime implicants.
19. Find minimal sum and minimal product for the following using K-map:

$$f(a, b, c, d) = \Sigma m(6, 7, 9, 10, 13) + dc(1, 4, 5, 11, 15)$$

20. Identify all prime implicants and essential prime implicants of the following functions using K-map:
    (i) $f(a, b, c, d) = \pi M(0, 2, 3, 8, 9, 10, 12, 14)$
    (ii) $f(a, b, c, d) = \Sigma m(0, 1, 2, 5, 6, 7, 8, 9, 10, 13, 14, 15)$

CHAPTER 2

Principles of Combinational Logic-2

2.1 QUINE McCLUSKEY MINIMIZATION TECHNIQUE

Karnaugh map method of simplification is convenient up to 5 or 6 variables. Beyond that it becomes unwieldy to handle. Quine and McCluskey developed an exact tabular method to simplify the Boolean expression. Quine-McCluskey minimization technique is an algorithm suitable for a computer solution. The principle used by Quine-McCluskey minimization technique is similar to K-map method in that the minterms whose binary equivalent differs only in one bit can be combined to reduce the minterms.

Let us explain Quine-McCluskey minimization technique through an example.

$$f(A, B, C, D) = \Sigma\ (0, 5, 7, 8, 9, 10, 11, 14, 15)$$

The solution is obtained by following the undermentioned steps.

(1) Arrange all the minterms, in a list of increasing order, so that groups of terms contain the same number of 1s. Group 0 contains no 1s. Group 1 contains only one 1 like {8}, i.e, 1000. Next group 2 contains only two 1s like {9} i.e., 1001, and next Group 3 contains only three 1s like {7}, i.e., 0111 and so on.

Table 2.1

Group	*Minterms*	*Variables*				
		A	*B*	*C*	*D*	
0	0	0	0	0	0	✓
1	8	1	0	0	0	✓
2	5	0	1	0	1	✓
	9	1	0	0	1	✓
	10	1	0	1	0	✓
3	7	0	1	1	1	✓
	11	1	0	1	1	✓
	14	1	1	1	0	✓
4	15	1	1	1	1	✓

The relation $a + \bar{a} = 1$ can be applied to pairs of minterms which are adjacent to each other.

(2) A new table is created by comparing the minterms in one group with the minterms in the next group such that they differ in only one position. Eliminated variable bit positions are indicated by the dash. Compare minterm {0} in group 0 with minterm {8} in group 1. Variable A only varies between them. $A\ B\ C\ D$ is written as –000. Now group 0 and group 1 have been compared. Next group 1 minterm {8} is compared with group 2 minterms {5} {9} 10}.

Minterm {8} and minterm {5} differ by more than 1 bit. Hence, next minterm {8} is compared with minterm {9}. The comparison gives the result 1 0 0–. Similarly, minterm {8} is compared with minterm {10} and we get the result as 1 0 –0. Next group 2 minterms are compared with group 3 minterms. New table is created as follows. After comparison, we check each minterm in Table 2.1.

Table 2.2

Group	*Minterms*	*Variables*				
		A	*B*	*C*	*D*	
0	0, 8	–	0	0	0	
1	8, 9	1	0	0	–	✓
1	8, 10	1	0	–	0	✓
2	5, 7	0	1	–	1	
	9, 11	1	0	–	1	✓
	10, 11	1	0	1	–	✓
	10, 14	1	–	1	0	✓
3	7, 15	–	1	1	1	
	11, 15	1	–	1	1	✓
	14, 15	1	1	1	–	✓

The combined minterms are grouped together as shown in Table 2.2. Each combination results in a new minterm group. If a minterm does not combine with another, then it is not checked. Then that minterm or minterm group is a prime implicant.

(3) All of the adjacent minterm groups shown in the Table 2.2 are compared to see that if groups of four are possible. The dashes in the group of two must be in the same bit position and only one variable change is allowed.

Minterms {0, 8} in group 0 does not combine with minterms {8, 9} and {8, 10} in group 1. Minterm {8, 9} of group 1 combine with {10, 11} of group 2 because dashes are in the same position and there is only one variable change between them. Similarly minterms {8, 10} of group 1, combines with only minterms {9,11} of groups. Again group 2 minterms are combined with group 3 minterms and new table with group of 4 is created as shown in Table 2.3.

Table 2.3

Group	Minterms	Variables			
		A	B	C	D
0	8, 9, 10, 11	1	0	–	–
	8, 10, 9, 11	1	0	–	–
1	10, 11, 14, 15	1	–	1	–
	10, 14, 11, 15	1	–	1	–

Now let us check those minterm groups which have combined with other groups. The minterm groups which are not combined with any other group is not checked.

(4) Repeat the process given in step 3. The new table is created. The same process is repeated until no further combination of minterm groups possible.

(5) All non-checked minterm groups are prime implicants.

(6) All of the prime implicant (PIs) are formed into a PI table as shown in Table 2.4. It lists all the minterms combined in the original equation across the top of the table.

Table 2.4

PI terms	Decimal form	Minterms								
		0	5	7	8	9	10	11	14	15
$\overline{B}\,\overline{C}\,\overline{D}$	0, 8	⊗			×					
$\overline{A}BD$	5, 7		⊗	×						
BCD	7, 15			×						×
$A\overline{B}$	8, 9, 10, 11				×	⊗	×	×		
AC	10, 11, 14, 15						×	×	⊗	×

Non-checked minterm groups are {0, 8}, {5, 7}, {7, 15}, {8, 9, 10, 11} and {10, 11, 14, 15). These PI terms are part of PI table.

(7) Minterm group {0, 8} consists minterm 0 and 8. A x is placed below the 0 and 8 columns. Similarly, other minterm groups that are part of PI table are considered by placing x across the minterm columns as shown in Table 2.4.

Now circle those minterms that are contained in only one PI. If minterms are circled, those minterm groups are EPIs. In minterm group {0, 8}, minterm 0 is circled, hence minterm group {0, 8} is EPI. In a similar way, minterm groups {5, 7}, {8, 9, 10, 11} and {10, 11, 14, 15,} are EPIs. The minterms 7 and 15 contained in minterm group {7, 15} are covered in other minterm groups. Hence, {7, 15} is just PI.

The solution for the problem is written as

$$f\{A, B, C, D) = A\overline{B} + AC + \overline{A}BD + \overline{B}\,\overline{C}\,\overline{D}$$

We can verify the above result obtained with Quine McCluskey method with that of K-map as shown in Fig 2.1.

$$f(A, B, C, D) = \Sigma\ (0, 5, 7, 8, 9, 10, 11, 14, 15)$$

K-map is drawn as shown in Fig 2.1.

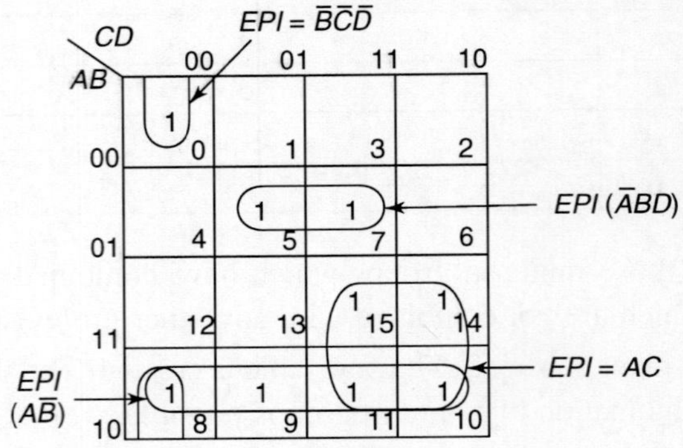

Fig 2.1 K-map for $f(A, B, C, D) = \Sigma(0, 5, 7, 8, 9, 10, 11, 14, 15)$

From K-map, we observe that there are 4 EPIs, the solution is written as

$$f(A, B, C, D) = A\overline{B} + AC + \overline{A}BD + \overline{B}\,\overline{C}\,\overline{D}$$

This is same as the result obtained with Quine-McCluskey method.

2.2 QUINE McCLUSKEY TECHNIQUE USING DON'T-CARE TERM

Let us take an example through which concepts can be explained. Simplify the function,

$$f(w, x, y, z) = \Sigma(1, 3, 13, 15) + \Sigma d(8, 9, 10, 11)$$

The same rules, applied for K-map with don't-care terms, are applicable to Quine-McCluskey method as well.

(1) List the minterms and don't-care terms according to the number of 1s. Don't-care terms are indicated by a * symbol. They are not indicated as PIs by themselves

Table 2.5

Group	Minterms	Variables				
		w	x	y	z	
1	1	0	0	0	1	✓
	8*	1	0	0	0	✓
2	3	0	0	1	1	✓
	9*	1	0	0	1	✓
	10*	1	0	1	0	✓
3	11*	1	0	1	1	✓
	13	1	1	0	1	✓
4	15	1	1	1	1	✓

(2) Compare terms in one group including don't-care terms with terms in the next group, looking for only one variable change. For finding PIs, let us treat don't-care terms as 1.

Table 2.6

Group	Minterms	Variables					
		w	x	y	z		
1	1, 3	0	0	–	1		✓
	1, 9*	–	0	0	1		✓
	8*, 9*	1	0	0	–		✓
	8*, 10*	1	0	–	0		✓
2	3, 11*	–	0	1	1	1	✓
	9*, 11*	1	0	–	1		✓
	9*, 13	1	–	0	1		✓
	10*, 11*	1	0	1	–		✓
3	11*, 15	1	–	1	1		✓
	13, 15	1	1	–	1		✓

(3) Repeat step 2, creating an additional table (Table 2.7) indicating groups of four minterms or don't-care terms. Continue this process until no further grouping is possible.

(4) Construct PI table and determine EPIs.

Table 2.7

Group	Minterms	Variables			
		w	x	y	z
1	1, 3, 9*, 11*	–	0	–	1
	8*, 9*, 10*, 11*	1	0	–	–
2	9*, 13, 11*, 15	1	–	–	1

Table 2.8

PI terms	Decimal	Minterms			
		1	3	13	15
$\bar{x}z$	1, 3, 9*, 11*	⊗	⊗		
wz	9*, 11*, 13, 15			⊗	⊗

Table 2.7 represents groups of four minterms/don't-care terms. The group of minterms {8*, 9*, 10*, 11*} contains only don't-care terms and is therefore not a prime implicant.

Table 2.8 indicates that both PIs {1, 3, 9*, 11*} and {9*, 11*, 13, 15} contain unique terms as circled and therefore are EPIs. The simplified equation is written as, $f(w, x, y, z) = \bar{x}z + wz$.

2.3 REDUCED PRIME IMPLICANT TABLES

We will consider an example to explain the concept of reduced prime implicant. Simplify

$$f(a, b, c, d) = \Sigma\, m(3, 4, 5, 7, 10, 12, 14, 15) + \phi\ (2)$$

Table 2.9

Group	Minterms	Variables				
		a	b	c	d	
1	2*	0	0	1	0	✓
	4	0	1	0	0	✓
2	3	0	0	1	1	✓
	5	0	1	0	1	✓
	10	1	0	1	0	✓
	12	1	1	0	0	✓
3	7	0	1	1	1	✓
	14	1	1	1	0	✓
4	15	1	1	1	1	✓

Comparing the minterms of one group with minterms of next higher group, we get group of two minterms. This process is continued till we complete comparison of all groups.

Group of two minterms is shown in Table 2.10 We observe that group of four minterms is not possible as there is no comparison possible between different groups. Hence, all the groups of two mintems become PIs. Then PI table is formed as shown in Table 2.11.

Table 2.10

Group	Minterms	Variables			
		a	b	c	d
1	2*, 3	0	0	1	–
	4, 5	0	1	0	–
	4, 12	–	1	0	0
	2*, 10	–	0	1	0
2	3, 7	0	–	1	1
	5, 7	0	1	–	1
	10, 14	1	–	1	0
	12, 14	1	1	–	0
3	7, 15	–	1	1	1
	14, 15	1	1	1	–

We observe that in Table 2.10, no group of minterms is checked. Therefore, all minterms are PIs. In PI table, all the minterms in the original equation except don't-care term appear.

Table 2.11

PI terms	*Decimal*	*Minterms*							
		3	4	5	7	10	12	14	15
$\bar{a}\bar{b}c$	2*, 3	×							
$\bar{a}b\bar{c}$	2*, 10					×			
$\bar{a}b\bar{c}$	4, 5		⊗	⊗					
$b\bar{c}\bar{d}$	4, 12		⊗				⊗		
$\bar{a}cd$	3, 7	⊗			⊗				
$\bar{a}bd$	5, 7			×	×				
$ac\bar{d}$	10, 14					⊗		⊗	
$ab\bar{d}$	12, 14						×	×	
bcd	7, 15				×				×
abc	14, 15							⊗	⊗

We observe that no minterm column has single minterms. Hence, there is no obvious EPI.

Now, let us look for EPIs. EPIs should cover all the minterms given in the problem. Let us start with minterm group {2*, 3}. 2* is a don't-care term, so it is not considered. Minterm 3 is also part of {3, 7}. Hence, minterm {2*, 3} is only PI. {3, 7} is EPI and minterms are circled. Similarly, minterms group {2*, 10} is only PI because 2* is a don't care term and minterm 10 is part {10, 14}. Hence, {10, 14} is EPI and minterms are circled.

Next {4, 5} is EPI and is circled. After this {4, 12} is EPI and the minterms are circled. Now, let us consider group of minterm {3, 7}. This is also EPI and the minterms are circled. Next {5, 7} is considered and both the minterms 5 and 7 are covered in {4, 5} and {3, 7}. Hence, {5, 7} is PI. Next {10, 14} is considered and is taken as EPI and the minterms are circled. Next in group {12, 14}, both the minterms are already covered in {4, 12} and {10, 14} and hence it is only PI. Next group of minterms {7, 15} and {14, 15}, the minterms 7 and 14 are already covered. Only minterm 15 in both the groups is yet to be covered. Hence, out of these two groups {7, 15} and {14, 15}, any one can be considered EPI. Let us take {14, 15} as EPI. Now, we observe that all the minterms have been covered in the five EPIs. Hence,

$$f\{a, b, c, d\} = \bar{a}b\bar{c} + b\bar{c}\bar{d} + \bar{a}cd + ac\bar{d} + abc$$

Thus, we see that the solution has been obtained by reducing the prime implicants. Out of 10 prime implicants, only 5 PIs have been considered EPIs.

Example 2.1 Simplify using the Quine-McCluskey minimization technique. Implement the simplified expression using basic gates.

$$v = f(a, b, c, d) = \Sigma(2, 3, 4, 5, 13, 15) + \Sigma\, d(8, 9, 10, 11)$$

(VTU – June 2013, VTU – June 2011)

Solution Let us list the minterms and don't care terms according to the number of 1s. Don't-care terms are indicated by a * symbol as shown in Table 2.12.

Table 2.12

Group	Minterms	Variables				
		a	b	c	d	
1	2	0	0	1	0	✓
	4	0	1	0	0	✓
	8*	1	0	0	0	✓
2	3	0	0	1	1	✓
	5	0	1	0	1	✓
	9*	1	0	0	1	✓
	10*	1	0	1	0	✓
3	11*	1	0	1	1	✓
	13	1	1	0	1	✓
4	15	1	1	1	1	✓

Compare terms in one group with the minterms of next group until no comparison is possible. Group of two minterms after comparison is shown in Table 2.13.

Table 2.13

Group	Minterms	Variables				
		a	b	c	d	
1	2, 3	0	0	1	–	✓
	2, 10*	–	0	1	0	✓
	4, 5	0	1	0	–	
	8*, 9*	1	0	0	–	✓
	8*, 10*	1	0	–	0	✓
2	3, 11*	–	0	1	1	✓
	5, 13	–	1	0	1	
	9*, 11*	1	0	–	1	✓
	9*, 13	1	–	0	1	✓
	10*, 11*	1	0	1	–	✓
3	11*, 15	1	–	1	1	✓
	13, 15	1	1	–	1	✓

Comparison of groups of two minterms results in group of 4 minterms. This is continued until no more comparison is possible. Group of minterms {2, 3} can be compared with {10*, 11*}. Comparison is possible where there is only one variable change between two adjacent groups.

The result is Table 2.14.

Table 2.14

Group	Minterms	Variables			
		a	b	c	d
1	2, 3, 10*, 11*	–	0	1	–
	2, 10*, 3, 11*	–	0	1	–
	8*, 9*, 10*, 11*	1	0	–	–
	8*, 10*, 9*, 11*	1	0	–	–
2	9*, 13, 11*, 15	1	–	–	1
	9*, 11*, 13, 15	1	–	–	1

Non-checked minterm groups in both Tables 2.13 and Table 2.14 are formed as PI table (Table 2.15)

Table 2.15

PI terms	Decimal form	Minterms					
		2	3	4	5	13	15
$\bar{a}\,b\,\bar{c}$	4, 5			⊗	⊗		
$b\,\bar{c}\,d$	5, 13				×	×	
$\bar{b}\,c$	2, 3, 10*, 11*	⊗	⊗				
$a\,d$	9*, 11*, 13, 15					⊗	⊗

In minterms columns, where there is single minterm, that particular group of minterms is circled. Hence, {4, 5}, {2, 3, 10*, 11*} and {9*, 11*, 13*, 15} are circled. {5, 13} is not circled because both the minterms are covered by other minterm groups. Hence, {5, 13} is only PI. EPIs are {4, 5} {2, 3, 10*, 11*} and {9*, 11*, 13, 15}. Hence, the final simplified expression is

$$f(a, b, c, d) = \bar{a}b\bar{c} + \bar{b}c + ad$$

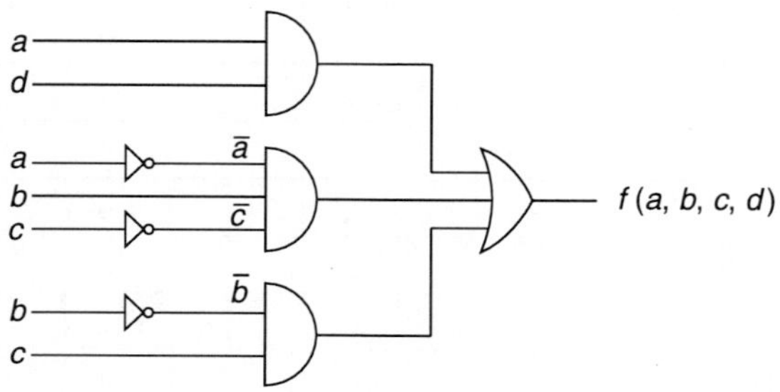

Fig 2.2 Implementation of logic circuit for *f*(*a*, *b*, *c*, *d*) using basic gates

Example 2.2 Minimize $f(a, b, c, d) = \pi(0, 6\ 7, 8, 9, 13) + \pi\ dc(5, 15)$ using Quine-McCluskey method. (VTU – Dec 2011)

Solution POS equation is converted into SOP equation and then list the minterms and don't-care terms according to the number of 1s.

SOP expression is written as,

$$f(a, b, c, d) = \Sigma(1, 2, 3, 4, 10, 11, 12, 14) + d(5, 15)$$

Table 2.16 shows the arrangement of minterms as per increasing number of 1s.

Table 2.16

Group	Minterms	Variables				
		a	b	c	d	
1	1	0	0	0	1	✓
	2	0	0	1	0	✓
	4	0	1	0	0	✓
2	3	0	0	1	1	✓
	5*	0	1	0	1	✓
	10	1	0	1	0	✓
	12	1	1	0	0	✓
3	11	1	0	1	1	✓
	14	1	1	1	0	✓
4	15*	1	1	1	1	✓

Compare minterms of one group with that of next higher group and the result is shown in Table 2.17.

Table 2.17

Group	Minterms	Variables				
		a	b	c	d	
1	1, 3	0	0	–	1	
	1, 5*	0	–	0	1	
	2, 3	0	0	1	–	✓
	2, 10	–	0	1	0	✓
	4, 5*	0	1	0	–	
	4, 12	–	1	0	0	
2	3, 11	–	0	1	1	✓
	10, 11	1	0	1	–	✓
	10, 14	1	–	1	0	✓
	12, 14	1	1	–	0	
3	11, 15*	1	–	1	1	✓
	14, 15*	1	1	1	–	✓

Table 2.18

Group	Minterms	Variables			
		a	b	c	d
1	2, 3, 10, 11	–	0	1	–
	2, 10, 3, 11	–	0	1	–
2	10, 14, 11, 15*	1	–	1	–
	10, 11, 14, 15*	1	–	1	–

When no more grouping is possible, PI table is prepared using non-checked minterm groups.

Table 2.19

PI terms	Decimal	Minterms							
		1	2	3	4	10	11	12	14
$\bar{a}\bar{b}d$	1, 3	⊗		⊗					
$\bar{a}\bar{c}d$	1, 5*	×							
$\bar{a}b\bar{c}$	4, 5*				×				
$b\bar{c}\bar{d}$	4, 12				⊗			⊗	
$ab\bar{d}$	12, 14							×	×
$\bar{b}c$	2, 3, 10, 11		⊗	⊗		⊗	⊗		
ac	10, 11, 14, 15*					⊗	⊗		⊗

{1, 3} covers {1, 5*}, {4, 12} covers {4, 5*}, {4, 12} and {10, 11, 14, 15*} cover {12, 14}.

Hence, minterm groups {1, 3}, {4, 12}, {2, 3, 10, 11} and {10, 11, 14, 15*} are the EPIs.

Simplified expression is

$$f(a, b, c, d) = ac + \bar{b}c + \bar{a}\bar{b}d + b\bar{c}\bar{d}$$

Example 2.3 Find essential prime implicants for the Boolean expression by using Quine-McCluskey method.

$$f(W, X, Y, Z) = \Sigma m(1, 3, 6, 8, 9, 10, 12, 13, 14), \qquad \text{(VTU – June 2013)}$$

Solution Table 2.20 shows the arrangement of minterms of the given Boolean expression as per increasing number of 1s.

Table 2.20

Group	Minterms	Variables			
		W	X	Y	Z
1	1	0	0	0	1
	8	1	0	0	0

Contd...

Contd...

2	3	0	0	1	1
	6	0	1	1	0
	9	1	0	0	1
	10	1	0	1	0
	12	1	1	0	0
3	13	1	1	0	1
	14	1	1	1	0

Compare minterms of one group with that of next higher group until all the groups have been compared and no further grouping is possible. The grouping of two minterms and comparison is shown in Table 2.21.

Table 2.21

Group	*Minterms*	*Variables*				
		W	*X*	*Y*	*Z*	
1	1, 3	0	0	–	1	
	1, 9	–	0	0	1	
	8, 9	1	0	0	–	✓
	8, 10	1	0	–	0	✓
	8, 12	1	–	0	0	✓
2	6, 14	–	1	1	0	
	9, 13	1	–	0	1	
	10, 14	1	–	1	0	✓
	12, 13	1	1	0	–	✓
	12, 14	1	1	–	0	✓

Again comparison is made between groups of two minterms and hence groups of four minterms are formed in Table 2.22.

Table 2.22

Group	*Minterms*	*Variables*			
		W	*X*	*Y*	*Z*
1	8, 9, 12, 13	1	–	0	–
	8, 10, 12, 14	1	–	–	0

Non-checked minterm groups form PI table. All the minterms given in the Boolean expression are placed across the table. From the PI table let us find EPIs. PI table is shown in Fig. 2.3.

Table 2.23

PI terms	Decimal	Minterms									
		1	3	6	7	8	9	10	12	13	14
$\overline{w}\overline{x}z$	1, 3	⊗	⊗								
$\overline{x}\overline{y}z$	1, 9	×					×				
$xy\overline{z}$	6, 14			⊗							⊗
$w\overline{y}z$	9, 13						×			×	
$w\overline{y}$	8, 9, 12, 13					⊗	⊗		⊗	⊗	
$w\overline{z}$	8, 10, 12, 14					⊗		⊗	⊗		⊗

Let us consider the PI terms for which the minterm column has a single minterm. The groups of minterm {1, 3} {6, 14} and {8, 10, 12, 14} have a single minterm each in the minterm column. Hence, all the three minterm groups {1, 3}, {6, 14} and {8, 10, 12, 14} are EPIs.

Next, let us circle the minterms 8, 9 and 12, 13 of the group {8, 9, 12, 13} and this group becomes EPI. The remaining PIs are {1, 9} and {9, 13}. All these minterms are covered in EPIs already mentioned above.

Hence, the essential prime implicants of the given Boolean expression are

$$w\overline{y},\ w\overline{z},\ xy\overline{z} \text{ and } \overline{w}\overline{x}z$$

Example 2.4 Obtain all the prime implicants of the following Boolean function using Quine-McCluskey method

$$f(a, b, c, d) = \Sigma(0, 2, 3, 5, 8, 10, 11)$$

Verify the result using K-map technique (VTU – Dec 2013)

Solution All the minterms given in the Boolean function are arranged in the order of increasing number of 1s. The arrangement is shown in Table 2.24.

Table 2.24

Group	Minterms	Variables				
		a	b	c	d	
0	0	0	0	0	0	✓
1	2	0	0	1	0	✓
	8	1	0	0	0	✓
2	3	0	0	1	1	✓
	5	0	1	0	1	
	10	1	0	1	0	✓
3	11	1	0	1	1	✓

Compare the minterms from one group to the next higher group so that there is only one variable change between them. It is continued until no further grouping is possible. The resulting table is shown in the Table 2.25.

Table 2.25

Group	Minterms	Variables				
		a	b	c	d	
0	0, 2	0	0	–	0	✓
	0, 8	–	0	0	0	✓
1	2, 3	0	0	1	–	✓
	2, 10	–	0	1	0	✓
	8, 10	1	0	–	0	✓
2	3, 11	–	0	1	1	✓
	10, 11	1	0	1	–	✓

Next, comparison is made between one group of two minterms with next higher group of two minterms until no further grouping is possible. The resulting groups of four minterms are shown in Table 2.26.

Table 2.26

Group	Minterms	Variables			
		a	b	c	d
0	0, 2, 8, 10	–	0	–	0
	0, 8, 2, 10	–	0	–	0
1	2, 3, 10, 11	–	0	1	–
	2, 10, 3, 11	–	0	1	–

Further grouping is not possible. Hence, the minterms shown in Table 2.26 become PIs.

Hence, PIs are placed in Table 2.27. In Table 2.26, in groups 0 minterms, both groups are same. Similarly, in group 1 minterms, both the groups are same.

Table 2.27

PI terms	Minterms
$\overline{a}b\overline{c}d$	5
$\overline{b}\,\overline{d}$	0, 2, 8, 10
$\overline{b}c$	2, 3, 10, 11

Hence, the prime implicants of the Boolean function $f(a, b, c, d) = \Sigma(0, 2, 3, 5, 8, 10, 11)$ are $\overline{a}b\overline{c}d$, $\overline{b}\,\overline{d}$ and $\overline{b}c$.

Now, let us verify this result using K-map technique. K-map is shown Fig. 2.3.

$$f(a, b, c, d) = \overline{a}b\overline{c}d + \overline{b}c + \overline{b}\,\overline{d}$$

This result obtained from Quine-McCluskey technique is verified with that obtained from K-map technique.

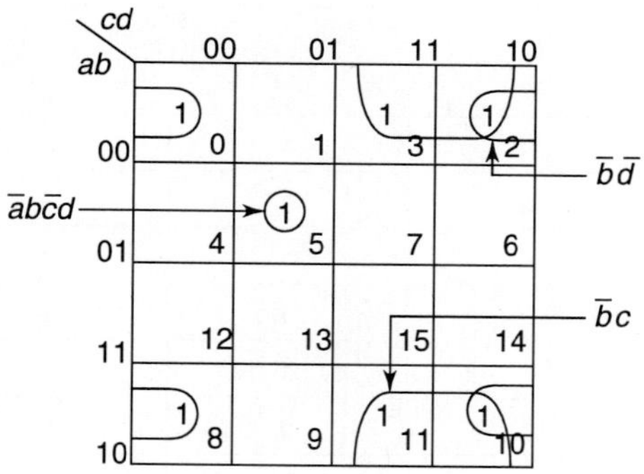

Fig. 2.3 K-map for Σ{0, 2, 3, 5, 8, 10, 11)

Example 2.5 Simplify the following function using Quine-McCluskey minimization technique:

$$T = f(a, b, c, d) = \Sigma\, m(0, 1, 2, 3, 6, 7, 8, 9, 14, 15)$$

(VTU – June 2010)

Solution All the minterms given in the Boolean function are arranged in the order of increasing number of 1s. The arrangement is shown in Table 2.28.

Table 2.28

Group	Minterms	Variables				
		a	*b*	*c*	*d*	
0	0	0	0	0	0	✓
1	1	0	0	0	1	✓
	2	0	0	1	0	✓
	8	1	0	0	0	✓
2	3	0	0	1	1	✓
	6	0	1	1	0	✓
	9	1	0	0	1	✓
3	14	1	1	1	0	✓
4	15	1	1	1	1	✓

Compare the minterms from one group with the minterms of next higher group so that there is only one variable change between them. This process is continued until no further grouping is possible. The result is shown in Table 2.29.

Table 2.29

Group	Minterms	Variables				
		a	*b*	*c*	*d*	
0	0, 1	0	0	0	–	✓
	0, 2	0	0	–	0	✓
	0, 8	–	0	0	0	✓
1	1, 3	0	0	1	1	✓
	1, 9	–	0	0	1	✓
	2, 3	0	0	1	–	✓
	2, 6	0	–	1	0	
	8, 9	1	0	0	–	✓
2	6, 14	–	1	1	0	
3	14, 15	1	1	1	–	

Next, comparison is made between one group of two minterms with another group of two minterms in the next higher group of two minterms until no further grouping is possible. The groups of four minterms are shown in Table 2.30.

Table 2.30

Group	Minterms	Variables			
		a	*b*	*c*	*d*
0	0, 1, 2, 3	0	0	–	–
	0, 1, 8, 9	–	0	0	–
	0, 2, 1, 3	0	0	–	–
	0, 8, 1, 9	–	0	0	–

Next, non-checked minterm groups form PI table which is shown in Table 2.31.

Table 2.31

PI terms	Decimal	Minterms								
		0	1	2	3	6	8	9	14	15
$\bar{a}c\bar{d}$	2, 6			×		×				
$bc\bar{d}$	6, 14					×			×	
abc	14, 15								⊗	⊗
$\bar{a}\bar{b}$	0, 1, 2, 3	⊗	⊗	⊗	⊗					
$\bar{b}\bar{c}$	0, 1, 8, 9	⊗	⊗				⊗	⊗		

In the PI table, circle the minterms of the groups for which there is only one minterm in the minterm column. Minterms of the groups {15, 14}, {0, 1, 2, 3} and {0, 1, 8, 9} are circled. Now, two PIs are remaining out of which any one we can choose as EPI. Let us choose {6, 14} as EPI because minterm 6 is not covered by the three EPIs. Hence, there are four EPIs.

Simplified expression is

$$f(a, b, c, d) = \bar{a}\bar{b} + \bar{b}\bar{c} + abc + bc\bar{d} \quad (1)$$

If we choose {2, 6} as EPI,

Simplified expression is

$$f(a, b, c, d) = \bar{a}\bar{b} + \bar{b}\bar{c} + abc + \bar{a}c\bar{d} \quad (2)$$

Both the solutions (i) and (ii) are valid solutions. In both the cases, all the minterms of the given Boolean function are covered.

Example 2.6 Simplify the following using Quine-McCluskey method. Use decimal notations.

$$f(a, b, c, d) = \Sigma\,(7, 9, 12, 13, 14, 15) + \Sigma d(4, 11)$$

Realize the simplified expression using only NOR gates. (VTU – June 2012)

Solution All the minterms given in the Boolean expression are arranged in the order of increasing number of 1s. Include don't-care terms also. The arrangement is shown in Table 2.32.

Table 2.32

Group	*Minterms*	*Variables*				
		a	*b*	*c*	*d*	
1	4*	0	1	0	0	✓
2	9	1	0	0	1	✓
	12	1	1	0	0	✓
3	7	0	1	1	1	✓
	11*	1	0	1	1	✓
	13	1	1	0	1	✓
	14	1	1	1	0	✓
4	15	1	1	1	1	✓

Compare the minterms from one group with the minterms of next higher group so that there is only one variable change between them. This process is continued until no further grouping is possible. The result is shown in Table 2.33.

Table 2.33

Group	*Minterms*	*Variables*				
		a	*b*	*c*	*d*	
1	4*, 12	–	1	0	0	
2	9, 11*	1	0	–	1	✓
	9, 13	1	–	0	1	✓
	12, 13	1	1	0	–	✓
	12, 14	1	1	–	0	✓

Contd...

Contd...

3	7, 15	–	1	1	1	
	11*, 15	1	–	1	1	✓
	13, 15	1	1	–	1	✓
	14, 15	1	1	1	–	✓

Next, comparison is made between one group of two minterms with another group of two minterms of next higher group until no further grouping is possible. The resulting groups of four minterms are shown in Table 2.34.

Table 2.34

Group	Minterms	Variables			
		a	*b*	*c*	*d*
1	9, 11*, 13, 15	1	–	–	1
	9, 13, 11*, 15	1	–	–	1
	12, 13, 14, 15	1	1	–	–
	12, 14, 13, 15	1	1	–	–

Next, non-checked minterm groups form the PI table which is shown in Table 2.35.

Table 2.35

PI terms	Decimal	Minterms					
		7	9	12	13	14	15
$b\bar{c}\bar{d}$	4*, 12			×			
bcd	7, 15	⊗					⊗
ad	9, 11*, 13, 15		⊗		⊗		⊗
ab	12, 13, 14, 15			⊗	⊗	⊗	⊗

In the PI table, circle the minterms of the groups for which there is only one minterm in the minterm column. We observe that the minterms of the following PIs are circled, {7, 15}, {9, 11*, 13, 15) and {12, 13, 14, 15}. They are EPIs which become part of solution.

$$f(a, b, c, d) = bcd + ad + ab$$

Minterm 12 of {4*, 12} is already covered in {12, 13, 14, 15}.

Now, we have to realize the simplified expression using only NOR gates. First let us realize using basic gates.

To convert the above circuit using NOR gates,

(i) if OR gates are present, their outputs must be bubbled.

(ii) if AND gates are present, the inputs to AND gates must be bubbled.

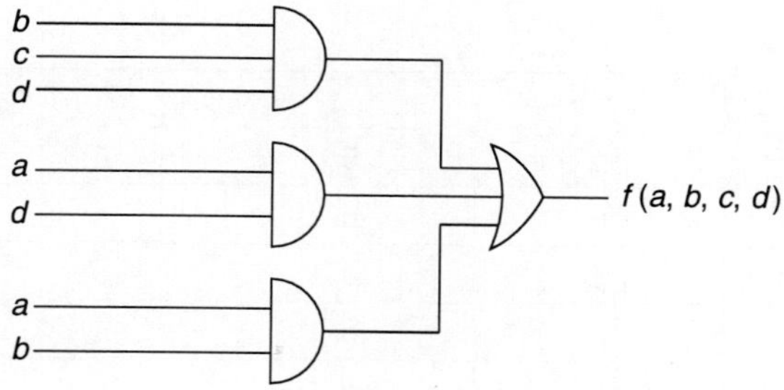

Fig. 2.4 Realization of *bcd* + *ad* + *ab* using basic gates

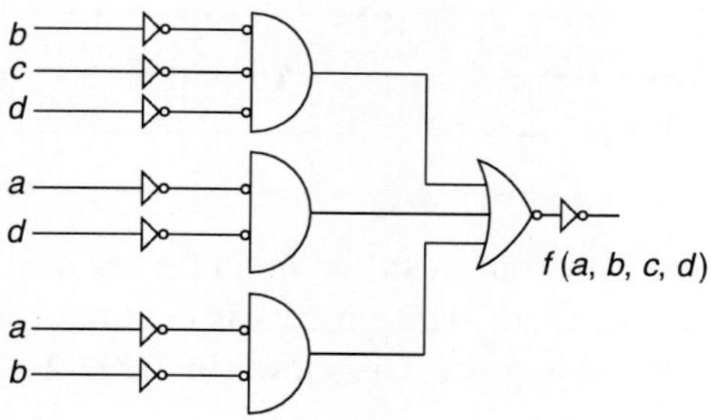

(a)

Figure 2.5 (a) and (b) shows the process of conversion to NOR and final realization using only NOR gates.

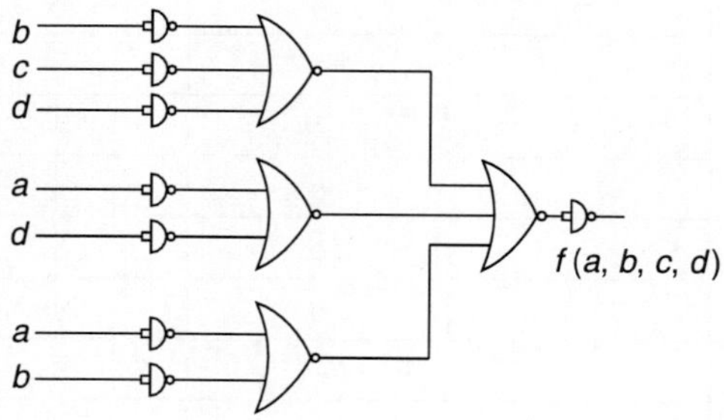

(b)

Fig. 2.5 Realization of *bcd* + *ad* + *ab* using only NOR gates

Example 2.7 Simplify $f(A, B, C, D) = \Sigma\,(0, 1, 2, 3, 10, 11, 12, 13, 14, 15)$ using Quine-McCluskey method.

(VTU – Dec 2012)

Solution All the minterms given in the Boolean expression are arranged in the order of increasing number of 1s. The arrangement is shown in Table 2.36.

Table 2.36

Group	Minterms	Variables				✓
		A	B	C	D	✓
0	0	0	0	0	0	✓
1	1	0	0	0	1	✓
	2	0	0	1	0	✓
2	3	0	0	1	1	✓
	10	1	0	1	0	✓
	12	1	1	0	0	✓
3	11	1	0	1	1	✓
	13	1	1	0	1	✓
	14	1	1	1	0	✓
4	15	1	1	1	1	✓

Compare the minterms from one group with the minterms of next higher group so that there is only one variable change between them. This process is continued until no further grouping is possible. The table resulting out of this process is shown in Table 2.37.

Table 2.37

Group	Minterms	Variables				
		A	B	C	D	
0	0, 1	0	0	0	–	
	0, 2	0	0	–	0	✓
1	1, 3	0	0	–	1	✓
	2, 10	–	0	1	0	✓
2	3, 11	–	0	1	1	✓
	10, 11	1	0	1	–	✓
	10, 14	1	–	1	0	✓
	12, 13	1	1	0	–	✓
	12, 14	1	1	–	0	✓
3	11, 15	1	–	1	1	✓
	13, 15	1	1	–	1	✓
	14, 15	1	1	1	–	✓

Comparison is made between one group of two minterms with another group of two minterms of next higher group until no further grouping is possible. The resulting groups of four minterms are shown in Table 2.38.

Table 2.38

Group	Minterms	Variables			
		A	B	C	D
0	0, 2, 1, 3	0	0	–	–
1	2, 10, 3, 11	–	0	1	–
2	10, 11, 14, 15,	1	–	1	–
	10, 14, 11, 15	1	–	1	–
	12, 13, 14, 15	1	1	–	1
	12, 14, 13, 15	1	1	–	–

Non-checked minterm groups form the PI table which is shown in Table 2.39.

Table 2.39

PI terms	Decimal	Minterms									
		0	1	2	3	10	11	12	13	14	15
$\overline{A}\,\overline{B}\,\overline{C}$	0, 1	×	×								
$\overline{A}\,\overline{B}$	0, 2, 1, 3	⊗	⊗	⊗	⊗						
$\overline{B}C$	2, 10, 3, 11			×	×	×	×				
AC	10, 11, 14, 15					⊗	⊗			⊗	⊗
AB	12, 13, 14, 15							⊗	⊗	⊗	⊗

Group {12, 13, 14, 15} has only one minterm in minterm column 12 and 13. So, this group {12, 13, 14, 15} becomes EPI. Out of remaining 4 PIs, if we choose groups {0, 2, 1, 3} and {10, 11, 14, 15} as EPIs, all of the minterms are covered. Hence, the simplified expression is

$$f(A, B, C, D) = AB + AC + \overline{A}\,\overline{B}$$

Example 2.8 Simplify the following Boolean function using Quine McCluskey method.

$$F(a, b, c, d) = \Sigma\,(1, 4, 6, 7, 8, 9, 10, 11, 15)$$

Solution All the minterms given in the Boolean function are arranged in the order of increasing number of 1s. The arrangement is shown in Table 2.40.

Table 2.40

Group	Minterms	Variables				
		a	b	c	d	
1	1	0	0	0	1	✓
	4	0	1	0	0	✓
	8	1	0	0	0	✓
2	6	0	1	1	0	✓
	9	1	0	0	1	✓
	10	1	0	1	0	✓

Contd...

Contd...

3	7	0	1	1	1	✓
	11	1	0	1	1	✓
4	15	1	1	1	1	✓

Compare the minterms from one group with the minterms of next higher group, so that there is only one variable change between them. This process is continued until no further grouping is possible. The table resulting out of this process is shown in Table 2.41.

Table 2.41

Group	*Minterms*	*Variables*				
		a	*b*	*c*	*d*	
1	1, 9	–	0	0	1	
	4, 6	0	1	–	0	
	8, 9	1	0	0	–	✓
	8, 10	1	0	–	0	✓
2	6, 7	0	1	1	–	
	9, 11	1	0	–	1	✓
	10, 11	1	0	1	+	✓
3	7, 15	–	1	1	1	
	11, 15	1	–	1	1	

Next, comparison is made between one group of two minterms with another group of two minterms of next higher group until no further grouping is possible. The resulting groups of four minterms are shown in Table 2.42.

Table 2.42

Group	*Minterms*	*Variables*			
		a	*b*	*c*	*d*
1	8, 9, 10, 11	1	0	–	–
	8, 10, 9, 11	1	0	–	–

Non-checked minterms are PIs. Now PI table is formed as shown in Table 2.43.

Table 2.43

PI terms	*Decimal*	*Minterms*								
		1	4	6	7	8	9	10	11	15
$\bar{b}\bar{c}d$	1, 9	⊗					⊗			
$\bar{a}b\bar{d}$	4, 6		⊗	⊗						
$\bar{a}bc$	6, 7			⊗	⊗					

Contd...

Contd...

bcd	7, 15				×					×
acd	11, 15								⊗	⊗
$a\bar{b}$	8, 9, 10, 11					⊗	⊗	⊗	⊗	

Now, we have to choose those minterm groups as EPIs for which in the minterm columns there is a single minterm. We observe that minterm groups {8, 9, 10, 11}, {1, 9} and {4, 6} are EPIs. Out of remaining three PIs, two PIs have to be chosen as EPIs such that all minterms in the given Boolean function are covered. {6, 7} and {11, 15} or {7, 15} and {11, 15} meet the criteria.

Hence, the simplified expression is

$$f(a, b, c, d) = \bar{b}\bar{c}d + \bar{a}b\bar{d} + \bar{a}bc + acd + a\bar{b}$$

or

$$f(a, b, c, d) = \bar{b}\bar{c}d + \bar{a}b\bar{d} + bcd + acd + a\bar{b}$$

2.4 MAP ENTERED VARIABLES

K-map technique is the best manual method for simplification of Boolean functions up to five variables, after which it becomes very difficult. Map Entered Variables (MEV) technique is useful for compressing K-map so that it allows a smaller map to manage more number of variables.

Each square in a K-map represents a minterm, a maxterm or a don't-care term whereas MEV K-map in addition permits a square to contain a single variable or a switching expression.

Consider for example, the simplification of the following function using MEV method.

$$f(a, b, c) = \Sigma\, m(0, 2, 3, 7)$$

Now, let us consider the variable c as map entered variable. Let us construct a special MEV truth table, with two minterm columns, one for MEV K-map and one for standard K-map. Because we are using one variable as MEV variable, two squares of standard K-maps are covered by one square of MEV K-map. A four-variable K-map has 16 squares. If one variable is considered MEV, then resulting MEV K-map will have 8 squares. If two variables are considered MEVs then MEV-K-map will have 4 squares.

Table 2.44

Decimal minterm		*Binary variables*			*Output*	*MEV*
MEV	*Standard*	*a*	*b*	*c (MEV)*	*f*	*entry*
0	0	0	0	0	1	$\bar{c}$
0	1	0	0	1	0	
1	2	0	1	0	1	1
1	3	0	1	1	1	
2	4	1	0	0	0	0
2	5	1	0	1	0	
3	6	1	1	0	0	c
3	7	1	1	1	1	

The procedure for loading K-map using MEV is as given below.

1. If the output variable is 0 for both standard minterms covered by a MEV map square, then a 0 is written in MEV map square.
2. If the output variable is 1 for both standard minterms covered by a MEV map square, then a 1 is written in MEV map square.
3. If for standard minterms covered by a MEV map square the output variable has the same value as MEV then MEV is written into MEV map square.

MEV	Output
0	0
1	1

4. If for standard minterms covered by a MEV map square, the output and MEV variables are complements, then complement of MEV is written into MEV map square.

MEV	Output
0	1
1	0

5. If, for both standard minterms covered by a MEV map square, the output variables are don't-care terms, a don't-care term is written in MEV map square.
6. If for standard minterms covered by a MEV map square, the output variable is a don't-care term in one case and a 0 in the other case, a 0 is written into MEV map square.

MEV	Output
0	*x* or *d*
1	0

MEV	Output
0	0
1	*x* or *d*

7. If the output variable is a don't-care term in one case and a 1 in the other, a 1 is written into MEV map square.

MEV	Output
0	*x* or *d*
1	1

MEV	Output
0	1
1	*x* or *d*

Now, Table 2.44 is constructed showing what to enter into MEV map squares. Output *f* is 1 and 0, for standard minterms 0 and 1. Hence, complement of MEV variable ($\overline{c}$) is written in MEV map square 0. Output *f* is 1 and 1 for standard minterms 2 and 3. Hence, a 1 is written in MEV map square 1. Output *f* is 0 and 0 for standard minterms 4 and 5. Hence, a 0 is written into MEV map square 2. Output *f* is 0 and 1, for standard minterms 6 and 7, hence MEV variable *C* is written in MEV map square 3. All these MEV entries are written in last column of Table 2.44.

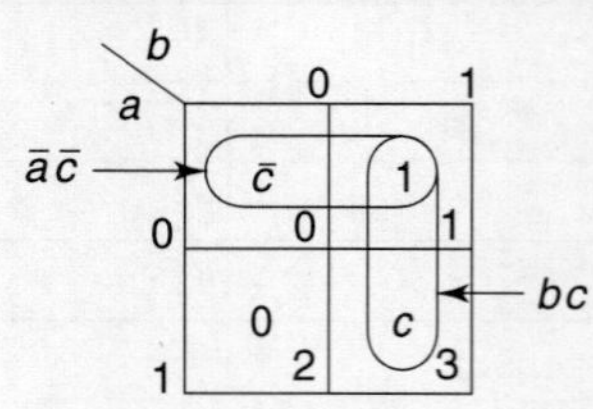

Fig. 2.6 MEV K-map for $\Sigma(0, 2, 3, 7)\, f(a, b, c) = \overline{a}\,\overline{c} + bc$

The MEV entry values are written in the MEV K-map as shown in Fig. 2.6.

There are two EPIs as seen in MEV K-map $f(a, b, c) = \bar{a}\bar{c} + bc$. Standard K-map is shown in Fig. 2.7. From this K-map we observe that the result is same as MEV K-map.

To read the simplified function from MEV K-map:

1. determine the EPIs consisting only 1s along with don't-care terms.
2. consider 1s as don't-care terms once step 1 is done.
3. group all identical MEV terms with 1s or don't-care terms to maximise the MEV EPI size.
4. determine the MEV EPIs by reading the K-map in the normal fashion. Then AND the MEV variable with the remaining map variables.

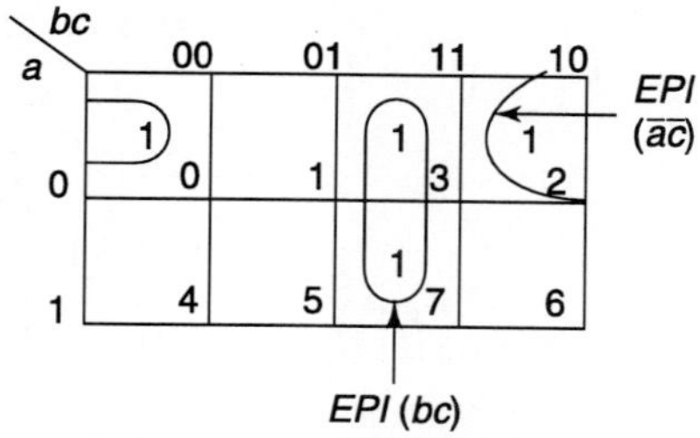

Fig. 2.7 K-map for Σ (0, 2, 3, 7) $f(a, b, c) = \bar{a}\bar{c} + bc$

Example 2.9 Simplify using MEV technique and implement using basic gates.

$$y = \overline{A}\,\overline{B}\,\overline{C}\,\overline{D} + \overline{A}\,\overline{B}\,\overline{C}D + A\overline{B}\,\overline{C}\,\overline{D} + A\overline{B}\,\overline{C}D + \overline{A}\,\overline{B}CD + \overline{A}BC\overline{D} + ABCD + ABC\overline{D},$$

(VTU – June 2011)

Solution The above function is written as

$Y = \Sigma$ (0, 1, 8, 9, 3, 6, 15, 14) and Table 2.45 is constructed for MEV.

Table 2.45

Decimal minterm		*Binary variable*				*Output*	*MEV map entry*
MEV	*Standard*	*a*	*b*	*c*	*d(MEV)*	*f*	
0	0	0	0	0	0	1	1
0	1	0	0	0	1	1	
	2	0	0	1	0	0	*d*
	3	0	0	1	1	1	
	4	0	1	0	0	0	0
	5	0	1	0	1	0	
	6	0	1	1	0	1	$\bar{d}$
	7	0	1	1	1	0	
	8	1	0	0	0	1	1
	9	1	0	0	1	1	
	10	1	0	1	0	0	0
	11	1	0	1	1	0	
	12	1	1	0	0	0	0
	13	1	1	0	1	0	
	14	1	1	1	0	1	1
	15	1	1	1	1	1	

Now MEV K-map is constructed as shown in Fig. 2.8.

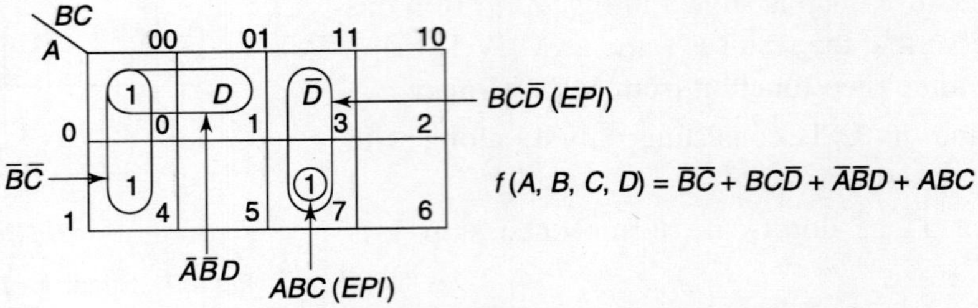

Fig. 2.8 MEV K-map for Σ (0, 1, 8, 9, 3, 6, 15, 14)

Example 2.10 Simplify the logic function given below using map entered variable (MEV) technique:

$$F(a, b, c, d) = \Sigma m\ (2, 9, 10, 11, 13, 14, 15),$$ (VTU – June 2010)

Solution Table 2.46 is constructed for the given Boolean function.

Table 2.46

Decimal minterm		*Binary variables*				*Output*	*MEV map entry*
MEV	*Standard*	*a*	*b*	*c*	*d(MEV)*	*f*	
0	0	0	0	0	0	0	0
0	1	0	0	0	1	0	
1	2	0	0	1	0	1	$\bar{d}$
1	3	0	0	1	1	0	
2	4	0	1	0	0	0	0
2	5	0	1	0	1	0	
3	6	0	1	1	0	0	0
3	7	0	1	1	1	0	
4	8	1	0	0	0	0	*d*
4	9	1	0	0	1	1	
5	10	1	0	1	0	1	1
5	11	1	0	1	1	1	
6	12	1	1	0	0	0	*d*
6	13	1	1	0	1	1	
7	14	1	1	1	0	1	1
7	15	1	1	1	1	1	

From Table 2.46, MEV map entries are written in the MEV K-map as shown in Fig. 2.9

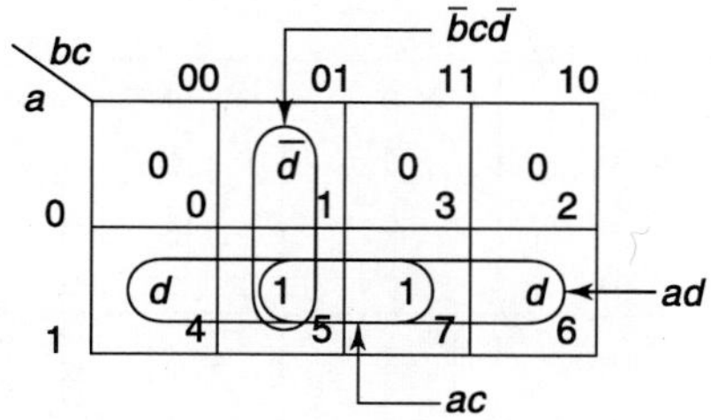

Fig. 2.9 MEV K-map for Σm (2, 9, 10, 11, 13, 14, 15)

From MEV K-map, we observe

$$f(a, b, c, d) = ac + ad + \bar{b}c\bar{d}$$

Example 2.11 Simplify the given function using MEV technique taking the least significant variable as the map entered variable.

$$f(a, b, c, d) = \Sigma(1, 3, 4, 6, 9, 11, 12, 14, 17, 19, 20, 22, 25, 27, 28, 30) + \Sigma d(8, 10, 24, 26).$$

(VTU – Dec 2013)

Solution Along with decimal minterms, the output function and MEV map entry are tabulated in Table 2.47.

Table 2.47

Decimal minterm		Binary variables					Output	MEV map entry
MEV	Standard	a	b	c	d	e(MEV)	f	
0	0	0	0	0	0	0	0	e
0	1	0	0	0	0	1	1	
1	2	0	0	0	1	0	0	e
1	3	0	0	0	1	1	1	
2	4	0	0	1	0	0	1	$\bar{e}$
2	5	0	0	1	0	1	0	
3	6	0	0	1	1	0	1	$\bar{e}$
3	7	0	0	1	1	1	0	
4	8	0	1	0	0	0	×	1
4	9	0	1	0	0	1	1	
5	10	0	1	0	1	0	×	1
5	11	0	1	0	1	1	1	
6	12	0	1	1	0	0	1	$\bar{e}$
6	13	0	1	1	0	1	0	
7	14	0	1	1	1	0	1	$\bar{e}$
7	15	0	1	1	1	1	0	

Contd...

Contd...

8	16	1	0	0	0	0	0	e
8	17	1	0	0	0	1	1	
9	18	1	0	0	1	0	0	e
9	19	1	0	0	1	1	1	
10	20	1	0	1	0	0	1	$\bar{e}$
10	21	1	0	1	0	1	0	
11	22	1	0	1	1	0	1	$\bar{e}$
11	23	1	0	1	1	1	0	
12	24	1	1	0	0	0	×	1
12	25	1	1	0	0	1	1	
13	26	1	1	0	1	0	×	1
13	27	1	1	0	1	1	1	
14	28	1	1	1	0	0	1	$\bar{e}$
14	29	1	1	1	0	1	0	
15	30	1	1	1	1	0	1	$\bar{e}$
15	31	1	1	1	1	1	0	

From Table 2.47 data, let us construct MEV K-map.

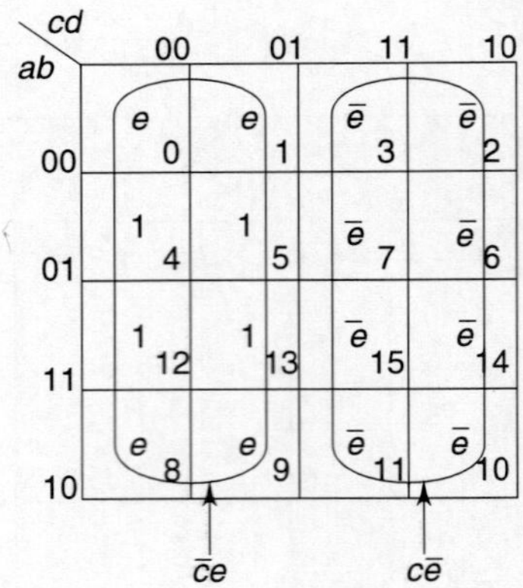

Fig. 2.10 MEV K-map for $f(a, b, c, d, e)$

From MEV K-map, we observe that

$$f(a, b, c, d, e) = \bar{c}e + c\bar{e} = c \oplus e$$

Example 2.12 Simplify the logic function given below using Variable Entered Mapping (VEM) technique.

$$f(A, B, C, D) = \Sigma m\,(0, 1, 3, 5, 6, 11, 13) + \Sigma d\,(4, 7) \qquad \text{(VTU – June 2013)}$$

Solution Table 2.48, is created from the data given.

Table 2.48

Decimal minterm		Binary variables				Output	MEV map entry
MEV	Standard	A	B	C	D (MEV)	f	
0	0	0	0	0	0	1	1
0	1	0	0	0	1	1	
1	2	0	0	1	0	0	D
1	3	0	0	1	1	1	
2	4	0	1	0	0	×	1
2	5	0	1	0	1	1	
3	6	0	1	1	0	1	1
3	7	0	1	1	1	×	
4	8	1	0	0	0	0	0
4	9	1	0	0	1	0	
5	10	1	0	1	0	0	D
5	11	1	0	1	1	1	
6	12	1	1	0	0	0	D
6	13	1	1	0	1	1	
7	14	1	1	1	0	0	0
7	15	1	1	1	1	0	

From Table entries, MEV K-map is constructed as shown in Fig. 2.11.

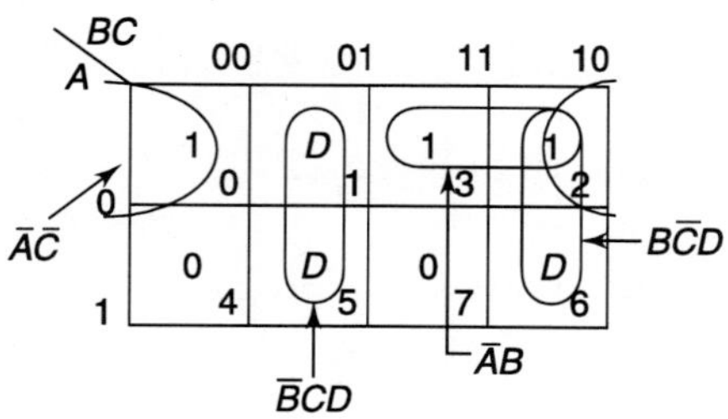

Fig. 2.11 MEV K-map for Σm (0,1,3,5,6,11,13) + d (4, 7)

From the MEV K-map, we observe that there are two EPIs, using 1s, i.e., {0, 2} and {2, 3}. Once, we complete forming groups using 1s and don't-care terms, if any, then look for groups 1s and MEVs. We find that {2, 6} is EPI and the expression in $B\bar{C}$ multiplied by MEV variable D, i.e., we get the EPI as $B\bar{C}D$. Next group is only Ds, i.e., group {1, 5}. We get EPI as $\bar{B}C$ multiplied by MEV variable D, i.e., EPI is $\bar{B}CD$.

Hence, the simplified expression is

$$f(A, B, C, D) = \bar{A}B + \bar{A}\,\bar{C} + B\bar{C}D + \bar{B}CD$$

Example 2.13 Simplify $f(a, b, c, d) = \Sigma m\ (2, 3, 4, 5, 13, 15) + dc\ (8, 9, 10, 11)$ taking least significant bit as map entered variable.

Solution Table 2.49 is created from the data given in the problem. d variable is taken as MEV.

Table 2.49

Decimal minterm		*Binary variables*				*Output*	*MEV map entry*
MEV	*Standard*	*a*	*b*	*c*	*d (MEV)*	*f*	
0	0	0	0	0	0	0	0
0	1	0	0	0	1	0	
1	2	0	0	1	0	1	1
1	3	0	0	1	1	1	
2	4	0	1	0	0	1	1
2	5	0	1	0	1	1	
3	6	0	1	1	0	0	0
3	7	0	1	1	1	0	
4	8	1	0	0	0	×	×
4	9	1	0	0	1	×	
5	10	1	0	1	0	×	×
5	11	1	0	1	1	×	
6	12	1	1	0	0	0	*d*
6	13	1	1	0	1	1	
7	14	1	1	1	0	0	*d*
7	15	1	1	1	1	1	

MEV K-map is constructed as shown in Fig. 2.12.

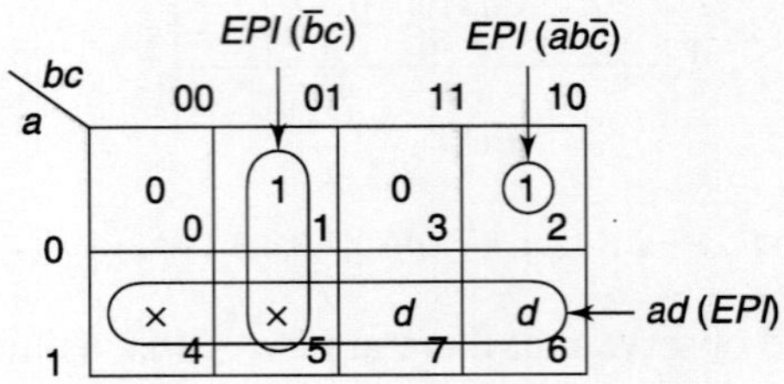

Fig. 2.12 MEV K-map for $\Sigma m\ (2, 3, 4, 5, 13, 15) + dc\ (8, 9, 10, 11)$

First group is {1, 5}. This becomes EPI. Next minterm {2} is EPI and third EPI is (4, 5, 6, 7).

Hence, the simplified expression is

$$f(a, b, c, d) = ad + \bar{b}c + \bar{a}b\bar{c}$$

Example 2.14 Simplify the function

$$f(a, b, c, d) = \Sigma m\,(2, 3, 4, 5, 13, 15) + dc\,(8, 9, 10, 11)$$

using a two variable MEV K-map. (VTU – Dec 2011)

Solution The given function is a four-variable function and to simplify it using a two-variable MEV K-map; we have to group 4 minterms. The data entry for MEV K-map is shown in Table 2.50.

Table 2.50

Decimal minterm		Binary variables				Output	MEV map entry
MEV	Standard	a	b	c (MEV)	d (MEV)	f	
0	0	0	0	0	0	0	c
0	1	0	0	0	1	0	
0	2	0	0	1	0	1	
0	3	0	0	1	1	1	
1	4	0	1	0	0	1	$\bar{c}$
1	5	0	1	0	1	1	
1	6	0	1	1	0	0	
1	7	0	1	1	1	0	
2	8	1	0	0	0	×	×
2	9	1	0	0	1	×	
2	10	1	0	1	0	×	
2	11	1	0	1	1	×	
3	12	1	1	0	0	0	d
3	13	1	1	0	1	1	
3	14	1	1	1	0	0	
3	15	1	1	1	1	1	

Two variable MEV K-map is shown in Fig. 2.13. For MEV 0 minterm, the output follows MEV variable c, hence MEV map entry is c Similarly, MEV 1 minterm, MEV 2 minterm and MEV 3 minterm contain $\bar{c}$, x and d respectively.

Hence, the simplified expression is,

$$f(a, b, c, d) = ad + \bar{b}c + \bar{a}\bar{c}$$

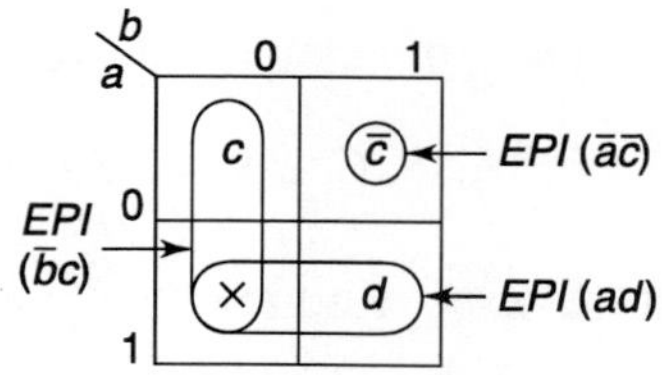

Fig. 2.13 MEV K-map for Σm (2, 3, 4, 5, 13, 15) + dc (8, 9, 10, 11

Example 2.15 Simplify the function $f(A, B, C, D) = \Sigma m$ (0, 1, 3, 5, 6, 11, 13) + d (4, 7) using two variable.

Solution As the function has four variables to simplify it, using two-variable MEV K-map, we have to group 4 minterms.

Table 2.51

Decimal minterm		Binary variables				Output		MEV map entry
MEV	Standard	A	B	C (MEV)	D (MEV)	f		
0	0	0	0	0	0	1	$\bar{C}+D$	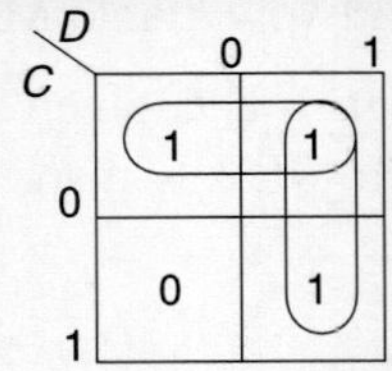
0	1	0	0	0	1	1		
0	2	0	0	1	0	0		
0	3	0	0	1	1	1		
1	4	0	1	0	0	×	1	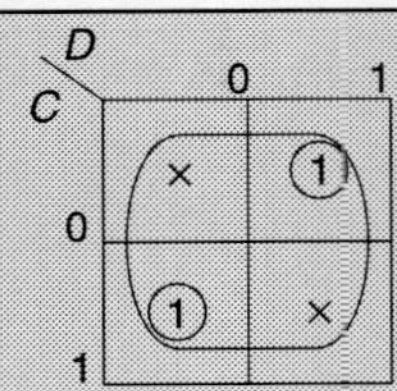
1	5	0	1	0	1	1		
1	6	0	1	1	0	1		
1	7	0	1	1	1	×		
2	8	1	0	0	0	0	CD	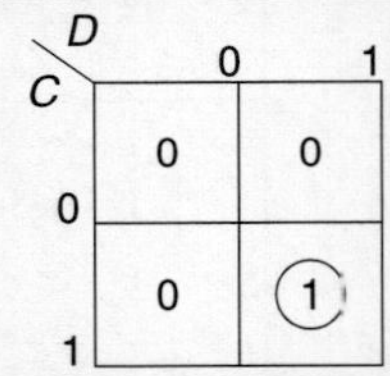
2	9	1	0	0	1	0		
2	10	1	0	1	0	0		
2	11	1	0	1	1	1		
3	12	1	1	0	0	0	$\bar{C}D$	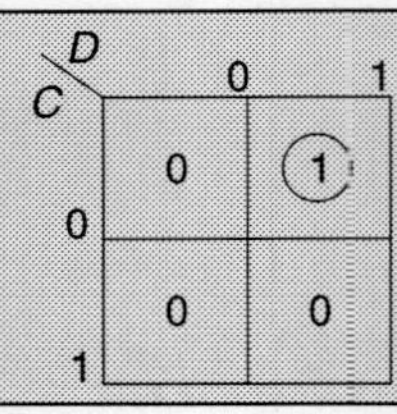
3	13	1	1	0	1	1		
3	14	1	1	1	0	0		
3	15	1	1	1	1	0		

MEV K-map is shown in Fig. 2.14.

Here, grouping is slightly different. First, there is a single 1 in MEV map square 1. Hence, this becomes $\bar{A}B$. Then, we may group the MEVs. Now, minterms 1 and 3 can be grouped together to give the expression $B\bar{C}D$. In minterms 0 and 2, D and CD are grouped together to give $\bar{B}CD$. Minterms 1 and 0 can be grouped to give $\bar{A}\,\bar{C}$ (taking only $\bar{C}$ from 0 minterm.

Hence, the simplified expression is

$$f(A, B, C, D) = \bar{A}B + \bar{A}\,\bar{C} + B\bar{C}D + \bar{B}CD$$

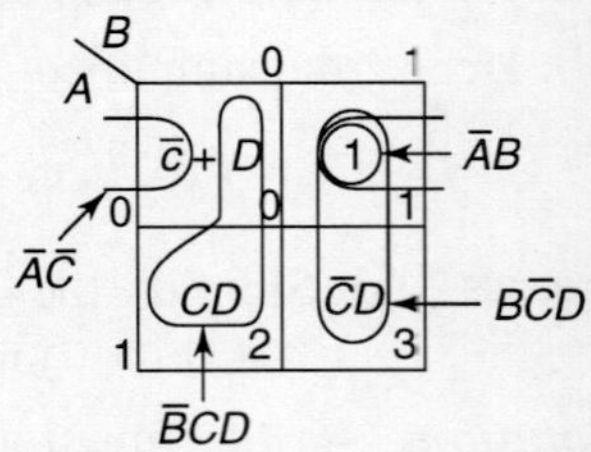

Fig. 2.14 MEV K-map for Σm (0, 1, 3, 5, 6, 11, 13) + d (4, 7)

Example 2.16 Reduce the given switching function using single variable map technique.

$$f(A, B, C, D) = \Sigma m\,(0, 1, 4, 7, 10, 14)$$

(VTU – Aug 2006)

Solution The given function is a four-variable function. It has to be simplified using single variable MEV K-map. So, we have to group 8 minterms.

Table 2.52

Decimal minterm		Binary variables				Output		MEV map entry
MEV	Standard	A	B (MEV)	C (MEV)	D (MEV)	f		
0	0	0	0	0	0	1	$\overline{B}\,\overline{C}+\overline{C}\,\overline{D}+BCD$	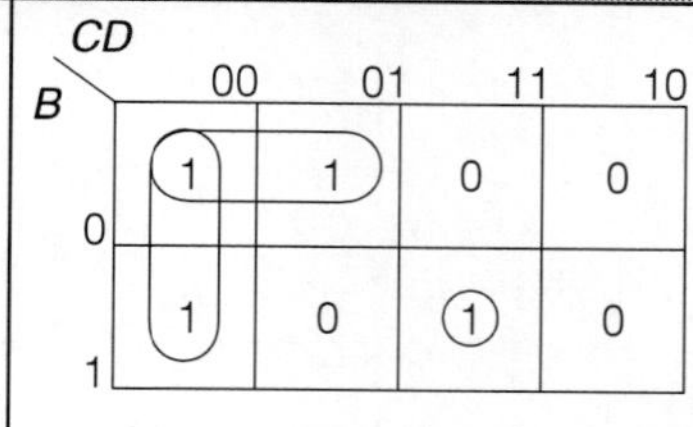
0	1	0	0	0	1	1		
0	2	0	0	1	0	0		
0	3	0	0	1	1	0		
0	4	0	1	0	0	1		
0	5	0	1	0	1	0		
0	6	0	1	1	0	0		
0	7	0	1	1	1	1		
1	8	1	0	0	0	0	$C\overline{D}$	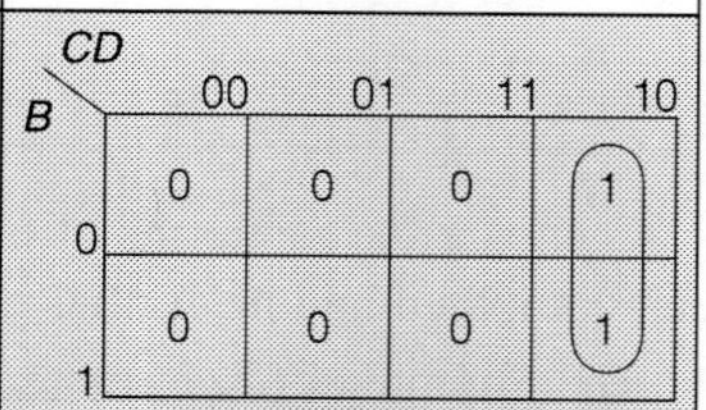
1	9	1	0	0	1	0		
1	10	1	0	1	0	1		
1	11	1	0	1	1	0		
1	12	1	1	0	0	0		
1	13	1	1	0	1	0		
1	14	1	1	1	0	1		
1	15	1	1	1	1	0		

MEV K-map is shown in Fig. 2.15.

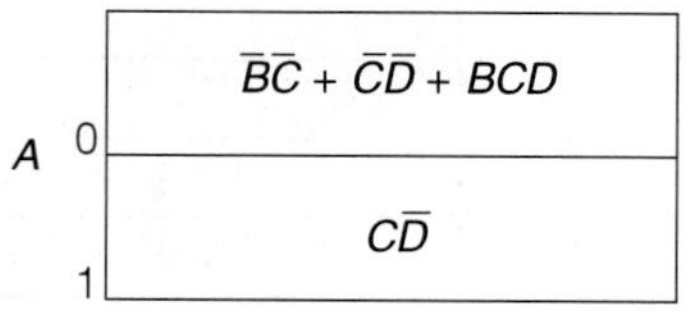

Fig. 2.15 MEV K-map for Σm (0, 1, 4, 7, 10, 14)

Hence, the simplified expression is

$$f(A, B, C, D) = \overline{A}\,\overline{B}\,C + \overline{A}\,\overline{C}\,\overline{D} + \overline{A}BCD + AC\overline{D}$$

From the single variable MEV K-map, $\overline{A}$ is multiplied with $\overline{B}\,\overline{C} + \overline{C}\,\overline{D} + BCD$ and A is multiplied with $C\overline{D}$.

Example 2.17 Find a minimal sum for the following Boolean function using decimal Quine-McCluskey method and prime implicant table reduction $F = \Sigma(1, 2, 3, 5, 6, 7, 8, 9, 12, 13, 15)$

(VTU – June 2014)

Solution Table 2.53 shows the arrangement of minterms of the given Boolean function as per increasing number of 1s.

Table 2.53

Group	Minterms	Variables				
		a	*b*	*c*	*d*	
1	1	0	0	0	1	✓
	2	0	0	1	0	✓
	8	1	0	0	0	✓
2	3	0	0	1	1	✓
	5	0	1	0	1	✓
	6	0	1	1	0	✓
	9	1	0	0	1	✓
	12	1	1	0	0	✓
3	7	0	1	1	1	✓
	13	1	1	0	1	✓
4	15	1	1	1	1	✓

Compare the minterms of one group with that of next higher group until all the groups have been compared and no further grouping is possible.

The grouping of two minterms and comparison is shown in Table 2.54.

Table 2.54

Group	Minterms	Variables				
		a	*b*	*c*	*d*	
1	1, 3	0	0	–	1	✓
	1, 5	0	–	0	1	✓
	1, 9	–	0	0	1	✓
	2, 3	0	0	1	–	✓
	2, 6	0	–	1	0	✓
	8, 9	1	0	0	–	✓
	8, 12	1	–	0	0	✓
2	3, 7	0	–	1	1	✓
	5, 7	0	1	–	1	✓
	5, 13	–	1	0	1	✓
	6, 7	0	1	1	–	✓
	9, 13	1	–	0	1	✓
	12, 13	1	1	0	–	✓
3	7, 15	–	1	1	1	✓
	13, 15	1	1	–	1	✓

Again comparison is made between groups of two minterms and groups of four minterms are formed as shown in Table 2.55.

Table 2.55

Group	Minterms	Variables			
		a	*b*	*c*	*d*
1	1, 3, 5, 7	0	–	–	1
	1, 9, 5, 13	–	–	0	1
	2, 3, 6, 7	0	–	1	–
	8, 9, 12, 13	1	–	0	–
2	5, 13, 7, 15	–	1	–	1

Again comparison is made between groups of four minterms. We find that no comparison is possible.

All non-checked minterm groups form prime implicant (PI) table. All the minterms given in the Boolean expressions are placed across the table. PI table is given in Table 2.56. From the PI table let us find EPIs and minimal SOP expression.

Table 2.56

PI terms	Decimal	Minterms										
		1	2	3	5	6	7	8	9	12	13	15
$\bar{a}d$	1, 3, 5, 7	×		×	×		×					
$\bar{c}d$	1, 9, 5, 13	×			×				⊗		×	
$\bar{a}c$	2, 3, 6, 7		×	×		⊗	×					
$a\bar{c}$	8, 9, 12, 13							⊗	×	×	×	
bd	5, 13, 7, 15				×		×				×	⊗

Let us consider the PI terms for which the minterm column has a single minterm. The group (1, 3, 5, 7) and (1, 9, 5, 13) has no single minterm.

Group (2, 3, 6, 7) has 6 as single minterm

Group (8, 9, 12, 13) has 8 as single minterm

Group (5, 13, 7, 15) has 15 as single minterm

Hence, these three groups, namely, (2, 3, 6, 7), (8, 9, 12, 13) and (5, 13, 7, 15), are EPIs and part of solution.

But between groups (1, 3, 5, 7) and (1, 9, 5, 13), minterm '1' is common to them and is not there as part of any other group. Hence, either group will form part of the solution.

Let us take the group (1, 9, 5, 13), as part of solution.

Hence, $f(a, b, c, d)$

$$= \bar{c}d + \bar{a}c + a\bar{c} + bd$$

If we consider (1, 3, 5, 7)

then $f(a, b, c, d) = \bar{a}d + \bar{a}c + a\bar{c} + bd$

Both are correct solutions.

Example 2.18 Using Quine-McCluskey method and prime implicant reduction, determine the minimal SOP expression for the following using decimal notation.

$$f(w, x, y, z) = \pi M(0, 4, 5, 9) * d(1, 7, 13)$$

The expression $f(w, x, y, z) = \pi M(0, 4, 5, 9) * d(1, 7, 13)$

can be writhen as $f(w, x, y, z) = \Sigma m(2, 3, 6, 8, 10, 11, 12, 14, 15) * d(1, 7, 13)$

Table 2.57 shows the arrangement of minterms of the above Boolean expression as per increasing number of 1s.

Table 2.57

Group	Minterms	Variables				
		w	x	y	z	
1	1*	0	0	0	1	✓
	2	0	0	1	0	✓
	8	1	0	0	0	✓
2	3	0	0	1	1	✓
	6	0	1	1	0	✓
	10	1	0	1	0	✓
	12	1	1	0	0	✓
3	7*	0	1	1	1	✓
	11	1	0	1	1	✓
	13*	1	1	0	1	✓
	14	1	1	1	0	✓
4	15	1	1	1	1	✓

Compare the minterms of one group with that of next higher group until all the groups have been compared and no further grouping is possible. The grouping of two minterms and comparison is shown in Table 2.58.

Table 2.58

Group	Minterms	Variables				
		w	x	y	z	
1	1*, 3	0	0	–	1	
	2, 3	0	0	1	–	
	2, 6	0	–	1	0	✓
	2, 10	–	0	1	0	✓
	8, 10	1	0	–	0	✓
	8, 12	1	–	0	0	✓

Contd...

2	3, 7*	0	–	1	1	✓
	3, 11	–	0	1	1	✓
	6, 7*	0	1	1	–	✓
	6, 14	–	1	1	0	✓
	10, 11	1	0	1	–	✓
	10, 14	1	–	1	0	✓
	12, 13*	1	1	0	–	✓
	12, 14	1	1	–	0	✓
3	7,* 15	–	1	1	1	✓
	11, 15	1	–	1	1	✓
	13*, 15	1	1	–	1	✓
	14, 15	1	1	1	–	✓

Again comparison is made between groups of two minterms and groups of four minterms are formed as shown in Table 2.59.

Table 2.59

Group	Minterms	Variables				
		w	x	y	z	
1	2, 6, 3, 7*	0	–	1	–	✓
	2, 6, 10, 14	–	–	1	0	✓
	2, 10, 3, 11	–	0	1	–	✓
	8, 10, 12, 14	1	–	–	0	
2	3, 7,* 11, 15	–	–	1	1	✓
	6, 7*, 14, 15	–	1	1	–	✓
	10, 11, 14, 15	1	–	1	–	✓
	12, 13*, 14, 15	1	1	–	–	

Again comparison is made between groups of four minterms and groups of eight minterms are formed as shown in Table 2.60.

Table 2.60

Group	Minterms	Variables			
		w	x	y	z
1	2, 6, 3, 7*, 10, 11, 14, 15	–	–	1	–

Non-checked minterms groups form Prime Implicant (PI) table. All the minterms given in the Boolean expression are placed across the table. PI table is given as Table 2.61. From the PI table let us find EPIs and minimal SOP expression.

Table 2.61

PI terms	Decimal	Minterms											
		1*	2	3	6	7	8	10	11	12	13*	14	15
$\bar{w}\bar{x}z$	1*, 3	⊗		×									
$w\bar{z}$	8, 10, 12, 14						⊗	×		×		×	
wx	12, 13*, 14, 15									×	×	×	×
y	2, 6, 3, 7*, 10, 11, 14, 15		⊗	×	⊗	⊗		×	⊗			×	×

Let us consider the PI terms for which the minterm column has a single minterm. The groups of minterms (1*, 3), (8, 10, 12, 14), (12, 13*, 14, 15) and (2, 6, 3, 7*, 10, 11, 14, 15) have all single minterms in the minterm column.

The group (1*, 3) has 1* as single minterm which is a don't-care term. The other minterm is covered by (2, 6, 3, 7*, 10, 11, 14, 15). Hence, this group (1*, 3) is eliminated.

The group (8, 10, 12, 14) has 8 as a single minterm in the minterm column. Here this group is EPI.

The group (12, 13*, 14, 15) has 13* as a single minterm in the minterm column which is a don't-care term. Other minterms (12, 14, 15) are covered by the group (8, 10, 12, 14) and (2, 6, 3, 7*, 10, 11, 14, 15). Hence, this group (12, 13*, 14, 15) is eliminated.

The group (2, 6, 3, 7*, 10, 11, 14, 15) has 2, 6, 7*, 11, 15 as single minterms in minterm column. Hence, this group (2, 6, 3, 7*, 10, 11, 15) forms as EPI.

Hence, there are two EPIs which form part of minimal SOP expression.

Hence, $f(w, x, y, z) = y + w\bar{z}$

Example 2.19 Using Quine-McCluskey tabulation method, obtain the set of prime implicants for the function

$$f(a, b, c, d) = \Sigma(0, 1, 4, 5, 9, 10, 12, 14, 15) + \Sigma\phi(2, 8, 13)$$

and hence obtain the minimal form of the given function employing decimal representation.

(VTU – July 2005)

Table 2.62 shows the arrangement of minterms of the given Boolean expression as per increasing number of 1s.

Table 2.62

Group	Minterms	Variables				
		a	b	c	d	
0	0,	0	0	0	0	✓
1	1	0	0	0	1	✓
	2*	0	0	1	0	✓
	4	0	1	0	0	✓
	8*	1	0	0	0	✓

Contd...

2	5	0	1	0	1	✓
	9	1	0	0	1	✓
	10	1	0	1	0	✓
	12	1	1	0	0	✓
3	13*	1	1	0	1	✓
	14	1	1	1	0	✓
4	15	1	1	1	1	✓

Compare the minterms from one group to the next higher group so that there is only one variable change between them. This procedure is continued until no further grouping is possible. The resulting table is shown in Table 2.63.

Table 2.63

Group	*Minterms*	*Variables*				
		a	*b*	*c*	*d*	
0	0, 1	0	0	0	–	✓
	0, 2*	0	0	–	0	✓
	0, 4	0	–	0	0	✓
	0, 8*	–	0	0	0	✓
1	1, 5	0	–	0	1	✓
	1, 9	–	0	0	1	✓
	2, 10	–	0	1	0	✓
	4, 5	0	1	0	–	✓
	4, 12	–	1	0	0	✓
	8, 9	1	0	0	–	✓
	8*, 10	1	0	–	0	✓
	8, 12	1	–	0	0	✓
2	5, 13*	–	1	0	1	✓
	9, 13	1	–	0	1	✓
	10, 14	1	–	1	0	✓
	12, 14	1	1	–	0	✓
3	13, 15	1	1	–	1	✓
	14, 15	1	1	1	–	✓

Next, comparison is made between one group of two minterms with next higher group of two minterms until no further grouping is possible. The resulting groups of four minterms is shown in Table 2.64.

Table 2.64

Group	Minterms	Variables				
		a	b	c	d	
0	0, 1, 8*, 9	–	0	0	–	✓
	0, 2*, 8*, 10	–	0	–	0	
	0, 4, 1, 5	0	–	0	–	✓
	0, 4, 8*, 12	–	–	0	0	✓
1	1, 9, 5, 13*	–	–	0	1	✓
	4, 12, 5, 13*	–	1	0	–	✓
	8*, 10, 12, 14	1	–	–	0	
2	12, 13*, 14, 15	1	1	–	–	

Next, comparison is made between minterms from one group to the next higher group so that there is only one variable change between them. This procedure is continued until no further grouping is possible. The resulting table is shown in Table 2.65.

Table 2.65

Group	Minterms	Variables			
		a	b	c	d
0	0, 1, 8, 9, 4, 12, 5, 13	–	–	0	–

From the four tables, non-checked group of minterms are tabulated in Table 2.66 they form prime implicants.

Table 2.66

PI terms	Minterms	Variables			
		a	b	c	d
$\bar{b}\bar{d}$	0, 2*, 8*, 10	–	0	–	0
$a\bar{d}$	8*, 10, 12, 14	1	–	–	0
ab	12, 13*, 14, 15	1	1	–	–
$\bar{c}$	0, 1, 8*, 9, 4, 12, 5, 13*	–	–	0	–

Let us consider the PI table where all the minterms in the given expression are placed across the table. The PI table is shown in Table 2.67.

Table 2.67

PI terms	Decimal	Minterms											
		0	1	2*	4	5	8*	9	10	12	13*	14	15
$\bar{b}\bar{d}$	0, 2*, 8*, 10	×		×			×		×				
$a\bar{d}$	8*, 10, 12, 14						×		×	×		×	
ab	12, 13*, 14, 15									×	×	×	×
$\bar{c}$	0, 1, 8*, 9, 4, 12, 5, 13	×	×		×	×	×	×		×	×		

Let us consider the PI terms for which the minterm column has a single minterm. The group of minterms (0, 2*, 8*, 10) has minterm 2*, as the single minterm is minterm column.

But minterm 2* is a don't-care term. Hence, this PI term can be eliminated. Next group of minterms (8*, 10, 12, 14) there is no single minterm is the minterm column. Hence, this PI term can be eliminated but if we observe carefully there is a minterm 10 which is available only in these two PI terms. Hence, we have to choose at least one PI term out of the two PI terms. Let us choose (0, 2*, 8*, 10). Hence, this PI term becomes part of the solution.

In PI term *ab*, the group of minterm (12, 13*, 14, 15), minterm 15 is single minterm in the minterm column. Hence, *ab* becomes EPI.

The group of minterms (0, 1, 8*, 9, 4, 12, 5, 13*) there are minterms (1, 4, 5, 9) are single minterms in the minterm column. Hence, this group becomes EPI.

Hence, $f(a, b, c, d) = \overline{b}\overline{d} + ab + \overline{c}$

Example 2.20 For the given Boolean function determine a minimal sum using MEV techniques using *a*, *b*, *c* as the map variables

$$f(a, b, c, d) = \Sigma(3, 4, 5, 6, 7, 8, 9, 12, 13, 15) \qquad \text{(VTU – June 2014)}$$

Solution Table 2.68 is created from the Boolean function given.

Table 2.68

Decimal minterm		Binary variables				Output	MEV map entry
MEV	Standard	a	b	c	d (MEV)	f	
0	0	0	0	0	0	0	0
0	1	0	0	0	1	0	
1	2	0	0	1	0	0	d
1	3	0	0	1	1	1	
2	4	0	1	0	0	1	1
2	5	0	1	0	1	1	
3	6	0	1	1	0	1	1
3	7	0	1	1	1	1	
4	8	1	0	0	0	1	1
4	9	1	0	0	1	1	
5	10	1	0	1	0	0	0
5	11	1	0	1	1	0	
6	12	1	1	0	0	1	1
6	13	1	1	0	1	1	
7	14	1	1	1	0	0	d
7	15	1	1	1	1	1	

From the Table 2.68 data, MEV K-map is constructed as shown in Fig. 2.16.

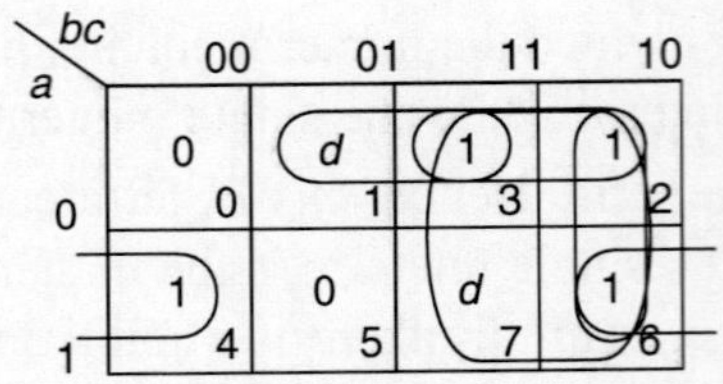

Fig. 2.16 K-Map for Example 2.20

$$f(a, b, c, d) = a\bar{c} + \bar{a}b + bd + \bar{a}cd$$

Example 2.21 Find a minimal sum for the following Boolean function using MEV technique with a, b, and c as the map variables $f(\alpha, \beta, a, b, c) = \alpha\overline{abc} + \alpha\overline{abc} + \alpha a\bar{b}c + \bar{\beta}abc + \beta\bar{a}\overline{bc} + \bar{a}bc$ $+ a\overline{bc}$ (VTU – June 2014)

Solution It is given that a, b and c are map variables. α and β are MEVs and they are ANDed with the cell variables.

The three variable K-map is shown in Fig. 2.17.

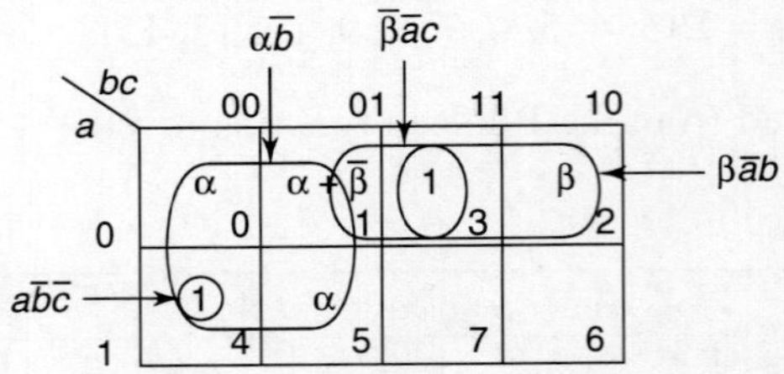

Fig. 2.17 K-map for Example 2.21

$$f(\alpha, \beta, a, b, c) = \alpha\bar{b} + \bar{\beta}\bar{a}c + \beta\bar{a}b + a\bar{b}\bar{c}$$

Example 2.22 Find the minimal sum and minimal product using MEV technique using a, b, c as map variables $f(a, b, c, d) = \Sigma m(3, 4, 5, 7, 8, 11, 12, 13, 15)$

Solution Table 2.69 is created from the data given in the Boolean function.

Table 2.69

Decimal minterm		*Binary variables*				*Output*	*MEV map entry*
MEV	*Standard*	*a*	*b*	*c*	*d (MEV)*	*f*	
0	0	0	0	0	0	0	0
0	1	0	0	0	1	0	
1	2	0	0	1	0	0	d
1	3	0	0	1	1	1	
2	4	0	1	0	0	1	1
2	5	0	1	0	1	1	
3	6	0	1	1	0	0	d
3	7	0	1	1	1	1	

Contd...

4	8	1	0	0	0	1	$\bar{d}$
4	9	1	0	0	1	0	
5	10	1	0	1	0	0	d
5	11	1	0	1	1	1	
6	12	1	1	0	0	1	1
6	13	1	1	0	1	1	
7	14	1	1	1	0	0	d
7	15	1	1	1	1	1	

From Table 2.69 data, MEV K-maps are constructed for minimal sum and minimal product as shown in Fig. 2.18 and Fig. 2.19 respectively.

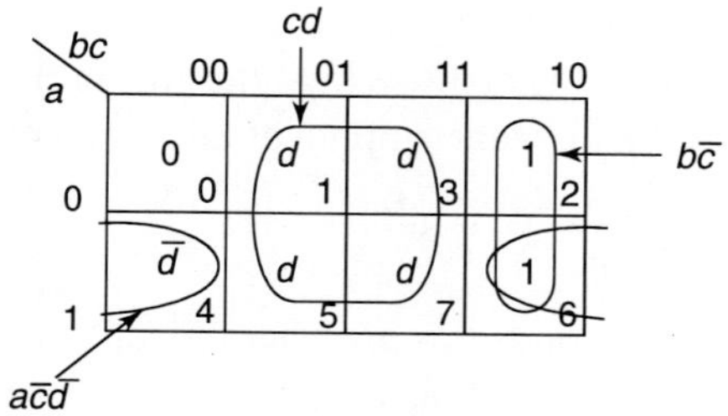

Fig. 2.18 MEV K-map for minimal sum for Example 2.22

$$f(a, b, c, d) = cd + b\bar{c} + a\bar{c}\bar{d}$$

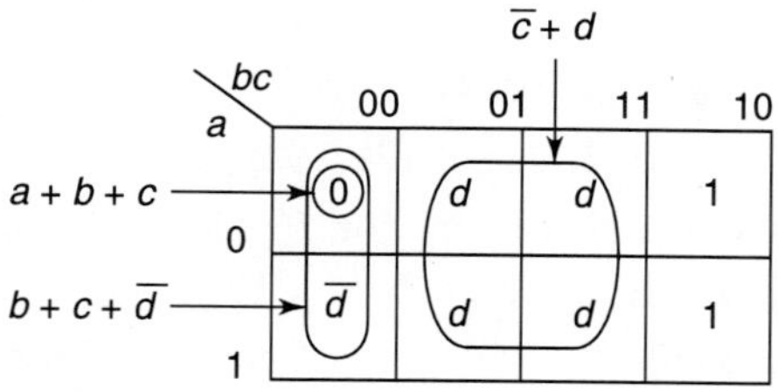

Fig. 2.19 MEV K-map for minimal product for example 2.22

$$f(a, b, c, d) = (a + b + c)\ (b + c + \bar{d})\ (\bar{c} + d)$$

EXERCISE

1. Simplify the following using tabulation method:

$$Y(A, B, C, D) = \Sigma m(1, 2, 3, 5, 9, 12, 14, 15) + d(4, 8, 11)$$

2. Simplify the following using Quine-McCluskey method:

$$f = \Sigma(0, 1, 2, 8, 10, 11, 14, 15)$$

3. Use Quine-McCluskey method to simplify the following function:

(i) $f(A, B, C, D, E) = \Sigma m(8, 9, 10, 11, 13, 15, 16, 18, 21, 24, 25, 26, 27, 30, 31)$

(ii) $f(A, B, C, D) = \Sigma m(1, 3, 5, 8, 9, 11, 15) + d(2, 13)$

4. Use Quine-McCluskey method to simplify the following function:

$$f(a, b, c, d) = \Sigma m(0, 1, 2, 3, 8, 9)$$

5. Using Quine-McCluskey tabulation method, obtain the set of prime implicants for the function $f(a, b, c, d) = \Sigma(0, 1, 4, 5, 9, 10, 12, 14, 15) + \Sigma\phi(2, 8, 13)$ and hence obtain the minimal form of the given function employing decimal representation.

6. Find a minimal sum for the following Boolean functions using decimal Quine-McCluskey method and prime implicants table reduction.

(i) $f(a, b, c, d) = \Sigma(1, 3, 5, 8, 9, 11, 12, 15)$

(ii) $f(a, b, c, d) = \Sigma(0, 3, 5, 7, 10, 11) + \Sigma d(4, 14)$

7. Find a minimal sum for the following incomplete. Boolean functions using Quine-McCluskey method and prime implicant table reduction.

(i) $f(a, b, c, d) = \Sigma\ (0, 1, 2, 3, 4, 6, 7, 9, 11, 12, 13, 15)$

(ii) $f(a, b, c, d) = a\bar{b} + c\bar{d} + \bar{c}$

8. Using Quine-McCluskey method and prime implicant table reductions, determine the minimal sums for the incomplete boolean function.

$$f(v, w, x, y, z) = \Sigma m(4, 5, 9, 11, 12, 14, 15, 27, 30) + dc(1, 17, 25, 26, 31)$$

9. Find all the prime implicants of the following functions using Quine-McCluskey method:

(i) $f(a, b, c, d) = \Sigma(0, 5, 6, 7, 9, 10, 12, 15)$

(ii) $f(a, b, c, d) = \Sigma(0, 1, 2, 6, 7, 9, 10, 12) + \Sigma d(3, 5)$

10. Find all the prime implicants of the function $f(a, b, c, d) = \pi(1, 3, 6, 7, 9, 11, 13, 14)$ by applying Quine-McCluskey algorithum on $\bar{f}$.

11. Determine the minimal SOP using tabulation method with only decimal notation.

$$f(A, B, C, D, E) = \Sigma(13, 15, 17, 18, 19, 20, 21, 23, 25, 27, 29, 31) + \Sigma\phi(1, 2, 12, 24)$$

12. Obtain all the prime implicants of the function

$$f(w, x, y, z) = \Sigma(0, 1, 2, 8, 10, 11, 14, 15)$$

13. Determine the minimal SOP using tabulation method with only decimal notation.

$$f(A, B, C, D, E) = \Sigma(13, 15,17, 18, 19, 20, 21, 23, 25, 27, 29, 31) + \Sigma\phi(1, 2, 12, 24)$$

14. Using Quine-McCluskey method and prime implicant reduction, determine the minimal SOP expression for the following using decimal notation:

$$f(w, x, y, z) = \pi M(0, 4, 5, 9) *d(1, 7, 13)$$

15. Write the map entered variable K-map for the Boolean function.

$$f(w, x, y, z) = \Sigma m(2, 9, 10, 11, 13, 14, 15)$$

16. Reduce the given switching function using single variable map technique.

$$f(A, B, C, D) = \Sigma m(0, 1, 4, 7, 10, 14)$$

17. Find the minimal sum and minimal product using MEV technique using a, b, c, as map variables.

$$f(a, b, c, d) = \Sigma m(3, 4, 5, 7, 8, 11, 12, 13, 15)$$

18. Simplify the function.

$$f(a, b, c, d) = \Sigma m(2, 3, 4, 5, 13, 15) + d(8, 9, 10, 11)$$

using two variable MEV K-map.

19. Reduce the given switching function using single variable map teachnique.

$$f(A, B, C, D) = \Sigma m(0, 1, 4, 7, 10, 14)$$

20. Simplify the function.

$f(A, B, C, D) = \Sigma m(0, 1, 3, 5, 6, 11, 13) + d(4, 7)$

using 3-veriable

MEV K-map.

CHAPTER 3

Analysis and Design of Combinational Logic-1

3.1 GENERAL APPROACH

Combinational logic circuits are decoders, encoders, multiplexers, arithmetic circuits, etc. The design of combinational logic starts with a problem statement and goes through six steps as mentioned in chapter 1. This is illustrated in the following examples.

Examples 3.1 Design a combinational circuit that will multiply two two-bit binary values.

Step 1 Let the two-bit variable be A_1A_0. Let another two-bit variable be B_1B_0. The product of two two-bit binary values can be maximum of four-bits. Let them be P_3, P_2, P_1, P_0.

Step 2 Let us construct the truth table using the above variables. Let A_1A_0 be 10 and B_1B_0 be 11. The product will be $(2 \times 3 = 6)$ 0110, i.e., $P_3P_2P_1P_0$.

	Inputs				Outputs			
	A_1	A_0	B_1	B_0	P_3	P_2	P_1	P_0
0	0	0	0	0	0	0	0	0
1	0	0	0	1	0	0	0	0
2	0	0	1	0	0	0	0	0
3	0	0	1	1	0	0	0	0
4	0	1	0	0	0	0	0	0
5	0	1	0	1	0	0	0	1
6	0	1	1	0	0	0	1	0
7	0	1	1	1	0	0	1	1
8	1	0	0	0	0	0	0	0
9	1	0	0	1	0	0	1	0
10	1	0	1	0	0	1	0	0
11	1	0	1	1	0	1	1	0
12	1	1	0	0	0	0	0	0
13	1	1	0	1	0	0	1	1
14	1	1	1	0	0	1	1	0
15	1	1	1	1	1	0	0	1

Fig. 3.1 Truth table for example 3.1

Let A_1A_0 be 11 and B_1B_0 be 01. The product will be $(3 \times 1 = 3)$ 0011. This is what in the truth table as S. No. 13. Like this A_1A_0 and B_1B_0 can have 16 different inputs. Truth table is constructed for the 16 different inputs.

Step 3 From the truth table, we can write the output SOP equations for P_3, P_2 P_1 and P_0.

$$P_3 = f(A_1, A_0, B_1, B_0) = \Sigma\ (15)$$

$$P_2 = f(A_1, A_0, B_1, B_0) = \Sigma\ (10, 11, 14)$$

$$P_1 = f(A_1, A_0, B_1, B_0) = \Sigma\ (6, 7, 9, 11, 13, 14)$$

$$P_0 = f(A_1, A_0, B_1, B_0) = \Sigma\ (5, 7, 13, 15)$$

Step 4 Next, we have to simplify the output SOP equations using K-maps. Each equation is of four variables. Hence, we will have K-map of 16 squares. For each output SOP equation there will be one K-map. The K-maps for each output are shown in Fig. 3.2.

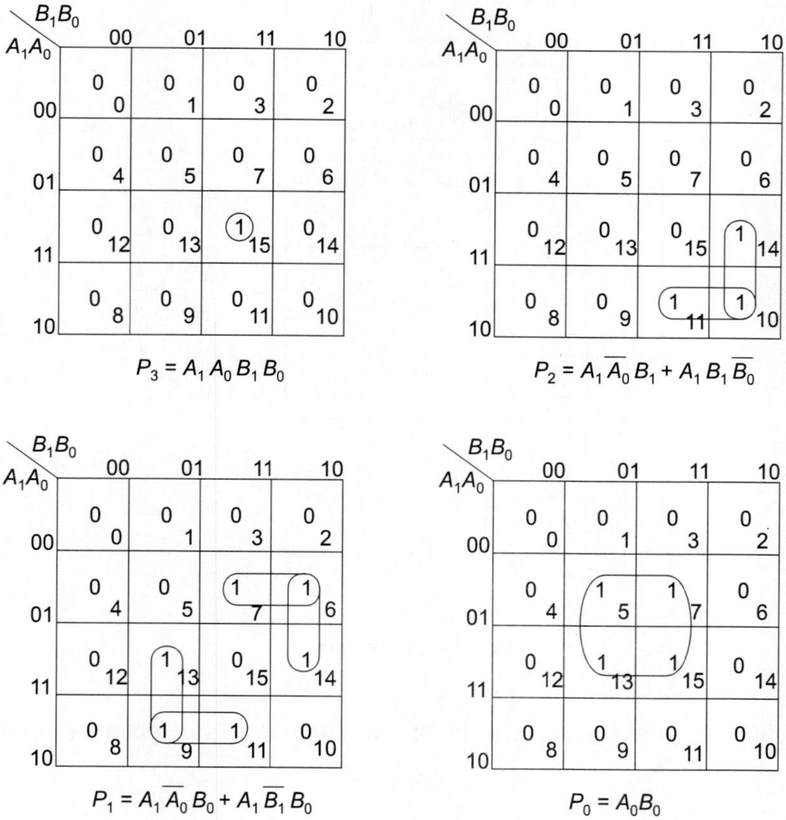

$$P_3 = A_1 A_0 B_1 B_0$$

$$P_2 = A_1 \overline{A_0} B_1 + A_1 B_1 \overline{B_0}$$

$$P_1 = A_1 \overline{A_0} B_0 + A_1 \overline{B_1} B_0 + \overline{A_1} A_0 B_1 + A_0 B_1 \overline{B_0}$$

$$P_0 = A_0 B_0$$

Fig. 3.2 K-maps for four outputs P_0, P_1, P_2 and P_3

Step 5 Based on the simplified output equations of P_3, P_2, P_1, P_0, we can draw the logic diagram using basic gates as illustrated below (Fig. 3.3).

Step 6 Once the logic diagram is drawn, one can build the circuit using the components mentioned in the logic diagram. When you give two-bit binary values as inputs to the circuit, the output will be the product of those two-bit binary values.

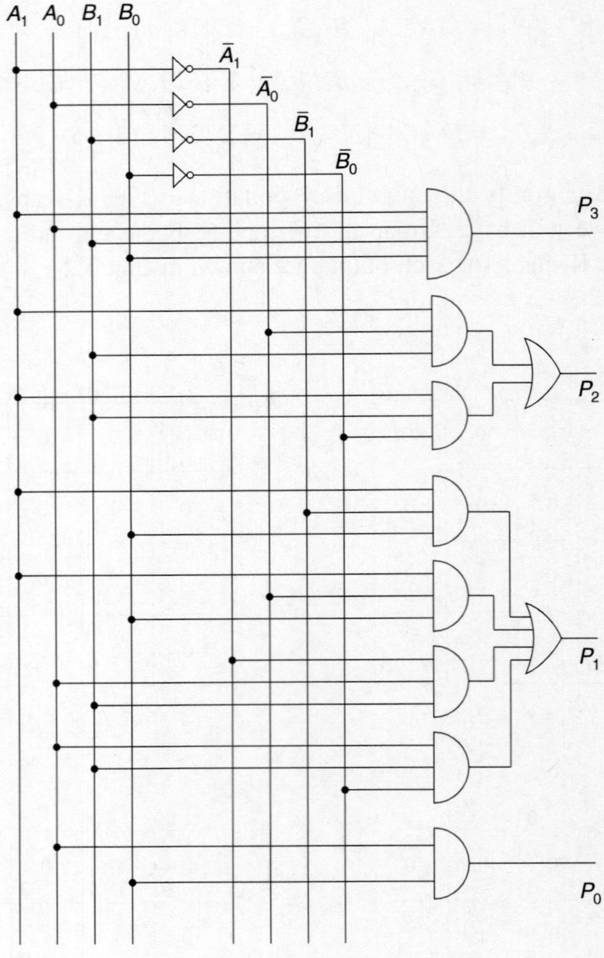

Fig. 3.3 Logic diagram

Example 3.2 Design a combinational logic circuit to output the 2s complement of a 4-bit binary number.

(i) Construct the truth table.

(ii) Simplify each output function using K-map and write reduced equations.

(iii) Draw the resulting logic diagram. (VTU – June 2010)

Solution

Step 1 Let the 4-bit binary number be $A_3\ A_2\ A_1\ A_0$. Let the 2's complement of the 4-bit binary number be $B_3\ B_2\ B_1\ B_0$.

Step 2 Let us construct the truth table using the above variables. For example, let us take the 4-bit binary number $A_3\ A_2\ A_1\ A_0$ as 0110. The 2's complement of 0110 is 1010. So $B_3\ B_2\ B_1\ B_0$ is 1010. Truth table is constructed for 16(= 2^4) different inputs as shown in Fig. 3.4.

	Inputs				Outputs			
	A_3	A_2	A_1	A_0	B_3	B_2	B_1	B_0
0	0	0	0	0	0	0	0	0
1	0	0	0	1	1	1	1	1
2	0	0	1	0	1	1	1	0
3	0	0	1	1	1	1	0	1
4	0	1	0	0	1	1	0	0
5	0	1	0	1	1	0	1	1
6	0	1	1	0	1	0	1	0
7	0	1	1	1	1	0	0	1
8	1	0	0	0	1	0	0	0
9	1	0	0	1	0	1	1	1
10	1	0	1	0	0	1	1	0
11	1	0	1	1	0	1	0	1
12	1	1	0	0	0	1	0	0
13	1	1	0	1	0	0	1	1
14	1	1	1	0	0	0	1	0
15	1	1	1	1	0	0	0	1

Fig. 3.4 Truth table for example 3.2

Step 3 From the truth table, we can write the output SOP equations for B_3, B_2 B_1 and B_0.

$$B_3 = f(A_3, A_2, A_1, A_0) = \Sigma\,(1, 2, 3, 4, 5, 6, 7, 8)$$

$$B_2 = f(A_3, A_2, A_1\ A_0) = \Sigma\,(1, 2, 3, 4, 9, 10, 11, 12)$$

$$B_1 = f(A_3, A_2, A_1, A_0) = \Sigma\,(1, 2, 5, 6, 9, 10, 13, 14)$$

$$B_0 = f(A_3, A_2, A_1, A_0) = \Sigma\,(1, 3, 5, 7, 9, 11, 13, 15)$$

Step 4 Next, we have to simplify the output SOP equations using K-maps. Each equation is of four variables. Hence, we will have K-maps of 16 squares each. For each output SOP equations, there will be one K-map. The K-maps for each output B_3, B_2, B_1 and B_0 are shown in Fig. 3.5.

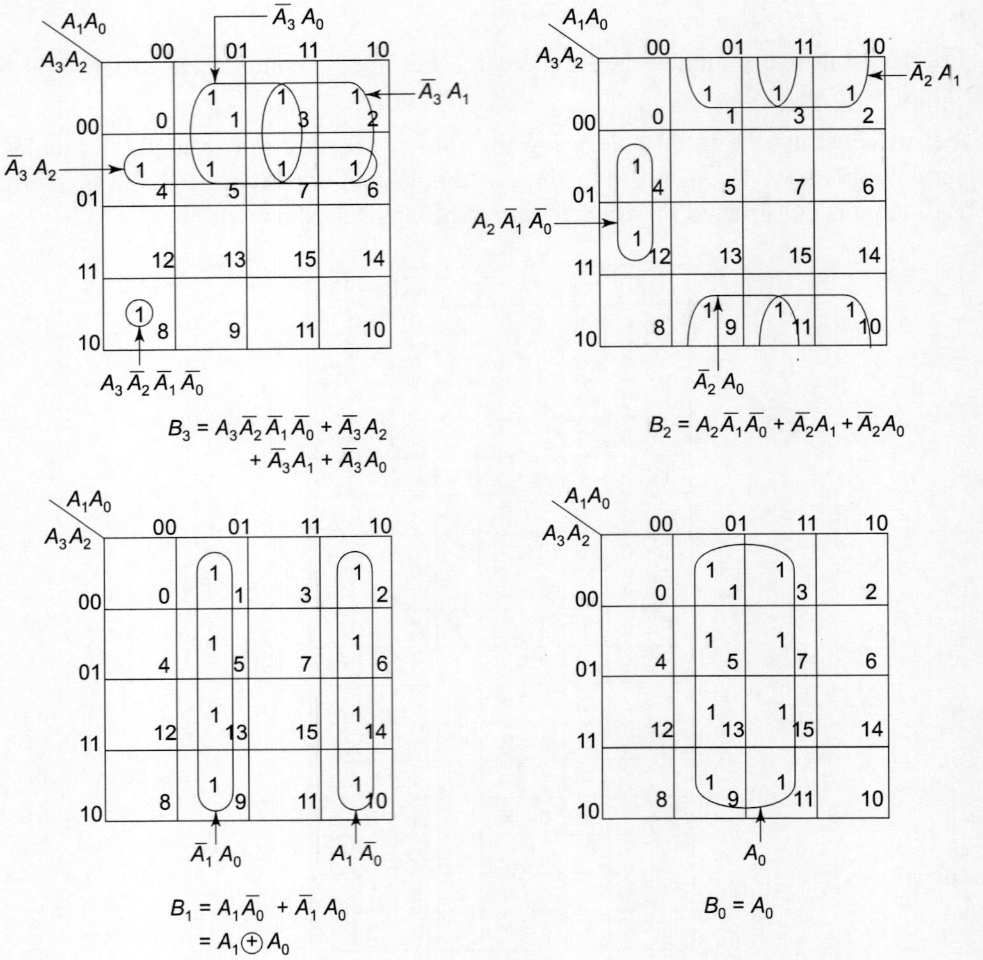

Fig. 3.5 K-maps for example 3.2

Step 5 Based on the simplified output equations obtained from K-maps as B_3, B_2, B_1 and B_0, the logic diagram is drawn using basic gates as shown in Fig. 3.6.

Step 6 Once the logic diagram is drawn, one can build the circuit using the components mentioned in the logic diagram.

Example 3.3 Design a combinational logic circuit that will convert a straight BCD to an Excess-3 BCD digit.

(i) Construct the truth table.

(ii) Simplify each output function using K-map and write the reduced equations.

(iii) Draw the resulting logic diagram. (VTU – June 2013)

Solution

Step 1 Let the BCD digits be $A_3\ A_2\ A_1\ A_0$ and the Excess-3 BCD digits be $E_3\ E_2\ E_1\ E_0$.

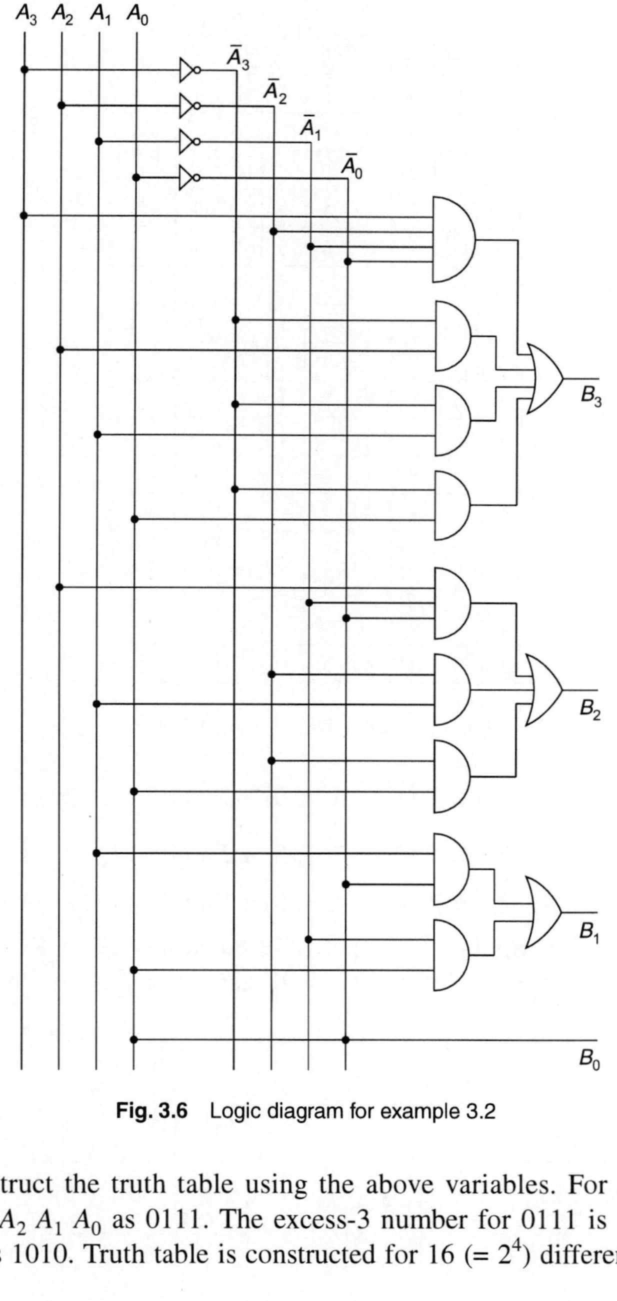

Fig. 3.6 Logic diagram for example 3.2

Step 2 Let us construct the truth table using the above variables. For example, let us take the BCD number $A_3\ A_2\ A_1\ A_0$ as 0111. The excess-3 number for 0111 is 1010 (0111 + 0011). Hence, $E_3\ E_2\ E_1\ E_0$ is 1010. Truth table is constructed for 16 (= 2^4) different inputs as shown in Fig. 3.7.

There is no BCD beyond 1001. Hence, for any 4-bit number beyond 1001, excess-3 BCD output does not exist.

Step 3 From the truth table, we can write the output SOP equations for E_3, E_2, E_1 and E_0.

$$E_3 = f(A_3, A_2, A_1, A_0) = \Sigma\,(5, 6, 7, 8, 9) + \Sigma d\,(10, 11, 12, 13, 14, 15)$$

	Inputs				Outputs			
	A_3	A_2	A_1	A_0	E_3	E_2	E_1	E_0
0	0	0	0	0	0	0	1	1
1	0	0	0	1	0	1	0	0
2	0	0	1	0	0	1	0	1
3	0	0	1	1	0	1	1	0
4	0	1	0	0	0	1	1	1
5	0	1	0	1	1	0	0	0
6	0	1	1	0	1	0	0	1
7	0	1	1	1	1	0	1	0
8	1	0	0	0	1	0	1	1
9	1	0	0	1	1	1	0	0
10	1	0	1	0	–	–	–	–
11	1	0	1	1	–	–	–	–
12	1	1	0	0	–	–	–	–
13	1	1	0	1	–	–	–	–
14	1	1	1	0	–	–	–	–
15	1	1	1	1	–	–	–	–

Fig. 3.7 Truth table for example 3.3

$$E_2 = f(A_3, A_2, A_1, A_0) = \Sigma\,(1, 2, 3, 4, 9) + \Sigma d\,(10, 11, 12, 13, 14, 15)$$

$$E_1 = f(A_3, A_2, A_1, A_0) = \Sigma\,(0, 3, 4, 7, 8) + \Sigma d\,(10, 11, 12, 13, 14, 15)$$

$$E_0 = f(A_3, A_2, A_1, A_0) = \Sigma\,(0, 2, 4, 6, 8) + \Sigma d\,(10, 11, 12, 13, 14, 15)$$

Step 4 Next, we have to simplify the output SOP equations using K-maps. Each equation is a function of four variables. Hence, we will have K-maps of 16 squares each. For

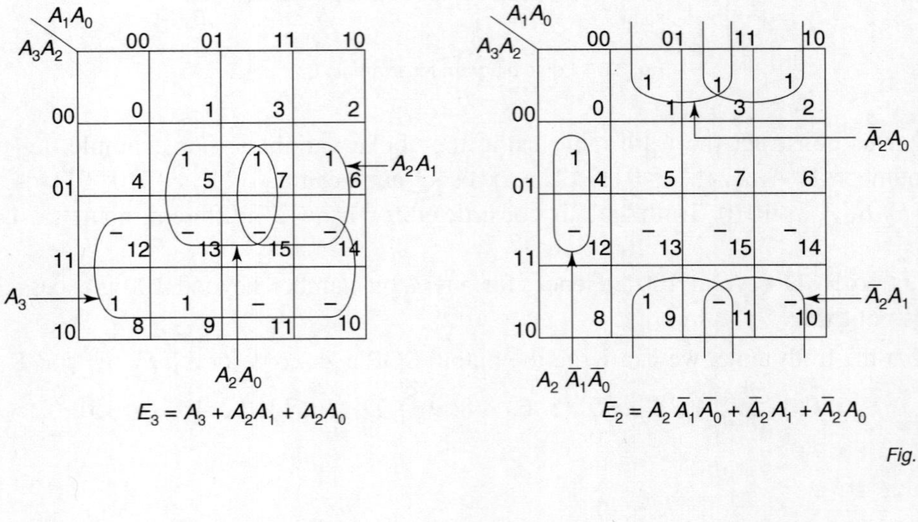

Fig. 3.8 Contd...

Fig. 3.8 Contd...

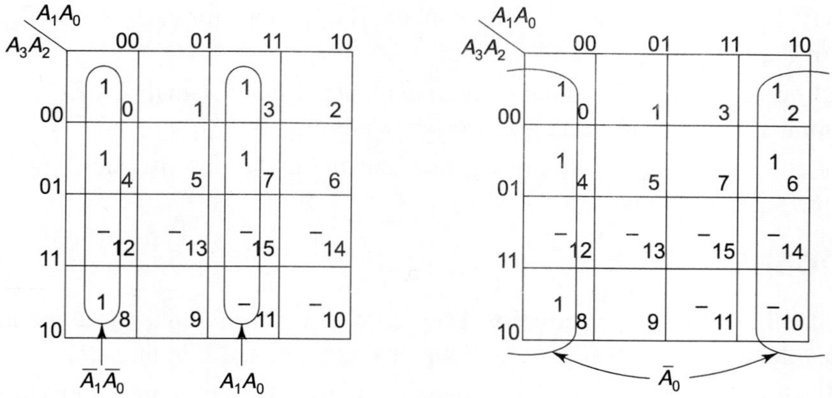

$E_1 = A_1A_0 + \bar{A}_1\bar{A}_0$ $\qquad$ $E_0 = \bar{A}_0$

Fig. 3.8 K-maps for example 3.3

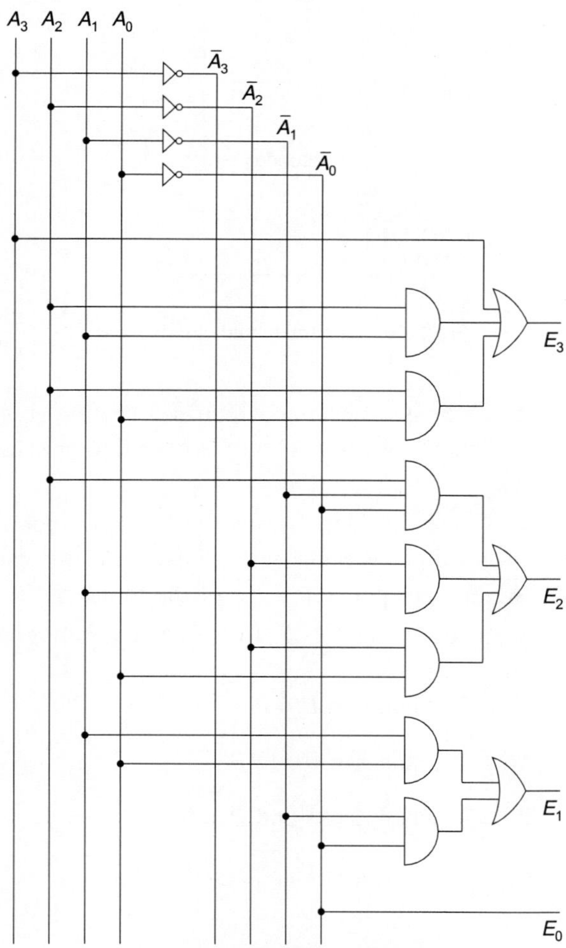

Fig. 3.9 Logic diagram for example 3.3

each output SOP equation, there will be one K-map. The K-maps for each output E_3, E_2, E_1 and E_0 are shown in Fig. 3.8.

Step 5 Based on the simplified output equations obtained from K-maps as E_3, E_2, E_1 and E_0, the logic diagram is drawn using basic gates as shown in Fig. 3.9.

Step 6 Once the logic diagram is drawn, one can build the circuit using the components mentioned in the logic diagram.

3.2 DECODERS

Decoders are combinational logic circuits. They convert a set of input variables into a set of output variables. Input represents a code and output represents a different code.

Figure 3.10 shows a general model of 2^n decoder. In this decoder, *n* inputs produce 2^n inputs. The 2^n output values range from 0 to $2^n - 1$. Decoders generally have enable or activate inputs to get the decoded output based on data inputs. Even if data inputs are present, decoded output will not be available, if enable input is not present.

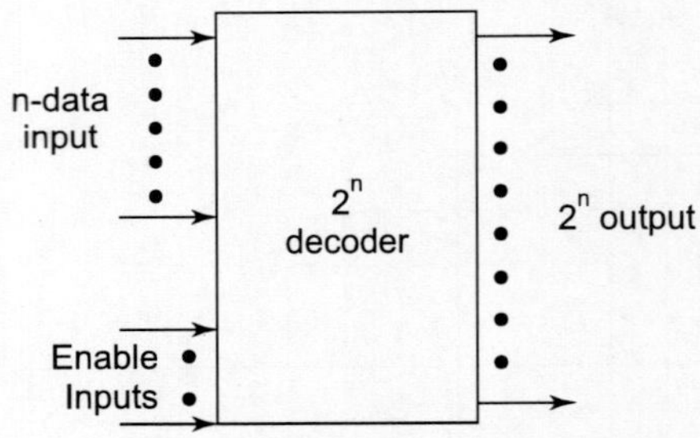

Fig. 3.10 General model of a decoder

Binary decoder: Binary decoder is a decoder which has an *n*-bit binary input code and one output out of 2^n output code. This is used when there is a need to activate only one of 2^n outputs based on *n*-bit input variables.

Figure 3.11 shows, 2-to 4-line decoder. In this decoder, two input variables are decoded into four output variables. Each output variable represents one of the minterms of the two input variables. Each of the four AND gates generates one of the minterms.

If enable input is 1, only one of the outputs Y_0 to Y_3 is active for a given set of input variables. If $EN = 1$,

$$Y_0 = 1, \text{ when } A = B = 0$$

$$Y_1 = 1, \text{ when } A = 0 \text{ and } B = 1$$

$$Y_2 = 1, \text{ when } A = 1 \text{ and } B = 0$$

$$Y_3 = 1, \text{ when } A = 1 \text{ and } B = 1$$

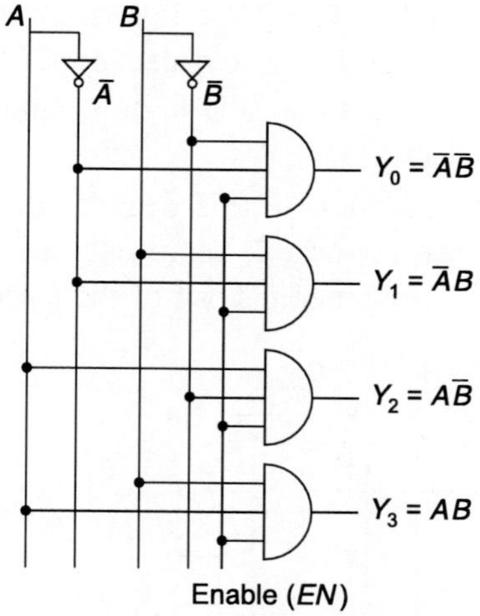

Fig. 3.11 2-to 4-line decoder

The corresponding AND gate output will be 1. If $EN = 0$, all the outputs will be 0. The truth table for the 2-to 4-line decoder is shown in Fig. 3.12.

Inputs			Outputs			
EN	*A*	*B*	Y_0	Y_1	Y_2	Y_3
0	×	×	0	0	0	0
1	0	0	1	0	0	0
1	0	1	0	1	0	0
1	1	0	0	0	1	0
1	1	1	0	0	0	1

Fig. 3.12 Truth table for 2-to 4-line decoder

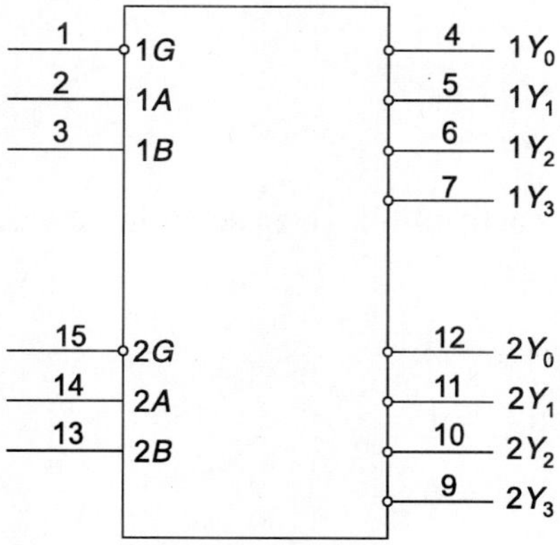

Fig. 3.13 Logic symbol for IC 74 × 139

Inputs			outputs			
G	*B*	*A*	Y_0	Y_1	Y_2	Y_3
1	×	×	1	1	1	1
0	0	0	0	1	1	1
0	0	1	1	0	1	1
0	1	0	1	1	0	1
0	1	1	1	1	1	0

Fig. 3.14 Truth table for 74 × 139

The 74 × 139 dual 2 to 4 Decoder: The 74 × 139 is commercially available dual 2 to 4 decoder. It has two independent and identical 2 to 4 decoders. The enable inputs and outputs of IC 74 × 139 are active low. Figure 3.13 shows the logic symbol and Fig. 3.14 shows the truth table for identical circuits of 74 × 139.

Figure 3.15 shows 3-to 8-line decoder. In this decoder three input variables are decoded into eight output variables. Each output variable represents one of the minterms of three input variables. Each of the eight AND gates generates one of the minterms.

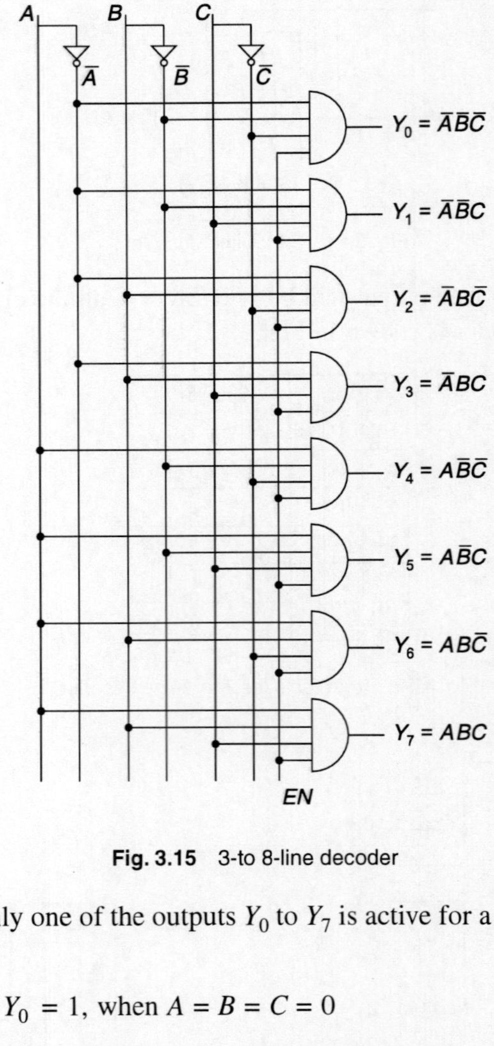

Fig. 3.15 3-to 8-line decoder

If enable input is 1, only one of the outputs Y_0 to Y_7 is active for a given set of input variables. If $EN = 1$,

$$Y_0 = 1, \text{ when } A = B = C = 0$$

$$Y_1 = 1, \text{ when } A = 0, B = 0 \text{ and } C = 1$$

$$Y_2 = 1, \text{ when } A = 0, B = 1 \text{ and } C = 0$$

$$Y_3 = 1, \text{ when } A = 0, B = 1 \text{ and } C = 1$$

$Y_4 = 1$, when $A = 1$, $B = 0$ and $C = 0$

$Y_5 = 1$, when $A = 1$, $B = 0$ and $C = 1$

$Y_6 = 1$, when $A = 1$, $B = 1$ and $C = 0$

$Y_7 = 1$, when $A = 1$, $B = 1$ and $C = 1$

If enable is 0, all the outputs will be 0. The truth table for 3-to 8-line decoder is shown in Fig. 3.16.

Inputs				Outputs							
EN	A	B	C	Y_0	Y_1	Y_2	Y_3	Y_4	Y_5	Y_6	Y_7
0	×	×	×	0	0	0	0	0	0	0	0
1	0	0	0	1	0	0	0	0	0	0	0
1	0	0	1	0	1	0	0	0	0	0	0
1	0	1	0	0	0	1	0	0	0	0	0
1	0	1	1	0	0	0	1	0	0	0	0
1	1	0	0	0	0	0	0	1	0	0	0
1	1	0	1	0	0	0	0	0	1	0	0
1	1	1	0	0	0	0	0	0	0	1	0
1	1	1	1	0	0	0	0	0	0	0	1

Fig. 3.16 Truth table for 3-to 8-decoder

The 74 × 138, Decoder: It is a commercially available 3-to 8-decoder. It has three data inputs (A, B, C), three enable inputs (G_1, G_2A, G_2B) and eight active low outputs ($Y_0 - Y_7$). The enable input G_1 is active high, and G_2A and G_2B are active low enable inputs. The logic symbol is shown in Fig. 3.17 and the truth table for 74 × 138 is shown in Fig. 3.18.

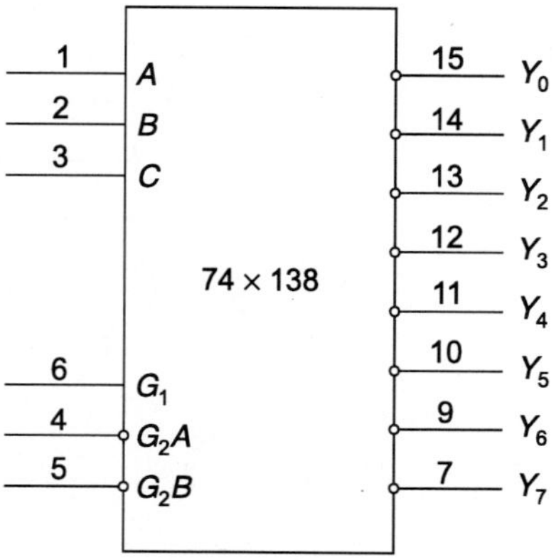

Fig. 3.17 Logic symbol for 74 × 138

Inputs						Outputs							
G_1	G_2A	G_2B	C	B	A	Y_0	Y_1	Y_2	Y_3	Y_4	Y_5	Y_6	Y_7
0	×	×	×	×	×	1	1	1	1	1	1	1	1
×	1	×	×	×	×	1	1	1	1	1	1	1	1
×	×	1	×	×	×	1	1	1	1	1	1	1	1
1	0	0	0	0	0	0	1	1	1	1	1	1	1
1	0	0	0	0	1	1	0	1	1	1	1	1	1
1	0	0	0	1	0	1	1	0	1	1	1	1	1
1	0	0	0	1	1	1	1	1	0	1	1	1	1
1	0	0	1	0	0	1	1	1	1	0	1	1	1
1	0	0	1	0	1	1	1	1	1	1	0	1	1
1	0	0	1	1	0	1	1	1	1	1	1	0	1
1	0	0	1	1	1	1	1	1	1	1	1	1	0

Fig. 3.18 Truth table for 74 × 138 decoder

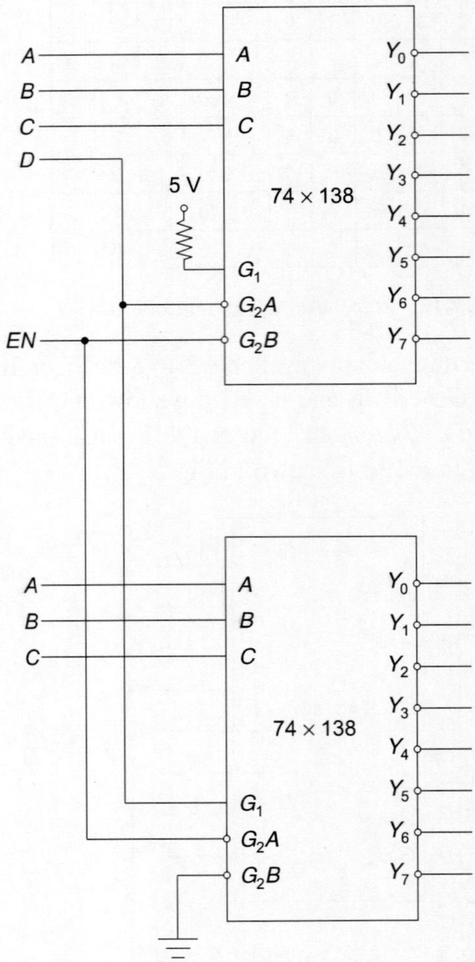

Fig. 3.19 4:16 decoder using two cascaded 3:8 decoder (74 × 138)

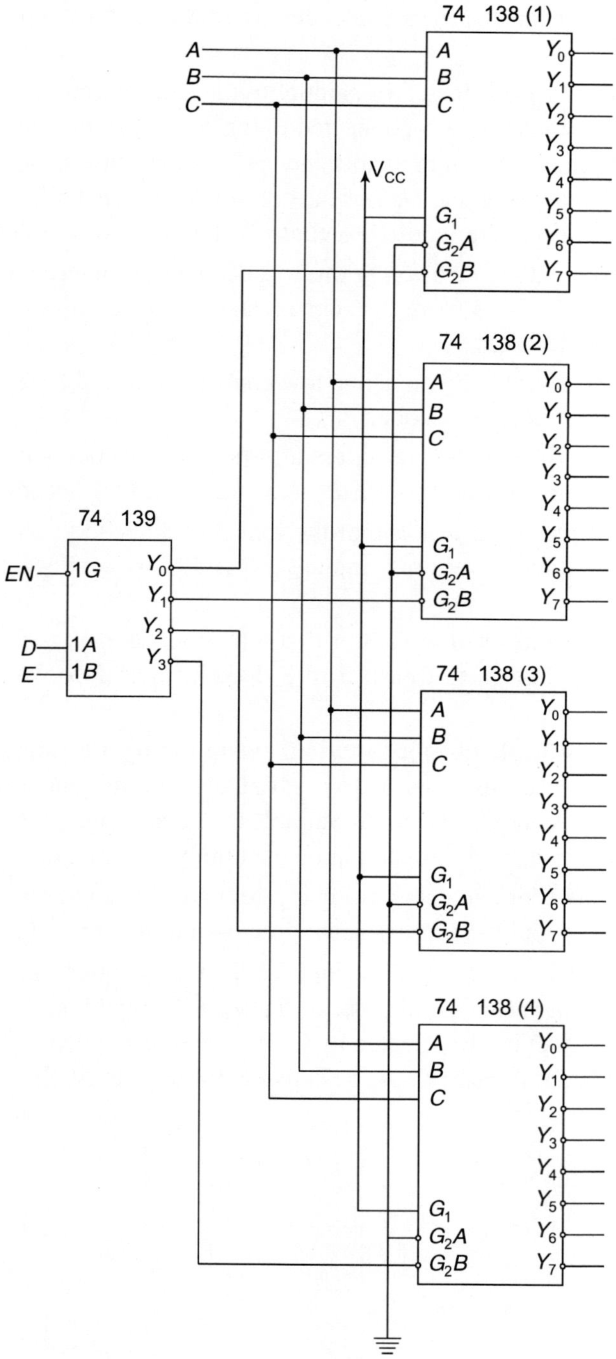

Fig. 3.20 5-to 32-decoder using four 74 × 138 decoders and one 74 × 139 decoder

Cascading binary decoders: Multiple 3 to 8 decoders can be connected to form 4 to 16 decoder or larger decoders. Consider the two 3 to 8 decoders cascaded to form a 4 to 16 decoder which is shown in Fig. 3.19.

Data inputs *A*, *B* and *C* are connected in parallel to the select inputs of both 3 to 8 decoders. Data input *D*, the most significant one is connected to the active low enable input. G_2A of the top 74 × 138 decoder and to the active high enable input G_1 of the bottom 74 × 138 decoder. G_1 is pulled up to V_{CC} on the top decoder and G_2B of the bottom decoder is pulled down to ground. The above type of cascading allows data input *D* to control which 3 to 8 decoder is to be enabled.

For the minterms (0, 1, 2, 3, 4, 5, 6, 7) the top decoder is enabled and for the minterms (8, 9, 10, 11, 12, 13, 14, 15) the bottom decoder is enabled. This allows decoding all possible minterms from four input variables.

The 4 to 16 decoder is enabled by an active low enable connected to G_2B of the top decoder and G_2A enable input of the bottom decoder.

Increasing the number of cascaded decoders allows larger decoders constructed. A 5 to 32 decoder can be formed by using four 3 to 8 decoders and one 2 to 4 decoder.

The 2 to 4 decoder is used to select one of the four 3 to 8 decoders by decoding two higher order inputs *D* and *E*. The three lower order inputs *A*, *B* and *C* are connected in parallel to all the four 3 to 8 decoders.

Y_0 of 2 to 4 decoder is connected to G_2B of first 3 to 8 decoder, Y_1 to second 3 to 8 decoder, Y_2 to third 3 to 8 decoder and Y_3 to fourth 3 to 8 decoder. The 5 to 32 decoder is shown in Fig. 3.20.

Realization of single or multiple output functions using binary decoders: A 3 to 8 decoder or 4 to 16 decoder can be used as three-or four-variable minterm generator respectively. They generate the minterms by decoding the input variables. The advangate of using the decoder to realize combinational functions is the reduction of the number of integrated circuits.

The combination of decoder and external logic gates can be used to realize single or multiple output functions. A decoder can have either active low output or active high output.

Active high output SOP function realization: When a decoder output is active high, it generates minterms for input variables. In order to realize SOP function, sum of selected product terms generated by the decoder has to be taken by ORing the selected decoder outputs. Figure 3.21 shows realization of function, $F = \Sigma m$ (2, 4, 6, 7) using 3:8 decoder with active high outputs.

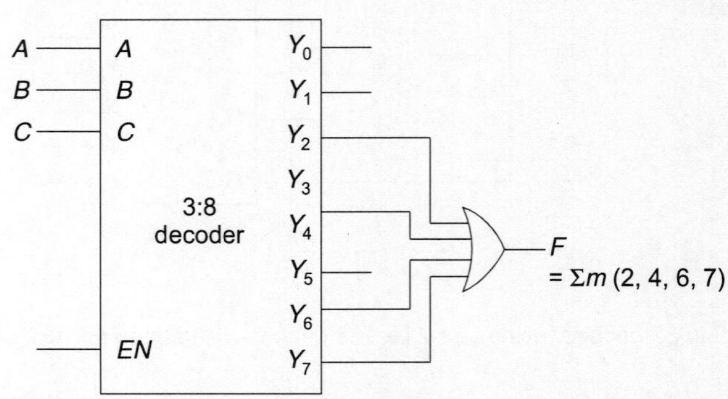

Fig. 3.21 Single output function realized using decoder and external gates

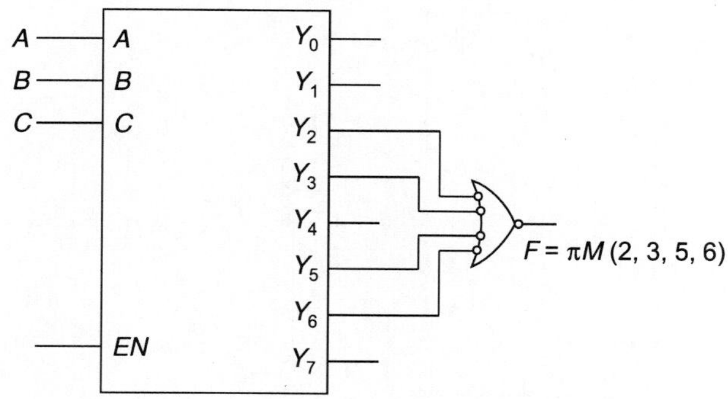

Fig. 3.22 Realization of POS function using decoder with active high output

Realization of POS function for active high output: When a decoder output is active high, POS function can be realized similar to SOP function except that the function output is complemented. This can be carried out using NOR gate instead of OR gate. Figure 3.22 shows realization of POS function, $F = \pi M\ (2, 3, 5, 6)$ using 3:8 decoder with active high output.

Realization of POS function for active low output: When a decoder output is active low, POS function can be realized using AND gate. The output of the decoder is in complemented form. It generates maxterms for input variables. Selected output will be logic *O*. POS function can be realized by taking product of selected maxterms. Figure 3.23 shows the realization of POS function.

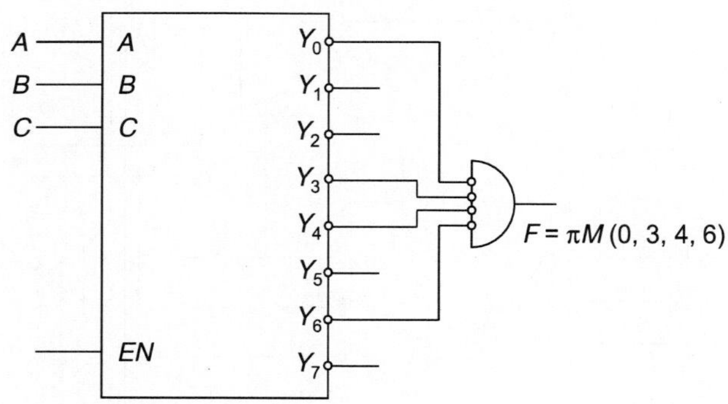

Fig. 3.23 Realization of POS function using decoder with active low output

Realization of SOP function for active low output: When decoder output is active low, SOP function can be realized similar to POS function except that the function output is complemented. This is carried out by using NAND gate instead of AND gate. Figure 3.24 shows realization of SOP function using 3:8 decoder with active low outputs.

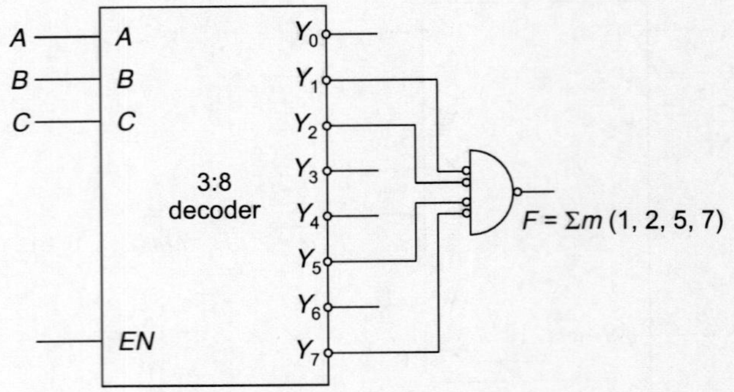

Fig. 3.24 Realization of SOP function using decoder with active low output

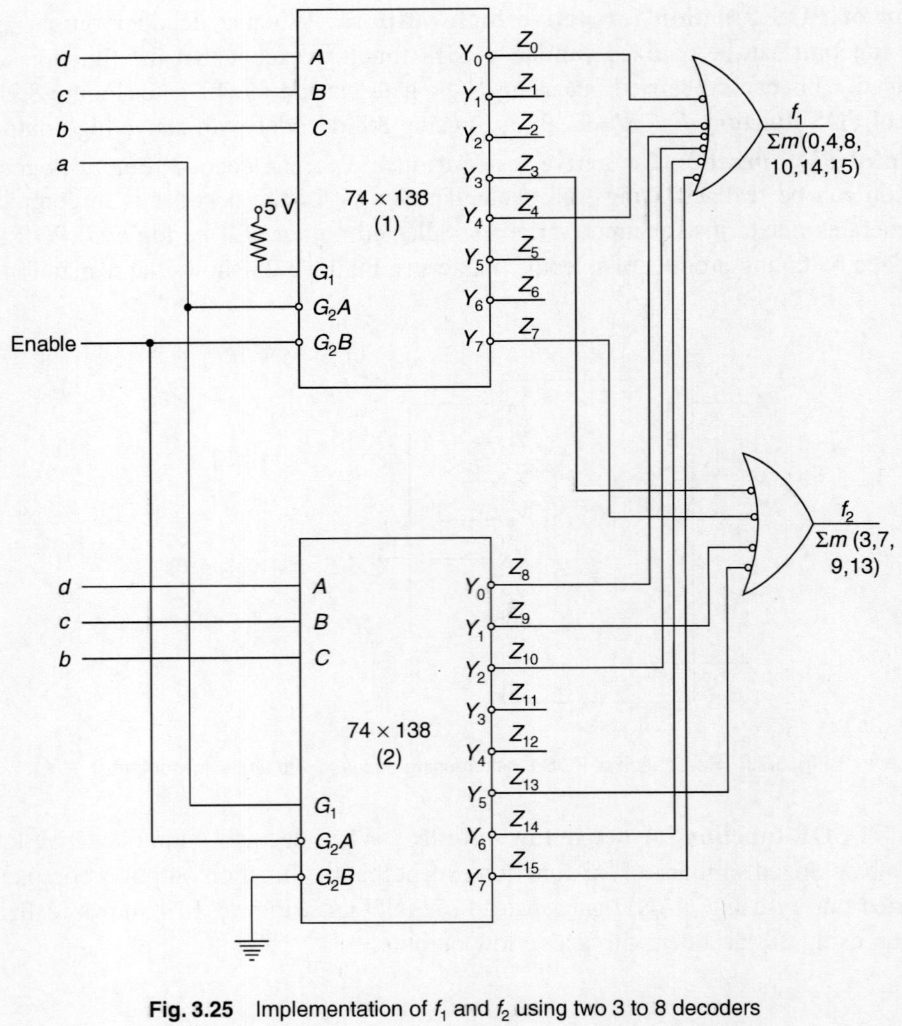

Fig. 3.25 Implementation of f_1 and f_2 using two 3 to 8 decoders

Example 3.4 Implement the multiple functions:

$f_1\ (a, b, c, d) = \Sigma\ (0, 4, 8, 10, 14, 15)$ and

$f_2\ (a, b, c, d) = \Sigma\ (3, 7, 9, 13)$ using two 3 to 8 decoders (VTU – Dec. 2013)

Solution The given functions consist of four input variables. Implementation of the function requires 4 to 16 decoder which can be realized using two 3 to 8 decoders. Figure 3.25 shows the implementation of f_1 and f_2 using two 3 to 8 decoders.

Instead of NOT – OR gates, we can also use NAND gates as explained earlier. It may be noted that a is the most significant variable and d is the least significant variable.

Example 3.5 Implement the following with a suitable decoder with active low enable input and active high output:

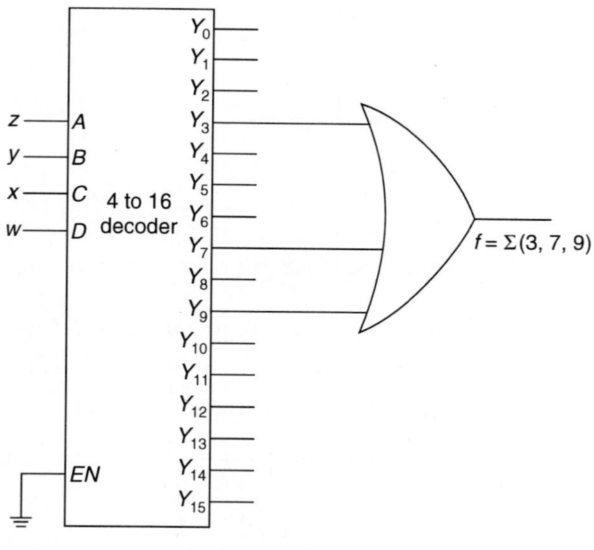

Fig. 3.26 Implementation of $f\,(w, x, y, z) = \Sigma\ (3, 7, 9)$

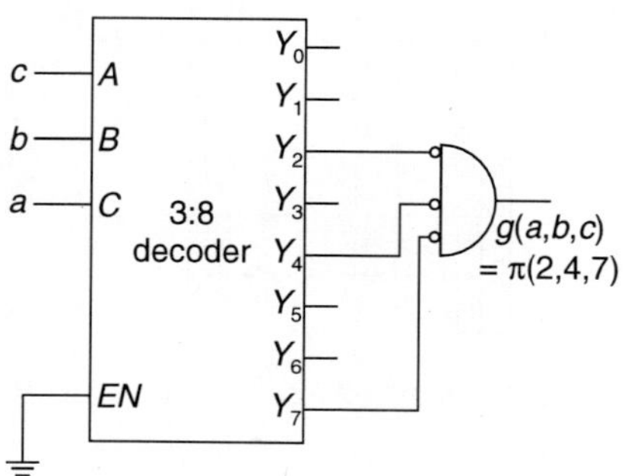

Fig. 3.27 Implementation of $g\ (a, b, c) = \pi\ (2, 4, 7)$

$$f(w, x, y, z) = \Sigma(3, 7, 9)$$

$$g(a, b, c) = \pi(2, 4, 7)$$

(VTU – Dec 2013)

$f(w, x, y, z)$ is a four-input variable function which requires 4 to 16 decoder. Figure 3.26 shows the implementation of for $f = \Sigma(3, 7, 9)$, using active high output decoder.

Implementation of $g(a, b, c) = \pi(2, 4, 7)$ requires 3 to 8 decoder. Figure 3.27 shows the implementation of $\pi(2, 4, 7)$.

The above function can also be implemented by converting the function to SOP form, i.e., $g(a, b, c) = \pi(2, 4, 7) = \Sigma(0, 1, 3, 5, 6)$. Its implementation is shown in Fig. 3.28.

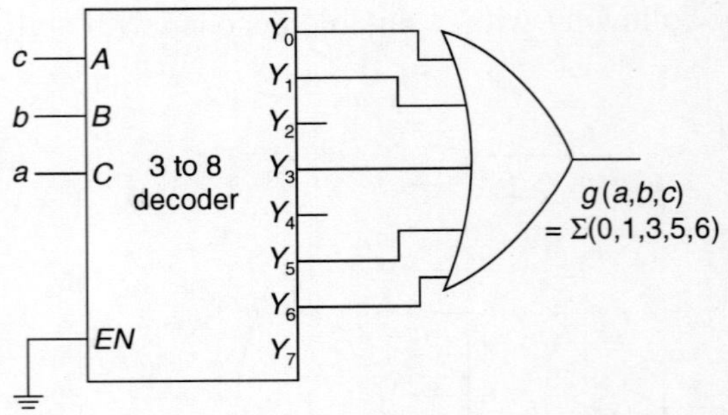

Fig. 3.28 Implementation of $g(a, b, c) = \Sigma(0, 1, 3, 5, 6)$

Example 3.6 Implement a full subtractor using a decoder and two NAND gates.

(VTU – July 2011, VTU – July 2013)

First, let us construct the truth table for full subtractor as shown in Fig. 3.29.

Inputs			Outputs	
A	B	B_{in}	D	B_{out}
0	0	0	0	0
0	0	1	1	1
0	1	0	1	1
0	1	1	0	1
1	0	0	1	0
1	0	1	0	0
1	1	0	0	0
1	1	1	1	1

Fig. 3.29 Truth table for full subtractor

From the truth table, the output functions of full subtractor are written as follows:

$$D = \Sigma(1, 2, 4, 7) \; B_{out} = \Sigma(1, 2, 3, 7)$$

Figure 3.30 is drawn as shown below.

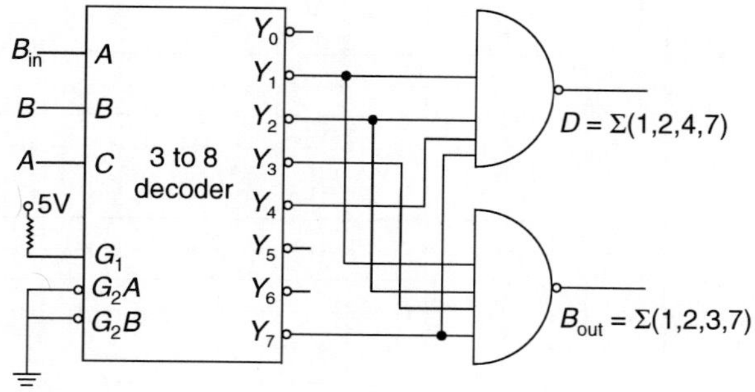

Fig. 3.30 Implementation of full subtractor

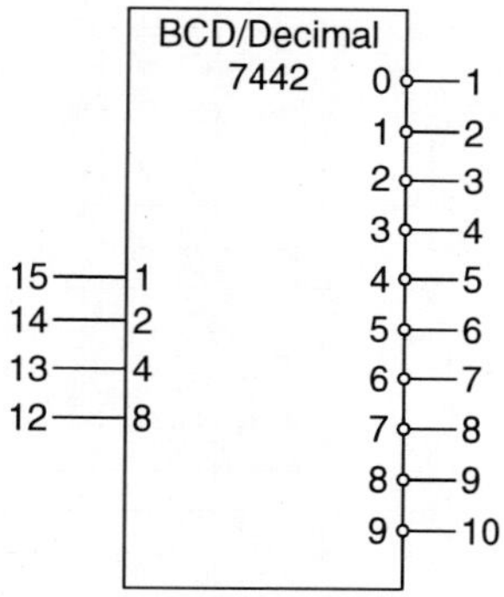

Fig. 3.31 Logic symbol

The output functions are implemented using 74 × 138 decoder and two NAND gates which is shown in Fig. 3.30.

3.3 BCD DECODERS

BCD decoders have four input lines and have 10 lines as output where each line corresponds to one input combination. Generally, the decoder will have active low output.

7442 is a BCD to decimal decoder IC. 7447 is a BCD to seven-segment decoder circuit. Fig. 3.31 shows the logic symbol of BCD to decimal decoder. Figure 3.32 shows the logic diagram of BCD to decimal decoder and Fig. 3.33 shows the truth table for BCD to decimal decoder.

BCD to 7 segment display decoder: Seven segment displays are used to give a visual indication of the output states of digital integrated circuits. BCD to seven segment display decoders are used to convert the BCD signal into a form suitable for driving these displays. Figure 3.34 shows the segments that are activated for display of different digits.

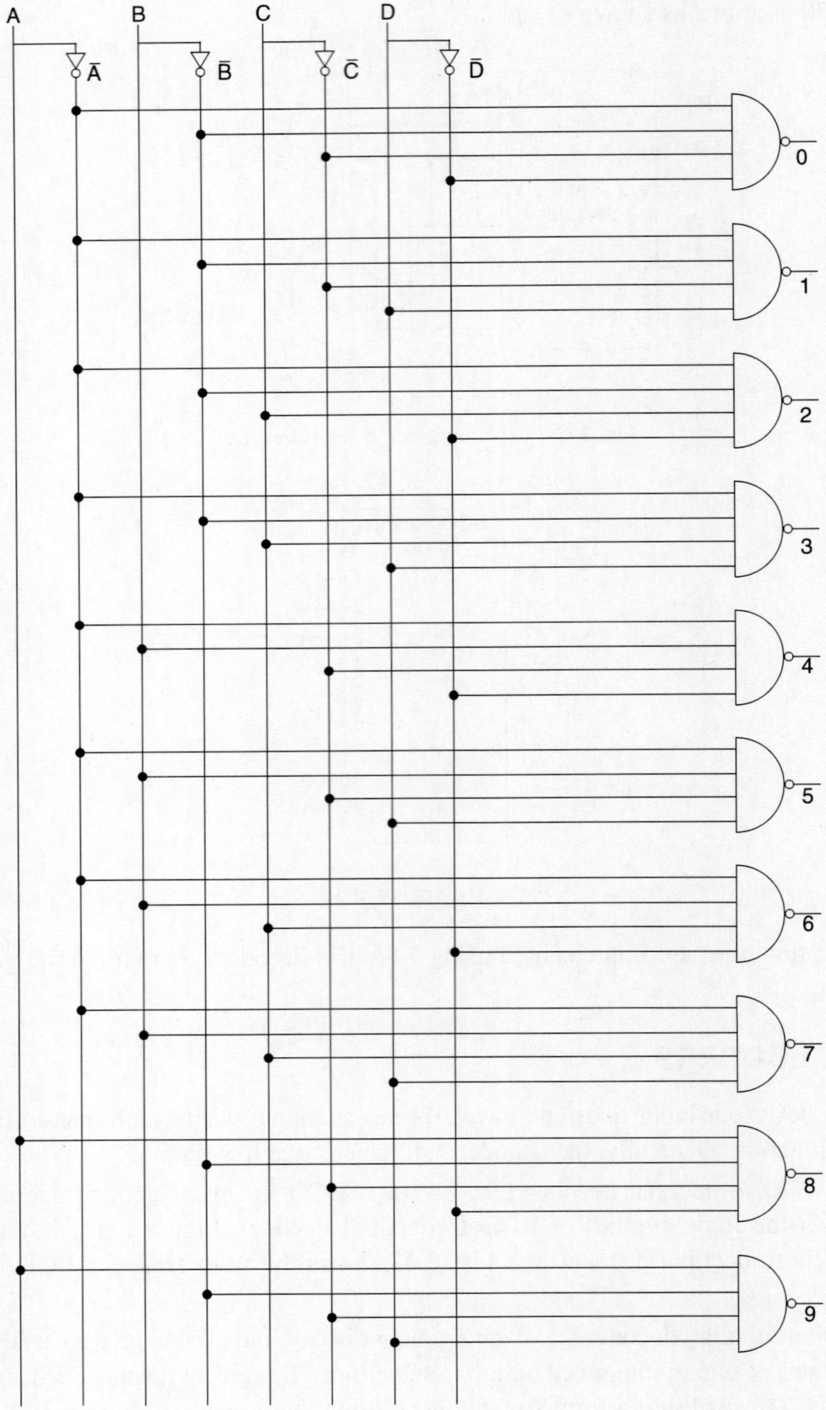

Fig. 3.32 Logic diagram of BCD to decimal decoder

Inputs				Outputs									
A	*B*	*C*	*D*	0	1	2	3	4	5	6	7	8	9
0	0	0	0	0	1	1	1	1	1	1	1	1	1
0	0	0	1	1	0	1	1	1	1	1	1	1	1
0	0	1	0	1	1	0	1	1	1	1	1	1	1
0	0	1	1	1	1	1	0	1	1	1	1	1	1
0	1	0	0	1	1	1	1	0	1	1	1	1	1
0	1	0	1	1	1	1	1	1	0	1	1	1	1
0	1	1	0	1	1	1	1	1	1	0	1	1	1
0	1	1	1	1	1	1	1	1	1	1	0	1	1
1	0	0	0	1	1	1	1	1	1	1	1	0	1
1	0	0	1	1	1	1	1	1	1	1	1	1	0

Fig. 3.33 Truth table for BCD to decimal decoder

Digit	Segments activated	Display
0	*a, b, c, d, e, f*	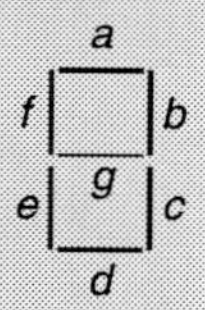
1	*b, c*	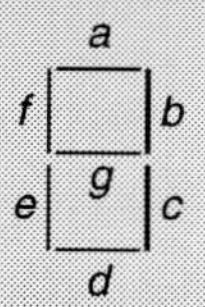
2	*a, b, d, e, g*	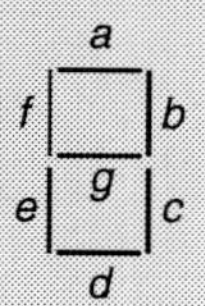
3	*a, b, c, d, g*	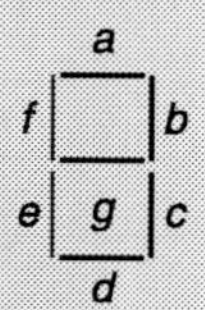
4	*b, c, f, g*	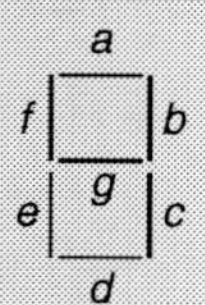

Fig. 3.34 Contd...

Fig. 3.34 Contd...

Digit	Segments	Display
5	*a, c, d, f, g*	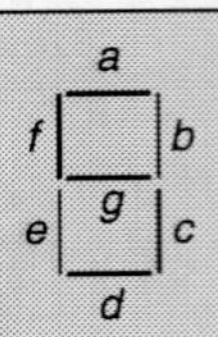
6	*a, c, d, e, f, g*	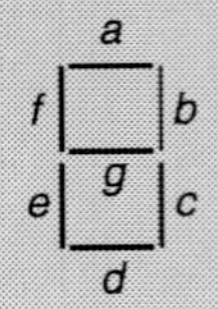
7	*a, b, c*	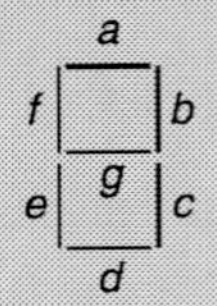
8	*a, b, c, d, e, f, g*	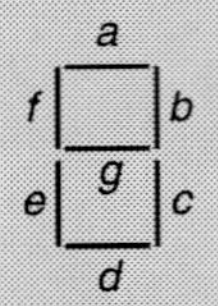
9	*a, b, c, d, f, g*	

Fig. 3.34 Segments to be activated for different digits

Inputs					Outputs						
Digit	*A*	*B*	*C*	*D*	*a*	*b*	*c*	*d*	*e*	*f*	*g*
0	0	0	0	0	1	1	1	1	1	1	0
1	0	0	0	1	0	1	1	0	0	0	0
2	0	0	1	0	1	1	0	1	1	0	1
3	0	0	1	1	1	1	1	1	0	0	1
4	0	1	0	0	0	1	1	0	0	1	1
5	0	1	0	1	1	0	1	1	0	1	1
6	0	1	1	0	1	0	1	1	1	1	1
7	0	1	1	1	1	1	1	0	0	0	0
8	1	0	0	0	1	1	1	1	1	1	1
9	1	0	0	1	1	1	1	1	0	1	1

Fig. 3.35 Truth table for BCD to common cathode 7 segment decoder

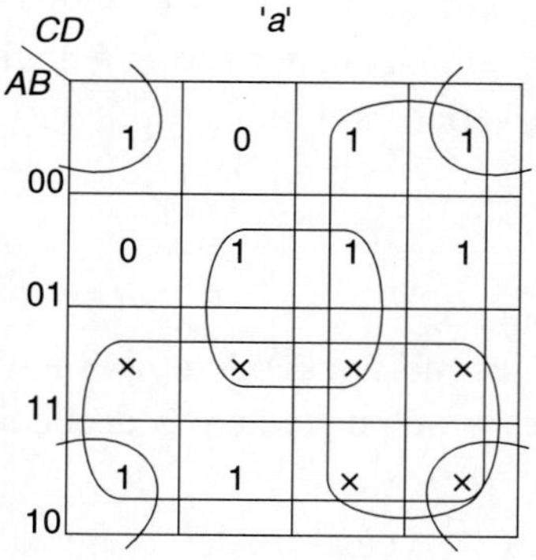

$a = A + C + BD + \bar{B}\bar{D}$

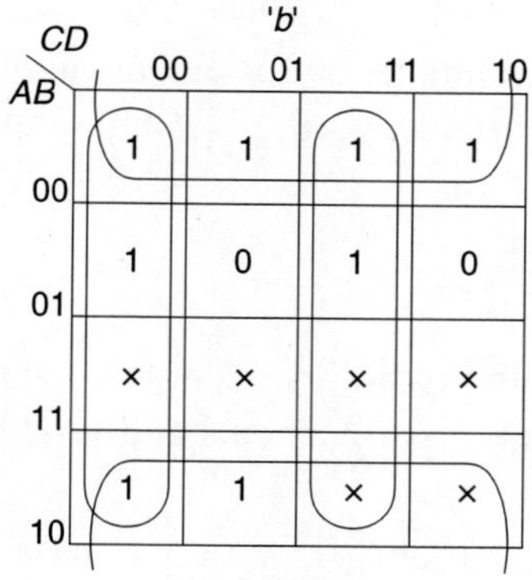

$b = \bar{B} + \bar{C}\bar{D} + CD$

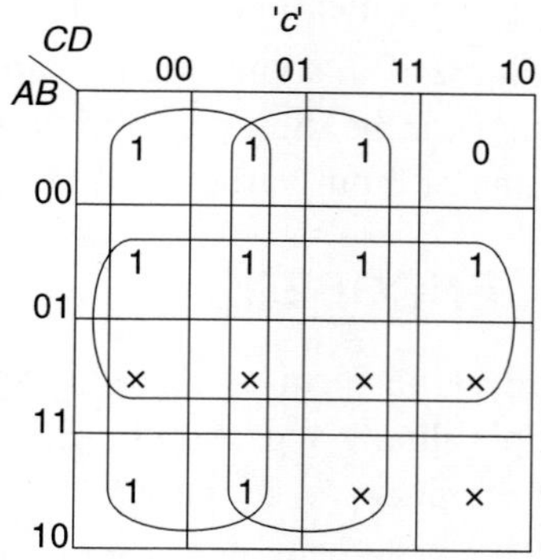

$c = B + \bar{C} + D$

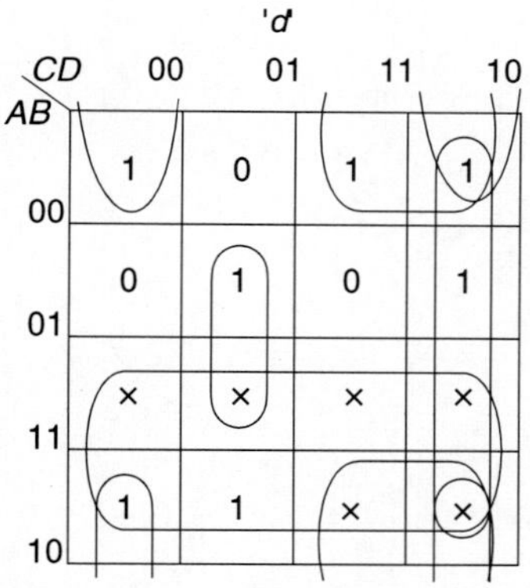

$d = \bar{B}\bar{D} + C\bar{D} + B\bar{C}D + \bar{B}C + A$

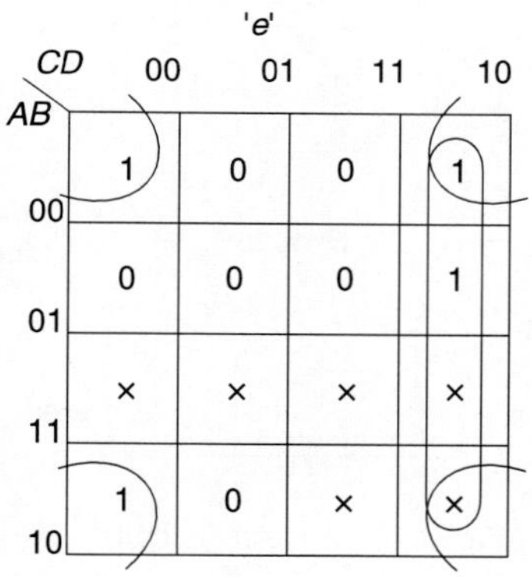

$e = \bar{B}\bar{D} + C\bar{D}$

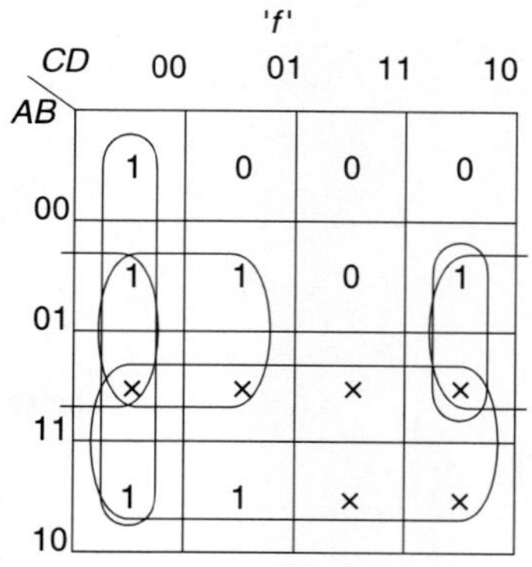

$f = A + \bar{C}\bar{D} + B\bar{C} + B\bar{D}$

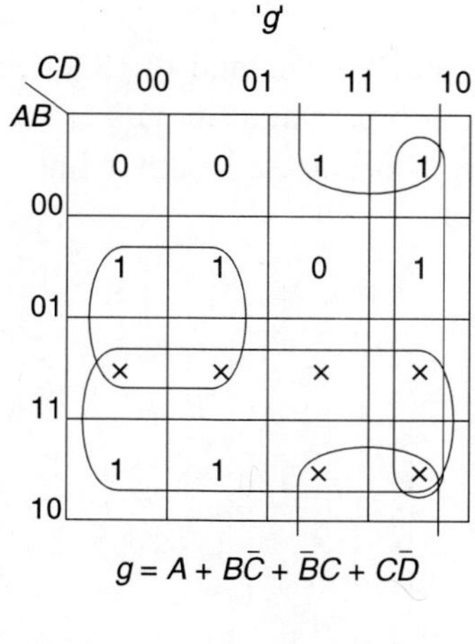

$g = A + B\bar{C} + \bar{B}C + C\bar{D}$

Fig. 3.36 K-map simplification

We can design the combinational logic circuit for common cathode 7 segment display by K-map simplification for each of the output variables *a*, *b*, *c*, *d*, *e*, *f* and *g* from the truth table.

Figure 3.36 shows the K-map simplification for output variables *a*, *b*, *c*, *d*, *e*, *f* and *g*. A logic diagram can be drawn using input variables *A*, *B*, *C*, *D* and output variables *a*, *b*, *c*, *d*, *e*, *f* and *g* in terms of input variables.

3.4 ENCODERS

Encoders perform a function that is inverse of decoders. Like decoders, encoders also have multiple inputs and outputs. Encoders have 2^n inputs and produces *n* outputs whereas decoders have *n* inputs and 2^n outputs.

Thus, encoders have more input variables than output variables. A typical model of encoder is shown in Fig. 3.37.

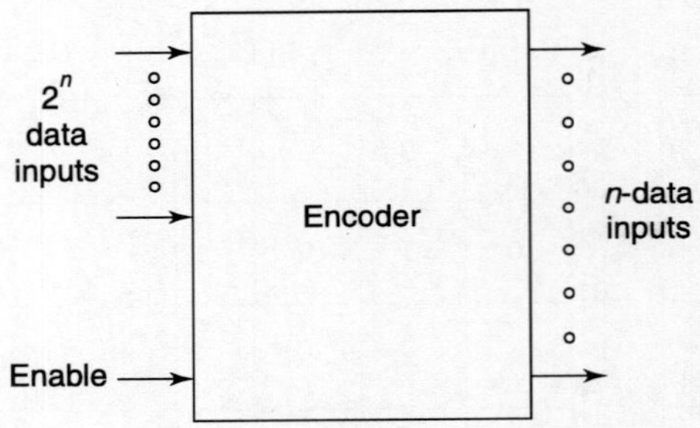

Fig. 3.37 A typical encoder

Decimal to BCD encoder: The decimal to BCD encoder has 10 input lines and four output lines.

Figure 3.38 shows the logic symbol for decimal to BCD encoder IC 74 × 147. It has nine input lines and four output lines. Both inputs and outputs are active low. There in no input line for decimal zero. When this condition occurs, all output lines are 1 indicating no valid BCD output.

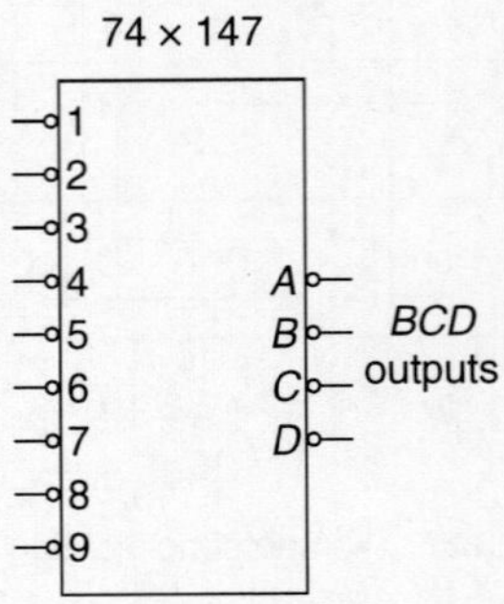

Fig. 3.38 Logic symbol for 3.38

Figure 3.39 shows the truth table for decimal to BCD encoder.

Decimal value	Inputs									Outputs			
	1	2	3	4	5	6	7	8	9	*D*	*C*	*B*	*A*
0	1	1	1	1	1	1	1	1	1	1	1	1	1
1	0	1	1	1	1	1	1	1	1	1	1	1	0
2	×	0	1	1	1	1	1	1	1	1	1	0	1
3	×	×	0	1	1	1	1	1	1	1	1	0	0
4	×	×	×	0	1	1	1	1	1	1	0	1	1
5	×	×	×	×	0	1	1	1	1	1	0	1	0
6	×	×	×	×	×	0	1	1	1	1	0	0	1
7	×	×	×	×	×	×	0	1	1	1	0	0	0
8	×	×	×	×	×	×	×	0	1	0	1	1	1
9	×	×	×	×	×	×	×	×	0	0	1	1	0

Fig. 3.39 Truth table for decimal to BCD encoder

Example 3.7 Draw the interfacing diagram of ten keypad interface to a digital system using decimal to BCD encoder. (VTU – Dec 2013)

Solution

Figure 3.40 shows the interfacing diagram of ten keypad interface.

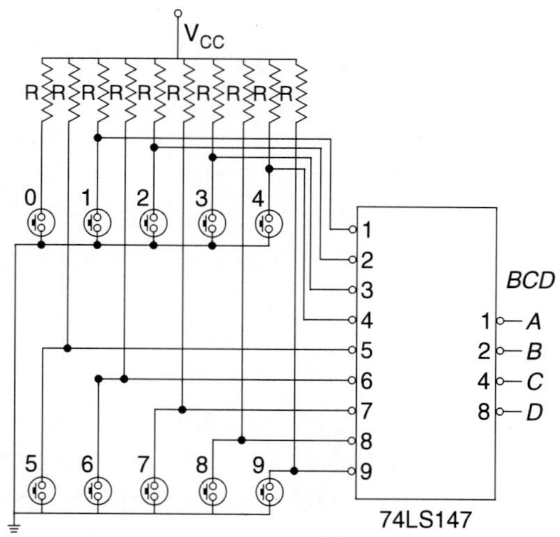

Fig. 3.40 Ten keypad interface diagram

Octal to binary encoder: Octal to Binary Encoder has eight inputs, and three outputs that generate the binary code corresponding to each input. It is assumed that only one input has a value of 1 at any given time.

Inputs								Outputs		
D_0	D_1	D_2	D_3	D_4	D_5	D_6	D_7	A	B	C
1	0	0	0	0	0	0	0	0	0	0
0	1	0	0	0	0	0	0	0	0	1
0	0	1	0	0	0	0	0	0	1	0
0	0	0	1	0	0	0	0	0	1	1
0	0	0	0	1	0	0	0	1	0	0
0	0	0	0	0	1	0	0	1	0	1
0	0	0	0	0	0	1	0	1	1	0
0	0	0	0	0	0	0	1	1	1	1

Fig. 3.41 Truth table of octal to binary encoder

Figure 3.41 shows the truth table of octal to binary encoder. Figure 3.42 shows the logic diagram of octal to binary encoder. This circuit has an ambiguity that when all the inputs are 0s, the outputs are 0s. When D_0 is 1, then also all outputs are 0s. This ambiguity can be resolved by providing an additional output that is valid condition.

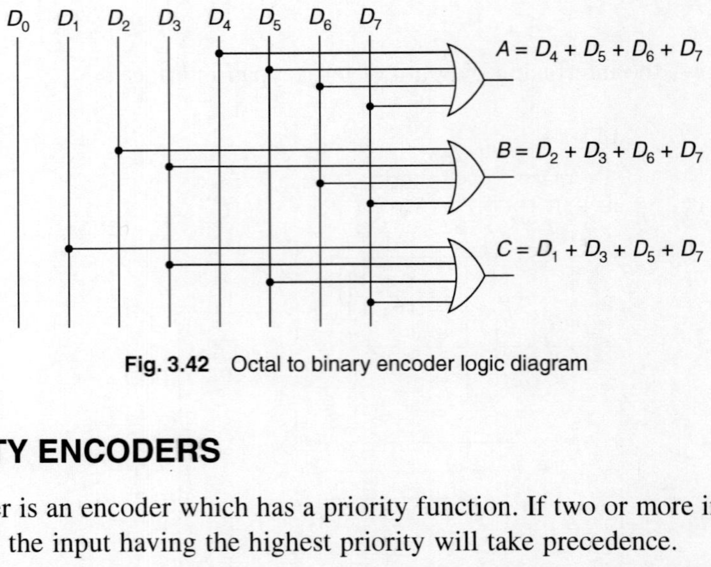

Fig. 3.42 Octal to binary encoder logic diagram

3.5 PRIORITY ENCODERS

A priority encoder is an encoder which has a priority function. If two or more inputs are equal to 1 simultaneously, the input having the highest priority will take precedence.

Figure 3.43 shows the condensed truth table of 4-bit priority encoder. This truth table is called condensed as the don't-care conditions are not explicitly mentioned either 0 or 1.

From truth table, it is seen that D_3 input has the highest priority and D_0 input has the lowest priority. When D_3 input is high, regardless of other inputs output is 11. D_2 input has the next priority. When $D_3 = 0$ and $D_2 = 1$, regardless of other lower priority inputs, output is 10.

The output for any input is generated only if higher priority inputs are 0. The output V (valid output indicator) indicates that one or more inputs are equal to 1. If all inputs are 0, V is equal to

0, and other two outputs (Y_1 and Y_0) are not used. Figure 3.44 shows K-map simplification. In the truth table, X indicates either 0 or 1.

After simplification of K-map, the logic diagram is drawn as shown in Fig. 3.45.

Inputs				Outputs		
D_0	D_1	D_2	D_3	Y_1	Y_0	V
0	0	0	0	×	×	0
1	0	0	0	0	0	1
×	1	0	0	0	1	1
×	×	1	0	1	0	1
×	×	×	1	1	1	1

Fig. 3.43 Truth table of 4-bit priority encoder

Example 3.8 Design a combinational circuit to find the 9's complement of a single digit BCD number. Realize the circuit using suitable logic gates. (VTU – June 2012)

Step 1 Let the single digit BCD number be ABCD. 9's complement of '0' is 9, of 5 is 4. Let the 9's complement be *WXYZ*.

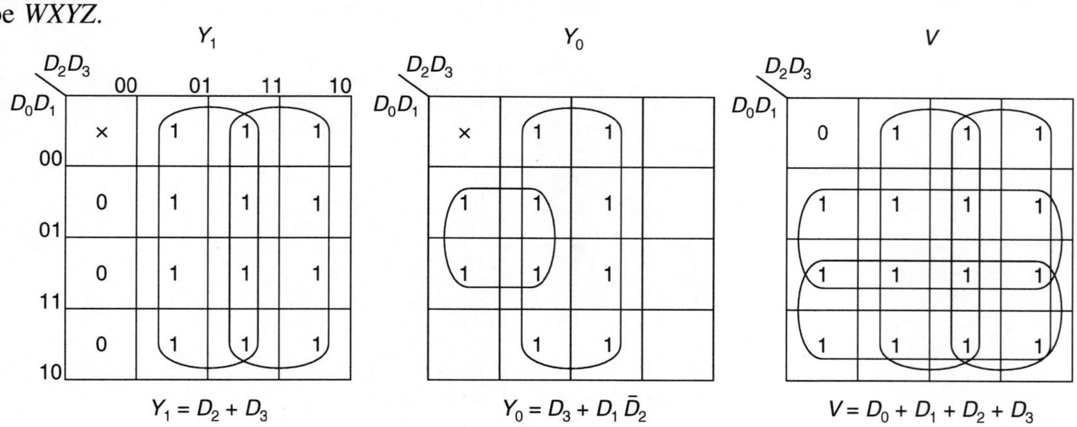

Fig. 3.44 K-map simplification

Step 2 Let us construct the truth table using the above variables, which is shown in Fig. 3.46.

BCD number is valid only up to 1001. Beyond 1001, the numbers are invalid. That is why for numbers above 1001, the 9's complement is shown as don't-care terms.

Step3 From the truth table, we can write the output SOP equations for W, X, Y and Z.

$$W = f(A, B, C, D) = \Sigma\,(0, 1) + \Sigma d\,(10, 11, 12, 13, 14, 15)$$

$$X = f(A, B, C, D) = \Sigma\,(2, 3, 4, 5) + \Sigma d\,(10, 11, 12, 13, 14, 15)$$

$$Y = f(A, B, C, D) = \Sigma\,(2, 3, 6, 7) + \Sigma d\,(10, 11, 12, 13, 14, 15)$$

$$Z = f(A, B, C, D) = \Sigma\,(0, 2, 4, 6, 8) + \Sigma d\,(10, 11, 12, 13, 14, 15)$$

Step 4 Next, we have to simplify the output SOP equations using K-maps. For each of the outputs W, X, Y and Z, there is one K-map. The K-maps for W, X, Y and Z are shown in Fig. 3.47.

Step 5 Based on the simplified output equations of W, X, Y and Z, we can draw the logic diagram using logic gates as shown in Fig. 3.48.

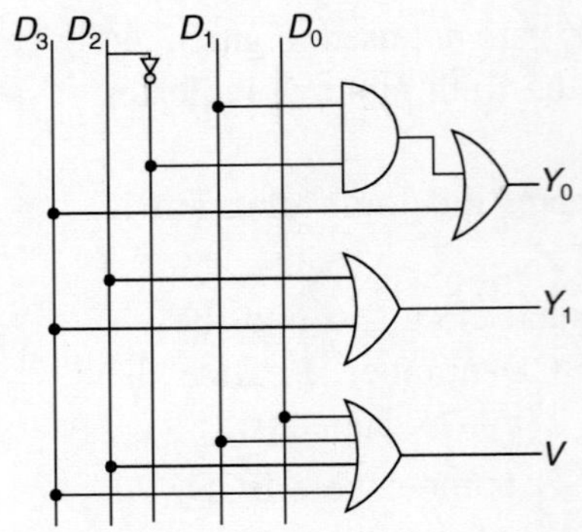

Fig. 3.45 Logic diagram of 4-bit priority encoder

	Inputs				Outputs			
Decimal No	*A*	*B*	*C*	*D*	*W*	*X*	*Y*	*Z*
0	0	0	0	0	1	0	0	1
1	0	0	0	1	1	0	0	0
2	0	0	1	0	0	1	1	1
3	0	0	1	1	0	1	1	0
4	0	1	0	0	0	1	0	1
5	0	1	0	1	0	1	0	0
6	0	1	1	0	0	0	1	1
7	0	1	1	1	0	0	1	0
8	1	0	0	0	0	0	0	1
9	1	0	0	1	0	0	0	0
10	1	0	1	0	–	–	–	–
11	1	0	1	1	–	–	–	–
12	1	1	0	0	–	–	–	–
13	1	1	0	1	–	–	–	–
14	1	1	1	0	–	–	–	–
15	1	1	1	1	–	–	–	–

Fig. 3.46 Truth table for example 3.8

Step 6 Once the logic diagram is drawn, one can realize the circuit using the components mentioned in the logic diagram.

Example 3.9 Implement the following function pairs using 74138 decoder.

$$f_1(a, b, c) = \Sigma(0, 2, 4): f_2(a, b, c) = \Sigma(1, 2, 4, 5, 7) \quad \text{(VTU – June 2012)}$$

Solution Implementation of the circuit is shown in Fig. 3.49.

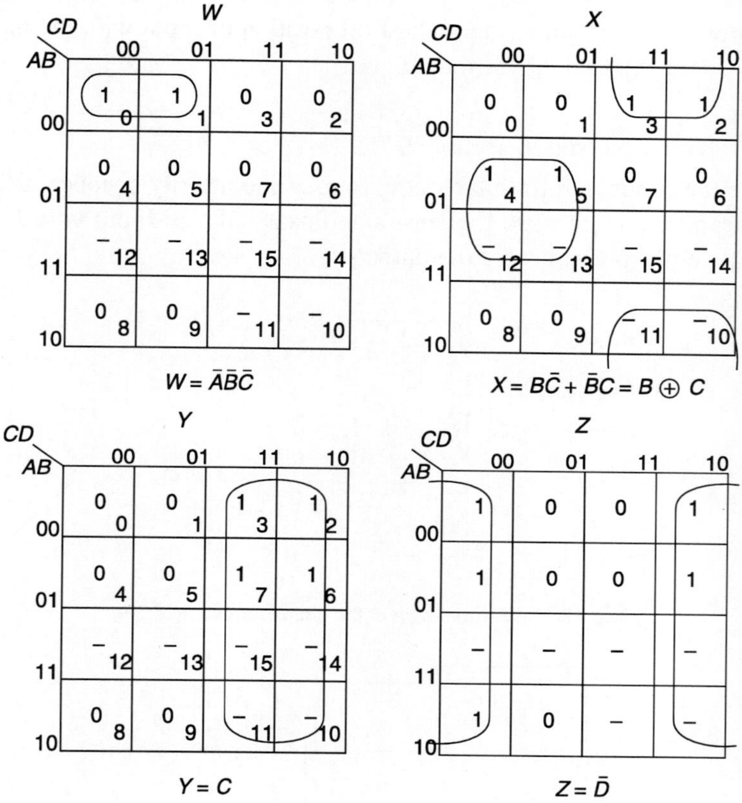

Fig. 3.47 K-maps for example 3.8

f_1 $(a, b, c) = \Sigma$ (0, 2, 4). In this function a is MSB and c is LSB. If we want to use minimum gate inputs, f_2 is realized by implementing $\bar{f}_2$ and inverting the output, $\bar{f}_2 = \Sigma$ (0, 3, 6). Implementation of the circuit is shown in Fig. 3.50.

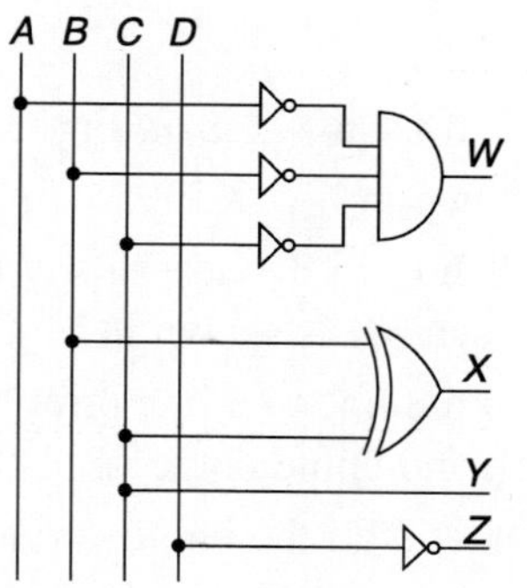

Fig. 3.48 Logic diagram for example 3.8

Example 3.10 Write the condensed truth table for a 4 to 2 line priority encoder with a valid output where the highest priority is given to the highest bit position or input with the highest index and obtain the minimal sum expressions for the outputs.

(VTU – Dec 2012)

Solution This problem is solved in section 3.5.

Example 3.11 Write the condensed truth table for a 4 to 2 line priority encoder with a valid output where the highest priority is given to the least significant input or input with lowest index and obtain the minimal sum expressions for the outputs.

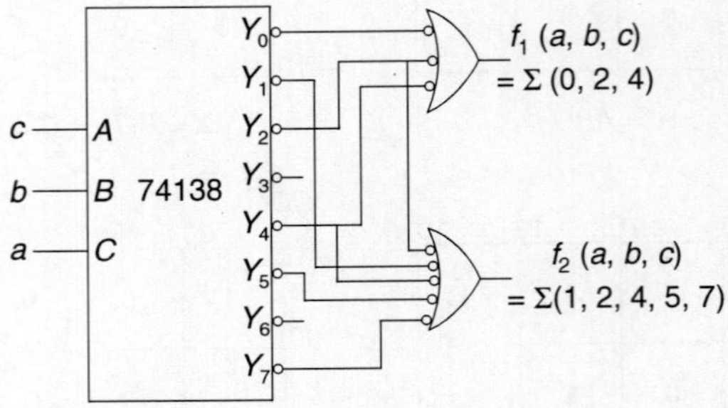

Fig.3.49 Implementation of the circuit for example 3.9

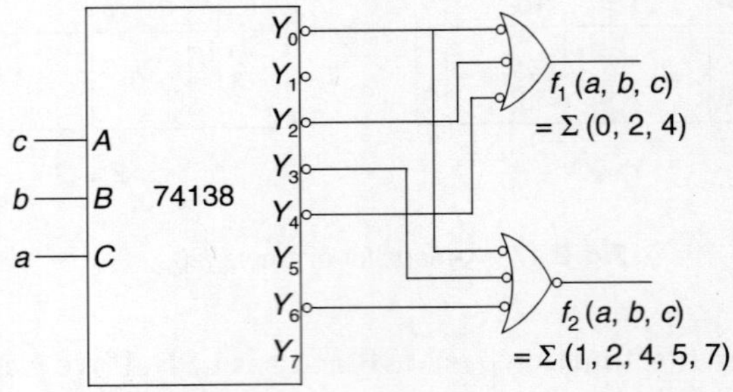

Fig. 3.50 Implementation of the circuit for example 3.9 using minimum gate inputs.

Solution The condensed truth table for a 4 to 2 line priority encoder giving highest priority to least significant input is shown in Fig. 3.51.

If one wants an explicit truth table, it is shown as in Fig. 3.52.

The K-maps for the outputs are shown in Fig. 3.53.

8 line to 3 line priority encoder: 8 line to 3 line priority encoder is available as 74148 in integrated circuit (IC) form. The logic symbol is shown in Fig. 3.54.

Figure 3.55 shows the truth table of a 8 line to 3 line priority encoder. When the enable input E_1 is high (1), the output lines are high and enble output E_0 is high.

If enable input E_1 is active low (0), and all the inputs are high, the output lines are high and enable output is low (0). It shows that none of the priority input lines have been activated.

It any one of the priority input lines is activated (i.e. 0), *GS* is low. *GS* low indicates that one of the inputs has been activated.

Cell Nos.	Inputs				Outputs		
	D_0	D_1	D_2	D_3	Y_1	Y_0	$V_{(valid)}$
0	0	0	0	0	0	0	0
8, 9, 10, 11, 12, 13, 14, 15	1	×	×	×	0	0	1
4, 5, 6, 7	0	1	×	×	0	1	1
2, 3	0	0	1	×	1	0	1
1	0	0	0	1	1	1	1

Fig. 3.51 Condensed truth table for example 3.11

Cell No.	Inputs				Outputs		
	D_0	D_1	D_2	D_3	Y_1	Y_0	V
0	0	0	0	0	0	0	0
8	1	0	0	0	0	0	1
9	1	0	0	1	0	0	1
10	1	0	1	0	0	0	1
11	1	0	1	1	0	0	1
12	1	1	0	0	0	0	1
13	1	1	0	1	0	0	1
14	1	1	1	0	0	0	1
15	1	1	1	1	0	0	1
4	0	1	0	0	0	1	1
5	0	1	0	1	0	1	1
6	0	1	1	0	0	1	1
7	0	1	1	1	0	1	1
2	0	0	1	0	1	0	1
3	0	0	1	1	1	0	1
1	0	0	0	1	1	1	1

Fig. 3.52 Complete truth table for example 3.11

Example 3.12 Realize 16:4 encoder using two 8:3 priority encoders. (VTU – June 2012)

Solution Figure 3.56 shows how two 8:3 priority encoders are used to realize a 16:4 priority encoder. $\overline{E}_0$ signal is connected to the $\overline{E}_1$ input of the next lower priority encoder. $\overline{E}_1$ input of the highest priority encoder is used as enable input for the 16:4 encoder. This ensures that only one encoder is enabled at a time. The outputs A_0, A_1 and A_2 of both the encoders are ANDed to produce active low outputs $\overline{A}_0$, $\overline{A}_1$ and $\overline{A}_2$. *GS* signals are ANDed to provide active low $\overline{GS}$ signal for 16:4 priority encoder. There are 16 inputs combining both the encoders. $\overline{GS}$ signal of the highest priority encoder is used as $\overline{A}_3$ signal. Hence, there are 16 inputs and four outputs $\overline{A}_0$, $\overline{A}_1$, $\overline{A}_2$ and $\overline{A}_3$.

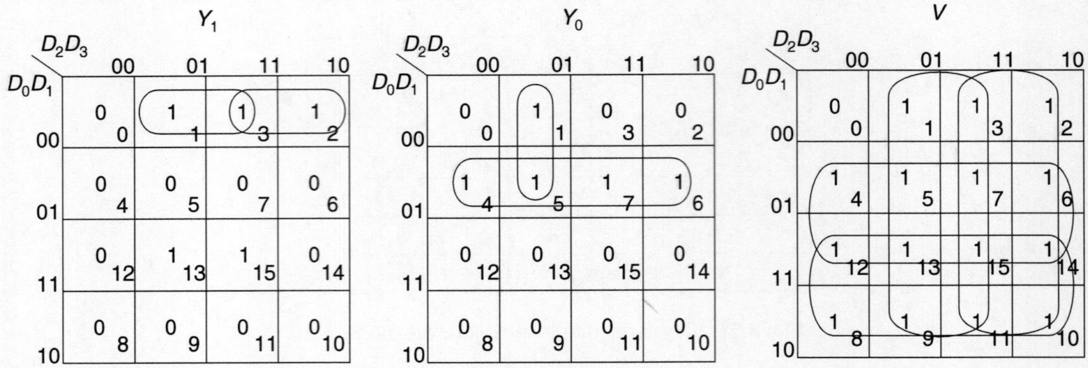

$Y_1 = \bar{D}_0\bar{D}_1D_3 + \bar{D}_0\bar{D}_1D_2$ $\quad$ $Y_0 = \bar{D}_0D_1 + \bar{D}_0\bar{D}_2D_3$ $\quad$ $V = D_0 + D_1 + D_2 + D_3$

Fig. 3.53 K-maps for example 3.11

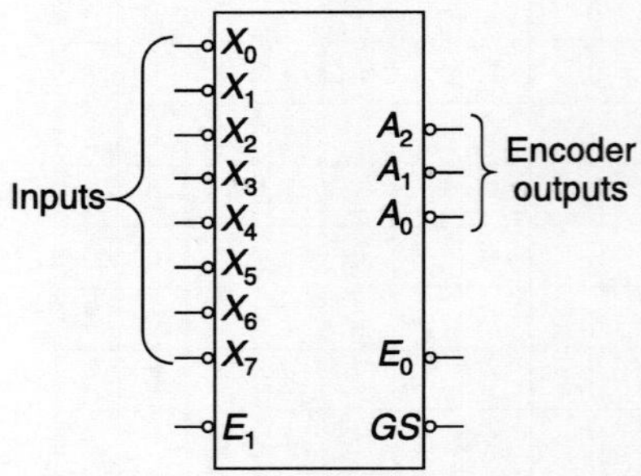

Fig. 3.54 Logic symbol of 8-line to 3-line priority encoder

Inputs									Outputs				
E_1	X_0	X_1	X_2	X_3	X_4	X_5	X_6	X_7	A_2	A_1	A_0	GS	E_0
1	×	×	×	×	×	×	×	×	1	1	1	1	1
0	1	1	1	1	1	1	1	1	1	1	1	1	0
0	0	1	1	1	1	1	1	1	1	1	1	0	1
0	×	0	1	1	1	1	1	1	1	1	0	0	1
0	×	×	0	1	1	1	1	1	1	0	1	0	1
0	×	×	×	0	1	1	1	1	1	0	0	0	1
0	×	×	×	×	0	1	1	1	0	1	1	0	1
0	×	×	×	×	×	0	1	1	0	1	0	0	1
0	×	×	×	×	×	×	0	1	0	0	1	0	1
0	×	×	×	×	×	×	×	0	0	0	0	0	1

Fig. 3.55 Truth table of 8 to 3 line priority encoder

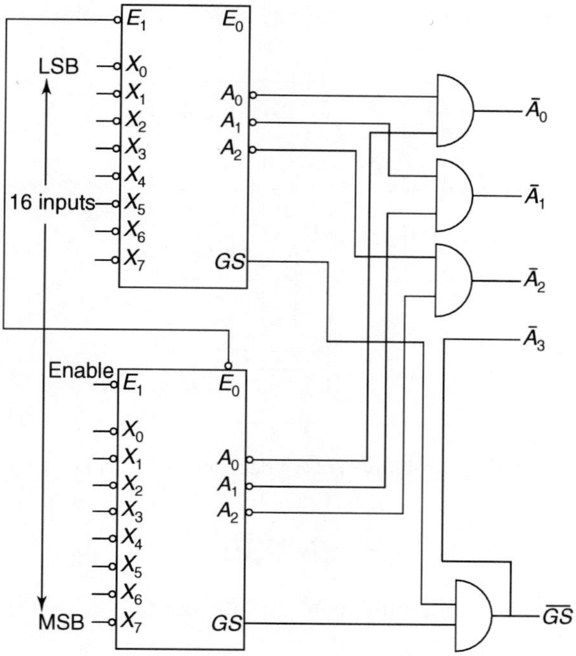

Fig. 3.56 16:4 Priority encoder using two 74148 and AND gates

Example 3.13 Develop the logic diagram of a 2 to 4 decoder with the following specifications: (i) active low enable input; (ii) active high encoded outputs. Draw the IEEE symbol.

(VTU – June 2014)

Solution The IEEE symbol for the above specifications is shown in Fig. 3.57.

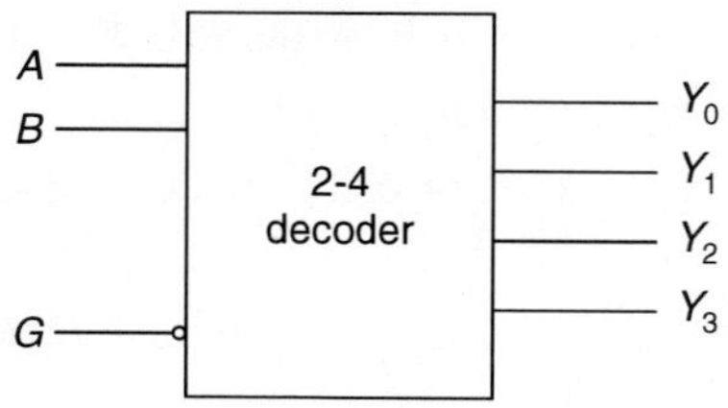

Fig. 3.57 IEEE symbol for Example 3.13

The truth table for 2 to 4 decoder with the above specifications is shown in Fig. 3.58.

Inputs			Output			
Enable	Select					
G	B	A	Y_0	Y_1	Y_2	Y_3
H	×	×	0	0	0	0
L	0	0	1	0	0	0
L	0	1	0	1	0	0
L	1	0	0	0	1	0
L	1	1	0	0	0	1

Fig. 3.58 Truth table for Example 3.13

The combinational circuit to realize the logic as per the truth table is shown in Fig. 3.59.

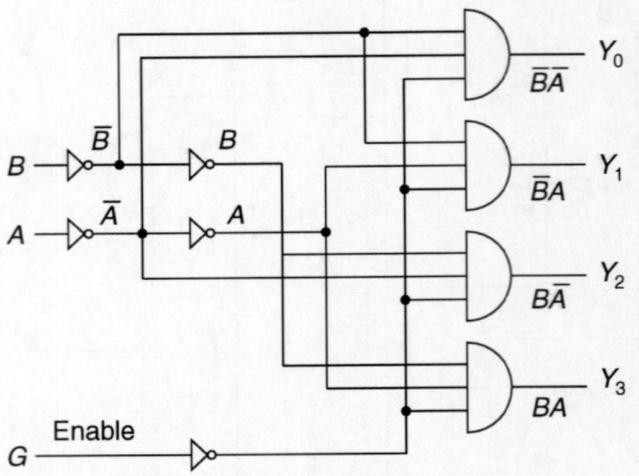

Fig. 3.59 Logic diagram of 2-4 decoder for Example 3.13

EXERCISE

1. Implement the following functions using 3:8 decoder:
   $F_1(A, B, C) = \Sigma m(0, 1, 4, 5, 7)$
   $F_2(A, B, C) = \Sigma m(2, 4, 6, 7)$
2. Design a 4:16 decoder using two 3:8 docoders and write truth table.
3. Explain a decimal to Binary Encoder using four OR gates. What is priority encoder?
4. What is an encoder? Explain an 8 to 3 encoder.
5. With the aid of block diagrams, clearly distinguish between a decoder and encoder.
6. Implement a full subtractor using a decoder and two NAND gates.
7. What is a decoder? Using gates, show how do you design a 3 to 8 line decoder?
8. Write a short note on priority encoder.
9. Implement the 32 input to 5 output priority encoder using four 74LS148 encoders and gates.
10. Draw the interfacing diagram of ten-key keypad interface to a digital system using decimal to BCD encoder.
11. Design a 5 to 32 decoder using one 2 to 4 and four 3 to 8 decoder ICS.
12. Draw the circuit for 3 to 8 decoder and explain.

CHAPTER 4

Analysis and Design of Combinational Logic-2

4.1 DIGITAL MULTIPLEXERS

Digital multiplexers provide digital equivalent of analog selector switch. A digital multiplexer connects one of n inputs to a single output line so that the logical value of the input is transferred to the output.

A 4 to 1 multiplexer requires 2 select inputs, an 8 to 1 multiplexer requires 3 select inputs and a 16 to 1 multiplexer requires 4 select inputs.

When analog selector is in position, as shown in Fig. 4.1, data is routed through source A to the output, through the selector switch. An enable switch is in series with the data output line which must be closed for data transfer.

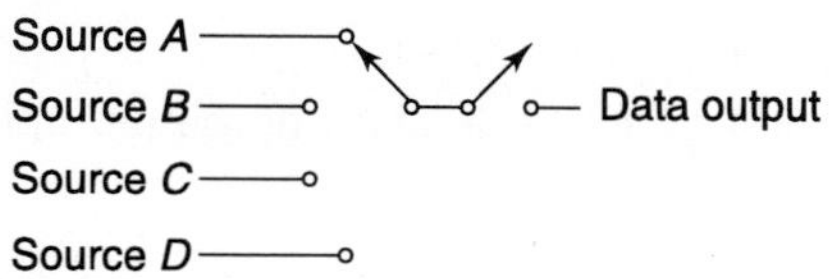

Fig. 4.1 Analog select switch

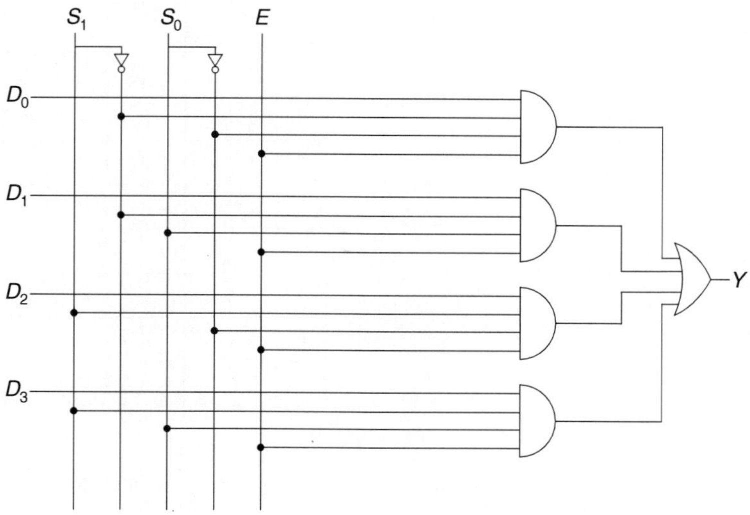

Fig. 4.2 Logic diagram of 4 to 1 multiplexer

E	S_1	S_0	Y
1	0	0	D_0
1	0	1	D_1
1	1	0	D_2
1	1	1	D_3
0	×	×	0

Fig. 4.3 Truth table for 4 to 1 multiplexer

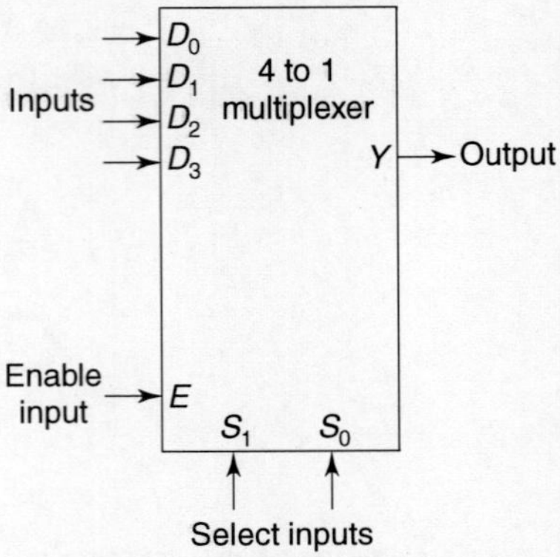

Fig. 4.4 Logic symbol

4 to 1 multiplexer: Figure 4.2 shows 4 to 1 line multiplexer. Each of the four lines, D_0 to D_3 is applied to one input of 4 input AND gates. Two selection lines are decoded to select a particular AND gate.

When S_1 S_0 = 00, the AND gate associated with D_0, has two of its inputs equal to 1, the third connected to D_0 and the fourth input to enable input E.

Only this AND gate output will be equal to 1, and all the other three AND gate outputs will be 0. Hence, the OR gate output Y will be corresponding to D_0. Thus, whatever the input D_0 will be transferred to output when S_1, S_0 = 00. Figure 4.3 shows the truth table for 4 to 1 multiplexer and Fig. 4.4 shows the logic symbol.

8 to 1 multiplexer: This has eight data inputs and one output and three select inputs and one enable input.

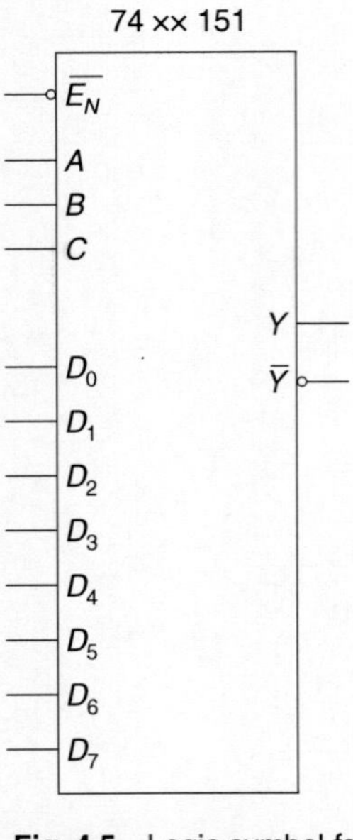

Fig. 4.5 Logic symbol for 74 xx 151

Inputs				Outputs	
Select			Enable		
C	B	A	$\overline{E_N}$	Y	$\overline{Y}$
×	×	×	1	0	1
0	0	0	0	D_0	$\overline{D_0}$
0	0	1	0	D_1	$\overline{D_1}$
0	1	0	0	D_2	$\overline{D_2}$
0	1	1	0	D_3	$\overline{D_3}$
1	0	0	0	D_4	$\overline{D_4}$
1	0	1	0	D_5	$\overline{D_5}$
D	1	0	0	D_6	$\overline{D_6}$
1	1	1	0	D_7	$\overline{D_7}$

Fig. 4.6 Truth table for 74 xx 151

A typical 8 to 1 multiplexer is 74 ×× 151. It has 8 inputs ($D_0 - D_7$) and two outputs (Y and $\overline{Y}$). Logic symbol of 74 ×× 151 is shown in Fig. 4.5. Truth table of 74 ×× 151 is shown in Fig. 4.6. Multiplexer acts as a data switch. Hence, it does not generate any data of its own, but passes external input data from the selected input to the outputThat is why the output column in the truth table represents data by D_n and $\overline{D}_n$.

Expanding multiplexers: Multiplexer ICs are available for different range of inputs such as 74150 (16 to 1 multiplexer), 74151 (8 to 1 mux) 74153 (dual 4 to 1 mux) and 74157 (dual 2 to 1 mux). Expanding the range of inputs is possible by interconnecting several multiplexers. For example, two 74 ×× 151 multiplexer (8 to 1) can be interconnected to form 16 to 1 multiplexer, two 74 ×× 150 multiplexers (16 to 1) can be interconnected to form (32 to 1) multiplexer.

Let us design a 16 to 1 multiplexer using two 8 to 1 multiplexers. Figure 4.7 shows a 16 to 1 multiplexer using two 74151 (8 to 1) multiplexers. Each 8 to 1 multiplexer has three select inputs

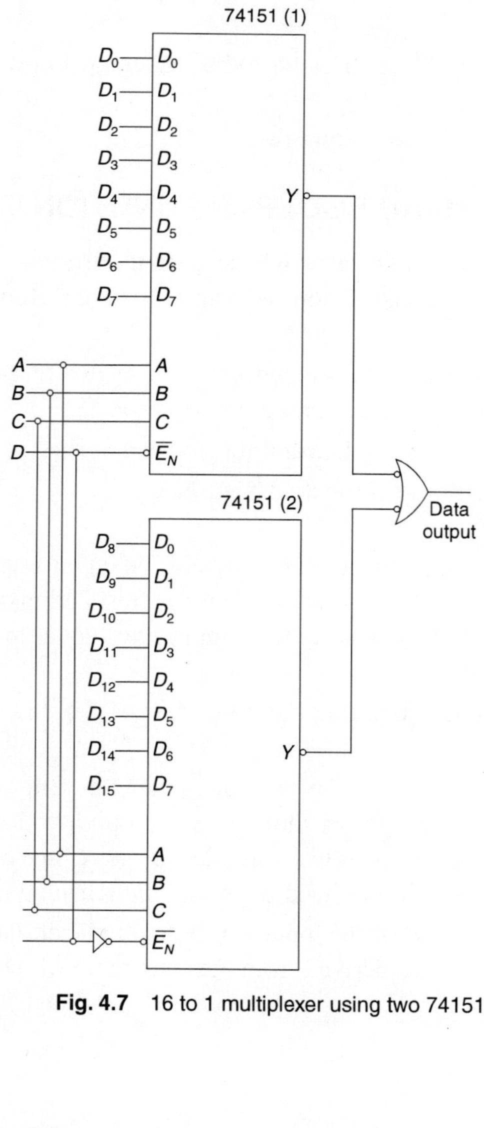

Fig. 4.7 16 to 1 multiplexer using two 74151 ICs

and a single enable. We need four select inputs to perform 16 to 1 multiplexing function. So, we can use the enable input of each IC as the fourth select bit. Select input D is directly connected to enable input of top IC and inverted and connected to bottom IC. When D is low, the top IC is enabled. The top multiplexer switches data lines D_0 to D_7 and the bottom IC switches data line D_8 to D_{15}.

Similarly, a 32 to 1 multiplexer can be realized using four 74151 (8 to 1 multiplexer) and one 74139 (dual 2 to 4 decoder) (Fig. 4.8).

A, B, C, D and E are select inputs to the multiplexer system. D and E are decoded by 74139 to determine which of the four 8 to 1 multiplexers will be enabled. Because only one of the four outputs from the decoder can be active, only one 8 to 1 multiplexer can be enabled a time.

Select inputs A, B and C are connected in parallel to the four 8 to 1 multiplexers. The top multiplexer switches inputs D_0 to D_7 to the output and the next multiplexer switches inputs D_8 to D_{15} to the output and so on. The four multiplexer active low outputs are ORed to provide the output D_0 to D_{31}.

In a similar manner a 32 to 1 multiplexer can also be realized using two 74150 ICs (16 to 1 multiplexers).

Figure 4.9 shows a 32 to 1 multiplexer using two 74150 ICs.

4.2 USING MULTIPLEXERS AS BOOLEAN FUNCTION GENERATORS

A multiplexer consists of a set of AND gates whose outputs are connected to OR gate as shown in Fig. 4.2. With this type of construction, we can realize any Boolean function using a multiplexer.

Each AND gate in a multiplexer can generate a minterm when the number of variables in the minterm is equal to the number of select lines on the multiplexer.

Let us go through some examples to understand the above concept.

Example 4.1 Realize the following Boolean function $f(A, B, C) = \Sigma(0, 1, 3, 5, 7)$ using 8:1 mux (74151). (VTU – June 2010)

Solution For a 8:1 mux, there are three select lines S_0, S_1, S_2. The function given is a three-variable function. The given minterms are selected by making their corresponding input lines equal to 1. Remaining minterms are not selected by making their input lines equal to 0. Figure 4.10 shows the realization of Boolean function.

Example 4.2 Realize the following Boolean function $f(A, B, C) = \Sigma(0, 1, 3, 5, 7)$ using 4:1 mux (74153). (VTU – June 2010)

Solution This is the same function as in the previous example. Only difference is that we have to use 4:1 mux instead of 8:1 mux. In 4:1 mux, there are only two select lines. Hence, two least significant variables are connected to select line, i.e., B and C are connected to S_1 and S_0 respectively. The inputs to multiplexer are derived from the implementation table.

The implementation table is the list of the inputs of the multiplexer and all the minterms are listed under them in two rows. These are derived from the truth table which is shown in Fig. 4.11

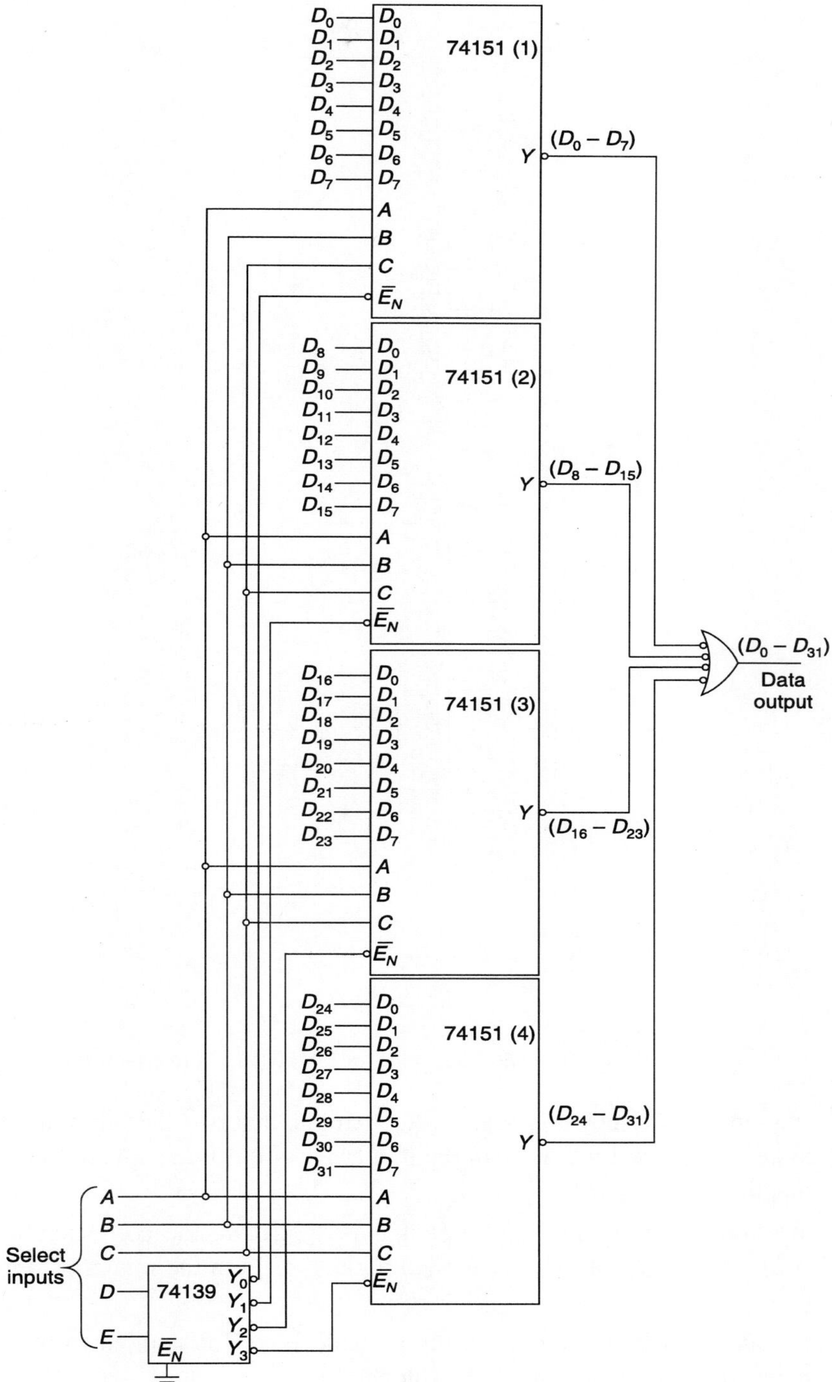

Fig. 4.8 32 to 1 multiplexer using four 8 to 1 multiplexers and one 2 to 4 decoder

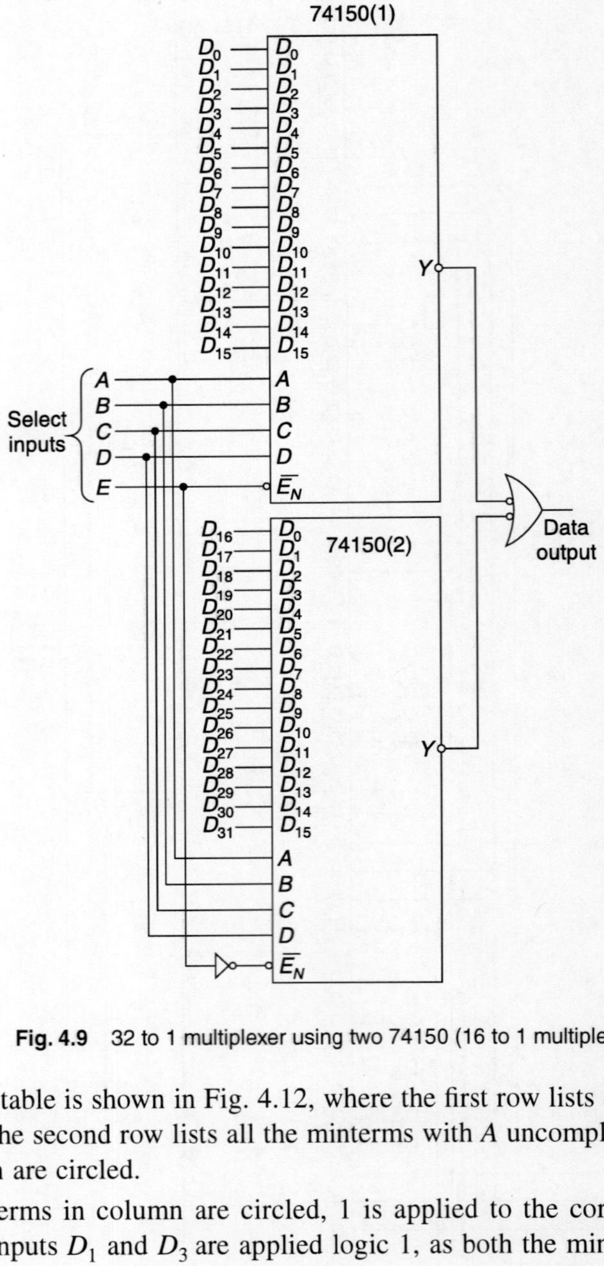

Fig. 4.9 32 to 1 multiplexer using two 74150 (16 to 1 multiplexers)

and implementation table is shown in Fig. 4.12, where the first row lists all minterms where A is complemented and the second row lists all the minterms with A uncomplemented. The minterms given in the function are circled.

If the two minterms in column are circled, 1 is applied to the corresponding multiplexer input. In this case, inputs D_1 and D_3 are applied logic 1, as both the minterms are circled under D_1 and D_3.

If both the minterms in a column are not circled, logic 0 is applied to the corresponding multiplexer input. In this case, the input D_2 is applied logic 0.

If the minterm in the first row is circled and minterm in the second row is not circled, $\bar{A}$ is applied to the corresponding multiplexer input. In this case, D_0 is applied $\bar{A}$.

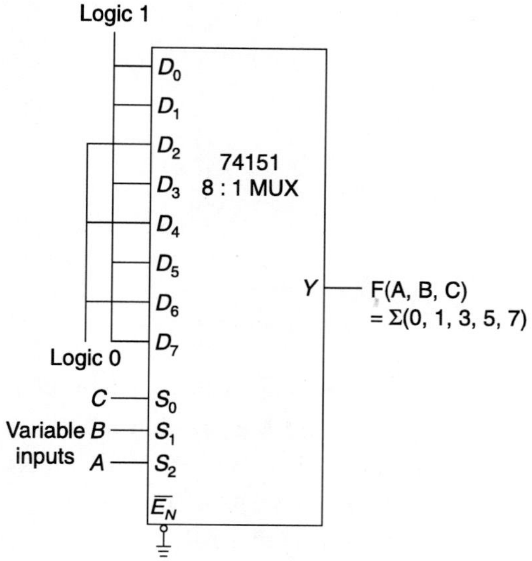

Fig. 4.10 Realization of Boolean function $f(A, B\ C), = \Sigma\ (0, 1, 3, 5, 7)$

Minterm	A	B	C	F
0	0	0	0	1
1	0	0	1	1
2	0	1	0	0
3	0	1	1	1
4	1	0	0	0
5	1	0	1	1
6	1	1	0	0
7	1	1	1	1

Fig. 4.11 Truth table

	D_0	D_1	D_2	D_3
$\bar{A}$	(0)	(1)	2	(3)
A	4	(5)	6	(7)
	$\bar{A}$	1	0	1

Fig. 4.12 Implementation table

If the minterm in the first row is not circled and the minterm in the second row is circled, then A is applied to the corresponding multiplexer input. Figure 4.13 shows the realization of the Boolean function using 4:1 mux. Instead of two least significant variables connected to select lines, we can connect two most significant variables to select lines, i.e., A and B can be connected to S_1 and S_0. C can be used as multiplexer input. Here the implementation table will be modified as shown in Fig. 4.14 using truth table.

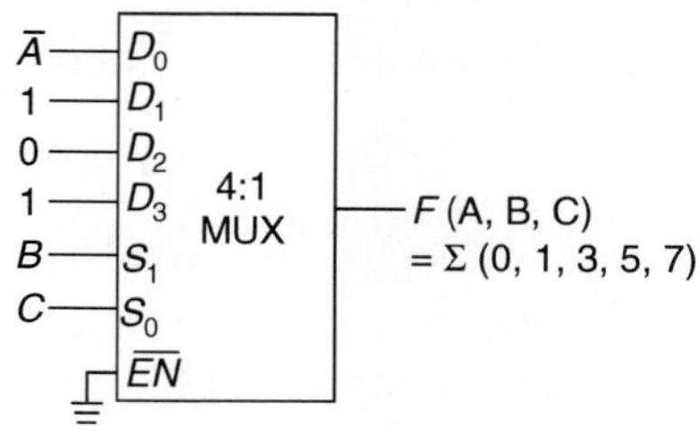

Fig. 4.13

Figure 4.15 shows the realization of Boolean function $f(ABC) = \Sigma\ (0, 1, 3, 5, 7)$. We see two different solutions for the same problem.

	D_0	D_1	D_2	D_3
$\bar{C}$	⓪	2	4	6
C	①	③	⑤	⑦
	1	C	C	C

Fig. 4.14 Implementation table

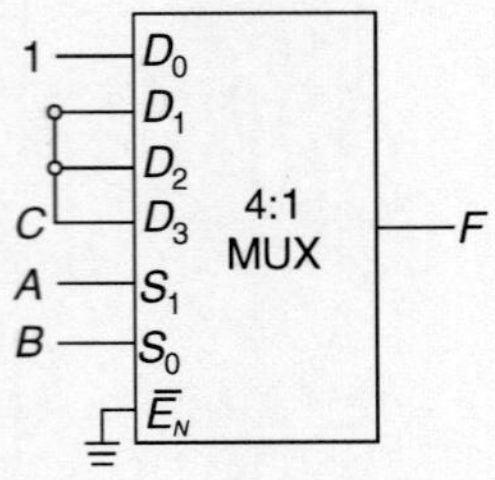

Fig. 4.15 Realization of Boolean function

Example 4.3 Implement $f(a, b, c) = \Sigma\,(1, 4, 5, 7)$ using 4:1 multiplexer. (VTU – June 2012)

Solution It is a three variable function and the 4:1 multiplexer has only two select lines. b and c variables are connected to S_1 and S_0. The implementation table is shown in Fig. 4.16 and implementation of the function $f(a, b, c)$ is shown in Fig. 4.17.

Example 4.4 Configure a 16 to1 MUX using 4 to 1 MUX. (VTU – Dec 2013)

Solution Here, all enable inputs are connected together and grounded. All the select inputs of first column 74153s are connected in parallel and they are S_1 and S_0.

For the second column 74153, the data inputs are from output of each of the multiplexer in the first column.

	D_0	D_1	D_2	D_3
$\bar{A}$	0	①	2	3
A	④	⑤	6	⑦
	A	1	0	A

Fig. 4.16 Implementation table

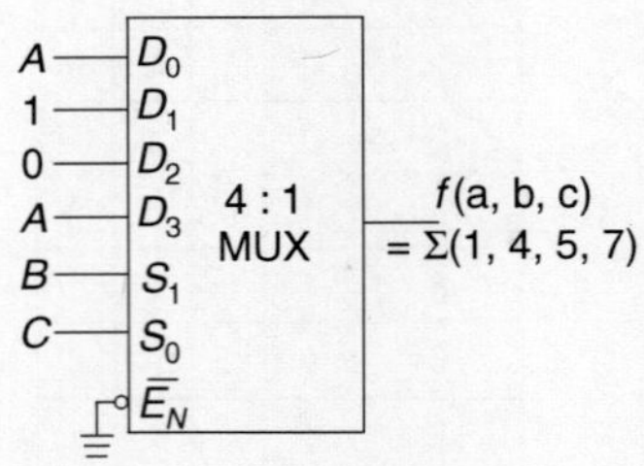

Fig. 4.17 Realization of Boolean function

For the 16 to 1 multiplexer 4 select lines are required, i.e., S_3, S_2, S_1 and S_0. S_3 and S_2 are connected to S_1 and S_0 of 2nd column multiplexer. We have configured a 16:1 MUX using 5, 4 to 1 multiplexers as shown in Fig. 4.18.

Example 4.5 Implement the following Boolean function with 8:1 multiplexer:

$$f(A, B, C, D) = \Sigma m\,(0, 2, 6, 10, 11, 12, 13) + d\,(3, 8, 14)$$

Solution This is a 4 variable problem. Hence, we need 16:1 multiplexer. If we have to use 8:1 multiplexer, one of the function variables has to be used as data input. Let us construct the implementation table and from that realize the function.

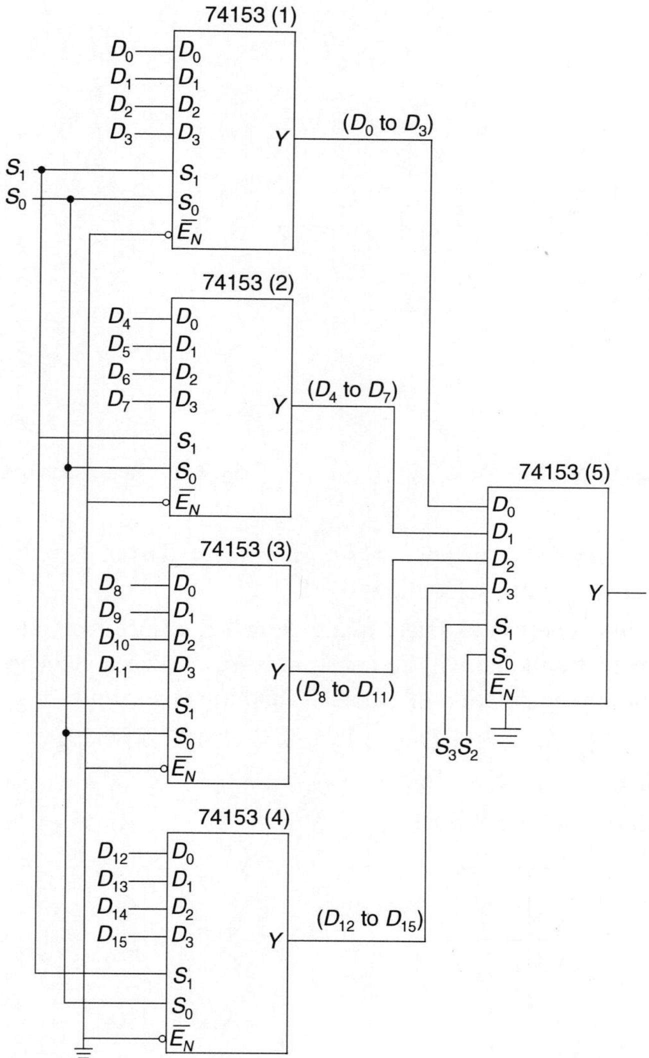

Fig. 4.18 A 16 to1 MUX using 4 to 1 MUX

Figure 4.19 shows the implementation table and Fig. 4.20 shows the realization of the Boolean function. Here, we have function variables *B*, *C*, *D* connected to select inputs S_2, S_1, S_0 respectively. Also the don't-care terms are considered 1s.

Example 4.6 Implement the following Boolean function using 4:1 multiplexer:

$$F(A, B, C) = \Sigma m\,(1, 3, 5, 6) \qquad \text{(VTU – June 2013)}$$

Solution Here, we connect *B*, *C* to select inputs S_1, S_0 and *A* as data input. Figure 4.21 shows the implementation table and Fig. 4.22 shows the implementation of the Boolean function using 4:1 multiplexer.

	D_0	D_1	D_2	D_3	D_4	D_5	D_6	D_7
$\bar{A}$	⓪	1	②	③	4	5	⑥	7
A	⑧	9	⑩	⑪	⑫	⑬	⑭	15
	1	0	1	1	A	A	1	0

Fig. 4.19 Implementation table

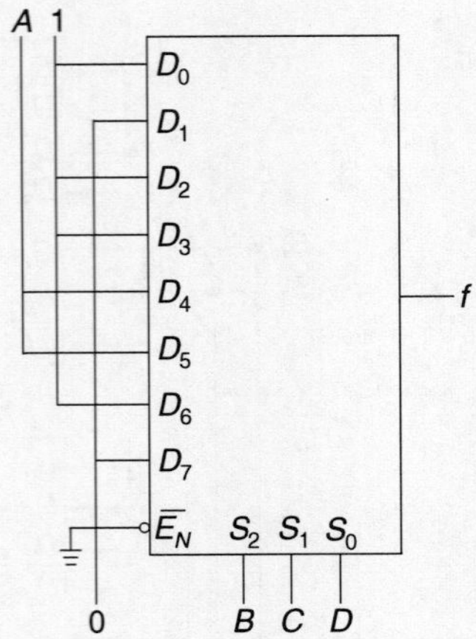

Fig. 4.20 Realization of Boolean function

Example 4.7 Implement the Boolean function $f(a, b, c, d) = \Sigma m\ (0, 1, 5, 6, 7, 9, 10, 15)$ using multiplexer with a, b connected to select lines S_1, S_0. (VTU – Dec 2011)

Solution Here a, b are connected to select inputs S_1 and S_0 respectively and c, d are connected as data inputs. Implementation table will be constructed c, d taken together as data inputs and is shown in Fig. 4.23 and implementation of Boolean function is shown in Fig. 4.24.

Example 4.8 Implement $f(a, b, c, d) = \Sigma m\ (0, 1, 5, 6, 7, 9, 10, 15)$ using

(i) 8:1 MUX with a, b, c as select lines.

(ii) 4:1 MUX with a, b as select lines. (VTU – July 2011)

	D_0	D_1	D_2	D_3
$\bar{A}$	0	①	2	③
A	4	⑤	⑥	7
	0	1	A	$\bar{A}$

Fig. 4.21 Implementation table

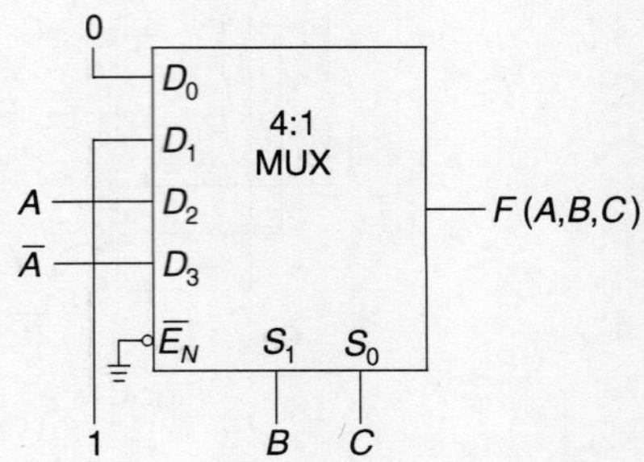

Fig. 4.22 Implementation of $F(A, B, C)$ using 4:1 multiplexer

Solution (i) Implementation table is constructed using a, b, c as select lines S_2, S_1 and S_0 respectively and d is connected as data input. Figure 4.25 shows the implementation table and Fig. 4.26 shows the implementation of Boolean function $f(a, b, c, d) = \Sigma m$ (0, 1, 5, 6, 7, 8, 10, 15).

(ii) This problem has been shown in Example 4.7.

	D_0	D_1	D_2	D_3
$\bar{c}\bar{d}$	(0)	4	8	12
$\bar{c}d$	(1)	(5)	(9)	13
$c\bar{d}$	2	(6)	(10)	14
cd	3	(7)	11	(15)
	$\bar{c}\bar{d} + \bar{c}d$ $\bar{c}$	$\bar{c}d + c\bar{d} + cd = \bar{c}d + c = c + d$	$\bar{c}d + c\bar{d} = c \oplus d$	cd

Fig. 4.23 Implementation table

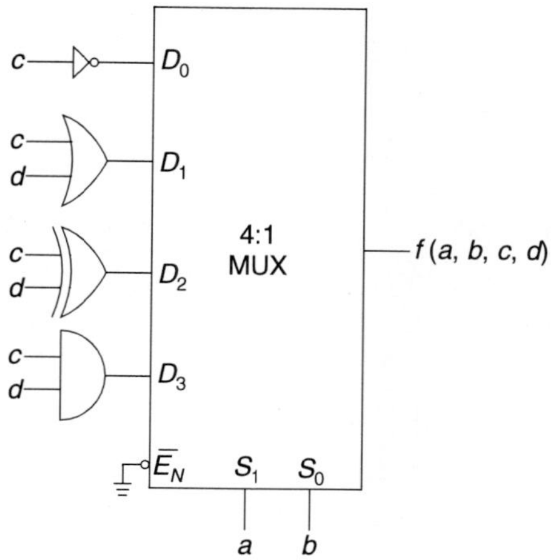

Fig. 4.24 Implementation of Boolean function

Example 4.9 Implement the following Boolean function with an 8:1 multiplexer with A, B and D connected to selection line S_2, S_1 and S_0 respectively

$$F(A, B, C, D) = \Sigma m\,(0, 1, 3, 4, 8, 9, 15). \qquad \text{(VTU – Jan 2006)}$$

Solution Here, C will be connected as data input. Hence, the implementation table is shown as in Fig. 4.27 and Fig. 4.28 shows the implementation.

	D_0	D_1	D_2	D_3	D_4	D_5	D_6	D_7
$\bar{d}$	(0)	2	4	(6)	8	(10)	12	14
d	(1)	3	(5)	(7)	(9)	11	13	(15)
	1	0	d	1	d	$\bar{d}$	0	d

Fig. 4.25 Implementation table

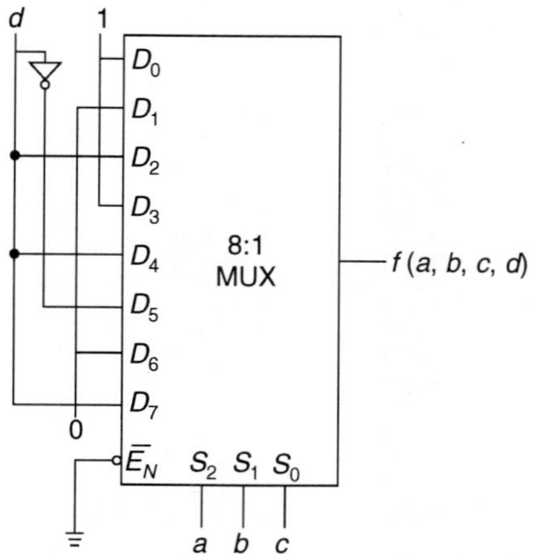

Fig. 4.26 Implementation of Boolean function

	D_0	D_1	D_2	D_3	D_4	D_5	D_6	D_7
$\bar{c}$	(0)	(1)	(4)	5	(8)	(9)	12	13
c	2	(3)	6	7	10	11	14	(15)
	$\bar{C}$	1	$\bar{C}$	0	$\bar{C}$	$\bar{C}$	0	C

Fig. 4.27 Implementation table

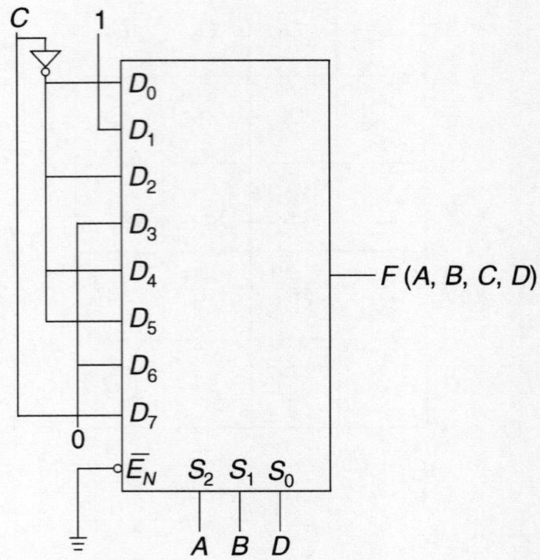

Fig. 4.28 Implementation of Boolean function

4.3 ADDERS AND SUBTRACTORS

Adding two single-bit binary values produces a sum and a carry output. This is called half add and the circuit that performs the function is called half adder.

In addition to two single binary values if a carry input is added together, a sum and a carry is produced and the circuit that performs this function is called full adder.

Inputs		Outputs	
A	B	Sum	Carry
0	0	0	0
0	1	1	0
1	0	1	0
1	1	0	1

Fig. 4.29 Truth table for half adder

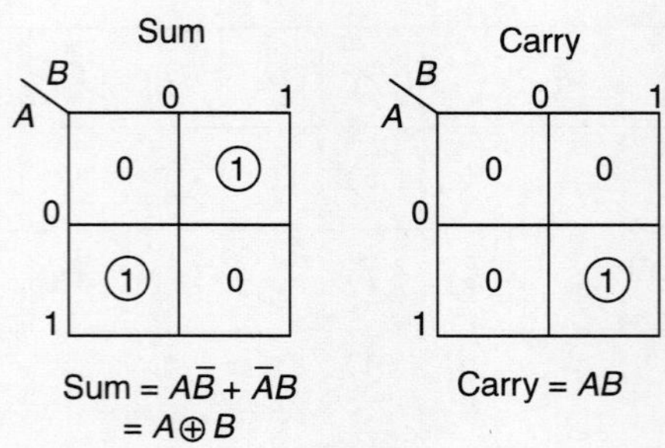

Fig. 4.30 K-map simplification for sum and carry

Half adder: The half adder has two binary input values, i.e., augend and addend. It has two binary outputs, i.e., sum and carry. Figure 4.29 gives the truth table for half adder and Fig. 4.30 shows K-map simplification for sum and carry.

Figure 4.31 shows the logic diagram for half adder.

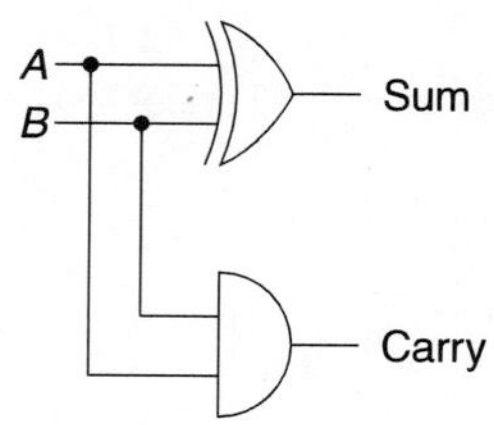

Fig. 4.31 Logic diagram for half adder

Input			output	
A	B	C_{in}	Sum	Carry
0	0	0	0	0
0	0	1	1	0
0	1	0	1	0
0	1	1	0	1
1	0	0	1	0
1	0	1	0	1
1	1	0	0	1
1	1	1	1	1

Fig. 4.32 Truth table for full adder

In practical addition, we have to add two single bits along with carry of previous digit addition. This is not possible using half adder.

Full adder: A full adder is arithmetic sum of three input binary values. It consists of three inputs and two outputs, i.e., sum and carry. The truth table for full adder is shown in Fig. 4.32.

Figure 4.33 shows the K-map simplification for full adder.

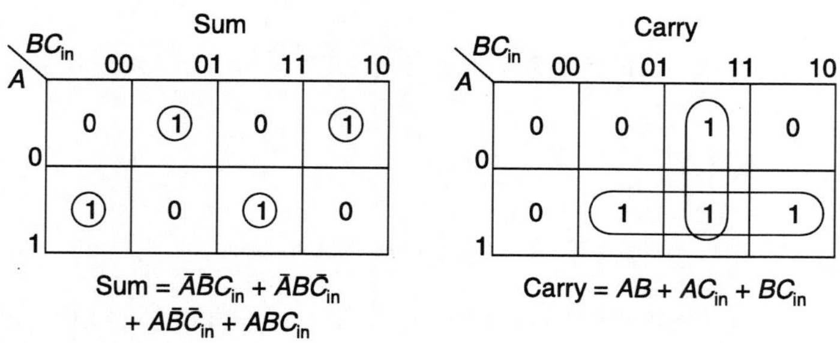

Fig. 4.33 K-map simplification for sum and carry of full adder

Figure 4.34 shows the logic diagram for sum and carry of full adder.

The sum of full adder can be written as,

$$\begin{aligned}\text{Sum} &= \bar{A}\bar{B}C_{in} + \bar{A}B\bar{C}_{in} + A\bar{B}\bar{C}_{in} + ABC_{in} \\ &= C_{in}(\bar{A}\bar{B} + AB) + \bar{C}_{in}(\bar{A}B + A\bar{B}) \\ &= C_{in}(A \odot B) + \bar{C}_{in}(A \oplus B)\end{aligned}$$

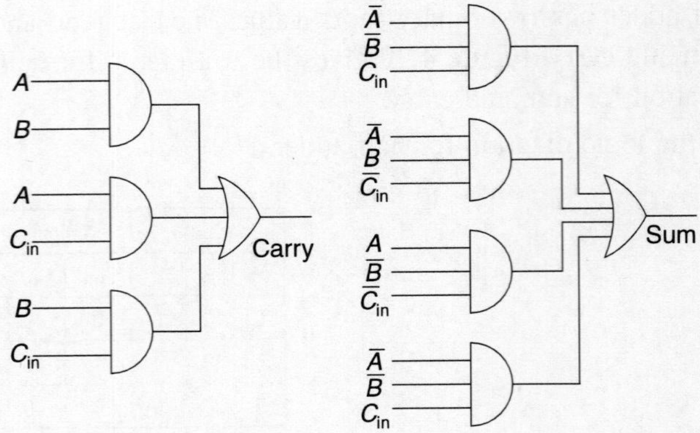

Fig. 4.34 Logic diagram for sum and carry of full adder

$$= C_{in}\,(\overline{A \oplus B}) + \overline{C}_{in}\,(A \oplus B)$$

$$= C_{in} \oplus (A \oplus B)$$

With this simplification, full adder can be implemented as shown in Fig. 4.35.

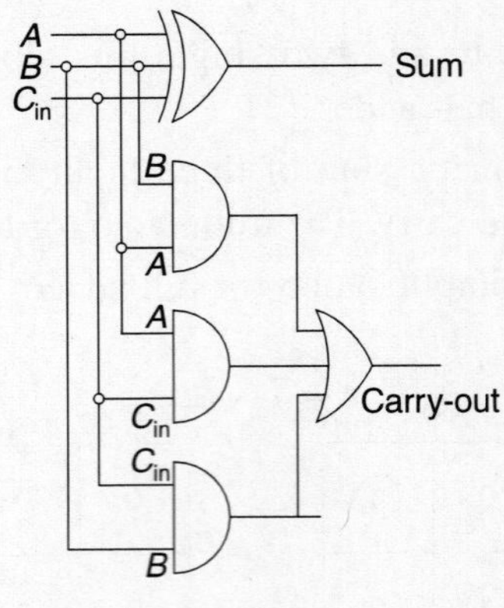

Fig. 4.35 Implementation of full adder

A full adder can also be implemented using two half adders and one OR gate. This is shown in Fig. 4.36. The sum output from the second half adder is the EX-OR of C_{in} and the output of the first half adder.

$$\text{Sum} = C_{in} \oplus (A \oplus B)$$

which has been proved to be equal to,

$$\overline{A}\,\overline{B}C_{in} + \overline{A}B\overline{C}_{in} + A\overline{B}\,\overline{C}_{in} + ABC_{in}$$

The carry output is

$$C_{out} = AB + C_{in}\,(A\overline{B} + \overline{A}B)$$

$$= AB + A\bar{B}C_{in} + \bar{A}BC_{in}$$

$$= AB\,(C_{in} + 1) + A\bar{B}C_{in} + \bar{A}BC_{in} \qquad [\because C_{in} + 1 = 1]$$

$$= ABC_{in} + AB + A\bar{B}C_{in} + \bar{A}BC_{in}$$

$$= AB + AC_{in}\,(B + \bar{B}) + \bar{A}BC_{in}$$

$$= AB + AC_{in} + \bar{A}BC_{in} \qquad [\because B + \bar{B} = 1]$$

$$= AB\,(C_{in} + 1) + AC_{in} + \bar{A}BC_{in} \qquad [\because C_{in} + 1 = 1]$$

$$= ABC_{in} + AB + AC_{in} + \bar{A}BC_{in}$$

$$= BC_{in}\,[A + \bar{A}] + AB + AC_{in}$$

$$= AB + BC_{in} + AC_{in} \qquad [\because A + \bar{A} = 1]$$

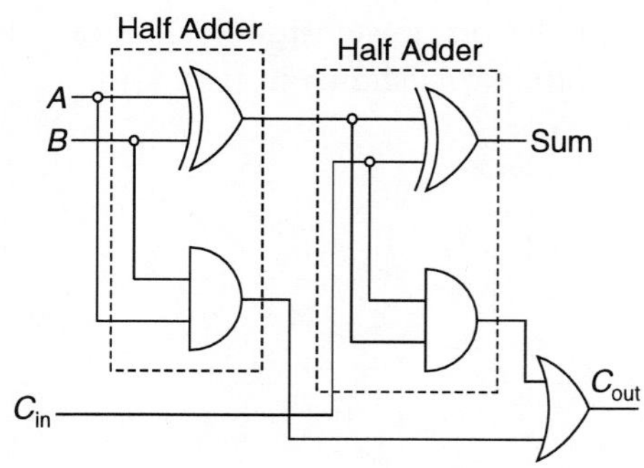

Fig. 4.36 Implementation of full adder with two half adders and an OR gate

Binary subtractor: A half subtractor is a combinational circuit that subtracts two bits and produces a difference and a borrow. The truth table for a half subtractor is shown in Fig. 4.37.

Inputs		outputs	
A	*B*	Difference	Borrow
0	0	0	0
0	1	1	1
1	0	1	0
1	1	0	0

Fig. 4.37 Truth table for half subtractor

A is the minuend and *B* is the subtrahand. Boolean expressions for difference and borrow are derived from truth table and by simplifying them using K-map as shown in Fig. 4.38.

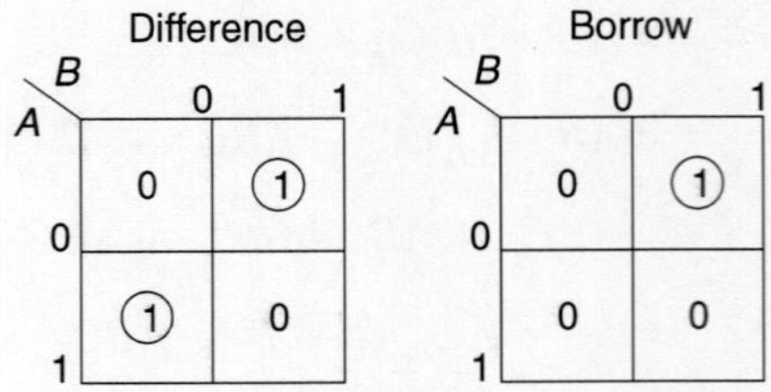

Difference $= A\bar{B} + \bar{A}B$
$= A \oplus B$

Borrow $= \bar{A}B$

Fig. 4.38 K-map simplification for half subtractor

Implementation of logic diagram for half subtractor is shown in Fig. 4.39. The limitation of half subtractor is that it has only two inputs whereas to include borrow-in it needs three inputs.

Full subtractor: A full subtractor is a combinational circuit that performs subtraction between two bits in addition to borrow input from lower significant stage. It has three inputs and two outputs. The truth table for full subtractor is shown in Fig. 4.40.

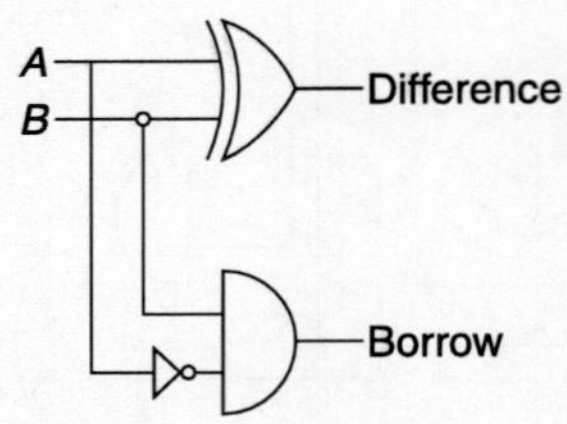

Fig. 4.39 Implementation of logic diagram for half subtractor

Inputs			outputs	
A	B	B_{in}	D	B_{out}
0	0	0	0	0
0	0	1	1	1
0	1	0	1	1
0	1	1	0	1
1	0	0	1	0
1	0	1	0	0
1	1	0	0	0
1	1	1	1	1

Fig. 4.40 Truth table for full subtractor

From truth table, output functions for difference and borrow can be simplified using K-map as shown in Fig. 4.41.

Figure 4.43 shows the implementation of logic diagram of full subtractor

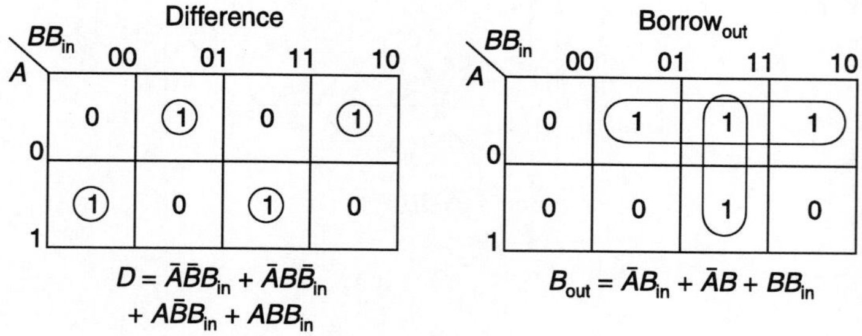

Fig. 4.41 K-map simplification for full subtractor

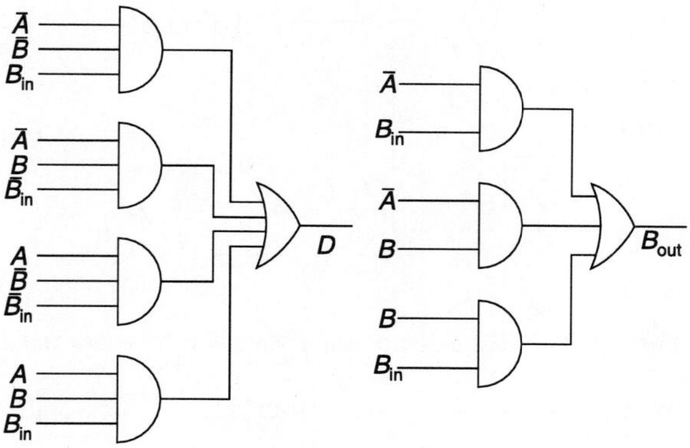

Fig. 4.42 Implementation of logic diagram of full subtractor

The Boolean function for difference (D) can also be written as

$$D = \bar{A}\bar{B}B_{in} + \bar{A}B\bar{B}_{in} + A\bar{B}\bar{B}_{in} + ABB_{in}$$

$$= B_{in}(\bar{A}\bar{B} + AB) + \bar{B}_{in}(\bar{A}B + A\bar{B})$$

$$= B_{in}(A \odot B) + \bar{B}_{in}(A \oplus B)$$

$$= B_{in}(\overline{A \oplus B}) + \bar{B}_{in}(A \oplus B)$$

$$= B_{in} \oplus (A \oplus B)$$

Now, we can implement the full subtractor as shown in Fig. 4.43.

Full subtractor can also be implemented using two half subtractors and one OR gate, which is shown in Fig. 4.45. Here, the difference output is the same as the difference output of full subtractor.

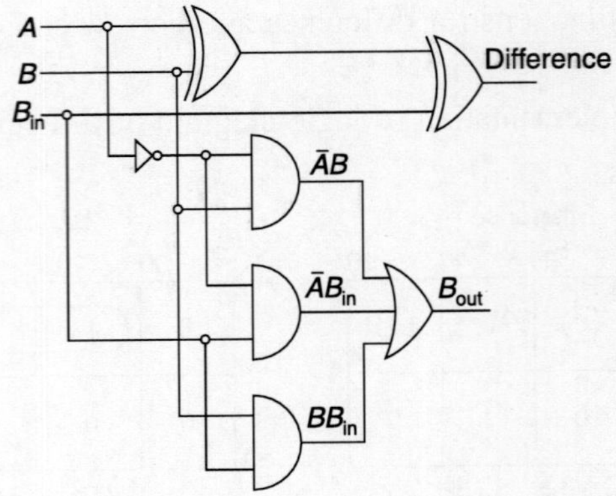

Fig. 4.43 Implementation of full subtractor

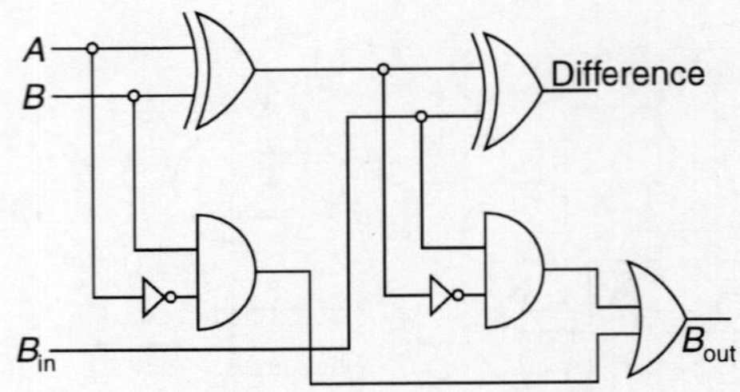

Fig. 4.44 Implementation of full subtractor using two half subtractors and an OR gate

The borrow output shown in Fig. 4.44 can be written as,

$$B_{out} = \bar{A}B + \overline{(A\bar{B} + \bar{A}B)}\, B_{in}$$

$$= \bar{A}B + (AB + \bar{A}\bar{B})\, B_{in}$$

$$= \bar{A}B + ABB_{in} + \bar{A}\bar{B}B_{in}$$

$$= \bar{A}B\,(1 + B_{in}) + ABB_{in} + \bar{A}\bar{B}B_{in} \qquad [\ \ 1 + B_{in} = 1]$$

$$= \bar{A}B + \bar{A}BB_{in} + ABB_{in} + \bar{A}\bar{B}B_{in}$$

$$= \bar{A}B + BB_{in}\,(\bar{A} + A) + \bar{A}\bar{B}B_{in}$$

$$= \bar{A}B + BB_{in} + \bar{A}\bar{B}B_{in} \qquad [\bar{A} + A = 1]$$

$$= \bar{A}B\,(1 + B_{in}) + BB_{in} + \bar{A}\bar{B}B_{in} \qquad [\ \ 1 + B_{in} = 1]$$

$$= \bar{A}B + \bar{A}BB_{in} + BB_{in} + \bar{A}\bar{B}B_{in}$$

$$= \bar{A}B + \bar{A}B_{in}\,(B + \bar{B}) + BB_{in}$$

$$= \bar{A}B + \bar{A}B_{in} + BB_{in} \qquad [\ \ B + \bar{B} = 1)$$

Hence, B_{out} is same as borrow out of full subtractor. Thus, we can implement full subtractor using two half subtractors and OR gate.

Example 4.10 Design a full adder using multiplexer. For a full adder

$$S = \Sigma m\ (1, 2, 4, 7)$$

$$C = \Sigma m\ (3, 5, 6, 7), \qquad \text{(VTU – July 2011)}$$

Solution In order to get a full adder using a single multiplexer, we can use 74153 a dual 4:1 MUX. We have to use implementation tables for *S* and *C* which are shown in Fig. 4.45 and Fig. 4.46. Truth table for full adder is shown in Fig. 4.47 and Fig. 4.48 shows the implementation of the circuit

	D_0	D_1	D_2	D_3
$\bar{C}_{n-1}$	0	(2)	(4)	6
C_{n-1}	(1)	3	5	(7)
	C_{n-1}	$\bar{C}_{n-1}$	$\bar{C}_{n-1}$	C_{n-1}

Fig. 4.45 Implementation table for sum

	D_0	D_1	D_2	D_3
$\bar{C}_{n-1}$	0	2	4	(6)
C_{n-1}	1	(3)	(5)	(7)
	0	C_{n-1}	C_{n-1}	1

Fig. 4.46 Implementation table for carry

A	B	C_{n-1}	S	C
0	0	0	0	0
0	0	1	1	0
0	1	0	1	0
0	1	1	0	1
1	0	0	1	0
1	0	1	0	1
1	1	0	0	1
1	1	1	1	1

Fig. 4.47 Truth table for full adder

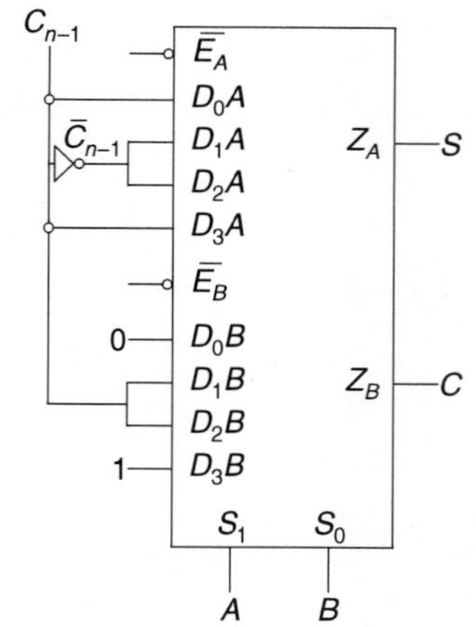

Fig. 4.48 Implementation of full adder using 74153

Example 4.11 Implement full subtractor using gates and write a truth table.

Solution Truth table for full subtractor is given in Fig. 4.49 and implementation of full subtractor using NAND gates is shown in Fig. 4.50.

A	B	B_{in}	D	B_{out}
0	0	0	0	0
0	0	1	1	1
0	1	0	1	1
0	1	1	0	1
1	0	0	1	0
1	0	1	0	0
1	1	0	0	0
1	1	1	1	1

Fig. 4.49 Truth table for full subtractor

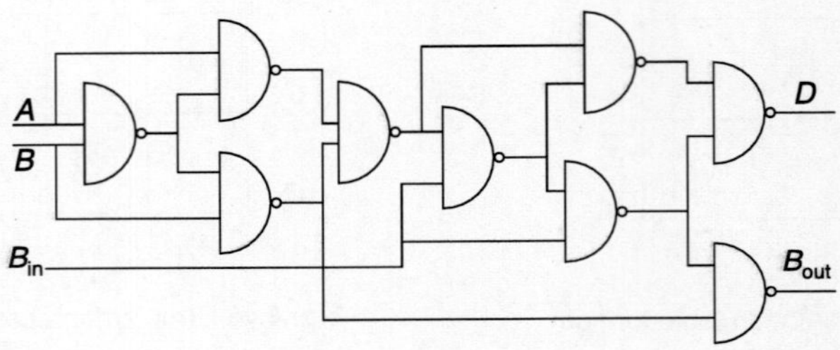

Fig. 4.50 Implementation of full subtractor using NAND gates

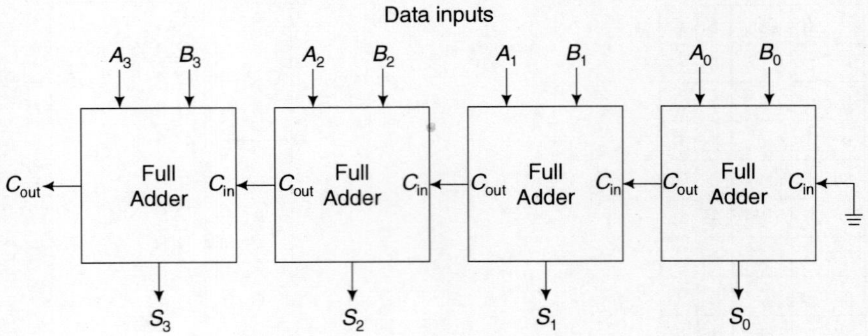

Fig. 4.51 Block diagram of 4 bit (parallel) cascaded adder

4.4 CASCADING FULL ADDERS

A full adder adds two one-bit numbers and a carry input. A full adder can be formed by using two half adders. An n-bit adder can be built by connecting in series n full adders, i.e., cascading n full adders.

Each carry-out from a full adder becomes the carry-in to the next higher order adder. Figure 4.51 illustrates cascading four full adders to form a 4-bit adder. In this adder, the carry-in input of the least significant full adder is grounded or we can use a half adder instead

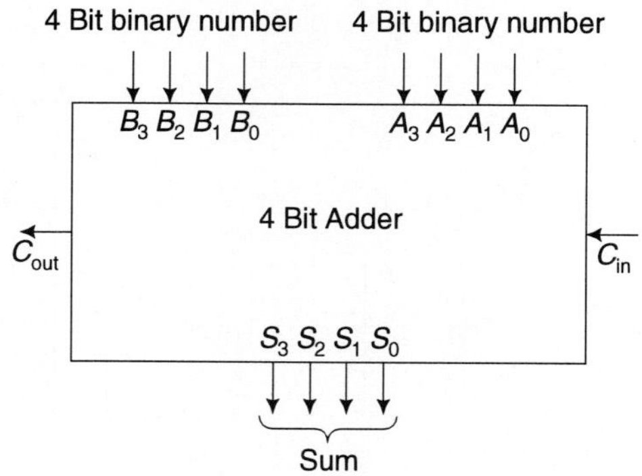

Fig. 4.52 Logic diagram of 4-bit parallel adder

because there is no carry-in for LSB. A_n and B_n are the binary inputs presented to the adders from external source.

Logic diagram of 4-bit parallel adder is shown in Fig. 4.52.

The designer must know how much time the logic requires for the addition of two binary numbers. This will facilitate knowing when to present new data inputs.

The add time required is determined by calculating the propagation delays through the full adders. The carries propagate from one full adder to the next higher order full adder.

The above type of addition is called ripple carry propagation. Total add delay time is the product of the number of stages in the adder multiplied by the carry-out propagation delay time.

High speed adders are available in integrated circuit form. They utilize look ahead carry or fast carry technique for reducing the propagation delay times through the adder.

The most common is a 4-bit parallel adder integrated circuit (7483/74283) that contains four full adders with look ahead carry circuitry.

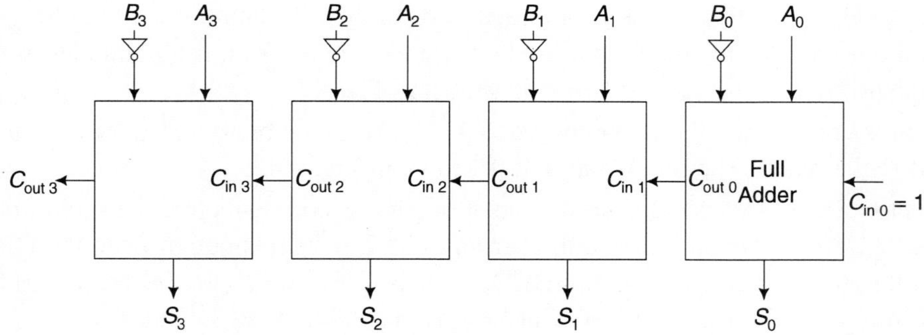

Fig. 4.53 4-bit parallel subtractor

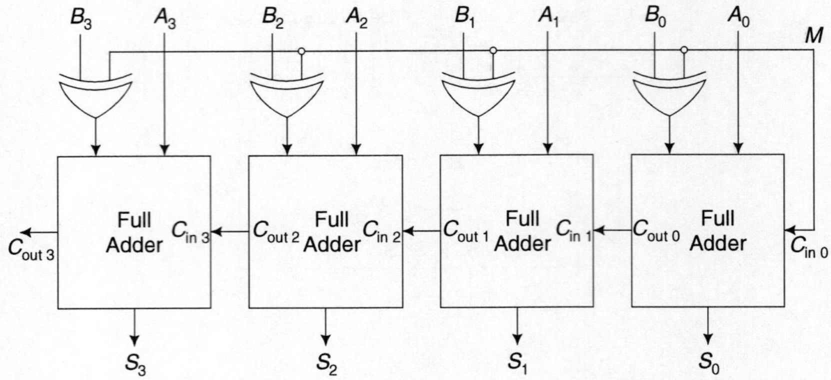

Fig. 4.54 Implementation of 4-bit adder/subtractor

Parallel subtractor: The subtractor $A - B$ can be done by taking 2's complement of B and adding it to A. This is carried out by taking 1's complement and adding one to the least significant pair of bits. The 1's complement can be implemented with inverters and one can be added to the input carry to get the sum as shown in Fig. 4.53.

Parallel adder/subtractor: The addition and subtraction operation can be combined into one circuit having one common binary adder. This is implemented by including an exclusive-OR gate with each full adder. This implementation is shown in Fig. 4.54. M is the mode input that controls the operation of the circuit. When $M = 0$, the circuit acts as an adder. One of the inputs to exclusive OR gate is M and the other input is only one of B_0, B_1, B_2 and B_3. The output of exclusive OR gate is $0 \oplus B_n = B_n$. Hence, the circuit acts a parallel 4-bit adder if the $C_{in0} = 0$.

If $M = 1$, the circuit acts as a subtractor. Here, one of the inputs to the exclusive OR gate is M and the other input is any one of B_0, B_1, B_2 and B_3. The output of exclusive OR gate is $1 \oplus B_n = \overline{B}_n$. Hence, B inputs are complemented and a 1 is added through the input carry. The circuit adds A to the 2's complement of B and hence this circuit acts as a subtractor if $M = 1$.

BCD adder: A BCD adder is a circuit that adds two binary coded decimal (BCD) digits and a sum is produced which is also in BCD. When you add two BCD numbers, if the sum is greater than 9, it is an invalid BCD number. We have to add 6 to the result, so that we get a BCD number.

In order to detect that the sum is greater than 9 or carry is 1, a circuit is to be designed. Let us construct the truth table for the output as shown in Fig. 4.55. From truth table let us simplify the Boolean expression using K-map which is shown in Fig. 4.56.

If the sum is greater than 9, the output y is 1. If C_{out} from the binary adder is 1, then also we add 0110 (6) to the result. The block diagram is shown in Fig. 4.57.

The detector circuit (two AND gates and one OR gate) decodes whether the sum of two BCD numbers is greater than 9 or the carry output from 7483 is 1. If this output from the OR gate is 1, the inputs for B_2 and B_1 for the bottom BCD adder is 1. B_0 and B_3 are 0s. Hence, 0110 (6) is added to the sum of the top BCD adder which is given to bottom BCD adder, as $A_3A_2A_1A_0$, In the bottom BCD adder, $A_3A_2A_1A_0$ is added to 0110 ($B_3B_2B_1B_0$) and the result is sum $S_3S_2S_1S_0$ of bottom 7483 IC. If the sum of top binary adder is less than 9 or the carry-out, C_{out}, is 0, then

Solution

Inputs				Outputs
S_3	S_2	S_1	S_0	Y
0	0	0	0	0
0	0	0	1	0
0	0	1	0	0
0	0	1	1	0
0	1	0	0	0
0	1	0	1	0
0	1	1	0	0
0	1	1	1	0
1	0	0	0	0
1	0	0	1	0
1	0	1	0	1
1	0	1	1	1
1	1	0	0	1
1	1	0	1	1
1	1	1	0	1
1	1	1	1	1

Fig. 4.55 Truth table for output of BCD addition

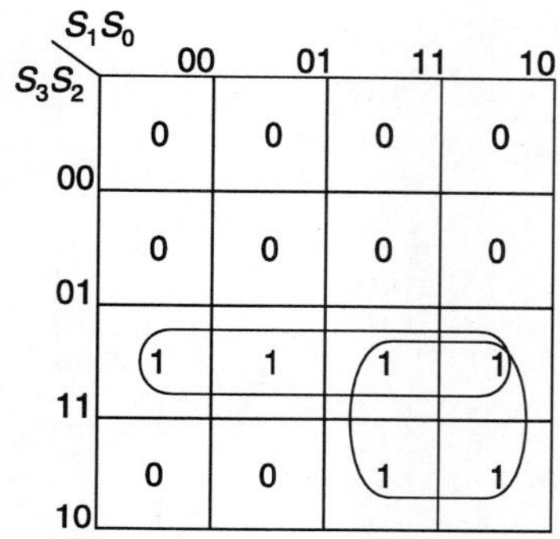

$Y = S_3S_2 + S_3S_1$

Fig. 4.56 K-map simplification

instead of 0110 (6) only 0000 is added to the sum. Hence, the sum of the bottom binary adder is same as top binary adder.

Example 4.12 Design a single decode BCD adder and explain the methodology in detail.

(Refer the explanation under the heading, BCD adder in section 4.4) (VTU – July 2011)

Example 4.13 Design a suitable BCD adder circuit using 7483 and provision has to be made for self-correction in case if the sum is not a valid BCD number. Justify your design with examples. (VTU – June 2012)

Solution (Refer the explanation under the heading BCD adder in section 4.4. Examples are given below.)

Let us consider the addition of two BCD numbers 0011 and 0101.

$$\begin{array}{r} 0011 \\ 0101 \\ \hline 1000 \\ \hline \end{array}$$

The sum is 1000 ($S_3S_2S_1S_0$) of top 7483. This is less than 9 and the carry output is also 0. Hence, the detector circuit carry output is 0. Hence, the sum of bottom 7483 is same as sum of top 7483, (i.e., 1000).

Now, let us consider addition of two BCD numbers 0101 and 0110.

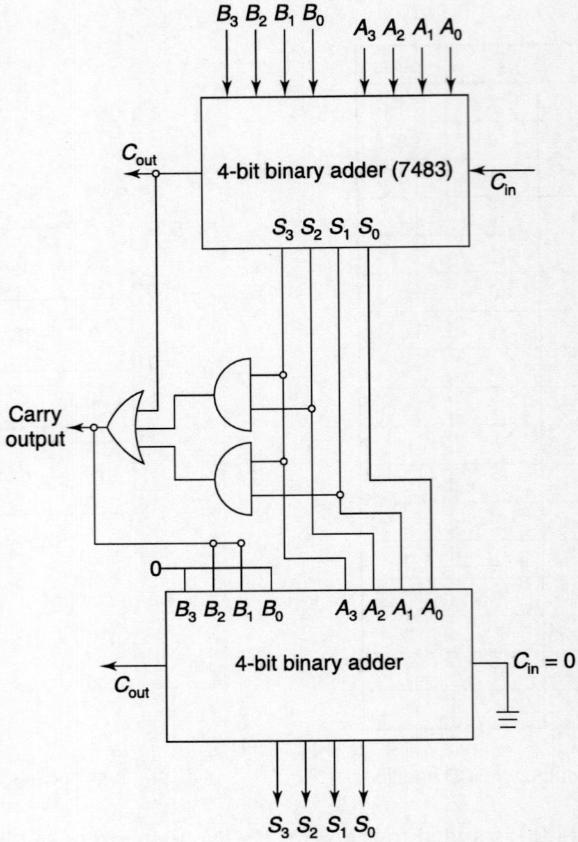

Fig. 4.57 Block diagram of BCD adder using 7483

0101
0110
1011

The sum is 1011 ($S_3S_2S_1S_0$) of top 7483 IC. This sum is (11) which is more than 9. Hence, the detector circuit carry output is 1. Therefore, bottom 7483 ICs inputs are 0110 ($B_3B_2B_1B_0$) and 1011 ($A_3A_2A_1A_0$).

Now 0110
1011
10001

Sum of the bottom IC 7483 is 0001 and the carry out is 1 and hence the output $S_3S_2S_1S_0$ = 0001, C_{out} = 1. Hence, 11 is the output.

Now let us consider another addition of two BCD numbers 1001 and 1000.

1001	(9)
1000	(8)
10001	(17)

The result is an invalid BCD number. Hence, correction is required.

The sum is less than 9, but carry is generated. Hence, we have to add (0110) to the result.

10001	Binary number for 17
0110	value of 6 to be added for corrections
10111	BCD for 17

Referring to Fig. 4.57, in the third case, carry generated by the top 7483 will be given to OR gate as one input and other two inputs of OR gate will be 0 because $S_3S_2 + S_3S_1$ will be 0 as $S_3 = 0$, $S_2 = 0$ and $S_1 = 0$. But the carry output of OR gate will be 1. Hence, (0110) will be added for correction as shown.

4.5 LOOK AHEAD CARRY ADDER

We have already seen that there is carry propagation delay in binary adder stages. If we can ensure that the sum and carry output of any stage is not dependent on the results of any previous stages, then the ripple effect is eliminated and speed of addition increases. This is called look ahead carry addition.

Consider the full adder circuit shown in Fig. 4.58.

$$P_i = A_i \oplus B_i$$

$$G_i = A_iB_i$$

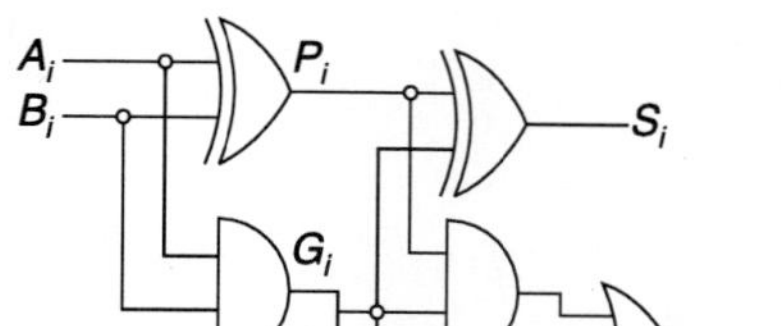

Fig. 4.58 Full adder circuit

The output sum and carry can be expressed as

$$S_i = P_i \oplus C_i \quad (1)$$

$$C_i + 1 = G_i + P_iC_i \quad (2)$$

Here, G_i is called carry generate and it produces a carry when both A_i and B_i are one, irrespective of input carry C_i. P_i is called carry propagate because it is the term associated with the propagation of the carry from C_i to C_{i+1}.

Now, the Boolean function for the carry output of each stage can be written by substituting $i = 1, 2, 3, 4$, etc., in equation (2).

$$C_2 = G_1 + P_1C_1$$

$$C_3 = G_2 + P_2C_2$$

$$= G_2 + P_2 (G_1 + P_1 C_1)$$

$$= G_2 + P_2 G_1 + P_2 P_1 C_1$$

(after substituting for $C_2 = G_1 + P_1 C_1$)

$$C_4 = G_3 + P_3 C_3$$

$$= G_3 + P_3 (G_2 + P_2 G_1 + P_2 P_1 C_1)$$

$$= G_3 + P_3 G_2 + P_3 P_2 G_1 + P_3 P_2 P_1 C_1$$

It is seen from the above expression for C_4, that C_4 does not depend on C_3 and C_2. Hence, it does not have to wait for C_3 and C_2 to propagate. All the carries C_2, C_3 and C_4 are propagated at the same time.

The Boolean functions for each output carry C_2, C_3, C_4, etc., are expressed in SOP form. Hence, they can be implemented using AND-OR logic or NAND-NAND logic.

Figure 4.59 shows the logic diagram of a look ahead carry generator.

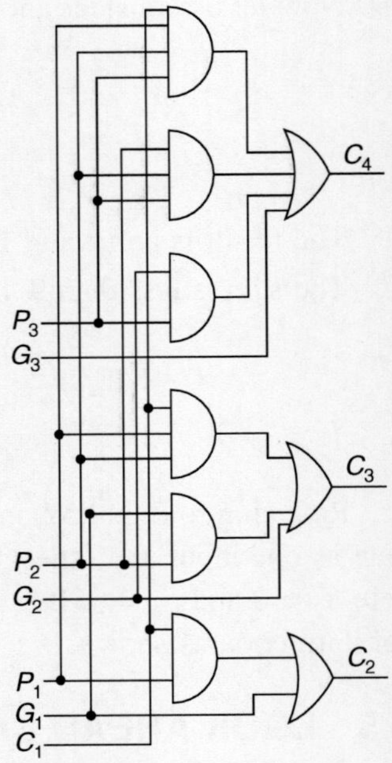

Fig. 4.59 Logic diagram of a look ahead carry generator

A 4-bit parallel adder can be constructed using a look ahead carry generator as shown in Fig. 4.60. Each sum output requires two exclusive-OR gates. The output of first exclusive-OR gate

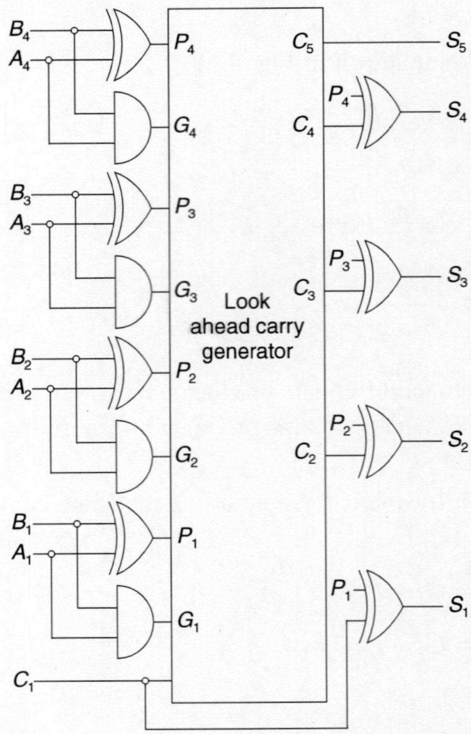

Fig. 4.60 4-bit parallel adder with look ahead carry generator

generates P_i and the AND gate generates G_i. The carries are generated using look ahead carry generator and they form the inputs to the second EX-OR gate. Other input to Ex-OR gate is P_i. The output of second EX-OR gate is the sum. The outputs S_2, S_3 and S_4 have equal propagation delay times.

IC 74182 is a look ahead carry generator.

4.6 BINARY COMPARATORS

Binary comparators are logic circuits that compare the relative magnitude of two binary numbers. If the two binary numbers are A and B, and if they are compared, three output conditions exist: $A = B$, $A > B$ and $A < B$.

Inputs		Outputs		
A	B	$A = B$	$A > B$	$A < B$
0	0	1	0	0
0	1	0	0	1
1	0	0	1	0
1	1	1	0	0

Fig. 4.61 Truth table of 1-bit comparator

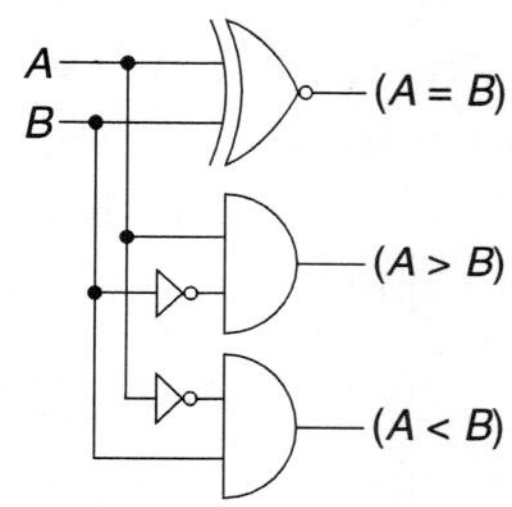

Fig. 4.62 Implementation of 1-bit comparator

Inputs				Outputs		
A		B				
a_1	a_0	b_1	b_0	$A = B$	$A > B$	$A < B$
0	0	0	0	1	0	0
0	0	0	1	0	0	1
0	0	1	0	0	0	1
0	0	1	1	0	0	1
0	1	0	0	0	1	0
0	1	0	1	1	0	0
0	1	1	0	0	0	1
0	1	1	1	0	0	1
1	0	0	0	0	1	0
1	0	0	1	0	1	0
1	0	1	0	1	0	0
1	0	1	1	0	0	1
1	1	0	0	0	1	0
1	1	0	1	0	1	0
1	1	1	0	0	1	0
1	1	1	1	1	0	0

Fig. 4.63 Truth Table for 2-bit comparator

One bit comparators: One bit comparators compare two one-bit numbers A and B and provide three outputs $A = B$, $A > B$ and $A < B$. The truth table is shown in Fig. 4.61.

This can be simplified using K-map or since this truth table is simple one we can straightaway write the output equations.

$$(A = B) = \overline{A}\,\overline{B} + AB \qquad [A = B = 1, \text{ where } A = B = 0 \text{ and } A = B = 1]$$

$$= A \odot B$$

$$A > B = A\overline{B} \qquad [\ A > B = 1, \text{ when } A = 1 \text{ and } B = 0]$$

$$A < B = \overline{A}B \qquad [\ A < B = 1 \text{ when } A = 0 \text{ and } B = 1]$$

Logic diagram is shown in Fig. 4.62.

Two-bit comparators: Two-bit comparators compare two 2-bit binary numbers and provide three outputs. The truth table is shown in Fig. 4.63.

The output functions are written as

$$(A = B) = \Sigma\,(0, 5, 10, 15)$$

$$(A > B) = \Sigma\,(4, 8, 9, 12, 13, 14)$$

$$(A < B) = \Sigma\,(1, 2, 3, 6, 7, 11)$$

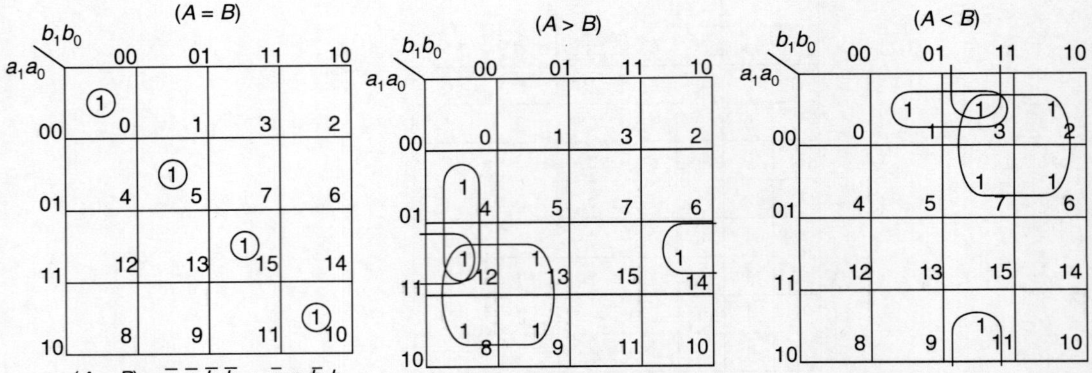

$(A = B) = \bar{a}_1\bar{a}_0\bar{b}_1\bar{b}_0 + \bar{a}_1 a_0 \bar{b}_1 b_0 + a_1\bar{a}_0 b_1\bar{b}_0 + a_1 a_0 b_1 b_0$

$(A > B) = a_1\bar{b}_1 + a_0\bar{b}_1\bar{b}_0 + a_1 a_0\bar{b}_0$

$(A < B) = \bar{a}_1 b_1 + \bar{a}_0 b_1 b_0 + \bar{a}_1\bar{a}_0 b_0$

Fig. 4.64 K-maps for ($A = B$), ($A > B$) and ($A < B$) of 2-bit comparator

We will simplify the above output functions using K-maps as shown in Fig. 4.64 and logic diagram is shown in Fig. 4.65.

$$(A = B) = \bar{a}_1\bar{a}_0\,\bar{b}_1\bar{b}_0 + \bar{a}_1 a_0\,\bar{b}_1 b_0 + a_1\bar{a}_0\,b_1\bar{b}_0 + a_1 a_0\,b_1 b_0$$

$$= \bar{a}_1\,\bar{b}_1\,(\bar{a}_0\bar{b}_0 + a_0 b_0) + a_1 b_1\,(\bar{a}_0\bar{b}_0 + a_0 b_0)$$

Solution

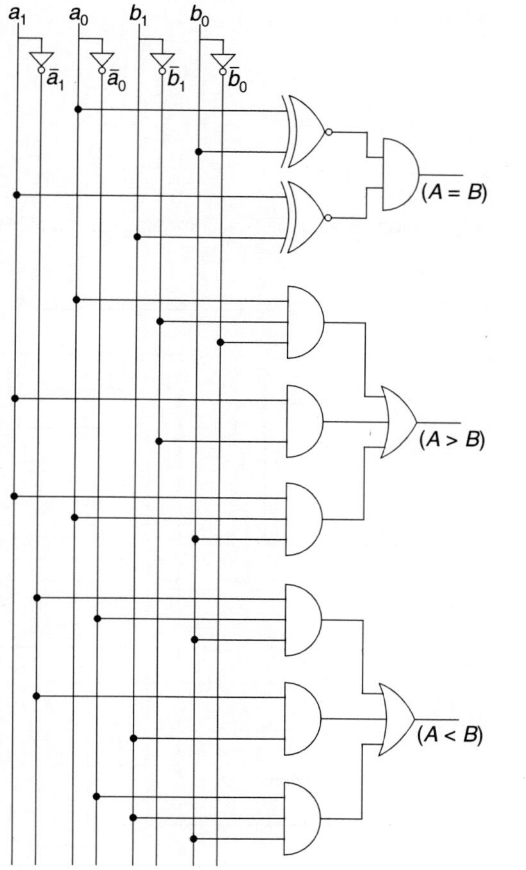

Fig. 4.65 Logic diagram for 2-bit comparator

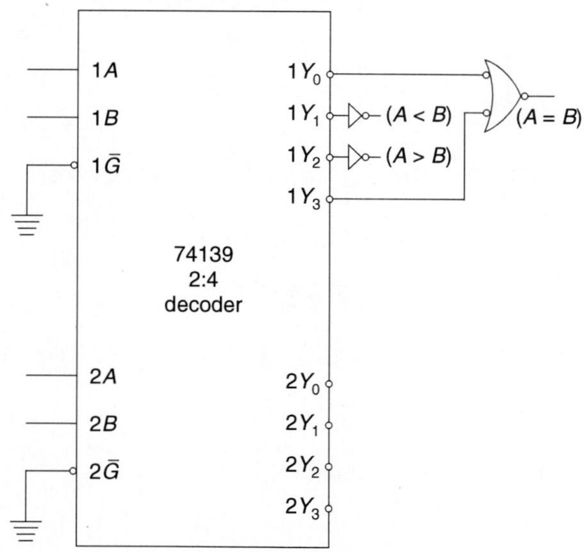

Fig. 4.66 Implementation of 1-bit comparator using 2:4 decoders

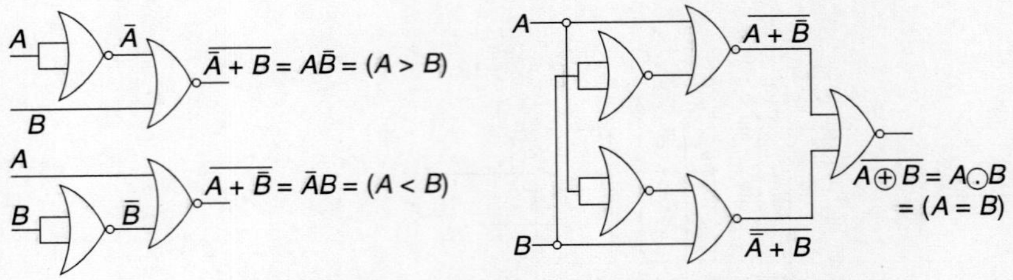

Fig. 4.67 Implementation of 1-bit comparator using NOR gates

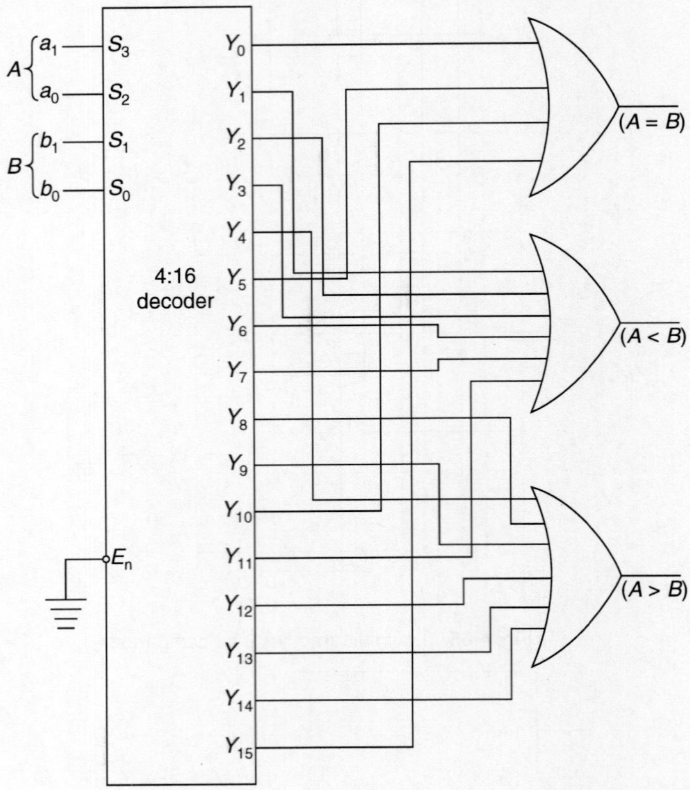

Fig. 4.68 Design of 2-bit comparator using 4:16 decoder

$$= (\bar{a}_0 \bar{b}_0 + a_0 b_0)\ (\bar{a}_1 \bar{b}_1 + a_1 b_1)$$

$$= (a_0 \odot b_0)\ (a_1 \odot b_1)$$

Example 4.14 Design a 1-bit comparator using 2:4 decoders. Also design the circuit using only NOR gates. (VTU – June 2012)

Solution

The three output equations for 1-bit comparator

$$(A = B) = \Sigma\,(0, 3) = \overline{A}\,\overline{B} + AB$$

$$(A > B) = \Sigma\,(2) = A\overline{B}$$

$$(A < B) = \Sigma\,(1) = \overline{A}B$$

Let us take commercially available 2:4 decoder 74139 IC. Fig. 4.66 shows the implementation of 1-bit comparator using 2:4 decoder. Fig. 4.67 shows implementation of 1-bit comparator using NOR gates.

Example 4.15 Design a 2-bit comparator using 4:16 decoder.

Solution From the truth table of 2-bit comparator, we have seen the three output functions as

$$(A = B) = \Sigma\,(0, 5, 10, 15)$$

$$(A > B) = \Sigma\,(4, 8, 9, 12, 13, 14)$$

$$(A < B) = \Sigma\,(1, 2, 3, 6, 7, 11)$$

Figure 4.68 shows the implementation of 2-bit comparator using 4:16 decoder.

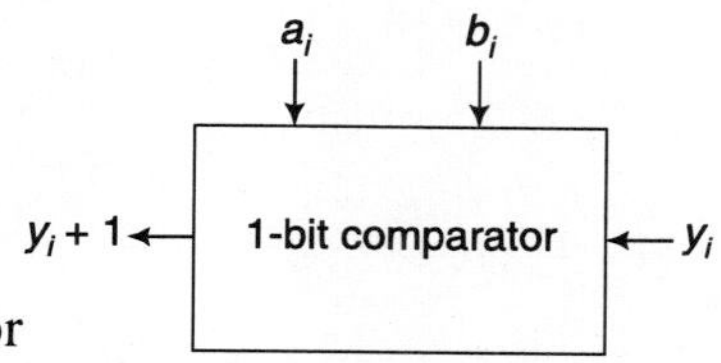

Fig. 4.69 Block diagram of 1-bit equality comparator

Example 4.16 Design a comparator to cheek if two n bit numbers are equal. Configure this cascaded stage of 1-bit equality comparator. (VTU – June 2010), (VTU – Dec 2012).

Solution 1-bit comparator has two inputs and three outputs. In a multistage comparator having 1-bit comparators, the 1-bit comparator of ith stage will have three inputs, i.e., two inputs a_i and b_i (two one-bit number of ith stage) and one input of y_i (equality of the previous stage) and one output y_{i+1}, which represents the equality of ith stage. If $y_i = 0$, the previous stage output is inequal. The block diagram of 1-bit equality comparator is shown in Fig. 4.69.

The truth table for the 1-bit equality comparator is shown in Fig. 4.70.

Inputs			Outputs
a_i	b_i	y_i	y_{i+1}
0	0	0	0
0	0	1	1
0	1	0	0
0	1	1	0
1	0	0	0
1	0	1	0
1	1	0	0
1	1	1	1

Fig. 4.70 Truth table of 1-bit equality comparator

Whenever $y_i = 0$, it clearly indicates that the previous stage is inequal. Hence, wherever, $y_i = 0$, y_{i+1} becomes 0. When $y_i = 1$, it indicates, that comparison of the previous stage is equal. Even if $y_i = 1$, if the two inputs of that stage are unequal, the output y_{i+1} becomes 0. Hence, in the above truth table, only in two cases, i.e., when a_i and b_i are both 0 and 1 and $y_i = 1$ then y_{i+1} becomes 1.

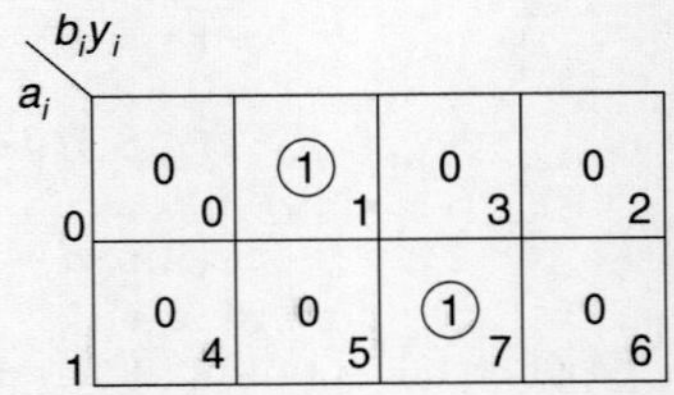

Fig. 4.71 Karnaugh map for 1-bit equality comparator

The output function y_{i+1} can be simplified using K-map as shown in Fig. 4.71.

The simplified output expression is written from K-map.

$$y_{i+1} = \bar{a}_i\bar{b}_i\, y_i + a_ib_iy_i$$

$$= y_i\, (\bar{a}_i\bar{b}_i + a_ib_i)$$

$$= y_i\, (a_i \odot b_i)$$

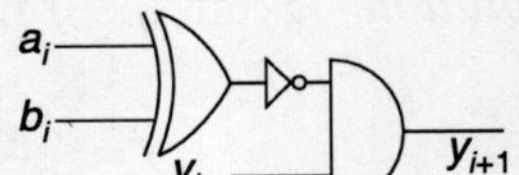

Fig. 4.72 Implementation of 1-bit equality comparator

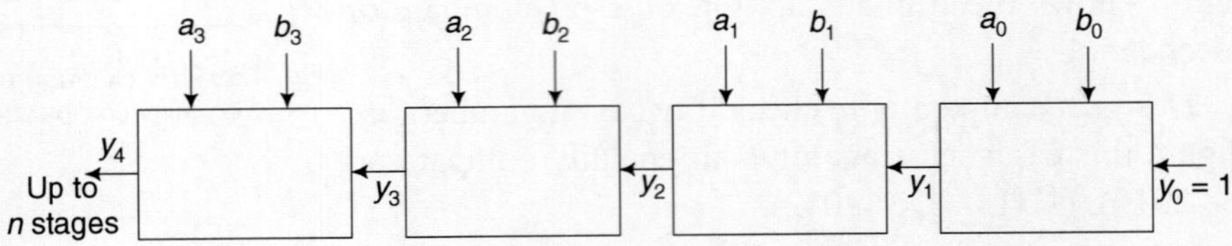

Fig. 4.73 *n*-stage equality comparator

$$= y_i\, \overline{(a_i \oplus b_i)}$$

The implementation of 1-bit equality comparator is shown in Fig. 4.72. *n* such stages been have cascaded to obtain *n*-bit equality comparator as shown in Fig. 4.73.

Example 4.17 Configure a 32 to 1 MUX using four 8 to 1 MUX.

Solution Figure 4.74 shows the configuration of 32 to 1 MUX using four 8 to 1 MUX. The 8 to 1 MUX are chosen using 2 to 4 decoder. For 32 to 1, MUX address selection bits are S_0, S_1, S_2, S_3 and S_4.

Example 4.18 Implement the following using multiplexers, whose data inputs could accept only either *a*, 0 or *a*, 1. A 16 to 1 MUX and 8 to 1 MUX with active low enable and with active high outputs are available:

(i) $f(a, b, c) = \Sigma\,(0, 2, 3, 6, 7)$

(ii) $f(a, b, c, d) = \Sigma\,(2, 5, 6, 9, 11, 14)$

(iii) $f(a, b, c, d, e) = \Sigma\,(1, 5, 8, 12, 19, 21, 27)$

Solution (i) $f(a, b, c) = \Sigma\,(0, 2, 3, 6, 7)$

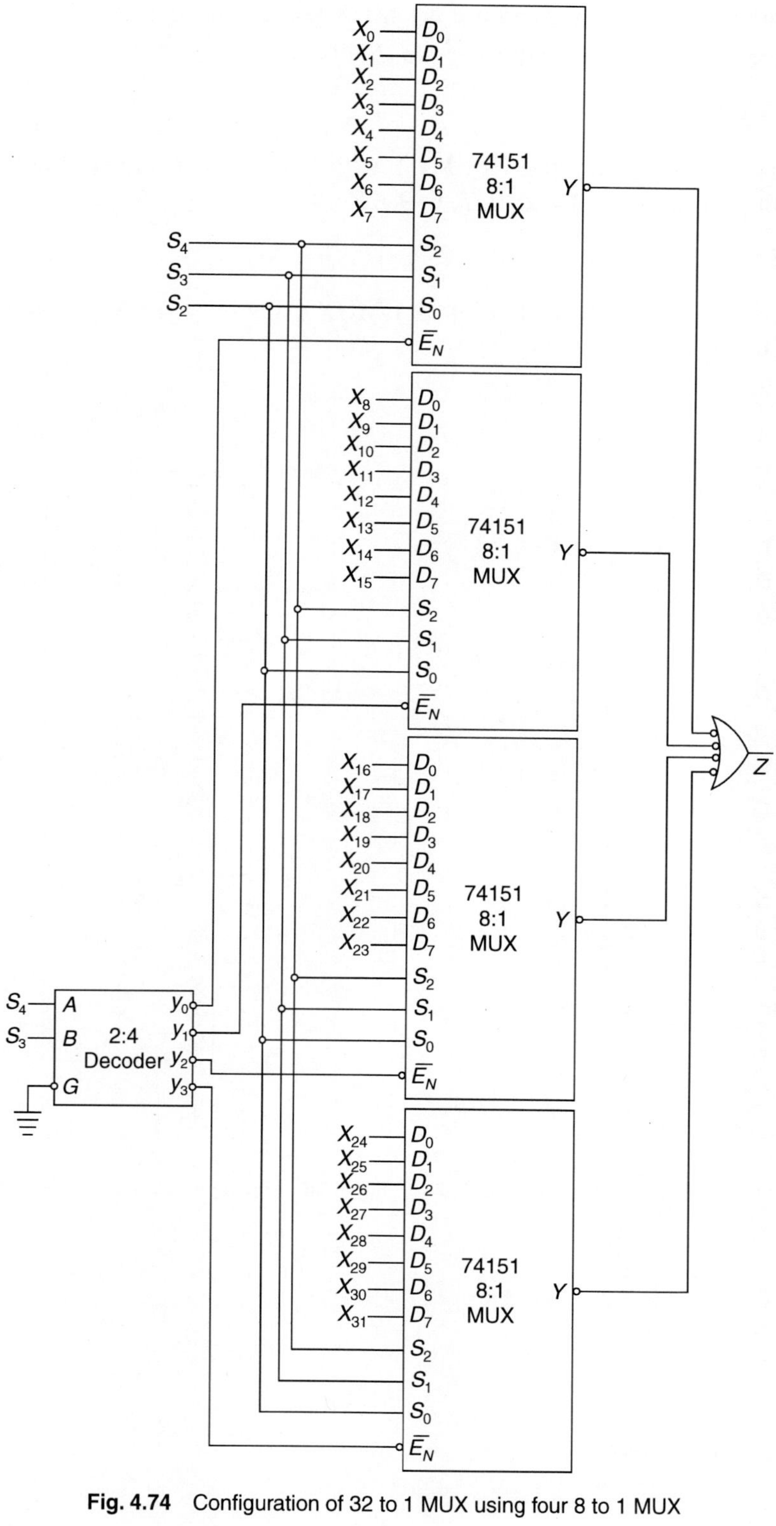

Fig. 4.74 Configuration of 32 to 1 MUX using four 8 to 1 MUX

This is a 3-variable function. We can use 8:1 MUX using 0 and 1 as data.

Figure 4.75 shows the implementation of $f(a, b, c) = \Sigma(0, 2, 3, 6, 7)$.

(ii) $f(a, b, c, d) = \Sigma(2, 5, 6, 9, 11, 14)$

This function can be realized using 16:1 MUX with 1 and 0 as data input. Figure 4.76 shows the implementation of $f(a, b, c, d) = \Sigma(2, 5, 6, 9, 11, 14)$.

(iii) $f(a, b, c, d, e) = \Sigma(1, 5, 8, 12, 19, 21, 27)$.

Figure 4.77 shows the implementation of 32:1 MUX using two 16:1 MUX. Here, data 0 and 1 are used for X_0 to X_{31} inputs.

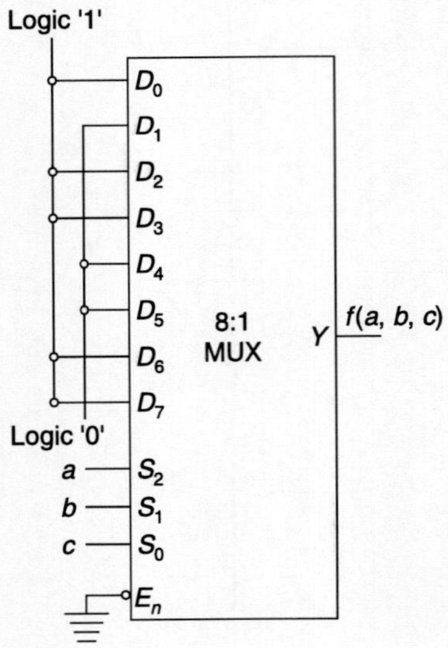

Fig. 4.75 Implementation of $f(a, b, c) = \Sigma(0, 2, 3, 6, 7)$

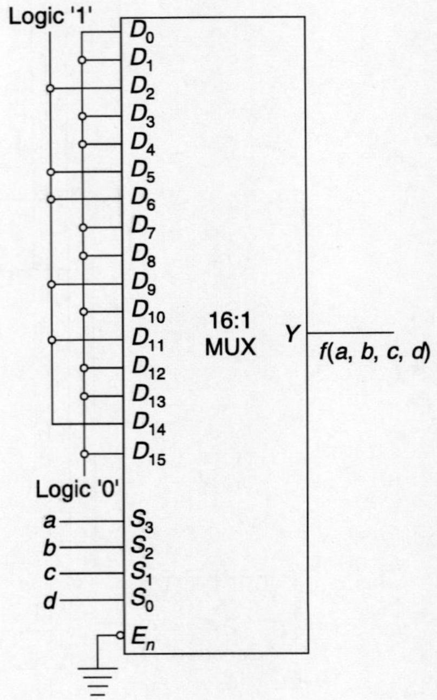

Fig. 4.76 Implementation of $f(a, b, c, d) = \Sigma(2, 5, 6, 9, 11, 14)$

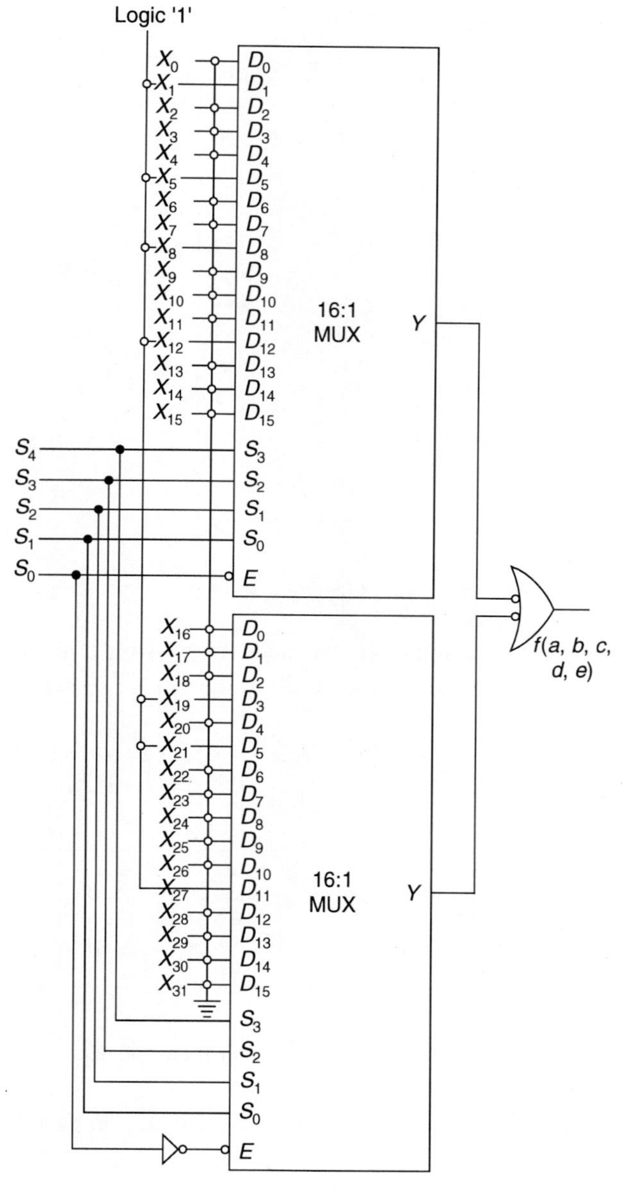

Fig. 4.77 Implementation of $f(a, b, c, d, e) = \Sigma(1, 5, 8, 12, 19, 21, 27)$

Example 4.19 Implement a 12-bit comparator using IC 7485. (VTU – June 2014)

Four-bit comparators are commercially available in IC form as 7485. It has two sets of inputs to be compared. Let us consider one set of four inputs as a_0, a_1, a_2, a_3 and the other set of four inputs as b_0, b_1, b_2, b_3. In addition, it has boundary inputs $a < b$, $a = b$ and $a > b$ to allow cascading of 4-bit comparators to configure $4n$-bit comparators.

The logic symbol of IC 7485 is shown in Fig. 4.78.

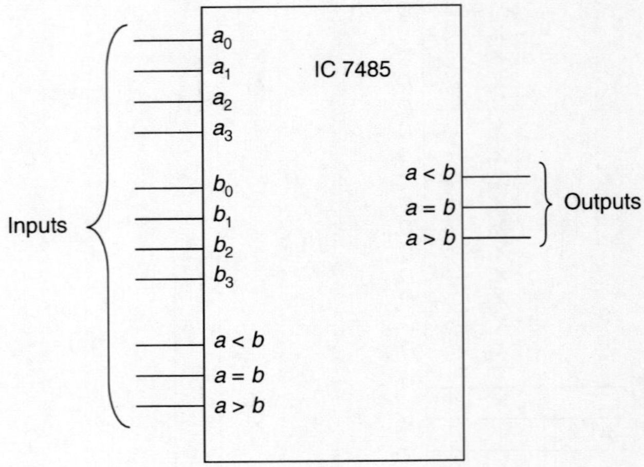

Fig. 4.78 4-bit IC comparator.

In order to implement 12 bit comparator, we need three 4-bit comparators. The boundary inputs and outputs of IC 7485 are used to cascade the three ICs as shown in Fig. 4.79.

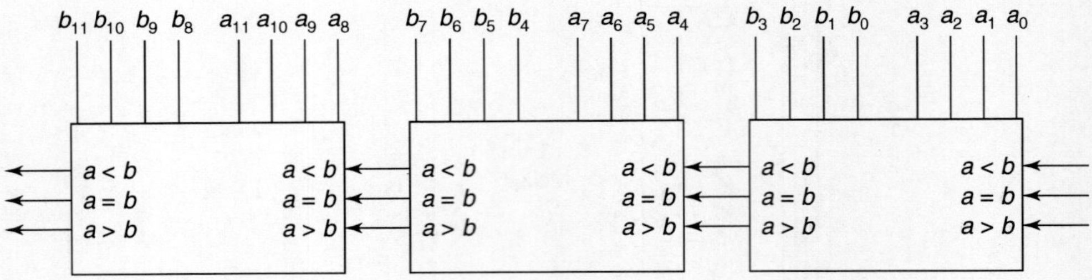

Fig. 4.79 A 12-bit comparators using three 7485 IC_s.

Example 4.20 Implement $u = ad + b\overline{c} + bd$, using 4-1 MUX using ab as select lines.

(VTU – June 2014)

Solution $u = ad + b\overline{c} + bd$. Let us draw the K-map for the above function. Normally, we derive simplified function from K-map. Here we draw K-map from the simplified function as shown in Fig. 4.80.

From the K-map, we can write the function

$$u = \Sigma(4, 5, 7, 9, 11, 12, 13, 15) \text{ as}$$

$$u = \overline{a}b\overline{c}\overline{d} + \overline{a}b\overline{c}d + \overline{a}bcd + a\overline{b}\overline{c}d + a\overline{b}cd + ab\overline{c}\overline{d} + ab\overline{c}d + abcd.$$

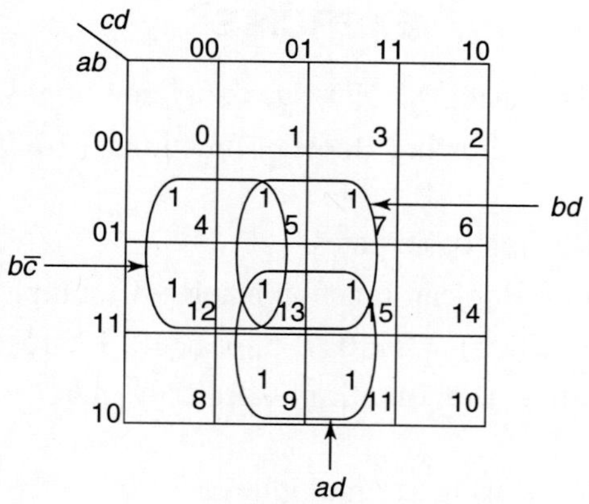

Fig. 4.80 K-map for $u = ad + b\bar{c} + bd = \Sigma\,(4, 5, 7, 9, 11, 12, 13, 15)$

$$= \bar{a}b\,(\bar{c}\bar{d} + \bar{c}d + cd) + ab\,(\bar{c}\bar{d} + \bar{c}d + cd) + a\bar{b}(\bar{c}d + cd)$$

$$= \bar{a}b\,(\bar{c}(\bar{d} + d) + cd) + ab\,(\bar{c}\,(\bar{d} + d) + cd) + a\bar{b}\,(d\,(\bar{c} + c))$$

$$= \bar{a}b\,(\bar{c} + cd) + ab(\bar{c} + cd) + a\bar{b}d$$

$$= \bar{a}b\,(\bar{c} + d) + ab(\bar{c} + d) + a\bar{b}d.$$

This can be written as

$$u = \bar{a}\bar{b}\,(0) + \bar{a}b\,(\bar{c} + d) + a\bar{b}\,(d) + ab\,(\bar{c} + d)$$

The above function can be implemented using 4-1 MUX as shown in Fig. 4.81.

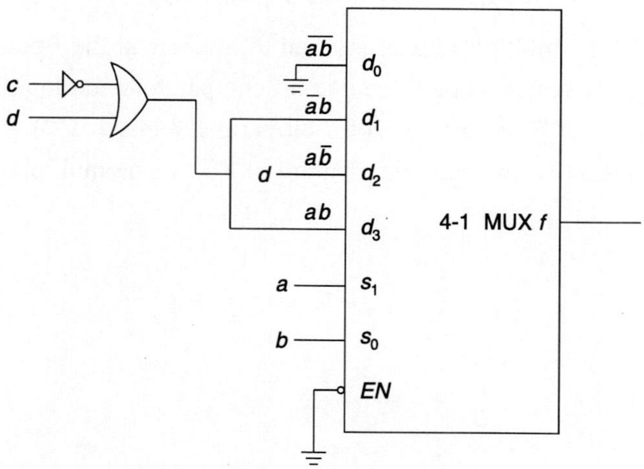

Fig. 4.81 Implementation of $u = ad + b\bar{c} + bd$ using 4-1 MUX

EXERCISE

1. Realize a 4:1 multiplexer using NAND gates only and briefly explain its working.
2. Realize using 74151 the following Boolean function, $f(ABCD) = \Sigma(0, 2, 4, 5, 7, 8, 10, 12, 13)$.
3. Realize a 4 to 1 MUX using basic gates.
4. Implement the following Boolean function using 8:1 multiplexer:
$$f(w, x, y, z) = \Sigma m(0, 1, 5, 6, 8, 10, 12, 15)$$
5. How would you realize the function. $ABCD + \overline{A}BC + B\overline{C}\,\overline{D}$ using an 8 to 1 multiplexer?
6. Construct 8:1 multiplexer using 2:1 multiplexer.
7. Realize an 8 to 1 line MUX using two 4 to 1 line MUX 74151.
8. Implement an 8 to 1 MUX using 4 to 1 MUX.
9. Give a 4 to 1 MUX implementation of the three variable function $f = \Sigma m(1, 4, 5, 7)$.
10. What is carry book ahead adder? Explain in detail.
11. Explain the concept of carry look ahead adder.
12. Realize a full subtractor using basic logic gates.
13. What is a high speed adder? Design a 4 bit carry look ahead adder circuit.
14. Show the construction of 4-bit parallel adder using IC 7483.
15. Implement the 4-bit parallel adder 74LS83 to perform both addition and subtraction. Give out the logic behind the implementation with example.
16. Realize using a 16:1 multiplexer, the function
$$f(D, C, B, A) = \Sigma(m_0, m_3, m_6, m_4, m_{12}, m_{15})$$
17. Show how IC 74151 multiplexer can be used to implement the Boolean function.
18. Design a 3-bit comparator using three one-bit comparators and logic gates.
19. Draw and explain the block diagram of n-bit parallel adder.
20. What is multiplexer? Draw the logic diagram of 8 to 1 line multiplexer.

CHAPTER 5

Sequential Circuits – 1

In sequential circuits, the output at a given time is dependent on the input at that time as well as on the earlier inputs. The sequential circuits are always associated with memory. Combinational circuit's operation is represented by truth table whereas the operation of sequential circuit is represented by its states. Sequential circuits are classified into synchronous sequential circuits and asynchronous sequential circuits. Synchronous circuits are controlled by a master clock and they change state as well as their outputs at specific clock instances. The operations of asynchronous circuits are not controlled by any clock pulses.

5.1 BASIC BISTABLE ELEMENT

Basic bistable element has two outputs Q and $\overline{Q}$ as shown in Fig. 5.1. It can store either 1 or 0. It consists of two cross coupled *not* gates, the output of one connected to the other involving feedback.

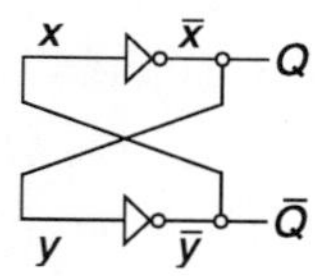

Fig. 5.1 Basic bistable element

It has two stable states. If it is assumed that $x = 0, \bar{x} = Q = y = 1$ and $\bar{y} = \overline{Q} = x = 0$. If it is assumed that $x = 1$, then $\bar{x} = Q = y = 0$ and $\bar{y} = \overline{Q} = x = 1$.

Thus, we observe that there are two stable states and the basic bistable element can store two binary numbers 0 or 1.

The binary number stored is called state of the element. Q output is called the state of the bistable element and is also called normal output and $\overline{Q}$ output is called complementary output. If it stores 1, it is said to be in '1' state or set. If it stores 0, it is said to be in '0' state or reset.

Basic bistable element has no inputs. When power is applied it becomes stable in one of the two states. It remains in that state until power is removed.

A flip-flop is a bistable device, with inputs that remain in a given state as long as the power is applied and until input signals are applied to cause its output to change. The process of storing 1 into a flip-flop is called setting the flip-flop and storing 0 is called resetting or clearing the flip-flop. The inputs to a flip-flop can be synchronous or asynchronous. Due to asynchronous or direct input, the flip-flop changes state immediately. A synchronous input does not immediately change the state of flip-flop but changes only when some control, usually called an enable or clock input also occurs.

5.2 LATCHES

Latches are storage devices that form one class of flip-flops. The timing of the outputs is not controlled. The output responds immediately to changes on the input lines. A special control signal called enable or clock is also provided with the latch. When enable signal is active, output responds to input changes.

***SR* Latch:** *SR* latch consists of two cross coupled NOR gates. It has two inputs *S*(set) and *R*(reset) and two outputs Q and $\overline{Q}$. It is shown in Fig. 5.2 and logic symbol for *SR* latch is shown in Fig. 5.3. Function table is shown in Fig. 5.4.

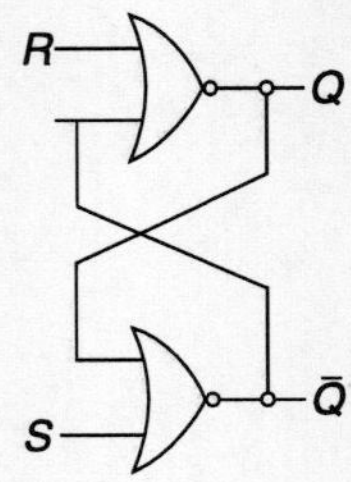

Fig. 5.2 SR latch using NOR gates

Inputs		Outputs	
S	R	Q^+	$\overline{Q^+}$
0	0	Q	$\overline{Q}$
0	1	0	1
1	0	1	0
1	1	unpredictable	

Fig. 5.4 Function table for SR latch

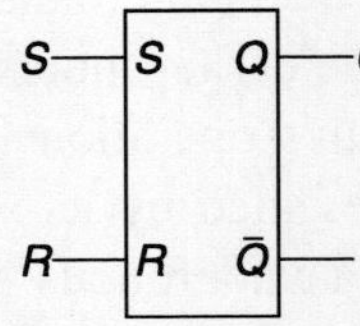

Fig. 5.3 Logic symbol for SR latch

In the function table Q denotes present state of the latch, i.e., Q is state at the time the input signals are applied. The response of the latch at Q and $\overline{Q}$ output terminals after applying the inputs is denoted by Q^+ and $\overline{Q}^+$. Q^+ is the next state of the latch.

Now, let us give inputs to the latch, i.e., $S = 0, R = 0$. Let us assume that initially $Q = 1$ and $\overline{Q} = 0$. When $Q = 1$ and $S = 0$, the inputs of the bottom NOR gate, the output is 0, i.e., $\overline{Q} = 0$.

Hence, the two inputs of the top NOR gate, are $\overline{Q} = 0$ and $R = 0$. The output of the top NOR gate is 1. Hence, we observe that the next state values of Q and $\overline{Q}$ remain same as their present states,

i.e., when $S = 0$ and $R = 0$ $\quad Q^+ = Q = 1, \overline{Q}^+ = \overline{Q} = 0$

For the same inputs $S = 0$ and $R = 0$, let us assume that initially $Q = 0$ and $\overline{Q} = 1$. Now the inputs of bottom NOR gate are $Q = 0$ and $S = 0$, and the output of the bottom NOR gate is 1, i.e., $\overline{Q}^+ = 1$. Inputs of the top NOR gate are $\overline{Q} = 1$ and $R = 0$ and the output of top NOR gate is 0, i.e., $Q^+ = 0$.

Hence, when $S = 0$ and $R = 0$, $Q^+ = Q = 0$ and $\overline{Q}^+ = \overline{Q} = 1$. Hence, we observe that the next state values of Q and $\overline{Q}$ remain the same as their present states.

Hence, we observe that first row of the function table, i.e., when $S = 0$ and $R = 0$, the output is $Q^+ = Q$ and $\overline{Q}^+ = \overline{Q}$.

As in the second row of the function table i.e. when $S = 0$ and $R = 1$, the output of top NOR gate is 0. Hence, the output is $Q^+ = 0$ and the output of bottom NOR gate is 1.

Hence, the above corresponds to second row of function table, i.e., when $S = 0$ and $R = 1$, $Q^+ = 0$ and $\overline{Q}^+ = 1$.

When $S = 1$ and $R = 0$, the output of bottom NOR gate is 0 and the output of top NOR gate is 1 as both the inputs are 0. Hence, the output $Q^+ = 1$ and $\overline{Q}^+ = 0$. This corresponds to the third row of the function table.

For the above three situations, the outputs Q^+ and $\overline{Q}^+$ are complementary. Consider the case when $S = 1$ and $R = 1$. This causes the outputs of both NOR gates to become 0. Hence, they are not complementary.

In this case, difficulty is encountered when the inputs return to 0. If one input returns to 0 before the other, the final state of the latch is determined by the order in which the inputs are changed. Hence, the output becomes unpredictable.

5.3 APPLICATION OF *SR* LATCH

A common problem involving switch is the occurrence of contact bounce. Figure 5.5 shows a switch contacts and the waveforms at the contact terminals.

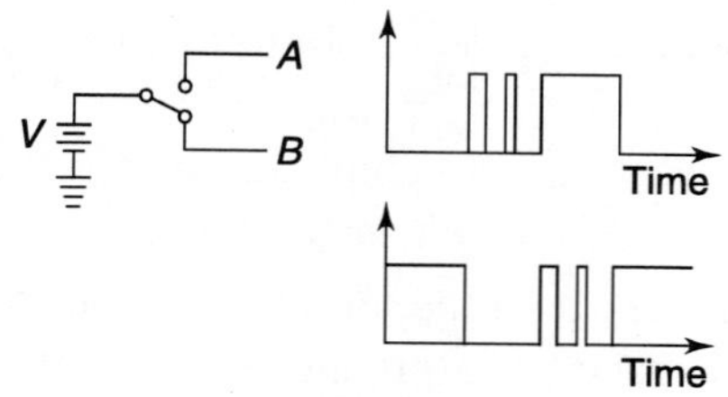

Fig. 5.5 Switch contact bounce effect and the waveforms

The centre contact of the switch in the lower position, the voltage at terminal *B* is +V volts. At the same time, the voltage at terminal *A* is 0 volts. Now, if we move the contact from lower position to upper position, the voltage at terminal *B* first becomes zero, followed by the voltage at terminal *A* becoming +V volts when the centre contact is in upper position.

Now, due to contact bounce, the centre contact of the switch leaves the upper terminal and after some time, it reaches back the upper terminal due to springiness of the contact. This happens quite a few times before the centre contact remains in the upper position.

In the present situation, because of contact bounce, the centre contact of switch leaves terminal *A* which causes the output at terminal to return to zero and then returns to terminal A so that the voltage at terminal *A* becomes +V volts. As already discussed this happens quite a few times making the voltage at terminal *A* to become +V volts and 0 volts alternately.

During the contact bounce, the centre contact does not return to terminal *B*. The output waveform is shown in Fig. 5.5 indicating the above action.

Similarly contact bounce again occurs, when the switch is moved from upper position to lower position. This kind of contact bounce is undesirable.

In case of push button keys on a keyboard, contact bounce may cause a system to respond in such a way as if a key has been pressed multiple times.

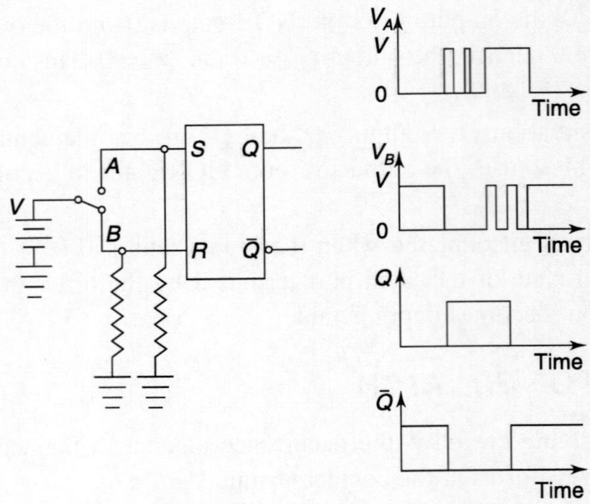

Fig. 5.6 Application of *SR* latch to eliminate contact bounce effect

An important application of *SR* latch is to eliminate the effect of contact bounce. Figure 5.6 shows the application of *SR* latch to eliminate contact bounce in switches.

Whenever the switch is open, i.e., both the terminals *A* and *B* are not connected to V volts, *S* and *R* inputs of *SR* latch are connected to ground, i.e., 0 volt, by the use of two pull down resistors.

Assume that the centre contact of the switch is connected to terminal *B*, *R* input is at V volts and *S* input is at 0 volts. Hence, the *SR* latch output is reset, i.e., $Q = 0$.

When the centre contact is moving towards terminal *A* both terminals *B* and *A* are not connected to V volts. Both inputs *S* and *R* are grounded and at 0 volt. Hence, *SR* latch output remains as earlier i.e., it is reset.

But when the centre contact reaches terminal *A*, it is at V_{volts} which becomes the input *S* and $R = 0$. Hence, *SR* latch output becomes set, i.e., $Q = 1$.

If the switch now opens due to contact bounce the input terminals *S* and *R* make the output remain unchanged. i.e., $Q = 1$ and $\overline{Q} = 0$.

Hence, we observe that the contact bounces has no effect and thus the effect of contact bounce is eliminated.

$\overline{S}\,\overline{R}$ latch: $\overline{S}\,\overline{R}$ latch consists of two cross coupled NAND gates as shown in Fig. 5.7. Logic symbol is shown in Fig. 5.8.

If $\overline{S} = 1$ and $\overline{R} = 0$, the output of top NAND gate is 0, i.e., $Q = 0$, and the output of bottom NAND gate is 1, i.e., $\overline{Q} = 1$. Hence, if $\overline{S} = 1$ and $\overline{R} = 0$, the latch is reset.

If $\overline{S} = 0$ and $\overline{R} = 1$, then the output of the latch is set, i.e., $Q = 1$.

If $\overline{S} = 1$ and $\overline{R} = 1$, then Q and $\overline{Q}$ remain same as before applying the inputs.

The above conditions are shown in the last three rows of function table (Fig. 5.9).

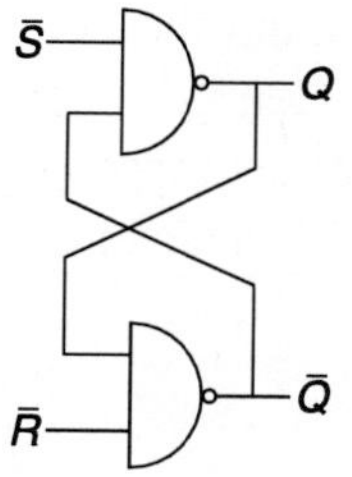

Fig. 5.7 $\overline{S}\overline{R}$ latch using Nand gates

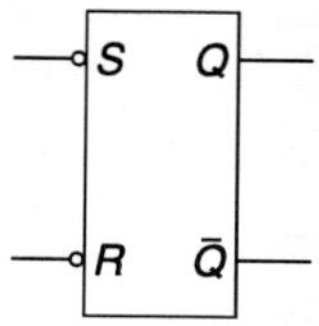

Fig. 5.8 Logic symbol for $\overline{S}\overline{R}$ latch

If both $\overline{S} = 0$ and $\overline{R} = 0$, then both outputs become 1. If the inputs subsequently return to 1 simultaneously, then unpredictable behaviour results.

Inputs		Outputs	
$\overline{S}$	$\overline{R}$	Q^+	$\overline{Q^+}$
0	0	unpredictable	
0	1	1	0
1	0	0	1
1	1	Q	$\overline{Q}$

Fig. 5.9 Function table

The Gated SR Latch: The inputs for both *SR* latch and $\overline{S}\overline{R}$ latch are asynchronous or direct. A change in inputs causes a change in output immediately. It is desirable to have the effect to occur at some predetermined time. For this, a gated *SR* latch or *SR* latch with enable is used. It consists of $\overline{S}\overline{R}$ latch with two additional Nand gates and a control input, *C* which is enable or clock input. The gated *SR* latch is shown in Fig. 5.10 and the logic symbol is shown in Fig. 5.11.

Fig. 5.10 The gated SR latch

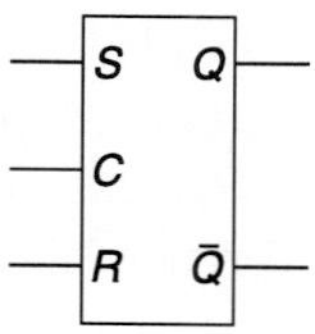

Fig. 5.11 Logic symbol for gated SR latch

If enable input, $C = 0$, the changes in *S* and *R* inputs don't have any effect in the output, i.e., output remains as the present state. If $C = 1$, the gated latch is enabled and behaves as a normal *SR* latch. The above conditions are shown in the function table as given in Fig. 5.12.

If $S = 1$ and $R = 0$, the top first NAND gate output becomes 0 and the bottom NAND gate output becomes 1. The inputs to $\overline{S}\overline{R}$ latch become $\overline{S} = 0$ and $\overline{R} = 1$. Hence, the output is set. This corresponds to the third row in the function table. Similarly, all other input combinations and their outputs are shown in the function table. Since the effects of S and R inputs are dependent on the enable signal, these inputs are called synchronous inputs.

Inputs			Outputs	
S	R	C	Q^+	$\overline{Q^+}$
0	0	1	Q	$\overline{Q}$
0	1	1	0	1
1	0	1	1	0
1	1	1		unpredictable
x	x	0	Q	$\overline{Q}$

Fig. 5.12 Function table for gated SR latch

The Gated *D* Latch: The gated D latch is similar to gated SR latch except that there is only one input D and is given as one input and other input is inverted D. The gated D latch is shown in Fig. 5.13 and logic symbol is shown in Fig. 5.14.

When the latch is disabled, i.e., $C = 0$, the latch remains in the earlier state.

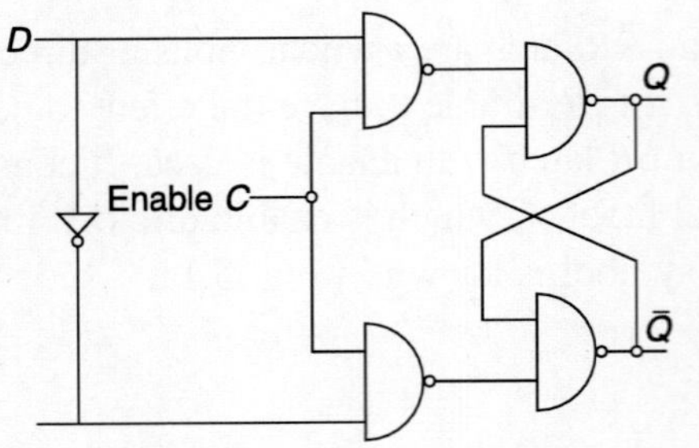

Fig. 5.13 The gated *D* latch

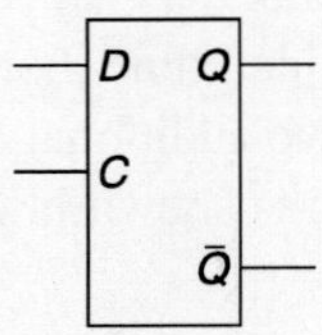

Fig. 5.14 Logic symbol for gated *D* latch

When the latch is enabled, i.e., $C = 1$, the output of the latch follows the D input. If $D = 0$, then the latch switches to or remains in 0 state. If $D = 1$, then the latch switches to or remains in 1 state. The function table for gated D latch is shown in Fig. 5.15.

Inputs		Outputs	
D	C	Q^+	$\overline{Q^+}$
0	1	0	1
1	1	1	0
x	0	Q	$\overline{Q}$

Fig. 5.15 Function table for gated *D* latch

Clocked *JK* Flip-flop: The uncertainty in the state of an *SR* flip-flop when $S = 1$ and $R = 1$ can be eliminated by converting it into a *JK* flip-flop. The data inputs are *J* and *K* which are ANDed with $\overline{Q}$ and Q respectively in order to obtain *S* and *R* inputs as shown in Fig. 5.16.

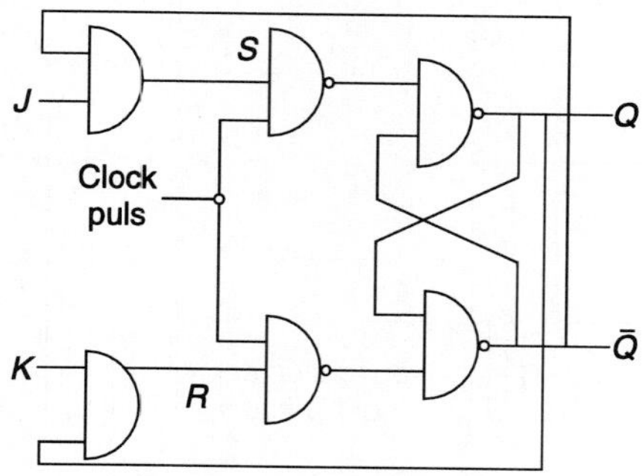

Fig. 5.16 (a) Clocked JK flip-flop

$J = K = 0$: When $J = K = 0$, $S = R = 0$, then no change in the output as per function table for SR flip-flop.

$J = 1$ and $K = 0$: Assume initially $Q = 1$ and $\overline{Q} = 0$, when $J = 1$ and $K = 0$, we observe that $S = 1$ and $R = 0$ and the *SR* flip-flop is in set state as per function table.

Assume initially $Q = 0$ and $\overline{Q} = 1$, when $J = 1$ and $K = 0$ then $S = 0$ and $R = 0$. As per function table for *SR* flip-flop, $Q = 1$ and $\overline{Q} = 0$, i.e., it is in set state.

$J = 0$ and $K = 1$: Assume initially $Q = 1$, $\overline{Q} = 0$, when $J = 0$ and $K = 1$, then we observe that $S = 0$ and $R = 1$, i.e., $Q = 0$ and $\overline{Q} = 1$, i.e., the flip-flop is in reset state.

Assume initially $Q = 0$ and $\overline{Q} = 1$. When $J = 0$ and $K = 1$, then we observe that $S = 0$ and $R = 0$ and hence $Q = 0$ and $\overline{Q} = 1$ and there is no change in the output.

$J = K = 1$: Assume initially $Q = 1$ and $\overline{Q} = 0$ when, $J = K = 1$, then we observe that $S = 0$ and $R = 1$. As per the function table of *SR* flip-flop, when $S = 0$ and $R = 1$, we get $Q = 0$, and $\overline{Q} = 1$, i.e., flip-flop toggles.

Race Around Condition: The clocked *JK* flip-flop shown in Fig. 5.16(a) is not practical. In this circuit the output is fedback to input and hence change in output results change in the input. Due to this when the clock pulse is high, and if both *J* and *K* are high then the output toggles continuously as shown in Fig. 5.16(b). This condition is called 'race around condition' and this must be avoided. In the 'race around condition' output transitions occur for $J = K = CP = 1$ in the intervals of the propagation delay time of the flip-flop. The solution to avoid race around condition in clocked *JK* latch is to use edge triggered or pulse triggered flip-flop.

Assume initially $Q = 0$ and $\overline{Q} = 1$, when $J = K = 1$, we observe that $S = 1$ and $R = 0$. As per the function table, in this condition $Q = 1$ and $\overline{Q} = 0$. Again we observe that flip-flop toggles.

Function table for clocked *JK* flip-flop is shown in Fig. 5.17 and logic symbol is shown in Fig. 5.18.

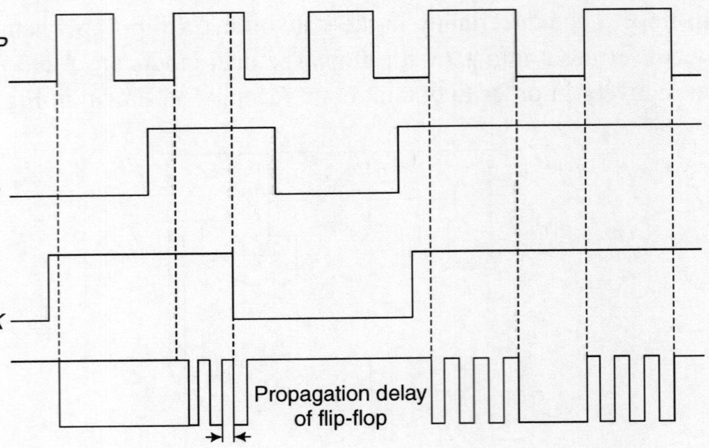

Fig. 5.16 (b) Race around condition in clocked *JK* flip-flop

Inputs			Outputs	
CP	J	K	Q^+	$\overline{Q^+}$
1	0	0	Q	$\overline{Q}$
1	0	1	0	1
1	1	0	1	0
1	1	1	$\overline{Q}$	Q

Fig. 5.17 Function table for clocked *JK* flip-flop

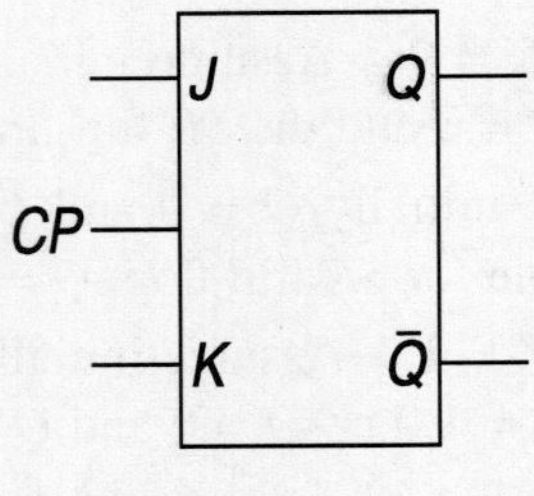

Fig. 5.18 Logic symbol for clocked *JK* flip-flop

Example 5.1 An edge triggered *D* flip-flop is connected as shown in Fig. 5.19. Assume that $Q = 0$ initially and sketch the waveform and determine the frequency of the signal at *Q* output.

Solution

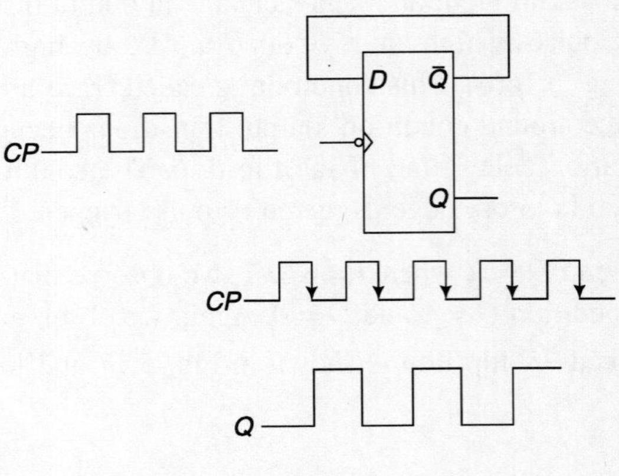

Fig. 5.19

Whenever negative edge triggers, we observe that Q output changes and $f_Q = \frac{f}{2}$ (clock pulse)

Comparison between combinational circuit and sequential circuit is given in the following table.

S.No.	Combinational circuit	Sequential circuit
1.	In combinational circuits, the output at a given time is dependent on the combination of input variables.	In sequential circuits, the output at a given time is dependent on the input as well as on the earlier inputs.
2.	Memory is not required in combinational circuits.	Memory is required to store the earlier inputs.
3.	The operation of combinational circuits is represented by truth table.	The operation of sequential circuit is represented by its states.
4.	Combinational circuits are faster as the delay is only due to propagation delay of gates.	The sequential circuits are relatively slower than combinational circuits.
5.	Combinational circuits are easier to design.	Sequential circuits are relatively difficult to design.
6.	Adders, subtractors, decoders, encoders, etc., are examples for combinational circuits.	Flip-flops, counters, registers, etc., are examples for sequential circuits.

5.4 THE MASTER-SLAVE FLIP-FLOPS

There are two other categories of flip-flops apart from latches. They are master-slave flip-flops or pulse triggered flip-flops and edge triggered flip-flops.

Some applications require that the output changes occur coincident with changes in the control input. The property of having the timing of flip-flop output in relation to a control input signal is achieved with master-slave and edge triggered flip-flops.

A master-slave flip-flop consists of two cascaded flip-flops. The first flip-flop is called master and the second as the slave.

5.5 THE MASTER-SLAVE *SR* FLIP-FLOP

Master-slave flip-flop is constructed from two gated *SR* latches and an inverter. Input lines S and R are used to set and reset the flip-flop. Figure 5.20 shows the master-slave *SR* flip-flop and its timing diagram. A clock signal C is applied to the control input. The change of the control signal from its low to high value, i.e., 0 to 1 is called the rising, leading or positive edge of the control signal. The transition from 1 to 0 is called falling, trailing or negative edge of the control signal.

When $C = 0$, the master is disabled. Hence, any changes in the S and R inputs are ignored. But due to the presence of inverter, slave is enabled. Slave will be in the same state of the master as Q_M and $\overline{Q}_M$ are connected to S and R inputs of the slave.

Now, let us say that the control input starts to rise, the slave is disabled at time t_1 by design while the master remains disabled.

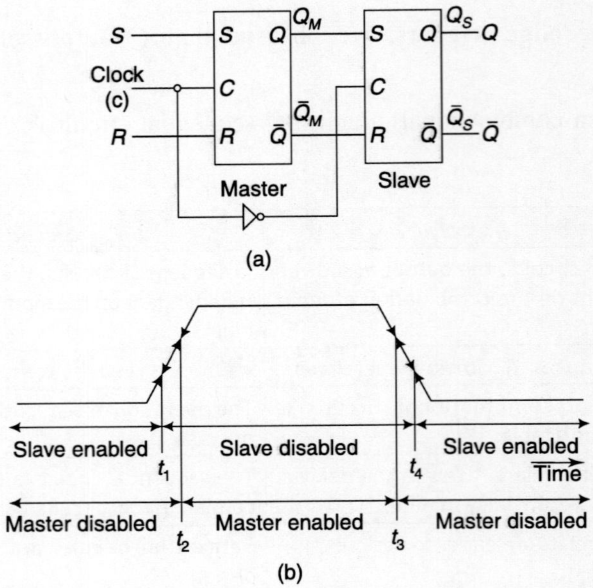

Fig. 5.20 Master-slave *SR* flip-flop and its timing diagram

At time t_2, the master is enabled. When $C = 1$, the master flip-flop responds to S and R inputs. Since the slave is disabled while the master is enabled, any changes in the output of the master will not have any effect on the salve.

When the control signal C is returned to its low at t_3, the master is disabled and its output is latched. At t_4, the slave is enabled and it takes on the state of the master.

For very short periods between t_1 and t_2 and between t_3 and t_4, both the master and slave are disabled. This is critical to the operation of master slave flip-flop.

The master can change its state any time when the control signal is 1. The slave changes its state only when the control signal goes from 1 to 0. Thus, the output of the master-slave flip-flop is synchronized to the trailing edge of the control signal.

The function table for master slave *SR* flip-flop is shown in Fig. 5.21 and the logic symbol is shown in Fig. 5.22.

Inputs			Outputs	
S	R	C	Q^+	$\overline{Q^+}$
0	0	⎍⎽	Q	$\overline{Q}$
0	1	⎍⎽	0	1
1	0	⎍⎽	1	0
1	1	⎍⎽	unpredictable	
x	x	0	Q	$\overline{Q}$

Fig. 5.21 Function table for master-slave *SR* flip-flop.

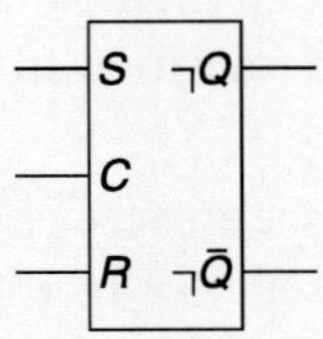

Fig. 5.22 Logic symbol for master-slave *SR* flip-flop

The pulse symbol ⎍ in the C column of the function table indicates that the master is enabled when the control signal is high and the state of the master is transferred to the slave at the end of pulse period.

Fourth row in the function table corresponds to the situation where both S and R are 1. Since master is a latch, it enters an unpredictable state and this state is transferred to the slave when the control signal goes from high to low. Hence, the output of the slave becomes unpredictable.

Since the behaviour of the master slave flip-flops is dependent upon the rising and falling edges of the control signal as well as when the control signal is high, they are also called pulse-triggered flip-flops.

The ¬ symbol in logic symbol is called the postponed output indicator. It means that the output change is postponed to the end of the pulse period. The timing diagram is shown in Fig. 5.23.

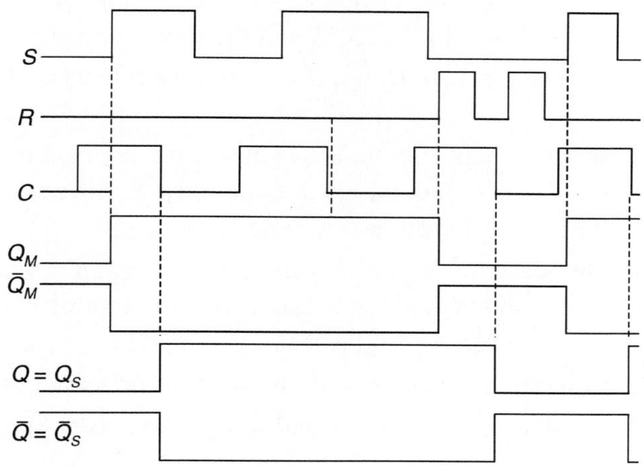

Fig. 5.23 Timing diagram for master slave *SR* flip-flop

5.6 THE MASTER-SLAVE *JK* FLIP-FLOPS

The output of master-slave flip-flop is unpredictable when both $S = R = 1$ and this can be avoided using master-slave JK flip-flop. This uses additional two AND gates apart from master-slave SR flip-flop as shown in Fig. 5.24.

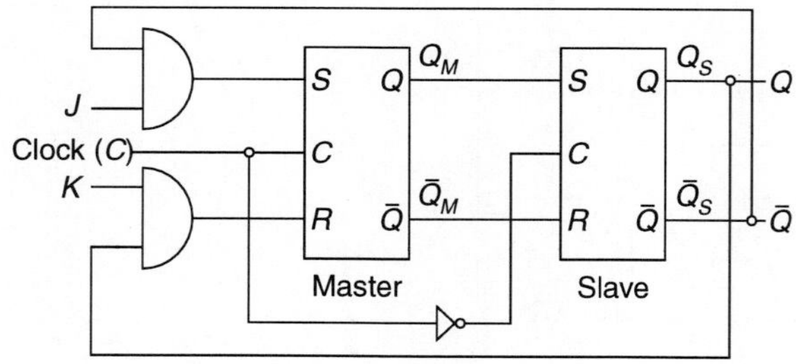

Fig. 5.24 Master-slave *JK* flip-flop

Assume the master-slave *JK* flip-flop is in state '1' clock = 0 and $J = K = 1$, i.e., $Q_S = Q = 1$ and $\overline{Q}_S = \overline{Q} = 0$. Hence, the output of *J* input AND gate is '0' and the output of *K* input AND gate is 1 i.e., $S = 0$ and $R = 1$. When $C = 0$, this cannot affect the state of the master.

If $C = 1$, then the master resets while the slave being disabled, it remains in '1' state. Again when $C = 0$, the slave is enabled and output master is transferred to slave, i.e., $Q_S = 0 = Q$.

Thus, when $J = K = 1$, the output of master-slave *JK* flip-flop is toggled.

Assume the output of master-slave *JK* flip-flop is in '0' state and $J = K = 1$ and $C = 0$.

Then $Q = Q_S = 0$ and $\overline{Q} = \overline{Q}_S = 1$. Now, the output of *J* input AND gate is '1' and the output of *K* input AND gate is 0.

At the input terminals of master, $S = 1$ and $R = 0$ when $C = 1$, the master sets, i.e., $Q_M = 1$ and this is transferred to slave when $C = 0$.

Thus, again when $J = K = 1$, the master-slave flip-flop is toggled. This is indicated by the fourth column in the function table as shown in Fig. 5.25 and the logic symbol is shown in Fig. 5.26.

Assume that the output of master-slave *JK* flip-flop is in '1' state and $C = 0$. Then $Q = Q_S = 1$ and $\overline{Q} = \overline{Q}_S = 0$.

If $J = 1$ and $K = 0$, then the outputs of both AND gates is 0. The input terminals of the master $S = R = 0$. When $C = 1$, the output of the master does not change. It remains in '1' state. When $C = 0$, the state of the master is transferred to slave and $Q_S = 1$.

If the output of the master-slave flip-flop is in 0 state, when $J = 1$, $K = 0$ and $C = 0$, $Q = Q_S = 0$ and $\overline{Q} = \overline{Q}_S = 1$. The output of *J* input AND gate is 1 and the output of *K* input AND gate is 0. At the input terminals of the master, $S = 1$ and $R = 0$.

When $C = 1$, the master is set and when $C = 0$, the state of the master is transferred to slave.

Thus, regardless of present state, when $J = 1$ and $K = 0$, the master-slave *JK* flip-flop enters '1' state upon occurrence of pulse signal.

Similarly, if $J = 0$ and $K = 1$, then the master-slave *JK* flip-flop enters '0' state after a pulse occurs.

When $J = K = 0$, the master-slave flip-flop retains its current state during a clock pulse.

Whenever $C = 0$, the state of the master-slave flip-flop does not change.

Inputs			Outputs	
J	*K*	*C*	Q^+	$\overline{Q^+}$
0	0	⎍	Q	$\overline{Q}$
0	1	⎍	0	1
1	0	⎍	1	0
1	1	⎍	$\overline{Q}$	Q
×	×	0	Q	$\overline{Q}$

Fig. 5.25 Function table for master-slave *JK* flip-flop

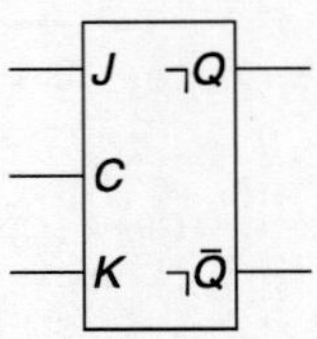

Fig. 5.26 Logic symbol for master-slave *JK* flip-flop

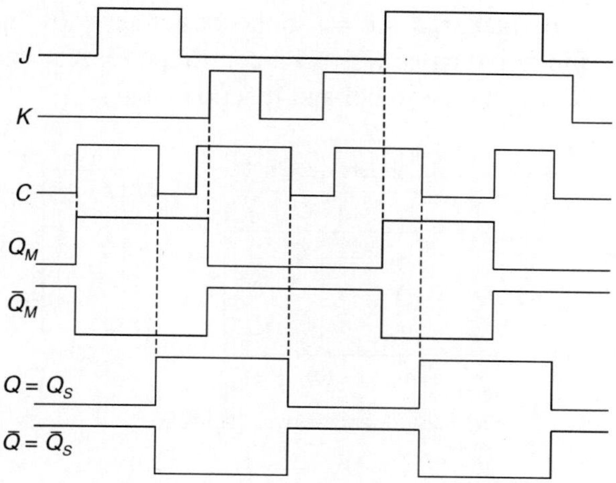

Fig. 5.27 The timing diagram for master-slave *JK* flip-flop

Postponed output indicator (¬) means that the output changes with the trailing edge of the clock.

The timing diagram is shown in Fig. 5.27.

0's and 1's catching: During the entire period when C = 1, the master of the master-slave flip-flop is enabled. If slave latch is in '1' state and K = 1, C = 1, then the master latch resets. Once the master latch is reset, when K = 1 a subsequent '1' on J input, when C = 1 does not cause the master to set. This is due to the fact that the slave does not change its state until C becomes 0. $\overline{Q}_S = 0$ keeps the output of J input AND gate at '0'. This is known as 0's catching.

Similarly, when the state of slave latch is in '0' state, when J = 1, C = 1, the master latch sets. A subsequent '1' on K input when C = 1, does not reset the master. This is known as 1's catching.

In many applications, the 0's and 1's catching is not desirable. Hence, J and K inputs should be held fixed during the entire period that the master is enabled.

The problem of 0's and 1's catching is also solved by the use of edge triggered flip-flops. Alternatively, the master-slave flip-flop with data lockout can also be used.

A master-slave *D* flip-flop: By placing an inverter between S and R inputs of a master-slave SR flip-flop, a master-slave D flip-flop is obtained which is shown in Fig. 5.28 along with logic symbol.

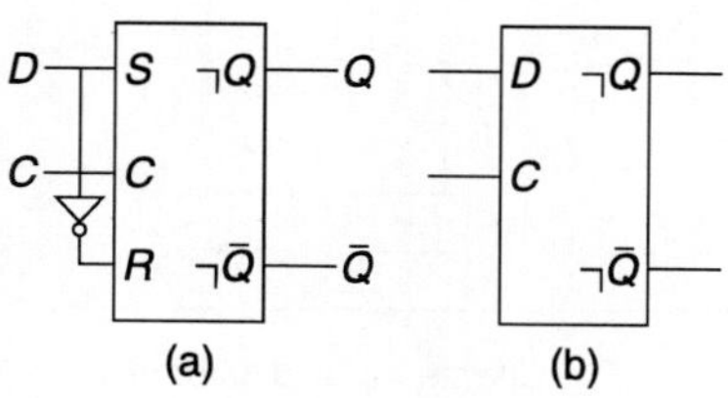

Fig. 5.28 Master-slave *D* flip-flop along with logic symbol

A master-slave *T* flip-flop: By making $J = K = T$ in the master-slave *JK* flip-flop, a master-slave *T* flip-flop is obtained. The flip-flop toggles with each control pulse. A master-slave *T* flip-flop is shown in Fig. 5.29 along with the logic symbol and function table.

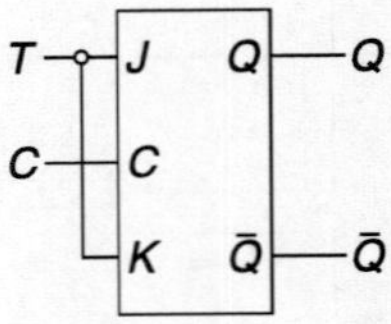

(a)

Inputs		Outputs	
T	C	Q^+	$\bar{Q}^+$
0	⎍	Q	$\bar{Q}$
1	⎍	$\bar{Q}$	Q
×	0	Q	$\bar{Q}$

(b)

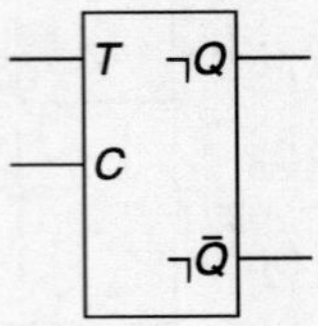

(c)

Fig. 5.29 Master-slave *T* flip-flop

5.7 EDGE TRIGGERED FLIP-FLOPS

Level Triggering: In the level triggering, when active level is maintained at the enable input, output changes according to the input. There are two types of level triggering latches positive level triggered and negative level triggered.

Positive level triggered: The output of latch responds to the input changes only when its enable input is '1' or high as shown in Fig. 5.30.

Negative level triggering: The output of latch responds to the input changes when its enable input is '0' or low as shown in Fig. 5.31.

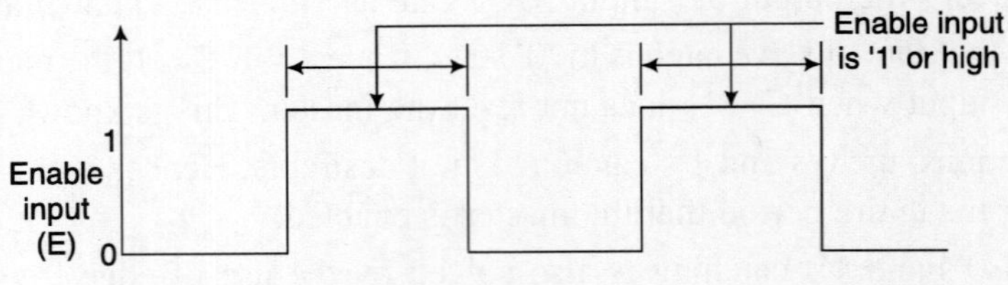

Fig. 5.30 Positive level triggering

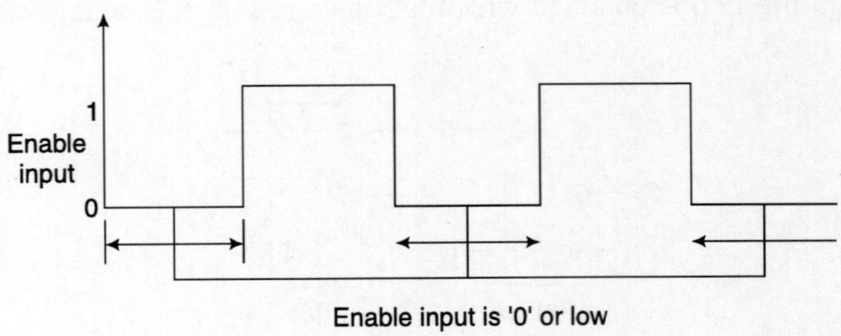

Fig. 5.31 Negative level triggering

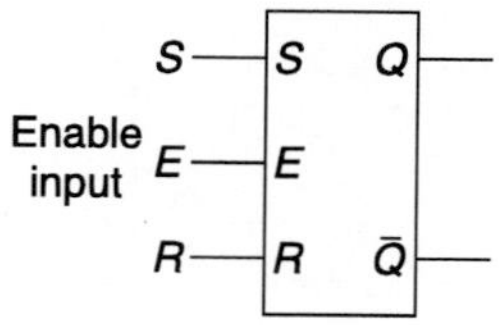

Fig. 5.32 Logic symbol for positive level triggering SR flip-flop

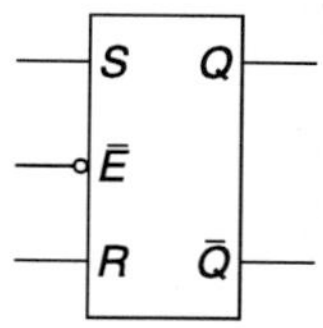

Fig. 5.33 Logic symbol for negative level triggering SR flip-flop

Logic symbols for both positive and negative triggered *SR* latches are shown in Fig. 5.32 and Fig. 5.33. For negative level triggering, an inverter has to be added to the enable input. In Fig. 5.33, the bubble indicates negative level triggering.

Edge triggering: In the edge triggering, the output responds to the changes in the input only at the positive or negative edge of the clock pulse.

Positive edge triggering: The output responds to the changes in the input at the positive edge of the clock pulse as shown in Fig. 5.34.

Negative edge triggering: The output responds to the changes in the input at the negative edge of the clock pulse as shown in Fig. 5.35.

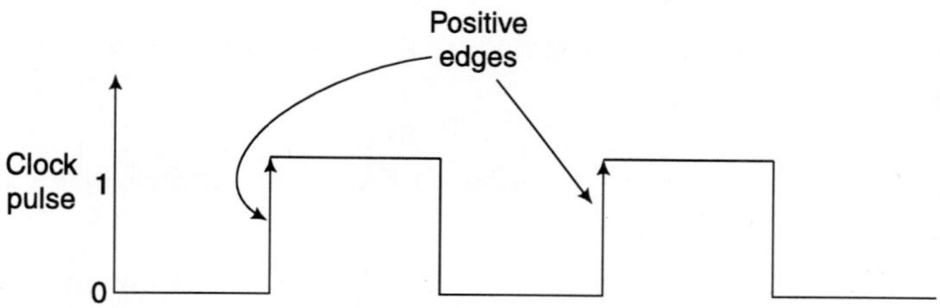

Fig. 5.34 Positive edge triggering

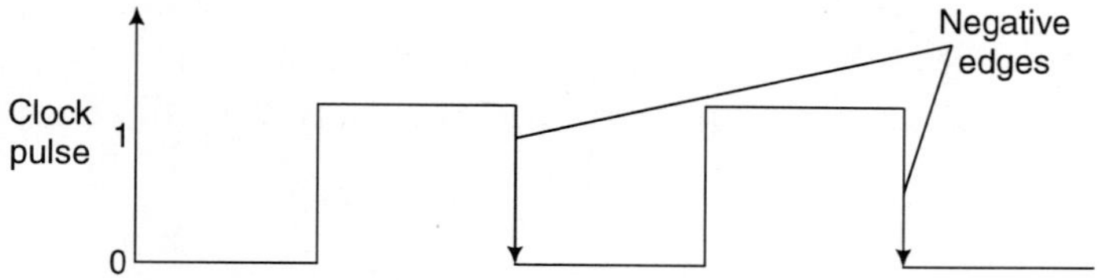

Fig. 5.35 Negative edge triggerring

Positive edge triggered *D* flip-flop: The logic diagram of positive edge triggered '*D*' flip-flop is shown in Fig. 5.36. Here, clock pulse is sent through edge detector circuit.

The *D* input goes directly to the *S* input and the complement of *D* input goes to *R* input. Due to this there are only two input conditions, available, i.e., one input condition $S = 0$ and $R = 1$ and other input condition is $S = 1$ and $R = 0$. The function table is shown in Fig. 5.37.

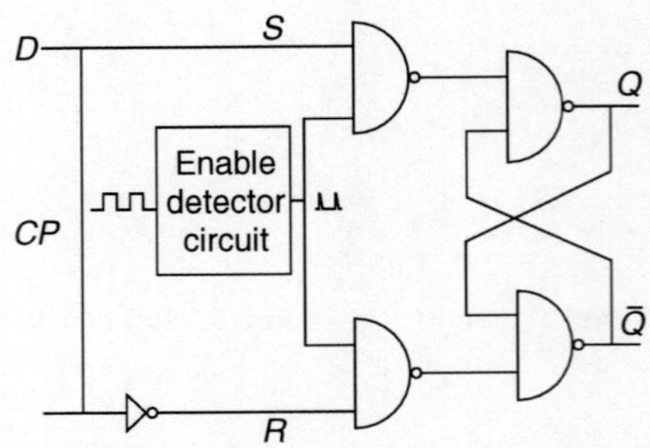

Fig. 5.36 Positive edge triggered '*D*' flip-flop

Inputs		Outputs	
D	*C*	Q^+	$\overline{Q^+}$
0	↑	0	1
1	↑	1	0
×	0	*Q*	$\overline{Q}$
×	1	*Q*	$\overline{Q}$

Fig. 5.37 Function table for positive edge triggered *D* flip-flop

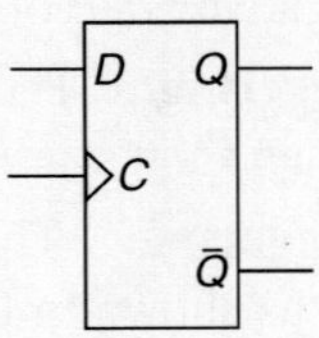

Fig. 5.38 Logic symbol for positive edge triggered *D* flip-flop

The logic symbol for position edge triggered *D* flip-flop is shown in Fig. 5.38. The symbol > is known as dynamic input indicator.

The behaviour of the positive edge triggered *D* flip-flop is similar to that of *D* latch, with difference being that the *D* input is transfered to the output only as a consequence of leading edge of the control signal. The positive edge of the control input has the effect of sampling the *D* input is shown by the ↑ symbol in function table. Figure 5.39 shows the timing diagram.

Looking at the function table for the positive edge triggered *D* flip-flop, we observe that Q^+ function follows *D* input at the positive edge of the clock pulse. However, the output Q^+ is delayed by one clock period. Thus, *D* flip-flop is also known as delay flip-flop.

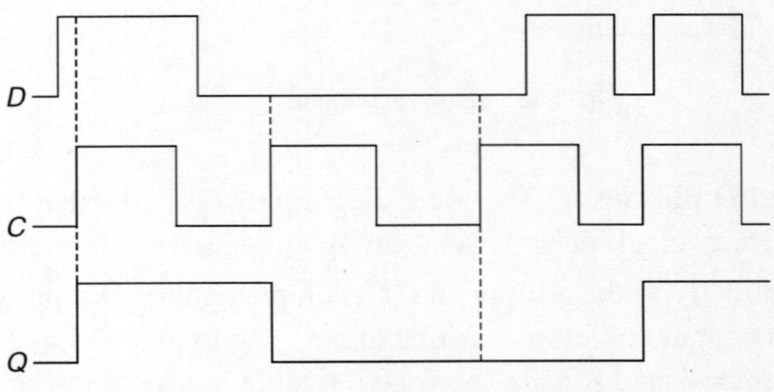

Fig. 5.39 Timing diagram of positive edge triggering *D* flip-flop

Negative edge triggered '*D*' flip-flop: In this case the falling edge, i.e., high to low transition of the control signal is used to sample *D* input rather than the rising edge. This is achieved by simply placing an inverter at the control input of the flip-flop.

The function table and logic symbol are shown in Figs. 5.40 and 5.41.

Inputs		Outputs	
D	C	Q^+	$\overline{Q}^+$
0	↓	0	1
×	↓	Q	$\overline{Q}$
×	1	Q	$\overline{Q}$

Fig. 5.40 Truth table for negative edge triggered *D* flip-flop

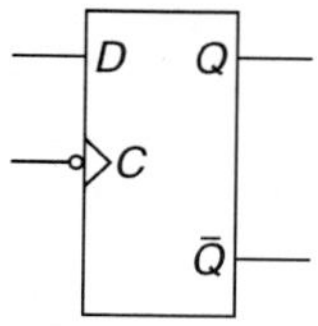

Fig. 5.41 Logic symbol for negative edge triggering *D* flip-flop

In the logic symbol for negative edge triggered '*D*' flip-flop. The inversion bubble and dynamic input indicator combination indicates negative edge triggering.

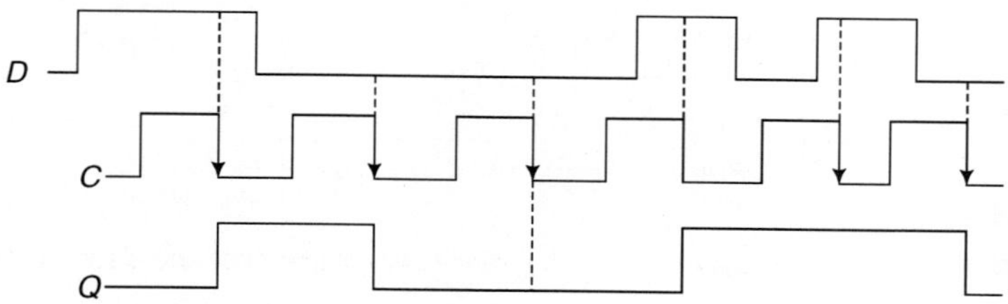

Fig. 5.42 Timing diagram for negative edge triggering '*D*' flip-flop

Asynchronous or Direct inputs: The information inputs of flip-flop are classified into synchronous and asynchronous inputs. All the inputs of edge triggered and master slave flip-flops are synchronous inputs, i.e., *SR*, *JK*, *D* and *T* are synchronous inputs. Many flip-flops have both synchronous and asynchronous inputs in the same device to provide flexibility. The asynchronous inputs called preset and clear are used to forcibly set and reset the flip-flop respectively, independent of control input. They are also called direct inputs.

These asynchronous inputs are particularly useful for bringing a flip-flop into a desired state prior to normal clocked operation.

Figure 5.43 shows *JK* flip-flop with active high preset and clear. An active high level on the preset input immediately sets the flip-flop as preset '1' input at the NOR gate makes its output to '0' which means $\overline{Q} = 0$ and $Q = 1$. An active high level on the clear input immediately resets the flip-flop.

The logic symbol for a *JK* flip-flop with active high preset and clear inputs is shown in Fig. 5.44. These inputs are active high and hence for synchronous operation, they both must be low. And the timing diagram is shown in Fig. 5.45. Assume $J = K = 1$. Hence, whenever preset is 1, $Q = 1$, irrespective of clock.

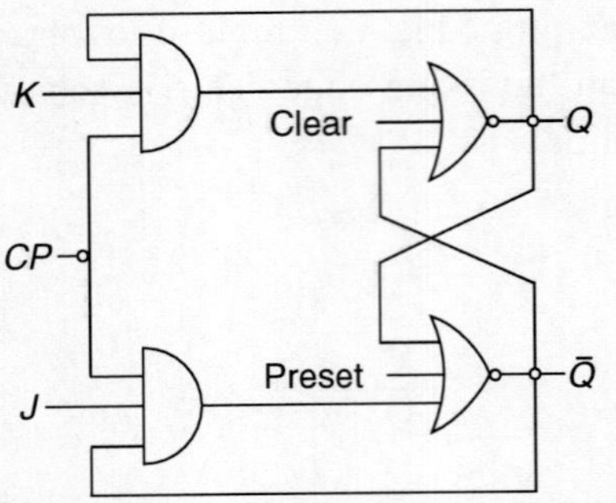

Fig. 5.43 *JK* flip-flop with active high preset and clear

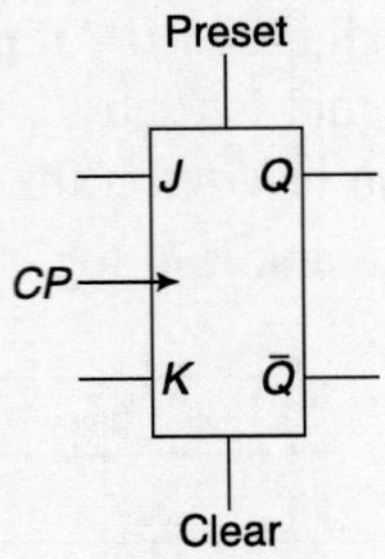

Fig. 5.44 Logic symbol for *JK* flip-flop with active high preset and clear input

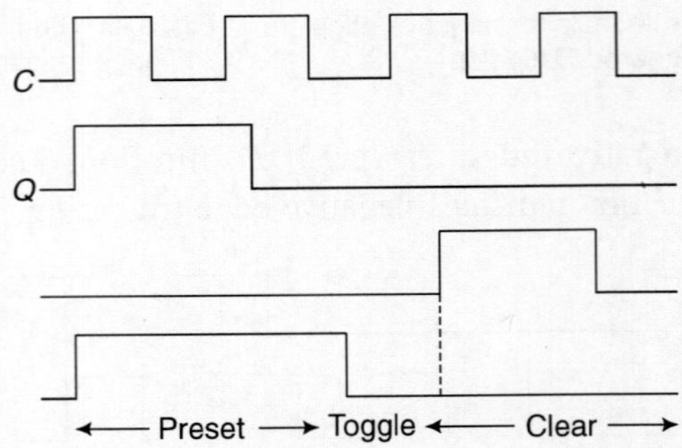

Fig. 5.45 Timing diagram for *JK* flip-flop with active high preset and clear inputs

But in many IC packages preset and clear inputs are active low, i.e., when both preset and clear are '0's, they will be asynchronous input. For synchronous operation, both preset and clear must be kept high. Figure 5.46 shows *JK* flip-flop with active low preset and clear inputs.

If clear input is active low, i.e., '0' and preset is 1, then $Q = 0$ and $\overline{Q} = 1$. If preset input is active low and clear is 1, then $\overline{Q} = 0$ and $Q = 1$. The synchronous operation is carried out when

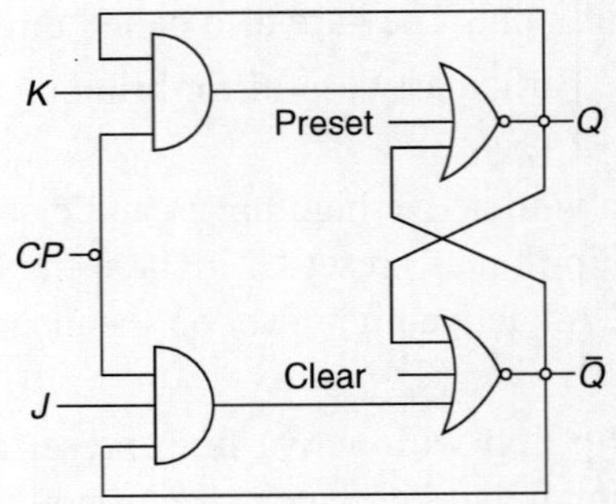

Fig. 5.46 *JK* flip-flop with action low preset and clear inputs and clear inputs

both clear and preset inputs are '1'. These are shown in function table which is given in Fig. 5.47 and the logic symbol is shown in Fig. 5.48.

Inputs					Outputs	
$\overline{PR}$	$\overline{CLR}$	J	K	C	Q^+	$\overline{Q}^+$
0	1	×	×	×	1	0
1	0	×	×	×	0	1
1	1	0	0	↑	Q	$\overline{Q}$
1	1	0	1	↑	0	1
1	1	1	0	↑	1	0
1	1	1	1	↑	$\overline{Q}$	Q
0	0	×	×	×	unpredictable	

Fig. 5.47 *JK* flip-flop with active low preset and clear inputs

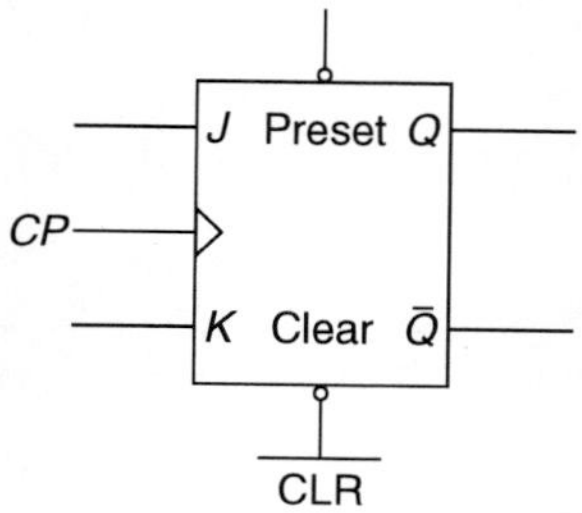

Fig. 5.48 Logic symbol for *JK* flip-flop with active low clear and preset inputs

Timing diagram of *JK* flip-flop with active low preset and clear inputs is shown in Fig. 5.49, when inputs $J = K = 1$.

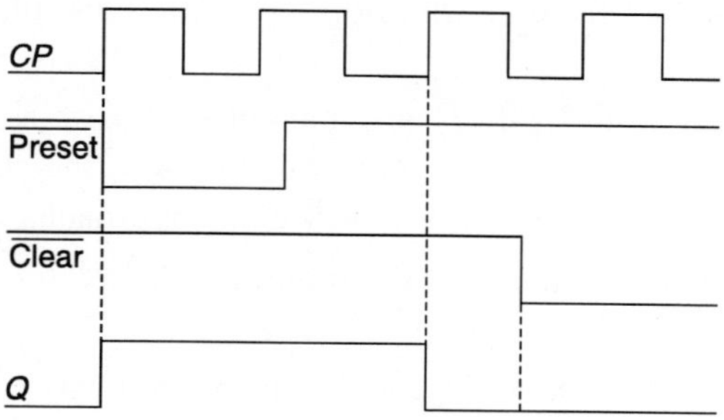

Fig. 5.49 Timing diagram for *JK* flip-flop with active low preset and clear input

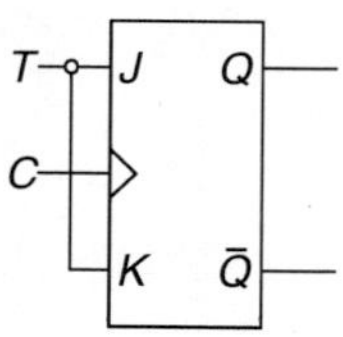

Fig. 5.50

Inputs		Outputs	
T	C	Q^+	$\overline{Q}^+$
0	↑	Q	$\overline{Q}$
1	↑	$\overline{Q}$	Q
×	0	Q	$\overline{Q}$
×	1	Q	$\overline{Q}$

Fig. 5.51

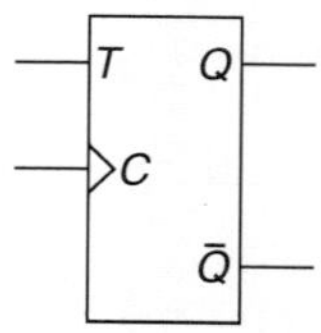

Fig. 5.52

Edge triggered T-flip-flop logic diagram, function table and logic symbol

Additional types of edge triggered flip-flops: Construction of a positive edge triggered *T* flip-flop is to tie together *J* and *K* inputs of a positive edge triggered *JK* flip-flop which is shown in Fig. 5.50 and function table and logic symbol are shown in Figs. 5.51 and 5.52 respectively

Master-slave flip-flops with data lockout: Master-slave configuration is used to get delayed outputs from flip-flops. However, to avoid 0's and 1's catching behaviour, the master should respond to inputs only on one edge of the control signal and transfer the content to the slave on the opposite edge of the control signal. These kinds of master slave flip-flops are said to have data lock out.

A positive edge triggered *JK* flip-flop is used for the master and an *SR* latch is used for the slave.

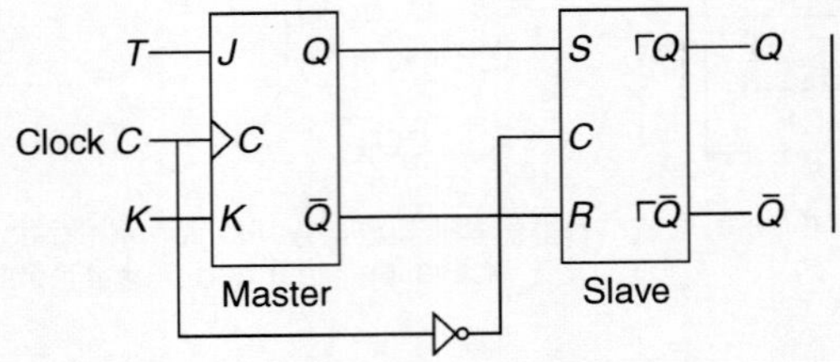

Fig. 5.53 Master-slave *JK* flip-flop with data lockout

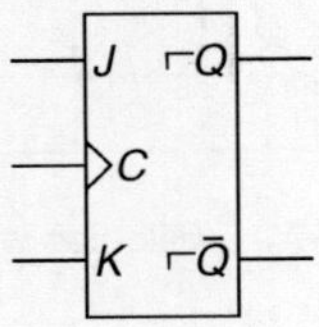

Fig. 5.54 Logic symbol

Figure 5.53 shows the master-slave *JK* flip-flop with data lockout and Fig. 5.54 shows the logic symbol for it.

Since master is edge triggered flip-flop, any changes on *J* or *K* inputs, when $C = 1$ are ignored. The content of the master is subsequently transferred to the slave on the negative edge of the control signal. We achieve the delayed output by this approach.

The dynamic input indicator indicates that the inputs are sampled on the positive edge of the control signal.

Postponed output indicators appear in the logic symbol since output is delayed as a consequence of the master-slave configuration.

Example 5.2 How do you convert *S-R* flip-flop to *J-K* flip-flop?

The excitation table for converting *SR* flip-flop to *J-K* flip-flop is shown in Fig. 5.55.

Inputs		Present state	Next state	Flip-flop Inputs	
J	K	Q_n	Q_{n+1}	S	R
0	0	0	0	0	×
0	0	1	1	×	0
0	1	0	0	0	×
0	1	1	0	0	1
1	0	0	1	1	0
1	0	1	1	×	0
1	1	0	1	1	0
1	1	1	0	0	1

Fig. 5.55 Excitation table for example 5.2

K-map is drawn for flip-flop inputs S and R as shown in Fig. 5.56 and is simplified and logic diagram is constructed as shown in Fig. 5.57.

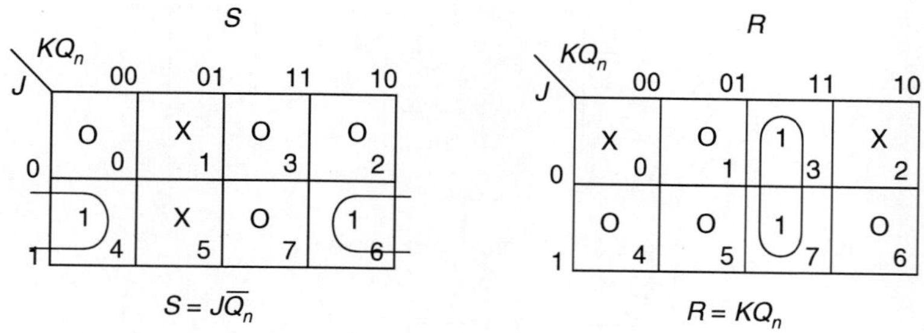

Fig. 5.56 K-map for example 5.2

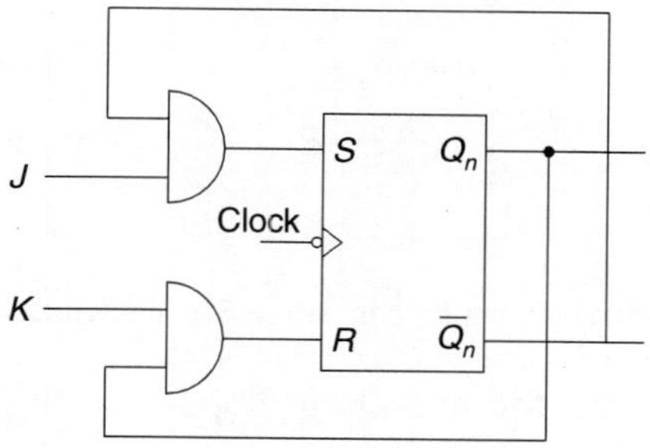

Fig. 5.57 Logic diagram for converting *SR* flip-flop to *JK* flip-flop.

Example 5.3 How do you convert *SR* flip-flop to *T* flip-flop?

Solution The excitation table for converting *SR* flip-flop to *T* flip-flop is shown in Fig. 5.58.

Input	Present state	Next state	Flip-flop Inputs	
T	Q_n	Q_{n+1}	S	R
0	0	0	0	x
0	1	1	x	0
1	0	1	1	0
1	1	0	0	1

Fig. 5.58 Excitation table for example 5.3

K-map is drawn for flip-flop inputs S and R as shown in Fig. 5.59 and is simplified and logic diagram is constructed as shown in Fig. 5.60.

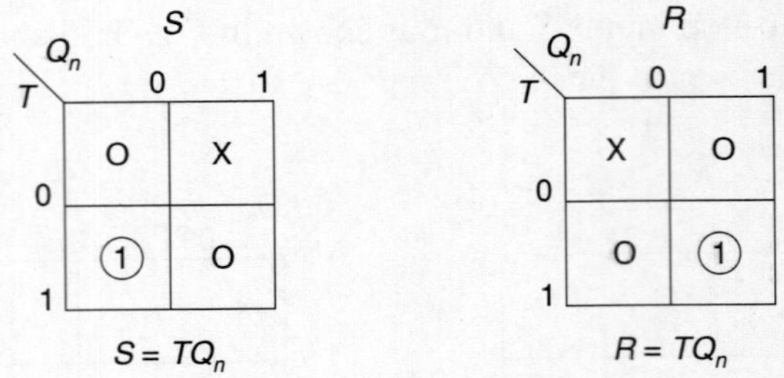

Fig. 5.59 K-map for Example 5.3

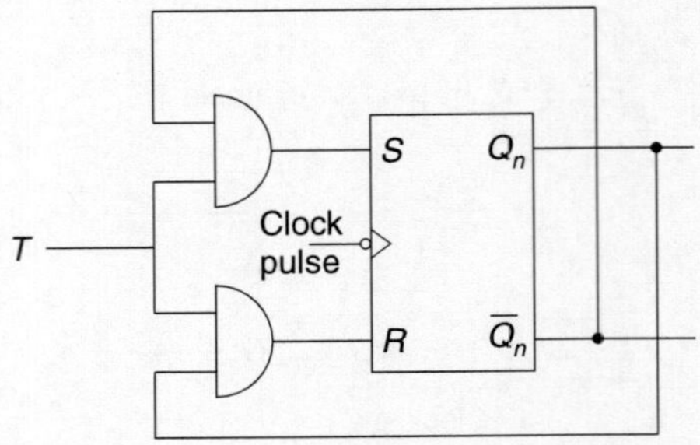

Fig. 5.60 Logic diagram for converting *SR* Flip-flop to *T* Flip-flop

Example 5.4 How do you convert *JK* flip-flop *D* flip-flop?

Solution The excitation table for converting *JK* flip-flop to *D* flip-flop is shown in Fig. 5.61.

Input	Present state	Next state	Flip-flop Inputs	
D	Q_n	Q_{n+1}	*J*	*K*
0	0	0	0	x
0	1	0	x	1
1	0	1	1	x
1	1	1	x	0

Fig. 5.61 Excitation table for example 5.4

K-map is drawn for flip-flop inputs *J* and *K* as shown in Fig. 5.62 and is simplified and logic diagram is constructed as shown in Fig. 5.63.

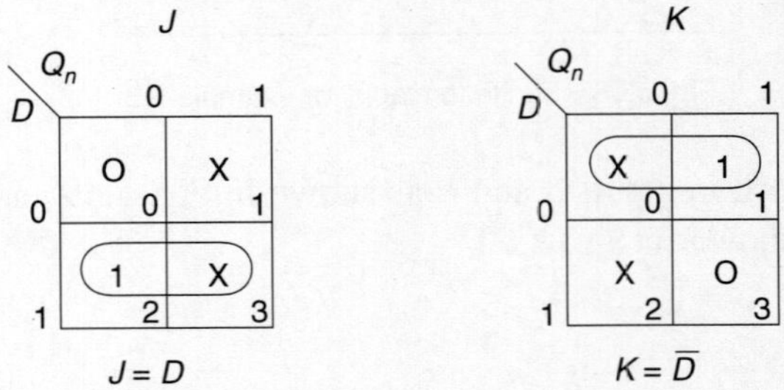

Fig. 5.62 K-map for example 5.4

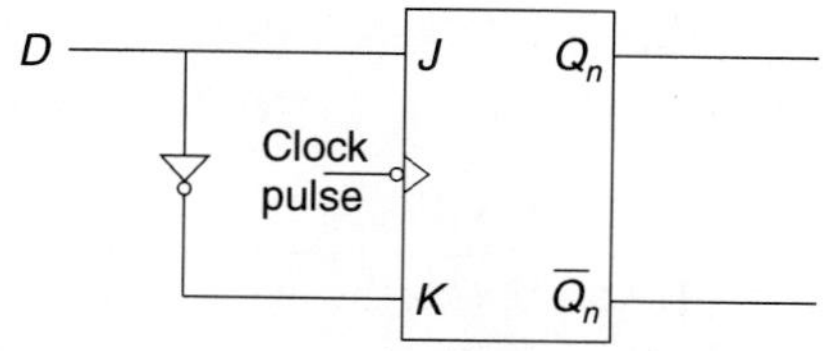

Fig. 5.63 Logic diagram for converting *JK* flop-flop to *D* flip-flop

Example 5.5 How do you convert *D* flip-flop to *T* flip-flop?

Solution The excitation table for converting *D* flip-flop to *T* flip-flop is shown in Fig. 5.64.

Input	Present state	Next state	Flip-flop Input
T	Q_n	Q_{n+1}	D
0	0	0	0
0	1	1	1
1	0	1	1
1	1	0	0

Fig. 5.64 Excitation table for example 5.5

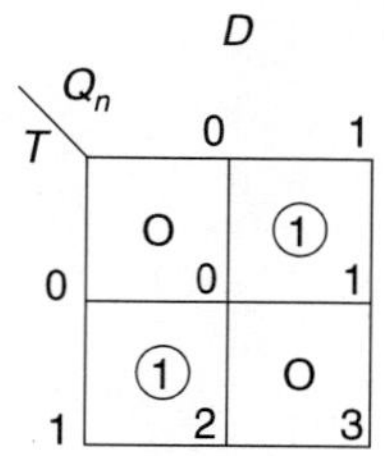

$$D = \overline{T}Q_n + T\overline{Q_n}$$
$$= T \oplus Q_n$$

Fig. 5.65 K-map for Example 5.5

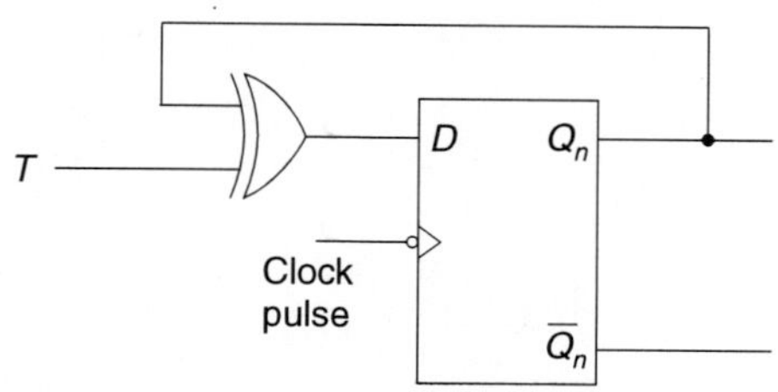

Fig. 5.66 Logic diagram for converting *D* flip-flop to *T* flip-flop.

K-map is drawn for flip-flop input *D* as shown in Fig. 5.65 and is simplified and logic diagram is constructed as shown in Fig. 5.66.

Example 5.6 How do you convert *JK* flip-flop to *S-R* flip-flop? (VTU – June 2014)

The excitation table for converting *JK* flip-flop to *SR* flip-flop is shown in Fig. 5.67.

Inputs	Present state	Next state	Flip-flop Inputs		
S	R	Q_n	Q_{n+1}	J	K
0	0	0	0	0	×
0	0	1	1	×	0
0	1	0	0	0	×
0	1	1	0	×	1
1	0	0	1	1	×
1	0	1	1	×	0
1	1	0	×	×	×
1	1	1	×	×	×

Fig. 5.67 Excitation table for example 5.6

K-map is drawn for flip-flop inputs *J* and *K* as shown in Fig. 5.68 and is simplified and logic diagram is constructed as shown in Fig. 5.69.

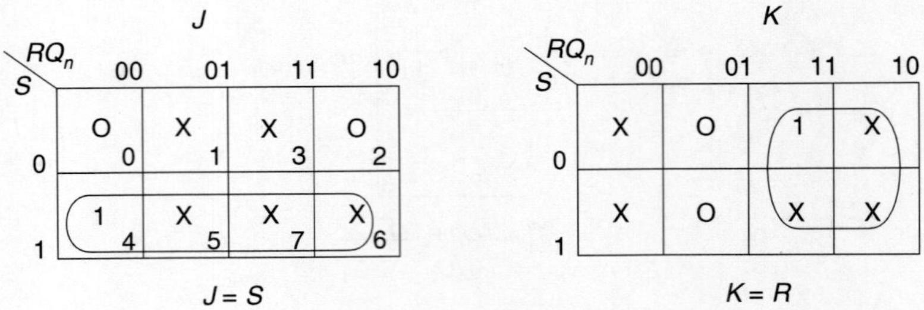

Fig. 5.68 K-map for example 5.6

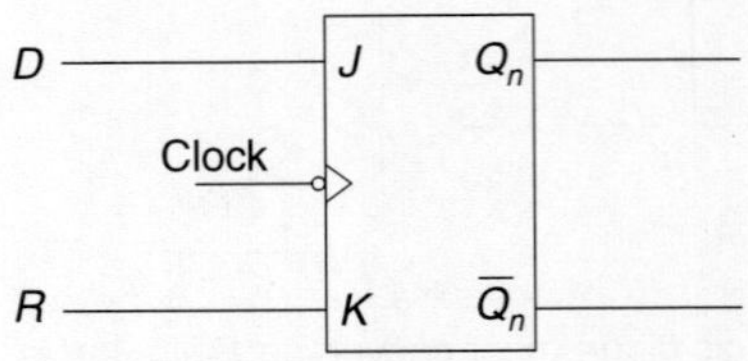

Fig. 5.69 Logic diagram for converting *JK* flip-flop to *SR* flip-flop.

EXERCISE

1. Explain the differences between combinational logic and sequential logic circuit.
2. Clearly distinguish between:
   (i) synchronous and asynchronous circuits.
   (ii) combinational and sequential circuits.
3. What is race around condition? Explain how it is eliminated using *JK* master-slave flip-flop.
4. Explain the working of:
   (i) *SR* latch, (ii) gated *SR* latch, (iii) gated *D* latch with the use of logic diagrams.
5. Explain different types of flip-flops along with their tables.
6. Explain the operation of *SR* flip-flop.
7. Explain the operation of simple *SR* flip-flop using NAND gates.
8. Explain the operation of basic *SR*. *FF* by using NOR gates only.
9. Give the details of a master-slave *S-R* flip-flop. Draw the logic diagram. Explain the flip-flop action during the control signal. Also give the function table.
10. Explain the construction of a master-slave *JK* flip-flop. Give the benefits of master-slave flip-flops.
11. Explain the operation of master-slave *JK* flip-flop along with its circuit diagram.
12. Explain different types of flip-flops along with their truth table. Also explain the race around condition in a flip-flop.
13. Explain the working of switch debouncer using SR latch.
14. With a neat logic diagram and timing waveforms, describe the operation of a master slave *JK* flip-flop.
15. Give the logic diagram of:
   (i) *SR* latch
   (ii) Gated *D* latch
   (iii) Master-slave *JK* flip-flop
   (iv) Master-slave *SR* flip-flop

CHAPTER 6

Sequential Circuits-2

6.1 CHARACTERISTIC EQUATIONS

Simplified function table of *SR* flip-flop, *JK* flip-flop, *D* flip-flop and *T* flip-flop are shown in Fig. 6.1. In these tables, control signal is not explicitly shown, but rather implicitly assumed. In the last row of the simplified function table, the dash indicates that the input combination $S = R = 1$ is not permitted since output is unpredictable. Only the next state values of Q, i.e., Q^+ are shown in the tables. $\overline{Q}$ values are opposite to those of Q.

S	R	Q^+
0	0	Q
0	1	0
1	0	1
1	1	–

(a)

D	Q^+
0	0
1	1

(c)

J	K	Q^+
0	0	Q
0	1	0
1	0	1
1	1	$\overline{Q}$

(b)

T	Q^+
0	Q
1	$\overline{Q}$

(d)

Fig. 6.1 Simplified function table of (a) *SR* flip-flop, (b) *JK* flip-flop, (c) *D* flip-flop, (d) *T* flip-flop

A variation of the simplified function tables, called next state tables is shown for four types of flip-flops in Fig. 6.2. The next state tables show the value of next state of flip-flops for each combination of values of the present state and input values. Since Q can have two values, each row of the simplified function table becomes two rows in the next state table.

The algebraic description of the next state table of a flip-flop is called the characteristic equation of the flip-flop.

S	R	Q	Q^+	
0	0	0	0	
0	0	1	1	
0	1	0	0	
0	1	1	0	
1	0	0	1	
1	0	1	1	
1	1	0	–	Inputs not allowed
1	1	1	–	

(a)

J	K	Q	Q^+
0	0	0	0
0	0	1	1
0	1	0	0
0	1	1	0
1	0	0	1
1	0	1	1
1	1	0	1
1	1	1	0

(b)

D	Q	Q^+
0	0	0
0	1	0
1	0	1
1	1	1

(c)

T	Q	Q^+
0	0	0
0	1	1
1	0	1
1	1	0

(d)

Fig. 6.2 Next state tables of (a) *SR* flip-flop, (b) *JK* flip-flop, (c) *D* flip-flop (d) *T* flip-flop

The algebraic description is obtained by constructing K-map for Q^+ in terms of present state and input variables. K-maps for all four types of flip-flops and their characteristic equations are shown in Fig. 6.3. The inputs that cause an undefined output are regarded as don't-cares since these inputs are assumed to not occur. The constraining equation $SR = 0$ indicates that S and R cannot be 1 simultaneously.

The characteristic equations only specify the functional behaviour of the flip-flops.

6.2 REGISTERS

A register is simply a collection of flip-flops taken as an entity. The basic function of a register is to hold information within a digital system so as to make it available to the logic circuits during computation.

Each of the flip-flops can store a 0 or 1. Hence, the register can store a combination of 0'S and 1'S. Each of the combinations is known as the state or content of the register.

Registers that are capable of moving information positionwise upon the occurrence of a clock signal are called shift registers. They are classified as unidirectional or bidirectional.

There are two basic ways in which transfers from the registers are done either in serial or in parallel. There are four possible ways registers can transfer information: (i) serial in/serial out, (ii) serial in/parallel out, (iii) parallel in/parallel out, and (iv) parallel in/serial out.

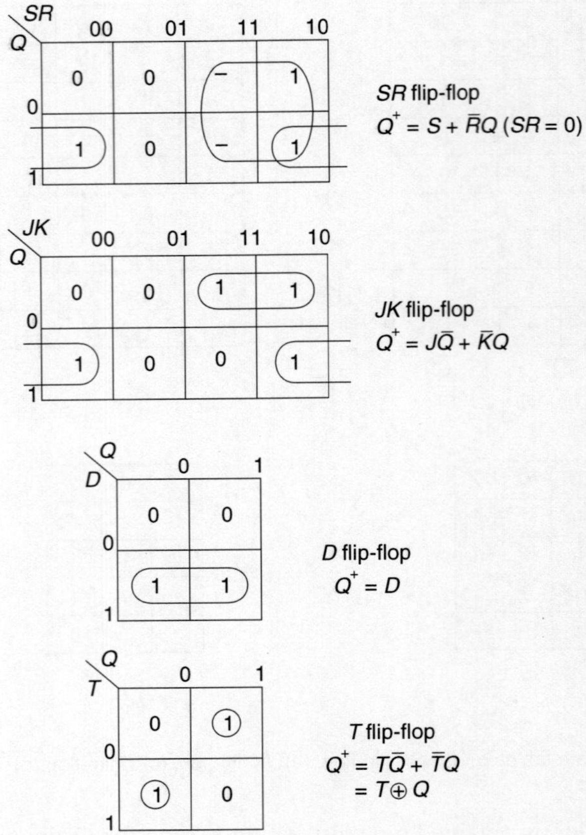

Fig. 6.3 K-maps and characteristic equations

Serial in serial out unidirectional shift right register: It is shown in Fig. 6.4. The Q output of each flip-flop of the serial in/serial out shift right register is connected to the D input of the flip-flop to its right.

The control inputs of all the flip-flops are connected together to a common clock. Thus, upon the occurrence of a positive edge of the clock signal, the content of each flip-flop is shifted one position to the right.

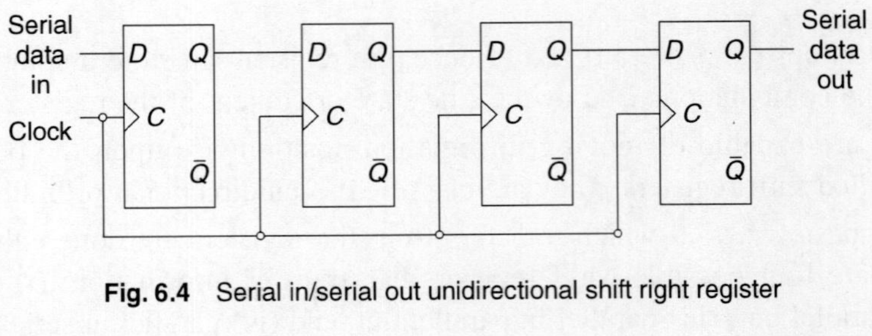

Fig. 6.4 Serial in/serial out unidirectional shift right register

The content of the leftmost flip-flop after the clock signal depends on the signal value on the serial data in-line and the content of the rightmost flip-flop prior to the clock signal is lost.

The output from the shift register occurs at the rightmost flip-flop on the serial data outline.

If the initial content of the shift register is 1101 and a '0' applied to the serial data in line prior to the positive edge of the clock signal, then the content of the register becomes 0110 after the positive edge of the clock signal.

Circular shift register: In some applications the information within a register must be preserved, but only a reorientation of information is required.

To achieve this, serial data outline is connected to the serial data in line. This register is known as circular shift register which is shown in Fig. 6.5.

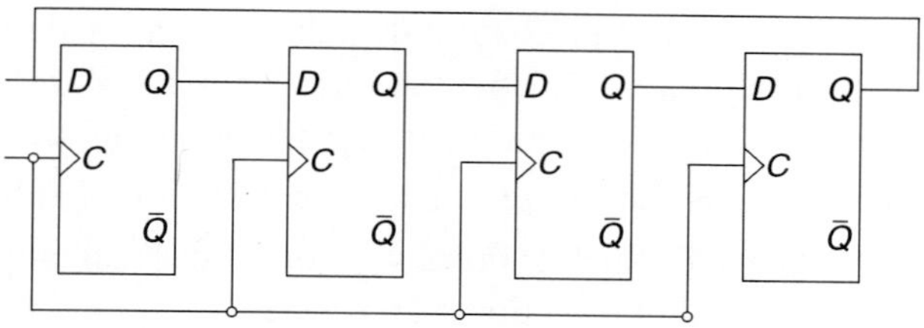

Fig. 6.5 Circular shift register

The content of the register is shifted one position to the right upon the occurrence of each clock signal, but the state of the leftmost flip-flop is replaced by the state of the rightmost flip-flop.

Assume that the initial content of the register is 1101 and the output of the rightmost flip-flop is connected to the input of the leftmost flip-flop.

After the occurrence of the positive edge of the clock signal, the register will contain 1110.

A flip-flop is simultaneously read into while being read by another flip-flop. Thus, we use edge triggered or pulse triggered, i.e., master slave flip-flops. Latches are not used in such applications since their outputs are subject to change during the entire period in which they are enabled.

Serial in parallel out unidirectional shift registers: In this shift registers, the outputs are provided from each flip-flop. This is shown in Fig. 6.6. Once the information is shifted into the register the information output is available as an entity, i.e., parallel out at the flip-flop output terminals.

Since information is transferred into this register serially and after an appropriate number of shifts made available in parallel, this type of register provides for serial to parallel conversion of information.

Parallel in, serial out unidirectional shift register: This is shown in Fig. 6.7. The operation of the register is controlled by the $\overline{\text{Load}}$/Shift line. When a logic '0' signal is given to this line, signals on the parallel data in lines I_a, I_b, I_c, I_d are transferred into the register upon the occurrence of a position edge signal.

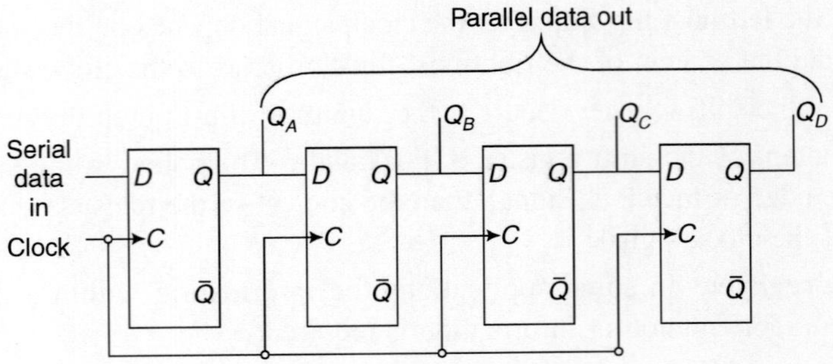

Fig. 6.6 Serial in / parallel out shift register

When a logic '1' signal appears on the $\overline{\text{Load}}$/Shift line, the AND gate which has serial data in will have other input as 1 and through OR gate, the serial data in will reach the D input. Thus, the D flip-flops will function as a unidirectional shift register providing the serial output.

In this way, the register provides for parallel to serial conversion of information.

By taking the outputs from each of the flip-flops, we can get parallel output. Thus, the register functions as a parallel in parallel out unidirectional shift register.

In addition, it can also function as a serial-in, parallel-out unidirectional shift register and as a serial-in, serial-out unidirectional shift register.

Thus, the circuit shown in Fig. 6.7, will cater to four different possible configurations of serial in/serial out and serial in/parallel out, parallel in/parallel out and parallel in/serial out.

Universal shift registers: Bidirectional shift registers are capable of shifting their contents either, left or right depending on the control inputs. These registers are called universal shift registers which is shown in Fig. 6.8.

Depending upon the signal values on the select lines of the multiplexers, there are four different modes of operations. The select lines are called mode control lines. The four modes of the register are (i) it can retain or hold its current state, (ii) shift right, (iii) shift left and (iv) it can be loaded in parallel.

Each of these operations is based on the occurrence of a positive edge on the clock line. The register can be cleared asynchronously if a logic '0' is applied to the 'clear' line.

The table is shown in Fig. 6.9, which indicates different modes and the corresponding register operation. If select lines S_1 S_0 are 00, then hold operation is carried out. Under this condition the I_0 is connected to f which is given to D input. But $I_0 = Q_A$ because Q_A is connected to I_0 input of the first multiplexer. Hence, whatever value Q_A has, will be applied to D.

Upon the occurrence of the positive edge of the clock signal, D input of the first flip-flop will be available as Q_A i.e., the flip-flop retains its state or holds its output value. Similarly, the other flip-flops retain states.

If the select lines S_1 S_0 of the multiplexess are 01, the register performs the shift right operation. Under this condition I_1 input of each multiplexer is connected to its f output. The input

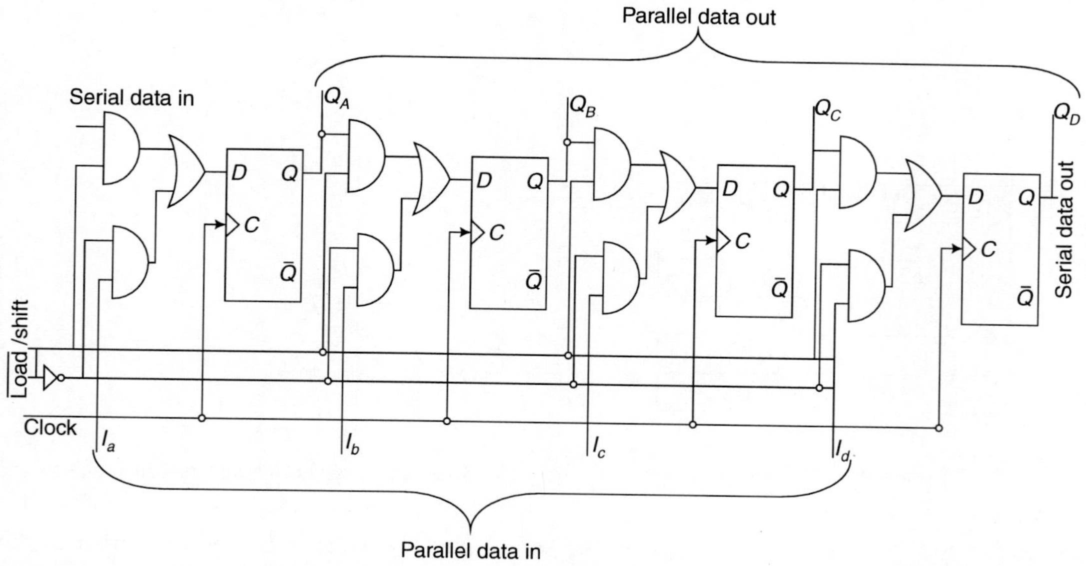

Fig. 6.7 Serial in/serial out, serial in/parallel out, parallel in/serial out, parallels in/parallel out unidirectional shift register

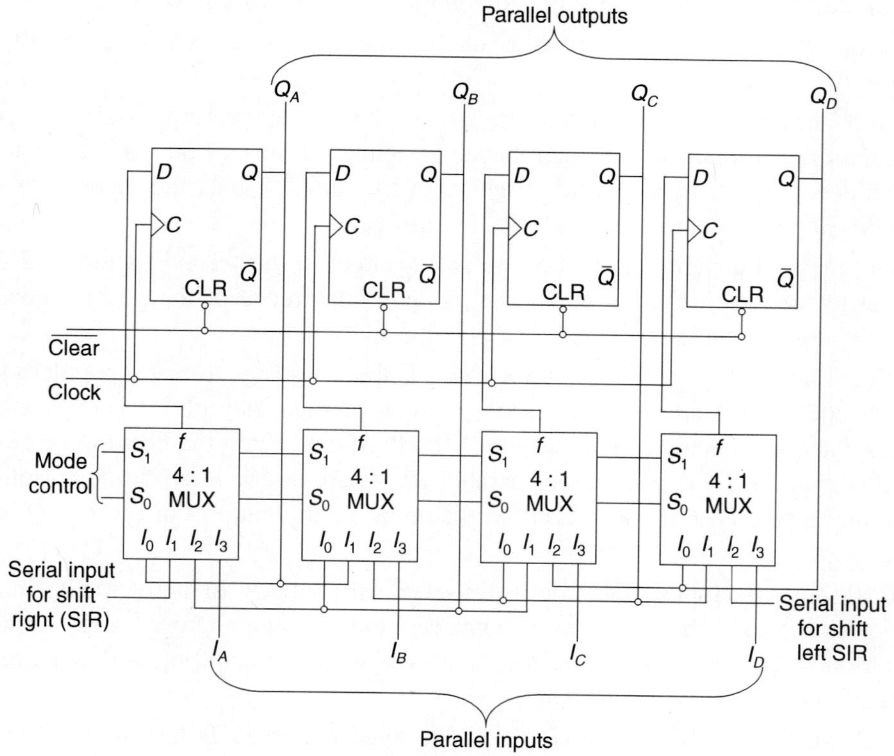

Fig. 6.8 Universal shift register

Select lines		Register operation
S_1	S_0	
0	0	Hold
0	1	Shift right
1	0	Shift left
1	1	Parallel load

Fig. 6.9 Mode table

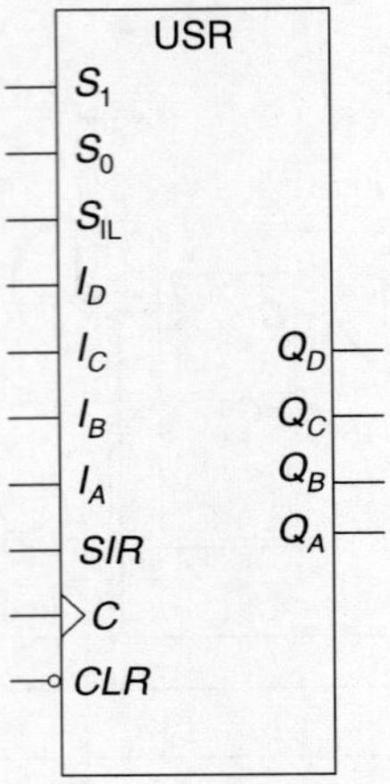

Fig. 6.10 Logic symbol for universal shift register

to the leftmost D flip-flop is the signal on the serial input for shift right line, the input to the second leftmost D flip-flop is the output of leftmost D flip-flop.

The input to the third leftmost D flip-flop is the output of the second leftmost D flip-flop and the input to the fourth leftmost D flip-flop is the output of third leftmost D flip-flop.

Upon the occurrence of the positive edge of the clock signal, the register shifts its content one position to the right.

If the select lines S_1 S_0 of the multiplexers are 10, the register performs shift left operation. Under this condition, I_2 input of each multiplexer is connected to its f output. The input to the rightmost D flip-flop is the signal on the serial input for shift left line, the input to the second rightmost D flip-flop is the output of rightmost D flip-flop.

The input to the third rightmost D flip-flop is the output of the second rightmost D flip-flop and the output to the fourth rightmost D flip-flop upon occurrence of the positive edge of the clock signal, the register shifts its content one position to the left.

If the select lines S_1 S_0 of the multiplexers are 11, the register performs a parallel input and parallel output operation. Under this condition, I_3 input of each multiplexer is connected to its 'f' output and that is connected to D input of all 'D' flip-flops. Upon the occurrence of positive edge of clock signal, all D inputs, i.e., all parallel inputs are available at the output of all flip-flops. All parallel inputs I_A, I_B, I_C and I_D are available as parallel outputs at Q_A, Q_B, Q_C and Q_D, respectively.

Figure 6.10 shows the logic symbol of the universal shift register. In these circuits, the control lines for the clock inputs of the flip-flops are connected together and appropriate logic is included to provide various capabilities, e.g., unidirectional or bidirectional shifting and handling ability of the information of input and output lines.

Example 6.1 Design a 4-bit register using positive edge triggered D flip-flops to operate as indicated in the table given below. (VTU – Dec 2013)

Mode select		Register operation
a_1	a_0	
0	0	Hold
0	1	Synchronous clear
1	0	Complement contents
1	1	Circular shift right

Solution

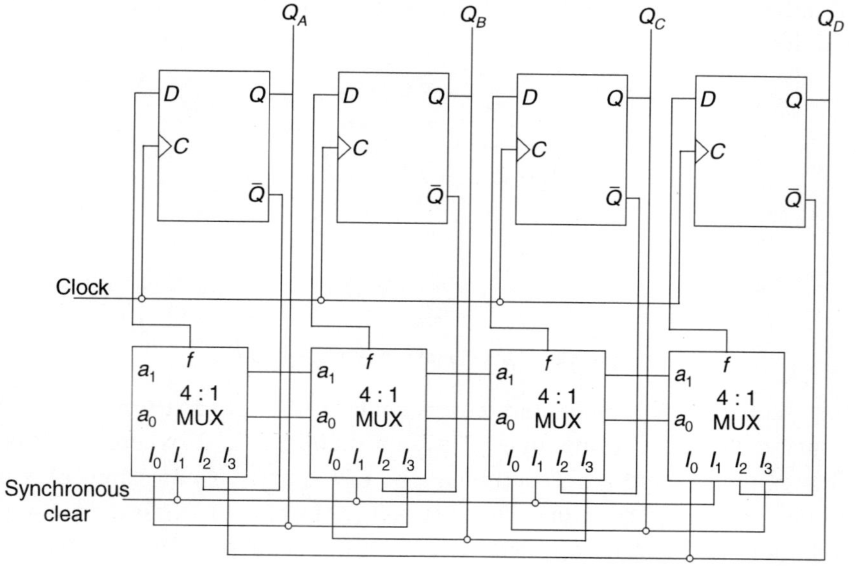

Fig. 6.11 4-bit register for example 6.1

Figure 6.11 shows a 4-bit '*D*' flip-flop register for the example 6.1. When $a_1 a_0$ = 0 0 all the *Q* outputs are connected to I_0 inputs of the corresponding multiplexers and '*f*' outputs of the multiplexers are connected to the corresponding *D* inputs and upon occurrence of positive edge of the clock signal, *D* inputs are shifted to *Q* outputs of the flip-flops. Hence, the output remains same or it in hold state.

When $a_1 a_0$ = 01, all I_1 inputs of the multiplexers are connected together and connected to synchronous clear signal. All the *f* outputs are connected to '*D*' inputs. Upon occurrence of positive edge of the clock signal, all flip-flop get cleared as all *D* inputs are '0'.

When $a_1 a_0$ = 10 all I_2 inputs of the multiplexers are connected to the corresponding $\overline{Q}$ outputs of flip-flops. '*f*' outputs of all multiplexers are connected to *D* inputs. Upon occurrence of positive edge of the clock signal all '*D*' inputs which are $\overline{Q}$ outputs will be transferred to *Q* outputs. Thus, all *Q* outputs will have complemented outputs.

When $a_1 a_0$ = 11, all I_3 inputs of the multiplexers are connected to '*f*' outputs which are in turn connected to '*D*' inputs. I_3 inputs are connected to next left flip-flop *Q* outputs. Hence, all the output of '*D*' flip-flops will be shifted right upon occurrence of positive edge of the clock signal.

6.3 COUNTERS – BINARY RIPPLE COUNTERS

A counter is a register whose primary function is to produce a specified output sequence. Each of the 0 – 1 combinations that are stored in the collection of flip-flops that comprise the counter, i.e., the output pattern is known as the state of the counter.

The total number of states is called its modulus. If a counter has *n* distinct states, it is called a modulus-*n* counter or mod-*n* counter. The order in which the states appear is referred to as its counting sequence. The counting sequence is depicted by a state diagram as shown in Fig. 6.12. Each node *Si* indicates one of the states of the counter and the arrows in the graph denote the order in which the states occur.

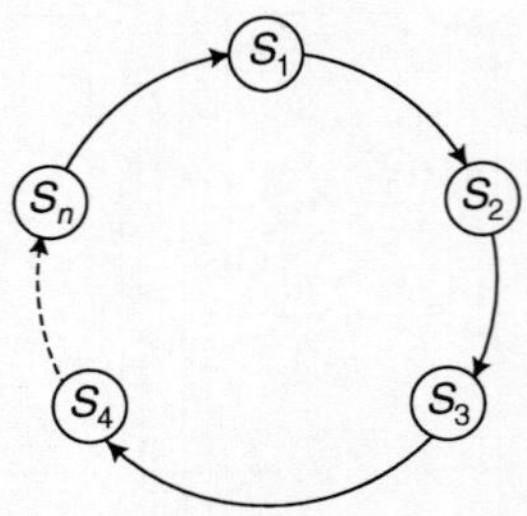

Fig. 6.12 State diagram of a mod-*n* counter

If counting sequence of the counters corresponds to that of binary numbers, the counters are called binary counters. The modulus of a binary counter is 2^n where *n* is the number of flip-flops in the counter. There are 2^n combinations of 0's and 1's consisting of *n* bits. For the case of binary up counter, the counting sequence 000…0 to 111…1. After reaching its maximum count, the counting sequence is repeated. The counting sequence for a binary down counter is 111… 1 to 000…0.

A four bit binary up-counter implemented with positive edge triggered *T* flip-flops is shown in Fig. 6.13. Each positive edge, i.e., from logic '0' to logic '1' on *C* input causes the flip-flop to toggle. Modulus of the counter is $2^4 = 16$ as this is four bit up counter and counting seuence is 0000 to 1111.

The input to the counter is a count enable signal and a series of count pulses applied to the *C* input of the leftmost flip-flop, i.e., the lowest order binary digit. The control input, i.e., *C* of the remaining flip-flops is connected to $\overline{Q}$ output of the previous order flip-flop.

The output of the counter appears at *Q* output terminals of four flip-flops.

With the count enable or *T* inputs held at logic '1' the output of each flip-flop toggles for every positive edge of the clock input, i.e., 0 to 1 transition of its clock inputs.

The second, third and fourth flip-flops change states on the 1 to 0 transition of the *Q* outputs of previous order flip-flops which correspond to the 0 to 1 transition of $\overline{Q}$ outputs. Figure 6.14 shows the timing diagram of 4-bit binary counter or modulus 16 counter

The counter is assumed to be initially in its 0000 states and count enable signal is logic '1' . This is shown in timing diagram as $Q_0\ Q_1\ Q_2\ Q_3$ output. Upon the occurrence of the positive edge of the first count pulse, Q_0 flip-flop changes its state.

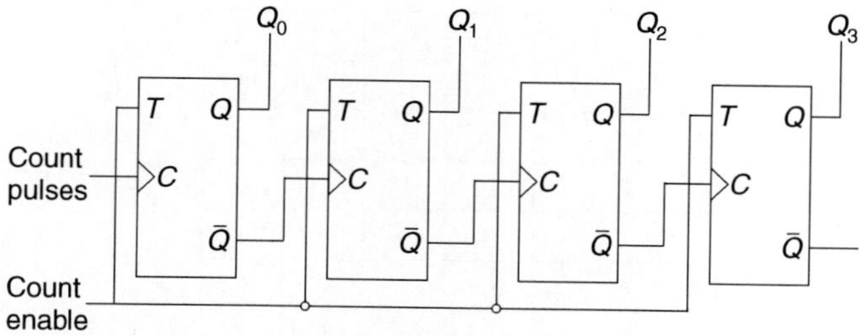

Fig. 6.13 4-bit binary ripple counter

Figure 6.14 should be modified as shown below.

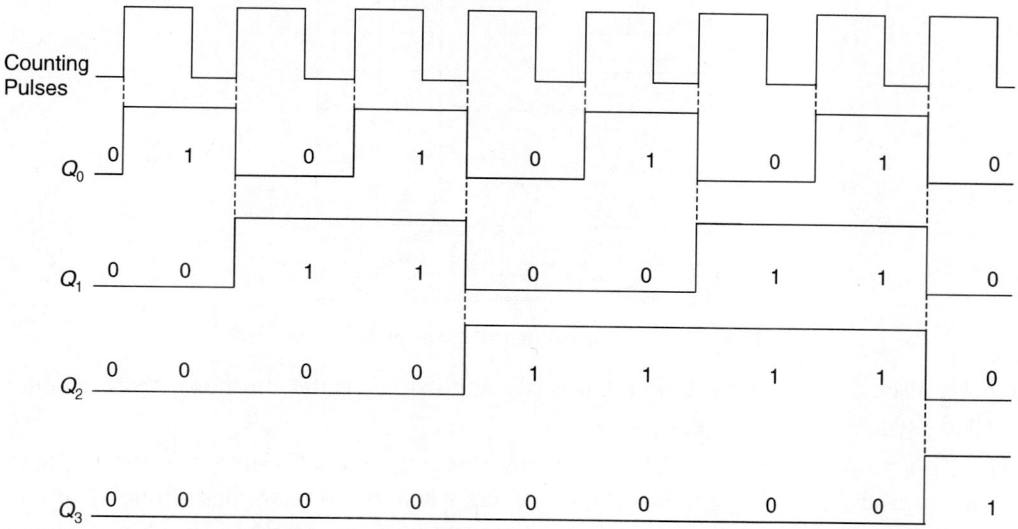

Fig. 6.14 Timing diagram of 4-bit binary up counter

Since $\overline{Q}_0$ output terminal goes from logic 1 to logic 0, flip-flop Q_1 is not affected by the input pulse. Now, the state of the counter, i.e., $Q_3\ Q_2\ Q_1\ Q_0$ is 0001 as observed in the timing diagram.

When the positive edge of the second count pulse arrives, Q_0 flip-flop again toggles. It returns to its 0 state. Since $\overline{Q}_0$ output goes from logic 0 to logic 1, a positive edge appears at the control input of Q_1 flip-flop and it causes Q_1 flip-flop to toggle. The change in Q_1 flip-flop does not affect Q_2 flip-flop since a negative edge occurs at its control input. Now at the end of second count pulse, the state of the counter, i.e., $Q_3\ Q_2\ Q_1\ Q_0$ is 0010 as observed in the timing diagram.

At the end of third count pulse, the state of the counter is 0011. Like this, the binary counting sequence continues until the count 1111 is reached as shown in Fig. 6.15.

At that time a count pulse causes Q_0 flip-flop to return to its 0 state. Consequently, this causes Q_1 flip-flop return to its '0' state. This, in turn, causes Q_2 flip-flop to return to its '0' state and finally Q_3 flip-flop returns to its '0' state. Thus, the state of the counter becomes 0000. If any more count pulses are applied to the counter then, the counting sequence is repeated.

These binary counters are called ripple counters because a change in state of Q_{i-1} flip-flop is used to toggle Q_i flip-flop. The effect of the count pulse must ripple through the counter. Since

Count pulse	Q_3	Q_2	Q_1	Q_0
0	0	0	0	0
1	0	0	0	1
2	0	0	1	0
3	0	0	1	1
4	0	1	0	0
5	0	1	0	1
6	0	1	1	0
7	0	1	1	1
8	1	0	0	0
9	1	0	0	1
10	1	0	1	0
11	1	0	1	1
12	1	1	0	0
13	1	1	0	1
14	1	1	1	0
15	1	1	1	1

Fig. 6.15 Counting sequence of 4 bit binary up counter

the clock pulses are not applied simultaneously applied to all the flip-flops, these counters are also called asynchronous counters.

There is a propagation delay t_{pd} between input and output of a flip-flop, the rippling behaviour affects the overall time delay. The worst case occurs when the counter goes through from its state 1111 to 0000. Since the toggle signals must propagate through the entire length of the counter.

In this case, the worst case setting time is $4 \times t_{pd}$. In general, for a n bit binary ripple counter the worst case setting time is $n \times t_{pd}$.

Example 6.2 Design a 4-bit binary ripple up counter using negative edge triggered *JK* flip-flops.

Solution If *J* and *K* inputs of *JK* flip-flop are tied together, the flip-flop behaves like a *T* flip-flop and it toggles at every negative edge of the clock input or 1 to 0 transition of the clock input.

A 4-bit binary ripple up counter using negative edge triggered *JK* flip-flop is shown in Fig. 6.16.

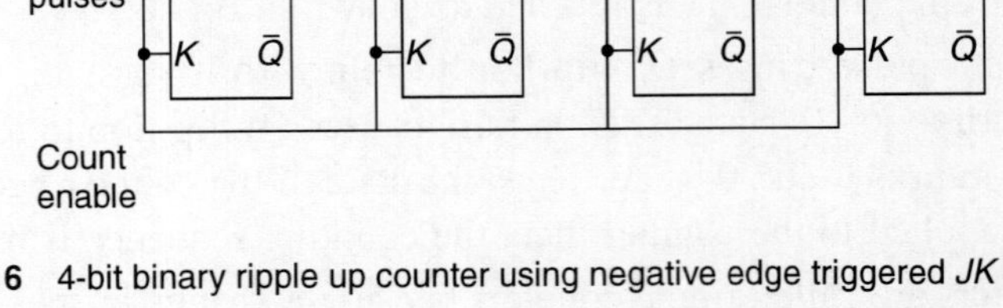

Fig. 6.16 4-bit binary ripple up counter using negative edge triggered *JK* flip-flops

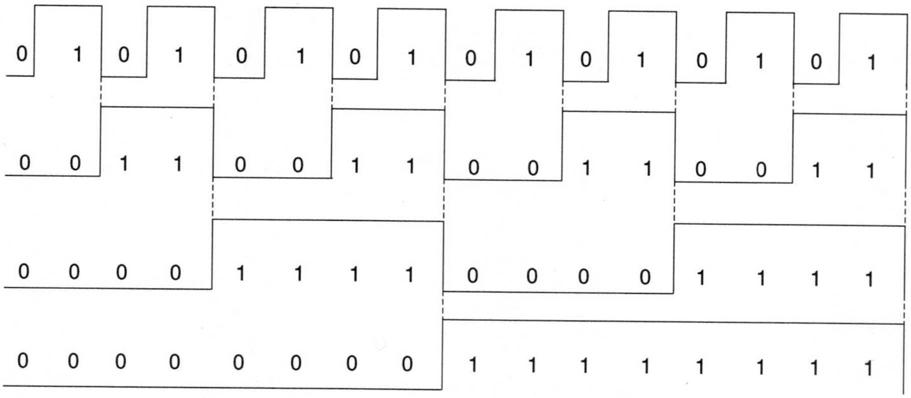

Fig. 6.17 Timing diagram of 4-bit binary ripple up counter using negative edge triggered *JK* flip-flop

Clock	Q_1	Q_2	Q_3	Output of reset logic *Y*
0	0	0	0	1
1	0	0	1	1
2	0	1	0	1
3	0	1	1	1
4	1	0	0	1
5	1	0	1	1
–	1	1	0	0
–	1	1	1	0

(a)

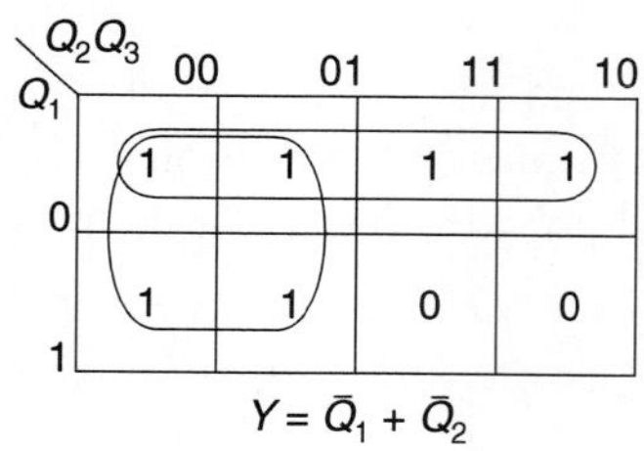

(b)

Fig. 6.18 Truth table for mod-6 ripple counter using *T* flip-flops and reset logic

Q output of each *JK* flip-flop is connected to the clock input of the next *JK* flip-flop. The *J* and *K* inputs of all the flip-flops are tied together and applied the count enable input. Count pulses are applied to the clock input of the first *JK* flip-flop.

This counter counts in the similar manner as shown in the timing diagram in Fig. 6.17. Again let us assume that initially $Q_3\, Q_2\, Q_1\, Q_0$ is at 0000 and the counter counts up to 1111 and finally returns to 0000 state and counting sequence repeats.

All flip-flops toggle their states at 0 to 1 transition of their clock signals.

Example 6.3 Design mod-6 ripple counter using *T* flip-flops.

Solution Number of flip-flops required for mod-6 counter, i.e., for 6 states is

$$2^n > N; 2^3 > 6; \therefore\ n = 3$$

Truth table for the counter is shown in Fig. 6.18 (a) and reset logic is shown in Fig. 6.18 (b). Implementation of mod-6 ripple counter using *T* flip-flop is shown in Fig. 6.19.

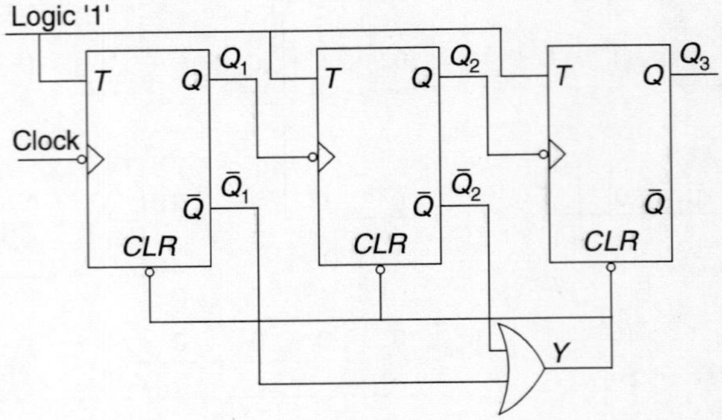

Fig. 6.19 Logic diagram of mod-6 ripple counter using *T* flip-flops

Example 6.4 Design a 4-bit binary ripple up counter using positive edge triggered *D* flip-flops without a count enable line.

Solution Fig. 6.20 shows the 4-bit binary ripple up counter using positive edge triggered *D* flip-flops. It also shows a single '*D*' flip-flop with its $\overline{Q}$ connected to its *D* input and the inputs *D* and clock *C* and its outputs *Q* and $\overline{Q}$. Let us assume initially $\overline{Q} = 1$ and hence $D = 1$. Now clock signal goes from 0 to 1 transition, *Q* becomes 1 and hence $\overline{Q} = 0$ and hence $D = 0$. But when next clock signal goes from 0 to 1 transition, *Q* becomes 0 and this process repeats.

When four '*D*' flip-flops are connected as shown in Fig. 6.20, the binary ripple up counter behaves as per the timing diagram shown in Fig. 6.21.

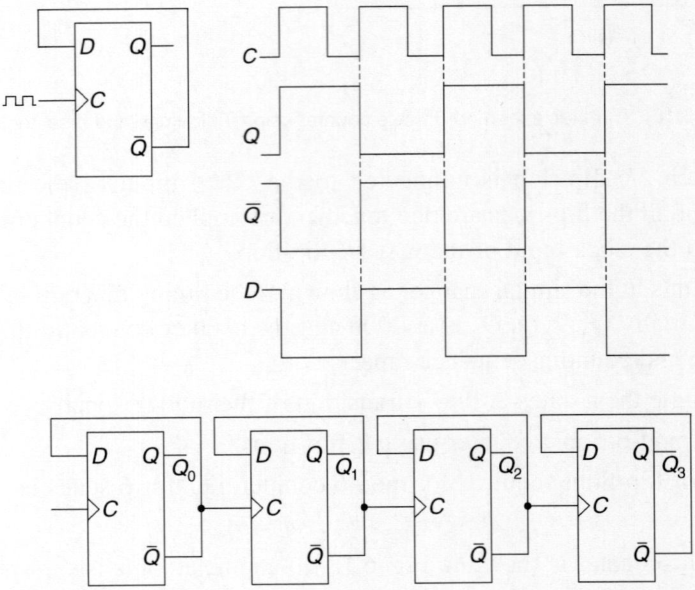

Fig. 6.20 4-bit binary ripple up counter using positive edge triggered *D* flip-flops

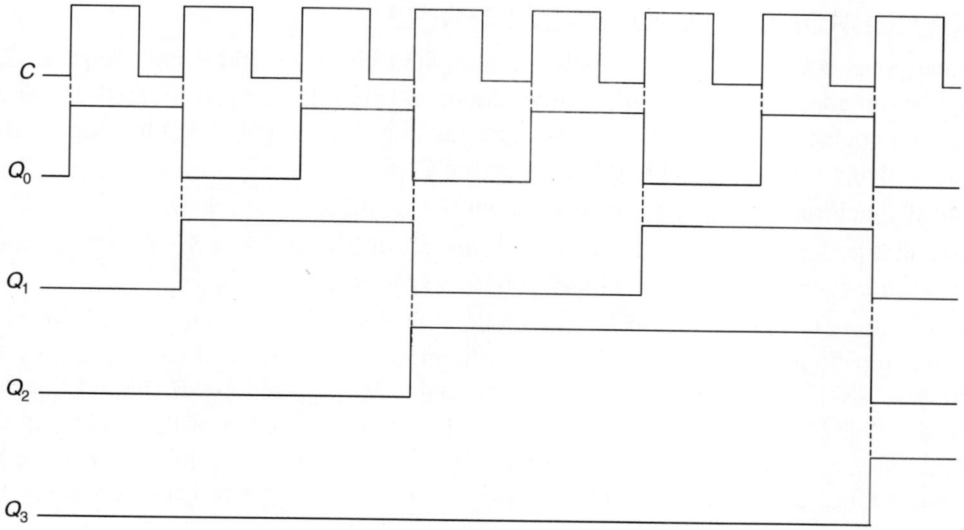

Fig. 6.21 Timing diagram for example 6.4

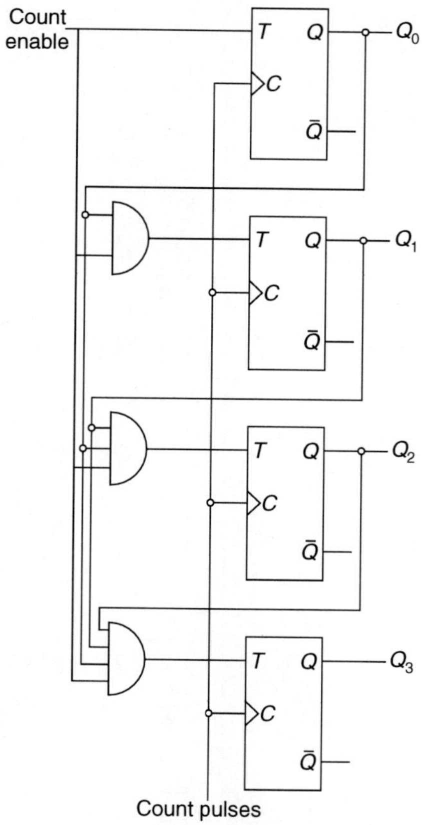

Fig. 6.22 4-bit synchronous binary counter

6.4 SYNCHRONOUS BINARY COUNTERS

For synchronous counters, the count pulses are applied directly to the control inputs, *C*, of all flip-flops simultaneously. The settling time associated with the ripple counters is avoided in synchronous counters. In synchronous counters, all flip-flops change simultaneously after the propagation delay time associated with a single flip-flop.

A 4-bit synchronous binary counter is shown in Fig. 6.22.

The count pulses are applied to the control input *C* of each clocked flip-flop. If count enable is logic '1', the counter follows the binary counting sequence.

The flip-flop Q_0 toggles with every clock pulse. The other flip-flops toggle, whenever all the lower order flip-flops are at 1. The flip-flop Q_3 toggles when its lower flip-flops Q_0, Q_1 and Q_2 are at 1. The AND gate has 4 inputs, i.e., count enable, Q_0, Q_1 and Q_2. If these 4 inputs are 1, then the flip-flop Q_3 toggles upon the occurrence of the positive edge of the count pulse. Since the count pulses are applied directly to each flip-flop, the only delay occurs between application of the count pulse and availability of the new count output is the propagation delay time of a flip-flop.

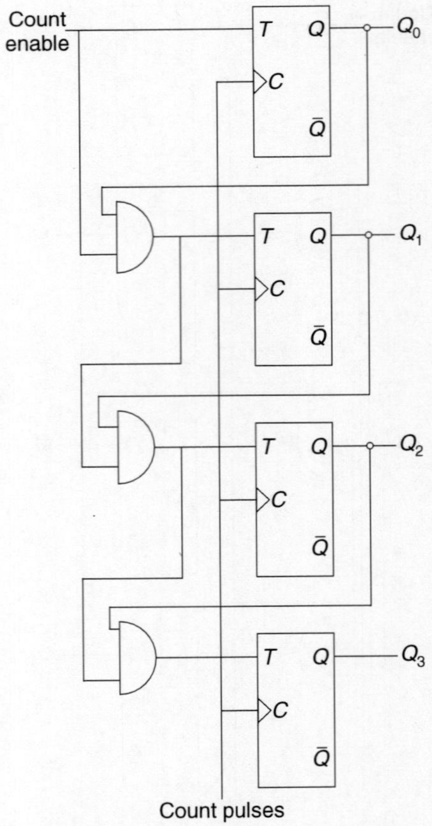

Fig. 6.23 4-bit synchronous counter with 2 input AND gates

There are three inputs to the AND gate connected to Q_3 flip-flop. There are m inputs to the AND gate connected to Q_m flip-flop. If the number of flip-flops is large, the lower order flip-flops must drive a large number of AND gates. This may introduce loading problems. Figure 6.23 shows the same 4-bit synchronous binary counter but with AND gates which have only two inputs and the output of each flip-flop is only needed as an input to the next stage AND gate.

The two inputs to AND gate are the output of the previous flip-flop and output of the previous AND gate. The synchronous counters are faster than asynchronous counters. It is the gate delays and flip-flop propagation delay in a synchronous counter that determine the rate at which count pulses can be applied.

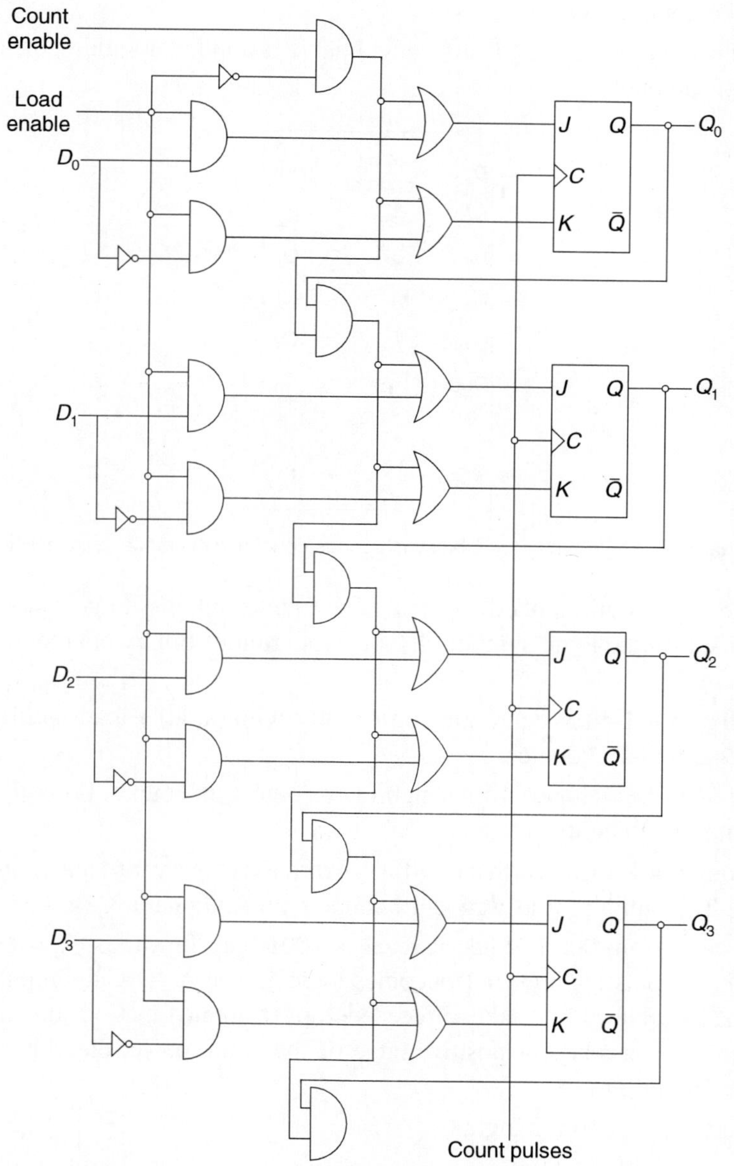

Fig. 6.24 4-bit synchronous counter with parallel load facility

A mod 2^n counter can be used as a mod-m counter where $m < 2^n$, if we provide a facility to parallel load an initial binary number.

JK flip-flops are used instead of *T* flip-flops to facilitate the handling of parallel load inputs as shown in Fig. 6.24.

Two enable signals are used. One facilitates parallel loading of data inputs D_0, D_1, D_2 and D_3 and the other facilitates counting. Both load and count operations are synchronized with the positive edges of the count pulse. If a logic 1 is on load signal, regardless of the signal value on the count enable line, the data inputs D_0, D_1, D_2 and D_3 are entered into the four flip-flops of the counter upon the occurrence of positive edge of count pulse. Thus, load function takes precedence over the count function.

If load enable is applied a logic '0' and count enable is applied a logic 1, the counter behaves as a normal binary up counter.

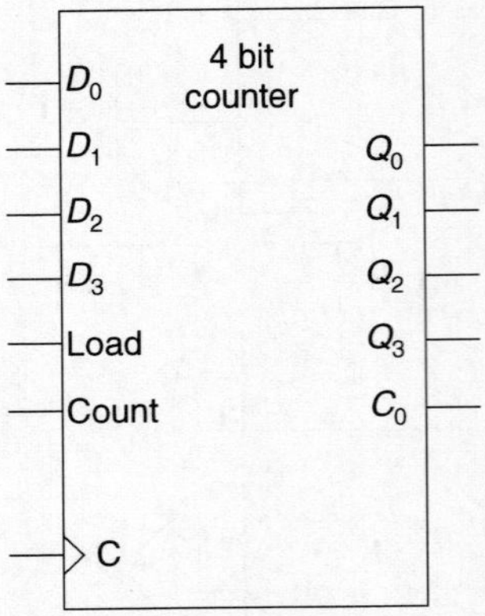

Fig. 6.25 Logic symbol of 4-bit synchronous counter with parallel load facility

If both enable signals are applied logic '0' the counter retains its current state as *J* and *K* are 0. Figure 6.25 shows the logic symbol of 4-bit synchronous binary counter with parallel load facility.

Example 6.5 Configure a 4-bit synchronous up counter with parallel load facility to count form 0000 to 1001, i.e., a mod-10 counter.

Solution Figure 6.26 shows how a 4-bit synchronous binary up counter is configured to function as a mod-10 counter, i.e., decimal counter.

The normal counting sequence is that of 4-bit synchronous binary up counter when count enable is applied logic 1. To configure it as a mod-10 counter, an AND gate is used to detect 1001.

The counter starts from 0000. When it reaches 1001, i.e., flip-flops $Q_0 = Q_3 = 1$, the AND gate output to which inputs $Q_0 = Q_3 = 1$ becomes logic 1. The AND gate output is connected to load enable. If load enable = 1, it takes precedence over count function, the counter is loaded with 0000. Upon the occurrence of positive edge of the count pulse, the values on the parallel inputs are D_0, D_1, D_2 and D_3.

D_0, D_1, D_2 and D_3 are applied logic 0.

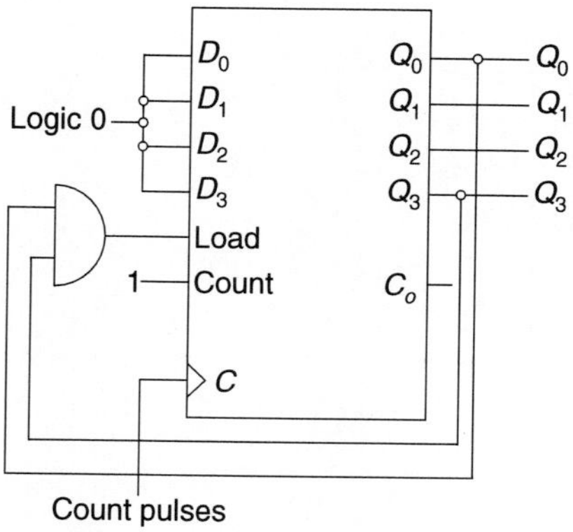

Fig. 6.26 Mod 10 counter

Count	Q_3	Q_2	Q_1	Q_0
0	0	0	0	0
1	0	0	0	1
2	0	0	1	0
3	0	0	1	1
4	0	1	0	0
5	0	1	0	1
6	0	1	1	0
7	0	1	1	1
8	1	0	0	0
9	1	0	0	1
0	0	0	0	0

Fig. 6.27 Counting sequence of mode 10 counter

Now, the counting sequence is 0000, 0001......1001, 0000, etc., as shown in Fig. 6.27. Thus, the counter becomes a decade counter or mod-10 counter.

There is a carry output C_0 which becomes logic 1 whenever the counter state is 1111 and counter is in its count mode.

Example 6.6 Configure an 8-bit synchronous binary up counter using two 4-bit synchronous counters.

Solution The connections necessary to construct an 8-bit binary counter is shown in Fig. 6.28. When the state of the top 4-bit binary counter is 1111, its carry output signal C_0 is 1. This C_0 output signal is applied to the count enable input of the bottom 4-bit binary counter that is used for four most significant binary digits of the 8-bit binary counter. Upon the occurrence of the positive edge of the next count pulse, the top 4-bit counter returns to 0000 state, while the bottom 4 bit counter is incremented by 1.

Example 6.7 Design a 4-bit synchronous down counter using T flip-flops.

Solution A 4-bit synchronous binary up counter has the Q output of Q_0 flip-flop toggling for every count pulse and $\overline{Q}$ output of Q_0 flip-flop toggles for every count pulse.

The two inputs of the AND gates are $\overline{Q}$ output of previous order flip-flop and the output of AND gate of previous stage. The 4-bit synchronous binary down counter is shown in Fig. 6.29 and the counting sequence is shown in Fig. 6.30.

Example 6.8 Design a 4-bit synchronous binary up/down counter using. T flip-flops, having a count enable input and a up/$\overline{\text{down}}$ control input.

Solution Figure 6.31 shows the 4-bit synchronous binary up/$\overline{\text{down}}$ counter. There are two 2 input AND gates. The inputs of the top AND gate are count enable and up/$\overline{\text{down}}$ enable and the inputs of bottom AND gate are count enable and inverted up/$\overline{\text{down}}$ enable. Thus, the top AND gate is used for up enable and the bottom AND gate is used for down enable. Both up enable and down enable are applied to the OR gate and through that to T input. Depending on the up enable or down enable input, the synchronous counter count up or counts down.

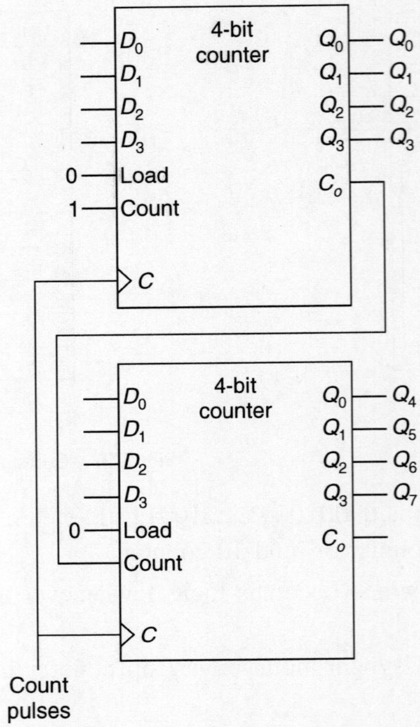

Fig. 6.28 8-bit synchronous binary up counter

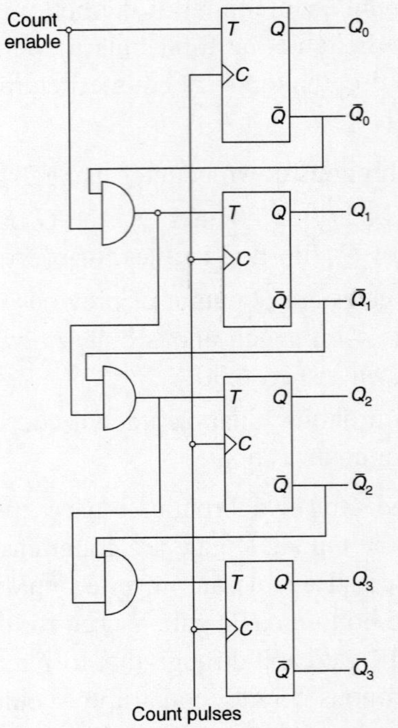

Fig. 6.29 4-bit synchronous binary down counter

Counting sequence of up counter					Counting sequence of down counter			
Count pulse	Q_3	Q_2	Q_1	Q_0	$\overline{Q}_3$	$\overline{Q}_2$	$\overline{Q}_1$	$\overline{Q}_0$
0	0	0	0	0	1	1	1	1
1	0	0	0	1	1	1	1	0
2	0	0	1	0	1	1	0	1
3	0	0	1	1	1	1	0	0
4	0	1	0	0	1	0	1	1
5	0	1	0	1	1	0	1	0
6	0	1	1	0	1	0	0	1
7	0	1	1	1	1	0	0	0
8	1	0	0	0	0	1	1	1
9	1	0	0	1	0	1	1	0
10	1	0	1	0	0	1	0	1
11	1	0	1	1	0	1	0	0
12	1	1	0	0	0	0	1	1
13	1	1	0	1	0	0	1	0
14	1	1	1	0	0	0	0	1
15	1	1	1	1	0	0	0	0

Fig. 6.30 Counting sequence of binary up/down counter

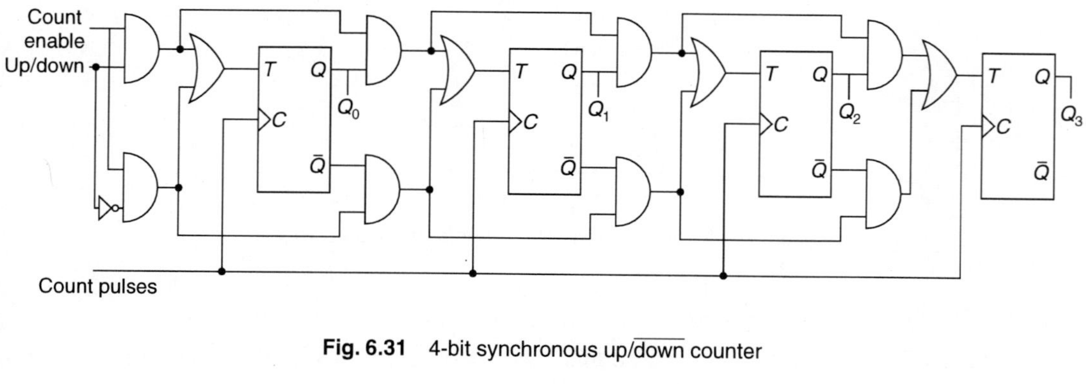

Fig. 6.31 4-bit synchronous up/$\overline{\text{down}}$ counter

Example 6.9 Design a mod-6 synchronous counter to sequence the first 6 states from 0000 to 0101 and repeat using a 4-bit synchronous counter with parallel load facility.

Solution Once the counter output reaches 0101, it has to be reset, i.e., Q_2 and Q_0 outputs are ANDed and applied to load input. Once the load input is 1, then 0000 is loaded into the counter. Fig. 6.32 shows the mod-6 synchronous counter.

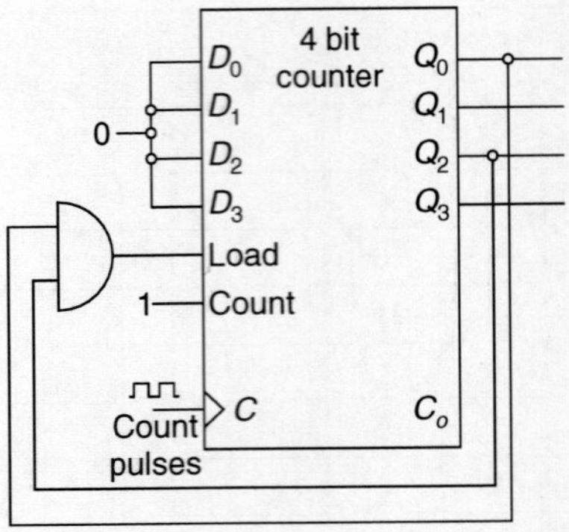

Fig. 6.32 Mod-6 synchronous counter

Example 6.10 Design a mod-4 synchronous counter to sequence last 5 states from 1100 to 1111 and repeat from 1100.

Solution When the count 1111 is reached, 1100 has to be reloaded. Reaching the count 1111 is indicated by $C_0 = 1$ and this is used as the load input. When load input is 1, 1100 is loaded at $D_3\ D_2\ D_1\ D_0$. This is depicted in Fig. 6.33.

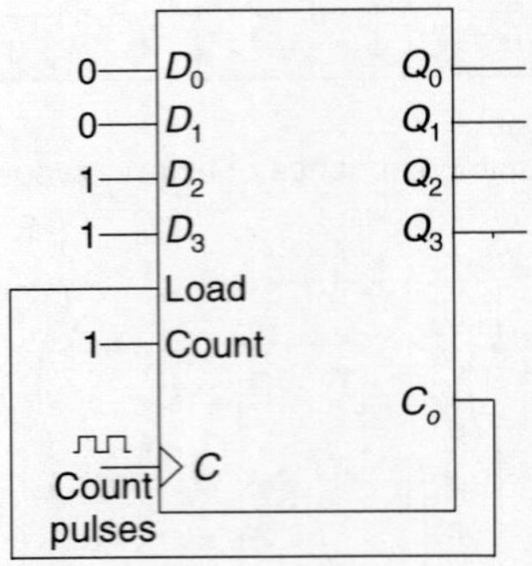

Fig. 6.33 Mod-4 synchronous counter for example 6.10

Example 6.11 Design a mod-88 synchronous counter by using two 4 bit binary counters.

Solution Mod-88 synchronous counter counts from 0000 to 87 decimal. Hence, there are 88 states.

$$87D = 01010111\ B$$

When the output reaches 01010111, the counters must be reset to 0000. This mod-88 synchronous counter is shown in Fig. 6.34.

Here Q_3, Q_4 and Q_6 outputs are ANDed and applied to both load inputs. C_0 output of top counter is given to count input of bottom counter. Top counter count input is 1. D_0, D_1, D_2 and D_3 of both counters are given 0.

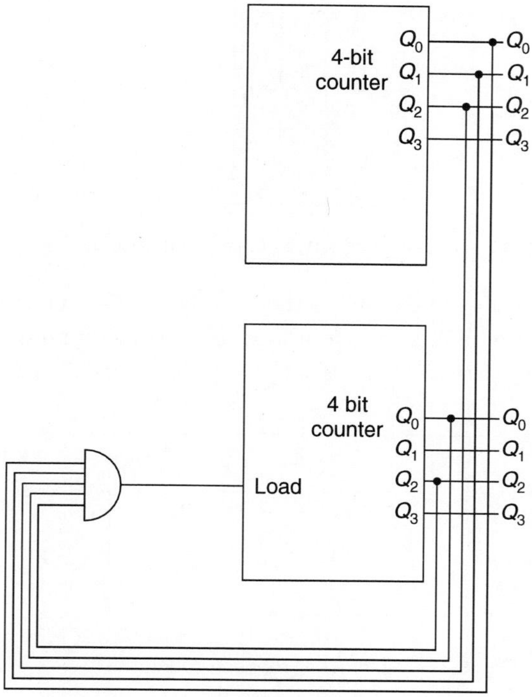

Fig. 6.34 Mod-88 synchronous counter

6.5 COUNTER BASED ON SHIFT REGISTERS

Non-binary counters based on shift registers are the ring counter and switch-tail counter. A ring counter is a circular shift register which is initialised such that only one of its flip-flops is in the '1' state. While other flip-flops are in their '0' states. Figure 6.35 shows a ring counter. This configuration serves as a mod-4 ring counter.

Upon the occurrence of each count pulse, a signal 1 is shifted to its adjacent flip-flop. A ring counter consisting of n flip-flops has only 'n' states in its counting sequence.

The counting sequence of mod-4 ring counter is shown in Fig. 6.36.

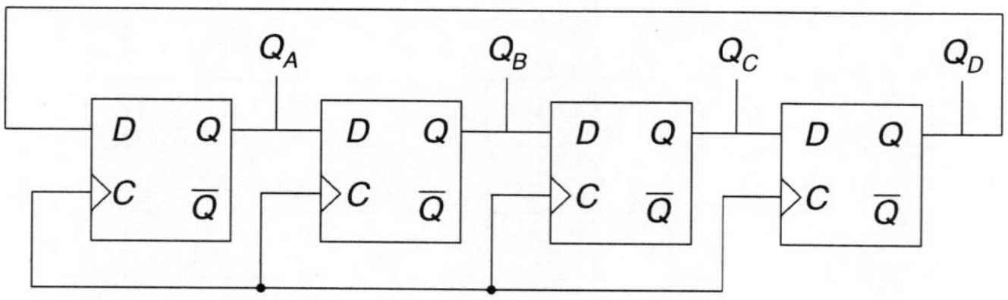

Fig. 6.35 Mod-4 ring counter

Q_A	Q_B	Q_C	Q_D
1	0	0	0
0	1	0	0
0	0	1	0
0	0	0	1
1	0	0	0

Fig. 6.36 Counting sequence of mod-4 ring counter

Johnson counter: A variation of ring counter is the switch-tail counter. It is also called twisted ring counter or Johnson counter which is shown in Fig. 6.37. The counting sequence is shown in Fig. 6.38 assuming the counter starts in $Q_A\ Q_B\ Q_C\ Q_D$ = 0000 state.

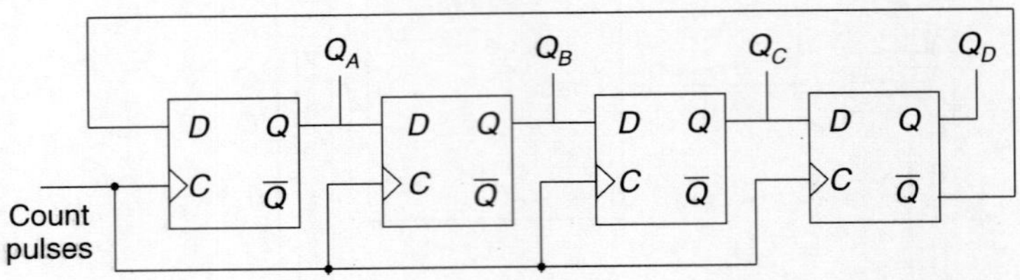

Fig. 6.37 4-bit mod-8 Johnson counter

In Johnson counter, the complement of the rightmost flip-flop serves as the input to the leftmost flip-flop in the shift-right register configuration. As a consequence, $2n$ state occur in the counting sequence of an n-stage counter. For a 4 bit Johnson counter, 2 × 4 = 8 states occur in the counting sequence which is shown in Fig. 6.38 along with AND gates required for detecting the state.

Q_A	Q_B	Q_C	Q_D	AND gate inputs required for detecting the state	
$\underline{0}$	0	0	$\underline{0}$	$\overline{Q_A}$	$\overline{Q_D}$
$\underline{1}$	$\underline{0}$	0	0	Q_A	$\overline{Q_B}$
1	$\underline{1}$	$\underline{0}$	0	Q_B	$\overline{Q_C}$
1	1	$\underline{1}$	$\underline{0}$	Q_C	$\overline{Q_D}$
$\underline{1}$	1	1	$\underline{1}$	Q_A	Q_D
$\underline{0}$	$\underline{1}$	1	1	$\overline{Q_A}$	Q_B
0	$\underline{0}$	$\underline{1}$	1	$\overline{Q_B}$	Q_C
0	0	$\underline{0}$	$\underline{1}$	$\overline{Q_C}$	Q_D
0	0	0	0		

Fig. 6.38 Counting sequence of Johnson counter along with AND gate inputs required for detecting the state

Unlike the ring counter, to detect any particular state in the counting sequence of a twisted ring counter, it is necessary to incorporate some logic elements. The timing sequence for a 4-bit Johnson counter is shown in Fig. 6.39.

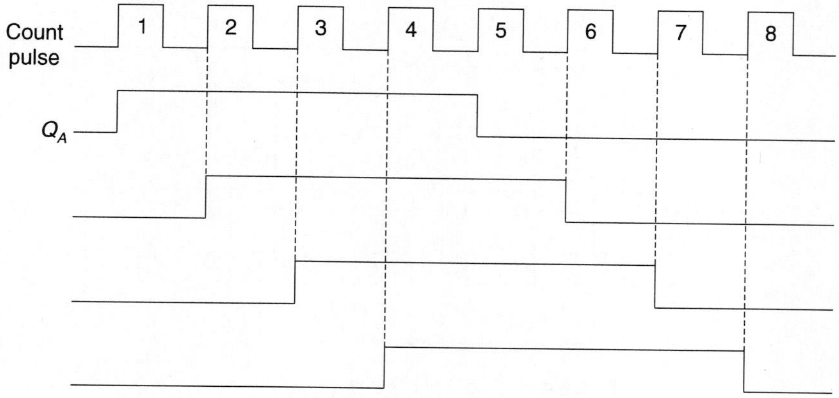

Fig. 6.39 Timing sequence for 4-bit Johnson counter

Fig. 6.40 shows a 4-bit Johnson counter with decoder. Referring to the counting sequence, the underlined pairs of bits uniquely determine a state. Thus, only a two-input AND gate is required to obtain a decoded output. A twisted ring counter having the above configuration always has an even number of states in its counting sequence.

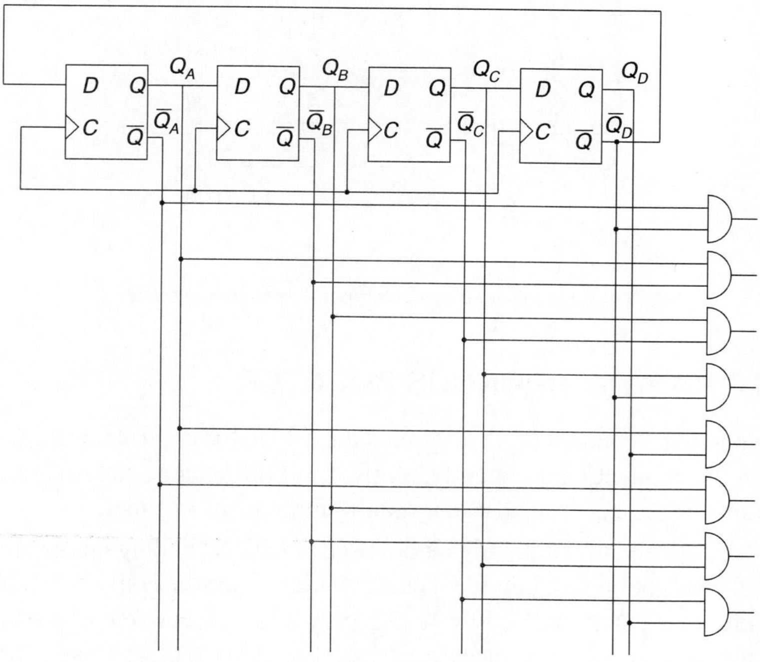

Fig. 6.40 Johnson counter with decoder

A twisted ring counter having an odd number of states is shown in Fig. 6.41. In this variation the state consisting of all 1's is eliminated from the counting sequence as shown in Fig. 6.42. This is achieved by connecting $\overline{Q}_C\,\overline{Q}_D$ to the input of the leftmost *D* flip-flop. Again each state is decoded by the use of two input AND-gates.

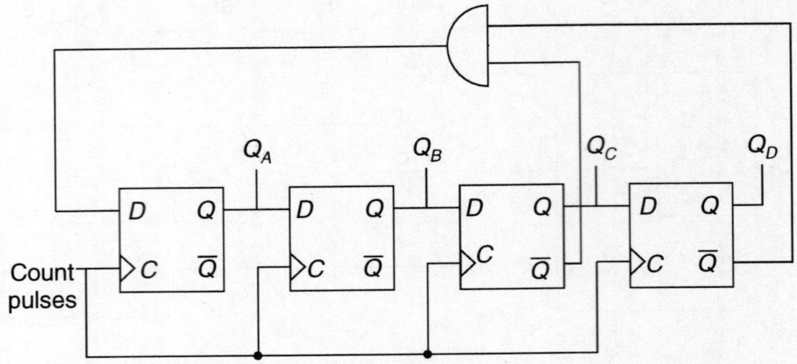

FIG. 6.41 Mod-7 twisted ring counter

Q_A	Q_B	Q_C	Q_D	AND gate inputs	
0	0	0	0	$\overline{Q}_A$	$\overline{Q}_D$
1	0	0	0	Q_A	$\overline{Q}_B$
1	1	0	0	Q_B	$\overline{Q}_C$
1	1	1	0	Q_C	$\overline{Q}_D$
0	1	1	1	$\overline{Q}_A$	Q_B
0	0	1	1	$\overline{Q}_B$	Q_C
0	0	0	1	$\overline{Q}_C$	Q_D
0	0	0	0		

Fig. 6.42 Counting sequence of mod-7 twisted ring conter

6.6 DESIGN OF A SYNCHRONOUS COUNTER

In synchronous counter, the count pulses are applied directly to the control inputs, *C* of the clocked flip-flops that form the counter. Consequently, all the flip-flops change states simultaneously and the changed state of the counter is available in minimum amount of time.

Counters can be designed to output any random sequence. Depending on the application other types of counters also might be required like counter which sequences only even numbers or only odd numbers or one that counts according to the grey code. A counter is a pattern generator in which the counting sequence produces a series of various patterns. Non-binary counting sequences may often be desirable. Synchronous counters can be designed using *JK* flip-flops, *D* flip-flops, *T* flip-flops or *SR* flip-flops.

6.7 DESIGN OF SYNCHRONOUS MOD-6 COUNTER USING CLOCKED *JK* FLIP-FLOPS

Let us assume a counting sequence as shown in Fig. 6.43 to illustrate the design of mod-6 counter using *JK* flip-flops.

Q_1	Q_2	Q_3
0	0	0
0	1	0
0	1	1
1	1	0
1	0	1
0	0	1
0	0	0

Fig. 6.43 A mod-6 counting sequence

A general structure of the three clocked *JK* flip-flops that have the count pulses applied directly to their control inputs *C* as shown in Fig. 6.44. The function of the combinational logic circuit is to generate proper signals for *J* and *K* inputs of the clocked flip-flops so that the specified next state in the counting sequence is available upon the occurrence of the triggering edge of a count pulse. Proper logic circuit has to be designed.

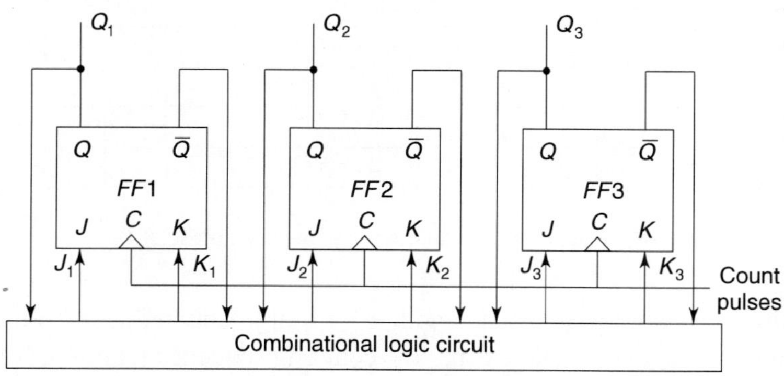

Fig. 6.44 General structure of a mod-6 counter using *JK* flip-flops

In order to do this, we need an application table for clocked *JK* flip-flop which is derived from its next state table. Application table gives the *J* and *K* inputs required for a particular output change. Both function table and application table are shown in Fig. 6.45.

Logic structure of the combinational logic circuit can be described by Boolean expressions for each of the six inputs to the flip-flop in terms of Boolean variables Q_1, Q_2 and Q_3 that are the present state of the counter.

J	K	Q^+	$\overline{Q^+}$
0	0	Q	$\overline{Q}$
0	1	0	1
1	0	1	0
1	1	$\overline{Q}$	Q

Function table

Q	Q^+	J	K
0	0	0	–
0	1	1	–
1	0	–	1
1	1	–	0

Application table for a clocked *JK* flip-flop

Fig. 6.45

In order to obtain these expressions, a truth table for the combinational logic circuit called an excitation table is constructed. Excitation table consists of three sections, namely, present state, next state and flip-flop inputs. It gives the flip-flop inputs for generation of the next states from the present states as shown in Fig. 6.46. We will write all possible states for a 3-flip-flop counter in the present state.

Present state			Next state			Flip-flop inputs					
Q_1	Q_2	Q_3	Q_1^+	Q_2^+	Q_3^+	J_1	K_1	J_2	K_2	J_3	K_3
0	0	0	0	1	0	0	–	1	–	0	–
0	0	1	0	0	0	–	1	0	–	0	–
0	1	0	0	1	1	1	–	–	0	0	–
0	1	1	1	1	0	–	1	–	0	1	–
1	0	0	+	–	+	–	–	–	–	–	–
1	0	1	0	0	1	–	0	0	–	–	1
1	1	0	1	0	1	1	–	–	1	–	0
1	1	1	–	–	–	–	–	–	–	–	–

Fig. 6.46 Excitation table for counting sequence of Fig. 6.43

Excitation table shows all possible states with a 3-flip-flop counter as the present states. For every present state, the next state is taken as per the counting sequence required. Next state which does not figure in the desired sequence is marked as don't-care.

From the excitation table for the synchronous mod-6 counter, the logic signals that must be applied to the three flip-flops in order to get a desired next state for a particular present state.

For example, for the present state $Q_1\ Q_2\ Q_3 = 000$, the next state $Q_1^+\ Q_2^+\ Q_3^+ = 010$, i.e., Q_1 must remain in its '0' state. As shown in the application table, Q to remain in '0' state, $J_1 = 0$, $K_1 = –$. Hence, these two inputs become the first two entries (J_1 and K_1) in the first row of the flip-flop input section. Similarly, flip-flop Q_2 must go from '0' state to '1' for which $J_2 = 1$ and $K_2 = –$ from the application table. Flip-flop Q_3 must remain in its '0' state for which $J_3 = 0$ and $K_3 =$ – as per the application table. The remaining entries in the flip-flop input section are determined in a similar manner.

The inputs to the combinational logic circuit correspond to the present state section of the excitation table and the outputs correspond to the flip-flop input section of the excitation table. Hence, the truth table for combinational logic circuit is the first and third section of the excitation table.

Using these two sections, six K-maps drawn for each of the flip-flop inputs as shown in Fig. 6.47.

Using the flip-flop input values, and the present state, we can implement the mod-6 synchronous counter as shown in Fig. 6.48.

6.8 DESIGN OF A SYNCHRONOUS MOD-6 COUNTER, USING CLOCKED *D, T* AND *SR* FLIP-FLOPS

6.8.1 Design of a Synchronous mod-6 Counter Using Clocked *D* Flip-flop

Referring to the *D* flip-flop next state table shown in Fig. 6.49, *D* flip-flop application table is shown in Fig. 6.50.

Let us assume the counting sequence of the counter for mod-6 synchronous counting using *D* flip-flops as shown in Fig. 6.51. For mod-6 synchronous counter, we need at least 3-flip-flops.

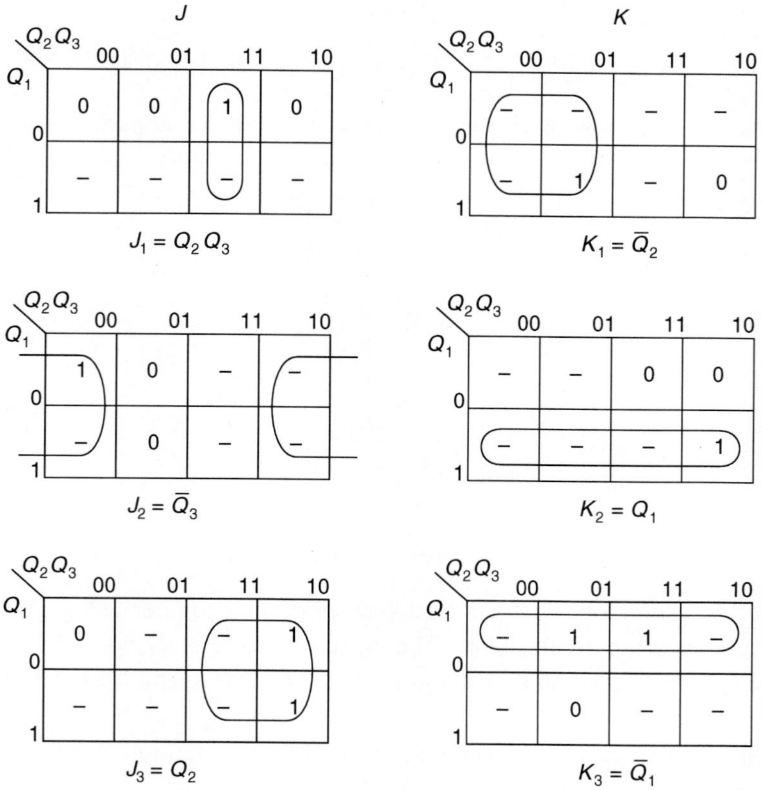

Fig. 6.47 K-maps for the simplification of flip-flop inputs

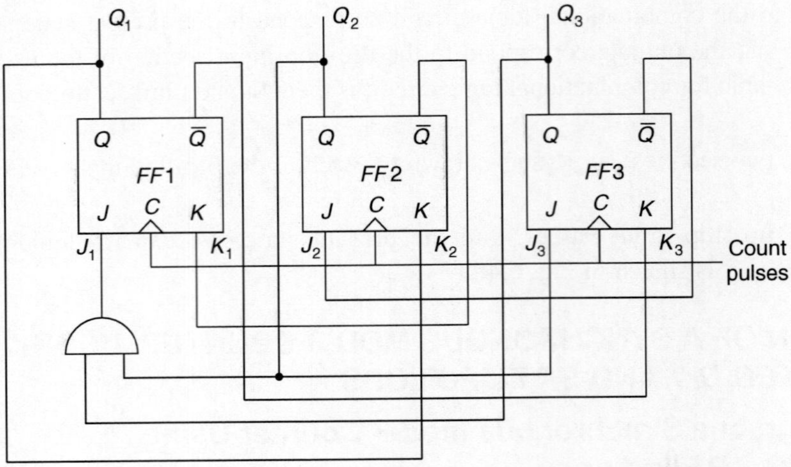

Fig. 6.48 Implementation of mod-6 synchronous counter using clocked *JK* flip-flop.

D	Q	Q⁺
0	0	0
0	1	0
1	0	1
1	1	1

Fig. 6.49 Next state table of *D* flip-flop

Q	Q⁺	D
0	0	0
0	1	1
1	0	0
1	1	1

Fig. 6.50 Application table of *D* flip-flop

Q_1	Q_2	Q_3
0	0	0
0	1	0
0	1	1
1	1	0
1	0	1
0	0	1
0	0	0

Fig. 6.51 Desired counting sequence.

We can write the excitation table for mod-6 synchronous counter using *D* flip-flop similar to design of the counter using *JK* flip-flops. The excitation table is shown in Fig. 6.52. From the excitation table, let us now draw the K-maps to simplify the expression for the *D* inputs as shown in Fig. 6.53.

The implementations of mod-6 synchronous counter using *D* flip-flops is shown in Fig. 6.54.

Present state			Next state			Flip-flop inputs		
Q_1	Q_2	Q_3	Q_1^+	Q_2^+	Q_3^+	D_1	D_2	D_3
0	0	0	0	1	0	0	1	0
0	0	1	0	0	0	0	0	0
0	1	0	0	1	1	0	1	1
0	1	1	1	1	0	1	1	0
1	0	0	–	–	–	–	–	–
1	0	1	0	0	1	0	0	1
1	1	0	1	0	1	1	0	1
1	1	1	–	–	–	–	–	–

Fig. 6.52 Excitation table for design of mod-6 counter using *D* flip-flops

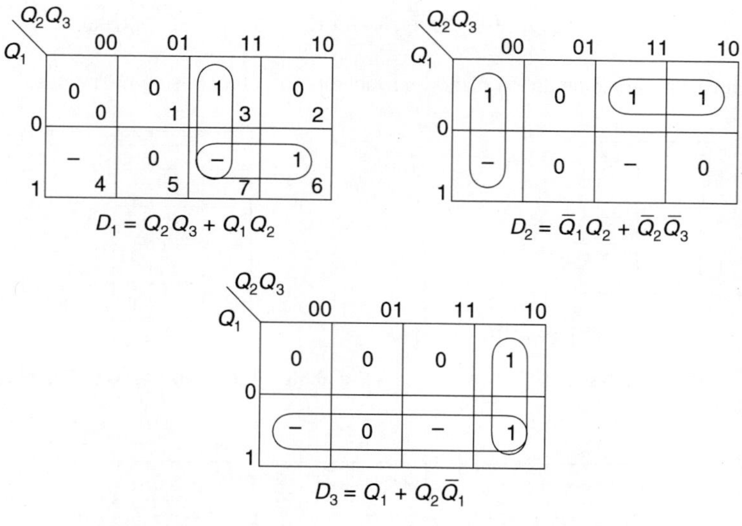

Fig. 6.53 K-maps for mod-6 synchronous counter using *D* flip-flops

6.8.2 Design of a Synchronous Mod-6 Counter Using T Flip-flops

As earlier, we need three flip-flops to design a mod-6 counter. The next state table and the application table of *T* flip-flops are shown in Fig. 6.55 and Fig. 6.56 respectively.

The excitation table for design of a mod-6 synchronous counter using clocked *T* flip-flops is shown in Fig. 6.57. The counting sequence is considered same as earlier.

The K-maps for the inputs to *T* flip-flops is shown in Fig. 6.58.

Using the flip-flop input values, and the present states, we can implement the mod-6 synchronous counter using *T* flip-flops as shown in Fig. 6.59.

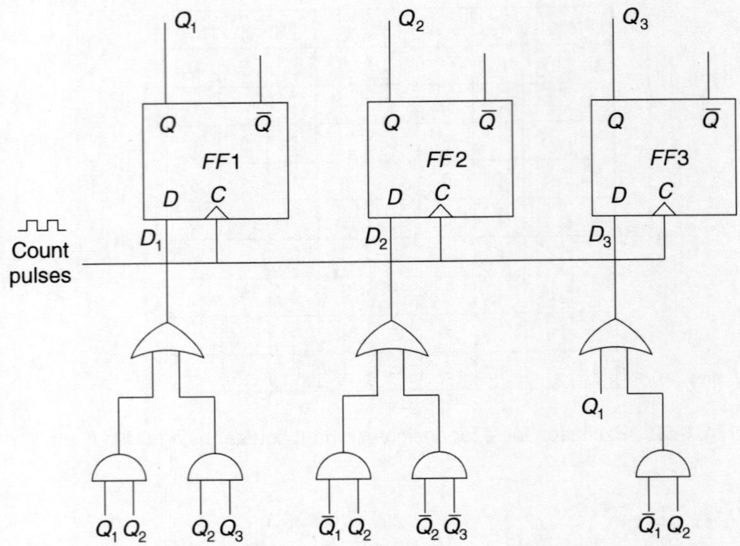

Fig. 6.54 Implementation of mod-6 synchronous counter using *D* flip-flops.

T	*Q*	Q^+
0	0	0
0	1	1
1	0	1
1	1	0

Fig. 6.55 Next state table of *T* flip-flop

Q	Q^+	*T*
0	0	0
0	1	1
1	0	1
1	1	0

Fig. 6.56 Application table of *T* flip-flop

Present state			Next state			Flip-flop inputs		
Q_1	Q_2	Q_3	Q_1^+	Q_2^+	Q_3^+	T_1	T_2	T_3
0	0	0	0	1	0	0	1	0
0	0	1	0	0	0	0	0	1
0	1	0	0	1	1	0	0	1
0	1	1	1	1	0	1	0	1
1	0	0	–	–	–	–	–	–
1	0	1	0	0	1	1	0	0
1	1	0	1	0	1	0	1	1
1	1	1	–	–	–	–	–	–

Fig. 6.57 Excitation table for mod-6 synchronous counter using *T* flip-flops

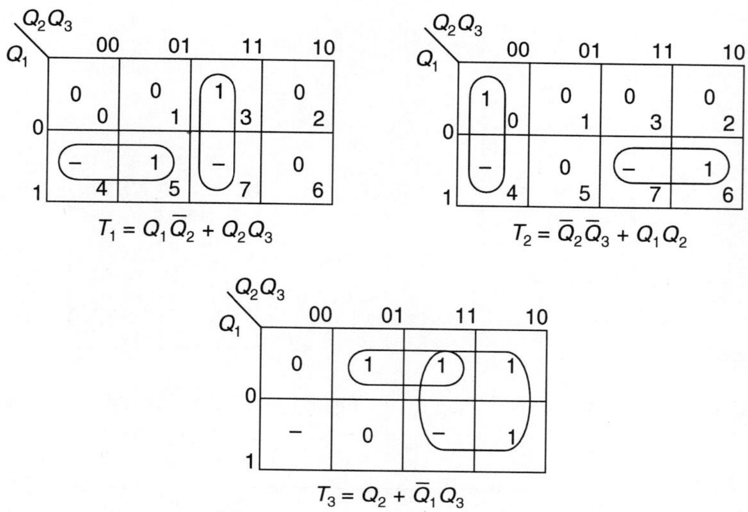

Fig. 6.58 K-maps for Fig. 6.57

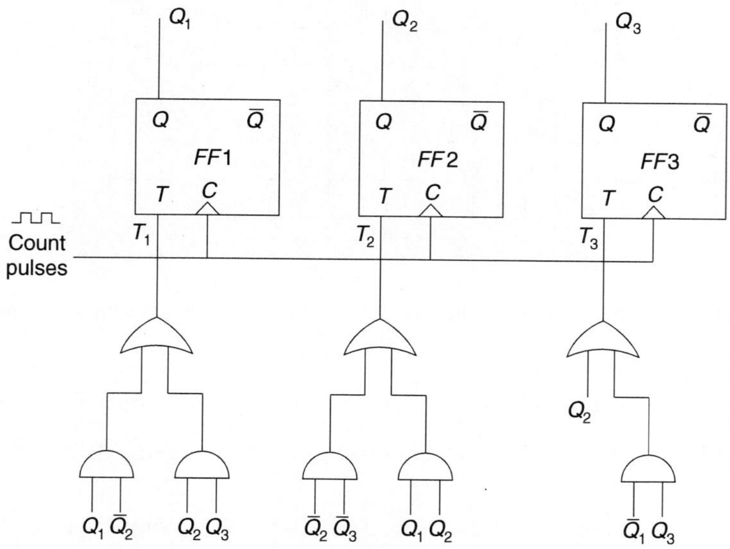

Fig. 6.59 Implementation of mod-6 synchronous counter using *T* flip-flops

6.8.3 Design of a Synchronous Mod-6 Counter Using *SR* Flip-flops

The next state table and the application table of *SR* flip-flop are shown in Fig. 6.60 and Fig. 6.61 respectively. We need minimum of three flip-flops to design a mod-6 counter. The excitation table for design of a mod-6 counter using clocked *SR* flip-flops is shown in Fig. 6.62. The counting sequence is same as earlier.

S	R	Q	Q^+
0	0	0	0
0	0	1	1
0	1	0	0
0	1	1	0
1	0	0	1
1	0	1	1
1	1	0	–
1	1	1	–

Unpredictable

Fig. 6.60 Next state table of *SR* flip-flop

Q	Q^+	S	R
0	0	0	–
0	1	1	0
1	0	0	1
1	1	–	0

Fig. 6.61 Application table of *SR* flip-flop

Present state			Next state			Flip-flop inputs					
Q_1	Q_2	Q_3	Q_1^+	Q_2^+	Q_3^+	S_1	R_1	S_2	R_2	S_3	R_3
0	0	0	0	1	0	0	–	1	0	0	–
0	0	1	0	0	0	0	–	0	–	0	1
0	1	0	0	1	1	0	–	–	0	1	0
0	1	1	1	1	0	1	0	–	0	0	1
1	0	0	–	–	–	–	–	–	–	–	–
1	0	1	0	0	1	0	1	0	–	–	0
1	1	0	1	0	1	–	0	0	1	1	0
1	1	1	–	–	–	–	–	–	–	–	–

Fig. 6.62 Excitation table for design of mod-6 synchronous counter using *SR* flip-flops

K-maps for inputs of SR flip-flops are drawn as shown in Fig. 6.63.

The implementation of mod-6 synchronous counter using *SR* flip-flops is shown in Fig. 6.64.

Example 6.12 Design and implement a divide by 10 asynchronous counters using $T\ FF^S$.

(VTU – Dec 2012)

Solution Firstly, we have to determine the number of flip-flops required to implement a divide by 10 counter. There will be 0 to 9 states, i.e., totally 10 states. $2^n > N$ i.e. $2^4 > 10$. Hence, we need four flip-flops.

Next, let us write the truth table for the above counter using *T* flip-flop as shown in Fig. 6.65 (a). We have to design a reset logic which will reset when we reach 1001 state. This is carried out using K-maps in Fig. 6.65(b). Figure 6.66 shows the implementation of divide by 10 asynchronous counter using *T* flip-flop.

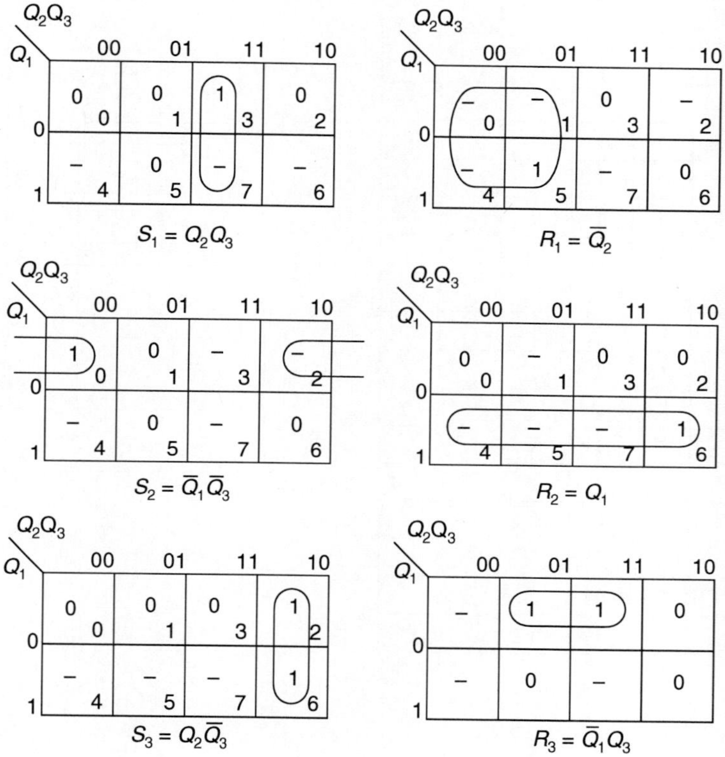

Fig. 6.63 K-maps for excitation table of Fig. 6.62

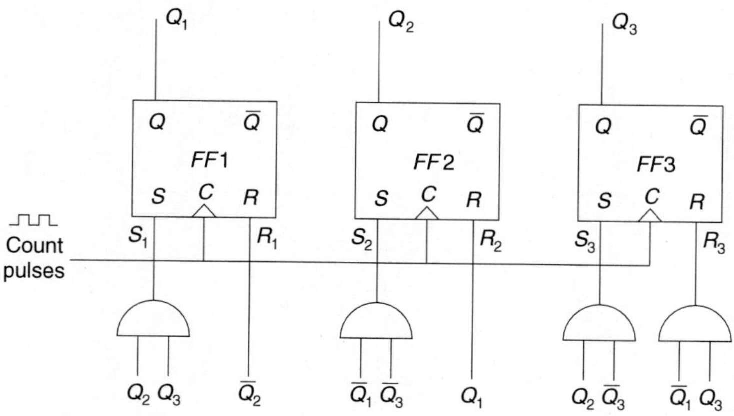

Fig. 6.64 Implementation of mod-6 synchronous counter using *SR* flip-flops

Clock	Q_A	Q_B	Q_C	Q_D	Output of reset logic Y
0	0	0	0	0	1
1	0	0	0	1	1
2	0	0	1	0	1
3	0	0	1	1	1
4	0	1	0	0	1
5	0	1	0	1	1
6	0	1	1	0	1
7	0	1	1	1	1
8	1	0	0	0	1
9	1	0	0	1	1
–	1	0	1	0	0
–	1	0	1	1	0
–	1	1	0	0	0
–	1	1	0	1	0
–	1	1	1	0	0
–	1	1	1	1	0

(a)

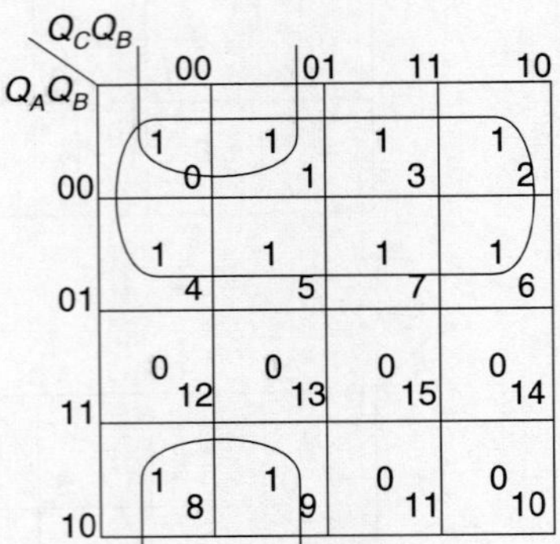

$$Y = \overline{Q}_A + \overline{Q}_B\,\overline{Q}_C$$

(b)

Fig. 6.65 Truth table and K-map for divide by 10 asynchronous counter

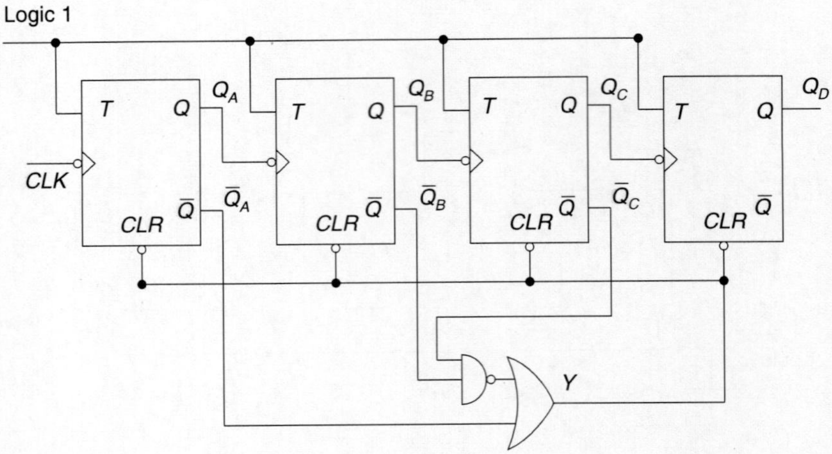

Fig. 6.66 Divide by 10 asynchronous counter using *TFFs*

Example 6.13 Design and implement a synchronous *BCD* counter using *JK, FFs.*

(VTU – Dec 2012)

Solution A *BCD* counter will count from 0 to 9. Number of flip-flops required is 4 [i.e., $2^4 > 10$]. Using *JK* flip-flop application table, excitation table for the design of synchronous *BCD* counter is constructed as shown in Fig. 6.67.

Present state				Next state				Flip-flop inputs							
Q_1	Q_2	Q_3	Q_4	Q_1^+	Q_2^+	Q_3^+	Q_4^+	J_1	K_1	J_2	K_2	J_3	K_3	J_4	K_4
0	0	0	0	0	0	0	1	0	–	0	–	0	–	1	–
0	0	0	1	0	0	1	0	0	–	0	–	1	–	–	1
0	0	1	0	0	0	1	1	0	–	0	–	–	0	1	0
0	0	1	1	0	1	0	0	0	–	1	0	0	1	0	1
0	1	0	0	0	1	0	1	0	–	–	0	0	–	1	0
0	1	0	1	0	1	1	0	0	–	–	0	1	0	0	1
0	1	1	0	0	1	1	1	0	1	1	0	–	0	1	0
0	1	1	1	1	0	0	0	1	0	0	1	0	1	0	1
1	0	0	0	1	0	0	1	–	0	0	–	0	–	1	0
1	0	0	1	0	0	0	0	0	1	0	–	0	–	0	1
1	0	1	0	–	–	–	–	–	–	–	–	–	–	–	–
–	–	–	–	–	–	–	–	–	–	–	–	–	–	–	–
1	1	1	1	–	–	–	–	–	–	–	–	–	–	–	–

Fig. 6.67 Excitation table for design of *BCD* counter

Next step is drawing K-maps to get flip-flop inputs J_1, K_1, J_2, K_2, J_3, K_3, J_4 and K_4 which are shown in Fig. 6.68.

Implementation of synchronous *BCD* counter using *JK* flip-flops is shown in Fig. 6.69.

Example 6.14 Draw the circuit of a 3-bit asynchronous, down counter using negative edge triggered *JK* flip-flops and draw the timing waveform. (VTU – Dec 2011)

Solution The down counter will count downward from a maximum count to zero. Figure 6.70 shows the 3-bit synchronous down counter using *JK* flip-flops. Clock or count pulse is connected to the clock input of the first flip-flop. The $\vec{Q}$ output of the first flip-flop is connected to the clock input of 2nd flip-flop and $\vec{Q}$ output of 2nd flip-flop is connected to the clock input of 3rd flip-flop. *J* and *K* inputs of all flip-flops are tied to logic '1'. Hence, the output will toggle for each negative edge of the clock input.

Figure 6.71 shows the timing diagram for 3-bit synchronous down counter.

Example 6.15 Design and implement synchronous counter to count the sequence 0 – 3 – 2 – 5 – 1 – 0 using negative edge triggered *JK* flip-flops.

Solution There are 5 states. Hence, the flip-flops required = 3, i.e., $2nd > N$; $N = 5$

Hence, $n = 3$

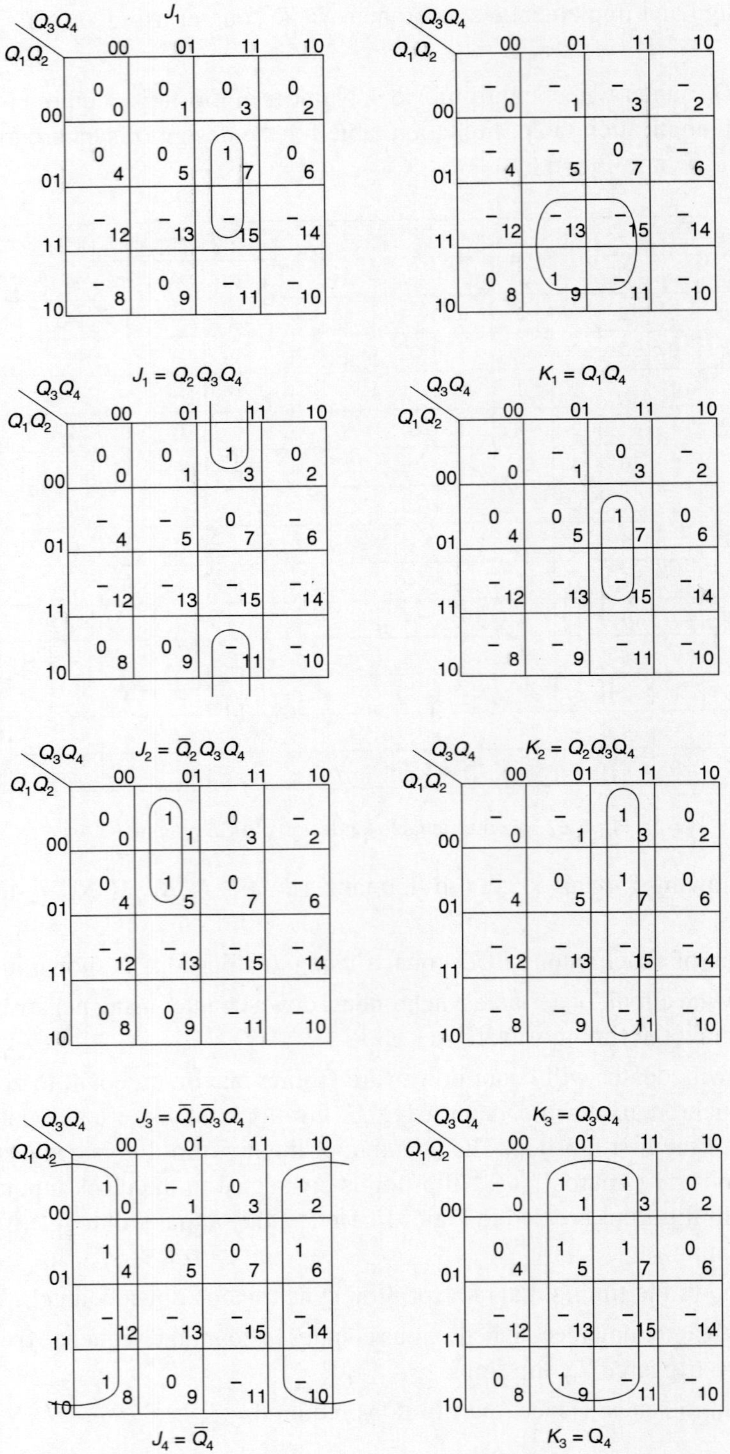

Fig. 6.68 K-maps for example 6.13

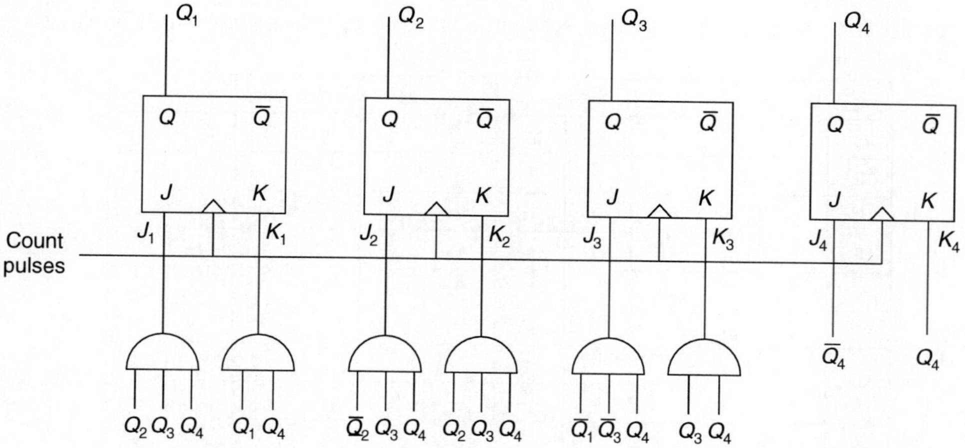

Fig. 6.69 Implementation of synchronous *BCD* counter using *JK* flip-flops

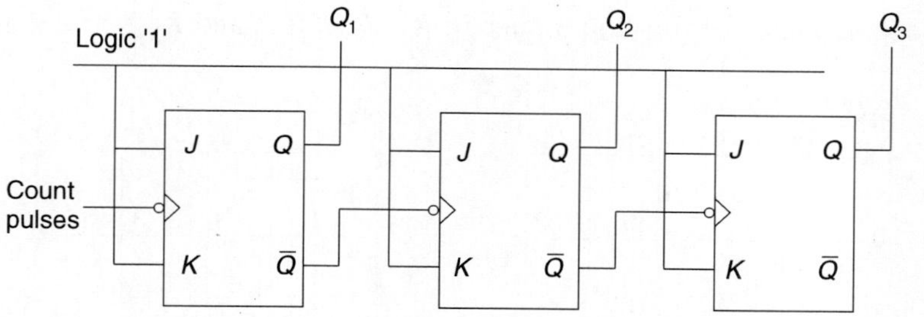

Fig. 6.70 3-bit asynchronous down counter using negative edge triggered *JK* flip-flops

Fig. 6.71 Timing diagram of 3-bit synchronous down counter

Next excitation table for the required sequence is constructed as shown in Fig. 6.72.

Present state			Next state			Flip-flop inputs					
Q_1	Q_2	Q_3	Q_1^+	Q_2^+	Q_3^+	J_1	K_1	J_2	K_2	J_3	K_3
0	0	0	0	1	1	0	–	1	–	1	–
0	0	1	0	0	0	0	–	0	–	–	1
0	1	0	1	0	1	1	–	–	1	1	–
0	1	1	0	1	0	0	–	–	0	–	1
1	0	0	–	–	–	–	–	–	–	–	–
1	0	1	0	0	1	–	1	0	–	–	0
1	1	0	–	–	–	–	–	–	–	–	–
1	1	1	–	–	–	–	–	–	–	–	–

Fig. 6.72 Excitation table for synchronous counter to count the sequence 0 – 3 – 2 – 5 – 1 – 0

Fig. 6.73 shows K-maps for flip-flop inputs J_1, K_1, J_2, K_2, J_3 and K_3.

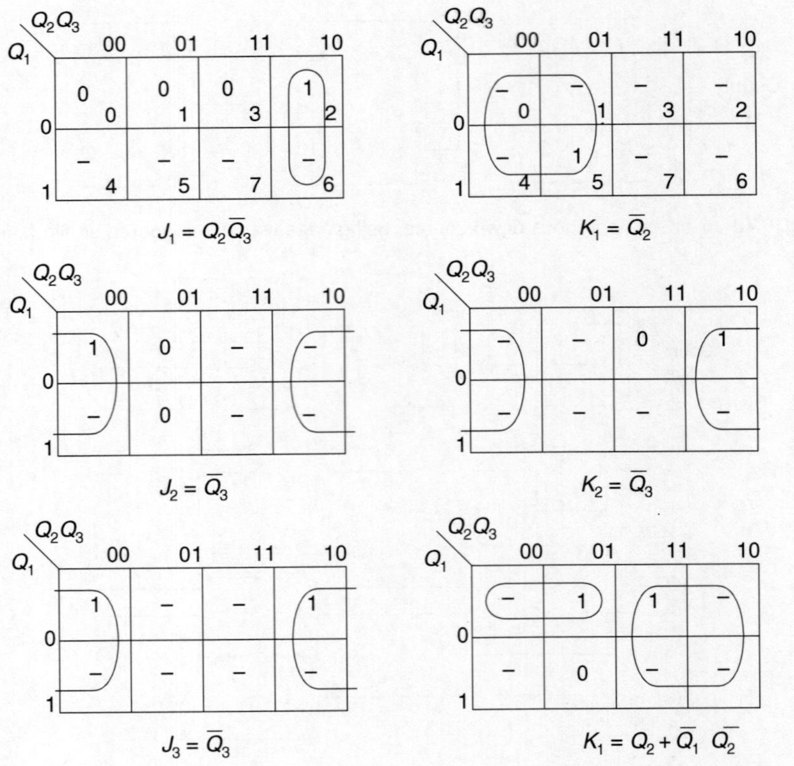

Fig. 6.73 K-maps for example 6.15

Implementation of synchronous counter to count the sequence 0 -3 -2 -5 -1 -0 is shown in Fig. 6.74.

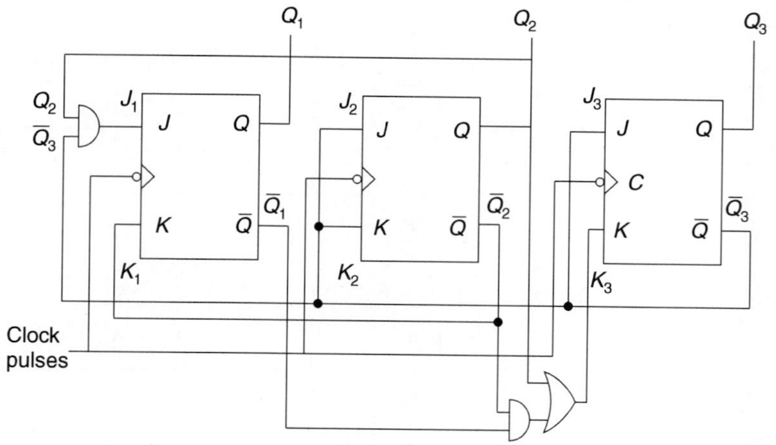

Fig. 6.74 Implementation of synchronous counter using negative edge triggered *JK* flip-flops

Example 6.16 Design a mod-5 synchronous counter using *JK* flip-flops and implement it. Also draw the timing diagram. (VTU – July 2011)

Solution As this is a mod-5 counter, we need three flip-flops.

$2nd > N$; $2^3 > N$; $N = 5$. Hence, three flip-flops are required.

The excitation table for the mod-5 synchronous counter is shown in Fig. 6.75.

Present state			Next state			Flip-flop inputs					
Q_1	Q_2	Q_3	Q_1^+	Q_2^+	Q_3^+	J_1	K_1	J_2	K_2	J_3	K_3
0	0	0	0	0	1	0	–	0	–	1	–
0	0	1	0	1	0	0	–	1	–	–	1
0	1	0	0	1	1	0	–	–	0	1	–
0	1	1	1	0	0	1	–	–	1	–	1
1	0	0	0	0	0	–	1	0	–	0	–
1	0	1	–	–	–	–	–	–	–	–	–
1	1	0	–	–	–	–	–	–	–	–	–
1	1	1	–	–	–	–	–	–	–	–	–

Fig. 6.75 Excitation table for example 6.16

K-maps simplification to get the flip-flop inputs is shown in Fig. 6.76.

Implementation of mod-5 synchronous counter using *JK* flip-flops is shown in Fig. 6.77 and the timing diagram is shown in Fig. 6.78.

Example 6.17 Design mod-11 asynchronous counter using *JK* flip-flops. (VTU – June 2012)

Solution For mod-11 asynchronous counter, there are 11 states. $2^n > N$, i.e., $2^n > 11$, i.e., $n = 4$

K-map for J_1, K-map for K_3, K-map for K_3 must be modified as shown here.

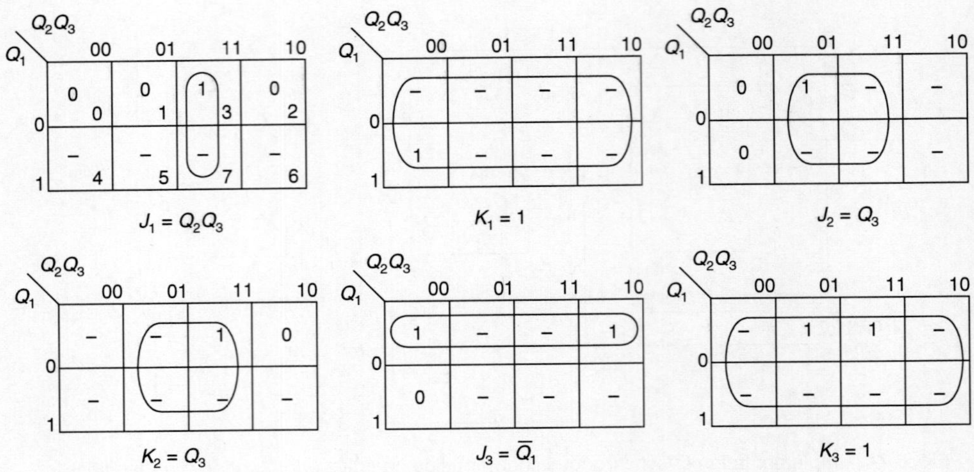

Fig. 6.76 K-maps for example 6.16

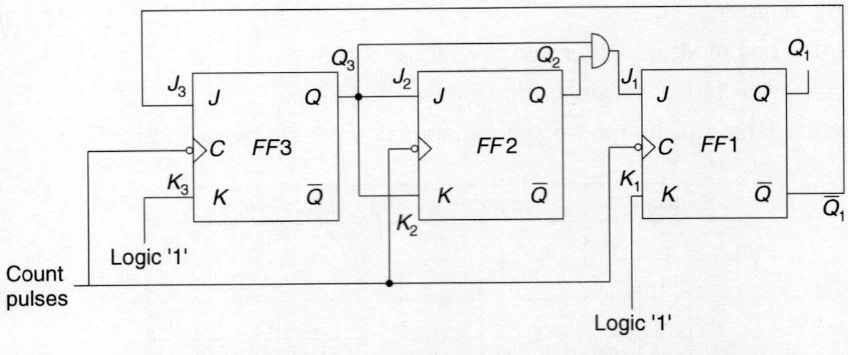

Fig. 6.77 Implementation of mod-5 synchronous counter using *JK* flip-flops

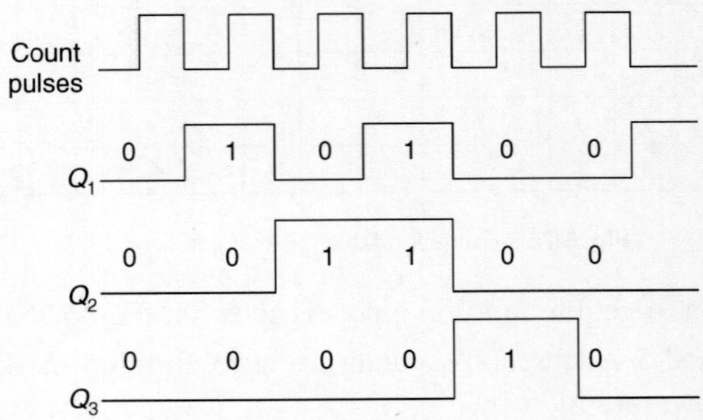

Fig. 6.78 Timing diagram for example 6.16

Four flip-flops are required.

As the requirement is for asynchronous counter, we need to write the truth table for the mod-11 asynchronous counter which is shown in Fig. 6.79.

Clock	Q_D	Q_C	Q_B	Q_A	Output of reset logic Y
0	0	0	0	0	1
1	0	0	0	1	1
2	0	0	1	0	1
3	0	0	1	1	1
4	0	1	0	0	1
5	0	1	0	1	1
6	0	1	1	0	1
7	0	1	1	1	1
8	1	0	0	0	1
9	1	0	0	1	1
10	1	0	1	0	1
–	1	0	1	1	0
–	1	1	0	0	0*
–	1	1	0	1	0
–	1	1	1	0	0
–	1	1	1	1	0

} Invalid states

Fig. 6.79 Truth table for mod-11 asynchronous counter

The reset input of each *JK* flip-flop is active low input. By applying logic '0' to *CLR* inputs of all flip-flops, we can reset the counter, i.e., again this counting sequence repeats, i.e., the counter counts from 0 to 10 (11 states) and it is reset and hence the counter is made to repeat the sequence form 0 to 10. Reset logic is made to '0' for invalid states, i.e., $Y = 0$ and at that state counter resets.

Reset logic is derived by K-map simplification. K-map is shown in Fig. 6.80.

Implementation of mod-11 asynchronous counter using *JK* flip-flops is shown in Fig. 6.81. Here, reset logic output Y is connected to *CLR* inputs of all flip-flops.

Example 6.18 Design a synchronous 5421 code sequence using positive edge triggering *D* flip-flop with minimum combinational circuits. (VTU – June 2012)

Solution The 5421 code sequence is shown in Fig. 6.82. For example, decimal 7 is represented by

1010, i.e.,

$$1 \times 5 + 0 \times 4 + 1 \times 2 + 0 \times 1 = 5 + 2 = 7$$

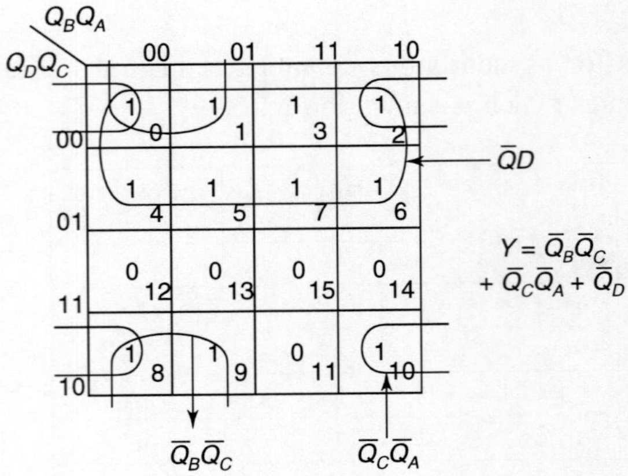

Fig. 6.80 K-map for example 6.17

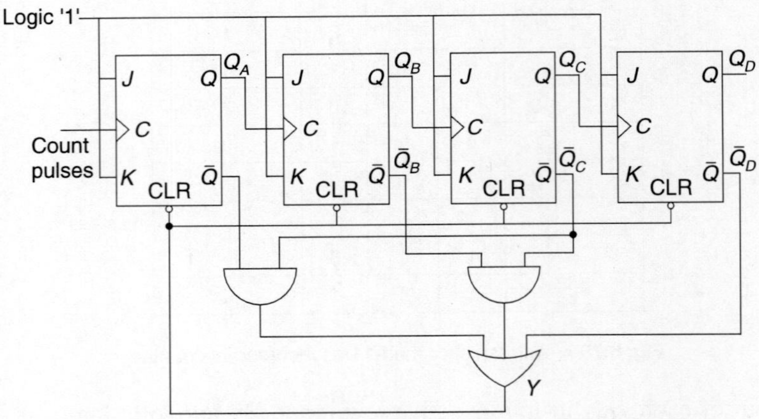

Fig. 6.81 Implementation of mod-11 asynchronous counter using *JK* flip-flops

Decimal	5	4	2	1
0	0	0	0	0
1	0	0	0	1
2	0	0	1	0
3	0	0	1	1
4	0	1	0	0
5	1	0	0	0
6	1	0	0	1
7	1	0	1	0
8	1	0	1	1
9	1	1	0	0

Fig. 6.82 The 5421 code sequence

The state diagram of 5421 code sequence is shown in Fig. 6.83.

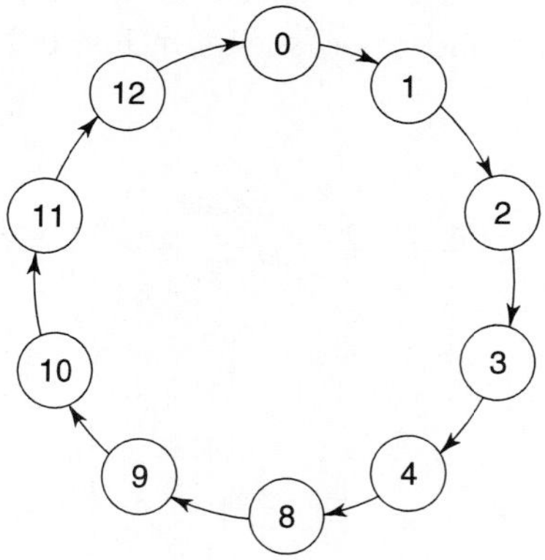

Fig. 6.83 The state diagram of 5421 sequence

Present state				Next state				Flip-flop inputs			
Q_1	Q_2	Q_3	Q_4	Q_1^+	Q_2^+	Q_3^+	Q_4^+	D_1	D_2	D_3	D_4
0	0	0	0	0	0	0	1	0	0	0	1
0	0	0	1	0	0	1	0	0	0	1	0
0	0	1	0	0	0	1	1	0	0	1	1
0	0	1	1	0	1	0	0	0	1	0	0
0	1	0	0	1	0	0	0	1	0	0	0
0	1	0	1	–	–	–	–	–	–	–	–
0	1	1	0	–	–	–	–	–	–	–	–
0	1	1	1	–	–	–	–	–	–	–	–
1	0	0	0	1	0	0	1	1	0	0	1
1	0	0	1	1	0	1	0	1	0	1	0
1	0	1	0	1	0	1	1	1	0	1	1
1	0	1	1	1	1	0	0	1	1	0	0
1	1	0	0	0	0	0	0	0	0	0	0
1	1	0	1	–	–	–	–	–	–	–	–
1	1	1	0	–	–	–	–	–	–	–	–
1	1	1	1	–	–	–	–	–	–	–	–

Fig. 6.84 Excitation table for example 6.18

K-maps for flip-flop inputs D_1, D_2, D_3 and D_4 are drawn as shown in Fig. 6.85 and implementation of synchronous counter is shown in Fig. 6.86.

Example 6.19 Design a counter using *JK* flip-flops whose sequence is (0, 1, 4, 6, 7, 5, 0 ...) by obtaining minimal sum equations. (VTU – June 2012)

Solution The sequence shows that there are six different states and hence, we will get a mod-6 synchronous counter. Figure 6.87 shows the state diagram for the count sequence. We need minimum three flip-flops.

The excitation table is constructed using application table for *JK* flip-flops.

K-maps for the flip-flop inputs are drawn as shown in Fig. 6.89. Implementation of synchronous counter for the given sequences is shown in Fig. 6.90.

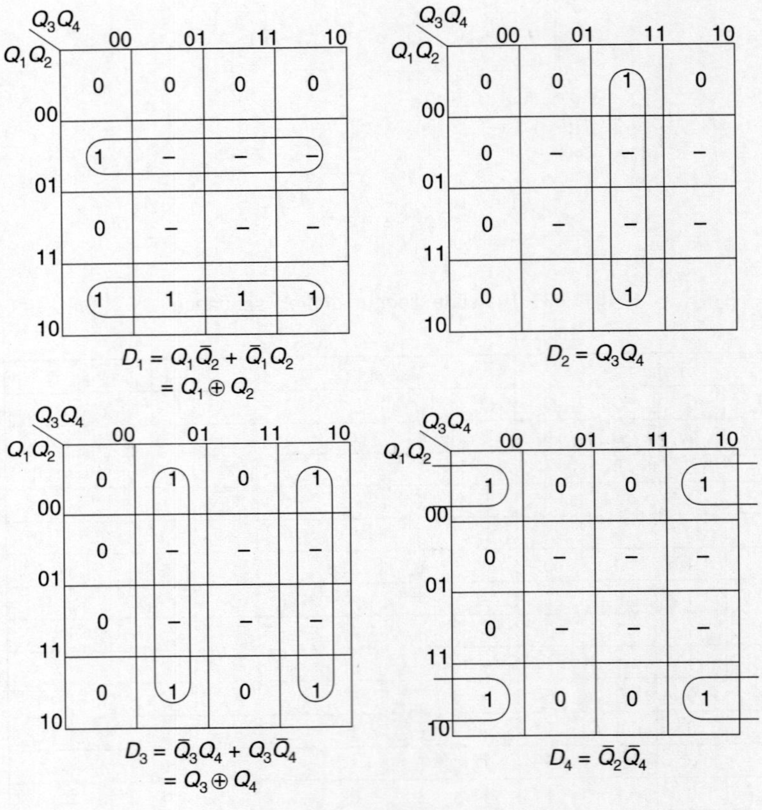

Fig. 6.85 K-maps for D_1, D_2, D_3 and D_4

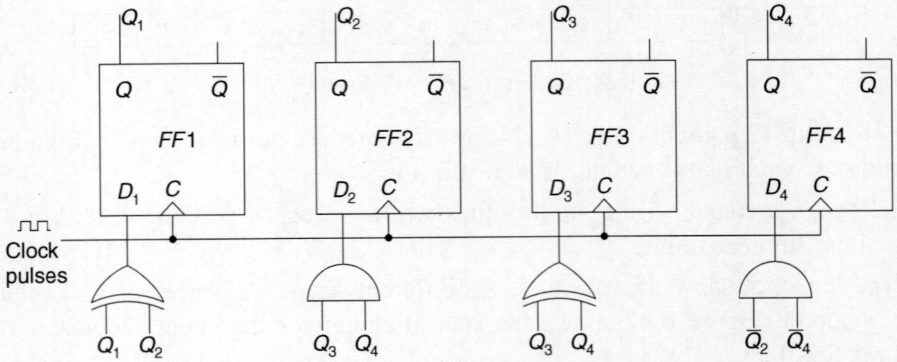

Fig. 6.86 Implementation of 5421 code sequencer

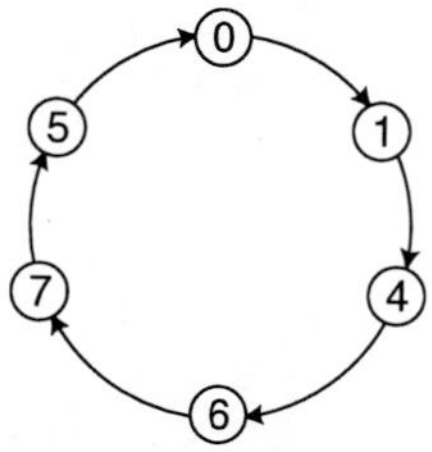

Fig. 6.87 State diagram for example 6.19

Present state			Next state			Flip-flop inputs					
Q_1	Q_2	Q_3	Q_1^+	Q_2^+	Q_3^+	J_1	K_1	J_2	K_2	J_3	K_3
0	0	0	0	0	1	0	–	0	–	1	–
0	0	1	1	0	0	1	–	0	–	–	1
0	1	0	–	–	–	–	–	–	–	–	–
0	1	1	–	–	–	–	–	–	–	–	–
1	0	0	1	1	0	–	0	1	–	0	–
1	0	1	0	0	0	–	1	0	–	–	1
1	1	0	1	1	1	–	0	–	0	1	–
1	1	1	1	0	1	–	0	–	1	–	0

Fig. 6.88 Excitation table for example 6.19

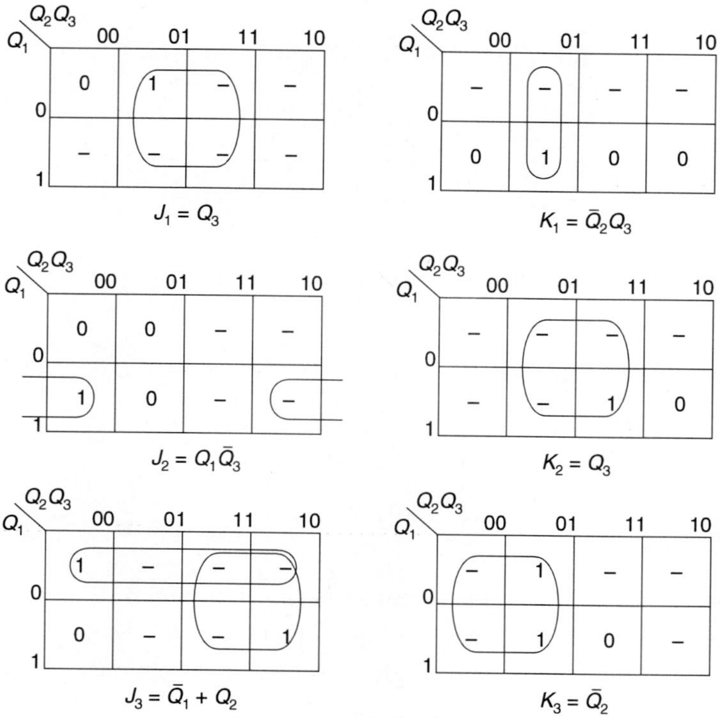

Fig. 6.89 K-maps for example 6.19

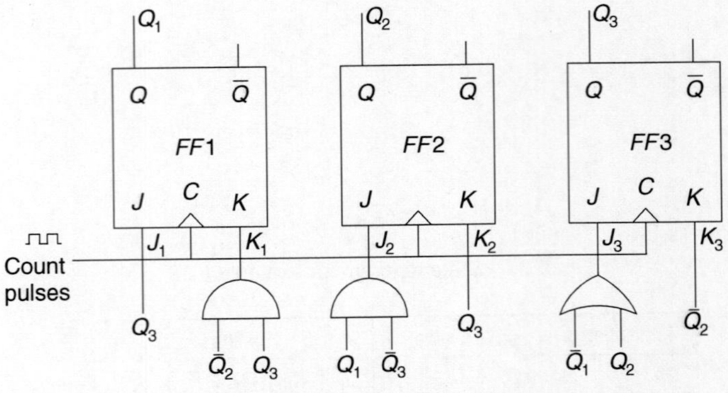

Fig. 6.90 Implementation of synchronous counter for example 6.19

Example 6.20 Design a synchronous mod-3 counter with the following binary sequence using clocked *JK* flip-flops. Count sequence: 0, 1, 2, 0, 1, 2 ... (VTU – Jan 2006)

0	0
0	1
1	0
1	1

Count sequence

Solution The excitation table is shown in Fig. 6.91 and K-maps are shown in Fig. 6.92.

Present state		Next state		Flip-flop inputs			
Q_1	Q_2	Q_1^+	Q_2^+	J_1	K_1	J_2	K_2
0	0	0	1	0	–	1	–
0	1	1	0	1	–	–	1
1	0	0	0	–	1	0	–

Fig. 6.91 Excitation table for example 6.20

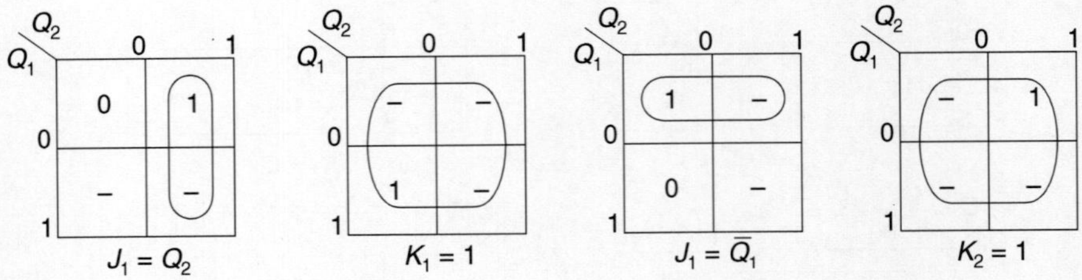

Implementation of mod-3 synchronous counter is shown in Fig. 6.92.

Example 6.21 Realize a 3-bit binary synchronous up counter using *JK* flip-flop. Write the excitation table, transition table and logic diagram. Include preset and clear options. (VTU – Aug 2007)

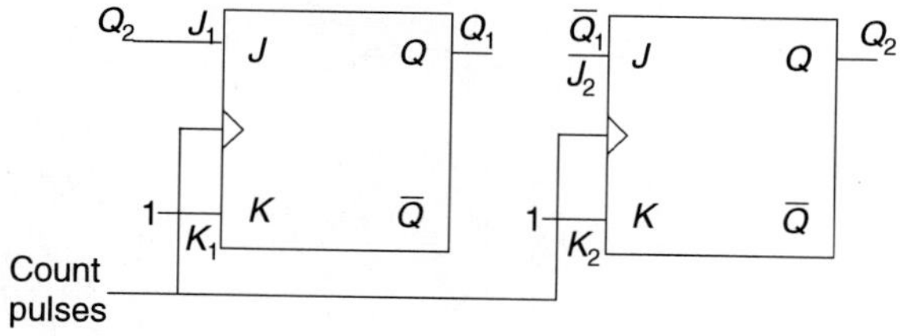

Fig. 6.92 Mod-3 synchronous counter

Solution For a 3-bit binary synchronous up counter, we need 3 flip-flops. Excitation table for *JK* flip-flop is shown in Fig. 6.93.

Q	Q^+	J	K
0	0	0	×
0	1	1	×
1	0	×	1
1	1	×	0

Fig. 6.93 Excitation table for *JK* flip-flop

Transition table is constructed as shown in Fig. 6.94.

Present state			Next state			Flip-flop inputs					
A	B	C	A^+	B^+	C^+	J_A	K_A	J_B	K_B	J_C	K_C
0	0	0	0	0	1	0	×	0	×	1	×
0	0	1	0	1	0	0	×	1	×	×	1
0	1	0	0	1	1	0	×	×	0	1	×
0	1	1	1	0	0	1	×	×	1	×	1
1	0	0	1	0	1	×	0	0	×	1	×
1	0	1	1	1	0	×	0	1	×	×	1
1	1	0	1	1	1	×	0	×	0	1	×
1	1	1	0	0	0	×	1	×	1	×	1

Fig. 6.94 Transition table for example 6.21

Flip-flop inputs are simplified using K-maps as shown in Fig. 6.95.

Using K-map values, we can draw the logic diagram as shown in Fig. 6.96.

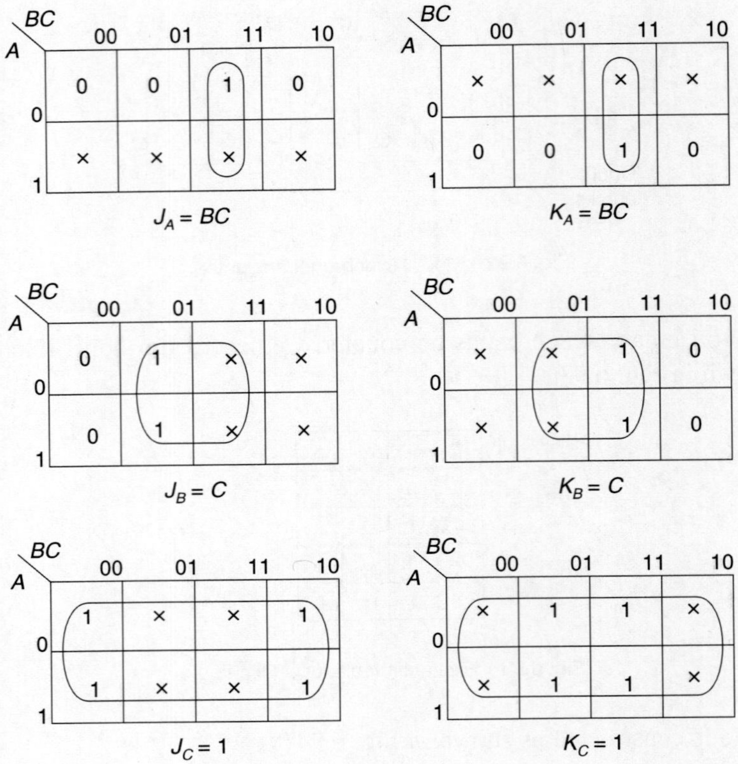

Fig. 6.95 K-maps for example 6.21

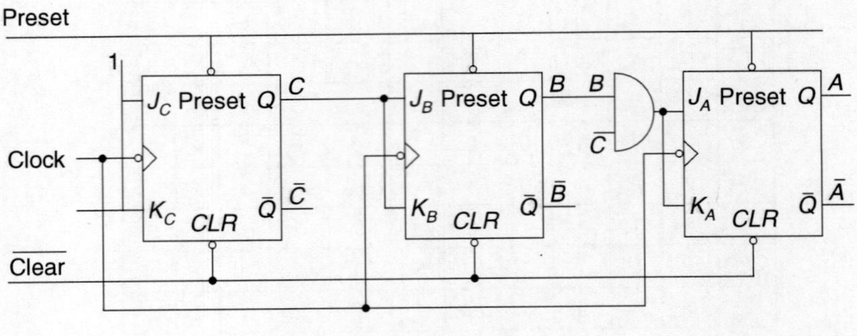

Fig. 6.96 Logic diagram for example 6.21

EXERCISE

1. Give the logic diagram of 4-bit bidirectional shift register with parallel load capability and briefly explain its operations.
2. Explain 4-bit shift register in detail and give its timing diagram.
3. Write short note on universal shift register.
4. Explain with suitable logic and timing diagram:
   (i) Serial in serial out
   (ii) Parallel-in parallel-out.
5. Explain the operation of 4-bit bidirectional shift register with the help of neat diagram.
6. Discuss BCD ripple counter with state diagram, logic diagram and timing diagram.
7. Explain Johnson counter with its circuit diagram and timing diagram. Give its state diagram.
8. Draw the block diagram of a mod-7 twisted ring counter and explain its operation. Give the count sequence table and the decoding logic used to identify the various states.
9. Design mod-4 nipple up counter with initial state is $(011)_2$. Draw timing diagram for the same.
10. Design mid-6 synchronous counter by using *JK FF*. Give excitation table of *FF*, state diagram, state table and waveforms for same.
11. Design a counter that has a repeated sequence of 06 states listed bellow. Give its state diagram.

Sequence		
0	0	0
0	0	1
0	1	0
1	0	0
1	0	1
1	1	0

12. Design mod-6 synchronous counter and describe its working with neat waveforms.
13. Design mod-3 center using *JK* flip-flops. Sketch the waveforms for outputs when clock is applied and verify its operations.
14. Draw the circuit and explain a synchronous mod-6 counter using *JK* flip-flops.
15. Draw a mod-4 synchronous down counter using *JK* flip-flop and implement it.
16. Write short notes on:
    (a) ripple counter
    (b) ring counter
17. Design a synchronous mod-3 counter with the following binary sequence using clocked *JK* flip-flops count sequence: 0, 1, 2, 0, 1, 2 ...

18. Design a synchronous mod-8 binary sequence counter using positive edge triggered T flip-flops with minimal combinational circuits.
19. Design a synchronous counter using negative edge triggered JK flip-flops to sequence $0 \rightarrow 5 \rightarrow 7 \rightarrow 4 \rightarrow 2 \rightarrow 0$ using minimal combinational gating.

CHAPTER 7

Sequential Design-1

7.1 INTRODUCTION

In clocked synchronous sequential circuits clock signal is connected simultaneously to the control inputs of all the flip-flops in the memory block of the circuit. A general configuration of a clocked sequential circuit is shown in Fig. 7.1. The change in states of flip-flops occurs together because all the flip-flops are simultaneously clocked.

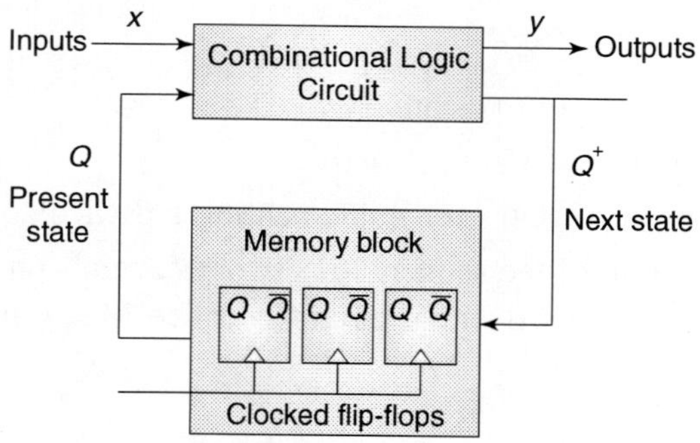

Fig. 7.1 Configuration of a clocked sequential circuit

Let us define

Q = the present state of the circuit

Q^+ = the next state of the circuit

X = the present inputs

Y = the outputs

As shown in Fig. 7.1.

The next state is a Boolean function of the present inputs and the present state.

$$Q^+ = f(x, Q)$$

The outputs are also a function of the present inputs and the present state.

$$Y = f(X, Q)$$

The synchronous clocked sequential networks are represented by two models, namely, Moore model and Mealy model.

Moore Model: The output of the circuit depends only on the present state of the flip-flops. Moore model is shown in Fig. 7.2.

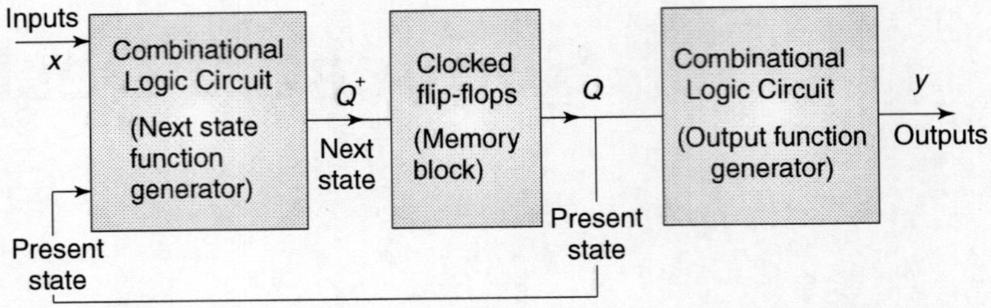

Fig. 7.2 Moore model of a clocked synchronous sequential circuit

Here the inputs are used to determine the next state and are not used to change the outputs, The outputs are derived from the present state of the flip-flops only. Therefore, for a Moore model,

$$Q^+ = f(x, Q)$$

$$Y = f(Q)$$

(i) Its output is a function of present state only.

(ii) The changes in input do not affect the output.

(iii) It requires more number of states for implementing a particular function.

Mealy Model: When the output of the sequential network depends on both the present state of the flip-flops and on the inputs, the sequential circuit is called Mealy model which is shown in Fig. 7.3.

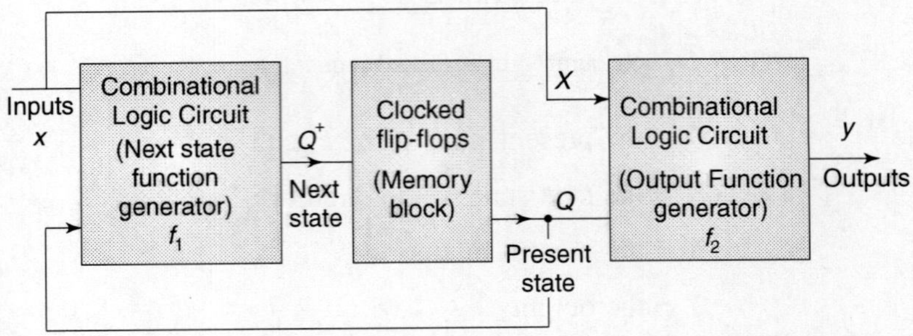

Fig. 7.3 Mealy model of a clocked synchronous sequential circuit

As shown in Fig. 7.3 the output is derived from the combination of present state of the flip-flops and input of the circuit.

For a Mealy model,

$$Q^+ = f_1(X, Q)$$

$$Y = f_2(X, Q)$$

(i) The output is a function of both the present state and the present input.
(ii) The changes in the input affects the output of the circuit.
(iii) It requires less number of states for implementing a particular function.

7.2 STATE MACHINE NOTATION

In the sequential machine, the Boolean variables are input variable, output variable, state variable and excitation variable.

Input variable is the variable that originates outside the sequential machine and is given as input to the machine.

Output variable is the variable that comes out of the sequential machine and taken as output from the sequential machine.

State variable is the variable that defines the state of the sequential machine. Output of the flip-flops in the memory block defines the state. Hence, the state variable is output of the flip-flop.

Excitation variable is the variable that forms as the input to the flip-flop. Excitation variable results as the output of the input combinational logic circuit operating on the input variable and the state variable.

Figure 7.4 shows a synchronous sequential circuit. Referring to the circuit, we define the above variables.

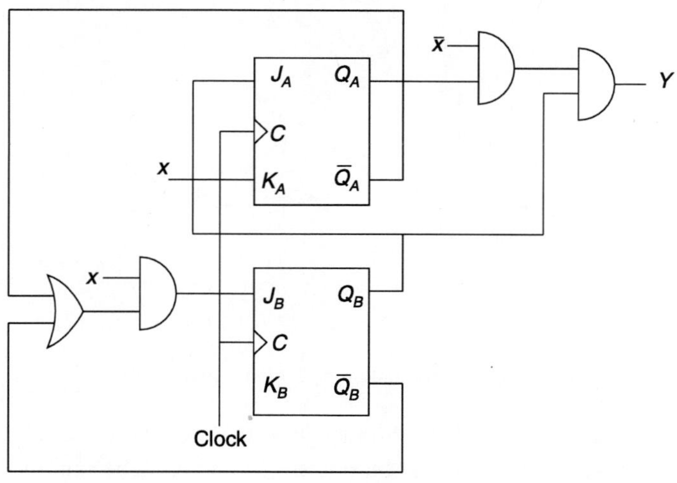

Fig. 7.4 A synchronous sequential circuit

Referring to Fig. 7.4, X is the input variable, Q_A and Q_B are state variables, Y is the output variable, $X(\overline{Q}_A + \overline{Q}_B)$ is the excitation variable.

State and state variable: As defined earlier state variable is the output of flip-flops. State is a particular combination of outputs of flip-flops.

$$2^n = N$$

where n is the number of state variables.

N is the maximum number of states.

State and state variables are related by the above equation.

Present state and next state: State variable Q_A is represented before the arrival of clock pulse and state variable Q_A^+ is represented after the arrival of the clock pulse.

Present state is defined as the states of all the variables at sometime t before the arrival of next clock.

Next state is defined as the status of all the state variables at sometime $t + 1$, i.e., after the arrival of the clock pulse.

State Diagram: A state diagram is defined as a pictorial representation of the behaviour of a sequential circuit. Figure 7.5 shows a state diagram for Mealy circuit. In this state diagram a circle represents a state and the transition between states is represented by directed lines connecting the circuit, i.e., the states. A directed line connecting two circles is connecting two states, i.e., present state and next state. A directed line connecting a circle with itself indicates that the next state is same as the present state. The binary number or the variable inside each circle identifies the state, i.e., there are four circles representing four states, i.e., 00, 01, 10 and 11 or *a*, *b*, *c* and *d*.

The directed lines are labelled with two binary numbers separated by a symbol '/'. The input values that cause of the state transition is labelled first and the output value during the present state is labelled after the symbol '/'. For example, 0/1 on the directed line means 0 is the input value that causes the state transition and 1 is the output value during the present state.

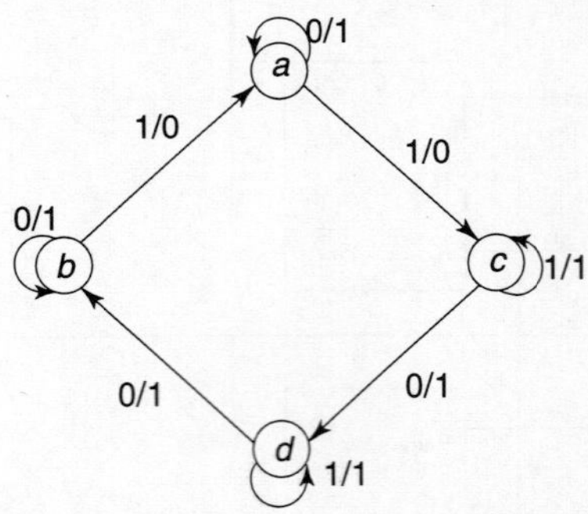

Fig. 7.5 State diagram for mealy circuit

Figure 7.6 shows the state diagram for a Moore circuit. Here also the circle represents a state. Inside a circle both the present state and the output are indicated. The output is indicated below the present state because the output depends only on the present state and not on the input.

For example, $\left(\frac{a}{1}\right)$ represents the present state *a* or 00 and 1 represents the output. The directed lines are labelled with only one binary number representing the state of input that causes the state transition.

State Table: Even though the state diagram provides pictorially the description of the behaviour of a sequential circuit, in order to implement the circuit, it is desirable to translate the information

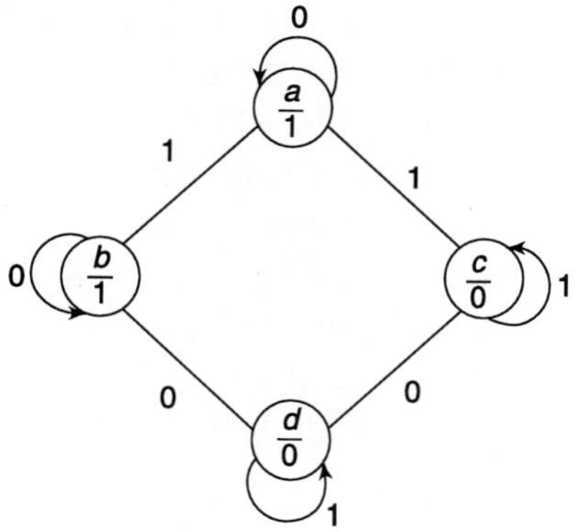

Fig. 7.6 State diagram for a Moore circuit

contained in the state diagram into a tabular form called state table. The state diagram shown in Fig. 7.5, is given as a state table as shown in Fig. 7.7.

Present state	Next state		Output	
	$X = 0$	$X = 1$	$X = 0$	$X = 1$
Q_AQ_B	Q_AQ_B	Q_AQ_B	Y	Y
a	a	c	1	0
b	b	a	1	0
c	d	c	1	1
d	b	d	1	1

Fig. 7.7 State table for Fig. 7.5

It represents the relationship between input, output and flip-flop states. There are three sections in a state table, namely present state, next state and output. The present state designates the state of flip-flops before the arrival of clock pulse. The next state is the state of the flip-flop after the application of clock pulse. The output gives the values of output variables during the present state. Next state and output sections have two columns representing two input conditions $X = 0$ and $X = 1$.

The state diagram shown in Fig. 7.6 is represented by the state table shown in Fig. 7.8.

Present state	Next state		Output
	$X = 0$	$X = 1$	Y
Q_AQ_B	Q_AQ_B	Q_AQ_B	
a	a	c	1
b	b	a	1
c	d	c	0
d	b	d	0

Fig. 7.8 State table for Fig. 7.6

This table is similar to the table shown in Fig. 7.7, i.e., it also has three sections, namely, present state, next state and output. The only difference is that it has only one column under output section, since the output does not depend on input as this is a Moore circuit.

Transition Table: The state diagram and state table represent states using symbols or names. In the transition table, specific values are assigned to each state. Assignment of values to state variables is called state assignment. Similar to state table, transition table also represents relation between present state, next state, output and input. Figure 7.9 shows the transition table corresponding to state table shown in Fig. 7.7. Q_AQ_B are the state variables. $Q_AQ_B = 00$ represents one state, $Q_AQ_B = 01$ represents second state, $Q_AQ_B = 10$ represents third state and $Q_AQ_B = 11$ represents fourth state.

Present State		Next state		Output	
		$X = 0$	$X = 1$	$X = 0$	$X = 1$
Q_A	Q_B	Q_AQ_B	Q_AQ_B	Y	Y
0	0	00	10	1	0
0	1	01	00	1	0
1	0	11	10	1	1
1	1	01	11	1	1

Fig. 7.9 Transition table corresponding to state table of Fig. 7.7

7.3 SYNCHRONOUS SEQUENTIAL CIRCUIT ANALYSIS

The operation of synchronous sequential circuit is complex relative to combinational logic circuit. The procedure to analyze the synchronous sequential circuit is as per the following steps:

1. Write the state variables
2. Identify the flip-flop types
3. Write the flip-flop input equations
4. Construct K-maps using the flip-flop input equations.
5. Construct excitation table using the function table of the corresponding flip-flops.
6. Write the state diagram from the excitation table.

Example 7.1 Analyze the synchronous sequential circuit shown in Fig. 7.10. (VTU – Dec 2013)

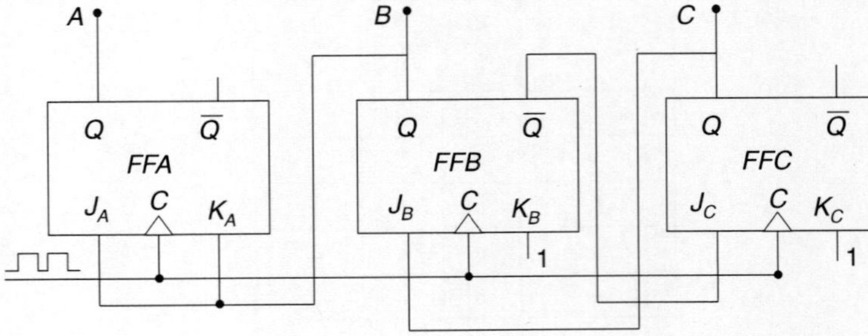

Fig. 7.10

Solution:

Step 1: Write the state variables, i.e., flip-flop outputs, i.e., state variables are *A*, *B*, *C*.

Step 2: Identify flip-flop types. In this case *JK* flip-flops

Step 3: Write the flip-flop input equations

$$J_A = K_A = B$$

$$J_B = C,\ K_B = 1$$

$$J_C = \overline{B},\ K_C = 1$$

Step 4: Construct K-maps using the flip-flop input equations as shown in Fig. 7.11.

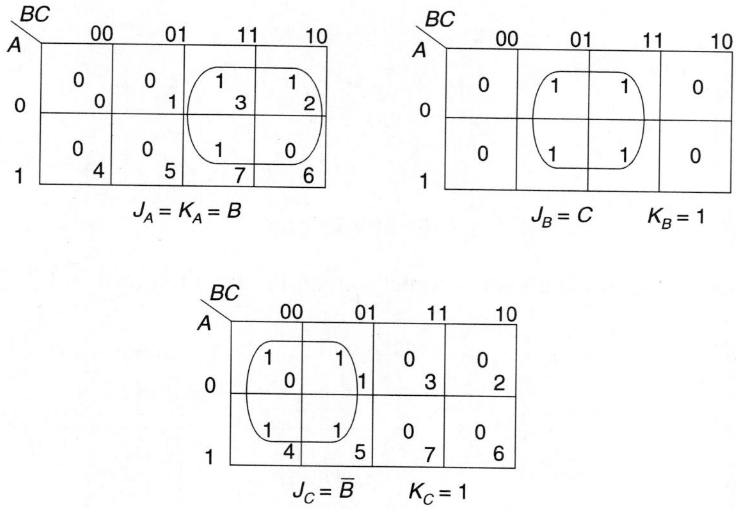

Fig. 7.11 K-maps for Fig. 7.10

Step 5: Construct the excitation table using the function table of *JK* flip-flop.

Present state			Next state			Flip-flop inputs					
A	B	C	A^+	B^+	C^+	J_A	K_A	J_B	K_B	J_C	K_C
0	0	0	0	0	1	0	0	0	1	1	1
0	0	1	0	1	0	0	0	1	1	1	1
0	1	0	1	0	0	1	1	0	1	0	1
0	1	1	1	0	0	1	1	1	1	0	1
1	0	0	1	0	1	0	0	0	1	1	1
1	0	1	1	1	0	0	0	1	1	1	1
1	1	0	0	0	0	1	1	0	1	0	1
1	1	1	0	0	0	1	1	1	1	0	1

(a)

J	K	Q^+
0	0	Q
0	1	0
1	0	1
1	1	$\overline{Q}$

(b)

Fig. 7.12 (a) Excitation table (b) Function table of *JK* flip-flop

The excitation table entries are made using K-map entries and *JK* flip-flop function table values, i.e., flip-flop inputs from K-map and next state values using present state and function table values.

Step 6: Write the state diagram from the excitation table entries as shown in Fig. 7.13.

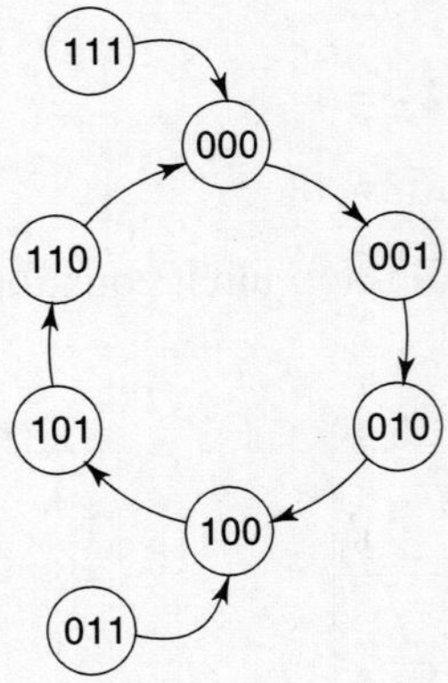

Fig. 7.13 State diagram

Example 7.2 Analyze the following synchronous sequential circuit shown in Fig. 7.14.

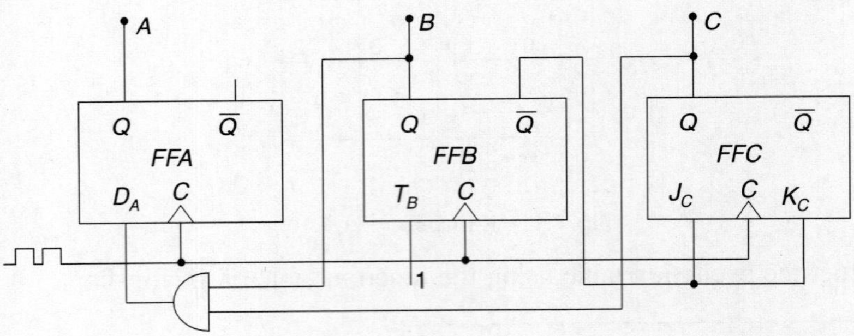

Fig. 7.14

1. The state variables are *A*, *B*, *C*.
2. Flip-flops are *D*, *T* and *JK*. Three different flip-flops are there in this circuit.
3. The flip-flop input equations are

$$D_A = BC$$

$$T_B = 1$$

$$J_C = K_C = \overline{B}$$

4. K-maps are constructed for the flip-flop inputs as shown in Fig. 7.15.

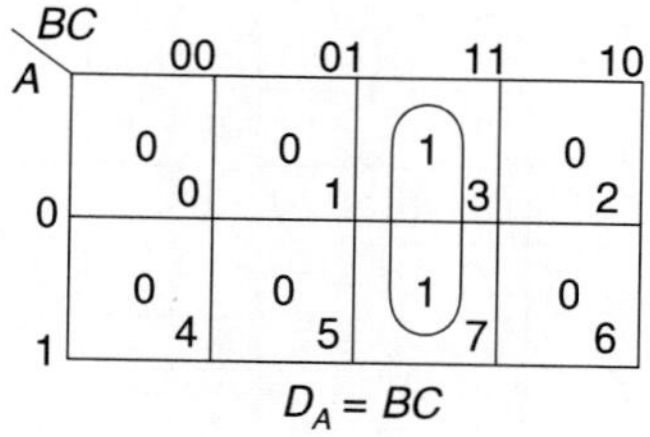

Fig. 7.15

There is no need for K-map as T_B and J_C and K_C are straightforward.

$$T_B = 1\ ,\ J_C = K_C = \overline{B}$$

5. Using function table of *D*, *T* and *JK* flip-flops, excitaion tables of flip-flops are written as shown in Fig. 7.15(a) and Fig. 7.15(b).

D	Q^+
0	0
1	1

T	Q^+
0	Q
1	$\overline{Q}$

J	K	Q^+
0	0	Q
0	1	0
1	0	1
1	1	$\overline{Q}$

Fig. 7.15(a) Function tables of flip-flops *D*, *T* and *JK*

Q	Q^+	D
0	0	0
0	1	1
1	0	0
1	1	1

Q	Q^+	T
0	0	0
0	1	1
1	0	1
1	1	0

Q	Q^+	J	K
0	0	0	×
0	1	1	×
1	0	×	1
1	1	×	0

Fig. 7.15(b) Excitation tables of flip-flops *D*, *T* and *JK*

6. Excitation table is written using the function table of three flip-flops and K-maps as shown in Fig. 7.16.

Present state			Next state			Flip-flop inputs			
A	B	C	A^+	B^+	C^+	D_A	T_B	T_C	K_C
0	0	0	0	1	1	0	1	1	1
0	0	1	0	1	0	0	1	1	1
0	1	0	0	0	0	0	1	0	0
0	1	1	1	0	1	1	1	0	0
1	0	0	0	1	1	0	1	1	1
1	0	1	0	1	0	0	1	1	1
1	1	0	0	0	0	0	1	0	0
1	1	1	1	0	1	1	1	0	0

Fig. 7.16 Excitation table for example 7.2

7. State diagram is written from the values of excitation table as shown in Fig. 7.17. The counter sequence is $0 \to 3 \to 5 \to 2 \to 0$.

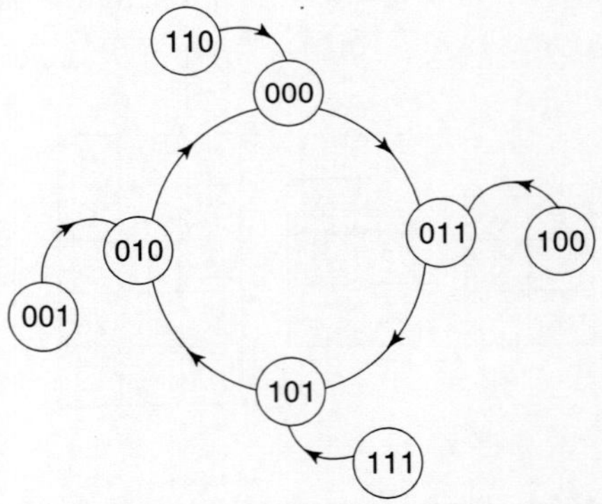

Fig. 7.17 State diagram for example 7.2

Example 7.3 Analyze the following synchronous sequential circuit shown in Fig. 7.18.

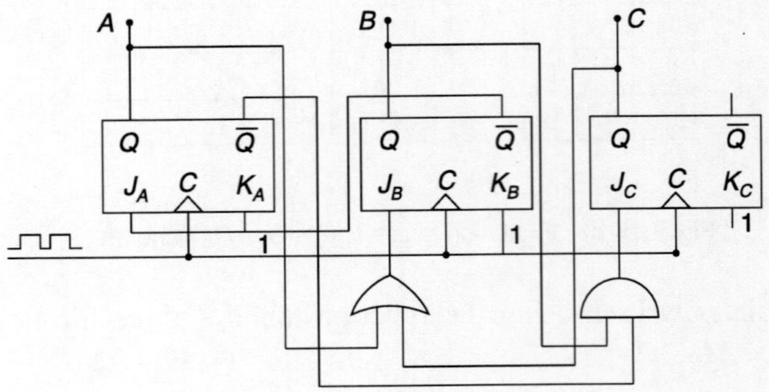

Fig. 7.18

1. The state variables, i.e., flip-flop output are A, B and C.
2. Flip-flops are of type JK
3. The flip-flop input equation are;

$J_A = \overline{B}$ $K_A = 1$ $J_C = B\overline{A}$ $K_C = 1$

$J_B = A + C$ $K_B = 1$

4. K-maps are constructed for flip-flop input as shown in Fig. 7.19.

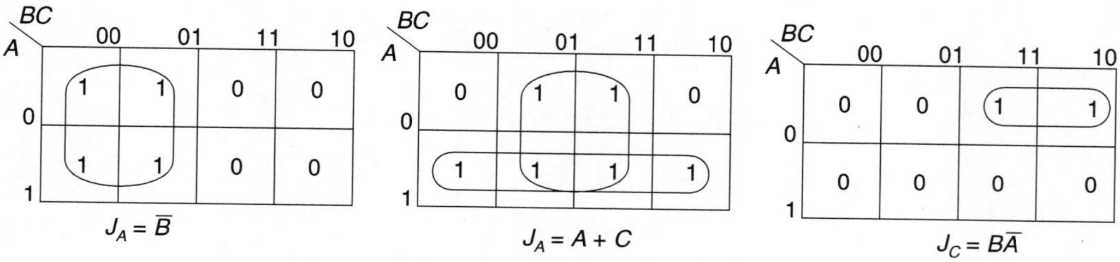

Fig. 7.19 K-maps for example 7.3

5. Excitation table is written using the function table of the JK flip-flops and K-maps as shown in Fig. 7.20.

Present state			Next state			Flip-flop inputs					
A	B	C	A^+	B^+	C^+	J_A	K_A	J_B	K_B	J_C	K_C
0	0	0	1	0	0	1	1	0	1	0	1
0	0	1	1	1	0	1	1	1	1	0	1
0	1	0	0	0	1	0	1	0	1	1	1
0	1	1	0	0	0	0	1	1	1	1	1
1	0	0	0	1	0	1	1	1	1	0	1
1	0	1	0	1	0	1	1	1	1	0	1
1	1	0	0	0	0	0	1	1	1	0	1
1	1	1	0	0	0	0	1	1	1	0	1

(a)

J	K	Q^+
0	0	Q
0	1	0
1	0	1
1	1	$\overline{Q}$

(b)

Fig. 7.20 (a) Excitation table (b) Function table for *JK* flip-flop

6. State diagram is written as shown in Fig. 7.21. The counter sequence is shown in Fig. 7.21.

Example 7.4 Analyze the folowing synchronous sequential circuit shown in Fig. 7.22.

1. The state variables are A, B and C
2. Flip-flops are of JK type
3. The flip-flop input equations are:

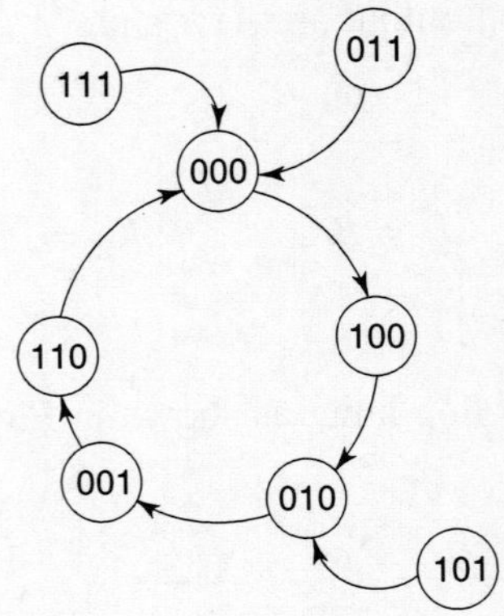

Fig. 7.21 State diagram for example 7.3

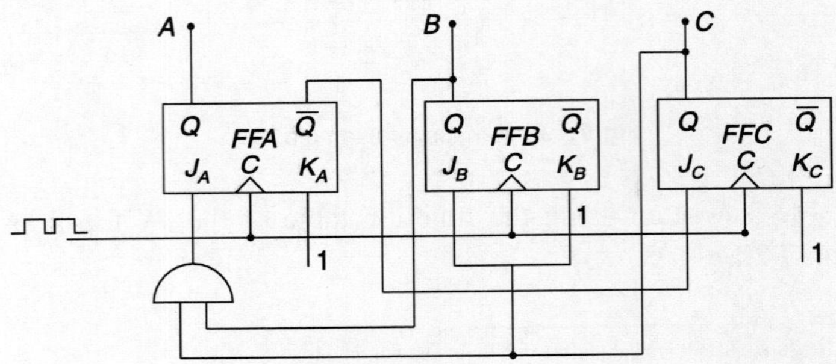

Fig. 7.22

$$J_A = BC \qquad J_B = C \qquad J_C = \overline{A}$$
$$K_A = 1 \qquad K_B = C \qquad K_C = 1$$

4. K-maps are constructed for flip-flop inputs as shown in Fig. 7.23.

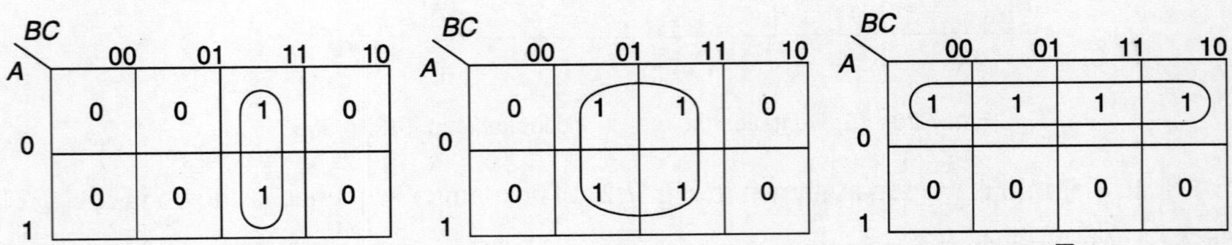

Fig. 7.23 K-maps for example 7.4

5. Excitation table is written using the function table of the *JK* flip-flops and K-maps as shown in Fig. 7.24.

Present state			Next state			Flip-flop inputs					
A	B	C	A^+	B^+	C^+	J_A	K_A	J_B	K_B	J_C	K_C
0	0	0	0	0	1	0	1	0	0	1	1
0	0	1	0	1	0	0	1	1	1	1	1
0	1	0	0	1	1	0	1	0	0	1	1
0	1	1	1	0	0	1	1	1	1	1	1
1	0	0	0	0	0	0	1	0	0	0	1
1	0	1	0	1	0	0	1	1	1	0	1
1	1	0	0	1	0	0	1	0	0	0	1
1	1	1	0	0	0	1	1	1	1	0	1

Fig. 7.24 Excitation table for example 7.4

6. State diagram is written from the values of Excitation table as shown in Fig. 7.25. The counter sequence is 0-1-2-3-4-0.

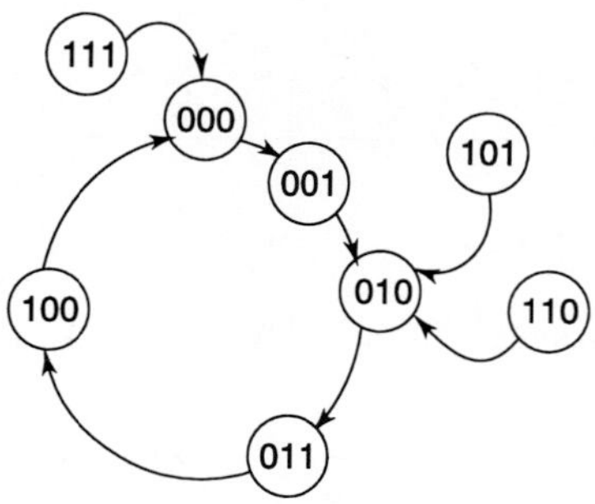

Fig. 7.25 State diagram for example 7.4

Example 7.5 Construct state tables for the following state diagrams shown in Fig. 7.26 and Fig. 7.27. (VTU – June 2005)

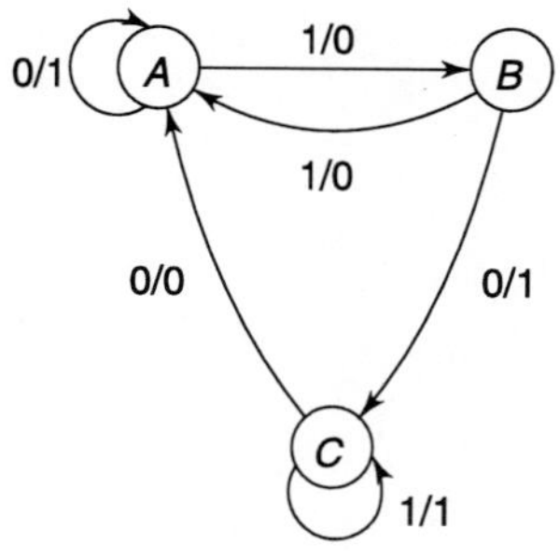

Fig. 7.26

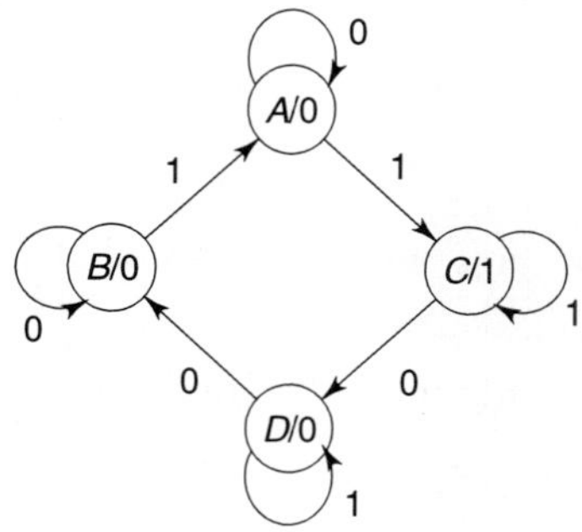

Fig. 7.27

The state diagrams are converted into tabular form, i.e., into state tables as shown in Fig. 7.28 and Fig. 7.29.

Present state	Next state		Output	
	$X = 0$	$X = 1$	$X = 0$	$X = 1$
ab	*ab*	*ab*	*y*	*y*
A	*A*	*B*	1	0
B	*C*	*A*	1	0
C	*A*	*C*	0	1

Fig. 7.28 State table for Fig. 7.26

Present state	Next state		Output
	$X = 0$	$X = 1$	
ab	*ab*	*ab*	*y*
A	*A*	*C*	0
B	*B*	*A*	0
C	*D*	*C*	1
D	*B*	*D*	0

Fig. 7.29 State table for Fig. 7.27

Example 7.6 Analyze the following synchronous circuit shown in Fig. 7.30.

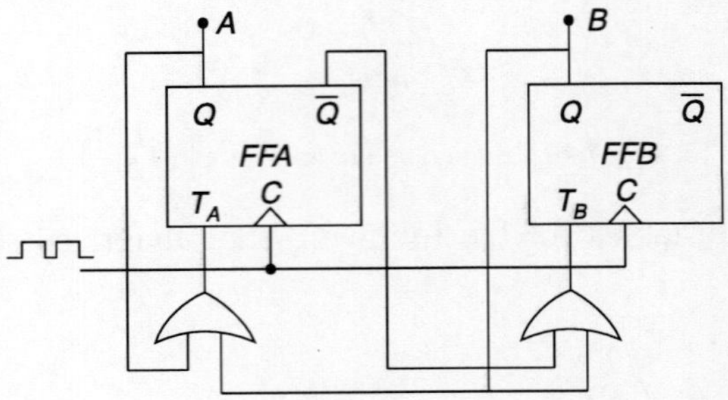

Fig. 7.30

1. Flip-flop outputs are *A* and *B*.
2. Here, we have *T* flip-flops
3. Flip-flop input equations are

$$T_A = A + B \qquad T_B = \overline{A} + B$$

4. K-maps are constructed for flip-flop inputs as shown in Fig. 7.31.

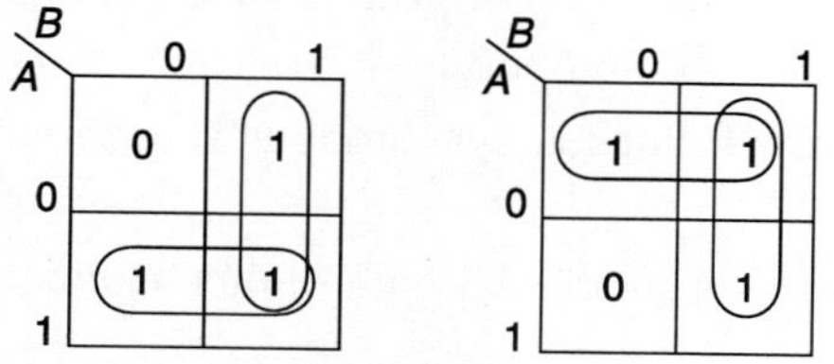

$T_A = A + B$ $\qquad$ $T_B = \bar{A} + B$

Fig. 7.31 K-maps for example 7.6

5. Excitation table is written using *T* flip-flop function table and the K-maps as shown in Fig. 7.32.

Present state		Next state		Flip-flop inputs	
A	B	A^+	B^+	T_A	T_B
0	0	0	1	0	1
0	1	1	0	1	1
1	0	0	0	1	0
1	1	0	0	1	1

(a)

T	Q^+
0	Q
1	$\bar{Q}$

(b)

Fig. 7.32 Excitation table (b) function table of T flip-flop for example 7.6

6. State diagram is constructed using the values in excitation table as shown in Fig. 7.33.

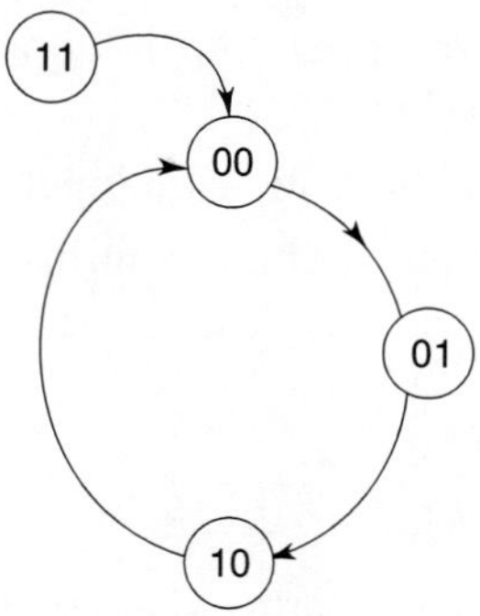

Fig. 7.33 State diagram for example 7.6

Here, the counter sequence is $0 \rightarrow 1 \rightarrow 2 \rightarrow 0$.

The state 3(11) is an invalid state. If the counter goes to invalid state. 3(11), it goes into the valid state 00 upon the arrival of next clock pulse. This kind of counters are called self correcting counters because the counters go into valid state from invalid state automatically. During the analysis of clocked synchronous sequential circuits so far we have seen simple circuits without inputs and decoded outputs. The states of the flip-flops were the outputs. Let us now analyze the circuits which have inputs and decoded outputs.

Let us consider the analysis of clocked synchronous sequential circuits using some typical circuits.

Example 7.7 Analyze the following clocked synchronous sequential Moore circuit shown in Fig. 7.34.

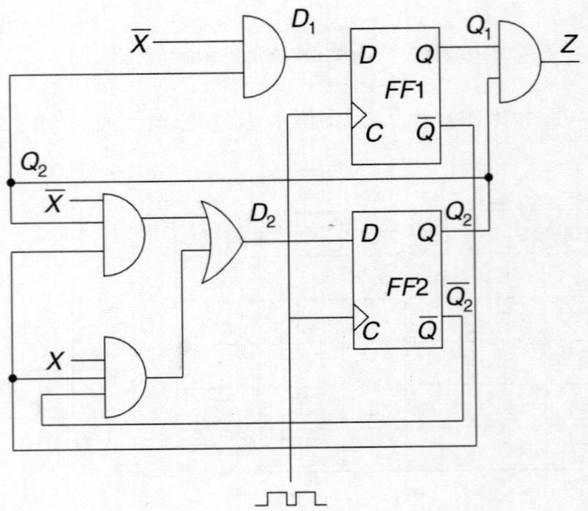

Fig. 7.34

Let us go through the following procedure to analyse completely to obtain the state diagram.

1. Excitation and output expression: First step is to write the equations for the flip-flop excitation expression and output expression.

According to the given sequential circuit, flip-flop inputs are D_1 and D_2 and the output is Z.

Hence, the excitation expressions are written in terms of present state and external input variables.

$$D_1 = \overline{X}Q_2$$

$$D_2 = \overline{X}\overline{Q}_1Q_2 + X\overline{Q}_1\overline{Q}_2$$

The output expression is also written in terms of present state and external input. In case of Moore circuit, output is expressed only in terms of present state.

2. Transition Equation: Next step is to write the transition equation. The transition equation is the next state expression which is derived from the characteristic equation of the flip-flops.

The characteristic equation for a D flip-flop gives the next state of flip-flop for the given excitation at its input terminals, i.e.,

$$Q^+ = D$$

By substituting the excitation expression into its characteristic equation, we can obtain the transition equation.

The characteristic equations for $FF1$ and $FF2$ are:

$$Q_1^+ = D_1$$

$$Q_2^+ = D_2$$

Hence, the transition equations are:

$$Q_1^+ = \overline{X}Q_2$$

$$Q_2^+ = \overline{X}\overline{Q}_1Q_2 + X\overline{Q}_1\overline{Q}_2$$

3. Transition Tables: The third step is to write the transition table. The transition table is the tabular representation of the transition equations and output equations. The table consists of three sections, namely, present state variables (Q_1 and Q_2), next state variables (Q_1^+ and Q_2^+) and the output variable Z.

The transition table can be written with the help of K-maps for Q_1^+ and Q_2^+. K-maps are constructed in terms of X, Q_1 and Q_2, i.e., external input and the present state as shown in Fig. 7.35.

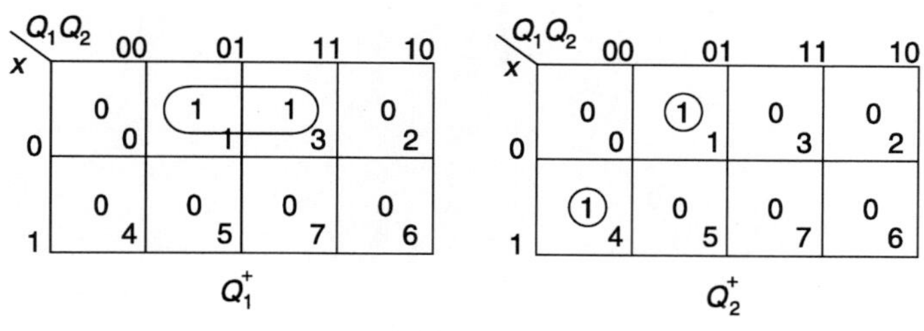

Fig. 7.35 K-maps for example 7.7

Using K-map values and the output expression, we can write the transition table as shown in Fig. 7.36.

Present state		Next state				Output
		$X = 0$		$X = 1$		
Q_1	Q_2	Q_1^+	Q_2^+	Q_1^+	Q_1^+	$Z = Q_1Q_2$
0	0	0	0	0	1	0
0	1	1	1	0	0	0
1	0	0	0	0	0	0
1	1	1	0	0	0	1

Fig. 7.36 Transition table for example 7.7

4. State Tables: The fourth step is to write the state table from the entries of transition table. The transition table can be converted into state table by writing alphanumeric symbols to represent the state instead of binary codes as shown in Fig. 7.37. The state 00 is assumed to be '*a*', 01 as '*b*', 10 as '*c*' and 11 as '*d*'.

Present state	Next state	Output	
	$X = 0$	$X = 1$	
Q_1Q_2	$Q_1^+Q_2^+$	$Q_1^+Q_2^+$	Z
a	*a*	*b*	0
b	*d*	*a*	0
c	*a*	*a*	0
d	*c*	*a*	1

Fig. 7.37 State table for example 7.7

5. State Diagram: The fifth step is to construct state diagram based on the values in the state table as shown in Fig. 7.38.

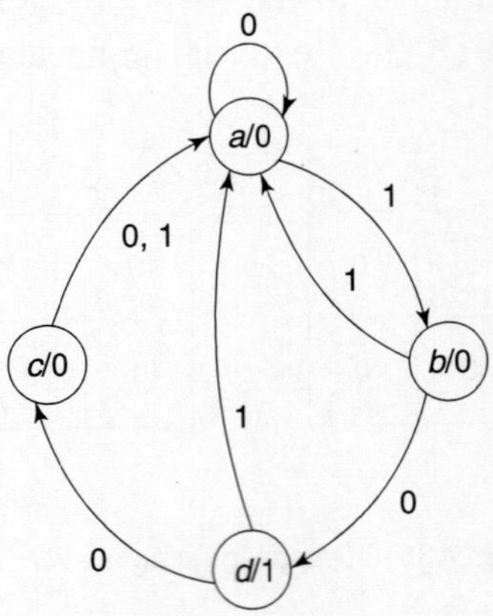

Fig. 7.38 State diagram for example 7.7

From *c*, there is a directed line ponting to *a*, but this indicates both 0 and 1 as present state. On both conditions, state '*c*' is changed to state '*a*'.

Example 7.8 Derive transition table, state table and state diagram for Moore sequential circuit shown in Fig. 7.39. (VTU – July 2005)

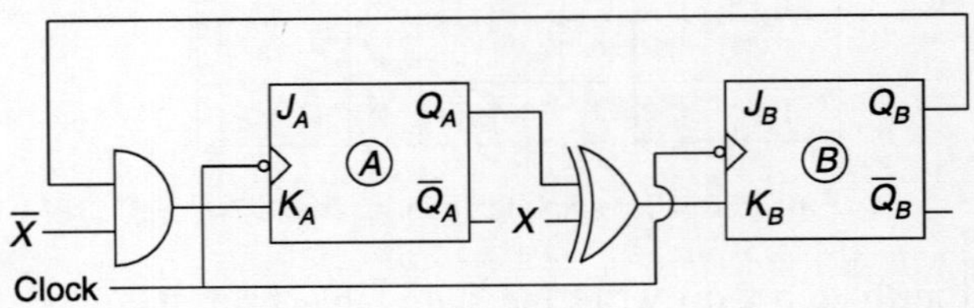

Fig. 7.39

1. Excitation and Output Expression:

$$K_A = \bar{X}Q_B$$

$$K_B = X\bar{Q}_A + \bar{X}Q_A$$

2. Transition Equation: The characteristic equation for *JK* flip-flop is:

$$Q^+ = J\bar{Q} + \bar{K}Q$$

Therefore,

$$Q_A^+ = J_A\bar{Q}_A + \bar{K}_A Q_A$$

$$Q_B^+ = J_B\bar{Q}_B + \bar{K}_B Q_A$$

Hence, the transition Equations are

$$Q_A^+ = J_A\bar{Q}_A + \overline{\bar{X}Q_B}\, Q_A$$

$$= (X + \bar{Q}_B)\, Q_A \quad \text{as there is no input at } J_A$$

$$Q_B^+ = \overline{(X\bar{Q}_A + \bar{X}Q_A)}\, Q_B$$

$$= (\overline{X\bar{Q}_A})\,(\overline{\bar{X}Q_A})\, Q_B$$

$$= [(\bar{X} + Q_A)\,(X + \bar{Q}_A)]\, Q_B$$

3. Transition Tables:

Q_A^+:

X \ Q_AQ_B	00	01	11	10
0	0	0	0	1
1	0	0	1	1

Q_B^+:

X \ Q_AQ_B	00	01	11	10
0	0	1	0	0
1	0	0	1	0

Fig. 7.40 K-maps for example 7.8

Present state		Next state				Output
		$X = 0$		$X = 1$		
Q_A	Q_B	Q_A^+	Q_B^+	Q_A^+	Q_B^+	Y
0	0	0	0	0	0	0
0	1	0	1	0	0	0
1	0	1	0	1	0	0
1	1	0	0	1	1	0

Fig. 7.41 Transition table for example 7.8

4. State Table:

Present state	Next state		Output
	$X = 0$	$X = 1$	
$Q_A Q_B$	$Q_A^+ Q_B^+$	$Q_A^+ Q_B^+$	Y
a	a	a	0
b	b	a	0
c	c	c	0
d	a	d	0

Fig. 7.42 State table for example 7.8

5. State Diagram:

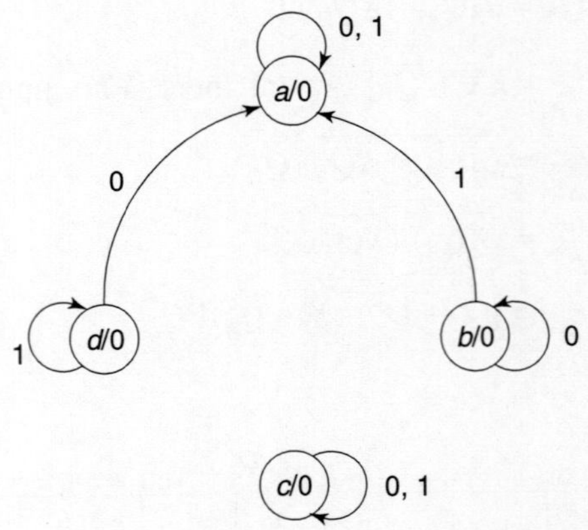

Fig. 7.43 State diagram fir example 7.8

Example 7.9 Construct the excitation table, transition table, state table and state diagram for the Moore sequential circuit shown in Fig. 7.44. (VTU – June 2010; June 2011; Dec 2011; Dec 2013)

Excitation and output expression:

Excitation expression,

$$J_A = B$$

$$K_A = \overline{X}B$$

$$J_B = \overline{X} \quad K_B = X \oplus A$$

Output expression,

$$y = A \oplus B = \overline{A}B + A\overline{B}$$

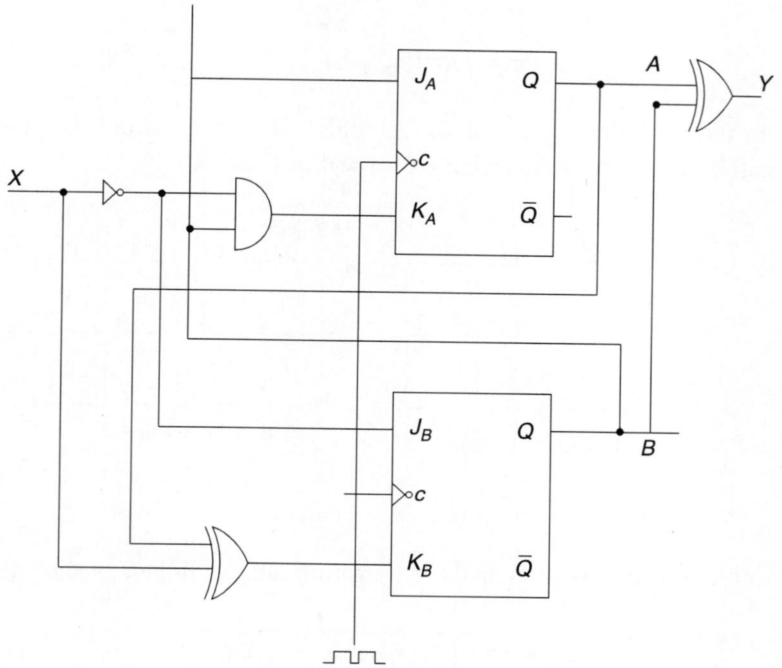

Fig. 7.44

2. Excitation table is derived from excitation expression and the output expression:

Present state		X = 0				X = 1				Output
		Excitation				Excitation				
A	B	J_A	K_A	J_B	K_B	J_A	K_A	J_B	K_B	Y
0	0	0	0	1	0	0	0	0	1	0
0	1	1	1	1	0	1	0	0	1	1
1	0	0	0	1	1	0	0	0	0	1
1	1	1	1	1	1	1	0	0	0	0

Fig. 7.45 Excitation table for example 7.9

3. Transition Equation: The characteristic equation for *JK* flip-flop is:

$$Q^+ = J\overline{Q} + \overline{K}Q$$

$$\therefore \quad A^+ = Q_A^+ = J_A\overline{Q}_A + \overline{K}_A Q_A$$

$$= B\overline{A} + \overline{\overline{X}B}\,A$$

$$= B\overline{A} + (X + \overline{B})\,A$$

$$B^+ = Q_B^+ = J_B\overline{Q}_B + \overline{K}_B Q_B$$
$$= \overline{X}\overline{B} + \overline{X \oplus A}\ B$$

K-maps: From the transition equations for A^+ and B^+ let us construct K-maps for A^+ and B^+ using present state A and B input X, which are shown in Fig. 7.46.

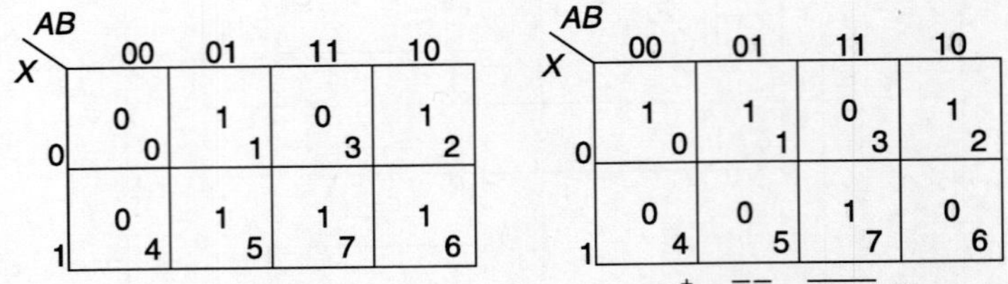

$A^+ = B\overline{A} + (X + \overline{B})A$

$B^+ = \overline{X}\overline{B} + \overline{X \oplus A}\ B$

Fig. 7.46 K-maps for example 7.9

5. Transition Table: From the K-maps, the transition table is drawn as shown in Fig. 7.47.

Present state		Next state				Output
		X = 0		X = 1		
A	B	A^+	B^+	A^+	B^+	$Y = A \oplus B$
0	0	0	1	0	0	0
0	1	1	1	1	0	1
1	0	1	1	1	0	1
1	1	0	0	1	1	0

Fig. 7.47 Transition table for example 7.9

6. State Table: We assign $a = 00$, $b = 01$, $c = 10$ and $d = 11$. Now we construct the state table from the transition table. State table is shown in Fig. 7.48.

Present state AB	Next state		Output
	X = 0	X = 1	
	A^+B^+	A^+B^+	Y
a	b	a	0
b	d	c	1
c	d	c	1
d	a	d	0

Fig. 7.48 State table for example 7.9

7. State Diagram: From the state table, we can draw state diagram as shown in Fig. 7.49. It is clearly seen that output depends only on the present state and not on the input. Hence, the given circuit is Moore sequential circuit.

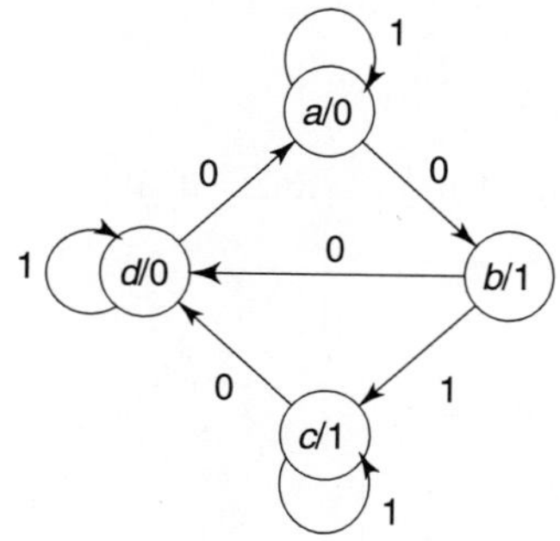

Fig. 7.49 State diagram for example 7.9

Example 7.10 For the logic diagram given in Fig. 7.50.

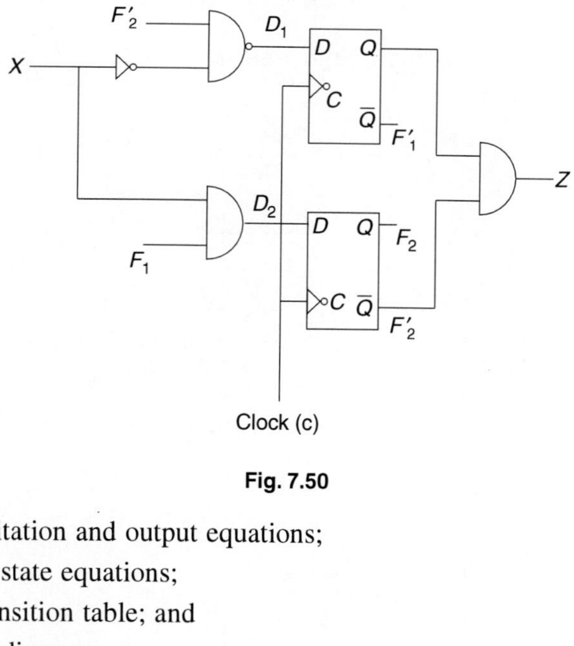

Fig. 7.50

(i) Derive the excitation and output equations;

(ii) Write the next state equations;

(iii) Construct a transition table; and

(iv) Draw the state diagram (VTU – Dec 2010)

Excitation and output equations:

Excitation expression $D_1 = \overline{\overline{X}\overline{F}_2} = X + F_2$

$D_2 = XF_1$

Output expression $Z = F_1\overline{F}_2$

2. Transition Equation (Next state equation): The characteristic equation for D flip-flop is:

$$Q^+ = D$$

$$F_1^+ = D_1 = \overline{\overline{X}\,\overline{F}_2} = X + F_2$$

$$F_2^+ = D_2 = XF_1$$

3. K-maps: Let us construct K-maps for F_1^+ and F_2^+ using present states F_1 and F_2 and input X. Fig 7.51 shows the K-maps.

F_1^+ (value, cell number):

X \ F_1F_2	00	01	11	10
0	0 (0)	1 (1)	1 (3)	0 (2)
1	1 (4)	1 (5)	1 (7)	1 (6)

F_2^+ (value, cell number):

X \ F_1F_2	00	01	11	10
0	0 (0)	0 (1)	0 (3)	0 (2)
1	0 (4)	0 (5)	1 (7)	1 (6)

Fig. 7.51 K-maps for example 7.10

4. Transition Table: From the K-maps, the transition table is constructed as follows in Fig. 7.52.

Present state		Next state				Output
		$X = 0$		$X = 1$		
F_1	F_2	F_1^+	F_2^+	F_1^+	F_2^+	$Z = F_1F_2^*$
0	0	0	0	1	0	0
0	1	1	0	1	0	0
1	0	0	0	1	1	1
1	1	1	0	1	1	0

Fig. 7.52 Transition table for example 7.10

5. State Table: We assign a = 00, b = 01, c = 10 and d = 11. We construct the state table as shown in Fig. 7.53.

Present state F_1F_2	Next state		Output
	$X = 0$	$X = 1$	
	$F_1^+F_2^+$	$F_1^+F_2^+$	Z
a	a	c	0
b	c	c	0
c	a	d	1
d	c	d	0

Fig. 7.53 State table for example 7.10

6. State diagram: From the state table we can draw the state diagram as shown in Fig. 7.54.

As output depends only on the present state and not on the input, this circuit is Moore sequential circuit.

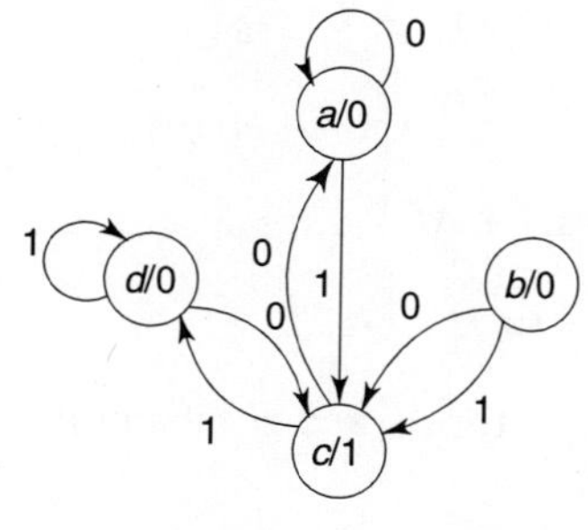

Fig. 7.54 State diagram for example 7.10

Example 7.11 Give output function, transition table and state diagram by analyzing the sequential circuit shown in Fig. 7.55. (VTU – Dec 2008)

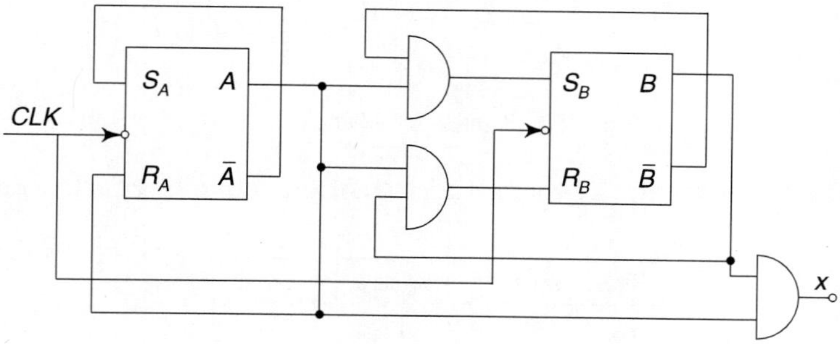

Fig. 7.55

1. Excitation and Output Equations:

$$S_A = \bar{A} \qquad R_A = A$$

$$S_B = A\bar{B} \qquad R_B = AB$$

$$X = AB$$

2. Transition Equation: The characteristic equation for *SR* flip-flop is:

$$Q^+ = S + \bar{R}Q$$

$$A^+ = Q_A^+ = S_A + \bar{R}_A Q_A$$

$$= \bar{A} + \bar{A}Q_A = \bar{A}(1 + Q_A)$$

$$= \bar{A}$$

$$B^+ = Q_B^+ = S_B + \overline{R}_B Q_B$$

$$= A\overline{B} + (\overline{AB})\, Q_B$$

$$= A\overline{B} + (\overline{A} + \overline{B})\, Q_B$$

$$= A\overline{B} + \overline{A}B + \overline{B}B$$

$$= A\overline{B} + \overline{A}B \qquad (\therefore\ \overline{B}B = 0)$$

$$= A \oplus B$$

3. K-maps: Let us construct K-maps for A^+ and B^+ using present states A and B shown in Fig. 7.56.

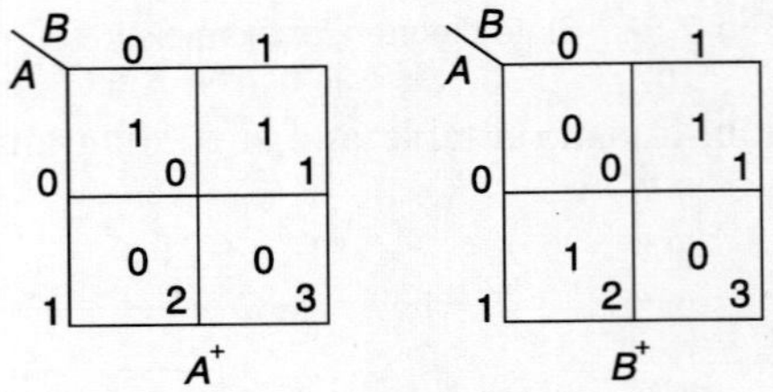

Fig. 7.56 K-maps for example 7.11

4. Transition Table: From the K-maps the transition table is constructed as shown in Fig. 7.57.

Present state		Next state		Output
A	B	A^+	B^+	$X = AB$
0	0	1	0	0
0	1	1	1	0
1	0	0	1	0
1	1	0	0	1

Fig. 7.57 Transition table for example 7.11

5. State Table: Let us assign $a = 00$, $b = 01$, $c = 10$ and $d = 11$. We construct the state table as shown in Fig. 7.58.

Present state	Next state	Output
AB	A^+B^+	X
a	c	0
b	d	0
c	b	0
d	a	1

Fig. 7.58 State table for example 7.11

6. State diagram: We can draw the state diagram from the state table as shown in Fig. 7.59.

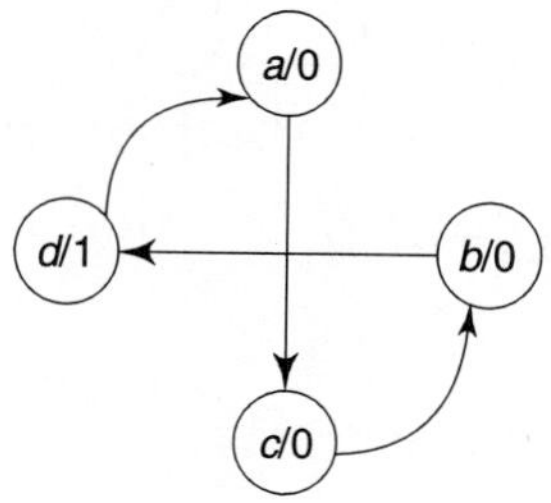

Fig. 7.59 State diagram for example 7.11

Example 7.12 Analyze the sequential circuit of Fig. 7.60 (clock not shown but is implicit)

(i) Write down the excitation and output functions.

(ii) Form the excitation and state tables.

(iii) Give a word description of the circuit operation. (VTU – July 2006)

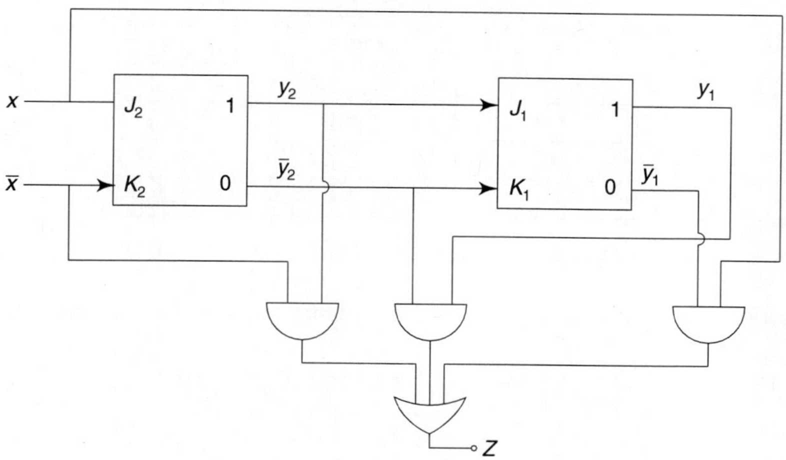

Fig. 7.60

1. Excitation and Output Functions:

$$J_2 = X \qquad K_2 = \overline{X}$$

$$J_1 = Y_2 \qquad K_1 = \overline{Y}_2$$

$$z = \bar{x}y_2 + \bar{y}_2 y_1 + \bar{y}_1 x$$

2. Transition Equations: The characteristic equation for *JK* flip-flop is:

$$Q^+ = J\overline{Q} + \overline{K}Q$$

$$Q_2^+ = J_2\overline{Q}_2 + \overline{K}_2 Q_2$$
$$= x\overline{Q}_2 + xQ_2$$
$$= x\overline{y}_2 + xy_2 = x(y_2 + \overline{y}_2) = x$$
$$Q_1^+ = J_1\overline{Q}_1 + \overline{K}_1 Q_1$$
$$= Y_2\overline{Q}_1 + \overline{Y}_2 Q_1$$
$$= Y_2\overline{Y}_1 + Y_2 Y_1$$
$$= Y_2(\overline{Y}_1 + Y_1)$$
$$= Y_2 \quad [\therefore\ Y_1 + \overline{Y}_1 = 1]$$ 1

3. Excitation Table: Excitation table is derived from excitation and output expressions as shown in Fig. 7.61.

Present state		$X = 0$ Excitation				$X = 1$ Excitation				Output Z	
Y_2	Y_2	J_2	K_2	J_1	K_1	J_2	K_2	J_1	K_1	$X = 0$	$X = 1$
0	0	0	1	0	1	1	0	0	1	0	1
0	1	0	1	0	1	1	0	0	1	1	1
1	0	0	1	1	0	1	0	1	0	1	1
1	1	0	1	1	0	1	0	1	0	1	0

Fig. 7.61 Excitation table for example 7.12

4. Transition Table: Transition table is constructed from transition equations (Fig. 7.62).

Present state		Next state $X = 0$		Next state $X = 1$		Output Z $X = 0$	Output Z $X = 1$
Y_2	Y_1	Y_2^+	Y_1^+	Y_2^+	Y_1^+		
0	0	0	0	1	0	0	1
0	1	0	0	1	0	1	1
1	0	0	1	1	1	1	1
1	1	0	1	1	1	1	0

Fig. 7.62 Transition table for example 7.12

State Table: State table is constructed from transition table by assigning $a = 00$, $b = 01$, $c = 10$ and $d = 11$. State table is shown in Fig. 7.63. From state table it is seen that when the sequential circuit remains in same state the output is '0'. When the flip-flop states are different, the output is 1.

Present state	Next state		Output Z	
	X = 0	X = 1	X = 0	X = 1
Y_2Y_1	$Y_2^+Y_1^+$	$Y_2^+Y_1^+$		
a	a	c	0	1
b	a	c	1	1
c	b	d	1	1
d	b	d	1	0

Fig. 7.63 State table for example 7.12

Example 7.13 Construct the state tables for the following state diagrams shown in Fig. 7.64 and Fig. 7.65.
(VTU – June 2008)

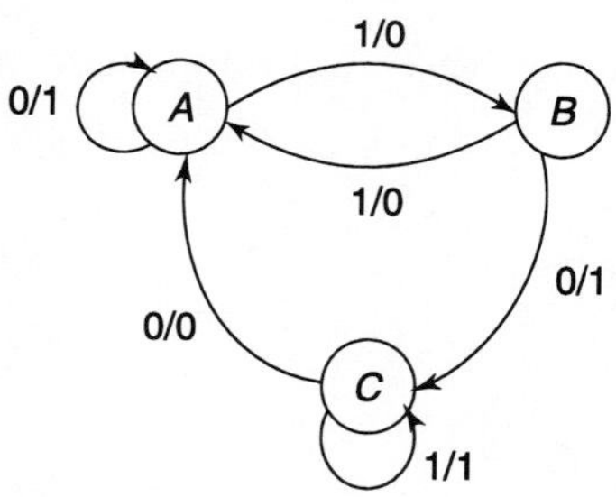

Fig. 7.64

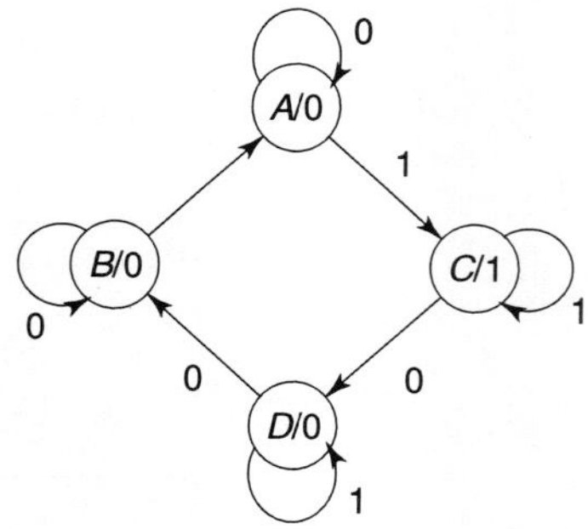

Fig. 7.65

Figure 7.66 shows state table for the circuit in Fig. 7.64. It is Mealy type sequential circuit. Figure 7.67 shows a state table for the circuit in Fig. 7.65. It is Moore type sequential circuit.

Present state	Next state		Output	
	X = 0	X = 1	X = 0	X = 1
A	A	B	1	0
B	C	A	1	0
C	A	C	0	1

Fig. 7.66 State table for Fig. 7.64

Present state	Next state		Output
	X = 0	X = 1	
A	A	C	0
B	B	A	0
C	D	C	1
D	B	D	0

Fig. 7.67 State table for Fig. 7.65

Example 7.14 Design a clocked sequential circuit that operates according to the state diagram shown in Fig. 7.68. Implement the circuit using *D* flip-flop (VTU – June 2008)

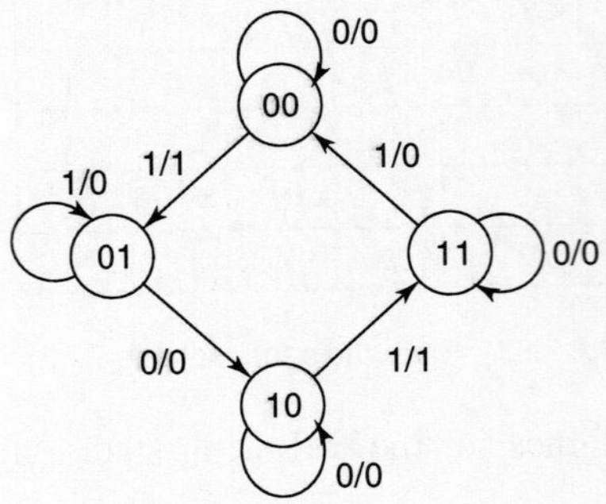

Fig. 7.68

As already state values have been assigned, we can straightaway write transition table as shown in Fig. 7.69.

Present state		Next state		Output	
		$X = 0$	$X = 1$	$X = 0$	$X = 1$
A	B	A^+B^+	A^+B^+	Y	Y
0	0	00	01	0	1
0	1	10	01	0	0
1	0	10	11	0	1
1	1	11	00	0	0

Fig. 7.69 Transition table for example 7.14

The transition table shows that there are four states the circuit goes through and therefore, we require 2 flip-flops (i.e., $2^2 = 4$ states). In this problem, we are using *D* flip-flops.

For *D* flip-flops, next states are nothing but the present states.

Karnaugh maps: We can use next states to determine flip-flop inputs.

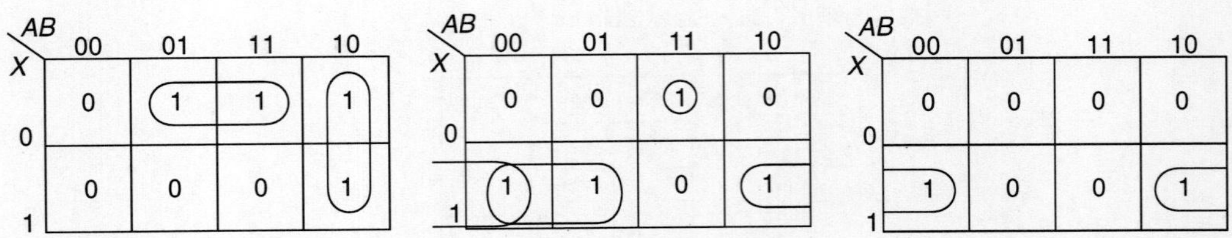

$A^+ = D_A$
$D_A = \overline{X}B + A\overline{B}$

$B^+ = D_B$
$D_B = X\overline{A} + X\overline{B} + \overline{X}AB$

xy
$y = X\overline{B}$

Fig. 7.70 K-maps

With these flip-flop input functions D_A and D_B and circuit output function Y, we draw the logic diagram as shown in Fig. 7.71.

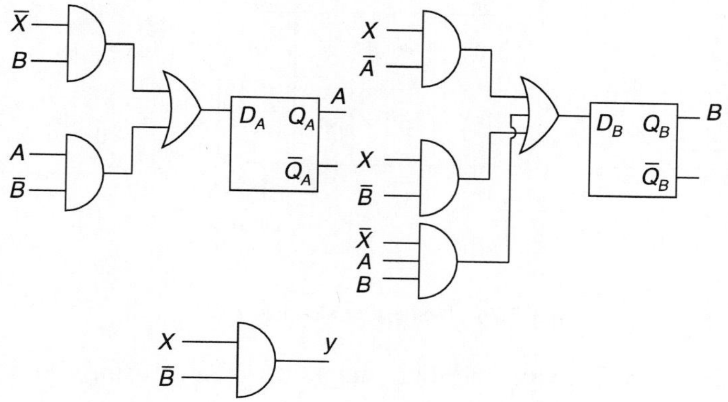

Fig. 7.71 Logic diagrams for example 7.14

Example 7.15 A sequential circuit has one input and one output. The state diagram is as shown below in Fig. 7.72. Design a sequential circuit using D flip-flop. (VTU – June 2012)

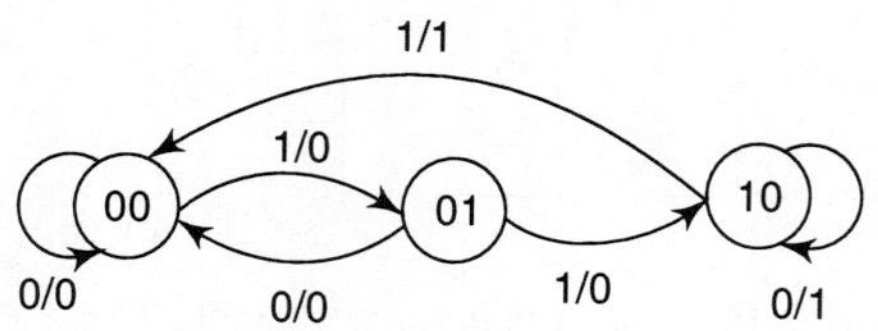

Fig. 7.72

The transition table for the state diagram shown in Fig. 7.72 in given is Fig. 7.73. State table is not needed as binary states are assigned values.

Present state		Next state		Output	
		X = 0	X = 1	X = 0	X = 1
A	B	A^+B^+	A^+B^+	Y	Y
0	0	00	01	0	0
0	1	00	10	0	0
1	0	10	00	1	1

Fig. 7.73 Transition table for example 7.15

K-Maps: From transition table, K-maps are drawn as shown in Fig. 7.74.

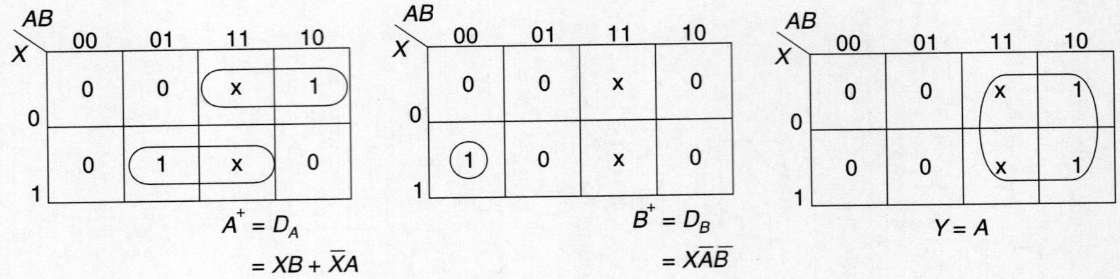

Fig. 7.74 K-maps for example 7.15

Login Diagram: From the K-maps, the logic diagram is drawn using flip-flop inputs D_A and D_B and the output Y.

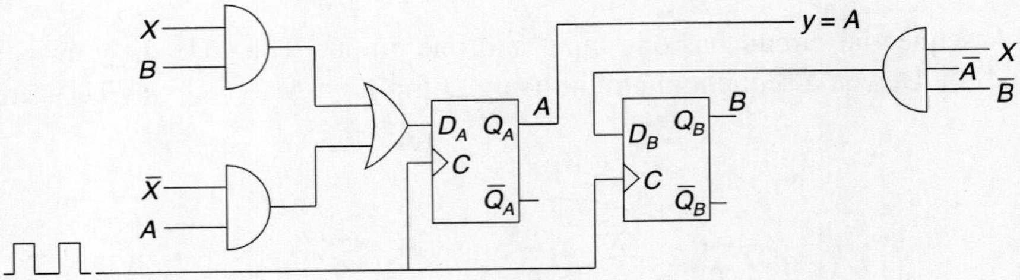

Fig. 7.75 Logic diagram for example 7.15

Example 7.16 A sequential network has one input and one output. The state diagram is shown in Fig. 7.76. Design the sequential circuit with T flip-flop. (VTU – June 2007)

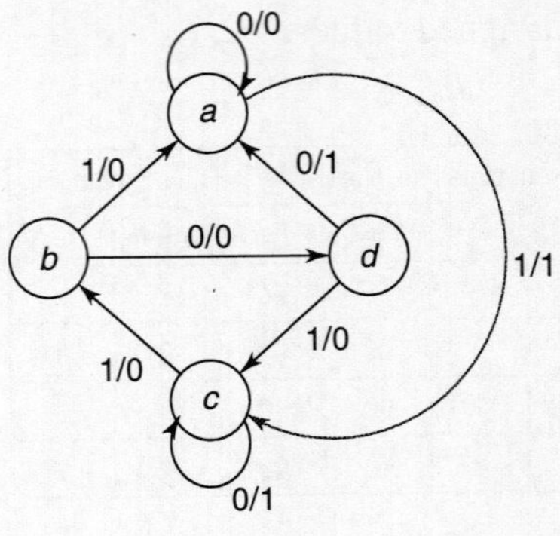

Fig. 7.76

State table is drawn using the state diagram.

Present state	Next state		Output	
	X = 0	X = 1	X = 0	X = 1
AB	A^+B^+	A^+B^+	Y	Y
a	a	c	0	1
b	d	a	0	0
c	c	b	1	0
d	a	c	1	0

Fig. 7.77 State table for example 7.16

From the state table, we can draw transition table by substituting $a = 00$, $b = 01$, $c = 10$ and $d = 11$. The transition table is shown in Fig. 7.78.

The application table for T flip-flop is shown in Fig. 7.78.

Present state		Next state		Output	
		X = 0	X = 1	X = 0	X = 1
A	B	A^+B^+	A^+B^+	Y	Y
0	0	00	10	0	1
0	1	11	00	0	0
1	0	10	01	1	0
1	1	00	10	1	0

Fig. 7.78 Transition table for example 7.16

Q_1	Q^+	T
0	0	0
0	1	1
1	0	1
1	1	0

Fig. 7.79 Application table for T flip-flop

The circuit excitation table with next state, and flip-flop inputs and output is shown in Fig. 7.80.

Present state		Next state		Flip-flop inputs		Output y	
		X = 0	X = 1	X = 0	X = 1	X = 0	X = 1
A	B	A^+B^+	A^+B^+	T_AT_B	T_AT_B	Y	Y
0	0	00	10	00	10	0	1
0	1	11	00	10	01	0	0
1	0	10	01	00	11	1	0
1	1	00	10	11	01	1	0

Fig. 7.80 Excitation table for example 7.16

K-maps are constructed using excitation table data. They are shown in Fig. 7.81.

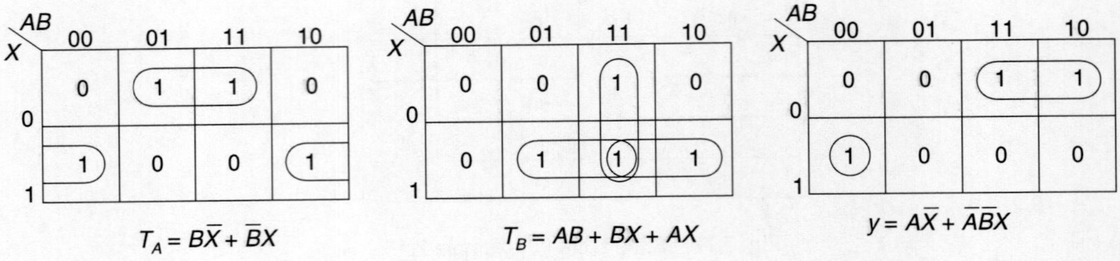

Fig. 7.81 K-maps for example 7.16

Flip-flop input function $T_A = B\overline{X} + \overline{B}X$

$T_B = AB + BX + AX$

Circuit output function $Y = A\overline{X} + \overline{A}\,\overline{B}X$

With flip-flop input functions T_A and T_B and output function Y, the logic diagram for the sequential circuit is shown in Fig. 7.82.

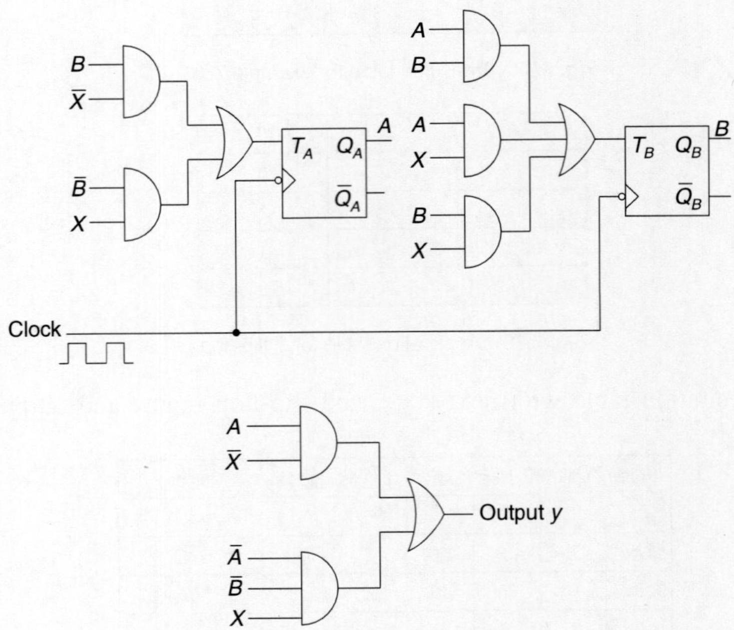

Fig. 7.82 Logic diagram for example 7.16

Example 7.17 Design a sequential machine using D flip-flops for realizing the state table below in Fig. 7.83. The machine is of a single input single output type.

Present state	Next state		Output Z	
	$X = 0$	$X = 1$	$X = 0$	$X = 1$
A	B	C	0	0
B	A	A	0	1
C	D	A	0	1
D	A	D	0	1

Fig. 7.83

Indicate the state transition diagram. Do the state assignment. Work out the excitation and the output logics.

(VTU – Jan 2005)

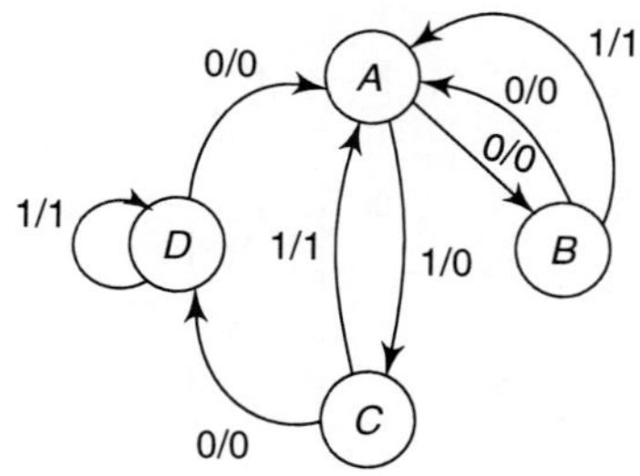

Fig. 7.84 State diagram for example 7.17

The state diagram is shown in Fig. 7.84. The state assignment is given as follows: A = 00, B = 01, C = 10 and D = 11. Using these state assignments, the state table is constructed as shown in Fig. 7.85(a) and transition table is as shown in Fig. 7.85(b).

Present state	Next state		Output Z	
	$X = 0$	$X = 1$	$X = 0$	$X = 1$
00	01	10	0	0
01	00	00	0	1
10	11	00	0	1
11	00	11	0	1

Fig. 7.85(a) State table for example 7.17

Present state		Input	Next state		Flip-flop input		Output Z
A	B	X	A^+	B^+	D_A	D_B	Z
0	0	0	0	1	0	1	0
0	0	1	1	0	1	0	0
0	1	0	0	0	0	0	0
0	1	1	0	0	0	0	1
1	0	0	1	1	1	1	0
1	0	1	0	0	0	0	1
1	1	0	0	0	0	0	0
1	1	1	1	1	1	1	1

Fig. 7.85(b) Transition table for example 7.17

Using *D* flip-flops, transition table is constructed as shown in Fig. 7.85(b). Now K-maps are drawn as shown in Fig. 7.86(a).

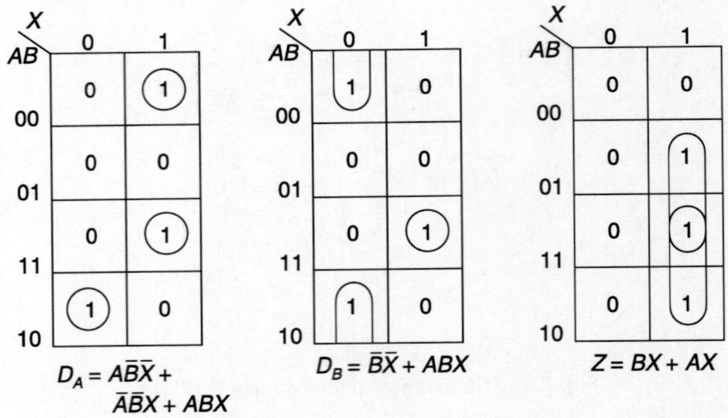

Fig. 7.86(a) K-maps for example 7.17

With flip-flop input function and output function, logic diagram is drawn as shown in Fig. 7.86(b).

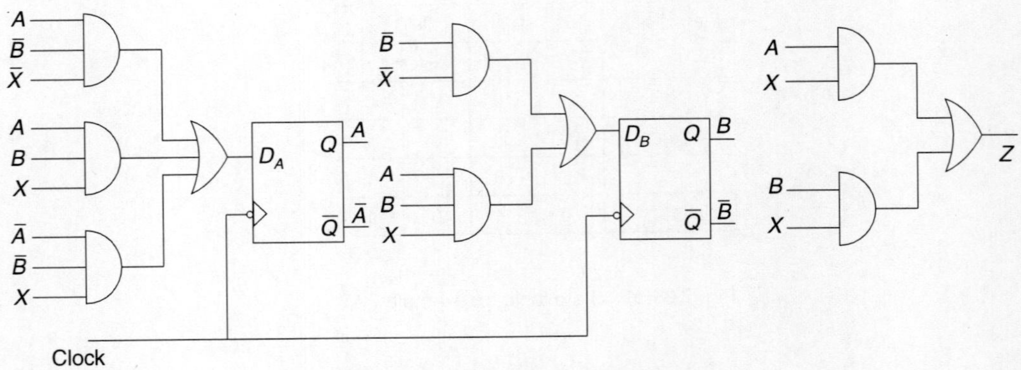

Fig. 7.86(b) Logic diagram for example 7.17

Example 7.18 A sequential circuit has one input and one output state diagram as shown in Fig. 7.87. Design the sequential circuit with *JK* flip-flop. (VTU – Dec 2012)

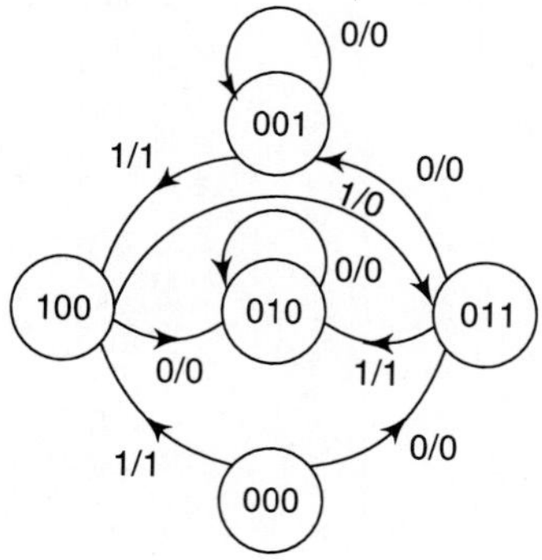

Fig. 7.87

The excitation table is constructed as shown in Fig. 7.88.

Present state input				Next state			Flip-flop inputs						Output
A	B	C	X	A^+	B^+	C^+	J_A	K_A	J_B	K_B	J_C	K_C	Y
0	0	0	0	0	1	1	0	×	1	×	1	×	0
0	0	0	1	1	0	0	1	×	0	×	0	×	1
0	0	1	0	0	0	1	0	×	0	×	×	0	0
0	0	1	1	1	0	0	1	×	0	×	×	1	1
0	1	0	0	0	1	0	0	×	×	0	0	×	0
0	1	0	1	–	–	–	–	–	–	–	–	–	0
0	1	1	0	0	0	1	0	×	×	1	×	0	0
0	1	1	1	0	1	0	0	×	×	0	×	1	1
1	0	0	0	0	1	0	×	1	1	×	0	×	0
1	0	0	1	0	1	1	×	1	1	×	1	×	0
1	0	1	0	–	–	–	–	–	–	–	–	–	×
1	0	1	1	–	–	–	–	–	–	–	–	–	×
1	1	0	0	–	–	–	–	–	–	–	–	–	×
1	1	0	1	–	–	–	–	–	–	–	–	–	×
1	1	1	0	–	–	–	–	–	–	–	–	–	×
1	1	1	1	–	–	–	–	–	–		–	–	×

Fig. 7.88 Transition table for example 7.18

K-maps are drawn for the excitation table data, i.e., for *JK* inputs and output *Y*, as shown in Fig. 7.89.

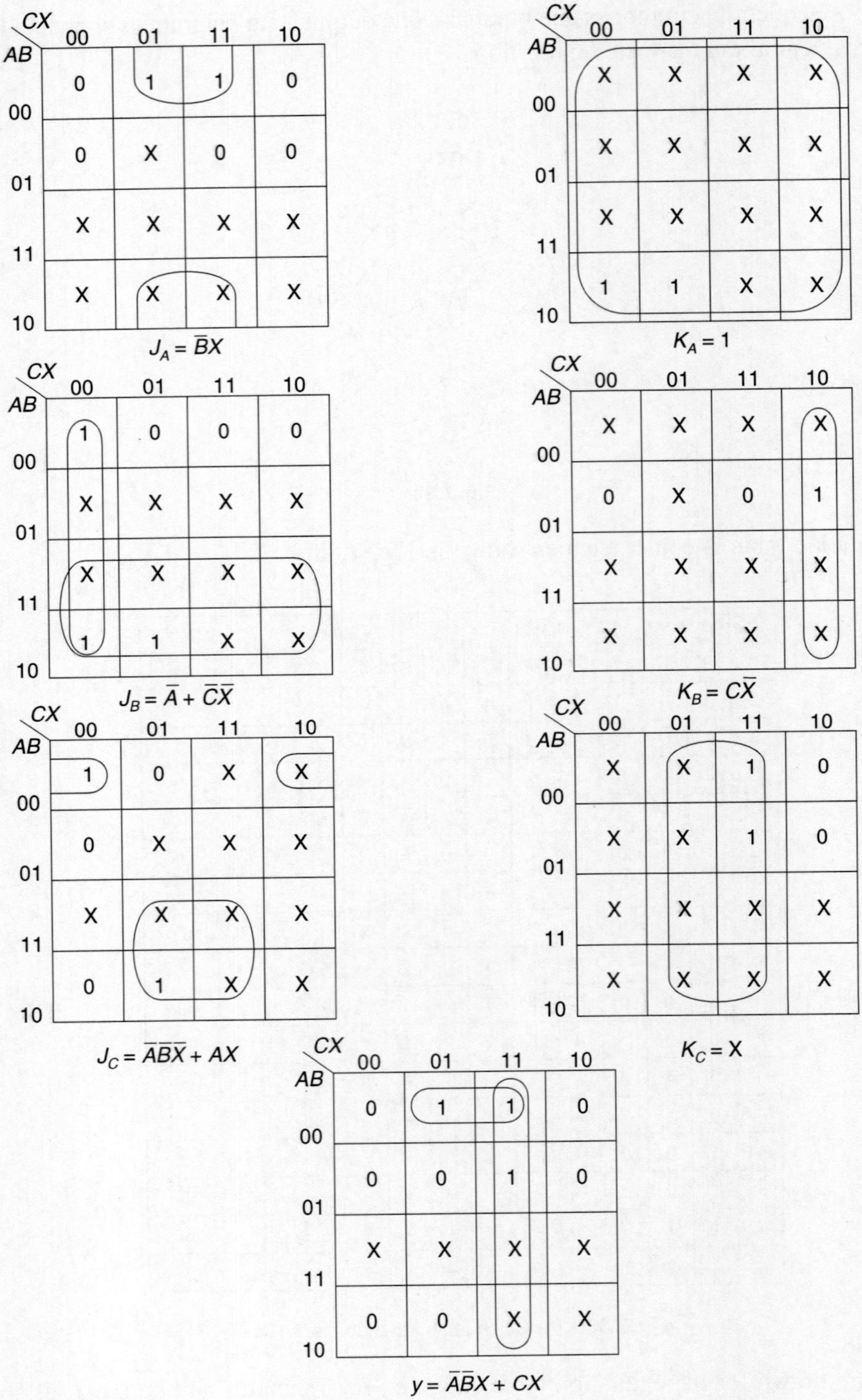

Fig. 7.89 K-maps for example 7.18

Logic diagram is drawn using flip-flop inputs functions and output function from the *K*-maps as shown in Fig. 7.90.

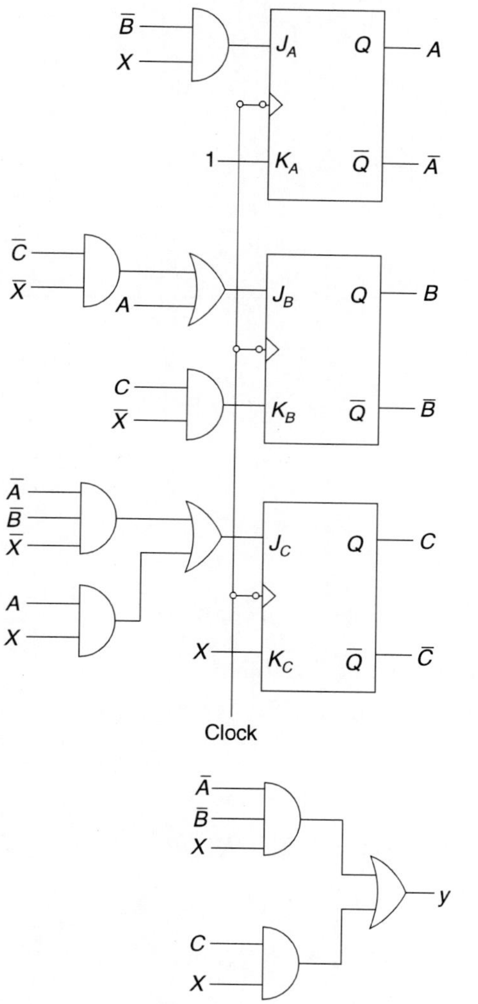

Fig. 7.90 Logic diagram for example 7.18

Example 7.19 A sequential circuit has two flip-flops *A* and *B*, two inputs *x* and *y* and an output *z*. The flip-flop input functions and the circuit output functions are as follows:

$$J_A = XB + \bar{y}\bar{B} \qquad K_A = x\bar{y}\bar{B}$$

$$J_B = x\bar{A} \qquad K_B = x\bar{y} + A$$

$$z = xyA + \bar{x}\bar{y}B$$

Obtain the logic diagram, state table and state equations, also state diagram.

(VTU – Dec 2012)

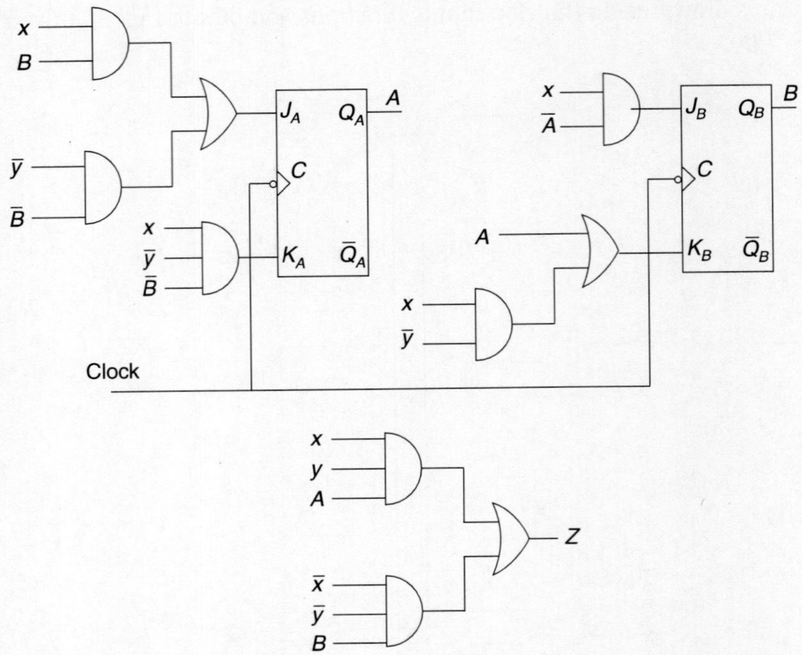

Fig. 7.91 Logic diagram

Logic diagram is drawn as shown in Fig. 7.91.

The transition equations for *JK* flip-flops can be derived from the characteristic equation for *JK* flip-flop.

$$Q^+ = J\bar{Q} + \bar{K}Q$$

$$\therefore \quad A^+ = Q_A^+ = J_A\bar{Q}_A + \bar{K}_A Q_A$$

$$= (xB + \bar{y}\bar{B})\,\bar{Q}_A + (\overline{x\bar{y}\bar{B}})\,Q_A$$

$$= xB\bar{Q}_A + \bar{y}\bar{B}\bar{Q}_A + (\bar{x} + y + B)\,Q_A$$

$$= xB\bar{Q}_A + \bar{y}\bar{B}\bar{Q}_A + \bar{x}Q_A + yQ_A + BQ_A$$

$$= xB\bar{A} + \bar{y}\bar{B}\bar{A} + \bar{x}A + yA + BA$$

$$B^+ = Q_B^+ = J_B\bar{Q}_B + \bar{K}_B Q_B$$

$$= (x\bar{A})\,\bar{Q}_B + (\overline{x\bar{y} + A})\,Q_B$$

$$= x\bar{A}\,\bar{Q}_B + (\overline{x\bar{y}})\,(\bar{A})\,Q_B$$

$$= x\bar{A}\,\bar{Q}_B + (\bar{x} + y)\,\bar{A}Q_B$$

$$= x\bar{A}\,\bar{Q}_B + \bar{x}\bar{A}Q_B + y\bar{A}Q_B$$

$$= x\bar{A}\,\bar{B} + \bar{x}\bar{A}B + y\bar{A}B$$

Now with the next state values the K-maps are drawn as shown in Fig. 7.92.

A^+

AB \ xy	00	01	11	10
00	1	0	0	1
01	0	0	1	1
11	1	1	1	1
10	1	1	1	0

B^+

AB \ xy	00	01	11	10
00	0	0	1	1
01	1	1	1	0
11	0	0	0	0
10	0	0	0	0

Fig. 7.92 K-maps for example 7.19

Present state		Next state				Output Z			
		xy = 00	xy = 01	xy = 10	xy = 11	xy = 00	xy = 01	xy = 10	xy = 11
A	B	A^+B^+	A^+B^+	A^+B^+	A^+B^+				
0	0	10	00	11	01	0	0	0	0
0	1	01	01	10	11	1	0	0	0
1	0	10	10	00	10	0	0	0	1
1	1	10	10	10	10	1	0	0	1

Fig. 7.93 Transition table for example 7.19

Let us construct state table from transition table as shown in Fig. 7.94 (a = 00, b = 01, c = 10 and d = 11)

Present state	Next state				Output Z			
	$\bar{X}\bar{Y}$	$\bar{X}Y$	XY	XY	$\bar{X}\bar{Y}$	$\bar{X}Y$	XY	XY
a	c	a	d	b	0	0	0	0
b	b	b	c	d	1	0	0	0
c	c	c	a	c	0	0	0	1
d	c	c	c	c	1	0	0	1

Fig. 7.94 State table for example 7.19

Now state diagram is drawn as shown in Fig. 7.95.

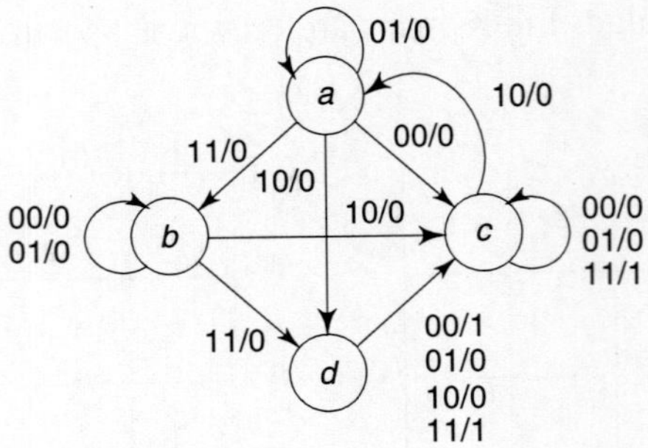

Fig. 7.95 State diagram for example 7.19

Example 7.20 For the state machine M_1 shown in Fig. 7.96, obtain

(i) state table
(ii) transition table
(iii) excitation table for T flip-flop
(iv) logic circuit for T excitation realization. (VTU – Dec 2007)

(i) From the state diagram, let us construct state table as shown in Fig. 7.96(a).

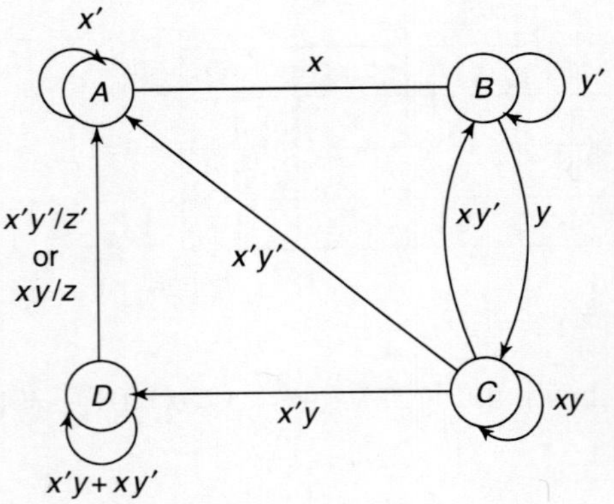

Fig. 7.96

Present state	Next state				Output (z)			
	$\bar{x}\bar{y}$ 00	$\bar{x}y$ 01	$x\bar{y}$ 10	xy 11	$\bar{x}\bar{y}$ 00	$\bar{x}y$ 01	$x\bar{y}$ 10	xy 11
A	A	A	B	B	0	0	0	0
B	B	C	B	C	0	0	0	0
C	A	D	B	C	0	0	0	0
D	A	D	D	A	0	0	0	1

Fig. 7.96(a) State table for example 7.20

Excitation table for T flip-flop is a shown in Fig. 7.97.

Q	Q^+	T
0	0	0
0	1	1
1	0	1
1	1	0

Fig. 7.97 Excitation table for T flip-flop

(ii) Using excitation table and state table, let us construct transition table as shown in Fig. 7.98. Here we assume $A = 00$, $B = 01$, $C = 10$ and $D = 11$

There is a requirement of two flip-flops as there are 4 states (A, B, C, D). Let the flip-flops be P and R.

Present state		Inputs		Next state		Flip-flop inputs		Output
P	R	X	Y	P^+	R^+	T_P	T_R	Z
0	0	0	0	0	0	0	0	0
0	0	0	1	0	0	0	0	0
0	0	1	0	0	1	0	1	0
0	0	1	1	0	1	0	1	0
0	1	0	0	0	1	0	0	0
0	1	0	1	1	0	1	1	0
0	1	1	0	0	1	0	0	0
0	1	1	1	1	0	1	1	0
1	0	0	0	0	0	1	0	0
1	0	0	1	1	1	0	1	0
1	0	1	0	0	1	1	1	0
1	0	1	1	1	0	0	0	0
1	1	0	0	0	0	1	1	0
1	1	0	1	1	1	0	0	0
1	1	1	0	1	1	0	0	0
1	1	1	1	0	0	1	1	1

Fig. 7.98 Transition table for example 7.21

(iii) Flip-flop inputs can be simplified using K-maps as shown in Fig. 7.99.

PR \ XY	00	01	11	10
00	0	0	0	0
01	0	1	1	0
11	1	0	1	0
10	1	0	0	1

$T_p = \bar{P}RY + RXY + P\bar{X}\bar{Y} + P\bar{R}\bar{Y}$

PR \ XY	00	01	11	10
00	0	0	1	1
01	0	1	1	0
11	1	0	1	0
10	0	1	0	1

$T_B = PR\bar{X}\bar{Y} + P\bar{R}\bar{X}Y + \bar{P}XY + RXY + \bar{P}RY + \bar{R}X\bar{Y}$

Fig. 7.99 K-map for example 7.21

(iv) Logic circuit for T excitation realization is as shown in Fig. 7.100.

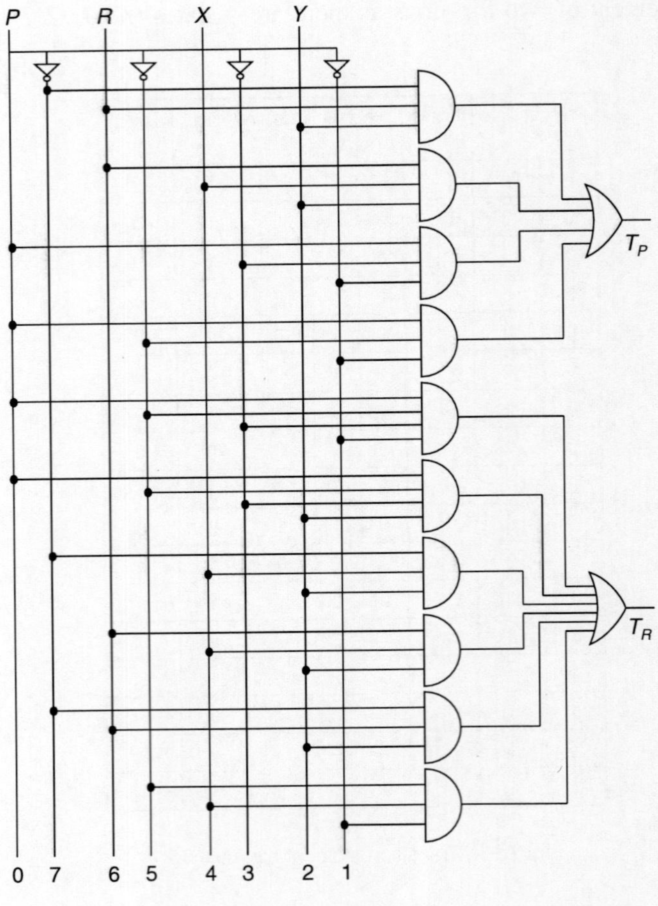

Fig. 7.100 Logic circuit for excitation realization

EXERCISE

1. Explain the Mealy model and Moore model of a clocked synchronous sequential network.
2. Analyze the synchronous circuit of the following figure (clock not shown but is implicit):

   (a) Write down the excitation and output functions.

(b) Form the excitation and state tables.

(c) Give a word description of the circuit operation.

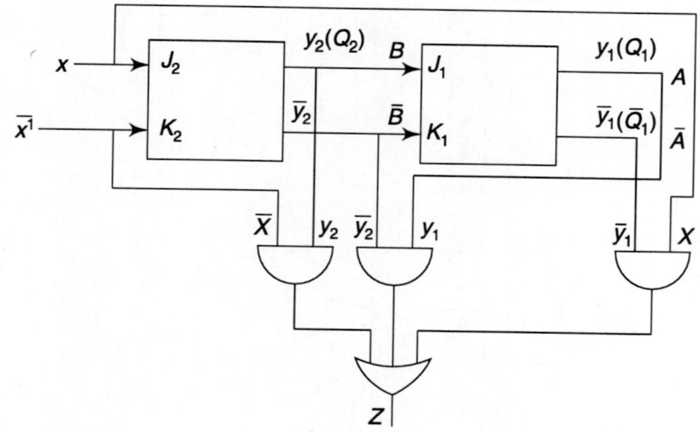

3. Construct the excitation table, transition table, state table and state diagram of a synchronous sequential circuit built wiring two positive edge triggered flip-flops A and B. The system inputs are x_1 and x_2 and the output is y. The flip-flop inputs and the circuit output are given by:

$$J_A = Bx_1 + \overline{B}\,\overline{x}_2 \qquad J_B = \overline{A}x_1$$

$$K_A = \overline{B}x_1\overline{x}_2 \qquad K_B = A + x_1\overline{x}_2y + Ax_1x_2 + B\overline{x}_1\overline{x}_2$$

4. Analyse the following synchronous sequential circuit with inputs x_1 and x_2 and output y:

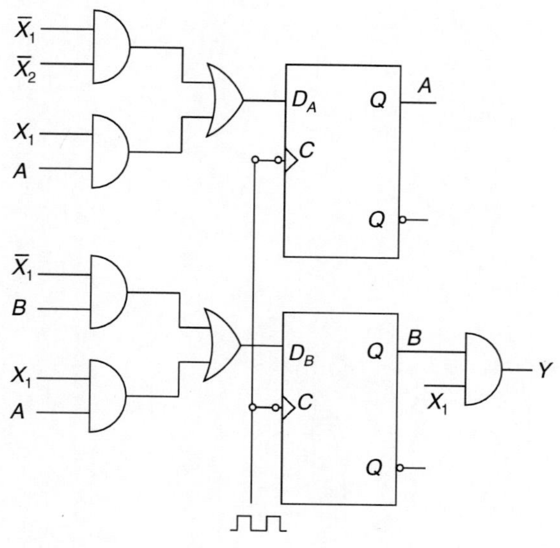

5. Analyze the given synchronous sequential circuit with input x and output y.

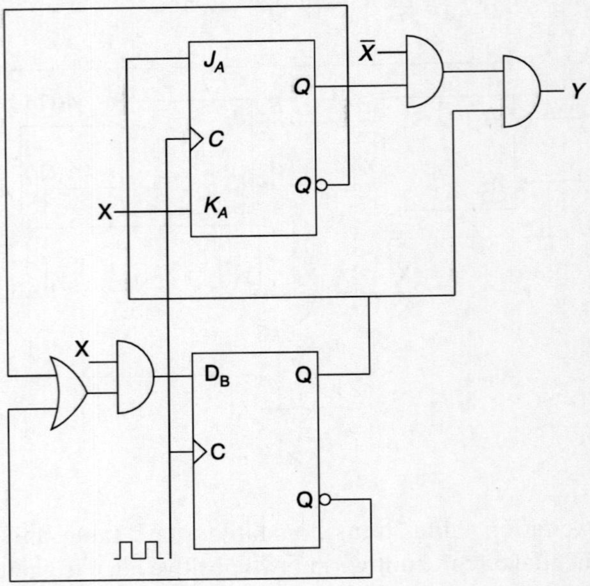

CHAPTER 8

Sequential Design-II

8.1 CONSTRUCTION OF STATE DIAGRAM

Construction of state diagram from problem statement and assignment of states is critical task in the design of sequential machine. The state diagram involves many attempts before the final state diagram is developed. It is similar to development of truth table in combinational logic circuits.

State diagram of an Up/Down Synchronous Decade Counter

Let us write a state diagram of an up/down synchronous decade counter. There has to be a control input which dictates whether the counter is in up control mode or down control mode. Let us call the control input as X. Decade counter will have 10 different states which needs four state variables. The 10 different states may be from 0000 to 1001 in the normal binary sequence. When $X = 0$, the counter is in count up mode and when $X = 1$, the counter is in countdown mode.

In commercially available up/down counters there will be two outputs. Similarly, let us have two outputs Y and Z in the synchronous decade up/down counter. Y will indicate the terminal output while counting up and Z will indicate terminal count while counting down. For the above mentioned conditions, we can draw the state diagram, as shown in Fig. 8.1.

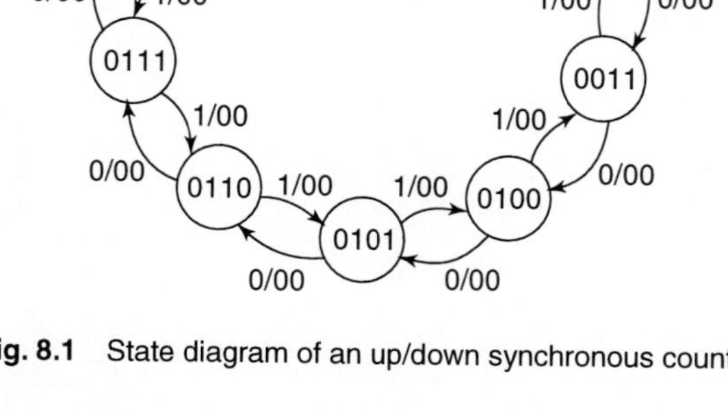

Fig. 8.1 State diagram of an up/down synchronous counter

Here, 0000, 0001, 0010, 0011, 0100, 0101, 0110, 0111, 1000, 1001 are ten states of decade counter. During up counting the counter starts from 0000 state and goes to 0001 state... and finally reaches 1001 and goes back to 0000 state. The input output representation is *X*/*YZ*. *X* is the control input which can take the value either 0 or 1. If it is the mode is count up and if it is 1, the mode is countdown.

As shown in the Fig. 8.1, if the input-output representation *X*/*YZ* is 0/00, then $X = 0$, i.e., the counter is counting up and output is 00, i.e., $YZ = 00$, i.e., that the counter is in any state other than the terminal count. It means that the up/down counter is in count up mode and is in anywhere from 0000 state to 1001 state. If *X*/*YZ* is 0/10, the control input $X = 0$ and the counter is counting up. *YZ* is 10, that means that the output $Y = 1$ and $Z = 0$ and the state is changing from 1001 to 0000. (terminal count). If *X*/*YZ* is 1/01, i.e., the control input is $X = 1$. It means that the counter is counting down and the output $Y = 0$ and $Z = 1$. Hence, the the state is changing from 0001 to 0000 (terminal count)

In the system shown, the output is a function of present state and input. Hence, the sequential circuit is a Mealy circuit.

State Diagram for Sequence Detectors

Design of sequential circuits with a desired relationship between the input and output sequences is required many a time. This requires development of sequence detectors. Some examples will illustrate this concept.

Example 8.1 Draw the state diagram of a Moore machine to output a 1 if the input has been 1 for three consecutive clock cycles.

Let us consider a particular sequence to illustrate the above problem. Let the input be *x* and the output be *y*.

Let $\quad x$ be 0 1 1 1 1 0 1 1 1 0 1 1 0 1 1 1 0 1

$\quad\quad y$ be 0 0 0 1 1 0 0 0 1 0 0 0 0 0 0 1 0 0

Fig. 8.2 Input-output sequence for example 8.1

In this case, a step by step approach is carried out. The state diagram is drawn step by step to finally arrive at a complete state diagram.

Step 1: From the sequence given, let us go from state to state. Let us start at state A. If $x = 0$, remains at state *A* and if $X = 1$, go to next state *B*, as shown in Fig. 8.3. If $x = 0$, output $y = 0$ and if $x = 1$, output $y = 0$.

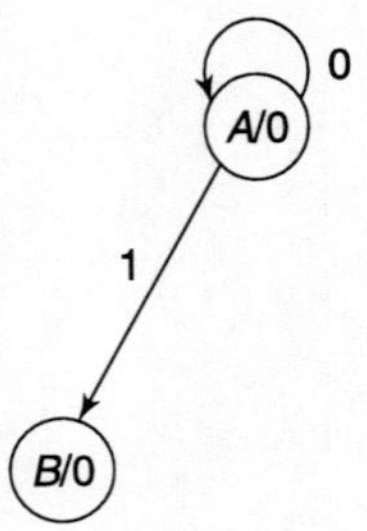

Fig. 8.3 State diagram after step 1

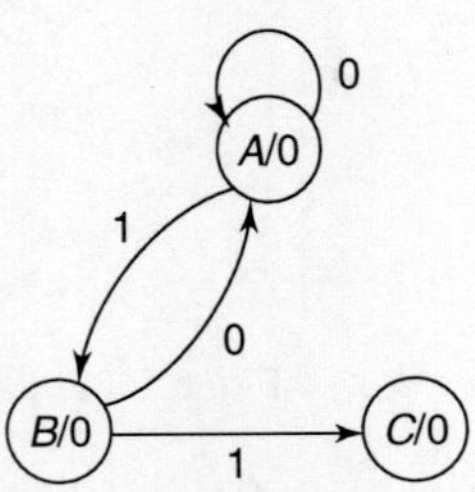

Fig. 8.4 State diagram after step 2

Step 2: At state *B*, if $x = 0$, go back to state *A* and if $x = 1$, go to state *C* indicating the occurrences of two 1's as shown in Fig. 8.4.

Step 3: Now at state *C*, if $x = 0$, we have to go back to state *A* and if $x = 1$, go to state *D* indicating the occurrences of three 1s at which point, the output *y* is 1. Since as given in the example. Since three 1s have occurred in three consecutive clock cycles, the output is 1 as shown in Fig. 8.5.

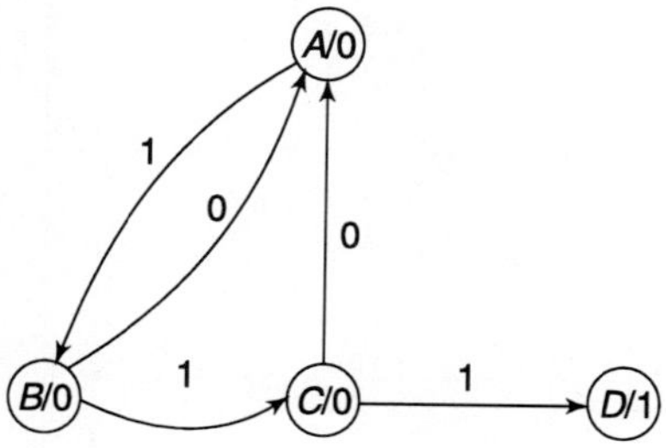

Fig. 8.5 State diagram after step 3

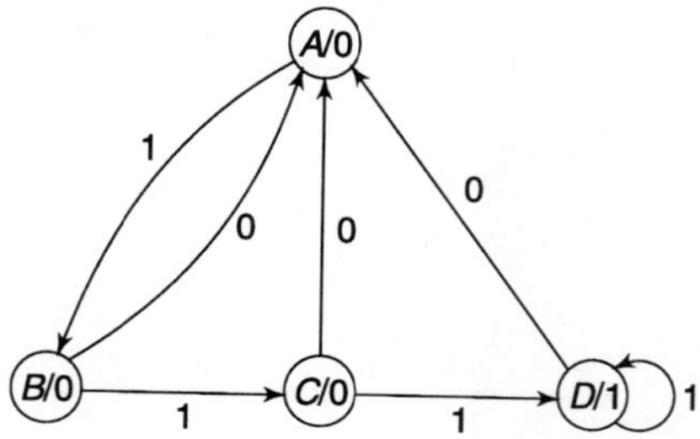

Fig. 8.6 Complete state diagram for example 8.1

Step 4: If it is at state *D*, and if $x = 0$, go back to state *A* and if $x = 1$, remain in state *D* indicating continuance of consecutive 1s as shown in Fig. 8.6.

Example 8.2 Construct a Mealy state diagram that will detect a serial sequence of 10110. When the input pattern has been detected, cause an output *Z* to be asserted high. (VTU – Dec 2007)

Let us have the input as *x* and the output as *z*. Let us have the input sequence as shown in Fig. 8.7. and the corresponding output sequence is also shown.

x – 1 0 1 1 0 1 0 1 1 0 1 0

z – 0 0 0 0 1 0 0 0 0 1 0 0

Fig. 8.7 Assumed input sequence for example 8.2

Step 1: Let us start at state *A*. If $x = 0$, remain at state *A* and if $x = 1$, go to state *B* as shown in Fig. 8.8.

Step 2: Let us start at state *B*. If $x = 1$, remain at state *B* and if $x = 0$, go to state *C* as shown in Fig. 8.9. In both cases output 1 is 0 because the required sequence is not complete.

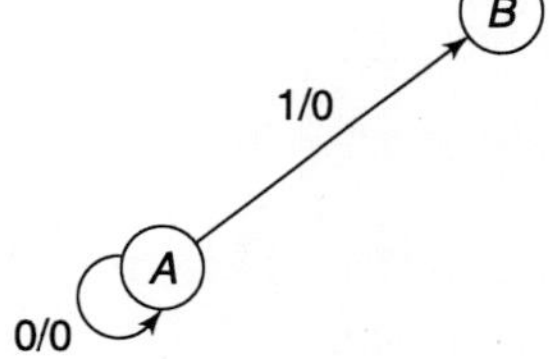

Fig. 8.8 State diagram after step 1

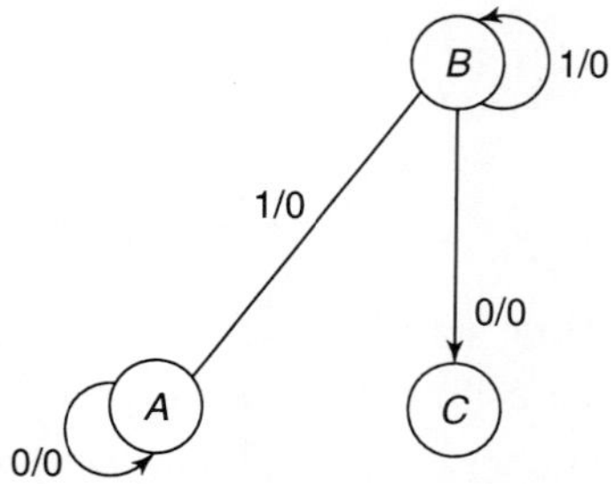

Fig. 8.9 State diagram after step 2

Step 3: Now let us start at state *C*. If $x = 1$, go to state *D* and if $x = 0$, go back to state *A* as the sequence has failed, i.e., it becomes 1, 0, 0 as shown in Fig. 8.10. We have to restart checking of input sequence again.

Step 4: Let us start at state *D*. If $x = 0$, go back to *C* and if $x = 1$, go to *E* as shown in Fig. 8.11.

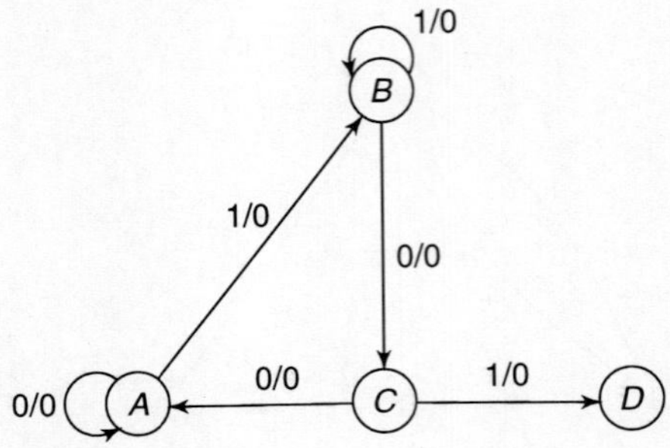

Fig. 8.10 State diagram after step 3

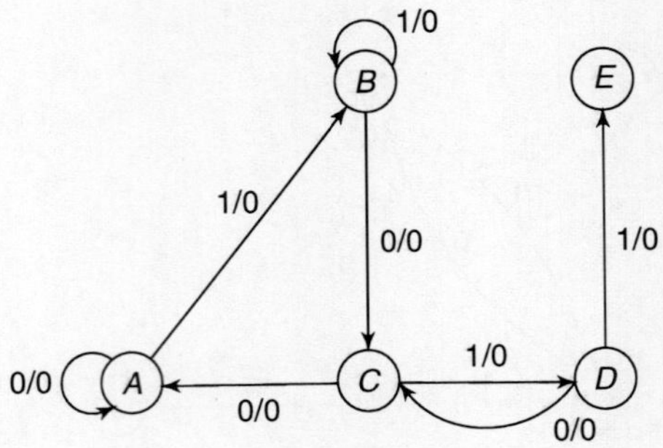

Fig. 8.11 State diagram after step 4

Step 5: Let us start at state *E*. If $x = 0$, go to state *C* with output $Z = 1$ as we have the sequence as required, i.e., 10110. If $x = 1$, go to state *B*.

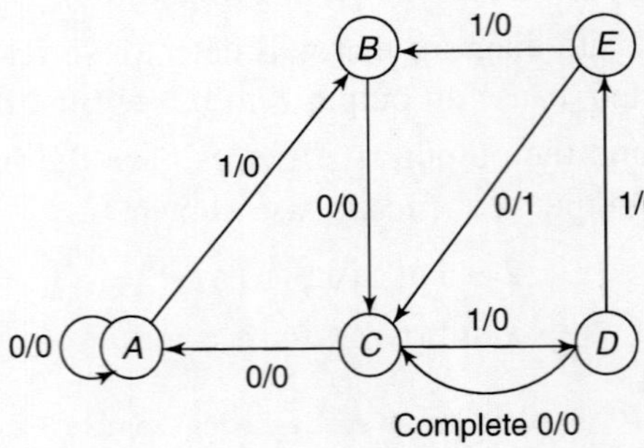

Fig. 8.12 State diagram for example 8.2

Example 8.3 Design a sequence detector for the following sequence 1, 0, 1, 1, 1 with overlap. Write the state diagram and logic diagram. (VTU – Dec 2012)

Let *x* be the input sequence and let the corresponding output sequence be *z* as shown in Fig. 8.13.

x 1 0 1 1 1 0 1 1 1

z 0 0 0 0 1 0 0 0 1

Fig. 8.13 Input and output sequence for example 8.3

Step 1: Let us start at state *A*. If $x = 0$, we remain at *A* and if $x = 1$, we have to go to state *B*. In both the cases, output is 0 since we have not completed the sequence.

Step 2: Now let us start at state *B*. If $x = 0$, we have to go to state *C* and if $x = 1$, we have to remain at state *B*. In both cases the output is 0 as we have not completed the required sequence.

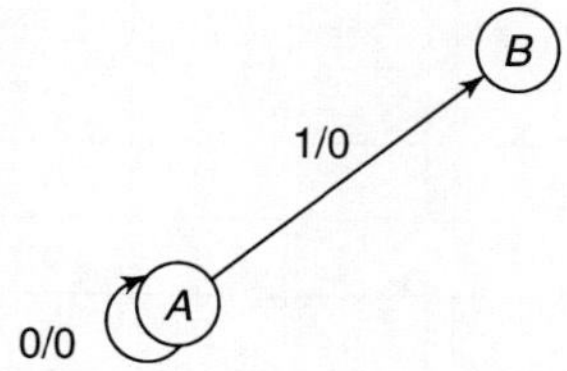

Fig. 8.14 State diagram after step 1

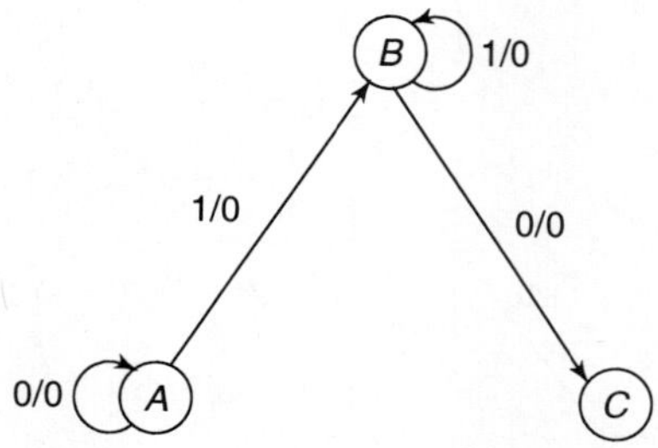

Fig. 8.15 State diagram after step 2

Step 3: Let us start at state *C*. If $x = 0$, we have to go back to state *A* as we have to restart checking the required sequence. If $x = 1$, we have to go to state *D* as shown in Fig. 8.16. In both the cases the output is 0.

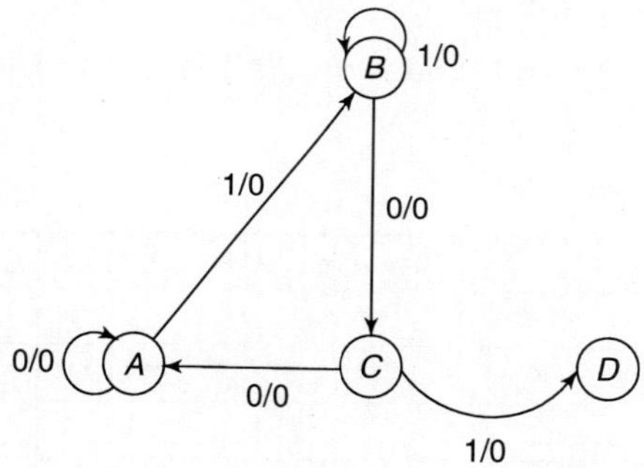

Fig. 8.16 State diagram after step 3

Step 4: Let us start at state *D*. If $x = 0$, we have to go back to *C*. If $x = 1$, go to state *E* as per the sequence (1011 ...) as shown in Fig. 8.17.

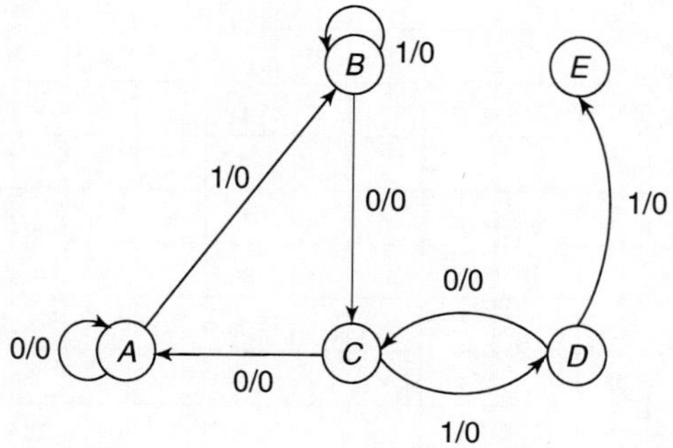

Fig. 8.17 State diagram after step 4

Step 5: Let us start at state *E*. If $x = 0$, we have to go to state *C*. If $x = 1$, we have to go to state *B* and the output will be 1 as shown in Fig. 8.18.

State table is constructed from the state diagram as shown in Fig. 8.19.

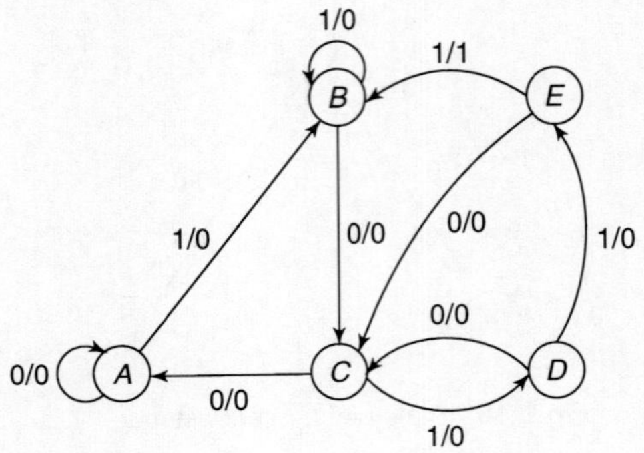

Fig. 8.18 Complete state diagram for example 8.3

Present state	Next state		Output
	$X = 0$	$X = 1$	Z
A	A	B	0
B	C	B	0
C	A	D	0
D	C	E	0
E	C	B	1

Fig. 8.19 State table for example 8.3

Let us give state assignment as follows:

$A = 000$, $B = 001$, $C = 010$, $D = 011$, and $E = 100$. Let us use D flip-flops to construct logic diagram.

Present state			Input	Next state			Flip-flop inputs			Output
P	R	S	X	P^+	R^+	S^+	D_P	D_R	D_S	Z
0	0	0	0	0	0	0	0	0	0	0
0	0	0	1	0	0	1	0	0	1	0
0	0	1	0	0	1	0	0	1	0	0
0	0	1	1	0	0	1	0	0	1	0
0	1	0	0	0	0	0	0	0	0	0
0	1	0	1	0	1	1	0	1	1	0
0	1	1	0	0	1	0	0	1	0	0
0	1	1	1	1	0	0	1	0	0	0
1	0	0	0	0	1	0	0	1	0	0
1	0	0	1	0	0	1	0	0	1	1
1	0	1	0	×	×	×	×	×	×	×
1	0	1	1	×	×	×	×	×	×	×
1	1	0	0	×	×	×	×	×	×	×
1	1	0	1	×	×	×	×	×	×	×
1	1	1	0	×	×	×	×	×	×	×
1	1	1	1	×	×	×	×	×	×	×

Fig. 8.20 Transition table for example 8.3 (continued in 11A) (60)

Using K-maps, flip-flop inputs can be simplified as shown in Fig. 8.21.

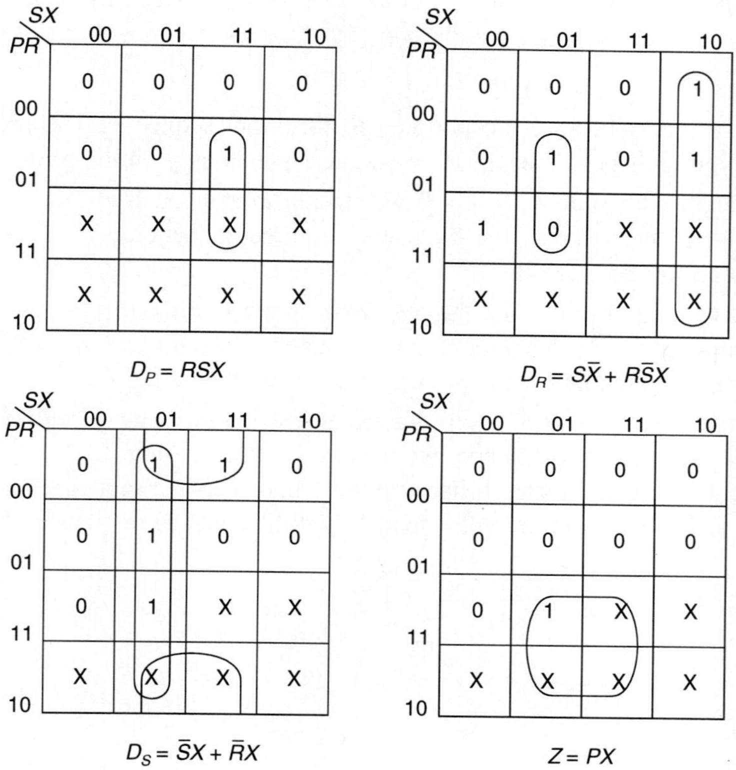

Fig. 8.21 K-maps for example 8.3

Logic diagram is constructed using flip-flop inputs and output expressions as shown in Fig. 8.22.

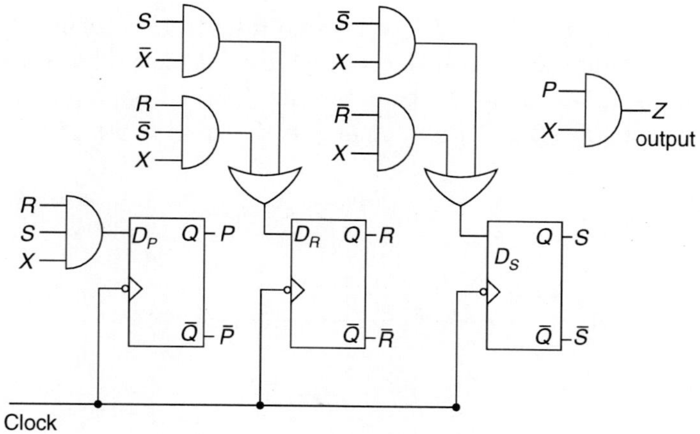

Fig. 8.22 Logic diagram for example 8.3

Example 8.4 Design a Moore type sequence detector to detect a serial input sequence of 101.

Let us have input as x and output as Z. Let us have the input sequence as shown below:

$$x = 1\ 0\ 1\ 1\ 0\ 1\ 0\ 1\ 1$$
$$z = 0\ 0\ 1\ 0\ 0\ 1\ 0\ 1\ 0$$

The output sequence will be corresponding to the input sequence. The problem is about designing Moore type sequence detector. Here output depends only on the present state.

Step 1: Let us begin with state A. If $x = 0$ we remain in state A. If $x = 1$, we would have detected the first bit in the required sequence. Hence, we have to go to next state B.

In both the cases, output is 0 since the required sequence has not been detected completely. Because Moore type sequence detector is required, the output is written below the present state inside the circle.

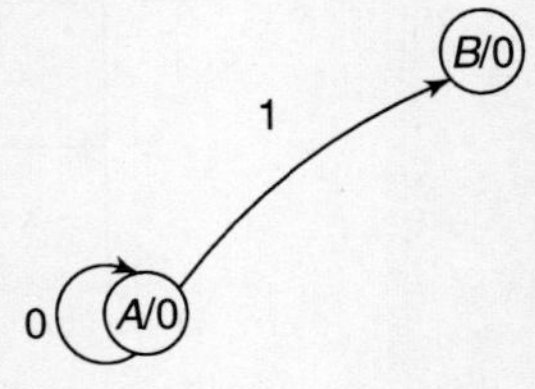

Fig. 8.23 State diagram after step 1

Step 2: Let us start from state B. If $x = 0$, we have detected the next bit in the required sequence (101). Hence, we have to go to next state C. If $x = 1$, we have to remain in state B because the 1 may start the sequence again. In both the cases the output z is 0 as we have not yet detected the full sequence as shown in Fig. 8.24.

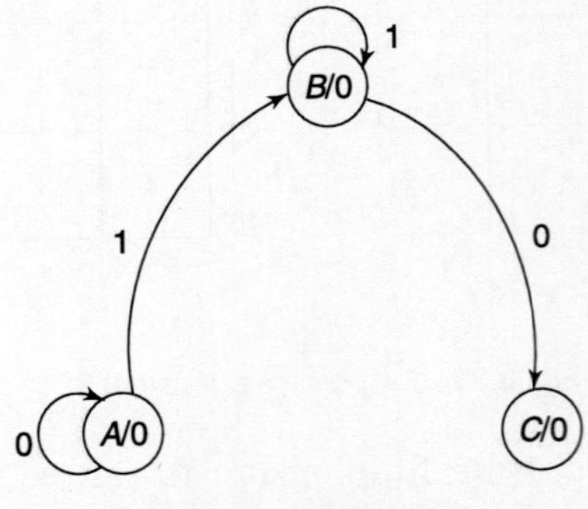

Fig. 8.24 State diagram after step 2

Step 3: Now let us start form C. If $x = 0$, we have to restart the checking of input sequence again. Hence, we have to return to state A. If $x = 1$, we have detected the correct sequence and output z is 1. If output is 1, we cannot go back to state B because the output in state B is 0. Hence, we have to create a new state D with output 1 as shown in Fig. 8.25.

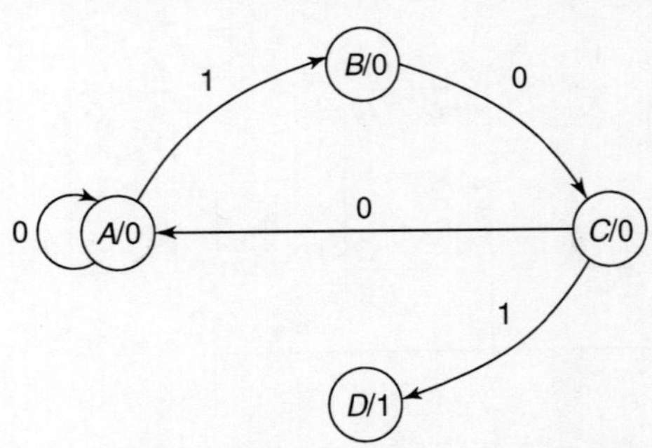

Fig. 8.25 State diagram after step 3

Step 4: Since the sequence has been detected, *D* is the last state. If $x = 0$, we would have detected the second bit in the overlapped sequence (1$\underline{0}$1). Hence, we have to go to state *C*.

If $x = 1$, we would have detected the first bit in the next sequence. Hence, we have to go to state *B* as shown in Fig. 8.26.

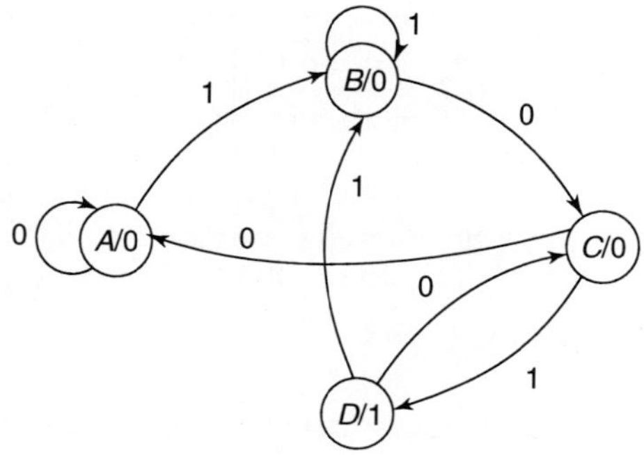

Fig. 8.26 Complete state diagram after step 4

Now, from the complete state diagram, we can construct state table as shown in Fig. 8.27.

Present state	Next state		Output Z
	X = 0	X = 1	
A	A	B	0
B	C	B	0
C	A	D	0
D	C	B	1

Fig. 8.27 State table for example 8.4

Since there are four states, we need two flip-flops. Now, we get transition table by assigning values to the states as follows: $A = 00$, $B = 01$, $C = 10$ and $D = 11$.

Present state		Next state				Output Z
		X = 0		X = 1		
A	B	A^+	B^+	A^+	B^+	
0	0	0	0	0	1	0
0	1	1	0	0	1	0
1	0	0	0	1	1	0
1	1	1	0	0	1	1

Fig. 8.28 Transition table

Next, we construct K-maps for A^+ and B^+ and Z.

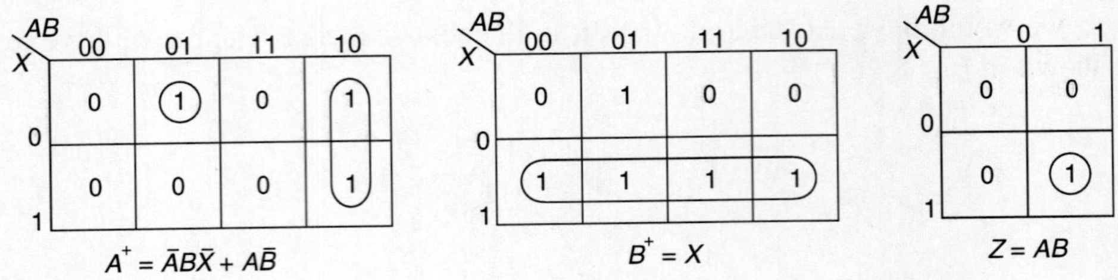

Fig. 8.29 K-maps for example 8

$$A^+ = \bar{A}B\bar{X} + A\bar{B}$$

Next, we construct logic diagram using K-map values as shown in Fig. 8.30.

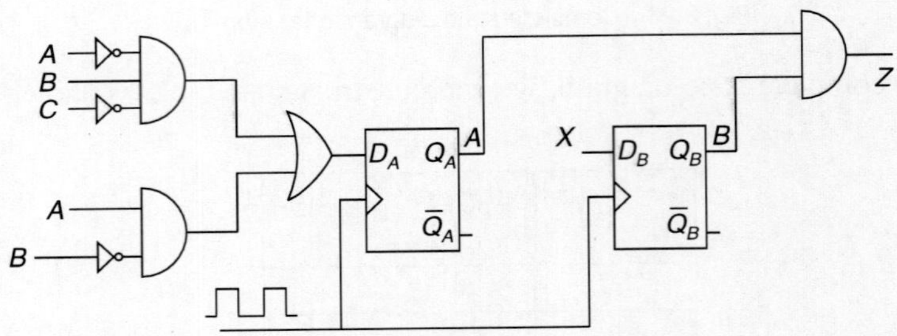

Fig. 8.30 Logic diagram of the sequence detector

Example 8.5 Construct Moore and Mealy state diagrams that will detect input sequence 10110, when input pattern is detected, z is asserted high. Give state diagrams for each state.

(VTU – Dec 2008)

In Example 8.2, a Mealy state diagram is constructed for the input sequence 10110. Here we will construct the state diagram for Moore sequential circuit.

Let us have input as x and the output as z. Let us have the input sequence as shown below.

$$x - 1\,0\,1\,1\,0\,0\,1\,0\,1\,1\,0\,0\,0$$

$$z - 0\,0\,0\,0\,1\,0\,0\,0\,0\,0\,1\,0\,0$$

Step 1: Let us start at state A. If $x = 0$, we have to remain at state A and if $x = 1$, we have to go to state B as shown in Fig. 8.31.

Step 2: Let us start at state B. If $x = 0$, we have to go to next state C. If $x = 1$, we have to remain in state B as shown in Fig. 8.32. In both the cases, the output is O because the sequence is not complete.

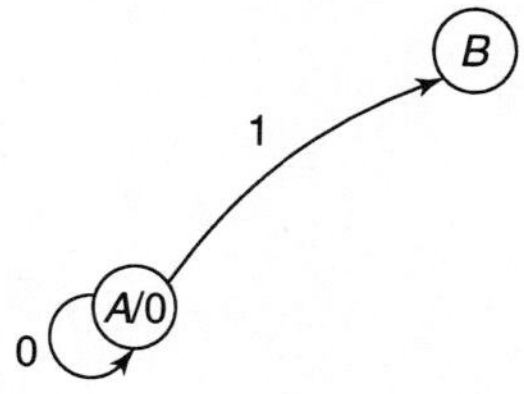

Fig. 8.31 State diagram after step 1.

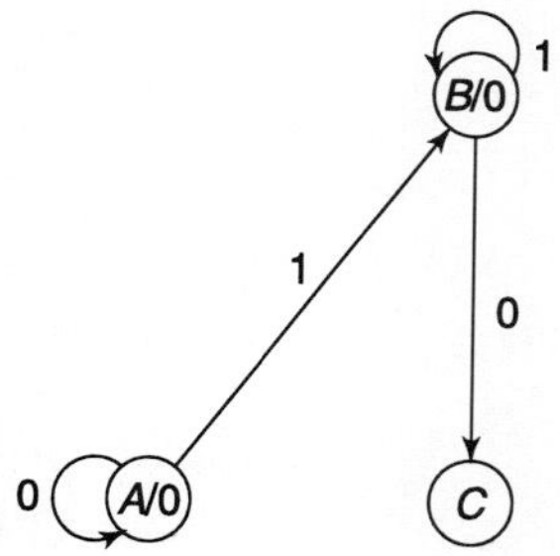

Fig. 8.32 State diagram after step 2

Step 3: Let us start at state C. If $x = 1$, we have to go to next state D and if $x = 0$, go back to state A as the sequence has failed. We have to restart checking the sequence. This is shown in Fig. 8.33.

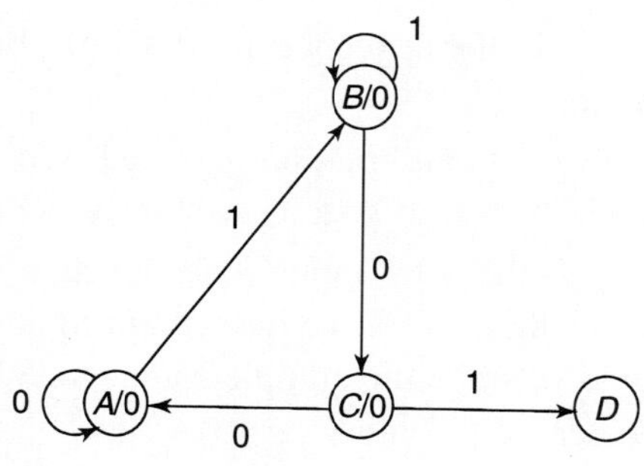

Fig. 8.33 State diagram after step 3

Step 4: Let us start at state D. If $x = 0$, go back to state C and if $x = 1$, go to state E as shown in Fig. 8.34. In both the cases, the output is O.

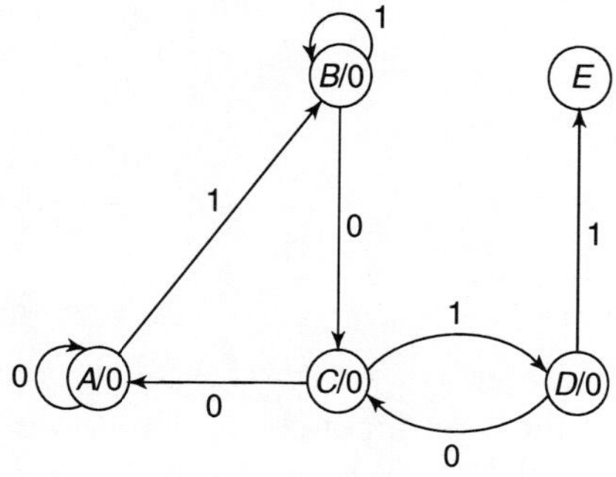

Fig. 8.34 State diagram after step 4

Step 5: Let us start at state E. If $x = 0$, we have the sequence completed (10110). We have to go to state C with output $z = 1$ as shown in Fig. 8.35. If $x = 1$, we have to go to state B.

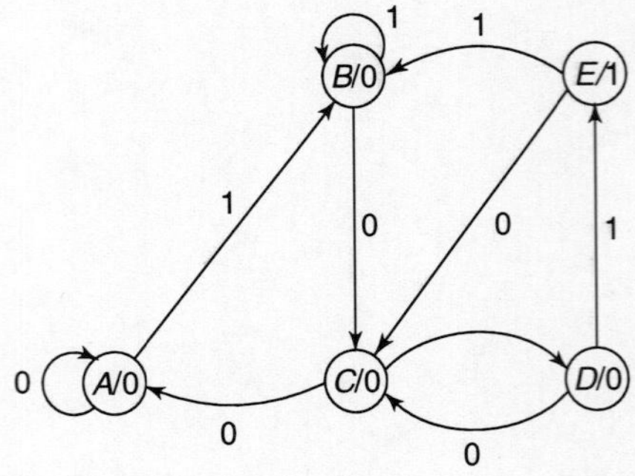

Fig. 8.35 Complete state diagram for example 8.5

Example 8.6 Draw the state diagram for an electronic combination lock Mealy machine which will open when the following 4-bit input combinations are punched in the sequence 1010, 0110, 0011, 1001.

The 4-bit input combinations are in the sequence 1010, 0110, 0011, 1001. Let the output be *Z* which must set to 1 to open the lock.

Step 1: Let us start from *A*. If the 4-bit combination punched is 1010, we will go to state *B*. If any other 4-bit code is punched, we will go to state *E* as shown in Fig. 8.36.

Step 2: Let us start from state *B*. If the 4-bit input code punched is 0110, we will go to state *C*. If the 4-bit code punched is other than 0110, we have to go to some state *F* as shown in Fig. 8.37. In both the cases the output is 0, since the complete sequence has not been carried out. At state *E* any state *S* will take the machine to state *F*.

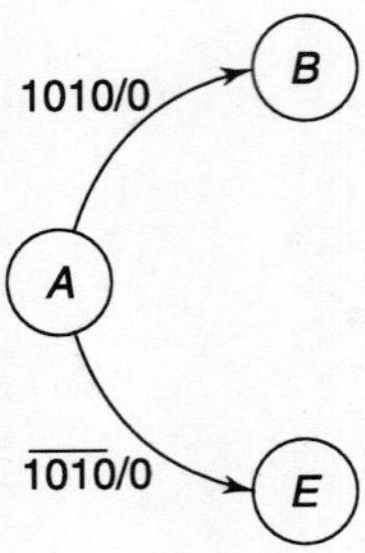

Fig. 8.36 State diagram after step 1

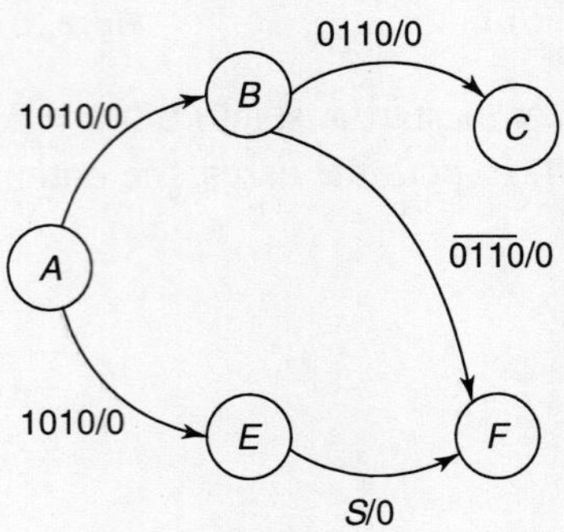

Fig. 8.37 State diagram after step 2

Step 3: Let us start at state *C*. If the 4-bit input code is 0011, we have to go to state *D*. If the 4-bit input code is anything other than 0011, then we have to go to state *G*. At state *F*, any state *S* takes the system to state *G*. The state diagram after step 3 is shown in Fig. 8.38.

Step 4: Let us start at state *D*. If the 4-bit input code is 1001, we will go to state *A* with output 1, i.e., we have completed the required sequence. For any code other than 1001, we will go to state *A* with output *O*.

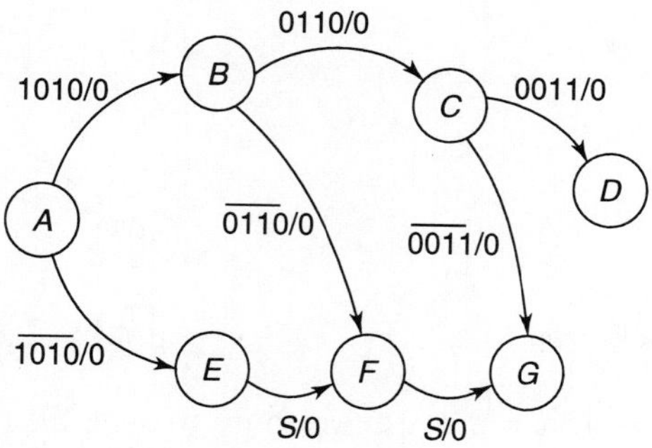

Fig. 8.38 State diagram after step 3

At state *G*, any state *S* will take the system back to state *A* with output *O*. This is shown in Fig. 8.39.

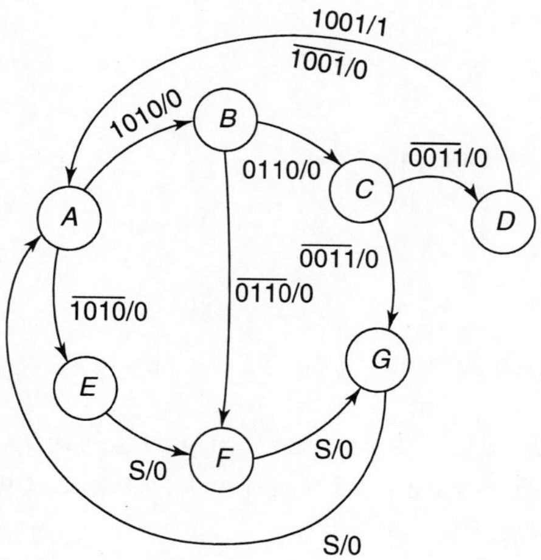

Fig. 8.39 Complete state diagram for example 8.6

Example 8.7 Draw the state diagram of a Moore machine whose output toggles whenever the 110 sequence is detected.

Let the input be *x* and the output be *z*. Let the input sequence be 1100110 and the corresponding output sequence will be 0010001.

x 1 1 0 0 1 1 0 0 0 1 1 0

z 0 0 1 1 1 1 0 0 0 0 0 1

Fig. 8.40 Input-output sequence

Step 1: Let us start at state *A*. If $x = 0$, we have to remain at state *A*. If $x = 1$, we have to go to state *B* as shown in Fig. 8.41.

Step 2: Let us start at state *B*. If $x = 0$, we have to go back to state *A*. If $x = 1$, we have to go to state *C* indicating that 11 has occurred as shown in Fig. 8.42.

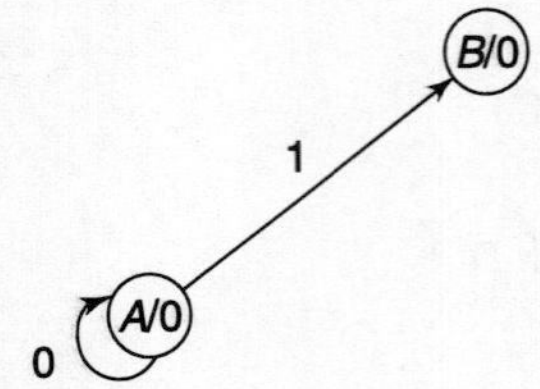

Fig. 8.41 State diagram after step 1

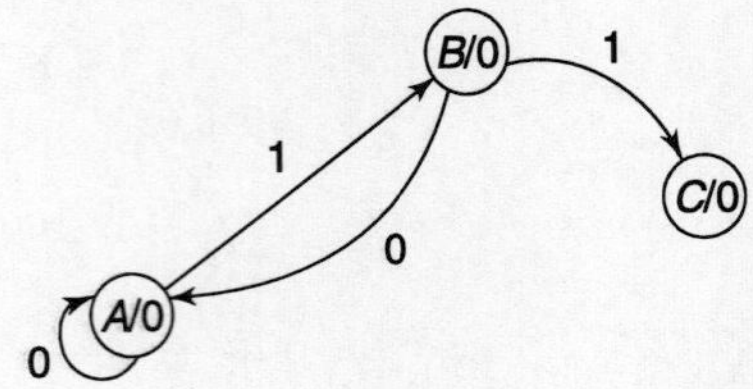

Fig. 8.42 State diagram after step 2

Step 3: Let us start at state *C*. If $x = 0$, we have to go to state *D* with output 1 since we have gone through the required sequence 110. If $x = 1$, we have to remain at state *C*.

Step 4: Let us start from state *D*. If $x = 0$, we have to remain at state *D*. If $x = 1$, we have to go to state *E*. The output at state *E* is 1 since the output must toggle whenever the sequence 110 is detected. Now we have not encountered the next sequence, the output has to be 1 only. This is shown in Fig. 8.44.

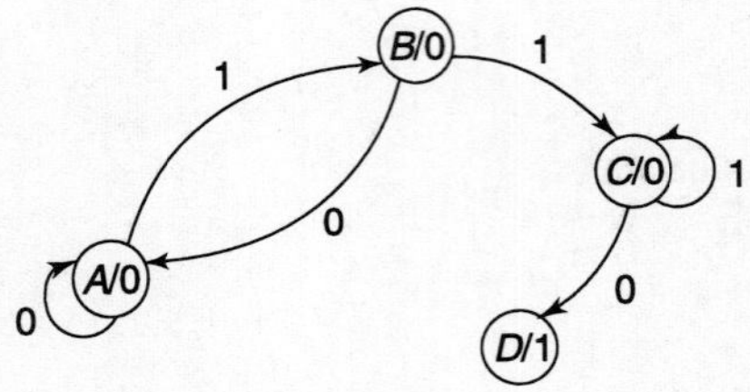

Fig. 8.43 State diagram after step 3

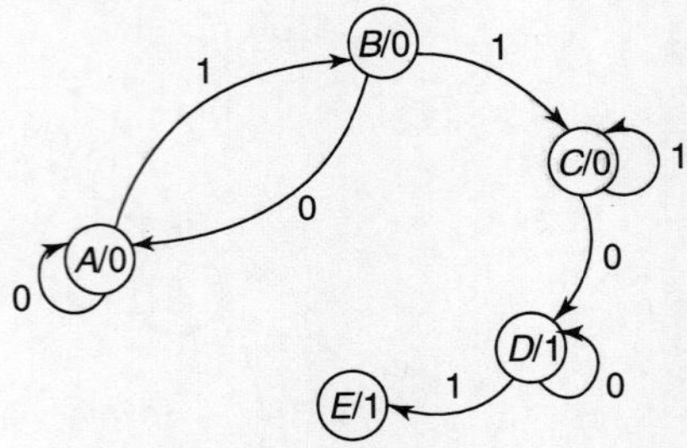

Fig. 8.44 State diagram after step 4

Step 5: Let us start at state *E*. If $x = 0$, we have to go back to *D* to start afresh the required sequence. If $x = 1$, we have to go to state *F* with output 1 (because it will toggle once the required sequence is encountered) as shown in Fig. 8.45.

Step 6: Let us now start from state *F*. If $x = 0$, a valid sequence 110 has been detected again hence we have to go to state *A*. The output will toggle if required sequence is encountered. When first time sequence 110 was encountered the output was 1 and second time when a valid sequence is detected the output will toggle, i.e., the output will be 0. This is shown in Fig. 8.46.

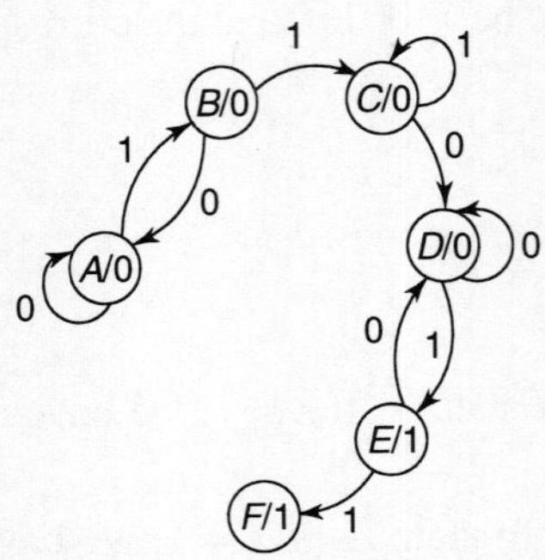

Fig. 8.45 State diagram after step 5

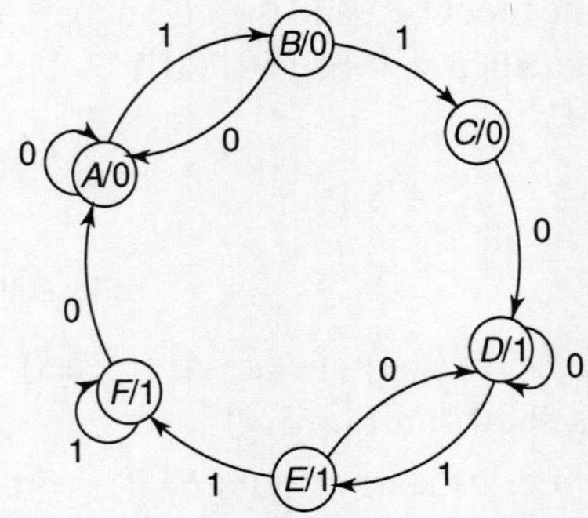

Fig. 8.46 Complete state diagram for example 8.7

Example 8.8 With a suitable example and appropriate state diagram, explain how to recognize a particular sequence EX 1011. (VTU – June 2013)

Let us take a Moore type sequence detector. The output depends only on the present state and not on the input. Let x be the input and z be the output.

Step 1: Let us start at state A. If $x = 0$, we have to remain in state A. If $x = 1$, we have to go to state B which is shown in Fig. 8.47.

Step 2: Let us start from state B. If $x = 0$, we have to go to state C. If $x = 1$, we have to remain in state B as shown in Fig. 8.48.

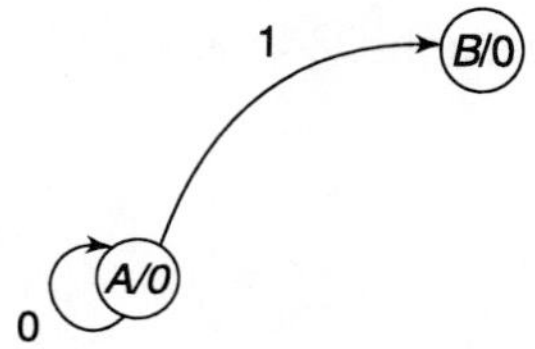

Fig. 8.47 State diagram after step 1

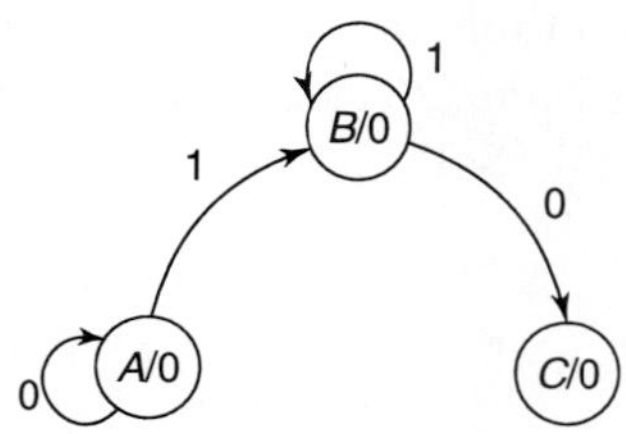

Fig. 8.48 State diagram after step 2

Step 3 Let us start from state C. If $x = 0$, we have to go back to state A. If $x = 1$, we have to go to state D. So far the sequence we have encountered is 1-0-1. This is shown in Fig. 8.49.

Step 4: Let us start from state D. If $x = 0$, we have to go to state A to refresh once again the input sequence. If $x = 1$, we have to go to state E and output is 1 as a valid sequence has been detected as shown in Fig. 8.50.

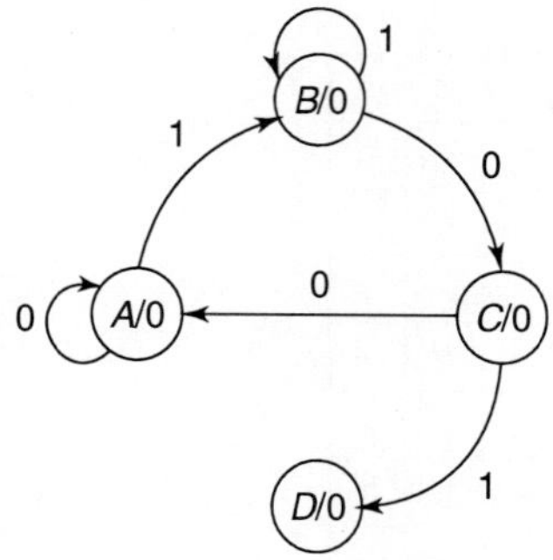

Fig. 8.49 State diagram after step 3

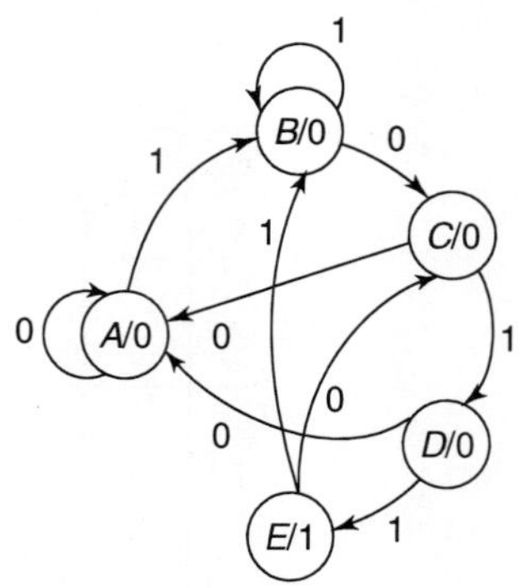

Fig. 8.50 Complete state diagram for example 8.8

Example 8.9 Design a sequence detector to detect the following sequence: 110 using JK flip-flops. Use Mealy machine.

Let x be the input and z be the output.

Step 1: Let us start from state A. If $x = 0$, we have to remain in state A. If $x = 1$, we have to go to the next state to detect the next bit in sequence. The next state is B. In both the cases, the output is O, since we have not detected complete sequence.

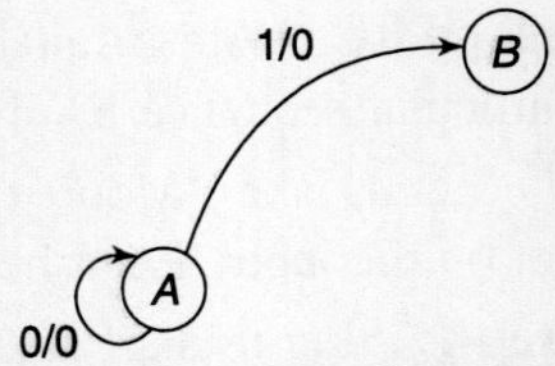

Fig. 8.51 State diagram after step 1

Step 2: Let us start form state B.

If $x = 0$, we have to go to state A to detect the first bit in the sequence. If $x = 1$, we have to go to state C as we have detected the second bit in the sequence as shown in Fig. 8.52.

Step 3: Let us start from state C. If $x = 0$, we have detected the last bit in the sequence, hence we have to go to the initial state to detect the next sequence. The output is 1 indicating that the sequence has been detected. If $x = 1$, we have go to state B because the '1' can start the sequence as shown in Fig. 8.53.

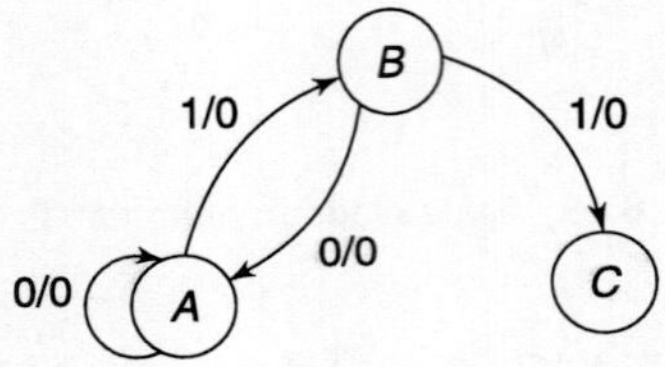

Fig. 8.52 State diagram after step 2

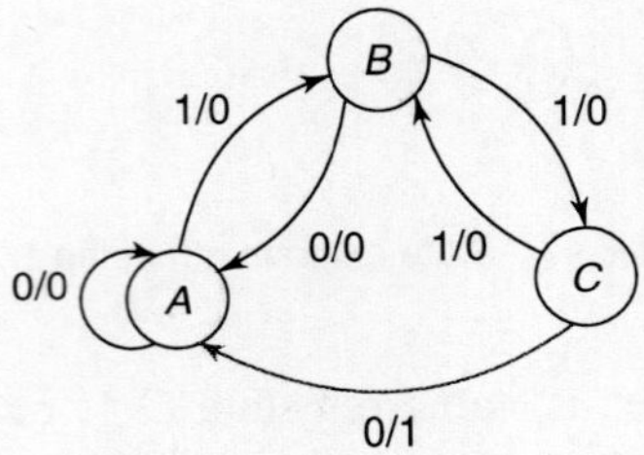

Fig. 8.53 State diagram after step 3

Assuming the state assignments $A = 00$ $B = 01$ $C = 10$ excitation table is constructed as shown in Fig. 8.54.

Input	Present state		Next state		Output	Flip-flop inputs			
X	A	B	A^+	B^+	Z	J_A	K_A	J_B	K_B
0	0	0	0	0	0	0	×	0	×
0	0	1	0	0	0	0	×	×	1
0	1	0	0	0	1	×	1	0	×
1	0	0	0	1	0	0	×	1	×
1	0	1	1	0	0	1	×	×	1
1	1	0	0	1	0	×	1	1	×

Fig. 8.54 Excitation table for example 8.9

Next using K-map simplification, flip-flop inputs are found which is shown in Fig. 8.55.

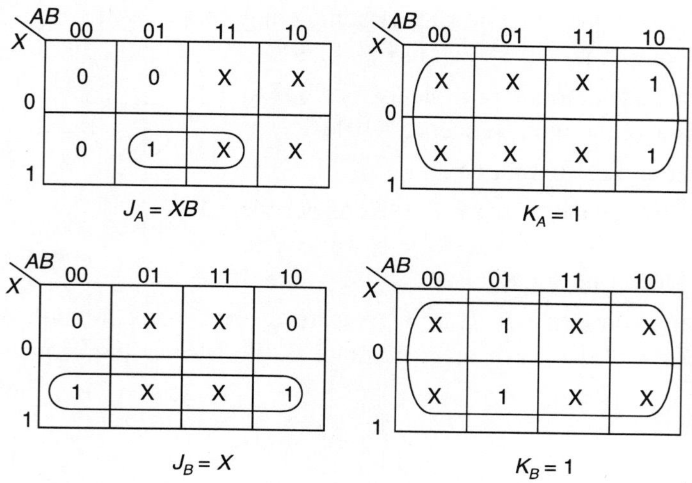

Fig. 8.55 K-maps for example 8.9

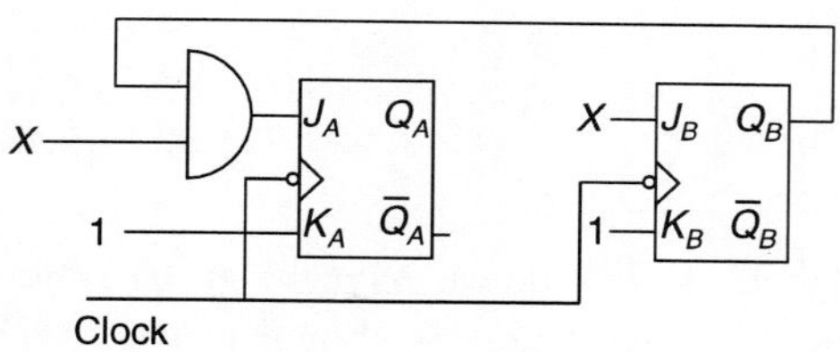

Fig. 8.56 Logic diagram for example 8.9

Example 8.10 Draw the state diagram of a Mealy machine whose output is 1 for every third input being 1 not necessarily consecutive but non-overlapping.

Let the input be x and the output be z.

Step 1: Let us start from state A. If $x = 0$, we have to remain at A. If $x = 1$, we have to go to state B as shown in Fig. 8.57.

Step 2: Let us start from state B. If $x = 0$, we have to remain at B and if $x = 1$, we have to go to state C as shown in Fig. 8.58.

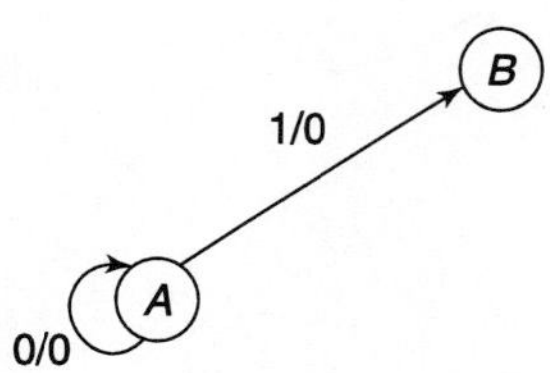

Fig. 8.57 State diagram after step 1

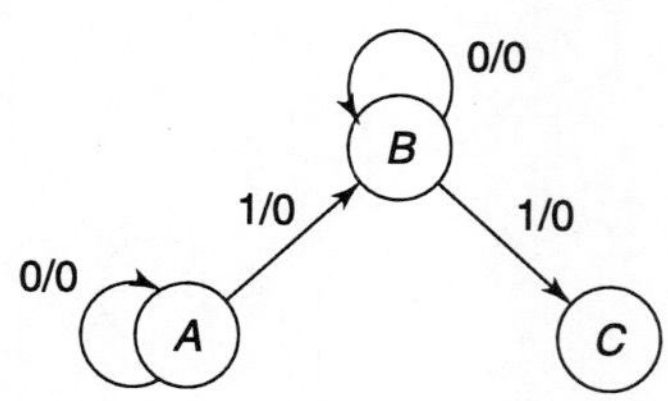

Fig. 8.58 State diagram after step 2

Step 3: Let us start form state *C*. If $x = 0$, we have to remain at *C* and if $x = 1$, it goes back to state *A* completing the sequence and the output is 1 as shown in Fig. 8.59.

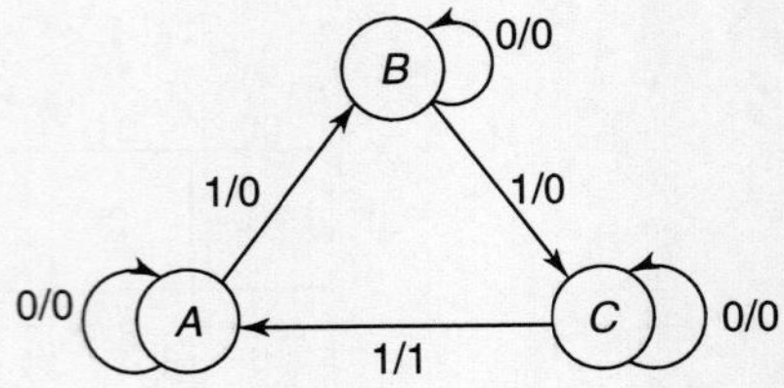

Fig. 8.59 Complete state diagram for example 8.10

Example 8.11 Draw the state diagram of a Mealy machine to output a 1 on detection of the input sequence 010110.

Let the input be x and the output be z.

Step 1: Let us start from state *A*. If $x = 0$, (i.e., as per the sequence), we have to go to state *B* and if $x = 1$, we have to remain in state *A* as shown in Fig. 8.60.

Step 2: Let us start from state *B*. If $x = 0$ we have to go back to state *A* as it has failed the sequence and if $x = 1$, we have to go to state *C* (i.e. as per the sequence 01) as shown in Fig. 8.61.

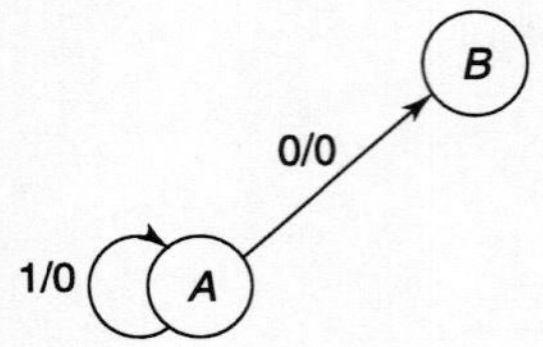

Fig. 8.60 State diagram after step 1

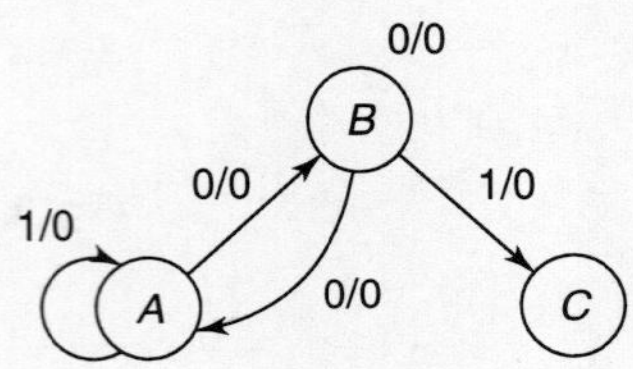

Fig. 8.61 State diagram after step 2

Step 3: Let us start from state *C*. If $x = 0$, we have to go to state *D* and if $x = 1$, we have to go back a to state as the sequence has failed as shown in Fig. 8.62. This is as per sequence (010...).

Step 4: Let us start from state *D*. If $x = 0$, we have to go back to state *A* as it fails the sequence. If $x = 1$, the input corresponds to the next valid bit in the sequence (0101...), it goes to state *E* as shown in Fig. 8.63.

Step 5: Let us start from state *E*. If $x = 0$, this is not a valid input bit in the sequence, we have to go to state *A* to start from the beginning. If $x = 1$, it goes to next state *F* as shown in Fig. 8.64.

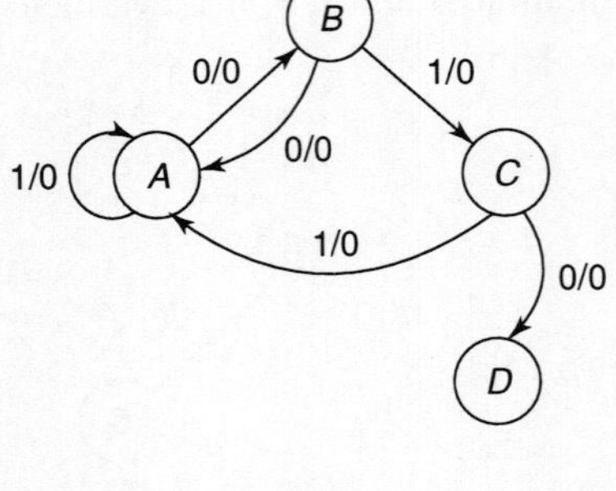

Fig. 8.62 State diagram after step 3

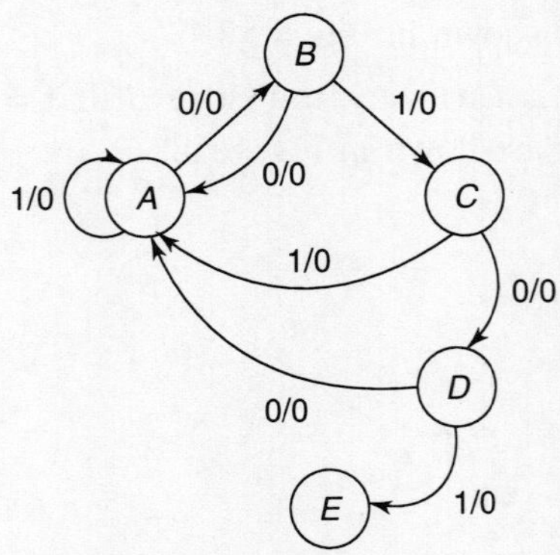

Fig. 8.63 State diagram after step 4

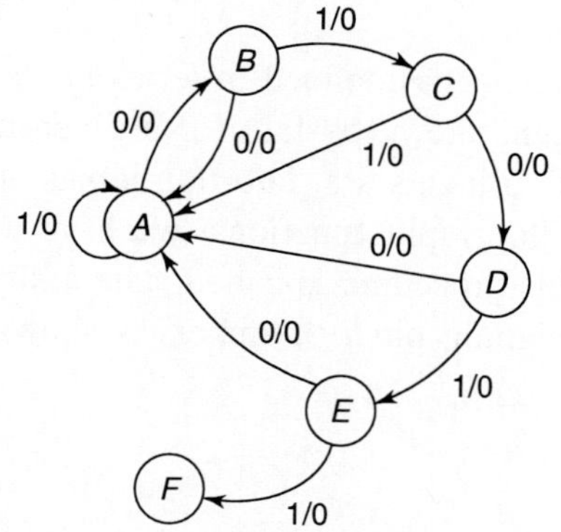

Fig. 8.64 State diagram after step 5

Step 6: Let us start from state F. If $x = 1$, this is not a valid input bit in the sequence, we have to go to state A. If $x = 0$, it goes to next state G as shown in Fig. 8.65. Here, the output is 1 as we have completed the sequence.

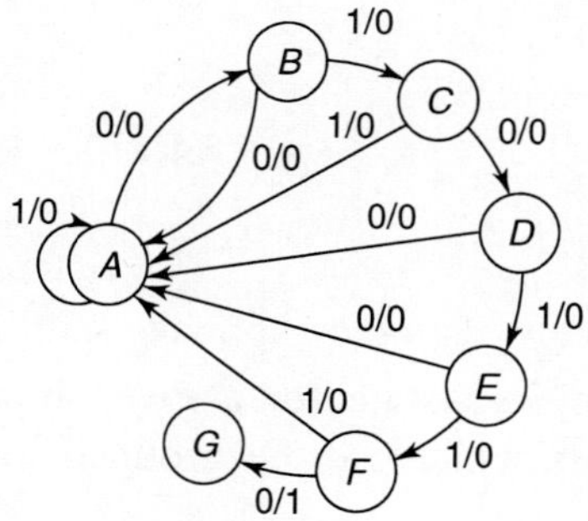

Fig. 8.65 State diagram after step 6

Step 7: Let us start form state G. If $x = 0$, it goes to state B, If $x = 1$ we have to go to state A to restart the process again. The complete state diagram is shown in Fig. 8.66.

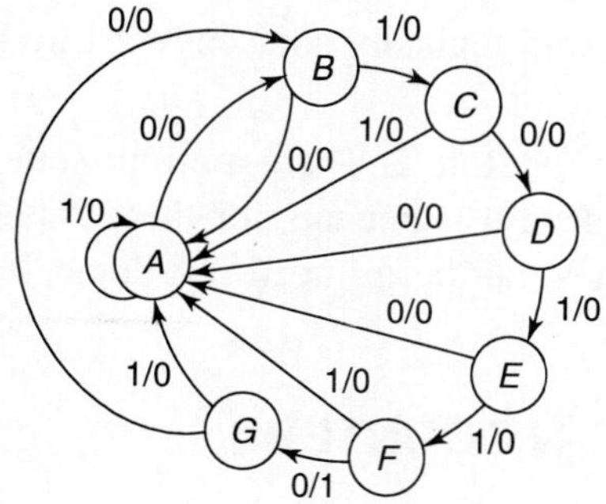

Fig. 8.66 Complete state diagram for example 8.11

State Assignment

The behaviour of the sequential circuits is defined in terms of their inputs, present states, next states and outputs. In order to generate next state for a given present state and inputs, it is necessary to know what the flip-flop inputs are. Flip-flop inputs are described by flip-flop input functions. To determine the flip-flop input functions, we have to represent the state diagram with states in binary numbers. This procedure is called state assignment, for example, the state diagram shown in Fig. 8.67. Assigning binary numbers is shown in Fig. 8.68 after assigning states with binary numbers.

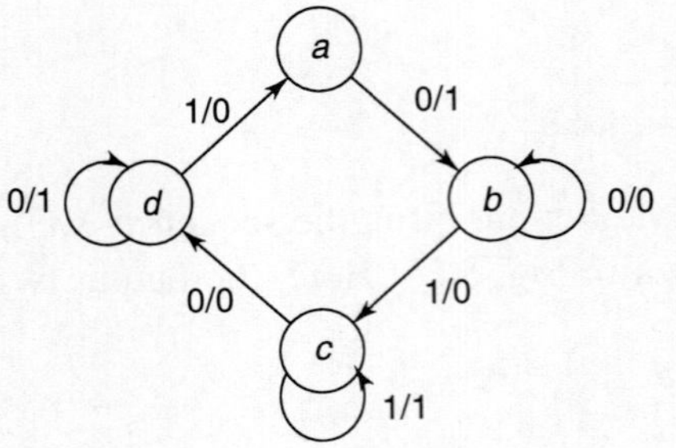

Fig. 8.67 State diagram

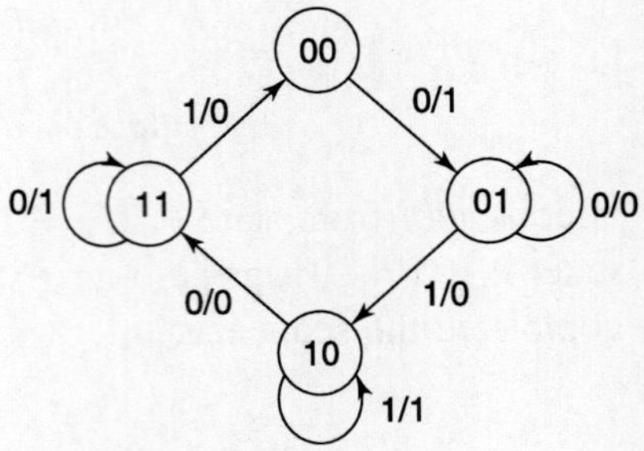

Fig. 8.68 State diagram with binary numbers

Rules for state assignments

There are two basic rules which specify as to how to make state assignments.

Rule 1: States having the same next state for a given input condition should have assignments which can be grouped into logically adjacent cells in a K-map.

Figure 8.69 shows an example for Rule 1. There are four states whose next state is same. Thus, state assignments for these states are 011, 100, 101 and 110 which can be grouped into logically adjacent cells in a K-map.

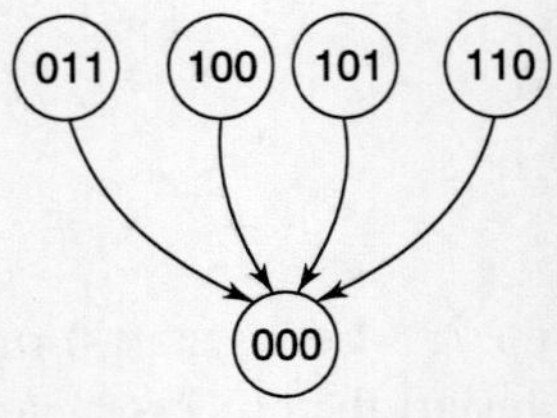

Fig. 8.69 Example using rule 1

Rule 2: States that are next states of a single state should have assignment which can be grouped into logically adjacent cells in a K-map.

Figure 8.70 shows an example for Rule 2. There are four states as next states to 000 state. Thus, state assignments for these states are 011, 100, 101, 110. Hence, they can be grouped into logically adjacent cells in a K-map.

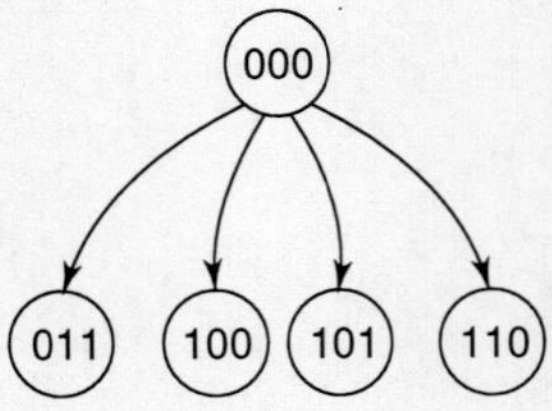

Fig. 8.70 Example for rule 2

8.2 DESIGN OF MODULO-N COUNTERS

There are design procedures for counters which are synchronous sequential machines. Many counters do not have any input. They go through a fixed sequence of states on successive clock pulses. There are some counters with inputs for count enable or up/down control, etc. When counters are designed, these inputs can be incorporated into the design.

The counter with n flip-flops is called Mod 2^n counter. If a counter has 3 flip-flops, it is called Mod-8 (2^3) counter and if it has 4 flip-flops, it is called Mod-16 (2^4) counter. These counters can be modified to produce counters with Mod number less than 2^n by allowing the counters to skip some states that are normally part of counting sequence.

Let us describe the procedures for design of Modulus-N counter using synchronous counters. This will be done using some examples.

Example 8.12 Design a synchronous counter using JK flip-flop to count the sequence 0, 1, 2, 3, 4, 5, 0, 1, 2. Use state diagram and state table. [VTU – Dec 2006]

The sequence is 0, 1, 2, 3, 4, 5. Let us draw the state diagram as shown in Fig. 8.71.

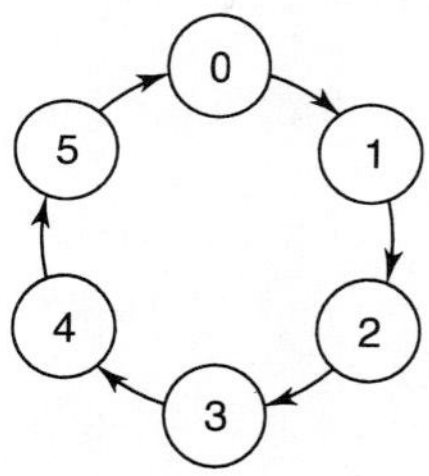

Fig. 8.71 State diagram for example 8.12

Number of flip-flops required is 'n'

i.e., $2^n \geq N$

Here $N = 6$

$\therefore$ $n = 3$

Hence, three flops are required.

we have to design a synchronous counter using JK flip-flops.

The excitation table for JK flip-flop is as shown in Fig. 8.72.

Q	Q^+	J	K
0	0	0	×
0	1	1	×
1	0	×	1
1	1	×	0

Fig. 8.72 Excitation table for JK flip-flop

From JK flip-flop excitation table, Transition table is constructed as shown in Fig. 8.73.

Present state			Next state			Flip-flop inputs					
Q_1	Q_2	Q_3	Q_1^+	Q_2^+	Q_3^+	J_1	K_1	J_2	K_2	J_3	K_3
0	0	0	0	0	1	0	×	0	×	1	×
0	0	1	0	1	0	0	×	1	×	×	1
0	1	0	0	1	1	0	×	×	0	1	×
0	1	1	1	0	0	1	×	×	1	×	1
1	0	0	1	0	1	×	0	0	×	1	×
1	0	1	0	0	0	×	1	0	×	×	1
1	1	0	×	×	×	×	×	×	×	×	×
1	1	1	×	×	×	×	×	×	×	×	×

Fig. 8.73 Transition table for example 8.12

Now using K-map, we can simplify the flip-flop input functions as shown in Fig. 8.74.

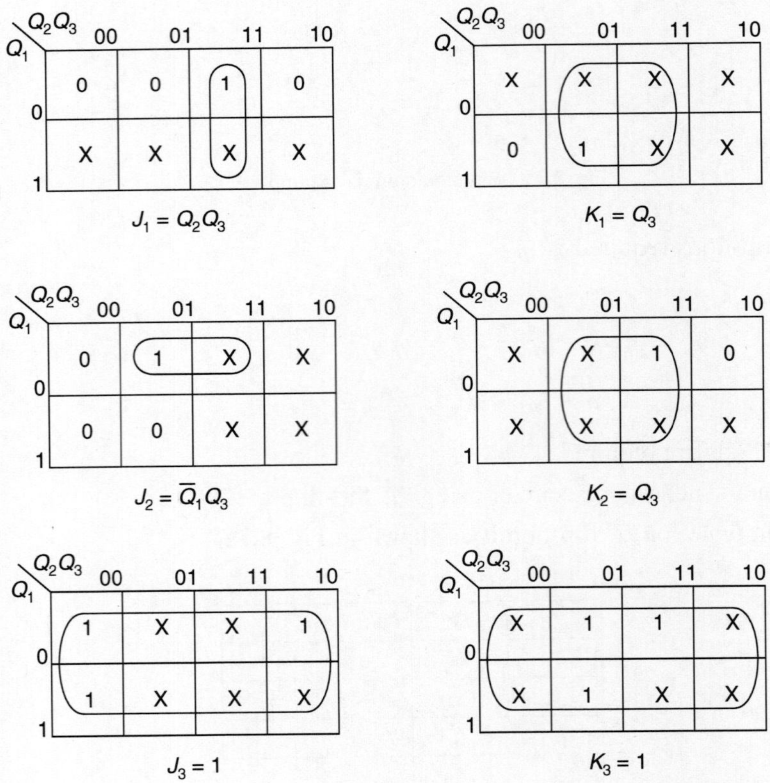

Fig. 8.74 K-maps for example 8.12

From K-map values, the logic diagram is constructed as shown in Fig. 8.75.

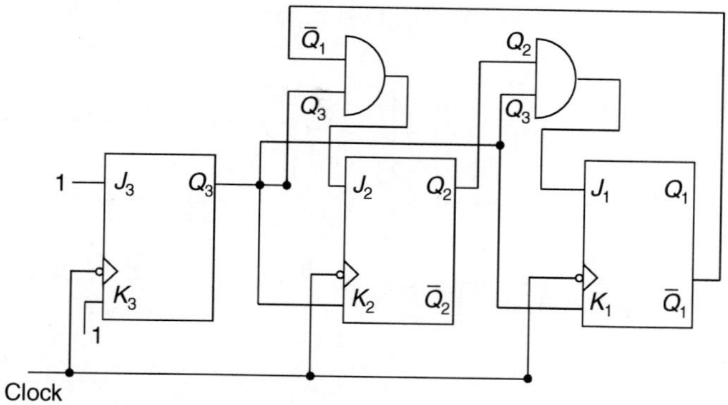

Fig. 8.75 Logic diagram for example 8.12

Example 8.13 Design a counter using *JK* flip-flops whose counting sequence is 000, 001, 100, 110, 111, 101, 000, etc. by obtaining its minimal sum equations. [VTU – June 2010; June 2008]

The sequence is 0, 1, 4, 6, 7, 5, 0, let us draw the state diagram as shown in Fig. 8.76.

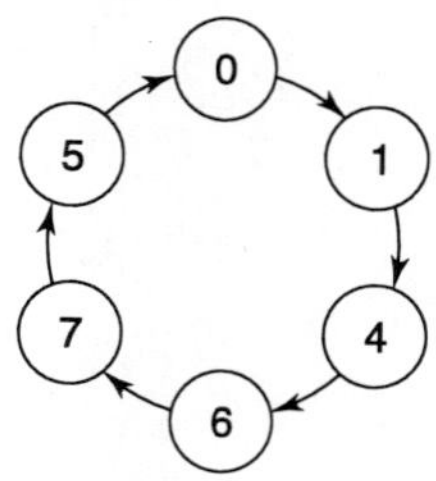

Fig. 8.76 State diagram for example 8.13

Number of flip-flops required is '*n*'

i.e., $$2^n \geq N$$

$$N = 6$$

$\therefore$ $$n = 3$$

Hence, three flip-flops are required.

We have to design a synchronous counter using *JK* flip-flops.

The excitation table for *JK* flip-flop is as shown in Fig. 8.77.

From *JK* flip-flop excitation table, transition table is constructed as shown in Fig. 8.78.

Q	Q^+	J	K
0	0	0	×
0	1	1	×
1	0	×	1
1	1	×	0

Fig. 8.77 Excitation table for *JK* flip-flop

Present state			Next state			Flip-flop inputs					
Q_1	Q_2	Q_3	Q_1^+	Q_2^+	Q_3^+	J_1	K_1	J_2	K_2	J_3	K_3
0	0	0	0	0	1	0	×	0	×	1	×
0	0	1	1	0	0	1	×	0	×	×	1
0	1	0	×	×	×	×	×	×	×	×	×
0	1	1	×	×	×	×	×	×	×	×	×
1	0	0	1	1	0	×	0	1	×	0	×
1	0	1	0	0	0	×	1	0	×	×	1
1	1	0	1	1	1	×	0	×	0	1	×
1	1	1	1	0	1	×	0	×	1	×	0

Fig. 8.78 Transition table for example 8.13

Now using K-map we can simplify the flip-flop input functions as shown in Fig. 8.79.

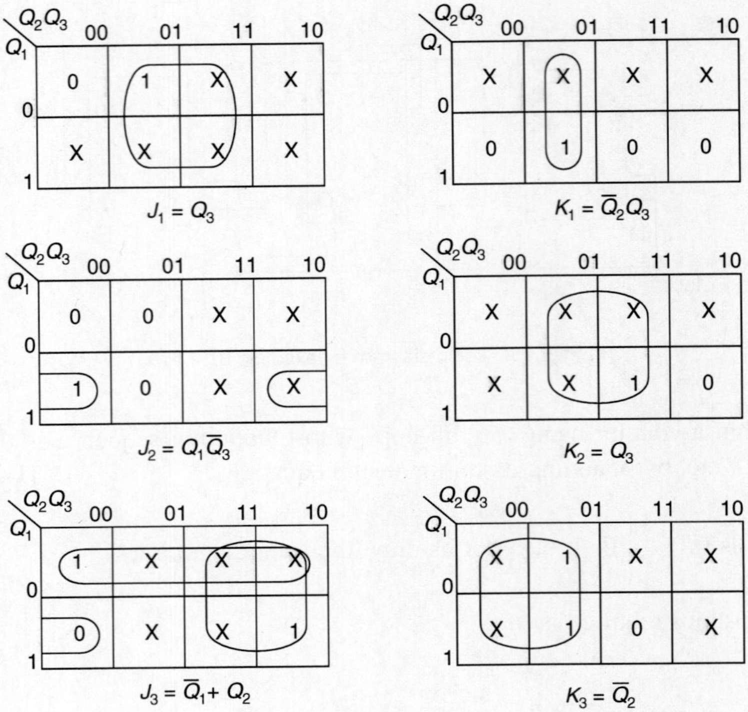

Fig. 8.79 K-maps for example 8.13

From K-map values, the logic diagram is constructed as shown in Fig. 8.80.

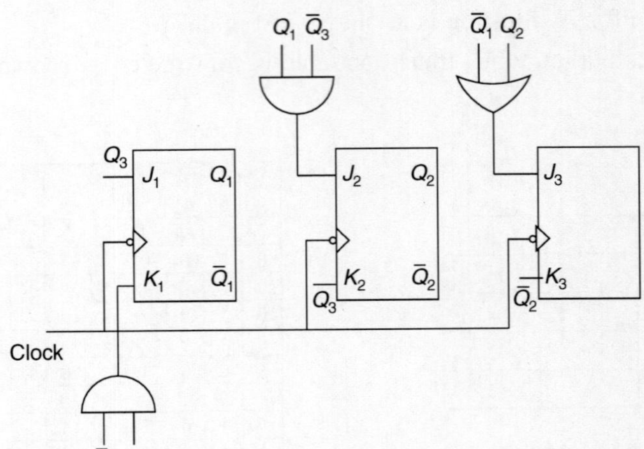

Fig. 8.80 Logic diagram for example 8.13

Example 8.14 Design a cyclic modulo-8 synchronous counter using *JK* flip-flop that will count the number of occurrences of an input; that is, the number of times it is 1. The input variable x must be coincident with the clock to be counted. The counter is to count in binary. [VTU – Jan 2008, Dec 2010]

The circuit is a cyclic modulo-8 synchronous counter using *JK* flip-flop. When input x is 1 it will start counting. For this counter, the state diagram is as shown in Fig. 8.81. When input $x = 0$, it will remain in the same state. If $x = 1$, the counter will go to next state. Excitation table for *JK* flip-flop is shown in Fig. 8.82.

Next transition table is constructed as shown in Fig. 8.83.

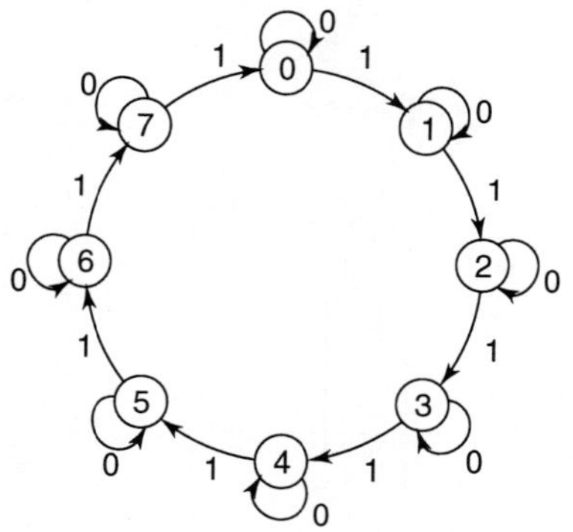

Fig. 8.81 State diagram for example 8.14

Q	Q^+	J	K
0	0	0	×
0	1	1	×
1	0	×	1
1	1	×	0

Fig. 8.82 Excitation table for *JK* flip-flop

Present state			Input	Next state			Flip-flop inputs					
A	B	C	X	A^+	B^+	C^+	J_A	K_A	J_B	K_B	J_C	K_C
0	0	0	0	0	0	0	0	×	0	×	0	×
0	0	0	1	0	0	1	0	×	0	×	1	×
0	0	1	0	0	0	1	0	×	0	×	×	0
0	0	1	1	0	1	0	0	×	1	×	×	1
0	1	0	0	0	1	0	0	×	×	0	0	×
0	1	0	1	0	1	1	0	×	×	0	1	×
0	1	1	0	0	1	1	0	×	×	0	×	0
0	1	1	1	1	0	0	1	×	×	1	×	1
1	0	0	0	1	0	0	×	0	0	×	0	×
1	0	0	1	1	0	1	×	0	0	×	1	×
1	0	1	0	1	0	1	×	0	0	×	×	0
1	0	1	1	1	1	0	×	0	1	×	×	1
1	1	0	0	1	1	0	×	0	×	0	0	×
1	1	0	1	1	1	1	×	0	×	0	1	×
1	1	1	0	1	1	1	×	0	×	0	×	0
1	1	1	1	0	0	0	×	1	×	1	×	1

Fig. 8.83 Transition table for example 8.14

Using K-maps we can simplify flip-flop input functions as shown in Fig. 8.84

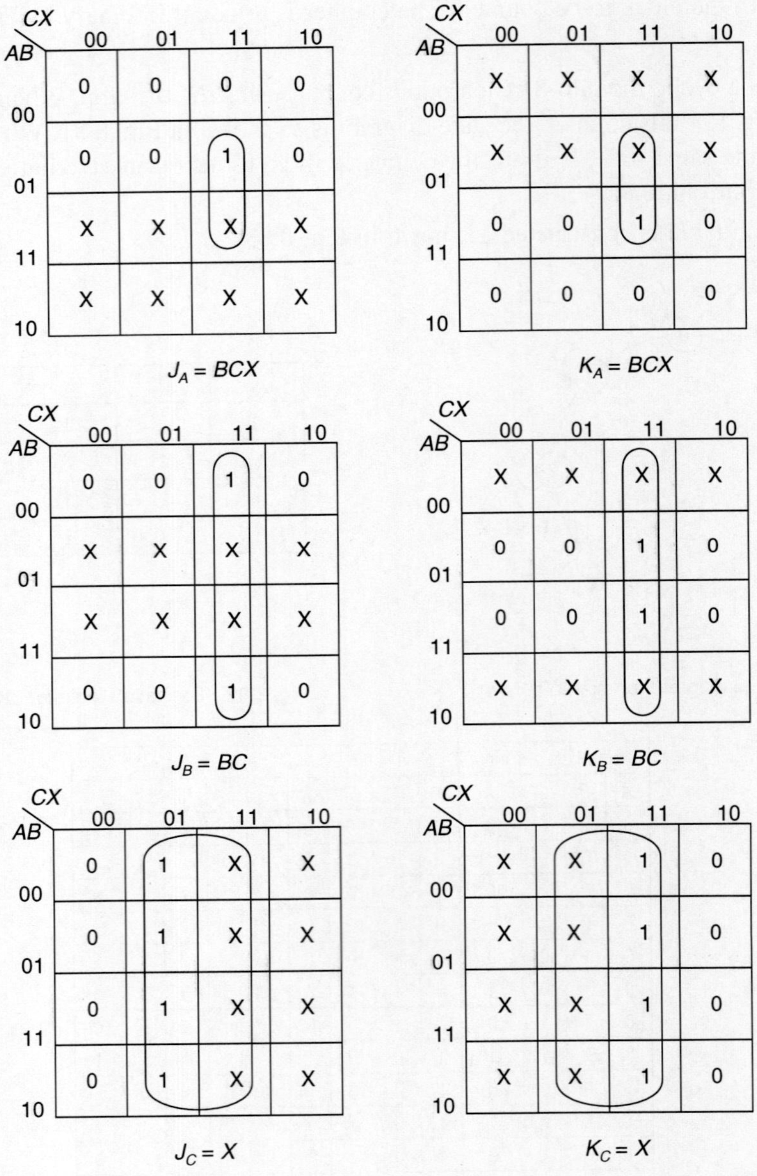

Fig. 8.84 K-maps for example 8.14

From the K-map values we can construct the logic diagram for cyclic modulo 8 synchronous counter as shown in Fig. 8.85.

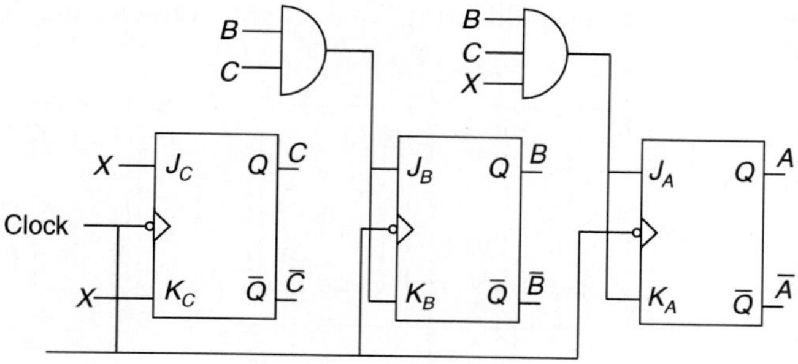

Fig. 8.85 Logic diagram for example 8.14

Example 8.15 Design a synchronous modulo-8 binary counter using D flip-flops starting from the state diagram.

The state diagram is shown in Fig. 8.86. The transition table for the state diagram is as shown in Fig. 8.87.

From the transition table values, K-maps are constructed as shown in Fig. 8.88.

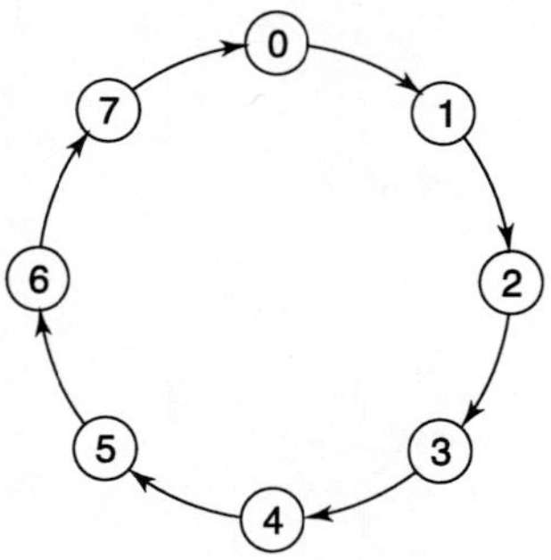

Fig. 8.86 State diagram for example 8.15

Present state			Next state			Flip-flop inputs		
A	B	C	A^+	B^+	C^+	D_A	D_B	D_C
0	0	0	0	0	1	0	0	1
0	0	1	0	1	0	0	1	0
0	1	0	0	1	1	0	1	1
0	1	1	1	0	0	1	0	0
1	0	0	1	0	1	1	0	1
1	0	1	1	1	0	1	1	0
1	1	0	1	1	1	1	1	1
1	1	1	0	0	0	0	0	0

Fig. 8.87 Transition table for example 8.15

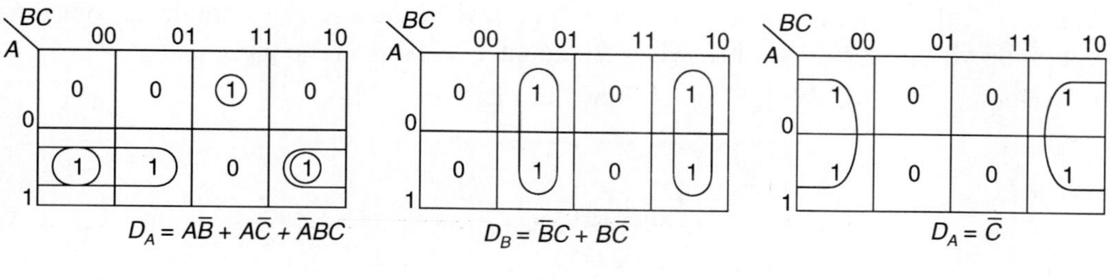

Fig. 8.88 K-maps for example 8.15

From the K-map values, the logic diagram for the synchronous modulo-8 binary counter is drawn as shown in Fig. 8.89.

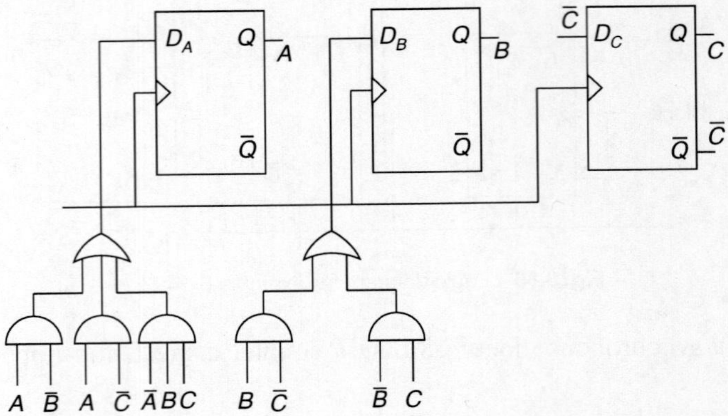

Fig. 8.89 Synchronous Modulo-8 binary counter for example 8.15

Example 8.16 Design a modulo-4 counter using *JK* flip-flops which will increment when two external inputs are coincident.

Let the two external inputs be X and Y and when they are coincident, i.e., when $X = Y$, the counter increments and will remain in the state in which it is presently if $x \neq y$. The state diagram is as shown in Fig. 8.90.

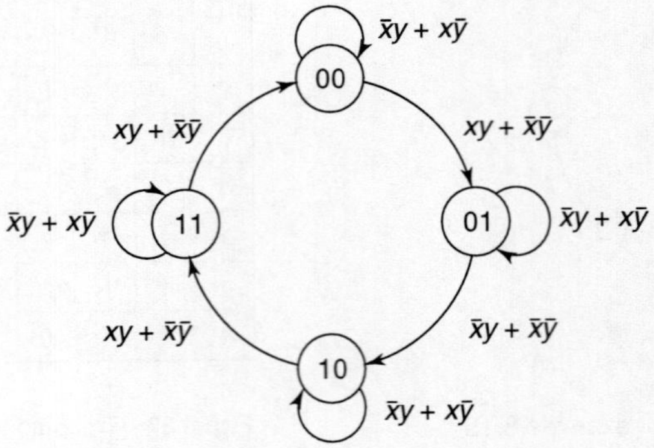

Fig. 8.90 State diagram for example 8.16

When $X = Y$, the condition will be XY or $\overline{X}\,\overline{Y}$, i.e., when the counter increments. When $X \neq Y$, the condition will be $\overline{X}Y$ or $X\overline{Y}$, i.e., when the counter remains in the present state.

The excitation table for *JK* flip-flop is shown in Fig. 8.91.

Q	Q^+	J	K
0	0	0	×
0	1	1	×
1	0	×	1
1	1	×	0

Fig. 8.91 Excitation table for *JK* flip-flop

Now the transition table with flip-flop inputs is constructed as shown in Fig. 8.92. Modulo-4 requires only two flip-flops (let us say A and B).

Present state		Input		Next state		Flip-flop inputs			
A	B	X	Y	A^+	B^+	J_A	K_A	J_B	K_B
0	0	0	0	0	1	0	×	1	×
0	0	0	1	0	0	0	×	0	×
0	0	1	0	0	0	0	×	0	×
0	0	1	1	0	1	0	×	1	×
0	1	0	0	1	0	1	×	×	1
0	1	0	1	0	1	0	×	×	0
0	1	1	0	0	1	0	×	×	0
0	1	1	1	1	0	1	×	×	1
1	0	0	0	1	1	×	0	1	×
1	0	0	1	1	0	×	0	0	×
1	0	1	0	1	0	×	0	0	×
1	0	1	1	1	1	×	0	1	×
1	1	0	0	0	0	×	1	×	1
1	1	0	1	1	1	×	0	×	0
1	1	1	0	1	1	×	0	×	0
1	1	1	1	0	0	×	1	×	1

Fig. 8.92 Transition table for example 8.16

From the transition table values, K-maps are constructed to simplify the flip-flop input functions as shown in Fig. 8.93.

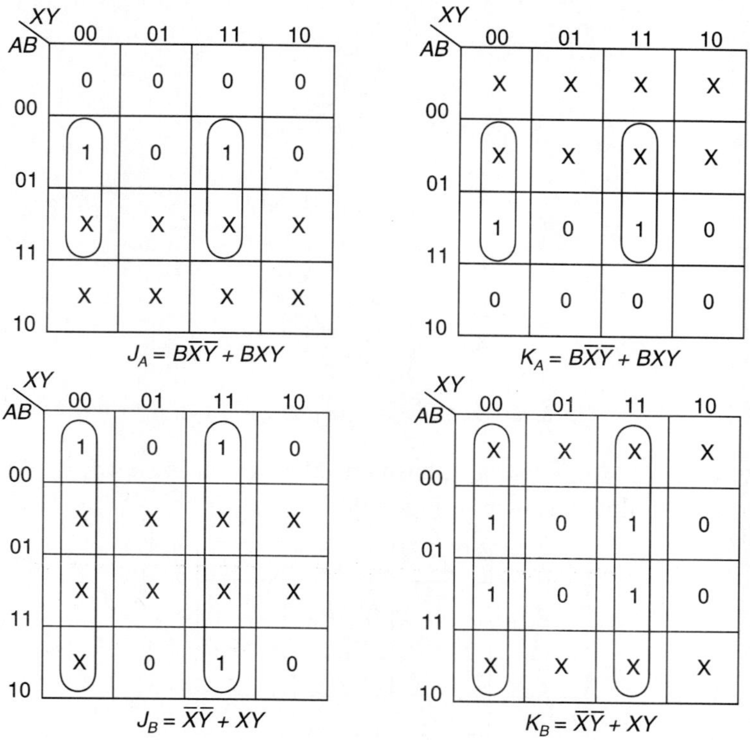

Fig. 8.93 K-maps for example 8.16

From the K-map values the logic diagram is drawn as shown in Fig. 8.94.

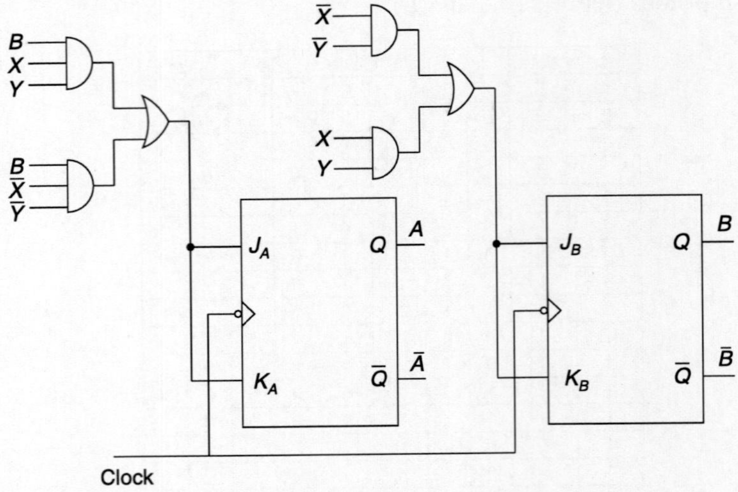

Fig. 8.94 Logic diagram for example 8.16

Example 8.17 Design a synchronous up/down modulo-8 counter using *SR* flip-flops.

Because this is a synchronous up/down counter we need a control input. Let us define a control input x which controls up/down counting. When $x = 0$, the counter counts up and when $x = 1$, the counter counts down. The state diagram for the modulo-8 up/down counter is as shown in Fig. 8.95.

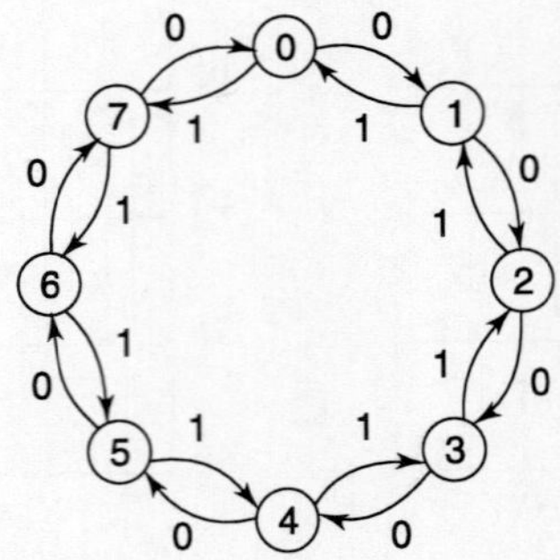

Fig. 8.95 State diagram for example 8.17

From the state diagram, we construct transition table which is shown in Fig. 8.97 and the excitation table for *SR* flip-flop is shown in Fig. 8.96.

Q	Q^+	S	R
0	0	0	x
0	1	1	0
1	0	0	1
1	1	x	0

Fig. 8.96 Excitation table for *SR* flip-flop

Present state			Input	Next state			Flip-flop inputs					
A	B	C	X	A^+	B^+	C^+	S_A	R_A	S_B	R_B	S_C	R_C
0	0	0	0	0	0	1	0	×	0	×	1	0
0	0	0	1	1	1	1	1	0	1	0	1	0
0	0	1	0	0	1	0	0	×	1	0	0	1
0	0	1	1	0	0	0	0	×	0	–	0	1
0	1	0	0	0	1	1	0	×	×	0	1	0
0	1	0	1	0	0	1	0	×	0	1	1	0
0	1	1	0	1	0	0	1	0	0	1	0	1
0	1	1	1	0	1	0	0	×	×	0	0	1
1	0	0	0	1	0	1	×	0	0	×	1	0
1	0	0	1	0	1	1	0	1	1	0	1	0
1	0	1	0	1	1	0	×	0	1	0	0	1
1	0	1	1	1	0	0	×	0	0	×	0	1
1	1	0	0	1	1	1	×	0	×	0	1	0
1	1	0	1	1	0	1	×	0	0	1	1	0
1	1	1	0	0	0	0	0	1	0	1	0	1
1	1	1	1	1	1	0	×	0	×	0	0	1

Fig. 8.97 Transition table for example 8.17

K-maps are constructed for flip-flop inputs as shown in Fig. 8.98.

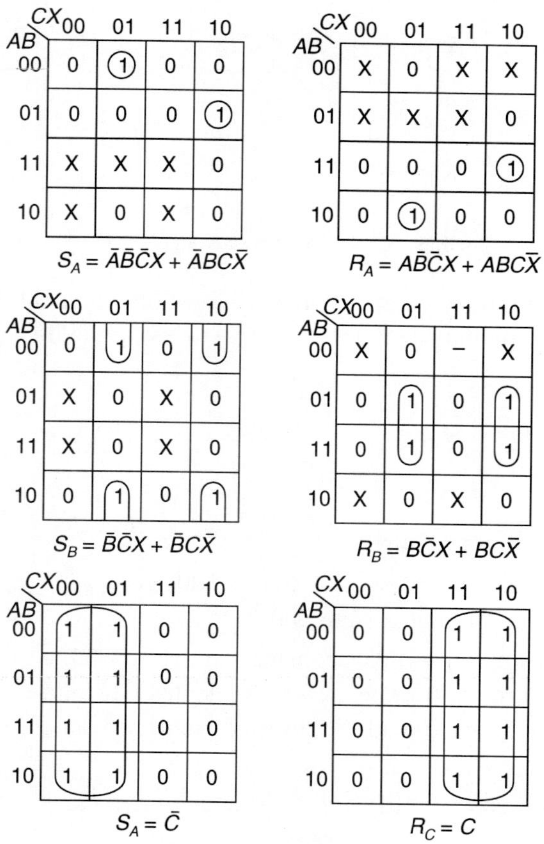

Fig. 8.98 K-maps for example 8.17

Using flip-flop inputs obtained from K-maps we can construct the logic diagram for synchronous up/down modulo-8 counter as shown in Fig. 8.99.

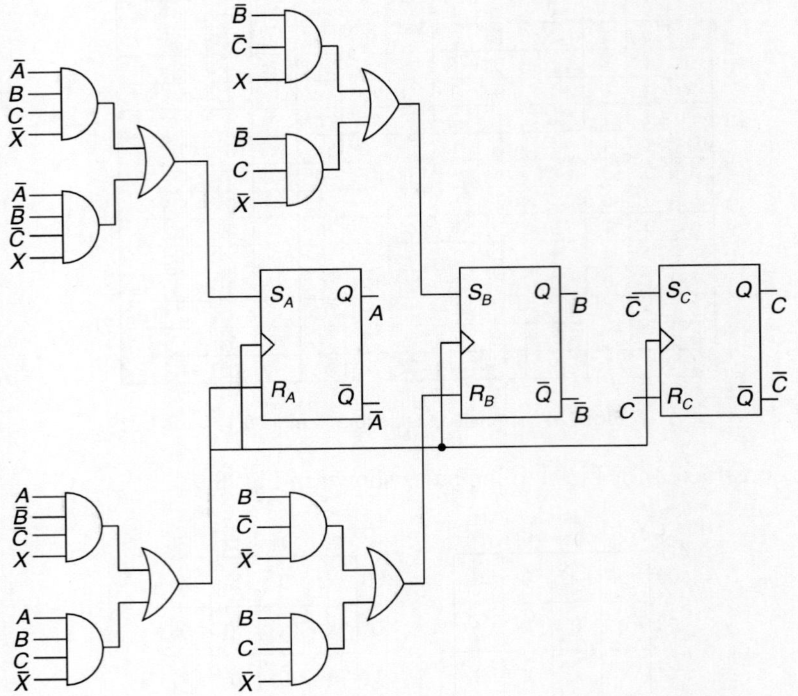

Fig. 8.99 Logic diagram for example 8.17

Example 8.18 Design a synchronous counter using *JK* flip-flops to count the sequence 0, 1, 2, 4, 5, 6, 0, 1, 2. Use state diagram and state table. [VTU – Jan 2007; June 2013]

No. of flip-flops required are $2^n \geq N$

$$2^n \geq 6$$

$$n = 3$$

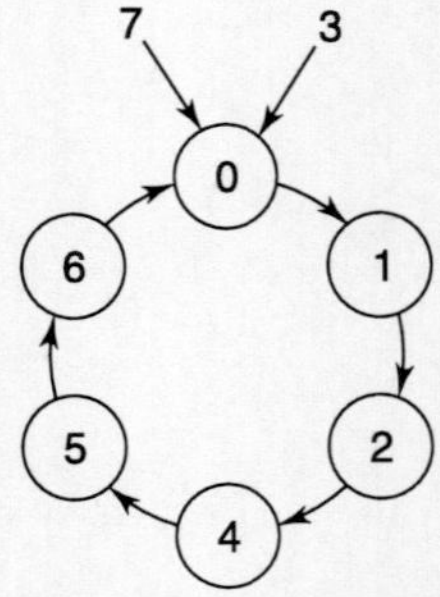

Fig. 8.100 State diagram for example 8.18

Therefore, three flip-flops are required.

The state diagram is drawn as shown in Fig. 8.100 Here, it is assumed that for states 3 and 7, the next state is 0.

Once state diagram is drawn, we can construct transition table as shown in Fig. 8.101. Here, next state is 000 for states 011 and 111. This is the assumption we have made when we have drawn state diagram.

Now using K-maps, we can simplify flip-flop input functions as shown in Fig. 8.102.

Present state			Next state			Flip-flop inputs					
A	B	C	A^+	B^+	C^+	JA	KA	JB	KB	JC	KC
0	0	0	0	0	1	0	×	0	×	1	×
0	0	1	0	1	0	0	×	1	×	×	1
0	1	0	1	0	0	1	×	×	1	0	×
0	1	1	0	0	0	0	×	×	1	×	1
1	0	0	1	0	1	×	0	0	×	1	×
1	0	1	1	1	0	×	0	1	×	×	1
1	1	0	0	0	0	×	1	×	1	0	×
1	1	1	0	0	0	×	1	×	1	×	1

Fig. 8.101 Transition table for example 8.18

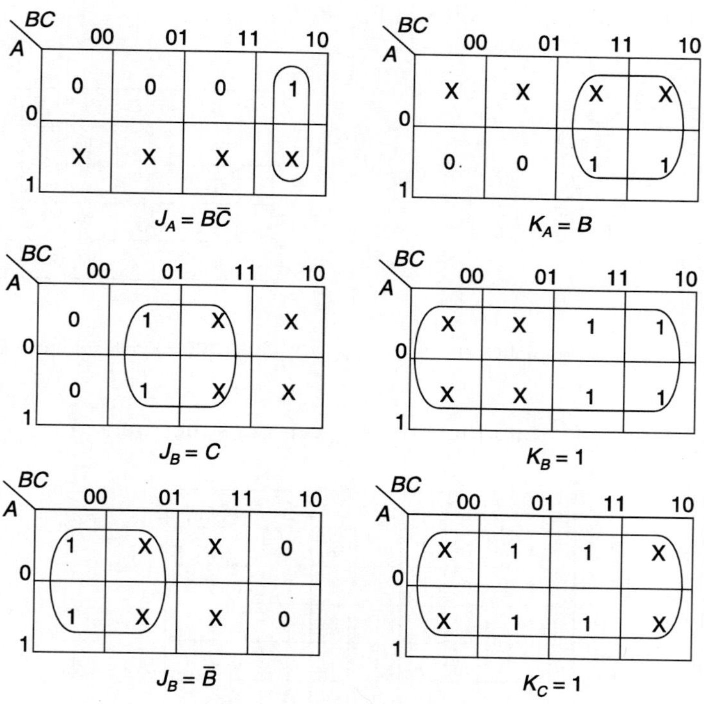

Fig. 8.102 K-maps for example 8.18

Using flip-flop input values, we can construct the logic diagram as shown in Fig. 8.103.

Example 8.19 Design divide by 6 counter, i.e., mod 6 counter using T flip-flop. Write state diagram, transition table and reduce the expression using K-map.

Mod 6 counter will have 6 states.

Number of flip-flops required

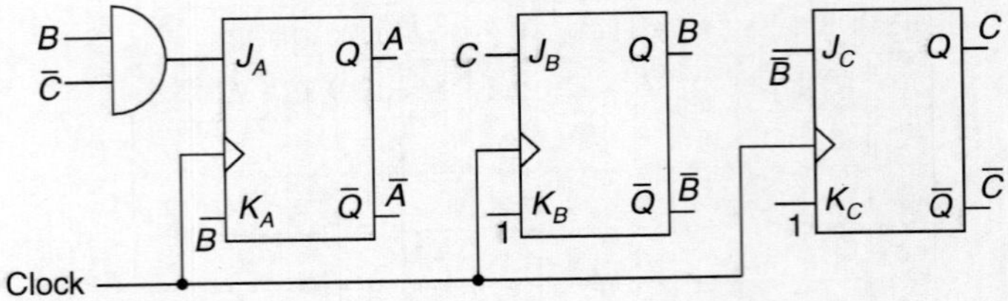

Fig. 8.103 Logic diagram for example 8.18

$$2^n \geq N$$

$$2^3 \geq 6$$

Hence, three flip-flops are required.

The state diagram is written as shown in Fig. 8.104.

Excitation table for T flip-flop is shown in Fig. 8.105.

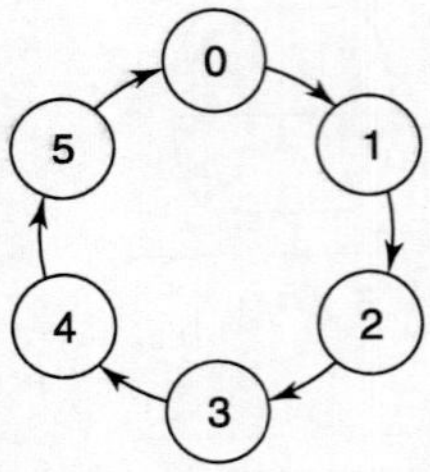

Fig. 8.104 State diagram for example 8.19

Q	Q^+	T
0	0	0
0	1	1
1	0	1
1	1	0

Fig. 8.105 Excitation table for T flip-flop

Using excitation table and state diagram, we can construct transition table as shown in Fig. 8.106.

Present state			Next state			Flip-flop inputs		
A	B	C	A^+	B^+	C^+	T_A	T_B	T_C
0	0	0	0	0	1	0	0	1
0	0	1	0	1	0	0	1	1
0	1	0	0	1	1	0	0	1
0	1	1	1	0	0	1	1	1
1	0	0	1	0	1	0	0	1
1	0	1	0	0	0	1	0	1

Fig. 8.106 Transition table for example 8.19

Flip-flop inputs can be obtained by K-map simplification as shown in Fig. 8.107.

Using K-map simplified values, we can construct the logic diagram for mod-6 counter as shown in Fig. 8.108.

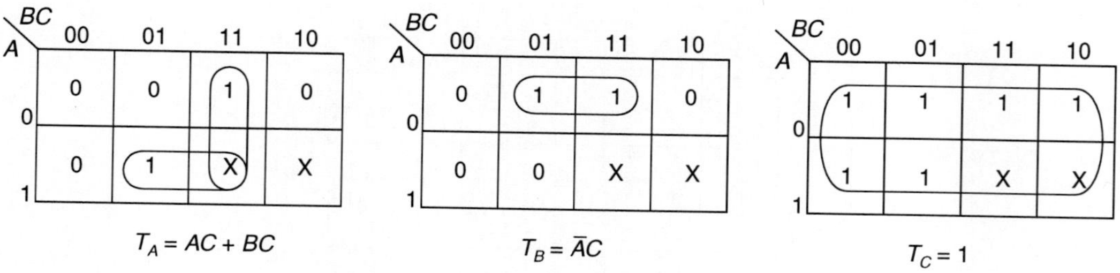

Fig. 8.107 K-maps for example 8.19

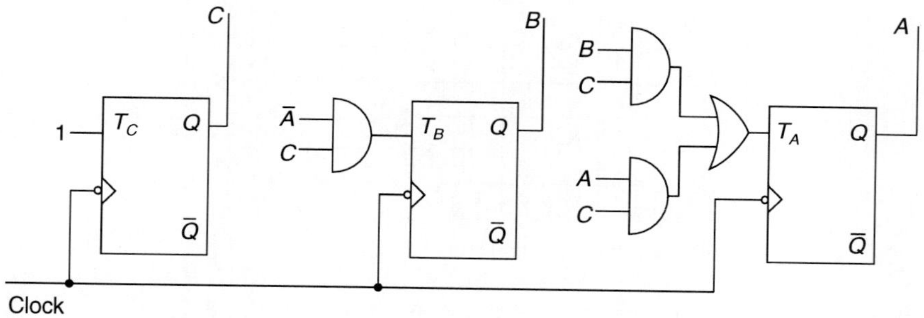

Fig. 8.108 Logic diagram for example 8.19

Example 8.20 Design a synchronous decade counter (Mod-10 counter) using T flip-flops. Write transition table, K-map, etc.

In order to have decade counter we need four flip-flops.

i.e.,

$$2^n \geq N$$

$$2^4 \geq 10$$

Excitation table for T flip-flop is shown in Fig. 8.109.

Q	Q^+	T
0	0	0
0	1	1
1	0	1
1	1	0

Fig. 8.109 Excitation table for T flip-flop

Using excitation table for T flip-flop, we can construct transition table as shown in Fig. 8.110.

Present state				Next state				Flip-flop inputs			
A	B	C	D	A^+	B^+	C^+	D^+	T_A	T_B	T_C	T_D
0	0	0	0	0	0	0	1	0	0	0	1
0	0	0	1	0	0	1	0	0	0	1	1
0	0	1	0	0	0	1	1	0	0	0	1
0	0	1	1	0	1	0	0	0	1	1	1
0	1	0	0	0	1	0	1	0	0	0	1
0	1	0	1	0	1	1	0	0	0	1	1
0	1	1	0	0	1	1	1	0	0	0	1
0	1	1	1	1	0	0	0	1	1	1	1
1	0	0	0	1	0	0	1	0	0	0	1
1	0	0	1	0	0	0	0	1	0	0	1
1	0	1	0	×	×	×	×	×	×	×	×
1	0	1	1	×	×	×	×	×	×	×	×
1	1	0	0	×	×	×	×	×	×	×	×
1	1	0	1	×	×	×	×	×	×	×	×
1	1	1	0	×	×	×	×	×	×	×	×
1	1	1	1	×	×	×	×	×	×	×	×

Fig. 8.110 Transition table for example 8.20

Flip-flop inputs can be simplified using K-maps as shown in Fig. 8.111.

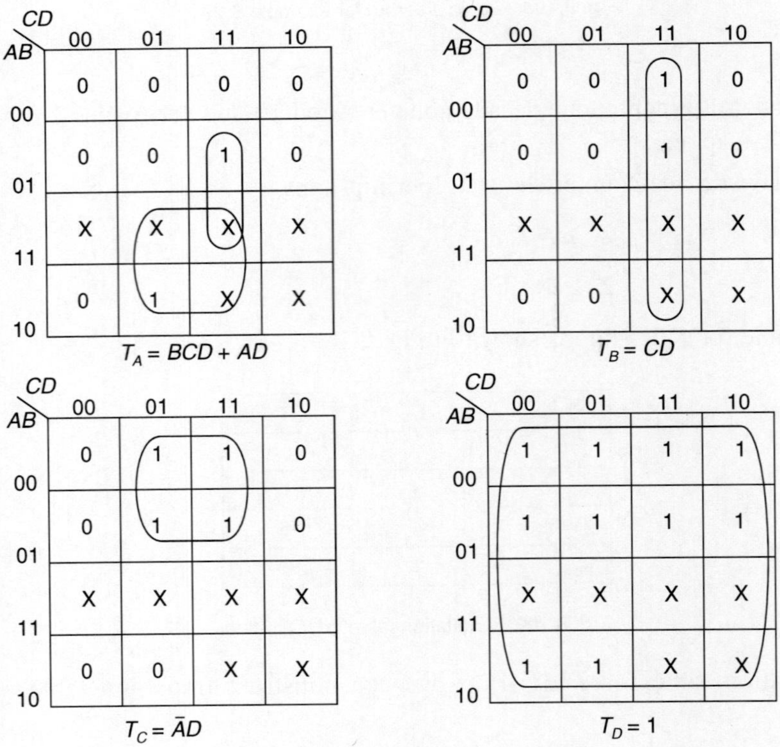

Fig. 8.111 K-maps for example 8.20

From K-map values, we can construct logic diagram as shown in Fig. 8.112.

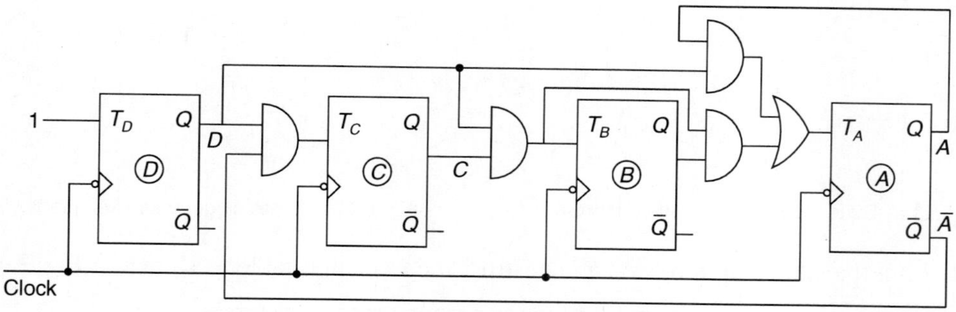

Fig. 8.112 Logic diagram for example 8.20

Lockout condition

There may be some unused states in a counter. For example, in a mod-8 counter there are eight states out of this eight, some states may be unused. In a counter, if the next state of unused state is another unused state and if the counter is not able to come out of unused state, it is said to be in lockout condition and the circuit in lockout condition is called bushless circuit.

Let us see the desired sequence as shown in Fig. 8.113(a) and the unused states as shown in Fig. 8.113(b).

(a) Desired sequence (b) Unused states

Fig. 8.113

The counter which never goes into lockout condition is called self-starting counter. To make sure that the counter will go to initial state from any unused state, additional logic circuit is necessary. To ensure that lockout does not occur, we have to design the counter such that next state from the unused states is forced to be the initial state as shown in Fig. 8.114.

Example 8.21 Design a synchronous counter for the following sequence $4 \rightarrow 6 \rightarrow 7 \rightarrow 3 \rightarrow 1 \rightarrow 4$ … Avoid lockout condition. Use *JK* flip-flops.

Step 1: Draw the state diagram for the given sequence $4 \rightarrow 6 \rightarrow 7 \rightarrow 3 \rightarrow 1 \rightarrow 4$ …

Here unused states are forced to go to used states, i.e., state 5 is forced to go to state 6. State 2 is forced to go to state 3 and state 0 is forced to go to state 1. This is done to avoid lockout condition. The state diagram for the given sequence is as shown in Fig. 8.115.

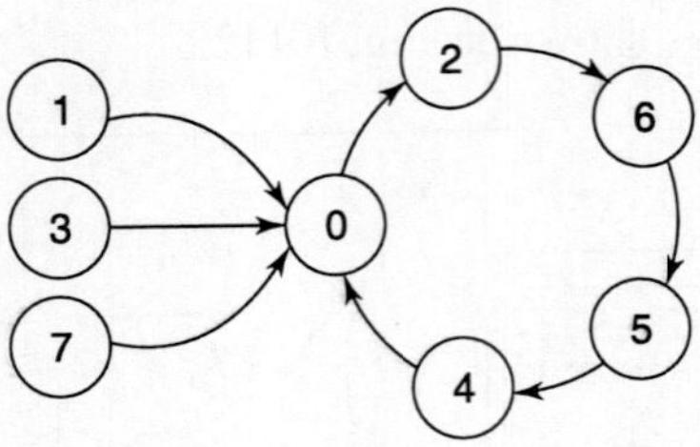

Fig. 8.114 State diagram for avoiding lockout

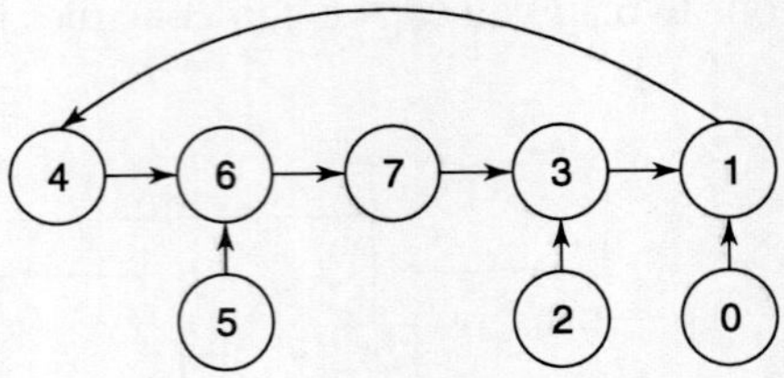

Fig. 8.115 State diagram for example 8.21

Step 2: From the state diagram, we can construct the transition table as shown in Fig. 8.116.

Present state			Next state			Flip-flop inputs					
A	B	C	A^+	B^+	C^+	J_A	K_A	J_B	K_B	J_C	K_C
0	0	0	0	0	1	0	x	0	x	1	x
0	0	1	1	0	0	1	x	0	x	x	1
0	1	0	0	1	1	0	x	x	0	1	x
0	1	1	0	0	1	0	x	x	1	x	0
1	0	0	1	1	0	x	0	1	x	0	x
1	0	1	1	1	0	x	0	1	x	x	1
1	1	0	1	1	1	x	0	x	0	1	x
1	1	1	0	1	1	x	1	x	0	x	0

Fig. 8.116 Transition table for example 8.21

Step 3: Using K-maps, we can obtain the simplified flip-flop inputs as shown in Fig. 8.117.

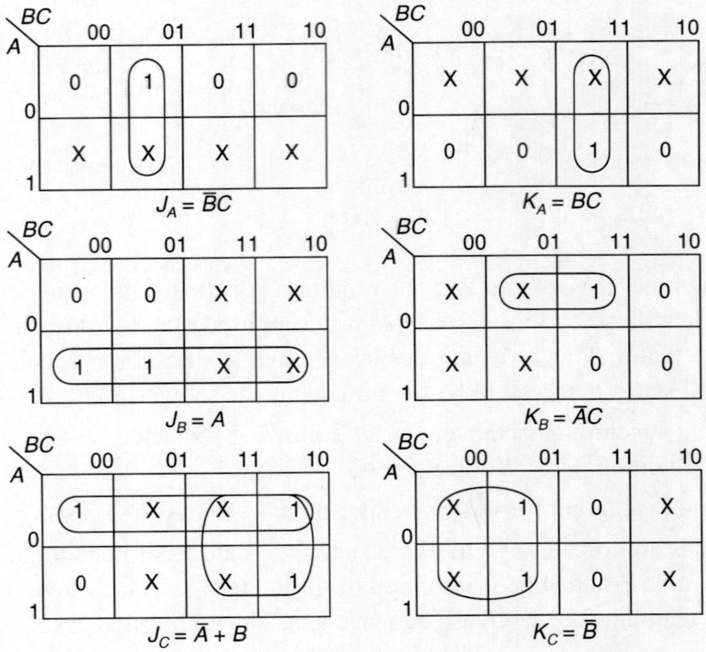

Fig. 8.117 K-maps for example 8.21

Step 4: Using flip-flop inputs after simplification from K-maps, we can construct logic diagram as shown in Fig. 8.118.

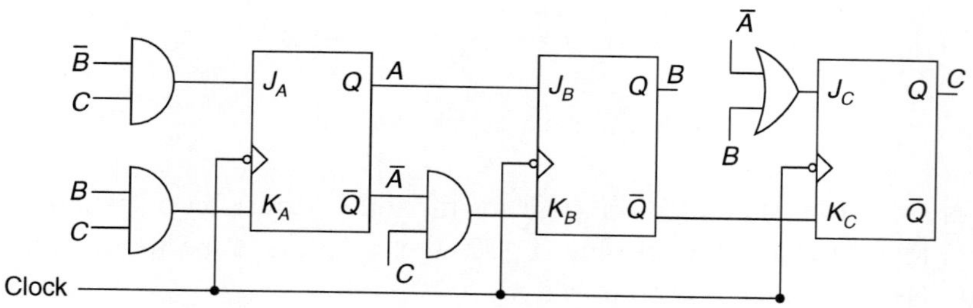

Fig. 8.118 Logic diagram for example 8.21

Example 8.22 Design a Mealy serial bit pattern detector that will detect the input sequence 01010 in a longer bit string. If the pattern is detected, then cause output Q to be active high. If an 011-bit pattern occurs within the same data string, cause output P to be active high. If the 011 pattern occurs, cause the state machine to initialize and start over looking for the 01010 patterns. Overlapping 01010 patterns can occur.

Let X be input string Q = Output if 01010 is detected

P = Output if 011 is detected

Let X = 0011001010111101010101

Q = 0000000001000000001010

P = 0001000000010000000000

For a given input string X, Q and P are outputs if 01010 and 011 are detected respectively as shown above.

Step 1: Let us start from state A. If $x = 0$, we have to go to state B. If $x = 1$, we have to remain in state A as shown in Fig. 8.119.

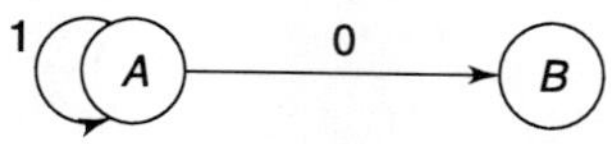

Fig. 8.119 State diagram after step 1

Step 2: Let us start from state B. If $x = 0$, we have to remain at state B. If $x = 1$, as per both input sequences, the second input bit is correct and we have to go to next state C as shown in Fig. 8.120.

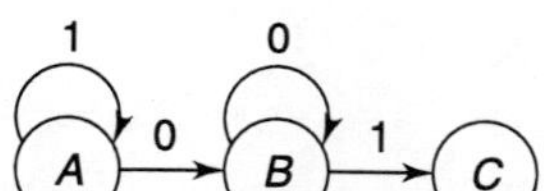

Fig. 8.120 State diagram after step 2

Step 3: Let us start from state C. This indicates that up to second input the sequence is correct for both patterns. If for third bit, $x = 0$, the correct 01010 pattern is in progress and we have to go to state D as shown in Fig. 8.121. If $x = 1$, then pattern 011 has been detected. Hence, $p = 1$ and we have to initialize i.e., go to state A.

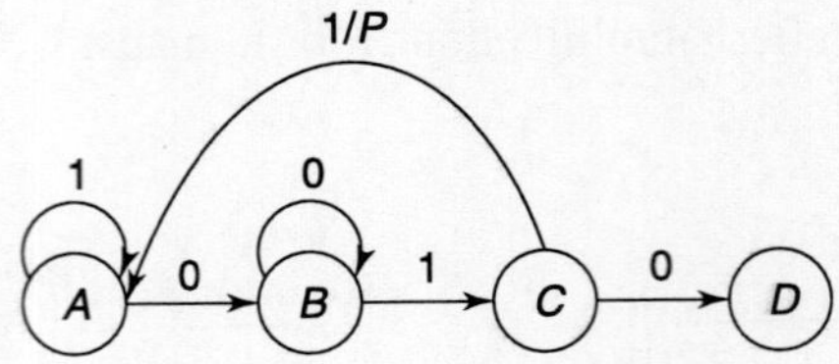

Fig. 8.121 State diagram after step 3

Step 4: Let us start from state *D*. This indicates the third correct bit of pattern 01010. If $x = 0$ we have to go to state *B* as shown in Fig. 8.122. If $x = 1$, this is the fourth correct bit in the sequence 01010. Hence, we have to go to state *E*.

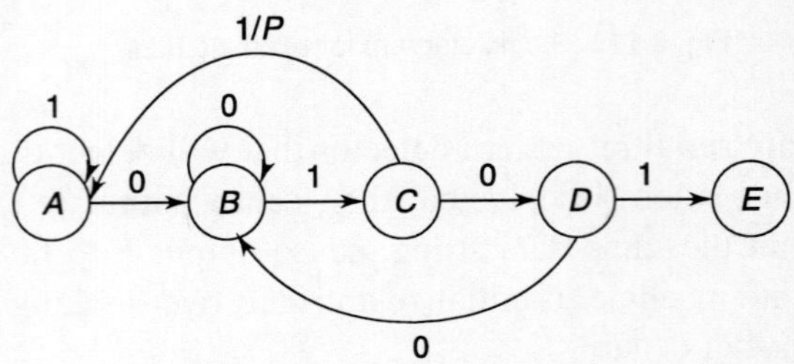

Fig. 8.122 State diagram after step 4

Step 5: Let us start from state *E*. If $x = 0$, the fifth correct bit has been detected and the output $Q = 1$ and the sequential machine goes to state *D*. This is done because it allows overlapping patterns. If $x = 1$, we have to go to state A as this indicates that the third correct bit of pattern 011 has been detected and output $p = 1$ as shown in Fig. 8.123.

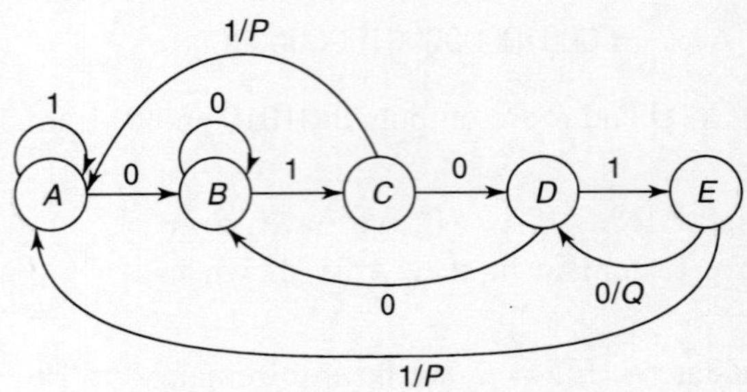

Fig. 8.123 Complete state diagram after step 5

EXERCISE

1. Draw the state diagram of a Mealy machine to detect the sequence 1101 assuming (a) overlapping is allowed and (b) overlapping is not allowed.
2. Draw the state diagram of a Moore machine that produces a 1 output if there have been four or more consecutive 1 inputs or two or more consecutive 0 inputs.

3. Draw the state diagram of a Moore machine that produces a 1 output if a sequence 10101 is detected.
4. Draw the state diagram of a Mealy machine to detect an input sequence 10110 which could overlap. An output 1 is to be generated when the sequence is detected.
5. Draw the state diagram of Mealy machine that produces a 1 output if the sequence 010 or 101 appears at the input with overlapping being allowed.
6. Draw the state diagrams of a Moore machine to output a 1 if two or more consecutive 1s or three or more consecutive 0s are detected at the output.
7. Draw the state diagram of Moore machine that produces a 1 output if there have been four or more consecutive 1 inputs or two or more consecutive 0 inputs.
8. Design a decade up/down counter using D flip-flops with two inputs x and y where x is assigned for direction of count and y for count enable.
9. Design a modulo-8 counter using JK flip-flops with two control inputs x, y such that
   (i) when $xy = 00$, count up even sequence
   (ii) when $xy = 01$, count down even sequence
   (iii) when $xy = 10$, count up odd sequence
   (iv) when $xy = 11$, count down odd sequence
10. Design a sequential machine using D flip-flops for realising the state table below. The machine is of a single input single output type.

Present state	Next state		Output Z	
	$X = 0$	$X = 1$	$X = 0$	$X = 1$
A	B	C	0	0
B	A	A	0	1
C	D	A	0	1
D	A	D	0	1

Indicate the state transition diagram. Do the state assignment. Workout the excitation and the output logics.